A DICTIONARY OF CLASSICAL REFERENCE
IN ENGLISH POETRY

A DICTIONARY
OF CLASSICAL REFERENCE
IN ENGLISH POETRY

Eric Smith

D. S. BREWER · BARNES & NOBLE

First published 1984 by D. S. Brewer
240 Hills Road, Cambridge
an imprint of Boydell & Brewer Ltd, PO Box 9,
Woodbridge, Suffolk IP12 3DF
and Barnes & Noble, 81 Adams Drive, Totowa,
New Jersey N. J. 07512, USA

Reprinted 1985

British Library Cataloguing in Publication Data
Smith, Eric
    A dictionary of classical reference in English
    poetry.
    1. English poetry — Dictionaries 2. Mythology,
    Classical, in literature — Dictionaries
    I. Title
    821'.009'37   PR 508.M9
    ISBN 0-85991-144-6

Library of Congress Cataloging in Publication Data
Smith, Eric, 1940-
    A dictionary of classical reference in English poetry
    Includes index.
    1. English poetry – Greek influences -- Dictionaries.
    2. English poetry – Roman influences -- Dictionaries.
    3. Classical literature -- Dictionaries.   4. Mythology,
    Classical, in literature -- Dictionaries.   5. Allusions --
    Dictionaries.   6. Classicism -- Dictionaries.   I. Title.
    PR 508.C68S63   1983   821'.009'15   83-12273
    ISBN 0-389-20430-7

          UK ISBN   0 85991 144 6
                    0 85991 218 3 (paperback)
          US ISBN   0 389 20430 7

Jacket illustration
The Renaissance of Venus by Walter Crane, 1877
(Reproduced by courtesy of the Trustees of the Tate Gallery)

Printed in Great Britain by Nene Litho
Bound by Woolnough Bookbinding
Both of Wellingborough, Northants

CONTENTS

PREFACE

This Dictionary contains virtually all the Classical references in some eighty English poets — subject to some qualification which I shall explain. In most cases there is a paragraph which defines the subject as it appears in the subsequent references, and these paragraphs are usually followed by indications of the main source for the subject. The second part of the book lists all the poets and poems cited, together with the references made. Thus, several purposes and approaches are possible. You might, for example, be interested in the substance and poetic use of a myth by one or more poets (possibly compared), in which case you would consult the first section; or you might be interested in the meaning of a line or series of lines, in which case you could consult either section; or, if you were concerned as to the frequency and nature of allusion in the work of a poet or in a poem, you would go to the second part, the author index.

For practical reasons, no dictionary such as this can be as comprehensive as might be wished for some purposes. Naturally, one would much prefer to give quotations rather than references, but economic constraints on length would result in much too limited a coverage if this method were followed. There has to be selection also. However, it is believed that these poets include all, or very nearly all, those commonly studied in schools and universities and read for pleasure. 'English' is interpreted in the light of what tends to occur in 'English' courses; it is not exclusively English or even solely British. The method of selection was based on a general estimate of stature and importance rather than any more objective means. Inevitably this creates particular problems with modern poetry, where reputations are not securely established. I have, therefore, confined myself to those who appear unquestionably significant poets and, with only one exception, I have not included living authors. I do not think that any of those included could have been omitted, but I am aware that claims could be made for including several others. As for the 'historical' end, I have, with a similar arbitrariness, started with Chaucer and excluded many pre-Elizabethan poets not widely read. Poetic drama is included where it is part of the *oeuvre* of a person who was primarily a poet. Shakespeare naturally could not have been excluded, and his dramatic and non-dramatic works are treated on the same footing. In the context of drama largely in verse, a few allusions in prose passages have been admitted. Classical allusion in poetic drama can, however, be exceedingly detailed — and much of it on a 'nonce' basis — and therefore I have tried to select according to the importance of the work involved. Where the profusion of references to one subject is great, allusions are grouped into sub-divisions, but these are not exclusive; therefore it may pay to look up references in sub-sections as well as in general sections.

'Classical' has been taken broadly to mean 'concerning Greece or Rome until c. 400 AD' — but neither the temporal nor the geographical limitation is precisely regarded. In particular, I have thought fit to include some common references (for example, to St Cecilia) which might well be thought to be 'Classical' but are barely so in fact; there is a sprinkling of Biblical allusions, chosen in the same manner. On the whole, covert and inexplicit allusions, unless quite obvious in their reference, are excluded, as are quotations from Classical authors. Generic and very mundane references — such as to the nymphs or to Cupid — have necessarily been curtailed. Most passing references having little definitive value (such as exclamations, imprecations, astronomical and 'sun-rise' material, and some catalogues of *exempla*) are omitted. Inevitably also, the treatment of complete English versions of Classical stories has to be partial, centreing on highlights and interesting detail; but main Classical sources for such stories are usually given. Translations are excluded, and the treatment of 'imitations' and 'paraphrases' varies according to interest and distance from the source. I have tried throughout to strike a balance between what reveals the meaning of the Classical, and what usage tells us of the English poet. What appears a matter of assembly, which could be entrusted to a machine, turns out to demand the exercise of critical judgment at every stage.

It should be noted that the Classical sources cited are those most readily accessible and most helpful in defining the subject; they may not be (but sometimes are) the actual sources of references in English, and their reliability may now, of course, be in dispute or refuted. That is often of no importance to their use by these poets. It is worth saying also that the defining paragraphs provide a minimum of background together with the details referred to in English poetry. These details may be heterogeneous, and the definition may appear disjointed as a result; it seemed preferable to indicate a Classical precedent for an apparently quirky and original detail, rather than to set out the Classical material *in toto* when much of it received no allusion.

Where they were available, standard one-volume line-numbered editions were adopted for the English texts.* A few doubtful passages and textual errors have been noted in parenthesis. However, it is not very often that textual problems are crucial in this area, and the same broadly applies to problems of attribution. A list of Classical texts has been given. For these the convenient Löeb bi-lingual editions were used wherever possible. The definitions inevitably owe a debt to

* References to Chaucer's works are to the edition of F. N. Robinson. This should be consulted for the line numbers. The works of Drayton are a selection only — to cite his complete

previous works of reference, particularly to Lemprière's long-lived *Classical Dictionary* (itself a source for some Nineteenth Century poets), to *The Handbook of Classical Mythology* by Edward Tripp, and to the *Oxford Classical Dictionary*. Where sources could be found, however, the definitions were constructed by reference to them, since in many cases these sources could have been used by English poets. Because of this, and because the emphasis is on that which has been used in English poetry, for some purposes fuller definitions in existing dictionaries may need to be consulted, particularly for historical background and sequence. This is not, after all, a Classical dictionary, but a work intended as a handbook for the enhanced appreciation of poetry at a time when Classical knowledge is far less widespread than it once was; although it is intended also to facilitate critical comparison of different versions of the same theme.

MAJOR CLASSICAL SOURCES AND TITLES USED

Works are normally cited by author only. Where there is the possibility of confusion, the work also is cited.

Aeschylus	*Plays (cited by title)*
Apollodorus	*The Library (and Epitome)*
Apollonius Rhodius	*Argonautica*
Aristotle	*The Poetics*
Caesar	*Civil Wars, Gallic Wars*
Catullus	*Poems*
Diodorus Siculus	*The Library of History*
Euripides	*Plays (cited by title)*
Herodotus	*History*
Hesiod	*Contest of Homer and Hesiod, Theogony,* *Works and Days*
Homer	*The Iliad, The Odyssey*
Homeric Hymns	*(Cited by number and addressee)*
Horace	*Epistles, Epodes, Odes, Satires*
Hyginus	*Astronomical Poems, Fables**
Juvenal	*Satires*
Livy	*History of Rome*
Lucan	*The Civil War*
Ovid	*Amores, Art of Love, Fasti, Heroides, Ibis,* *Metamorphoses, Tristia*
Pausanias	*Description of Greece*
Pindar	*Nemean Odes, Olympian Odes, Pythian Odes*
Plato	*Works (cited by title)*
Pliny	*Natural History*
Plotinus	*Enneads*
Plutarch	*Lives*
Polybius	*The Histories*
Sophocles	*Plays (cited by title)*
Statius	*The Thebaid*

* In *The Myths of Hyginus* trans. M. Grant (Kansas, 1960)

Major Classical Sources and Titles Used

Strabo	*The Geography*
Suetonius	*Lives of the Caesars*
Tacitus	*The Annals, The Histories*
Theocritus	*Poems*
Thucydides	*The History*
Tibullus	*Elegies of Lygdamus*
Virgil	*The Aeneid, Culex, Eclogues, Georgics*
Xenophon	*Anabasis, Cyropaedia, Hellenica*

SUBJECTS AND REFERENCES

Abradates King of *Susa* (*Seleucia*, on the borders of modern Iran and Iraq) in the 5th Century BC, and husband of Penthea. He went over to the Persians when they captured his wife and she was well-treated, but he was killed in his first battle for Cyrus II. Penthea stabbed herself on his corpse and Cyrus erected a monument to the couple.

(Xenophon *Cyropaedia* vii)
See also *Habradate*

Absyrtus Son of *Aeetes* of *Colchis*, and brother to *Medea*. When fleeing her father to join *Jason*, Medea mangled Absyrtus's body and strewed the pieces in the way of Aeetes. In other versions Absyrtus was killed by Jason before Medea's eyes, because he led the Colchian pursuit against the *Argonauts* who had the captured fleece. The murder aroused the anger of *Zeus*, who laid on a great storm, but Jason, Medea and the Argonauts were purified of the murder by *Circe*.

(Apollodorus I ix 24;
Apollonius Rhodius IV 452-81)
Herrick   *To His Book* 1-4
Shakespeare   *King Henry VI pt 2* V ii
56-9
Spenser   *Faerie Queene* V viii 47

Abydos A town on the *Hellespont*, opposite *Sestos*. The birthplace of *Leander*.
See also *Hero*
Donne   *Elegy* XVIII 60-3
Hood   *Hero and Leander* 3
Marlowe   *Hero and Leander* 1-5, 51-3

Academe, Academia The gymnasium outside *Athens*, where *Plato* taught in a grove of olive trees. It was dedicated to Academus, a mythological hero who revealed to *Castor* and *Pollux* where *Theseus* had concealed their sister *Helen*.

(Pausanias i 30;
Plutarch *Theseus* xxxii)
Milton   *Paradise Regained* iv 244-5

Acantha A nymph loved by *Apollo* and given immortality in the flower *Acanthus*.

Acanthus
See *Acantha*
Milton   *Paradise Lost* iv 695-7

Acarnania A country near Aetolia and Calydon in Western Greece.
Swinburne   *Atalanta in Calydon* 1244

Accius A prolific minor Roman poet and dramatic theorist born in 170 BC. Much of his dramatic work is free translation of the Greek tragedians. His idiosyncratic style, relying heavily on alliteration, antithesis and other verbal figures, was much admired in his day.

(Horace *Epistles* II i 56)
Jonson   *To Shakespeare* 31-7
The Poetaster I i

Acestes King of *Eryx* (the name of a river-god, his ancestor) in Sicily. He supported *Priam* in the Trojan War and entertained *Aeneas*, helping him to bury *Achises* and set up a shrine on Mt Eryx. In an archery competition, arranged by Aeneas, Acestes missed the target but was pronounced winner because his arrow burst into flame, a good omen.

(Virgil *Aeneid* V 519 ff, 746 ff)
Tennyson   *Religion Be Thy Sword* 5-8

Achates The proverbially 'faithful Achates', trusty companion of *Aeneas*, who accompanied him on his explorations on arrival in Libya.

(Virgil *Aeneid* i 316)
Byron   *Don Juan* i 159
Chaucer   *Legend of Good Women*
964-6, 1023-6
Marlowe   *Dido Queen of Carthage*
762-7

Achelaus, Achelous A river-god, the rival of *Hercules* for the hand of *Deianeira*. Achelous wrestled with Hercules for her, and changed himself into a serpent and a bull in order to win, but Hercules defeated him by breaking off one of the bull's horns (which was replaced by the horn of *Amalthea* and became a cornucopia).

(Apollodorus II vii 5;
Ovid *Metamorphoses* ix 4 ff)
Bridges   *Prometheus the Firegiver*
968-72
Chaucer   *Monk's Tale* 3293-3300
Swift   *The Progress of Marriage* 109 ff
Swinburne   *Atalanta in Calydon* 34-5,
53 ff

Acheron, Acherontic   A river of Epirus flowing into the Ionian Sea. Its deadness led to its being regarded as a river of *Hades* or hell. Acheron was the first river to be crossed by dead souls (ferried by *Charon*) and the name was often used for Hades itself.

(Homer *Odyssey* x 513-5;
Lucan iii 16; Pausanias I xvii;
Virgil *Aeneid* vi 106-8, 295ff,
vii 568-71)

Belloc	*When you to Acheron's ugly water come* 1ff
Byron	*Childe Harold* ii 7, 51
De La Mare	*I Wonder* 1-7
Drayton	*The Owl* 275-80, 281-6
	Polyolbion xxv 31ff
Dryden	*Albion and Albanius* ii
Fletcher G.	*Christ's Victory on Earth* 22
Jonson	*On the Famous Voyage* 141-5
Marlowe	*Hero and Leander* 187-91
Milton	*Comus* 602-4
	Paradise Lost ii 578
Shakespeare	*Macbeth* III v 14-9
	Midsummer Night's Dream III ii 357
	Titus Andronicus IV iii 43-5
Skelton	*Philip Sparrow*
Spenser	*Faerie Queene* I v 33

Acherusia, Acherusian   A lake near Memphis in Egypt. It was the supposed original location of the myth of *Charon* and *Styx* and was thence associated with rivers of the same name near Naples and in *Thesprotia*, Epirus.

(Diodorus Siculus I 96)
Drayton   *Polyolbion* xxv 31ff

Achilles   The Greek hero of the Trojan War, son of *Peleus* of *Thessaly* and a Nereid, *Thetis*. During his infancy, Thetis made him invulnerable, save for his heel, by washing him in the *Styx*. He was educated in war and music by the centaur *Chiron*, and he was armed by *Vulcan* at the request of Thetis. (There is an alternative version of his upbringing — see *Lycomedes*). When *Agamemnon* had stolen his mistress *Briseis*, Achilles refused to join him and the Greeks in war with *Troy*, but he was driven to do so in revenge for the slaying of his close friend *Patroclus* by *Hector*. He killed Hector after pursuing him three times round Troy, and he had his body dragged by the heels round the walls of the city before submitting to the prayers of Hector's aged father, *Priam*. Priam was accompanied in some accounts by his daughter *Polyxena*, with whom Achilles had been in love whilst Hector had opposed the match. After Hector's death, Achilles courted Polyxena but was killed by her brother *Paris*, who either succeeded with a long shot from within Troy, or ambushed him when he came to seek Polyxena's hand. In any case, the fatal wound was in his heel. As the Greeks prepared to sail home, the ghost of Achilles appeared from Hades and demanded the sacrifice of Polyxena on his tomb, since the victors were entitled to a share of the spoils. The sacrifice was duly performed by *Neoptolemus*, his son.

(Apollodorus *Epitome* 3; Homer
Iliad, *Odyssey*; Hyginus *Fabulae*
95, 101)

See also *Penthesilea, Telephus, Thersites*
— General

Auden	*The Shield of Achilles* 65-72
Brooke	*Fragment*
Browning E. B.	*The Fourfold Aspect* 37-46
Byron	*Childe Harold* ii 14
Chaucer	*Book of the Duchess* 326-34, 1055-75
	Man of Law's Tale 197-9
	Squire's Tale 236-40
	House of Fame 397-404, 1456-63
	Parliament of Fowls 290-5
Cleveland	*Upon an Hermaphrodite* 49-53
Coleridge	*Recantation* 79-82
Drayton	*The Barons Wars* ii 43
Dryden	*Conquest of Granada* II iii
Fletcher P.	*The Purple Island* i 9
Graves	*Penthesilea* 1-5, 7-10
Jonson	*Epistle to Elizabeth* 51ff
Keats	*Hyperion* i 27-30
Kingsley	*Elegiacs* 3-4
Lewis C. D.	*Transitional Poem* 18
Masefield	*The Spearman*
Shakespeare	*Troilus and Cressida* I iii 146-50, 316-9; II i 31-4; II iii 167-71; V v 30-4
Spenser	*Hymn in Honour of Love* 231-7

Muiopotmos 63-4
Stevenson   *Et Tu in Arcadia* 6-7
Swift   *The Virtues of Sid Hamet's Rod*
59 ff
— *Upbringing, heel*
Arnold   *Empedocles on Etna* I ii 57 ff
Butler S.   *Hudibras* I iii 139-44
Byron   *Don Juan* iv 4, viii 84
Coleridge   *To a Friend (Charles Lamb)*
7-12
Cowley   *Pindaric Ode* 8
Drayton   *Polyolbion* v 21-4
Pope   *Dunciad* ii 209-10
Southey   *Roderick* xvi 199-203
Spenser   *Ruins of Time* 427-31
Swift   *Ode to the King* 142
Swinburne   *Atalanta in Calydon* 405-9
— *Polyxena*
Byron   *The Deformed Transformed* I i
267 ff
— *Hector*
Chaucer   *Nun's Priest's Tale* 4331-8
Troilus and Criseyde v 1553 ff
Marlowe   *Tamburlaine* ii 3566-70
Marvell   *Elegy on the Death of Lord
Villiers* 97-104
Milton   *Paradise Lost* ix 13-16
Shakespeare   *Troilus and Cressida* V ix
4-6

Acidalia, Acidalian   The name of a fountain and hill in Boeotia. They were sacred to *Venus* and the *Graces* bathed there. The name was also used of Venus herself.
(Virgil *Aeneid* i 720)
Spenser   *Epithalamion* 305-10
Faerie Queene IV v 5, VI x 9,
115

Acontius   A young man of low origin who fell in love with *Cydippe* and yet was unable to come into her presence. He threw to her an apple from the Garden of *Venus*, having inscribed on it a declaration of her love for him; reading this message out loud in the Temple of *Diana*, Cydippe was bound by it, being in the presence of the goddess.
(Ovid *Heroides* xx-xxi)
Spenser   *Faerie Queene* II vii 55

Acrisius   The father of *Danae*.
Jonson   *Volpone* V i

Acropolis   The central hill and fortress of *Athens*, on which there were a wall and palace at least by the 12th Century BC. The Parthenon, a temple to *Athena*, was erected under the direction of *Phidias* the sculptor in 447 BC on the site of earlier temples; there were other shrines and temples on the hill.
Shelley   *Ode to Liberty* 74-5
Tennyson   *Timbuctoo* 31-6

Actea, Actaea   A *Nereid*.
Spenser   *Faerie Queene* IV ii 50

Actaeon   A hunter, son of *Aristaeus* and *Autonoë* who was a daughter of *Cadmus*. Actaeon came upon the naked *Diana* bathing with her train of nymphs on Mount *Citheron*, whereupon she turned him into a stag devoured by his own hounds (see *Melanchaetes*). There are other versions of his offence and death, as that he tried to violate Diana in her temple, that he claimed to rival her in hunting, or that she destroyed him as the agent of *Zeus*. (Zeus was enraged by Actaeon's courting of *Semele*, whom the god wanted for himself.) After Actaeon's death, his mentor *Chiron* erected a statue of the hunter to console the masterless hounds.
(Apollodorus III iv 4;
Diodorus Siculus iv 81
Ovid *Metamorphoses* iii 138 ff)
Bridges   *Prometheus the Firegiver* 944 ff
Clough   *Actaeon* 29-33
Daniel   *Civil Wars* ii 12
Whilst Youth and Error 7-12
Denham   *On John Fletcher's Works* 7-10
Drayton   *Rosamond and Henry II*
139-42
Jonson   *Cynthia's Revels* I i
Keats   *Endymion* i 511-3
Marlowe   *Edward II* 61 ff
Hero and Leander ii 260-3
Shakespeare   *Titus Andronicus* II i 61-4
Twelfth Night I i 19-23
Shelley   *Adonais* 274-9
Ode to Naples 77-82
Skelton   *Philip Sparrow*
Tennyson   *The Princess* iv 184-8

Actium   A small town at the Ambracian Gulf on the West coast of Greece. It was the site of *Mark Antony*'s camp and so of the naval battle offshore in 31 BC, in which *Augustus* decisively defeated Antony.

Dryden   *Conquest of Granada* V i
           All for Love II i
Prior   *Alma* i 486-7
Shakespeare   *Antony and Cleopatra* III
         vi 47 ff
Tennyson   *Antony to Cleopatra* 25-6

Ades   Also known as *Hades*, *Orcus* and *Pluto*; the god of the Underworld, meaning 'without light'.
Milton   *Paradise Lost* ii 963-4

Admetus
See *Alcestis*, *Amete*
Browning E. B.   *The Fourfold Aspect*
         49-50
Browning R.   *Aristophanes' Apology*
         193-8
         Balaustion's Adventure
         2598-2602
Milton   *Sonnet* xxiii 1-4
Spenser   *Faerie Queene* III xi 39
Swinburne   *Atalanta in Calydon* 1266

Adonian
See *Adonis*
Keats   *Lamia* i 316-20

Adonis   The son of *Myrrha* (by an incestuous union with her unwitting father Cinyras, king of Cyprus or Smyrna), Adonis was loved by *Venus*, who tried to lessen his passion for the dangerous sport of hunting. When nonetheless he was killed by a boar, he was changed into an anemone and *Proserpina* restored him to life on condition that he spend half the year in the Underworld with her and half the year on earth with Venus. This is taken to represent the alternation of the seasons and parallels the myths of (among others) *Thammuz*, *Osiris* and Proserpina herself. Gardens of Adonis were pots of seeds, hung on rooftops and tended by women at the period of mourning for the vegetation god Adonis (i.e. the sowing time or midsummer). The flowers of these plants faded rapidly and part of the rites consisted of casting them into a river or the sea. The rites were held at several places (notably *Athens* and *Alexandria*) and varied considerably. Essentially, they represented a life-cycle with renewal in

water, whilst the 'gardens' were often associated with surroundings of legendary beauty for the love of the Classical Venus and Adonis.

(Apollodorus III xiv 3-4;
Bion *Lament for Adonis*;
Ovid *Metamorphoses* x 503 ff, 708-49;
Plato *Phaedrus* 276; Pliny xix 19;
Theocritus *Idyll* xv)

See also *Adoun*, *Astarte*
— *and Venus*
Browning R.   *With Gerard de Lairesse*
         161 ff
De La Mare   *Youth* 11
Keats   *Endymion* ii 458-78, 516-29;
         iii 917-9
Lovelace   *Princess Louisa Drawing* 34-7
MacNeice   *Cock o' The North* iii
Marlowe   *Hero and Leander* i 11-15,
         91-3
         Jew of Malta 1811-4
Marvell   *Elegy on the Death of Lord*
         Villiers 105 ff
Milton   *Comus* 999-1002
Pope   *Summer* 61-2
         Winter 21-4
Shakespeare   *King Henry VI pt 1* I vi
         4-7
         The Passionate Pilgrim 4,
         6, 9
         Sonnet 53
         Taming of the Shrew
         Introduction 47-51
         Venus and Adonis 67-8,
         85-90, 421-4, 615-6,
         1055-6, 1167-8
Shelley   *Adonais* 10-14, 64, 316, 343-4,
         370-1, 492-5
         Scene from 'Tasso' 10-13
         Witch of Atlas 576-83
Spenser   *Faerie Queene* III i 34-8,
         vi 48-50
Swift   *A Love Song* 9-12
Swinburne   *St Dorothy*
Tennyson   *Lucretius* 85 ff
Wordsworth   *Love Lies Bleeding* 12-19
— *Gardens of Adonis*
Fletcher G.   *Christ's Victory on Earth*
         40
         Description of Encalpius
         39-40
Jonson   *Cynthia's Revels* V iii
Milton   *Paradise Lost* ix 439 ff

Spenser   *Colin Clout's Come Home
           Again 803-4
           Faerie Queene II x 71, III vi
           29, 46-7*

Adonis (River)   A Phoenicean river flowing
into the Mediterranean near Byblos, which was
sacred to *Adonis* or *Thammuz*. The waters,
being turned red by the mountains of Lebanon
through which it flowed, were said to be stained
by the blood of Adonis.
    Milton   *Paradise Lost* i 446ff

Adoun
See *Adonis*
    Chaucer   *Troilus and Criseyde* iii 715-20

Adrastus   King of *Argos*, who married his
daughters to *Polyneices* and *Tydeus* and set
out, with Polyneices, as leader of the *Seven
Against Thebes* to wrest the Theban throne
from *Eteocles* for Polyneices. The campaign
was a disaster in which all the principals except
Adrastus were killed. Although he returned in
revenge with the sons of the Seven and was
successful, his son *Aegilaus* was killed and
Adrastus died old and in grief.
                         (Apollodorus III 6-7)
See also *Thebes*
    Browning E. B.   *Queen Anelida 9*
    Chaucer   *Anelida and Arcite 57-63*
    Skelton   *Laud and Praise*

Adriane
See *Ariadne*
    Chaucer   *House of Fame 405-20
               Legend of Good Women
               267-8, 1968-72, 2114-8,
               2144-8, 2170-6, 2218ff,
               2459-64*

Aeacide, Aecides   Descendant(s) of *Aeacus*.
See *Peleus, Chiron*
    Chapman   *Amorous Contention of Phillis
               and Flora 63*
    Shakespeare   *Taming of the Shrew* III i
                   50-1
    Spenser   *Faerie Queene VI x 22*
    Swinburne   *Atalanta in Calydon 1260*

Aeacus   A son of *Jupiter* by Aegina, famed
as an ancient father of Greece. In answer to

his prayers during a plague, Jupiter repeopled
his country from its ants and thereafter Aeacus
was worshipped. His was father of *Peleus* by
Endeis and of Phocus by the Nereid *Psamanthe*.
His love of justice led to his being one of the
three judges in *Hades*.
                        (Apollodorus III xii 6)

Aeaea, Aeaean   A name for *Circe* after her
birthplace, Aea(e), an island off *Colchis* on
the eastern Euxine.
    Keats   *Endymion* iii 415-7
    Milton   *Comus 46-50*
    Shelley   *Ode to Naples 164-5*

Aeetes   King of *Colchos* and father of *Medea*
and *Absyrtus*. *Phrixus* had fled the wrath of
his stepmother *Ino*, flying to Colchos on a
golden ram. Aeetes, who was a friend of
Phrixus's father *Athamas*, gave the refugee his
daughter Chalciope, but later killed him, either
in jealousy for the fleece or because he believed
him to be a threat to the throne.
                          (Apollodorus I 9;
                       Apollonius Rhodius 2-3)
See also *Oetes*

Aegeus   A king of *Athens*, father of *Theseus*.
He married Aethra at the court of her father
Pittheus in western Peloponnesus and gave her
certain instructions if she should bear a son;
when he was strong enough to lift a huge stone
from the sword and sandals which he had
hidden under it, she should send the boy with
these tokens to him, so that he would recognise
him. This device was to conceal the son's
identity from rivals to the throne. Theseus in
due course revealed himself in this way to
Aegeus and thereby incurred the enmity of
Medea, with whom Aegeus was then living.
Aegeus subsequently drowned himself when
Theseus in error returned from his conquest
of the *Minotaur* with black sails — the agreed
sign of failure. The Sea was supposedly called
the 'Aegean' after this event.
                 (Apollodorus III xv 5-11 *Epitome* I;
                       Ovid *Metamorphoses* vii 402ff;
                                Plutarch *Theseus*)
See also *Egeus*
    Lewis C. D.   *Ariadne on Naxos*

Aegina   An island in the Aegean, named after

Aegina, mother of king *Aeacus* by *Zeus* in the form of a flame. Aeacus grew up there alone after his mother had died, supposedly from drinking water poisoned by the jealous *Hera*. At his plea Zeus turned the local ants into people (*Myrmidons*), over whom Aeacus held a long and peaceful reign — or perhaps the people, during a famine, developed their husbandry with the diligence of ants.

(Ovid *Metamorphoses* vi 103ff;
Pausanias II 29; Strabo VIII vi 16)
Byron   *The Curse of Minerva* 7ff
Spenser   *Faerie Queene* III xi 35

Aegle, Aegles   A nymph, daughter of Panopeus. In some accounts, *Theseus* fell in love with her after his desertion of *Ariadne*.

(Plutarch *Theseus* 20)
Shakespeare   *Midsummer Night's Dream*
II i 75-80

Aegon   A shepherd in pastoral poetry.

(Virgil *Eclogues* III 2;
Theocritus *Idylls* IV 26)
Pope   *Autumn* 5-6, 55

Aegyptus   King of Egypt and brother of Danaeus of *Argos*. One of the brothers had fifty daughters and the other had fifty sons. Danaeus ordered the daughters to kill the sons, with whom they had all married; but *Lynceus*, a son, escaped with the help of *Hypermnestra*, a daughter, and either killed Danaeus or was reconciled to him.
See also *Danaides, Egiste*

Aelian, Aelianus   Claudius Aelianus, Roman rhetorician and writer of the 2nd Century AD. He was famous particularly for his Greek moral teachings by animal fable.
Browning R.   *The Ring and the Book*
i 232-7, viii 511-6

Aemilian Way   The Via Aemilia, a road running north from Rome to Aequileia on the north Adriatic coast.
Milton   *Paradise Regained* iv 67-70

Aeneas   A Trojan prince, son of *Anchises* and *Venus*, married to *Creusa*, daughter of *Priam* of *Troy*, from whom he had a son *Ascanius* or *Iulus*. Aeneas was born on Mt *Ida*

and reared by nymphs. He fought bravely in the Trojan War under the command of Priam's son *Hector*. He was then alleged to have carried away Anchises on his shoulders, and led Ascanius by hand, as Troy burned, back to Mt Ida (Virgil *Aeneid* II 705ff). Subsequently Aeneas sailed away with twenty shiploads of followers with the intention of founding a city, initially in *Thrace*. Their adventures, and the conflict between *Venus* and *Juno* form the substance of Virgil's *Aeneid*, itself a myth of origin for the Roman Empire of which Aeneas, through his sons *Iulus* and Sylvius, was felt to be a direct ancestor. The sense of duty with which he was felt to have pursued this divine purpose led to the general appellation, from Virgil, of 'pi(o)us Aeneas'. The matter of Rome (i.e. its origin and legendary history) is, in selective fashion, depicted on a shield made by *Vulcan* and presented to Aeneas by Venus (Virgil *Aeneid* VIII). A story especially loved by poets is Aeneas's affair, conflicting with his duty, with *Queen Dido* (Virgil *Aeneid* IV). Subsequently (in *Aeneid* VI) he was guided into *Hades* by two doves, who led him to a magical golden bough.
See also *Eneas, Enyas*
— *General*
Browning E. B.   *The Battle of Marathon*
15-20, 900-4
Butler S.   *Hudibras* I i 475-8, I iii 490-3
Chaucer   *The House of Fame* 143-8
Cowley   *To Mr Hobbs* 5
Sitting and Drinking in the
Chair 3
Dryden   *The Hind and the Panther* iii
766ff
Jonson   *To William Roe* 12-4
Marlowe   *Tamburlaine* i 2174ff
Milton   *Paradise Lost* ix 13-19
Noyes   *Drake, Exordium*
Prior   *Carmen Seculare* 557-8
Down Hall 1-4
Ode Inscribed to the Queen
281-3
On Fleet 15-8
Shakespeare   *Cymbeline* III iv 55-9
Shenstone   *Economy* iii 123-8
Spenser   *Faerie Queene* III ix 41-3
Hymn in Honour of Love
231-7
Tennyson   *On a Mourner* 31-5

— *leaving Troy*
Jonson   *The New Inn* I i
Pope   *Temple of Fame* 207-9
Shakespeare   *Julius Caesar* I ii 100ff
        King Henry VI pt 2 V ii
        62-5
— *and the Golden Bough*
Denham   *Progress of Learning* 5-6
— *and Dido*
Marlowe   *Dido Queen of Carthage*
        719-25, 1039ff, 1175-80
Pope   *The Rape of the Lock* ii 92-5
Shakespeare   *Antony and Cleopatra* IV
        xiv 51-4
        Hamlet II ii 428ff
        King Henry VI pt 2 III ii
        114-7
        Midsummer Night's Dream
        I i 169ff
        The Tempest I ii 70-7
        Titus Andronicus II iii
        21-6, V iii 80-7
Wyatt   *Jopas' Song* 1-4

Aeneid   The epic poem (26-19BC) of Virgil, telling of the adventures of *Aeneas* in flight from fallen *Troy* until his arrival at *Latium*, where he married *Lavinia*, daughter of King *Latinus*, to be the ancestor of the Julian line of Roman Emperors.

Aeole
See *Aeolus*
Spenser   *Muiopotmos* 419-20

Aeolia, Aeolian   Of *Aeolus*, god of storms and winds, who lived on the floating island of Aeolia, north of eastern Sicily. There is some evidence for the existence of a Classical Aeolian harp or lyre (see Pindar *Pythian Ode* i), but English poetic references are, as a rule, to the wind-vibrated harp developed at the turn of the 16th-17th Centuries.
Shelley   *Oedipus Tyrannus* I i 171-2
        The Birth of Pleasure 4-7
Tennyson   *The Lover's Dream* i 463-7
Wordsworth   *The Prelude* vii 531-4

Aeolus   God of the winds, who occupied *Aeolia*. *Zeus* gave Aeolus command of the winds which he kept in a cave and released at will. Aeolus was also known as *Hippotades*,

being son of Hippotas, and he was father of the ill-fated *Canace*. He is an amalgam of various myths, and accounts of him differ. He was said to have tied up the winds in a bag and given them to *Ulysses* to aid his return to *Ithaca*, but Ulysses's men released them and were driven back to Aeolia.
    (Homer *Odyssey* X; Ovid *Metamorphoses*
        i 268ff, xiv 224ff *Heroides* xviii 46;
            Virgil *Aeneid* i 50-64)
See also *Eolus*
Bridges   *Prometheus the Firegiver*
        922-7
Crashaw   *Upon the Gunpowder Treason*
        29-30
Eliot T. S.   *Sweeney Erect* 5-7
Keats   *Endymion* iii 653-5, 951-4
Marvell   *Last Instructions to a Painter*
        543ff
Spenser   *Faerie Queene* I vii 9, III vi 44,
        IV ix 23
Young   *The Merchant* iii

Aeschines   A rival orator of *Demosthenes* in the 4th Century BC. Aeschines and Demosthenes were deeply involved in the political intrigues arising from the war between *Athens* and *Philip of Macedon*. The struggle between the orators was eventually won by Demosthenes and Aeschines retired from the political scene to teach rhetoric.
Skelton   *The Garland of Laurel*

Aeschylus   Aeschylus, the first Athenian tragic dramatist of stature, was born at Eleusis in 525BC and died at Gela in southern Sicily in 456BC. He fought at the Battle of *Marathon* in which his brother, *Cynegirus*, was killed, and he may also have been at *Plataea* and *Salamis*. He was associated with the new city of *Aetna* (founded 476BC to replace Catana on the slopes of the mountain) and wrote a lost play (*Women of Aetna*) in its honour. The author of some eighty tragedies, of which seven survive, he was probably largely responsible for the form and moods of Greek tragedy, including the importance of *hybris* (tragic pride). His *Persians* (402ff) includes the song 'Sons of Hellas, free your native land' as a battle song of Salamis.
Browning E. B.   *An Island* 26-7
        A Vision of Poets 301-9

7

Browning R. *Wine of Cyprus* 11
Aristophanes' Apology 120-2
Balaustion's Adventure 37-9, 76-7, 130-1
A Death in the Desert 279-86
Sordello i 65-8, iii 950-4
Jonson   *To Shakespeare* 31-7
Pope   *The Dunciad* iii 311-2
Swinburne   *Athens* ant. ii, ep. ii

Aesculapeus, Aesculapius   A deified mortal who became god of healing. He was son of *Apollo* and either Arsinoe of *Messenia* or *Coronis* of Epidaurus in eastern Peloponnesus — Epidaurus became the centre of his cult. The future god was born and reared in obscurity because, it was said, Coronis, while pregnant with him, lay with Ischys. For so insulting Apollo, he (or *Artemis*) killed her and Ischys, and turned the crow who had informed on them from white to black. Apollo rescued the unborn child and arranged for him to be reared by *Chiron* the Centaur, who later taught him healing arts. Aesculapius's undoing in his medical career lay in attempting to revive a dead patient (*Glaucus, Lycurgus, Hymenaeus*, or *Hippolytus* — the latter is most usual) with the help of some blood given to him by *Athene*. For this presumptuous act Zeus killed Aesculapius with a thunderbolt. In 234BC Aesculapius was transferred to Rome in the form of a huge snake in order to cure a plague, and he was then worshipped as a Roman god on the Tiberian island outside the city. Snakes and cocks were sacred to him. He is depicted with a very large beard.

(Apollodorus III x 3-4; Homer *Iliad* iv 193; Ovid *Metamorphoses* xv 626 ff; Pausanias II xxvi 3-10)

See also *Esculapius*
Herrick   *Upon Prudence Baldwin* 3-7
Jonson   *The Alchemist* IV i
To Dr Empiric 1-2
The Magnetic Lady V ii
Shakespeare   *Merry Wives of Windsor* II iii 27
Spenser   *Faerie Queene* I v 36, 39, 43

Aeson   The eldest son of Cretheus, king of Iolcus; Aeson was usurped in succession by

his half-brother *Pelias*. His son, by Alcimede or Polymede, was *Jason* whose existence was kept secret for twenty years until he led the Argonauts. Pelias forced Aeson to commit suicide or, it was also said, Aeson was restored to youth by Medea.

(Apollodorus I 9; Ovid *Metamorphoses* vii 285)
Carew   *To the Countess of Anglesey* 7-8
Davies, Sir J.   *Nosce Teipsum* xxxix 63-4
Drayton   *Henry to Rosamond* 85-9
Herrick   *To his Mistresses* 7-10
Jonson   *Volpone* I i
Lovelace   *To My Friend Mr E. R.* 40-4
Shakespeare   *Merchant of Venice* V i 12-14
Wordsworth   *Laodamia* 79-84

Aesop   The Thracian fabulist of the 6th Century BC, who started life as a slave. His life is appropriately surrounded by meaningful legend. He was supposed to have been ordered by King *Croesus* of *Lydia* to consult the Delphic oracle, but when he satirised it the Delphians threw him from a rock to his death. As a slave he was said to have been asked by a bidder what he could do and to have replied 'Nothing', because his fellow slaves replied 'Everything', leaving him no scope. The Fables are probably a compilation from several hands.

(Herodotus ii 134)
Clare   *Written in Prison* 11-13
Donne   *Epigram — Mercurius* 1-3
Satire V 88-9
Dryden   *The Hind and the Panther* ii 48-9, iii 6-7
Goldsmith   *Epilogue Spoken by Mr Lee Lewes* 27 ff
Kipling   *The Fabulists* 1-4
Marlowe   *Jew of Malta* 2139-43
Shakespeare   *King Henry VI pt 2* V v 25-6

Aesop, Aesopus   A Roman tragic actor and friend of *Cicero* in the 1st Century BC. He was a contemporary of *Roscius*, whose name is often linked as a comic actor with his.

(Horace *Epistles* II ii 82)
Jonson   *To Edward Alleyn* 1-8

Aethon   One of the four horses of the

chariot of *Apollo* in his guise as the sun.

> (Ovid *Metamorphoses* ii 153-5)
> Keats   *Endymion* iii 364-5

Aetius   Flavius Aetius, a patrician of the
5th Century AD, who was consul three times
and the right-hand-man of Emperor *Valentinian III*, who was uninterested in statecraft
or war. He was murdered by Valentinian in
454 AD, but the Emperor was assassinated in
revenge by followers of Aetius in 455.

> Lovelace   *To Fletcher Revived* 14ff

Aetna   The volcanic mountain in Sicily and
a town (also Catana) nearby. The eruptions,
which seem to have occurred, if occasionally,
from the earliest times, were attributed to the
giant *Typhon* or *Enceladus* within. Aetna was
also held to be the forge where *Vulcan* made
Jove's thunderbolts, and the home of the
Cyclopes.

> (Ovid *Metamorphoses* v 346ff;
> Pindar *Olympic Ode* iv 7;
> Virgil *Aeneid* iii 571ff, 674ff)

See also *Etna*
> Keats   *Otho the Great* V 5 120-5
> Meredith   *The Day of the Daughter of
> Hades*
> Shelley   *Ode to Liberty* 183-4
> Spenser   *Faerie Queene* I xi 44, II viii
> 20, 29; III ii 32
> Swift   *Ode to the King* 97-8
> Tennyson   *The Lover's Dream* iv 17-18

Aetnean

See *Aetna*
> Keats   *Endymion* ii 585-7
> Shelley   *Oedipus Tyrannus* I i 169-72

Affrycan

See *Africanus*
> Chaucer   *Parliament of Fowls* 29ff

African (Hannibal)
See *Hannibal*

Africanus (1) (Africane)   A title conferred
on the *Scipio* family, and in particular on
Publius Cornelius Scipio, Scipio Major (Scipio
The Great), the Roman general who lived from
236-184 BC, for his valour in the *Punic Wars*.
He was appointed to command Spain in 210 BC.

He defeated the Carthaginians and established
Roman authority in 206, only to see the Carthaginians rise again under *Hannibal* in 202.
In 204 as consul he invaded Africa, in spite of
the delaying tactics of *Fabius* (Cunctator), and
within a year captured Tunis. In 202 he finally
defeated Hannibal at Zama and was given the
title Africanus. Thereafter he was occupied
mainly as legate and in the internal politics of
Rome. Served with accusations of corruption
in later life, he loftily discounted them and
retired to a country estate near Naples. In
210 BC, at the fall of New Carthage, he gave
back a beautiful Spanish captive to her betrothed, Allucius.

> (Livy xxvi 50)

See also *Cipioun*
> Milton   *Paradise Regained* ii 199-200
> Spenser   *Sonnet 'Those prudent
> heads . . .'*

Africanus (2)   Aemilianus Numantinus
Scipio, adopted by the elder son of Scipio
The Great, achieved distinction in the Third
Punic and Numantine Wars in the 2nd Century
BC, when he ended Spanish resistance to Rome.
He was much admired by *Cicero*, who repr-
esented him as the ideal of wise statesmanship.
The commentary of *Macrobius* (5th Century
AD) on part of Cicero's *De Republica* was
very influential on medieval and later poetry;
it recounts the *Somnium Scipionis* in which
Scipio the Great appeared in a dream to his
descendant, foretold his future and instructed
him in the virtues needed for gaining life after
death.

See also *Cipioun*

Agamemnon   There are many, often conflicting, versions of Agamemnon's terrible
story. In the commonest (basically Homeric),
he and *Menelaus* were sons of *Atreus*, king of
Mycenae; they waged a lengthy battle for the
throne with *Thyestes*, who was ultimately
defeated by Agamemnon. Menelaus, who came
to rule *Sparta*, was married to *Helen*, and when
she was abducted by *Paris* he won Agamemnon's help to bring her back from *Troy*. Agamemnon married Helen's sister, *Clytemnestra*,
daughter of Tyndareus of Sparta, and there
followed the Trojan War, in which Agamemnon
commanded the Greeks. In his absence, Clytem-

nestra was unfaithful to Agamemnon and ingeniously planned his murder on his return. To achieve this, she gave him a net or tunic with tied sleeves as he emerged from the bath, and struck him down as he attempted to put the garment on or wrestled with the net. Their children, *Orestes* and *Electra*, became caught up in a duty of revenge with appalling consequences.

(Homer *Iliad* passim; *Odyssey* iv, xi 404 ff;
Aeschylus *Agamemnon* passim)

See also *Iphigenia*

Browning E. B.	*Aurora Leigh* v 139-41
Eliot T. S.	*Sweeney Among the Nightingales* 46-50
Marlowe	*Jew of Malta* 174-6
Masefield	*Clytemnestra* 4 ff
Shakespeare	*King Henry VI pt 3* II ii 146-9
	Troilus and Cressida I iii 54-5, III iii 274
Swinburne	*On the Cliffs* 152 ff
Thomas, Dylan	*Greek Play in a Garden* 4-8, 23-4
Yeats	*Leda and the Swan* 1 ff

Agamenoun
See *Agamemnon*
    Chaucer   *Troilus and Criseyde* iii 379-82

Aganippe, Aganippa   A fountain at the foot of Mt *Helicon*, sacred to the *Muses*, who were sometimes called Aganippedes.

(Ovid *Fasti* v 7; Pausanias IX xxix 5;
Virgil *Eclogues* x 12)

Drayton	*Endymion and Phoebe* 137 ff
	Polyolbion v 83-8
Milton	*Lycidas* 15-16
Pope	*A Rhapsody* 1-6
Sidney	*Astrophel and Stella* lxxiv 1-4

Agathon   An Athenian tragic poet, victor of the Lenaea contest of 416 BC, celebrated in Plato's *Symposium*, where he utters one of the speeches in praise of love. Only scanty fragments survive, but the many references to Agathon suggest that his importance was second only to the triad of *Aeschylus*, *Sophocles* and *Euripides*. With the latter he was friendly and, like Euripides, he spent his later years at the court of *Archelaus* in Macedonia.

(Plato *Symposium* 195 ff)

See also *Agaton*

Browning R.	*Aristophanes' Apology* 314-8
Shelley	*Fragment connected with Epipsychidion*
	Prince Athanase 224-9

Agaton
See *Agathon*
    Chaucer   *Legend of Good Women* 525-6

Agave (1)   The daughter of *Cadmus* and Hermione of *Thebes*, and mother of *Pentheus*. She was supposed to have killed her husband, Echion, during a Bacchic revel. Possibly out of her mind, she dismembered Pentheus, either because he spied on and tried to prevent a Bacchic revel, or because she mistook him for a wild animal. The madness was supposed to have been inflicted by the Gods as a punishment for her cursing the pregnancy of her sister *Semele* with *Dionysus* by Zeus. The connections made between these events vary.

See also *Leucothea*

Cowley	*On a Copy of Verses by my Lord Broghill* 2
Shelley	*Prometheus Unbound* iv 470-5
Spenser	*Faerie Queene* V viii 47
Swinburne	*Tiresias* 73-6

Agave (2)   A *Nereid*.

(Apollodorus I ii 6)
    Spenser   *Faerie Queene* IV ii 49

Agdestes, Agdistis   A Phrygian mountain and goddess or spirit whose cult centred there. Agdestis represented the elemental force of Nature and was sometimes identified with *Cybele*.

(Strabo XII v 3)
    Spenser   *Faerie Queene* II xii 47-8

Age of Gold
See *Golden Age*
    Milton   *On the Morning of Christ's Nativity* 135

Agenor   Son of *Neptune* and brother of *Belus*, Agenor was king of Phoenicia. He was father of *Cadmus*, *Europa* and *Phoenix*, the country's eponym; in later life he was blind.

(Apollodorus II i 4, III i 1;
Apollonius Rhodius ii 234ff)
Chaucer   *Legend of Good Women* 110-4
Drayton   *Polyolbion* xx 169-71
Shakespeare   *Taming of the Shrew* I i
162-5
Spenser   *Faerie Queene* IV xi 15
Swinburne   *Celaeus*

Ages of Man
See *Golden Age*

Agis   Agis III, king of *Sparta* in the 4th
Century BC. He had mixed fortunes in securing
Greek support against the Persians, raised an
army of mercenaries, and was heavily defeated
by Antipater at Megalopolis in 330BC.
Thomson   *Winter* 487-9

Aglaia
See *Graces*
Spenser   *Faerie Queene* VI x 22

Agraulus   The wife of *Cecrops*.
See *Herse*

Agrawlos
See *Agraulus*
Chaucer   *Troilus and Criseyde* iii 729-32

Agrippa Postumus   So called because he was
born to Julia, in 12BC, after the death of his
father, Marcus Agrippa, an influential friend
of *Augustus*. (Julia was a daughter of Augustus
by Scribonia, one of several wives.) On the
death of Augustus, Agrippa Postumus was put
up as his heir in rivalry to *Tiberius* — both had
been adopted sons of the Emperor — but died
within a very short time in mysterious circumstances. He combined physical beauty with
notorious depravity and sullenness.
(Tacitus, *Annals*)
Masefield   *Letter from Pontus*

Agrippina (1) (Vipsania)   The wife of
Germanicus, nephew, adopted son, and rival
of *Tiberius*, whom Agrippina suspected of
being involved in the poisoning of Germanicus.
Tiberius and she constantly quarrelled and in
due course he had her banished to Pandataria,
an island off *Cumae*, where she died in 33 AD.
Jonson   *Sejanus* II ii

Tennyson   *The Princess* ii 69-71

Agrippina (2) (The Younger)   The mother
of *Nero*, whom she caused to succeed her
uncle *Claudius* by having him adopted by
Claudius as guardian to his own son *Britannicus*, who was four years younger than Nero.
She may have poisoned Claudius, and was
herself assassinated by Nero, on the grounds
that he could not rule dependent on her, in
59 AD.
Gray   *Agrippina* 38-9

Aidoneus   'Ruler of many' — a name for
Dis or *Pluto*.
(Homeric Hymn XIII *To Demeter* 84)
Bridges   *Demeter* 713-4
Tennyson   *Demeter and Persephone* 35-9

Ajax   The answer to the prayer of *Heracles*
to *Zeus* to send his friend *Telamon* a son; an
eagle appeared and Ajax was so named ('eagle')
in consequence. Ajax shared with *Achilles* the
reputation of being the tallest, most handsome
and perhaps most heroic of the Greeks at *Troy*,
but he was also renowned for stupidity. He
fought *Hector* in a duel and the two parted in
mutual respect, exchanging a sword and a belt.
He lost control of his senses when *Odysseus*,
rather than he, was awarded the prize of
Achilles' sword on the latter's death, and he
destroyed a flock of sheep in his fury, believing
them to be his enemies. On returning to reason,
he killed himself with the sword received from
Hector. *Agamemnon* and *Menelaus* refused
to bury him, but relented on the advice of
Odysseus. Ajax had a particularly fine shield
apparently covered with seven layers of bull-
skin — to Ovid he is 'lord of the seven-fold
shield'.
(Apollodorus *Epitome* v 4-7; Ovid
Metamorphoses xii-xiii; Sophocles *Ajax*)
Butler S.   *Hudibras* I ii 299ff
Cleveland   *Upon a Miser* 29-30
Crabbe   *The Village* i 86ff
Jonson   *Epistle to Elizabeth* 51ff
Marvell   *The Unfortunate Lover* 45-8
Pope   *Essay on Criticism* 366ff
Prior   *On Fleet* 15-8
Shakespeare   *Antony and Cleopatra* IV
xiv 38-41
Cymbeline IV ii 253-4

King Henry VI pt 2 V i 26-7
King Lear II ii 119
Rape of Lucrece 1398-1400
Titus Andronicus I i 379-82
Troilus and Cressida I ii 28-9,
I iii 381, II i 31-4

Alastor   A non-specific avenging power or its victim.

(Aeschylus *Agamemnon* 1501;
Eumenides 236)
Shelley   *Alastor*

Alba   Alba Longa, a Latian city said to have been built by *Iulus* as his capital after he had succeeded *Aeneas* as king. It was known as Longa because it was built along the Alban hill.

(Livy i 3)
Spenser   *Faerie Queene* III ix 43

Albion   Albion, son of *Neptune*, established a kingdom in Gt Britain (excluding Ireland). The name is also given to the country, and the god is perhaps a mythologising of a name in fact owed to the white (*albus*) cliffs of Dover (which are often mentioned with the name and are not cited here).
Collins   *Ode to Liberty* 109, 129
Blake   *King Edward III* vi 55-60
Dryden   *Albion and Albanius* 1
Pope   *Spring* 6
Spenser   *Faerie Queene* II x 6,
IV xi 15-16

Alcaeus   A poet of *Lesbos*, contemporary with *Sappho* to whom he addressed poems, in the 6th Century BC.
Byron   *English Bards* 417-20
Coleridge   *The Picture* 170-1
Collins   *Ode to Liberty* 8-9
Pope   *Temple of Fame* 202-5
Wordsworth   *Departing Summer hath
Assumed* 37-9

Alcamenes   Greek sculptor of the 5th Century BC, a pupil and rival of *Phidias*.
Browning R.   *Aristophanes' Apology*
490-2

Alceste
See *Alcestis*

Chaucer   *The Franklin's Tale* 1442-4
Legend of Good Women
213-9, 510ff
Troilus and Criseyde v 1527ff

Alcestis   The second wife of *Admetus* and daughter of *Pelias*. Pelias promised his daughter to whomever could bring him a chariot drawn by a lion and a boar. The test was passed by Admetus — who owned the cattle which *Apollo* tended whilst in exile from heaven — with the help of Apollo. Alcestis gave her life to redeem Admetus from the fury of her brother Acastus, who was appalled by the killing of Pelias by his daughters, at the instigation of *Medea*. Alcestis was returned to life by *Persephone* or *Hercules*.

(Apollodorus I 8; Euripides *Alcestis*)
See also *Alceste*
Browning R.   *Aristophanes' Apology*
193-8
Balaustion's Adventure
569-72, 2598-2602
Milton   *Sonnet* xxiii 1-4
Wordsworth   *Laodamia* 79-84

Alcibiades   Athenian general and statesman of the 5th Century BC. He was a relative of *Pericles*, who acted as his guardian, and he became a pupil and close friend of *Socrates*. He was apparently self-indulgent and extravagant and his known weaknesses may have been a disadvantage to Socrates in the philosopher's trial for corruption of youth. He allied *Athens*, *Argos* and others against *Sparta*, but the alliance was defeated in 418BC. He began an expedition against Sicily but was recalled to Athens to stand trial for mutilation of the statues of *Hermes*. He escaped to Sparta and tried to provoke war with Greece, but he was subsequently reappointed in Athens, though he did not regain popular support. Regarded by the Athenians as a symbolic last hope in the Spartan wars, he was killed by the Spartans in 404BC. Before his death he was supposed to have dreamed that he saw his mistress, *Timandra*, bearing his severed head and painting it as that of a woman. At his death, she tried to bury him in her own clothes and was killed in the act.

(Plutarch *Alcibiades*;
Thucydides V-VIII)

Byron	*Don Juan* xv 11
Chaucer	*Book of the Duchess* 1055-75
	Franklin's Tale 1439-41
Daniel	*To my Brother and Friend John*
	Florio 96-8
MacNiece	*Autumn Journal* ix
	Autumn Sequel xix
Marlowe	*Edward II* 689-94
Yeats	*The Saint and the Hunchback*

Alcides   A name for *Hercules*, after his grandfather Alcaeus.

Byron	*Marino Faliero* II i 390-1
	Sardanapalus III i 218ff
Chapman	*Ovid's Banquet of Sense*
Cowley	*Nemean Ode* 6ff
Drayton	*Endymion and Phoebe* 30-4
Dryden	*Britannia Rediviva* 55-8
	Threnodia Augustalis 446ff
Fletcher P.	*Piscatory Eclogues* vii 20
	Purple Island xii 16, 66
Jonson	*On the Famous Voyage* 50-5
Lovelace	*To Fletcher Revived* 28-32
Marlowe	*Hero and Leander* ii 120
	Tamburlaine i 2310-1
Milton	*Paradise Lost* ii 539-44
	Paradise Regained iv 562-5
Pope	*Temple of Fame* 81-2
Prior	*On Beauty* 10ff
	The Wedding Night 1ff
Shakespeare	*The Merchant of Venice*
	II i 32-4
	Titus Andronicus IV ii 93-7
Spenser	*Faerie Queene* I vii 17, II x 31,
	vii 61, xii 7, IV i 23, V viii 31,
	VI xii 32
	Muiopotmos 65-72

Alcinous   King of Phaeacia, an island (now Kerkyra) in the Ionian Sea, who entertained *Ulysses* and was the father of Nausicaa. He was celebrated as a teller of tall stories and for the beauty of his palace and gardens, and his land abounded in fruit — pears, pomegranates, apples.

(Homer *Odyssey* vii 112ff; Pliny XIX xix 4; Virgil *Georgics* II 87)

Clough	*Trunks the Forest Yielded* 1ff
Fletcher P.	*Piscatory Eclogues* vii 21
Milton	*At a Vacation Exercise* 47-9
	Paradise Lost v 338-41,
	ix 439-41

Alcione
See *Halcyone*

Cowley	*My Heart Discovered* 31ff

Alciphron   The sophist author of a collection of 'Letters' by Athenians to courtesans in the 3rd Century BC.

Swinburne	*Dolores* 299-301

Alcmena, Alcmene   The mother, by *Zeus*, of *Hercules/Heracles*. Usually said to be the daughter of Electryon (son of *Perseus* and king of *Mycenae*) and Anaxo, Alcmena married her cousin *Amphitryon* but would not consummate the marriage until he avenged the death of her brothers in a cattle-raid. In the process he killed Electryon, whose brother (*Sthenelus*) usurped the throne and exiled Alcmena, who fled to *Thebes*. Amphitryon raised an army and crushed the invaders, but on coming to Alcmena he found that someone had preceded him to her bed. *Tiresias* explained that this was Zeus who had arranged to prolong his amours for three days and three nights by instructing *Mercury* to stop the rising of the sun (*Phoebus*) for this time. In due course — after complications wrought by *Hera* in jealousy of Zeus's infidelity — Alcmena produced twins, Heracles and *Iphicles*, one for each lover. After Amphitryon's death, she was said to have married *Rhadamanthus*.

(Euripides *Children of Heracles*;
Homer *Iliad* xix 96ff; Ovid
Metamorphoses ix 280ff, vi 103ff;
Pindar *Pythian Ode* ix;
Plautus *Amphitryon*)

Prior	*The Ladle* 101ff
	The Wedding Night 1ff
Spenser	*Faerie Queene* III xi 34
	Mother Hubberds Tale 1297-9

Alcyon, Alcyone
See *Halcyone*

Chapman	*Andromeda Liberata*
Chaucer	*Book of the Duchess* 107-14,
	136-46, 203-14

Alecto   One of the *Furies*.
See also *Eumenides*, (*Alete, Electo*)

Crashaw	*Sospetto D'Herode* 34
Dryden	*Oedipus* Song III 21-4
Fletcher P.	*The Purple Island* xii 35

Keats   *Endymion* ii 874-5
Shakespeare   *King Henry IV pt 2* V v 37
Skelton   *Philip Sparrow*

Aleian   A flat part of Cilicia on the south coast of Turkey, where it was said that *Bellerophon* fell after his attempted flight to heaven on *Pegasus*.

(Strabo xiv 5)
Milton   *Paradise Lost* vii 16-9

Alete
See *Eumenides, Alecto*
Chaucer   *Troilus and Criseyde* IV 22-4

Alexander III (The Great)   Born at *Pella*, the capital of Macedonia, and sometimes called 'Pellean', Alexander was king of Macedonia for nine brilliant years (336-323 BC). Nominated commander-in-chief by the Greek states he conquered Phoenicia, Palestine, Egypt, Tyre, Asia Minor, Persia and the Punjab. In 332, defeating Egypt, he reached the Temple of *Ammon* where priests obsequiously called him 'Son of Ammon'; in 335 he marched on *Thebes* and razed it to the ground; in 326 he crossed the Indus. He was an extravagant and heroic character, explorer, supreme military strategist and general; also a political and economic theorist of force and originality — he had been a pupil of *Aristotle*. In his life he was so worshipped that his sweat was taken to be perfume denoting divinity. He died, most probably of fever, though reputedly of drink, aged 33 in 323 BC.

(Plutarch *Alexander*)
See also *Alisandre (2), Alixandre, Darius III, Hephaestion, Pellean*
Arnold   *Iseult of Brittany* 143 ff
Auden   *An Island Cemetery* 13-16
Burns   *The Fornicator* 43-7
Byron   *The Age of Bronze* 28 ff, 35-8
Chaucer   *House of Fame* 1412-4
Dryden   *On the Death of Lord Hastings* 15-8
Graves   *Troublesome Fame* 1-4
Gray   *Lines Spoken by the Ghost of John Dennis* 51
Jonson   *Sejanus* I i
Keats   *Endymion* ii 24-5
    King Stephen I iv 33-4
    To J. H. Reynolds Esq. 5-9

Marlowe   *Doctor Faustus* 1035-8
    Jew of Malta 1400 ff
Marvell   *Appleton House* 427-8
Milton   *Paradise Regained* iii 82-7, iv 251-3
Pope   *Epistle to Dr Arbuthnot* 117
    Essay on Man iv 220
    Temple of Fame 151-2
Shakespeare   *Coriolanus* V iv 20-1
    Hamlet V i 207-8
    King Henry V III i 19-21
Spenser   *Faerie Queene* I v 48, II ix 45, IV i 22
Swinburne   *Song for the Centenary of Landor* 41
Tennyson   *Persia* 17-23, 26-32
Yeats   *Among School Children* vi
    The Saint and the Hunchback

Alexandria   The city, founded as a naval base by *Alexander the Great* in 331 BC on his conquest of Egypt. It was a great commercial and cultural centre under the Ptolomies and for a thousand years after its foundation. During the Roman Empire it was regarded as the second city to Rome.
See also *Alisaundre (1)*

Alexis   An unresponsive youth in pastoral poetry where he is beloved of the shepherd *Corydon*.

(Virgil *Eclogue* ii)
Pope   *Winter* 11-2

Alimeda   A *Nereid*.
Spenser   *Faerie Queene* IV ii 51

Alisaundre (1)
See *Alexandria*
Chaucer   *Canon Yeoman's Tale* 972-5

Alisaundre (2)
See *Alexander*
Chaucer   *Manciple's Tale* 226-34
    Monk's Tale 3837-50

Alixandre
See *Alexander*
Chaucer   *House of Fame* 914-20

Allectus   The first minister of *Carausius*, self-appointed emperor of Britain under

Diocletian. He assassinated Carausius in 293 AD, and in 296 was defeated in Hampshire by *Asclepiodatus*.

Spenser   *Faerie Queene* II x 57-8

Almageste
See *Ptolemy (2)*
   Chaucer   *The Miller's Tale* 3208-11
                Wife of Bath's Prologue 180-3, 324-7

Almena
See *Alcmena*
   Chaucer   *Troilus and Criseyde* iii 1427-8

Alpheus   An Arcadian river in which the nymph *Arethusa* bathed. Pursued by the amorous river-god, she was protected by a cloud of mist sent by *Diana* and transformed into a fountain in *Ortygia*. It was held that the River Alpheus passed beneath the Adriatic following the waters of his beloved Arethusa and emerging at the Sicilian island of Ortygia. Alpheus and Arethusa were invoked as muses of pastoral poetry.

          (Ovid *Metamorphoses* v 576 ff; Pausanias V 7)

Chapman   *Shadow of Night*
Coleridge   *Kubla Khan* 3-5
Cowley   *Coldness* 4
Keats   *Endymion* ii 948 ff, 1005-12
Milton   *Arcades* 28-31
        Lycidas 132-3
Pope   *Dunciad* ii 314-9
Shelley   *Arethusa* 14 ff, 73 ff
        Fragments Written for Hellas 8-9, 15-16
Spenser   *Faerie Queene* IV xi 21
Swinburne   *Song for the Centenary of Landor* 29

Althaea
See *Meleager*
   Shakespeare   *King Henry IV pt 2* II ii 85-7
                  King Henry VI pt 2 I i 227-30
   Swinburne   *Atalanta in Calydon* 247-302, 1583-7

Alysaunder
See *Alexander*

Chaucer   *Book of the Duchess* 1055-75

Amalthea, Almatheia   Amalthea, the she-goat nurse of *Zeus*, was by him made into a star (Capella — she-goat) and had wonderful horns filled with nectar and ambrosia, one of which (the *Cornucopia*) was filled with fruit and given to Zeus. According to some accounts, she was mother to *Dionysus* by *Ammon*. The very fertile part of Libya where this happened was shaped like a bull and so called Hesperonkeras. 'Amalthea's Horn' became proverbial for very fertile land. Yet another version concerns the legend of *Achelaus*.

        (Diodorus Siculus iii 67-70; Ovid *Fasti* v 121)

Burns   *To R.G. of F.* 29-30
Carew   *To my Friend G.N.* 57-60
Chapman   *Shadow of Night*
Keats   *Endymion* ii 446-9
Milton   *Paradise Lost* iv 275-9
        Paradise Regained ii 353-6
Spenser   *Mutability Cantos* vii 41

Amaryllis   A country girl in pastoral poetry, symbolic of pleasurable diversion and of the capricious moods of women.

        (Theocritus *Idylls* iii, iv 36; Virgil *Eclogues* i 5, 36, ii 14-15, iii 82)
Milton   *Lycidas* 64-6

Amasis   Amasis II rose from the ranks to become king of Egypt in the 6th Century BC: sent to quell a revolt against King Apries, he was preferred by the rebels and defeated Apries. He delighted in unconventional behaviour but reigned for 44 years, instituting notable legal reforms and constructing big temples and monuments.

        (Herodotus ii 161 ff)
Shelley   *The Witch of Atlas* 646-8

Amazon   A nation of women reputed to have lived before the Trojan War in Cappadocia, Western Turkey, and celebrated for their warlike habit and ferocity. They were held to have invaded Attica and been defeated by *Theseus* when he had carried off their queen *Antiope* (*Hippolyte*) the daughter of *Mars*.

        (Herodotus iv 110; Homer *Iliad* iii 184 ff; Virgil *Aeneid* v 311; Plutarch *Theseus* xxvii)

See also *Penthesilea*
    Chaucer   *Knight's Tale* 860-8
    Dryden   *Annus Mirabilis* 193-6
    Gray   *A Long Story* 29-30
    Shakespeare   *King Henry VI pt 3* I iv
                       111-5
                       King John V ii 154-8
    Spenser   *Faerie Queene* II iii 31

Amazonian   The leaves of the Indian fig-tree are likened to Amazonian shields.
                          (Pliny xii 11)
See *Amazon*
    Milton   *Paradise Lost* ix 1110-1

Ambracia   A city near *Actium*.
See also *Cleopatra*
    Byron   *Childe Harold* ii 45

Ambrosia, Ambrosial   The food, as nectar was the drink, of the gods. Ambrosia was supposed to have an overwhelming scent and to confer immortality on those who ate it. According to some accounts, it was stolen from the gods by *Tantalus*, for which he was doomed to live in hell tempted by food or water beyond his reach.
               (Homer *Odyssey* iv 445ff;
            Pindar *Olympian Ode* i 60ff)
    Keats   *Endymion* ii 809-10
    Milton   *Comus* 16-7, 837-40
                Paradise Lost v 55-7, ii 244-5,
                iv 218-20, v 641-2, vi 474-5,
                xi 279
                Paradise Regained iv 587-90
    Shelley   *Orpheus* 65-6
    Spenser   *Faerie Queene* III vi 18,
                IV Prologue 4
                *Hymn in Honour of Heavenly
                Love* 22-7
                Ruins of Time 398-9
                *Shepherd's Calender,
                November* 193-6

Amete
See *Admetus*
    Chaucer   *Troilus and Criseyde* I 659-65

Amfidius   Amfidius Tullus of *Antium*, the capital of the Volsci. The Volscian general first joined with the banished *Coriolanus* to plan a war on Rome, and then became jealous of the acclaim with which Coriolanus was received back to Rome. The position was reversed when Amfidius and Coriolanus were at Antium. Coriolanus' oratory was considered a danger and Amfidius procured his murder.
               (Plutarch *Coriolanus*)
See *Aufidius*

Amimone
See *Amymone*
    Drayton   *Rosamond and Henry IInd*
                153-8

Ammon   Ammon or Hammon was the Libyan name for *Zeus*, said to be the heavenly father of *Alexander the Great* (probably an alcoholic). He appeared to *Heracles* (or *Dionysus*) in the African desert and showed him a fountain with which to water his troops. A temple was then erected there with a ram's horns, and it was celebrated for its oracle (which identified Alexander's paternity). The ram was made a constellation. Ammon was identified with Ham or Cham, son of Noah.
            (Diodorus Siculus iii 67-70;
        Herodotus ii 55; Pindar *Pythian Ode*
                     iv 16; Strabo i 3)
    Milton   *Paradise Lost* iv 275-9
    Prior   *To Mr Howard* 5ff
    Spenser   *Faerie Queene* I v 48

Amphiareus   One of the *Seven Against Thebes* and a hunter in the *Calydonian Boar Hunt*. *Zeus* saved him from a humiliating death by clearing the ground with a thunderbolt — Amphiareus vanished. There were extended funeral rites and immortality was bestowed.
See also *Amphiorax, Eripyle*
    Browning E. B.   *Queen Anelida* 9
    Swinburne   *Atalanta in Calydon* 1260,
                1314

Amphimachus   Son of *Cteatus*, a Greek leader in the Trojan War and one of *Helen*'s suitors.
          (Homer *Iliad* ii 620, xiii 184-96)
    Shakespeare   *Troilus and Cressida* V v
                11-15

Amphion   A son of *Jupiter* by *Antiope*, born on Mt *Cithaeron* and brought up by a shepherd to avoid discovery by Antiope's father (Nicteus) and by *Dirce*, the first wife of *Lycus*, whom Antiope had superseded. Amphion was instructed in music by *Mercury* and moved stones by the power of his music so that they fell into place as the walls of the city of *Thebes*. Lycus and Dirce mistreated Antiope, and Amphion and his twin (Zethus) took revenge by killing Lycus and having Dirce dragged over rocks by a bull until she died. Amphion married *Niobe* and thus suffered the vengeance of the gods at Niobe's boast of the size of her family. He was killed or committed suicide, leaving a daughter, Chloris.

(Apollodorus III v 5-6; Ovid *Metamorphoses* vi 146-312)

Butler S.	*A Panegyric* 45-8
Byron	*Hints from Horace* 667-8
Chaucer	*Knight's Tale* 1542-8
	Manciple's Tale 113-8
	Merchant's Tale 1715-7
Cowley	*Ode on Wit* 4
Davies, Sir J.	*Orchestra* 133-40
Drayton	*Endymion and Phoebe* 204-5
	The Owl 82-6
Herrick	*Orpheus and Pluto* 23 ff
	To his Friend 3-7
Keats	*Endymion* iii 460-2, 1001-2
	Otho the Great V v 23-6
Lovelace	*To my Noble Kinsman T.S.* 13-18
Marlowe	*Doctor Faustus* 639-41
Marvell	*The First Anniversary* 49 ff
Noyes	*Tales from the Mermaid* v
Pope	*Temple of Fame* 85-8
	Ode for Music 35 ff
Shelley	*Revolt of Islam* 84-8
Sidney	*Astrophel and Stella* lxviii, lxxxiii
Skelton	*The Garland of Laurel*
Tennyson	*Amphion* 17-20, 49-52
Wordsworth	*The Power of Sound* 129-44

Amphionic
See *Amphion*
Shelley   *Hellas* 1002-7

Amphiorax
See *Amphiaraus*
Chaucer   *Anelida and Arcite* 57-63

Troilus and Criseyde v 1498-9
Wife of Bath's Prologue 740-6

Amphisbaena   A Libyan serpent with a head at either end, eyes like lamps, and a lethal bite.

(Lucan ix 719)

Milton	*Paradise Lost* x 519-26
Pope	*On Burnet and Ducket* 5-8
Shelley	*The Revolt of Islam* 3379-87
	Prometheus Unbound III iv 119

Amphitrion, Amphitrionide
See *Amphitryon, Hercules*
Drayton   *Fourth Eclogue* 65-6
Spenser   *Mutability Cantos* vii 36

Amphitrite   The daughter of *Nereus* or *Oceanus* and wife of *Neptune*, by whom she had *Triton*. When Neptune courted her, she fled to the protection of *Atlas*; one of Neptune's messengers (*Delphin*) discovered her and won her for the god, who placed the dolphin among the stars as reward.

(Hesiod *Theogony* 243, 254; Hyginus *Poetica Astronomica* II 17)

Browning R.	*Pan and Luna* 57-9
Hood	*Hero and Leander* 36
Keats	*Endymion* ii 106-9, iii 1003-5
Milton	*Comus* 920-1
Shelley	*Lines Written among the Euganean Hills* 94-9
Spenser	*Faerie Queene* III xi 42, IV xi 11

Amphitryon   A Theban, son of *Alcaeus* and grandson of *Perseus*. Amphitryon married his uncle Electryon's daughter, *Alcmena*, on condition that she remain a virgin until Electryon returned from battle with the Taphians of Aetolia. Amphitryon, perhaps accidentally, killed Electryon with a club and he and Alcmena fled to Thebes. When Amphitryon asked Alcmena why she would not lie with him, she said in surprise that she had done so the night before; *Tiresias* then revealed to him that *Zeus*, in the form of Amphitryon, had in fact spent three nights with her. When twins were born, the strong one, *Hercules*, was plainly sired by Zeus.

(Apollodorus II iv 5-11)

See also *Amphitrion*
Prior   *The Ladle* 101 ff

Amulius   A legendary king of *Alba*, who drove his brother Numitor from power and killed his sons. However, Numitor's grandsons − *Romulus* and *Remus* − killed Amulius and restored Numitor. Amulius had tried to prevent this succession through *Rhea Silvia* (Numitor's daughter) by devoting her to *Vesta* and virginity, but this plan was upset by *Mars*, who fathered Romulus and Remus.

(Livy i 3-4)

Macaulay   *Prophecy of Capys* 1

Amymone   A daughter of Danaus whose job it was to supply *Argos* with water during a drought. Whilst searching for water, she grew bored and hunted a deer for pleasure, throwing a javelin which accidentally hit a satyr. *Poseidon* rescued her from this passionate creature with his trident and himself had an affair with her. When he took his trident from the rock which it had struck, a river, to be named Amymone or *Lerna*, began to flow. Amymone had a son, Nauplius, by Poseidon.

(Apollodorus II i 4; Hyginus *Fabulae* 169; Ovid *Amores* I x 5 ff)

Daniel   *Complaint of Rosamond* 379 ff
Milton   *Paradise Regained* ii 181-8

Anacreon   The Greek poet of the 6th Century BC. He lived mainly at *Samos* under the tyrant *Polycrates*, though he visited *Athens* where he joined an artistic group surrounding *Hipparchus* and where a statue to him was erected. His poetry, of which only fragments survive, is known for its concise humour and celebration of love and wine. He was reputed to have choked to death on a grape pip, but this mode of dying was perhaps assigned to him in a cautionary manner. He was said to have had a love affair with a boy named Bathyllus and − though his dates are unknown − to have lived to a great age.

(Horace *Epode* xiv 9; Pliny vii 7)

Byron   *Don Juan* i 42
         Isles of Greece 11
Cowley   *Elegy on Anacreon* 79-80
Herrick *The Apparition of his Mistress* 32-7
         The Vision 1-4
Jonson   *Helen, Did Homer Never See* 5-8
         Inviting a Friend to Supper

29-33
Let me Be What I Am 1-2
Keats   *Fragments of 'The Castle-Builder'* 38-41
Moore   *To George Morgan* 3-5
Prior   *Cupid and Ganymede*
Spenser *Hymn of Heavenly Beauty* 210-1
Young   *The Merchant, Prologue*

Anactoria   A Lesbian woman loved by *Sappho* the poetess.

(Ovid *Heroides* xv 17)

Swinburne   *Anactoria* 1-4, 17 ff

Anaxagoras   Greek philosopher of the 5th Century BC who taught *Pericles*, *Sophocles* and *Euripides* in *Athens*. Anaxagoras believed that everything contained elements or 'seeds' of everything else, save for the prime mover, Mind; his geocentric cosmology included this principle, with heavenly bodies being rocks torn from earth. He was the first to explain eclipses. Tried for impiety, he was released through the agency of Pericles and died amid general acclaim.

Browning R.   *Aristophanes' Apology* 2077-9
Butler S.   *Hudibras* II iii 736-45
Lawrence   *Anaxagoras* 1-4

Anaxarete
See *Iphis*
Lovelace   *Princess Louisia Drawing* 22-5

Ancaeus   An *Argonaut* and participant in the *Calydonian Boar Hunt*, in which he died. He was the brother of *Cepheus (2)*, both being sons of *Lycurgus*.

(Apollodorus i 8)

Swinburne   *Atalanta in Calydon* 452, 1250

Anchises   A Dardanian king, the father of *Aeneas* from *Venus*. He was so handsome that the goddess joined him on Mt *Ida* and Aeneas was brought up by the nymphs there. He was carried through the flames of *Troy* by Aeneas at the end of the War and eventually died in Sicily. As he did not keep secret his relationship with Venus, it was said that he was killed or injured by an avenging thunderbolt from

Zeus. The Roman Emperors and legendary early kings of Britain were claimed to descend from Anchises.

> (Homer *Iliad* xiii 428-31;
> Homeric Hymn *To Aphrodite* (V);
> Virgil *Aeneid* ii 707-89)

See also *Anchises*

Auden	*Secondary Epic* 47ff
Browning E. B.	*The Battle of Marathon* 900-4
Chaucer	*Legend of Good Women* 943-5, 1086
Dryden	*Eleanora* 193ff
Milton	*Comus* 922-3
Pope	*Temple of Fame* 207-9
Shakespeare	*Julius Caesar* I ii 100ff
	King Henry VI pt 2 V ii 62-5
Spenser	*Faerie Queene* III ix 41

Anchyses
See *Anchises*

Chaucer   *House of Fame* 166-9, 439-46

Ancus   Ancus Martius, fourth king of Rome and grandson of *Numa*. In about the 7th Century BC he led the Romans against the Latians and Volsci, feeling this to be necessary in self-defence, though ending an era of peace.

> (Livy I-II)

Dryden   *Threnodia Augustalis* 465-71

Androgeus   The son of *Minos* of Crete and *Pasiphae*. He grew up in *Athens* and died young, either fighting the Cretan bull (see *Pasiphae*) or being killed by jealous gamesters. As a result Minos made war on Athens and the Athenian tribute of youth fed to the *Minotaur* was begun as his prize. Androgeus was a celebrated *victor ludorum* in Athens and games were named after him.

> (Apollodorus III xv 7)

Chaucer   *Legend of Good Women* 1894-8

Andromache, Andromachea
See *Hector*

Browning E. B.	*The Battle of Marathon* 890-5
Chaucer	*Nun's Priest's Tale* 4331-8
Rosetti D. G.	*Cassandra* 9-11
Shakespeare	*Troilus and Cressida* V

> iii 83-6

Skelton   *Philip Sparrow*

Andromeda   The beloved of *Perseus*, Andromeda was bound naked to a rock to be devoured by a monster on the orders of *Neptune* (because *Cassiope*, her mother, had boasted herself fairer than *Juno* or the *Nereids*). She was released by Perseus on condition that she marry him. *Cepheus*, Andromeda's father, agreed and Perseus turned the monster into rock by using *Medusa*'s head. *Minerva* made Andromeda a constellation at death.

> (Apollodorus ii 4; Ovid *Metamorphoses*
> iv 670ff; Pliny v 31)

Browning R.	*Pauline* 456-60
	With Francis Furini 141-3, 489-91
	Sordello ii 210-1
Chapman	*Andromeda Liberata*
Graves	*New Legends* 1ff
Hopkins	*Andromeda* 1, 9
Keats	*Endymion* iv 602-8
	If by Dull Rhymes 1-3
Kingsley	*Andromeda* 53ff, 80-2, 238ff, 262-4
Milton	*Paradise Lost* iii 557-60
Prior	*Prologue, Spoken at Court* 33-6
Rosetti D. G.	*Aspecta Medusa* 1-5
Spenser	*Ruins of Time* 645-9

Anna   Sister and confidante of *Dido*, Anna unwittingly constructed the pyre on which Dido committed suicide when deserted by *Aeneas*. After Dido's death, she travelled to Italy and was well received by Aeneas. This incited his wife *Lavinia* to jealousy and she plotted against Anna's life. Anna was, however, warned by the ghost of Dido and fled — to be drowned in the River Numicius, subsequently becoming a goddess.

> (Ovid *Fasti* III 601ff;
> Virgil *Aeneid* iv 9ff)

See also *Anne*

Marlowe	*Dido Queen of Carthage* 1137ff
Pope	*Rape of the Lock* ii 92-5
Shakespeare	*Taming of the Shrew* I i 147-9

Anne
See *Anna*

Chaucer   *Legend of Good Women*
1168 ff

Antaeus   A Libyan giant, son of *Terra* and *Neptune*. It was his boast that he would erect a temple of the skulls of his victims, and he received new strength from his mother, *Earth*, whenever he fell in wrestling. *Hercules* conquered him by crushing him held off the ground.

(Apollodorus II v 11)

See *Antheus*

Milton   *Paradise Regained* iv 562-6
Owen   *Antaeus* 1 ff
Yeats   *The Municipal Gallery Revisited* vi

Antenor   A respected Trojan counsellor of *Priam*. Before the onset of war, he intervened to save the lives of Greek envoys trying to secure the return of *Helen*. Subsequently he advocated sending Helen back to the Greeks, but was overruled by Priam and *Paris*. Late and medieval writers developed him into a traitor of almost proverbial status, from the facts that he urged the Greeks to make the wooden horse which proved the downfall of *Troy*, that he urged the appeasement of the enemy, and that, being the spokesman for peace, he was spared in the sack of Troy.

(Homer *Iliad* III, VII 347-54;
Ovid *Metamorphoses* xiii 196-204)

See *Anthenor*

Marlowe   *Dido Queen of Carthage* 403-6
Shakespeare   *Troilus and Cressida*
Prologue 16-9

Anteros   A god of harmonious love ('love returned') and tenderness, son of *Mars* and *Venus*.

Rosetti D. G.   *Hero's Lamp* 1 ff

Anthenor
See *Antenor*

Chaucer   *Book of the Duchess* 1114-20

Anthesterion   The name of the twelfth month (spring), given to the 'Anthesteria', a festival of *Dionysus*, which occurred then.

Swinburne   *Eros* 2

Antheus
See *Antaeus*

Chaucer   *Monk's Tale* 3293-300

Anthropophagi, Anthropophaginian   A carnivorous race of Scythians reputed to drink out of skulls and to use scalps as napkins.

(Pliny VII xi 12)

Shakespeare   *Merry Wives of Windsor*
IV v 9
Othello I iii 142-5

Antiates   The people of *Antium*, a Volscian town.

(Plutarch *Coriolanus*)

Anticyra   A town of Phocis, famed for its hellebore (variously identified), a medicine used for mental illness.

Cowper   *To the Rev. William Bull* 35-9

Antigone   With *Eteocles* and *Polyneices*, the incestuous offspring of *Oedipus* and his mother, *Jocasta*. When her brothers killed each other in struggling for the throne of *Thebes*, *Creon*, acting as regent, decreed that they should not be buried, being invaders. Antigone gave Polyneices funeral rites and Creon ordered her to be buried alive in her brother's tomb or in a cave, where she committed suicide. In another version, she was granted to *Haemon*, Creon's son, and produced a son who was recognised by a birthmark and rejected by Creon. Haemon killed Antigone and himself. (The name also of a niece of *Cressida*.)

(Apollodorus II 7; Hyginus *Fabulae*
lxxii; Sophocles *Antigone*)

See also *Argia, Seven Against Thebes*

Arnold   *Fragment of an 'Antigone'*
Browning R.   *Pauline* 63-5
Chaucer   *Troilus and Criseyde* ii 824-6
Meredith   *Antigone*
Swinburne   *Athens* str. 3

Antinous   An Ithacan suitor of *Penelope* in *Ulysses*'s absence at *Troy*. Antinous, a persistent villain, tried to persuade the suitors to kill her son *Telemachus*, and turned away the disguised Ulysses when he returned. Antinous was the first suitor to be killed once Ulysses appreciated the situation.

(Homer *Odyssey* xvi ff)

Davies, Sir J.   *Orchestra* 29 ff

Hopkins   *Escorial* 11

Antioch   The capital of the Seleucid Syrian empire, of which *Parthia* was a province until conquered by *Arsaces*. It was founded in 300BC by Seleucus I and named after his father. Greatly extended by successors, it was annexed by *Pompey* in 64BC to be the capital of the Syrian province of the Roman Empire, but made autonomous by *Caesar* in 47. In literature it is sometimes regarded as a degenerate place, perhaps because of its great commercial wealth and the pleasurable grove of Daphne nearby.

(Strabo xxx XVI ii 5)
Milton   *Paradise Regained* III 294-7

Antiochus (Epiphanes)   Antiochus Epiphanes VI, king of Syria from 175-163BC, conquered Egypt, destroyed Jerusalem and established ruthless control over Judea. In Jerusalem he stripped all precious metal from the temple, placed a pagan altar on top of the Jewish one, and gloated over his desecrations. His attempt to suppress Judaism led to a Macabean rebellion and a terrible death supposed to be divine punishment. Known as 'Epimanes' ('the maniac') he was an eccentric, respecting neither class nor age, jesting in the street and being a candidate in mock elections.

(Macabees *Polybius* xxvi, xxxiii)
Chaucer   *Monk's Tale* 3786-3810
Shakespeare   *Pericles, Prologue* I i 145-7,
II iv 5-10
Spenser   *Faerie Queene* I v 47

Antiopa, Antiope (1)   A daughter of Nycteus King of Thebes. She was pursued by *Jupiter* in the form of a satyr, by whom she was the mother of *Amphion* and Zethus. The *Muses* were sometimes said to be her daughters by *Pierus*.

(Ovid *Metamorphoses* vi 110ff)
See *Nyctimine*
Browning R.   *Filippo Baldinucci*
397-400
Milton   *Paradise Regained* ii 181-8
Spenser   *Faerie Queene* III xi 35

Antiopa, Antiope (2)   An Amazonian queen, daughter of *Mars*, also called *Hippolyta*. She was the wife of *Theseus* and mother of

Hippolytus. In some accounts Hippolyta is regarded as the sister of Antiope and is said to have died at *Megara* after defeat by Theseus. Her death was variously attributed to a stray arrow from her ally, *Penthesilea*, or to her being slain on threatening to kill the guests at Theseus' wedding to *Phaedra*.

(Apollodorus *Epitome* i 15-16, v 1;
Plutarch *Theseus*)
Shakespeare   *Midsummer Night's Dream*
II i 75-80

Antium   The capital of the Volsci until they were defeated by *Camillus* in the 4th Century BC. An important coastal resort, the birthplace of *Nero*.
Gray   *Agrippina* 160-1

Antoninus (Pius)   Roman Emperor (138-61AD), the successor to *Hadrian*. The title 'pius' was conferred on him by the Senate, possibly in recognition of his loyalty to Hadrian, who adopted him while still in power. The rule of Antoninus was unadventurous and peaceful, marked by a growth of centralised bureaucracy.
Shelley   *Queen Mab* ii 179-81

Antonius (Lucius)   Younger brother of *Mark Antony*. He held office in Asia and supported Mark. He was besieged by *Augustus* at Perusia but his life was spared and he was given a position in Spain.
Shakespeare   *Antony and Cleopatra* II
i 41-2

Antonius (Marcus)
See *Antony (Mark)*
Chaucer   *Knight's Tale* 2031-5
Legend of Good Women 508ff
Prior   *Alma* i 486-8
Spenser   *Faerie Queene* I v 49

Antony (Mark)   'Mark Antony' (Marcus Antonius), a distinguished cavalry officer who joined *Caesar*'s staff in 54BC and was placed in Italy whilst Caesar campaigned in Spain. He spoke an oration after the murder of Caesar in 44BC and formed a triumvirate with *Octavian* and *Lepidus*, defeating the murderers *Brutus* and *Cassius* at *Philippi* in 42BC. He was first married to *Fulvia*, whom he divorced. Whilst responsible for security in the East, he met *Cleopatra* with whom his relationship, in regard to ending his politically motivated second marriage to *Octavia* (Octavian's sister), was the cause of his downfall in the culmination of *Actium* 31BC. After this he committed suicide as Octavian advanced into *Alexandria* (30BC). A popular version had it that he committed suicide in the false belief that Cleopatra was dead, but lived long enough to see her, whereupon Cleopatra killed herself with an asp to save submitting to Octavian.

(Plutarch *Antony* lxxviff)

See also *Marcus*

Byron	*The Deformed Transformed* I i 230-6
	Don Juan vi 4, xv 53
Chaucer	*Legend of Good Women* 610-3, 624-5, 660-1
Collins	*Epistle to Sir Thomas Hanmer* 115-6
Cowley	*Brutus* 5
Dryden	*All for Love* I i; II i; III i
	Conquest of Granada I, V i
Hardy	*The Clasped Skeletons* 21-4
Prior	*On Beauty* 10ff
Shakespeare	*Antony and Cleopatra* I i 12-3, iv 4-7, 23, v 70-2; II ii 130-2, iii 39-41, vi 116-9; III ii 54-6, vi 3-6, 23-6, 47ff, x 17-21, xi 35-9, xii 3-4; IV xiv 51-4, 99-101; V i 17-8, 32-3, ii 355-6
	Cymbeline II iv 68-71
	Julius Caesar I ii 28-9; II i 156ff; III i 246-7, ii 217-9; IV iii 166-9
	Macbeth III i 53-6
Spenser	*Faerie Queene* V viii 2
Tennyson	*Antony and Cleopatra* 9-10
	Dream of Fair Women 141-2, 145-6

Antylegyus
See *Archilocus*

Chaucer	*Book of the Duchess* 1055-75

Aon A son of *Neptune*, the eponymous king of *Aonia* (Boeotia).

Spenser *Faerie Queene* IV xi 15

Aonia, Aonian An old name for Boeotia, a country north-west of *Athens*, in which stood Mt *Helicon*, seat of the *Muses*.
See *Aon*

Byron	*English Bards* 883-7
Milton	*Paradise Lost* i 12-15
Pope	*Messiah* 3-6
Shenstone	*Elegies* i 23-4
Swift	*Description of Mother Ludwell's Cave* 1-2
Young	*Night Thoughts* iv

Aornos, Aornus A gulf or lake, noted as birdless, near *Baiae* and Naples. It was also called *Avernus*, the entrance to *Hades* and one of the rivers of hell.

(Strabo I ii 18, I v 4-5;
Virgil *Aeneid* vi 242)

Browning E. B.	*Portuguese Sonnets* 11
Shelley	*Ode to Naples* 40-1

Apega A sort of Iron Maiden said to have been employed by the tyrant *Nabis*. It was a statue of a woman (named after his wife Apega) clad in nail-studded leather. When the victims entered its embrace the machine clasped them, torturing or killing them.

(Polybius xiii 7)

Southey *Hymn to the Penates* 229-34

Apelles A Greek painter of the 4th Century BC. He is particularly associated with *Alexander the Great*, who would allow him alone to paint him, and whom Apelles pictured with a thunderbolt.

(Pliny xxxv 36)

Byron	*Prophecy of Dante* IV 41-3
Carew	*Obsequies to a Lady* 25-8
Chaucer	*Physician's Tale* 14-18
Cowley	*On a Copy of Verses by my Lord Broghill* 5
Dryden	*To Sir Godfrey Kneller* 97
Pope	*The Dunciad* iii 102-4
Prior	*Protogenes and Apelles* 17-18
	To Mr Howard 5ff
Skelton	*Garland of Laurel*
Spenser	*Faerie Queene* IV v 12
Thomson	*Liberty* ii 215-9

Apemanthis, Apemantus A cynical philosopher and wit who associated with the misanthrope *Timon of Athens*.

(Plutarch *Antony* lxx)
Shakespeare *Timon of Athens* I i 62-3

Aphrodite
See *Venus*
    Auden   *Anthem for St Cecilia's Day*
          9-13
          Homage to Clio 17-18
          In Memory of Sigmund Freud
          111-2
    Browning E. B.   *The Dead Pan* 16
    Byron   *The Island* ii 131-2
    Graves   *Judgment of Paris* 1-4
    Lawrence   *Spiral Flame* 18-19
    Noyes   *Mount Ida* 138-44
    Praed   *The County Ball* 608-12
    Spenser   *Faerie Queene* II xii 13, 65
    Swinburne   *Atalanta in Calydon* 781ff
                 Sapphics 9ff
    Tennyson   *Oenone* 170-1, 181-3

Apicata   The wife of *Sejanus*.
    Jonson   *Sejanus* II i

Apicius   A proverbial Roman name for a glutton, of which M. Gavius — probably more of a gourmet in fact — in the 1st Century BC was the most famous example.

                   (Juvenal xi 3)
    Byron   *Vision of Judgment* xlvi
    Jonson   *The Staple of News*

Apis   An Egyptian god, worshipped in the form of a black ox or the spirit of *Osiris* therein. The ox was distinctively figured, with a star on its head, an eagle on its back and crescent moon on its side.
    Shelley   *Witch of Atlas* 625-8

Apius
See *Appius, Virginia*
    Chaucer   *The Physician's Tale* 126-9,
          140-1, 170-85

Apollo   The god of youth, poetry (particularly of an elevated or epic kind), music, prophecy, archery and healing. He is often identified with the Sun and called *Phoebus* ('bright one'). Apollo was son of *Zeus* and the Titaness *Leto*. He established his shrine at *Delphi*, where he had killed a huge dragon. The dragon was sometimes known as *Python*,

and accounts differ as to whether it was a marauder or guardian of the oracle. Like his sister *Artemis*, Apollo may be called *Cynthian*, after the Delian mountain of *Cynthus* where they were born. He spent a period in exile in *Thessaly* as a shepherd and so became regarded as a god of shepherds; this exile was imposed by Zeus because Apollo killed Zeus's thunderbearing *Cyclops* for striking dead Apollo's son *Aesculapius*, whose medical powers provoked jealousy among the gods. Apollo's association with laurel, which he wore on his head, arose partly from his attempted seduction of *Daphne*, who was turned into a laurel to escape his attentions. A less familiar role for Apollo is as introducer of plague as an instrument of divine anger. Like Artemis (*Diana*) he may be depicted driving a chariot (see *Phaethon*) or with a golden lyre. He was also associated with swans (see *Cycnus*).

          (Homer *Iliad* i 9-12; Homeric Hymn
        To Apollo iii, xxi; Ovid *Metamorphoses*
        ii 677ff; Virgil *Eclogues* vi 1-5)
See also *Coronis, Delos, Helios, Hyacinth*
— *General*
    Auden   *Under Which Lyre* 67-72
    Browning E. B.   *The Dead Pan* 12
    Byron   *English Bards* 265-7
    Chaucer   *Franklin's Tale* 1031-7
          House of Fame 1094ff,
          1229-32
          Troilus and Criseyde i 70,
          iv 1397-8, V 206-10
    Drayton   *The Muses' Elizium* ix 15-7,
          21-3, 32-7
    Graves   *The White Goddess* 2
    Keats   *Endymion* i 350-3, 789-90;
          iii 463-4, 785-8, 955-9; iv 11-12,
          774
          *Hence Burgundy, Claret and
          Wine* 13-18
          Hyperion iii 76-80, 113-20
          In drear-nighted December 9-12
          *I Stood Tiptoe upon a Little
          Hill* 218
          Otho the Great III ii 41-3
          To Apollo 1-12
          To George Felton Matthew
          79-86
    Marlowe   *Dido Queen of Carthage*
          1068-72
          Hero and Leander i 5-8

Meredith	*The Rape of Aurora*
Milton	*On the Morning of Christ's Nativity* 176-8
	Paradise Regained ii 188-91
	Sonnet xii 5-7
Pope	*Epistle to Dr Arbuthnot* 231
Shakespeare	*All's Well* II i 160-1
	Winter's Tale III i 143ff; IV iv 25-30; V i 37
Shelley	*Hellas* 230-4
	Hymn of Apollo 23-7, 31-6
	Lines Written Among the Euganian Hills 106-14
	Prometheus Unbound II v 10-11; III ii 40
	Witch of Atlas 289-94
Spenser	*Faerie Queene* II xii 13; III iv 41; IV xii 25; VI ii 25
Stevenson	*I whom Apollo Sometime Visited* 1-3
Suckling	*The Metamorphosis* 1-4
Swift	*Ode to Athenian Society* 208-10
	To Lord Harley 31-2
Swinburne	*Hymn to Proserpine* 4-8
Tennyson	*Lucretius* 124-6
Wordsworth	*The Waggoner* iv 108-13

— and Python
Arnold	*Empedocles on Etna* II i 201-7
Browning R.	*Sordello* i 927-32
Coleridge	*The Destiny of Nations* 435-7
Drayton	*The Muses Elizium* ix 65-8
Sidney	*Arcadia* xxvi 5 ff

— Poetry, Muses
Blake	*Imitation of Spenser* 1 ff
Byron	*The First Kiss of Love* 9-12
Drayton	*The Muses Elizium* ix 73-7
	Tom Himself and the Harp 11-15
Jonson	*Dedication of the King's new Cellar* 25-8
Keats	*Acrostic* 3-5
	Apollo to the Graces 1-3
	Endymion ii 723-9, iii 43
	Hyperion ii 292-5, iii 13, 42-3, 61-8
	Ode to Apollo 42-3
	On First Looking into Chapman's Homer 3-4
	Sleep and Poetry 56-61, 181-3
	The Fall of Hyperion i 204-8
	To Georgina Augusta Wylie 11-4
	To My Brother George 9-12,

43-5
Shelley	*Adonais* 249-51
Spenser	*Tears of the Muses* 1-2
Stevenson	*Still I love to Rhyme* 5-6

— Music
Campion	*To His Sweet Lute Apollo* 1ff
Davies Sir J.	*Nosce Teipsum* xxxix 51-2
Drayton	*Fourth Eclogue* 67-8
Keats	*Endymion* i 95-9, 139-41; ii 358-63
	I Stood Tiptoe Upon a Little Hill 47-52
	Lamia i 70-5, ii 78-81
	To Aubrey George Spencer 1-4
Marlowe	*Hero and Leander* ii 397-431
Milton	*At a Vacation Exercise* 37-8
	Comus 476-80
Shakespeare	*Love's Labour's Lost* IV iii 335-41; V iii 917
Wordsworth	*Sonnet: I heard (alas . . .)* 6-11

— Daphne, laurel
Chaucer	*Troilus and Criseyde* iii 539-44
Keats	*To a Young Lady who Sent Me a Laurel Crown* 5-7
	To Charles Cowden Clarke 44-5
Marlowe	*Dr Faustus* 1478-80
Milton	*Comus* 661-3
Sassoon	*Solar Eclipse* 8ff
Shakespeare	*Midsummer Night's Dream* II i 230-2
	Taming of the Shrew, Induction 55-87
Shelley	*Prometheus Unbound* II i 138-41
Vaughan	*Olor Iscanus* 1-2

— Hyacinth
| Drayton | *The Muses' Elizium* 57-60 |
| Milton | *On the Death of a Fair Infant* 23-8 |

Apollodorus   Apollodorus 'the Sicilian' – a friend of *Cleopatra*, who carried her in to *Caesar*, by her wish, in a bed-sack, so that he would be surprised. He was. The coquetry prompted his infatuation with her.

(Plutarch *Caesar* xlix)
| Shakespeare | *Antony and Cleopatra* II vi 69-70 |

Apollonian
See *Apollo*

Keats   *Endymion* ii 396-400

Apollonius (Tyana)
See *Lycius (Menippus)*
    Keats   *Lamia* ii 159-62, 291-300

Appian (Way)   The Via Appia, built by
Appius Claudius Caecus in 312 BC — the main
road south from Rome to Brindisi.
See *Via Appia*
    Milton   *Paradise Regained* iv 67-70

Appius Claudius   A Decemvir (one of ten
Patrician magistrates responsible for codifying
Roman law during the suspension of the constitution in 451 BC). He had some reputation
as a lawgiver and sharer of power with the
plebeians, but posterity regarded him as the
salacious tyrant who desired *Virginia*: he set
her up with one of his friends as the daughter
of a slave, so that he could have his will with
her, and then passed a judicial verdict excul-
pating himself. This story, influenced by that
of *Lucretia* and the *Tarquins*, symbolised the
civil disorder of the time; the army came to
support the girl's father Virginius (who had
killed his daughter in preference to her being
ravaged), Appius was imprisoned and committed suicide, the friend (Marcus) was killed,
and the Decemvirate was abolished. The order
of the Tribunes was restored.
                                        (Livy iii 44 ff)
See also *Apius*, *Verginius*
    Macaulay   *Virginia*

Apuleius   The author, in the 2nd Century
AD, of *The Golden Ass* or *Metamorphoses*,
the only extant Latin novel, rich in magical
and mythological lore. Apuleius was a prolific
author but few of his works survive.
    Graves   *Alice* 35-6

Apulia   Puglia, in south-west Italy, famed
for its wool and horses.
                                        (Pliny III xi)
See *Poilleys*

Aquarius   The Water-Carrier constellation,
said to represent *Ganymede*, cup-bearer to the
gods.
        (Ovid *Fasti* i 652; Virgil *Georgics* iii 304;
                Hyginus *Poetica Astronomica* ii 29)

Keats   *Endymion* iv 581-5

Aquilo, Aquilon
See *Boreas*
    Milton   *On the Death of a Fair Infant*
                8-9
    Shakespeare   *Troilus and Cressida* IV v
                6-9

Arabia   The country between the Arabian
and Persian Gulfs, of which the western part
(modern Jordan) was known as Arabia Petraea,
the north and centre (much of Saudi Arabia)
as Arabia Deserta, and the southern (Yemen
and South Saudi Arabia) as Arabia Felix. The
latter — Araby the Blest — was noted for spices
and herbs.
                        (Diodorus Siculus III 46)
    Milton   *Paradise Lost* iv 62-3

Arachne   A Lydian woman famous for her
weaving and needlework, in which she presumed to challenge *Minerva*. The goddess, in
her own tapestry, represented the contest
between herself and *Neptune* in the naming
of *Athens*, and other legends depicting the
power of the gods. Arachne in hers showed
other myths, particularly the amours of *Jove*
and the story of *Europa* and the Bull. Minerva
was enraged at her rival's flawless work and
tore it to pieces, striking Arachne with it, who
then hanged herself. The goddess then took
pity on her and gave her new life, but in the
form of a spider, so that she might go on
spinning her web.
                    (Ovid *Metamorphoses* vi 1-145)
    Chapman   *Hero and Leander* iv
    Coleridge   *The Silver Thimble* 49-51
    Denham   *Progress of Learning* 186-7
    Diaper   *Dryades* 504-11
    Drayton   *The Barons' Wars* vi 43
    Fletcher P.   *Purple Island* v 33
    Meredith   *A Garden Idyll*
    Spenser   *Faerie Queene* II vii 28,
                II xii 77
                    Muiopotmos 272 ff
    Wordsworth   *On Seeing a Needlecase in
                the Form of a Harp* 5-8

Aratus   A statesman and ruler of Sicyon, in
Achaia, in the 3rd Century BC. His career is
the story of ever-changing relationships be-

tween the lesser states of the Achaian Confederacy with bigger powers such as Macedon, Egypt and Sparta. When *Philip* of Macedon was called in to assist Aratus against Aetolia, he distrusted Aratus's power and was said to have poisoned him, as a result of which Aratus spat blood and uttered a cynical comment on the friendship of kings; more probably, however, he died of consumption.

    Browning E. B.   *The Battle of Marathon* 865-71
    Thomson   *Winter* 491-2

Arcadia, Arcadian
See *Arcady*
    Browning E. B.   *Flush or Faunus* 5 ff
    Butler S.   *The Emperor in the Moon* 103-7
    Cowper   *Hope* 9
        The Task iv 513-9
        The Winter Nosegay 9-12
    Goldsmith   *The Traveller* 319
    Keats   *Endymion* i 139-40, ii 488-90
    Milton   *Paradise Lost* ix 129-33
    Pope   *Windsor Forest* 159-62
    Swift   *A Love Song* 5-8
    Wordsworth   *Yarrow Revisited* xi 1-3

Arcady   The mountainous central Peloponnesus, named after *Arcas*, son of *Zeus* who reigned here in the then Pelasgia or Lycaonia. The people were shepherd-musicians and *Pan*, god of shepherds, lived among them. They were also warriors, and to ancient Greece it seemed a rude and barbarous land; the Romans idealised it, with less direct knowledge, into a paradise of nymphs and shepherds.

        (Homeric Hymn *To Pan* xix;
        Pausanias viii 1-2, 4)

See *Arcadia*
    Keats   *Ode on a Grecian Urn* 5-7
    Milton   *Arcades* 28-31
    Spenser   *Astrophel* 1-2
    Stevenson   *You Know the Way to Arcady* 1-4
    Tennyson   *In Memoriam* xxiii 22-4
    Wordsworth   *Look at the Fate of Summer Flowers* 14
    Yeats   *Song of the Unhappy Shepherd*

Arcas   Son of *Zeus* and *Callisto* (*Helice*), and eponymous king of *Arcadia*. Arcas nearly

killed his mother, who had been transformed into a bear by *Hera*; she was jealous of Zeus's affair with Callisto, which was enacted with Zeus disguised as *Artemis*, to whose train Callisto belonged. On his death, Arcas was made into the constellation of the Lesser Bear, with his mother as the Greater Bear being hunted by him. The Greeks sailed by the Great Bear and the Phoenicians by the Lesser Bear.

        (Apollodorus iii 8; Ovid *Fasti* iii 107;
        Pausanias viii 4)

See also *Cynosura*
    Milton   *Comus* 341-2
    Prior   *First Hymn to Callimachus* 39 ff

Archelaus   A 5th Century BC Greek philosopher, pupil of *Anaxagoras* and reputed teacher of *Socrates*.
    Drayton   *Endymion and Phoebe* 1 ff

Archemorus   A warning was issued by an oracle that Archemorus (or Ophaltes), son of *Lycurgus*, should not touch the ground before he could walk. His nurse, *Hypsipyle*, laid him on a bed of parsley whilst giving directions to the *Seven Against Thebes* on how to find a fountain, and the baby was bitten by a snake and died. This was taken to be an omen and the Seven named the baby Archemorus ('Beginner of Doom').

        (Apollodorus III vi 4;
        Hyginus *Fabulae* lxxiv)

See *Archymois*

Archilocus
See *Polyxena*

Archimedean
See *Archimedes*
    Shelley   *Letter to Maria Gisborne* 15-19

Archimedes   The Greek mathematician and inventor, 287-212 BC. He was said to have invented, among other things, elaborate instruments of war used against the Romans in the siege of Syracuse, a mirror which burned the enemy, a complex planetarium and a screw for raising water. His discovery of specific gravity in the displacement of water reputedly came to him in the bath, from which he emerged to run home naked crying 'Eureka'. Many popular stories gathered round him, but he has been recognised as a strikingly original mathematical theorist. He was supposed to have been killed whilst so deeply engrossed in a problem that he was unaware that Syracuse was in enemy hands.

(Livy xxiv 34; Plutarch *Marcellus*)
Jonson   *The Magnetic Lady* I i
Milton   *Sonnet* xxi 5-7
Wordsworth   *The Excursion* viii 220ff
                    The Prelude xi 435

Architas   A Greek philosopher and mathematician of the 5th Century BC, accredited with inventing the screw and the pulley.
Jonson   *Expostulation with Inigo Jones* 5-6

Archymoris
See *Archemorus*
Chaucer   *Troilus and Criseyde* v 1498-9

Arctos   Constellations of Ursa, the Bear, supposed to be Arcas and his mother.
See *Arcas*
Shelley   *Rosalind and Helen* 1302-3

Ardea   A Rutulian city close to Rome, attacked repeatedly by the Volsci and the Gauls. During a siege here in the 6th Century BC, the fatal boast of the excellence of wives took place which is the background to the Rape of *Lucretia*.

(Livy I lvii)
See also *Tarquinius Superbus*
Chaucer   *Legend of Good Women* 1694-1702
Shakespeare   *Rape of Lucrece* 1-7

Ares   The Greek equivalent to the Roman *Mars*, God of War. Ares was son of *Zeus* and had many liaisons and offspring.
Tennyson   *Tiresias* 11-13, 93-5, 108ff

Arethusa, Arethuse   A nymph, daughter of *Oceanus*, and of one of *Diana*'s train. She was pursued by the god of the River *Alpheus*, who fell in love with her, and she was transformed into a fountain by Diana. Alpheus was said to continue to pursue her beneath the Adriatic, and the two waters to merge near Syracuse. Alpheus and Arethusa were invoked as muses

of pastoral poetry. (The association with *Faunus* in *Faerie Queene* II ii 7ff appears to be Spenser's own.)

(Moschus *Lament for Bion*; Ovid *Metamorphoses* v 576ff; Pausanias V 7; Strabo VII ii 4; Virgil *Eclogues* x 1)
See *Alpheus*
Keats   *Endymion* ii 1005-12
Marlowe   *Dr Faustus* 1341-7
Meredith   *Daphne*
Milton   *Arcades* 28-31
                Lycidas 85-7
Pope   *The Dunciad* ii 314-9
                Windsor-Forest 195ff
Shelley   *Fragments Written for Hellas* 8-9, 15-16
Skelton   *Arethusa* 1-3, 37-45, 73-8, 82-7
                Philip Sparrow
Spenser   *Faerie Queene* II ii 7-8
Wordsworth   *The Prelude* xi 464-6

Argia   Daughter of *Adrastus* and wife of Polyneices; for burying her husband's body she was executed by *Creon*. In some versions, she escaped.   (Aeschylus *Seven Against Thebes*; Hyginus *Fabulae* lxxi; Statius *Thebaid* xii)
See *Antigone*
Skelton   *Garland of Laurel*

Argive
See *Argos*
Tennyson   *In Memoriam* xxiii 22-4

Argo   The ship — named after its builder or the city of *Argos* in the Peloponnesus — which carried *Jason* and his companions to recapture the *Golden Fleece*. This was held by *Aeetes*, King of *Colchis*. The task of recapturing the Fleece was suggested by Jason's uncle, *Pelias*, usurper to the throne of Iolchis, to dispose of Jason; an oracle had told Pelias that one such as Jason must eventually overthrow him. In this quest, the Argo was nearly overwhelmed as it passed through the Bosphorous, but was guided by a dove.

(Apollodorus I ix; Apollonius Rhodius; Ovid *Metamorphoses* vii; Pindar *Pythian Ode* iv 67ff)
See also *Bisaltis*
Milton   *Paradise Lost* ii 1016-8
Pope   *Ode for Music* 37-41

Prior   *Carmen Seculare* 472-3
           On the Coronation of James
           II, 15-16
Shelley   *Hellas* 1072-3
Spenser   *Faerie Queene* II xii 44
Wordsworth   *Memorials of a Tour 1820*
           xi 7-14
Yeats   *Two Songs from a Play* i

Argolic, Argolis
See *Argos*
Spenser   *Mutability Cantos* vii 33

Argonauts   The heroes who manned *Jason's* ship, *Argo*. They were variously listed, but included *Heracles*, *Hylas*, *Orpheus*, Jason, the *Dioscuri*, and, usually, *Meleager* and Mopsus. The starting point of their voyage is unknown.
           (Ovid *Metamorphoses* vi 720-1;
           Apollonius Rhodius i)
Arnold   *The Strayed Reveller* 257-60
Chapman   *Shadow of Night*
Keats   *Endymion* i 346-8
Spenser   *Amoretti* 44
           Faerie Queene IV i 23

Argonautycon   The Argonautica of Valerius Flaccus (1st Century AD), a derivative account of the Argonautic expedition.
Chaucer   *Legend of Good Women*
           1453-7

Argos   The capital of *Argolis* in the eastern Peloponnesus, supposed to have been founded by *Inachus* (the name of its main river) and subsequently united with Mycenae. It was said to have been built by *Cyclopes*. Inachus' daughter, *Io*, became the ancestress of the thrones of *Thebes*, *Crete* and Argos. Rulers of Argos celebrated in literature include Danaus, *Perseus*, *Atreus* and *Agamemnon*. In the 7th Century BC under *Pheidon*, Argolis was the principal power of Greece and 'Argive' or 'Argolic' was for long used to refer to Greece generally. Argos was a centre for the cult of Hera (*Juno*).
Browning E. B.   *Queen Anelida* 8
Lovelace   *Cupid Far Gone* 25-30

Argus (1)   Argus Panoptes, the all-seeing man, in the earliest mention had four eyes, but was later given a hundred, all over his head or body. His parentage was disputed, but he was called Arestorides because said to be a son of Arestor. It was his many eyes rather than his adventures (including such escapades as dressing in the hide of a bull to terrorise *Arcadia*, and killing the monster *Echidna*) which made him notable. He was lulled to sleep and killed by *Mercury* after being set by *Hera* to watch *Io*, who was in the form of a cow. Hera then placed his eyes in the tail of the peacock, with which she is often associated.
           (Apollodorus II i 2-3;
           Ovid *Metamorphoses* i 622-723)
Bridges   *Demeter* 575
Chaucer   *Knight's Tale* 1385-90
           Merchant's Tale 2111-5
           Wife of Bath's Prologue 357-60
           Troilus and Criseyde iv 1459
Daniel   *Complaint of Rosamund* 500
Diaper   *Dryades* 504-11
Donne   *Second Anniversary* 199-200
           The Will 2-4
Drayton   *Rosamund and Henry II* 163-6
Fletcher G.   *Christ's Victory on Earth*
           36
Hood   *The Two Swans* 15
Keats   *As Hermes Once* 1-5
           Endymion ii 675-7
           The Cap and Bells 246-9
Marlowe   *Hero and Leander* i 386ff
Milton   *Paradise Lost* xi 129-31
Pope   *The Dunciad* ii 340-4, iii 343-5
           Lines from Alcander X 2-4
Shakespeare   *Love's Labour's Lost* III i
           185ff
           Troilus and Cressida I ii
           28-9
Sidney   *Arcadia* viii 13-4
Spenser   *Faerie Queene* I iv 17, III ix 7
           Muiopotmos 88-96
           Shepherd's Calendar July
           153-5, *September* 203, *Oc-*
           tober 11-12

Argus (2)   A son of *Phrixus*, and builder of the ship, Argo.
           (Apollodorus I ix 16)
Chaucer   *Legend of Good Women*
           1453-7

Argus (3)   *Ulysses's* favourite dog.

(Homer *Odyssey* xvii 300ff)
Byron   *Don Juan* iii 23
MacNeice   *Day of Returning* ii
Pope   *Argus* 10-15

Ariadne   The daughter of *Minos*, king of *Crete*, Ariadne fell in love with *Theseus* and provided him with a clue of thread to get himself out of the *Minotaur*'s Labyrinth. He married her and made her pregnant, but then abandoned her at *Naxos* and married her sister, *Phaedra*. Ariadne was consoled, and perhaps loved, by *Bacchus* who gave her a crown, made into a constellation after her death.
(Apollodorus *Epitome* 8-15; Ovid *Heroides* x,
                Metamorphoses viii 183ff)
See also *Adriane, Adryane*
    Belloc   *In Praise of Wine* 120-4
    Cowley   *The Heart Fled Again* 3
    Drayton   *Eclogue* ix 216-22
    Eliot T. S.   *Sweeney Erect* 5-7
    Hood   *Hero and Leander* 108
    Keats   *Endymion* ii 441-4
                Isabella 93-6
                Lamia i 57-8
                Sleep and Poetry 334-6
    Lewis C. D.   *Ariadne on Naxos*
    Lovelace   *Princess Louisa Painting*
                18-21
    MacNeice   *Autumn Sequel* xx vi
    Shakespeare   *Midsummer Night's Dream*
                II i 75-80
                Two Gentlemen of Verona
                IV iv 163-7
    Shenstone   *Economy* iii 30-2
    Spenser   *Faerie Queene* VI x 13

Ariconian   Of Aricia, an ancient town near Rome, where *Theseus* built a temple to *Diana*.
    Diaper   *Dryades* 64-70

Arimaspi, Arimaspian   A one-eyed people said to have marauded *Scythia* and stolen her gold, which was guarded by griffins. Arimaspias was also the name of a gold-bearing river in Scythia.
    (Aeschylus *Prometheus Bound*, 804-7;
        Herodotus iii 116, iv 13; Strabo I 2)
    Milton   *Paradise Lost* ii 743-7

Arion   A lyrical poet of *Lesbos* who made a fortune in Italy and, on returning to Lesbos,

was the object of a murder plot by the seamen. He threw himself into the sea after playing a swan-song and was rescued by a dolphin which transported him back to Corinth. Here King *Periander* had the sailors executed. *Apollo* placed Arion and the Dolphin among the stars.
    (Herodotus i 23-4; Ovid *Fasti* ii 79ff)
See also *Delphinus, Orion*
    Browning R.   *Fifine at the Fair* 1294ff
    Drayton   *The Barons' Wars* iii 48
    Keats   *Endymion* ii 358-60
    Milton   *Lycidas* 164
    Shakespeare   *Twelfth Night* I ii 15-16
    Shelley   *The Witch of Atlas* 481-5
    Spenser   *Amoretti* 38
                Faerie Queene IV xi 23
    Wordsworth   *The Power of Sound*
                129-44
    Young   *Ocean*
                Sea-piece, Dedication

Arisbe   Daughter of Macar, a legendary king of *Lesbos* who was said to be a son of *Helios*.
    Swinburne   *Dolores* 299-301

Aristaeus   A rustic deity, son of *Apollo* by an affair with *Cyrene* (thereby fulfilling a prophecy that the girl's name would become that of a city). Aristaeus was brought up by *Cheiron* and instructed in husbandry, apiary in particular. When he chased a beautiful *Dryad*, she stepped on a snake and died, and, shortly afterwards, Aristaeus's bees fell mortally sick. On Cyrene's advice, he bound *Proteus* and consulted him as oracle. Proteus revealed that the Dryad had been *Eurydice* and that the other Dryads wished death on his bees. The situation was redeemed by Aristaeus making copious sacrifice of bulls to *Orpheus*. Aristaeus married *Autonoe*, daughter of *Cadmus*, and *Actaeon* was his son. Subsequent events included the founding of the city of Cyrene.
    (Apollonius Rhodius ii 500ff;
                Virgil *Georgics* iv 315ff)
    Browning R.   *The Ring and the Book*
                ix 1345-8
    Cowper   *The Task* v 135-7
    Kipling   *The Bees and the Flies* 1-8

Aristarchus   A Greek grammarian of *Samothrace* in the 2nd Century BC. He was famous for his savage revision of earlier writers, including *Homer*.

See also *Aristorchus*

Aristeides
See *Aristides*

> Browning R.   *Aristophanes' Apology*
> 457-51

Aristides   Aristides 'The Just' was an Athenian statesman of the 5th Century BC who fought at *Marathon* and was celebrated for his poverty, honesty and generosity. He was ostracised in 482 BC by his rival, *Themistocles*; according to tradition, he wrote his own name on the shell which was used in the ballot for those to be expelled, replacing that of an illiterate peasant who objected to his nickname 'The Just'.

> (Plutarch *Aristides* vii)

See also *Aristeides*

> Browning E. B.   *The Battle of Marathon*
> i 35-6
> Dryden   *Britannia Rediviva* 33-61 x
> Pope   *Temple of Fame* 172-3
> Thomson   *Summer* 1491-3
> *Winter* 458-63

Aristippus   i) A philosopher-associate of *Socrates* and ii) the grandson of this man. Little is known of either. Aristippus junior taught a form of hedonism and this is associated also with his grandfather, who was taken to be the founder of the Cyrenaic belief, an early kind of Epicureanism.

> Byron   *Don Juan* ii 207
> Moore   *Morality* 36-43

Aristoclides   King of Orchomenos in *Arcadia*. Aristoclides killed his beloved *Stymphalis* (and her father) because he could not win her love. The Arcadians rose up against him and killed him in revenge.

> Chaucer   *Franklin's Tale* 1387-94

Aristogiton   With *Harmodius*, the would-be assassin of *Hippias* and his brother *Hipparchus* in 514 BC. The plot misfired and Hippias escaped death. Harmodius was killed by troops and Aristogiton was executed. Hippias, who was not popular, was subsequently expelled; the plotters then received posthumous tributes

from the people and were remembered as those who had slain the relatively harmless Hipparchus.

> (Herodotus v 55)
> Swinburne   *Athens* ep. 1
> Wordsworth   *The Prelude* x 198-202

Aristophanes   The father of Greek comedy who lived c457-385 BC. The main victims of his satire were men in public life (especially noisy innovators) and his satire is essentially conservative. From the eleven of his plays which are extant (less than a quarter of his work) it is clear that his strength lay in an extraordinary versatility of mood and an ability to universalise temporal particulars.

> Browning E. B.   *A Vision of Poets* 322-34
> Browning R.   *Aristophanes' Apology*
> 600 ff, 621-3, 1449-55
> Butler S.   *Hudibras* II ii 310-4
> Coleridge   *Lines to a Comic Author* 4 ff
> Jonson   *To Shakespeare* 51-4
> Pope   *Epistle to Henry Cromwell* 102-3

Aristorchus
See *Aristarchus*

> Marlowe   *Edward II* 2385-6

Aristotle   The Greek philosopher (384-322 BC) was a pupil of *Plato* and subsequently tutor to *Alexander the Great* from 342, though he saw little of him after his accession in 336. At that time Aristotle returned from Macedon to *Athens* and set up a school, the *Lyceum*, teaching as he walked about ('peripatetic'); a school in the more usual sense he could not run, since he was born at Stagirus and as a foreigner could not hold Athenian property. His works are mainly notes for the peripatetic school and cover diverse fields including ethics, poetics, zoology, politics and logic (which he virtually founded as a science). To literary theory he brought his love of order and empirical commonsense and in his *Poetics* laid down the principles of Classical drama with observation of 'unities'. The practical basis for these prescriptions tended to be overlooked in later literary history.

See also *Stagyrite*, *Pythias*

> Browning E. B.   *The Ring and the Book*
> viii 487-8
> Byron   *Don Juan* i 120, 201, xv 32

Chaucer	*Canterbury Tales (General Prologue)* 293-6
	Squire's Tale 23-4
	House of Fame 753-9
Denham	*Progress of Learning* 35-9
Dryden	*Sophonisba, Prologue at Oxford* 27-30
Goldsmith	*The Logicians Refuted*
Milton	*Paradise Regained* iv 251-3
Moore	*The Grecian Girl's Dream* 44-5
Pope	*Essay on Criticism* 271-2, 645-8
Shakespeare	*Taming of the Shrew* I i 31-3
	Troilus and Cressida II ii 163-7
Yeats	*Among School Children* vi

Arminius A Roman general in the auxiliary forces who resisted Rome's conquest of Germany but was defeated by *Germanicus* in 16 AD. The people turned against him and poisoned him in 19 AD. He had a brother in the Roman army and on one occasion the two came near to single combat.

(Strabo vii 1; Tacitus *Annals* ii 10)

Praed	*Arminius* 2-5, 19-24
Shelley	*Ode to Liberty* 196-202

Arne A daughter of *Aeolus*. *Neptune*, in the form of a bull, fell in love with her.

Spenser	*Faerie Queene* III xi 42

Arpies
See *Harpies*

Chaucer	*Monk's Tale* 3288-92

Arrian, Arrianus
See *Epictetus*

Arnold	*To a Friend* 6-8

Arsaces The first of the Parthian kings, coming probably from *Scythia*. He invaded *Parthia* in 250 BC and thereafter, with his successors (the Arsacids) laid the foundations of the Parthian Empire, with *Ecbatana* as its capital.

(Strabo xi 9)

Milton	*Paradise Regained* iii 294-7

Artemis The virgin goddess of the moon, chastity, woods, wild animals, the hunt, women, childbirth; also known as *Diana*, *Cynthia* and *Phoebe*. She was daughter of *Zeus* and sister of *Apollo*. *Asteria* and *Latona* were her children. The Romans identified her with their wide-ranging fertility goddess Diana. She was permitted by Zeus to have a train of sixty *Oceanides* and twenty other nymphs, all virgins, and such an entourage frequently accompanies her in poetry. She may be depicted with hunting dogs, bow and arrows, and hunting boots, and she is often seen bathing at a fountain. Worshipped at crossroads, she was sometimes called Trivia or, because identified with the moon and *Proserpina*, Triformis. Her temple at *Ephesus* was reckoned to be one of the wonders of the world. Dittany and poppy were among the plants sacred to her.

(Apollodorus *Epitome* iii 21-2;
Homeric Hymn *To Apollo* iii;
Strabo xiv i 20-3)

See also *Delia, Luna, Actaeon*

Arnold	*Fragment of an 'Antigone'* 54 ff
Auden	*Homage to Clio* 17-18
Bridges	*Prometheus the Firegiver* 944 ff
Browning R.	*Artemis Prologises* 1 ff, 10-12, 13-14
	Gerard de Lairesse 230-5
Clough	*Actaeon* 29-33
Collins	*The Passions, an Ode for Music* 20-3, 74-5
Jonson	*Cynthia's Revels* V iii
Lewis C. D.	*Transitional Poem* 31
Milton	*Sonnet* xii 5-6
Swinburne	*Atalanta in Calydon* 38-40

Artemis, Artemesia A 4th Century BC queen of *Caria* who was married to her brother *Mausolus*, and to whom she erected a monument, the Mausoleum, after his death. This was accounted one of the wonders of the world. She drank his ashes in her drink after his cremation and died of grief two years after his death.

(Strabo XIV ii 16)

Chaucer	*Franklin's Tale* 1451-2
Gray	*Lines spoken by the Ghost of John Dennis* 50
Hardy	*In St Paul's a While Ago*
Tennyson	*The Princess* ii 67

Ascalaphus, Ascallaphus A son of *Acheron* ordered by *Pluto* to guard *Proserpine*. Proserpine was allowed to return to earth provided she had eaten nothing in Pluto's kingdom, but

Ascalaphus revealed that she had eaten a pomegranate. As a result she was sentenced to alternate periods of six months with Pluto and with her mother *Demeter*. Proserpine then changed him into an owl by dowsing him with water from *Phlegethon* – or, in another version, Demeter imprisoned him behind a stone (removed by *Hercules*) in hell.

> (Apollodorus I v 3, II vi 12; Ovid *Metamorphoses* v 533 ff)

See also *Escaphilo*

Drayton   *The Owl* 97 ff, 281-6, 286-90

Ascanius

See *Iulus, Aeneas*

Browning E. B.   *The Battle of Marathon* 900-4
Chaucer   *House of Fame* 174-88
    Legend of Good Women 940-2, 1140-4
Drayton   *Polyolbion* i 335 ff
Dryden   *To the Duchess of Ormond* 160-2
Marlowe   *Dido Queen of Carthage* 96-9, 612-7
Shakespeare   *King Henry VI pt 2* III ii 114-7

Asclepioda, Asclepiodotus   A general sent by the Caesar *Constantius* to subdue *Allectus* in Britain in 296 AD, while *Diocletian* was Emperor.

Spenser   *Faerie Queene* II x 58

Asclepios, Asklepios

See *Aesculapius*

Browning R.   *Artemis Prologises* 13-14, 101-3, 113-7
    Balaustion's Adventure 372-6

Ascraean   Coming from Ascra, a Boeotian town, the birthplace of *Hesiod*.

Drayton   *The Muses' Elizium* iii 116-20
Moore   *The Philosopher Aristippus* 38-42

Ashtaroth

See *Astarte, Astoreth*

Milton   *On the Morning of Christ's Nativity* 200-1

Asia   An *Oceanid*, daugher of *Oceanus* and *Tethys*. Asia was, by some accounts, the mother, by *Iapetus*, of *Atlas, Prometheus* and *Epimetheus*. She represented, with Africa and Europe, one of the three parts of the known world.

> (Apollodorus I ii)

Keats   *Hyperion* ii 53-9
Shelley   *Prometheus Unbound* I i 120-3, 807 ff, 826-7, II i 203-6, v20-8, III iii 48 ff

Asopus (1)   A son or sons of *Neptune*, after whom several rivers were named. The daughters included *Aegina* and *Salamis*.

> (Apollodorus III xii 6; Diodorus Siculus IV 72)

See *Sisyphus, Aegina*

Arnold   *Fragment of an 'Antigone'* 61-4
    The Strayed Reveller 135-42
Spenser   *Faerie Queene* IV xi 14

Asopus (2)   A Persian river near *Thermopylae* and *Plataea*.

Shelley   *Hellas* 688-91

Aspasia   A Greek teacher of rhetoric and the arts. Aspasia was the mistress of *Pericles* and was accused of influencing him towards war. She was a friend of *Sophocles* and recalled as such by *Plato*.

> (Plato *Menexenus* 236)

Moore   *Aspasia*
    The Grecian Girl's Dream 46-7
Swinburne   *Song for the Centenary of Landor* 37
Tennyson   *The Princess* ii 322-5

Asphodel, Asphodels   A Mediterranean lily connected by the Greeks with *Hades* and the Elysian Fields, and also with *Persephone*. It was held to have therapeutic properties.

> (Homer *Odyssey* xi 539, xxiv 13; Pliny xxii 67 ff)

Milton   *Comus* 837-8
Pope   *Letter to Cromwell* 2-4
    Ode for Musick 72-5
Shelley   *Arethusa* 82-4
    Letter to Maria Gisborne 10-11
    The Sensitive Plant i 49-59
    Witch of Atlas 275-7
Tennyson   *Demeter and Persephone*

150-1
The Lotos-Eaters 169-70

Assaracus A mythical Trojan king, son of Tros and grandfather of *Anchises*, *Aeneas's* father.

(Homer *Iliad* xx 232;
Virgil *Aeneid* i 284)
Spenser *Faerie Queene* II ix 56-7, x 9

Astarte A Syrian goddess identified with the Greek *Aphrodite*, and representing the female principle to many Eastern peoples. She had temples at Sidon, Tyre and Carthage, and is referred to in the Bible as Ashtoreth. Associated with the planet *Venus*, she was shown with a crescent moon upon her head. When her lover *Thammuz* was killed by a boar, she persuaded the gods to allow him to spend half the year with her and half in the underworld, a myth paralleling those of Adonis and of Proserpina. Probably they all represent a vegetation myth in which the death of the year is lamented.

See also *Astoreth*
Browning R.   *Popularity* 26-30
Byron   *Manfred* II iii 98-102
Hardy   *The Collector Cleans His Picture* 29-30
Meredith   *The Comic Spirit*
Milton   *Paradise Lost* i 438-9
Swinburne   *Dolores* 392-6

Asteria Daughter of the Titans *Phoebe* and *Coeus*, Asteria was the mother of *Hecate*. Subsequently, when pursued by Zeus she leaped into the sea and became a quail (*ortyx*). On the site of this event arose an island, Asteria or *Ortygia* (2). The same story is also told of *Latona*.

(Apollodorus I iv; Hesiod *Theogony* 404-12;
Ovid *Metamorphoses* vi 103 ff)
See also *Delos*
Spenser *Faerie Queene* III xi 33

Astery
See *Asteria*
Spenser *Muiopotmos* 113-23

Astoreth
See *Astarte*, *Ashtoroth*
Milton   *Paradise Lost* i 438-9

Astraea, Astraean Goddess of Justice, daughter of *Saturn* and *Rhea*, or Saturn's brother *Titan* by *Aurora*. She lived on earth in the Golden Age of Justice, but fled from the wickedness of man and thereafter exercised her powers from heaven. Poets live in constant hope of her return to earth. She is depicted with scales in one hand and a sword in the other. Her flight from man is also reflected in representations of Peace.

See also *Justice*
(Hesiod *Theogony* 409 ff;
Ovid *Metamorphoses* i 149-50)
Byron   *Love's Last Adieu* 37-8
Campion   *Ev'ry Dame Affects Good Fortune*
Carew   *Coelum Britannicum* 687-90
Upon My Lord Chief Justice 15 ff
Drayton   *Endymion and Phoebe* 859-60
Fletcher P.   *The Locusts* iv 23
Purple Island i 51
Milton   *On the Death of a Fair Infant* 50-1
On the Morning of Christ's Nativity 141-4
Moore   *Rhymes on the Road* III 13-14
Prior   *Carmen Seculare* 257-8
Shakespeare   *King Henry VI pt 1* I vi 4-7
Skelton   *Laud and Praise*
Spenser   *Daphnaida* 218-9
Faerie Queene V i 5, 11
Swift   *Paulus, The Answer* 30-5
Tennyson   *I Dare not Write an Ode* 3-4
The Princess ii 420
Thomson   *To the Memory of Lord Talbot* 73-6
Wordsworth   *Memorials of a Tour 1820* xxv 75-8

Astraeus One of the Titans, a son of Crius and Eurybia, who made war against *Jupiter*. Astraeus was father by *Eos* of the winds *Boreas*, *Zephyrus* and *Notus*. The marriage of Eos and Astraeus was regarded as incestuous.
(Hesiod *Theogony* 375-82)
Spenser *Faerie Queene* IV xi 13

Astyages The last king of Media, of the 6th Century BC, who was defeated by his grandson *Cyrus*. He dreamed that his daughter would produce a son who would defeat him, and the dream proved correct.

(Herodotus i)

Butler S.   *Hudibras* III i 691-3

Atalanta   A virgin huntress suckled by a bear and brought up by hunters in *Arcadia* or Boeotia. *Jason* declined her request to join the *Argo* because he feared she would provoke dispute (as she was notoriously to do in the *Calydonian Boar Hunt*). When her father wished her to marry, though pledged to virginity, she countered the idea by challenging all suitors to a race with her, believing herself invincible. So she generally proved, and beheaded all whom she defeated. One young man, *Melanion* or *Hippomenes*, did defeat her: he prayed to *Aphrodite* in advance and she gave him three apples of the *Hesperides*, with which he diverted Atalanta as she ran. The oracle had foretold disaster for Atalanta if she married. She linked herself with the winner, but he had omitted to give thanks to Aphrodite. Stopping to make love in a temple, of *Zeus* or *Cybele*, the couple were turned into lions by the goddess.

(Apollonius Rhodius i 769-73;
Apollodorus I viii 2-3;
Ovid *Metamorphoses* x 560ff)

See also *Athalante*, *Atlante*, *Meleager*

Chaucer   *Troilus and Criseyde* V 1474-7
Graves   *New Legends* 7-11
Shakespeare   *As You Like It* III ii 135-9
Spenser   *Amoretti* 77
Faerie Queene II vii 54
Swinburne   *Atalanta in Calydon* 43-5,
205-10, 646ff, 969-1038,
1252ff, 1289ff, 1701-5,
1900-5

Ate   Daughter of *Jupiter*, Ate was goddess of evil. She caused envy among the gods and so was banished from heaven by Jupiter.

(Apollodorus III xii 3;
Homer *Iliad* xix 91-136)

See also *Discord*

Lamb   *The Female Orators* 17-18
Shakespeare   *Julius Caesar* III i 271
King John II i 2-3
Much Ado About Nothing
II i 221ff
Spenser   *Faerie Queene* II vii 55, IV i 19

Athalante
See *Atalanta*
Chaucer   *Parliament of Fowls* 286-7
Knight's Tale 2069-72

Athalus
See *Attalus III*
Chaucer   *Book of the Duchess* 662-4

Athamante
See *Athamas*
Chaucer   *Troilus and Criseyde* IV 1534ff

Athamas   Son of *Aeolus* and king of Boeotian *Thebes*. He married Nephele, from whom he had a son *Phrixus* and daughter *Helle*. He then married *Ino* (*Leucothea*), daughter of *Cadmus*, believing, or pretending to believe, that Nephele was mad. From Ino he had two sons, *Learchus* and *Melicerta*. Ino was subject to the enmity of *Juno*, as the former was descended from *Venus* and the goddesses were opposed. She was also jealous of Phrixus and Helle, since they were in the line of succession, and her persecution of the son and daughter led them to escape on the golden ram. Juno then made Athamas mad, so that he mistook Ino for her lioness and her children for lion's whelps. He shot or dashed Learchus to pieces, while Ino jumped from a cliff with Melicerta into the sea.

(Apollodorus I ix 2)

See also *Athamante*
Bridges   *Prometheus the Firegiver*
931-6
Spenser   *Faerie Queene* V viii 47

Athena
See *Athene*, *Minerva*
Byron   *Childe Harold* ii 2

Athenai
See *Athens*
Browning R.   *Aristophanes' Apology*
75ff

Athene
See *Minerva*, *Pallas*
Tennyson   *Tiresias* 38ff
Yeats   *Michael Robartes and the Dancer*
Two Songs from a Play i

Athenian
Collins   *Epistle to Sir Thomas Hanmer* 47-8
           The Persians 99
Milton   *Sonnet* viii 13-14

Athens   The Greek city which became a cultural centre in the 6th Century BC and defeated the Persians to become the major military and economic power in the 5th Century BC; by then she was the heart of an extensive empire. Sparta and Macedonia, both fearful of Athenian power, then became her main enemies. In 409 BC the Spartans, under *Lysander*, captured the city and tore down the walls to the sound of the flutes of city girls. By the end of the 4th Century *Alexander the Great* (Macedonia) had made inroads into the empire and the cultural creativity and importance of Athens began to decline. She conducted repeated skirmishes with the Macedonians, supported by various allies, and was defeated in 262 BC. She regained independence as a much-reduced power and was taken over by the Romans under *Sulla* in 86 BC.
                   (Plutarch *Lysander* xv)
See also *Acropolis*
Collins   *Lines on the Music of the Grecian Theatre* 3-4
Drayton   *The Owl* 223-4
MacNeice   *Autumn Sequel* xix
Milton   *Paradise Lost* ix 670-2
           Paradise Regained iv 238-43
Shelley   *Hellas* 682-6, 1084-7
           Ode to Liberty 61-5, 72-5
           Queen Mab ii 162ff
Spenser   *Muiopotmos* 305ff
Swinburne   *Athens, an Ode*

Athos   A celebrated Macedonian mountain on the eastern promontory of Kalkidice. Though nearly 100 miles away it was said to overshadow the island of *Lemnos* at sunset and was sacred to *Zeus*. It was severed from the mainland by a canal cut by *Xerxes* early in the 5th Century BC. A sculptor, Dinocrates, offered to hew Athos into a statue of *Alexander*, with a city in one hand, but Alexander turned down the idea.
        (Plutarch *Alexander* 72; Herodotus vii, 22-4; Aeschylus *Agamemnon* 289)
Browning E. B.   *Aurora Leigh* v 139-70

Byron   *The Age of Bronze* 13-18
        Childe Harold ii xxvii
Cleveland   *To Prince Rupert* 109-12
Marvell   *The Character of Holland* 97-8
Shelley   *Revolt of Islam* 2101-4

Atilius
See *Regulus*
Shelley   *Ode to Liberty* 97-8

Atlanta
See *Atalanta*
Donne   *Elegy* xix 35-8
Suckling   *His Dream* 7-10

Atlantean
See *Atlas*
Milton   *Paradise Lost* ii 305-7

Atlantides   Daughters of *Atlas*, including *Maia*, *Electra*, *Merope* and *Alcyone*. They were also called *Hesperides*, after their mother Hesperis, and *Pleiades* when their mother was taken to be the Oceanid Pleione.
Shelley   *The Witch of Atlas* 55-7

Atlantis   A large island supposed to have been in the Atlantic off Gibraltar. It was held to have been the ruling power of the known world until the rise of *Athens*, but in due course became submerged. As an ideal land its constitution as a commonwealth was the subject of a discourse by *Plato*.
        (Plato *Critias*; Timaeus 24e ff)
Auden   *Atlantis* 35-9
MacNeice   *Leaving Barra* 9-13
Shelley   *Hellas* 65-71, 992-5

Atlas   Atlas, king of Mauritania, was a Titan, the owner of flocks and gardens which he placed in the care of a dragon. *Perseus*, carrying the head of *Medusa*, changed Atlas into the African mountain which was believed to be so high that it touched heaven. Atlas was said to bear the world on his shoulders, perhaps as a punishment for assisting the Giants in war with the Gods. From this burden *Hercules* eased him, in gratitude for giving him knowledge of astronomy as a reward for restoring to him his seven daughters, the *Atlantides* when they had been abducted by *Busiris* of Egypt.

(Hesiod *Theogony* 508 ff; Ovid
Metamorphoses iv 631 ff;
Virgil *Aeneid* iv 246 - 50, 481)

Belloc	*In Praise of Wine* 56 ff
Browning R.	*Prince Hohenstiel-Schwangau* 715 - 8
Byron	*On the Death of Mr Fox* 12 - 16
Davies Sir J.	*Orchestra* 449 - 51
Denham	*Cooper's Hill* 51 - 2
Dryden	*Threnodia Augustalis* 26 ff
Fletcher P.	*Purple Island* x
Herbert, Lord	*A Description* 36 - 7
Keats	*Endymion* ii 689 - 90, iii 682 - 5
	Hyperion ii 73 - 4
	To Charles Cowden Clarke 62 - 3
Lamb	*Leisure* 13 - 14
Marlowe	*Dido Queen of Carthage* 1068 - 72
	Tamburlaine i 463 - 5
Milton	*Paradise Lost* iv 985 - 7, xi 402
Pope	*Temple of Fame* 59 - 60
Shakespeare	*Antony and Cleopatra* I iv 23
	King Henry VI pt 3 V i 34 ff
Shelley	*Witch of Atlas* 55 - 7
Spenser	*Faerie Queene* II vii 54, III i 57
	Sonnet 'To you, right noble lord'
Thomson	*Autumn* 798
Wyatt	*Jopas' Song* 1 - 4

Atreus   Son of *Pelops* and Hippodamia. Atreus (with his brother *Thyestes*) killed Pelops's bastard son Chrysippus, of whom Hippodamia was jealous; he was banished, but was rescued by the King of Mycenae. Atreus married Aerope, princess of Crete, to save her from slavery, and became father (or in another version, grandfather) of *Agamemnon* and *Menelaus*. Atreus and Thyestes were at enmity over the succession and the latter became lover of Aerope; they had several children. Atreus then banished Thyestes but decided to further his revenge by pretending a reconciliation in which he asked Thyestes to a banquet; here he served up Thyestes' dismembered sons, whose heads and hands were displayed to the father afterwards. Thyestes fled to Sicyon, where he had a son, Aegisthus, by his own daughter, Pelopia. Atreus found Thyestes and tried to persuade his unnatural son to kill him, but Aegisthus refused to do so and in fact slew Atreus. Although Thyestes then succeeded to the throne, he was ousted by Agamemnon, who was in turn killed by Aegisthus, who was then slain by Agamemnon's son *Orestes*. This appalling and intricate cycle of events was explained as the working-out of the family curse and the crime of Pelops.

(Apollodorus *Epitome* II viiff;
Hyginus *Fabulae* 83 ff)

Crashaw	*Sospetto d'Herode* 42

Atrides   *Agamemnon* and *Menelaus*, generally said to be sons of *Atreus*.

Prior	*Alma* ii 91 ff
	Carmen Seculare 454 - 5

Atropos   The oldest of the three sisters, the *Fates* or *Parcae*. (The others being *Clotho* and *Lachesis*.) She is represented blind, or with a black veil and a pair of scissors with which she cuts indiscriminately the thread of life spun by her sisters. Sources differ as to whether they were omnipotent or subject to *Zeus*.

(Hesiod *Theogony* 217 - 22; Pausanias II
xi 4; Plato *Republic* x 616 - 7)

Browning R.	*Apollo and the Fates* 21 - 5
Byron	*Don Juan* ii 64
Chaucer	*Troilus and Criseyde* iv 1208, 1546 - 7
Gray	*Lines Spoken by the Ghost of John Dennis* 3 - 4
Keats	*Endymion* iii 580 - 1
Milton	*Epitaph on the Marchioness of Winchester*
	Lycidas 75 - 6
Shakespeare	*King Henry IV pt 2* II iv 188 - 9
Sidney	*Arcadia* lxxiii, 109 - 11
Skelton	*On the Dolorous Death of the Earl of Northumberland* 120 ff
Spenser	*Faerie Queene* IV ii 48

Attalus III   King of Pergamum in the 2nd Century BC. Attalus had a short and eccentric reign (devoted to gardening and sculpture) until his death in 138 BC when he was still very young. Rome had intervened to save his uncle, Attalus II, from a Bithynian invasion and in a famous will the young king bequeathed his kingdom to the Romans. It was also believed (wrongly) that he invented the game of chess.

Attheon
See *Actaeon*
> Chaucer   *Knight's Tale* 2065-8, 2297-2303

Attica   The south-eastern promontory of Greece, of which *Athens* was the capital. 'Attic' is also used generally of Greek culture.
> Collins   *Ode to Simplicity* 11, 35
> Gray   *Ode on the Spring* 5
> Keats   *Fragments of 'The Castle-Builder'* 58-61
> *Ode on a Grecian Urn* 41-3
> Milton   *Paradise Regained* iv 243-6
> *Sonnet* xx 9-10

Attic Bird
See *Nightingale*

Atticus   Titus Pomposius 'Atticus', a friend and correspondent of *Cicero*, was given the name because he spent much of his time in *Athens*. He refused all invitations to political office and lived the life of a gentleman scholar, made possible by a wealthy family. It is possible that he had clandestine political influence — he certainly observed the political scene — but he committed suicide in his thirties during illness. Like the retired *Scipio*, he was seen by later ages as a type of the cultured and leisured man.
> Pope   *Windsor Forest* 257-8

Attila   King of the Huns, who conquered many surrounding tribes to make himself supreme in Central Europe in the 5th Century AD. He attacked northern Italy, desecrating ancient cities, in 452 but died in 453 the night after his wedding. 'Attila the Hun' became a byword for arrogant assurance in pursuit of national causes.
> Chaucer   *Pardoner's Tale* 579-81
> Lawrence   *Attila* 1-3

Attis, Atys   A Phrygian shepherd loved by the goddess *Cybele*. She made him take an oath of celibacy, which he broke with a nymph, and Cybele then drove him to madness in which he castrated himself or, in another version, was turned into a pine tree.
> (Ovid *Metamorphoses* x 104;
> Pausanias VII xvii 9-11)

> Meredith   *The Empty Purse*

Atys   A Lydian prince (and part of Lydia, named after him), son of *Croesus*. As Croesus had a dream that Atys had been killed, he forbade Atys all arms and kept all arms from the house in case they should fall on him. He was, however, persuaded to let him hunt a wild boar which was ravaging neighbouring *Mysia*. *Adrastus*, a Phrygian prince who was made his guardian, went with him and killed him, possibly by accident, instead of the boar. Thus the dream was fulfilled.
> (Herodotus I vii, xxxivff)
> Housman   *Atys* 8-15

Aufidius
See *Amfidius*
> Shakespeare   *Coriolanus* I i 226-7, IV vi 66-7, V iv 31ff

Aufidus   A major river (Ofanto) virtually crossing southern Italy, flowing into the Adriatic Sea, and having *Cannae* near its mouth. It is mentioned by *Horace* as known to him almost from birth.
> (Horace *Satires* I i 58; Odes IV ix)
> Belloc   *In Praise of Wine* 37-44

Auge, Augea   Daughter of *Neaera* and princess of Tegea. Auge was raped by *Hercules* and produced a son, *Telephus*, who was brought up in the woods. Aleus, her father, in his rage ordered Nauplius (a son of *Neptune*) to kill her. Nauplius relented and sold her to King Teuthras of *Mysia*, who adopted her as his daughter and subsequently promised her to whoever could free his land from its enemies. This turned out to be Telephus. Incest was avoided by intervention of the gods, who put a snake between mother and son. In other versions Nauplius is omitted; Auge is put to sea in a chest with Telephus and is found by Teuthras.
> (Apollodorus II vii, III ix; Pausanias VIII iv; Hyginus *Fabulae* 99, 100)
> Graves   *To Ogmian Hercules* 4-8

Augean   Belonging to the wealthy family of King Augeus of Elis, in particular his stables. Augeus had an enormous stock of beasts and they kept both land and stables deep in dung.

It was the fifth of *Hercules'* labours to clean out the stables in one day. Augeus broke his bargain to pay him and Hercules, though driven away, returned to defeat his forces and possibly to kill Augeus.

(Apollodorus II v 5)

Butler S.	*Hudibras* I ii 457-8
Chapman	*Bussy d'Ambois* IV i 182-8
Cowley	*Ode Upon his Majesty's Restoration* 3-5
Herrick	*To His Saviour* 1-2

Augusta (1)   A Roman name for London, depicted as married to *Albion*.

Dryden	*Albion and Albanius* I
	MacFlecknoe 64-7
Pope	*Windsor-Forest* 335-6, 377-8
Shenstone	*Elegies* i 1-2

Augusta (2)
See *Livia (1)*

Jonson	*Sejanus* II i

Augustan
See *Augustus*

Byron	*Manfred* III iv 29-30

Augustus (Octavian)   *Julius Caesar*'s great-nephew and adopted son; the first Roman Emperor from 27 BC until his death in AD 14, when he was declared a god. 'Augustus' was a title conferred by the Senate on Octavian in 27 BC as a mark of respect; it was a semi-religious term meaning virtually 'divine' (as opposed to 'humanus'). Partly because of his own successful exploits earlier, the Augustan era became one of relative peace in which culture and civil improvements flourished. It was the age of *Virgil*, *Horace* and Propertius. The celebrated patron of the arts, *Maecenas*, enjoyed the close trust of the Emperor. The turning-point towards this settled period was the battle of Actium in 31 BC, in which Augustus defeated *Antony* and *Cleopatra*, who had violated the agreements sealed by the marriage of *Octavia* (Augustus's sister) and Antony. A fitting text for Augustus's reign is his apotheosis in Horace's twelfth *Ode*.
See also *Octavian, Octavianus*

Auden	*Secondary Epic* 47 ff
Denham	*Progress of Learning* 73-6
Graves	*Rhea* 13-14

	Troublesome Fame 11-14
Dryden	*Astraea Redux* 320-3
	MacFlecknoe 3-6
Johnson	*On Colley Cibber* 1
MacNeice	*Memoranda to Horace* iii
Pope	*Temple of Fame* 229-31
Prior	*Carmen Seculare* 54-5
	Ode Inscribed to the Queen 1 ff
Shakespeare	*Antony and Cleopatra* III xi 35-9
	Cymbeline V v 81-2, 458-61
Spenser	*Shepherds Calendar October* 61-2
	Sonnet 'That Mantuan Poet's . . .'
	Sonnet 'Those prudent heads . . .'
Yeats	*The Saint and the Hunchback*
Young	*Epistle to Lord Lansdowne* 1-2
	The Best Argument for Peace
	The Old Man's Relapse

Augustan   Of the age of Augustus or characteristic of that age.

Collins	*Lines to a Friend about to Visit Italy* 11-12

Aurelian   The Roman Emperor Lucus Aurelianus (215-75 AD) rose from humble birth to command the troops of *Claudius* II and to be Emperor himself c. 270. He defeated a number of barbaric tribes and put down *Zenobia*, the self-styled Empress of the East, in 273; the victory was followed by a triumphal procession of all his victims, led by Zenobia (whom, however, he permitted to retire in peace). He was murdered in a military plot in 275. His reign was brief, but he was a ruthless man who went far to restore the Empire to the unity from which it had fallen.

Chaucer	*Monk's Tale* 3541-8
Tennyson	*The Princess* ii 69-71

Aurelius   Marcus Aurelius, Roman Emperor from 161-180 AD. An austere, highly educated administrator rather than a general or emperor of imagination, but also an important Stoic philosopher. His twelve books of *Meditations* have survived the centuries for their just mixture of Stoic philosophy and personal reflection expressed in a concise manner.

Pope   *Temple of Fame* 165-7

Aurora   Aurora (*Eos*), goddess of dawn and morning, was daughter of *Hyperion* and *Thea*, or of *Titan* and *Terra*. She was married to *Tithonus* and took as her lovers *Cephalus* (Aeolides), son of *Aeolus*, and also *Orion*. She was raped by *Apollo*. Dawn is represented in a roseate chariot, opening gates in the East with a rosy hand. She wore a white veil and her horses were white. Dawn is frequently described in terms of the rising of Aurora from the bed of Tithonus.

(Hesiod *Theogony* 371-4;
Ovid *Metamorphoses* ii 113-5, vii 672ff)
See also *Leucothea*

Arnold   *Fragment of an 'Antigone'* 54ff
Byron   *Don Juan* ii 142
Chaucer   *Legend of Good Women* 774-5
Hood   *The Departure of Summer* 24-7
Keats   *Endymion* ii 695-7, iii 111-5
        To George Felton Matthew 20-2
Meredith   *The Rape of Aurora*
Milton   *L'Allegro* 18-9
        Paradise Lost v 5-6
Shakespeare   *Romeo and Juliet* i 132-5
Shelley   *Witch of Atlas* 576-83
Spenser   *Faerie Queene* I ii 7, iv 16,
        xi 51, III x 1, iii 20
        Muiopotmos 49-52
Wordsworth   *The Prelude* vii 500-2

Ausonia, Ausonian   Italy, supposed to be named Ausonia after *Ulysses*'s son Auson, but the name may well be 'Oscan', the name of an ancient people there.

Keats   *Endymion* iv 14-15
Milton   *Paradise Lost* i 739-40
Pope   *Temple of Fame* 202-5
Shelley   *Ode to Naples* 171-3
Marlowe   *Tamburlaine* i 1062-6

Auster   See *Notus*

Autonoe   A *Nereid*.   (Apollodorus I ii 6)
Spenser   *Faerie Queene* IV xi 50

Avernus   A river of *Hades*.
See *Aornos*
Marlowe   *Tamburlaine* i 333-6, 1656-61
Spenser   *Faerie Queene* I v 31

Azotus   Ashdod, formerly a Syrian town off the Mediterranean coast, one of the five principal cities of the Philistines. It was a centre for the worship of *Dagon*, and its temple was destroyed by Judas Macabeus and Jonathan in the 2nd Century BC.
Milton   *Paradise Lost* i 262-4

Babiloigne
See *Babylon*
Chaucer   *Summoner's Tale* 2079-82
        Monk's Tale 3333-40
        Legend of Good Women 706-8

Babylon   The capital of the Babylonian province of the Assyrian Empire (and of Assyria under the Nebuchadnezzars) in modern Iraq. It was celebrated for its size and defences, which included immense walls and a hundred brazen gates. In 539BC it was captured by *Cyrus*, who diverted the River Euphrates and marched along the bed of the river. Thereafter, the city became part of the Persian Empire.
(Herodotus i 178-83, 188-91)
See *Babiloigne*, *Semiramis*
Keats   *Endymion* iii 847-9
Milton   *Paradise Regained* iii 240-4
Spenser   *Faerie Queene* IV i 22

Bacchae
See *Bacchanal*
Lawrence   *Late at Night* 21ff

Bacchanal, Bacchanalian   The orgy of followers of *Dionysus* (*Bacchus*), or the name given to these revellers.
See *Bacchae*, *Maenad*
Arnold   *Bacchanalia* 24-31
Cowper   *On the Death of Mrs Throckmorton's Bullfinch* 61-6
        Truth 461-2
Pope   *Ode for Musick* 111
Shakespeare   *Midsummer Night's Dream* V i 48-9
Shelley   *Lines Written During the Castlereagh Administration* 16-20
        Ode to Liberty 171-3, 196-202
Swinburne   *Atalanta In Calydon* 112ff

Wordsworth   *River Duddon* xx 7 ff

Baccheion   The Temple of *Dionysus* (*Bacchus*) at Syracuse.
    Browning R.   *Balaustion's Adventure* 337-8, 348-9

Bacchic
See *Bacchus*
    Shelley   *Prometheus Unbound* III iii 154

Bacchus   The Roman name for the god *Dionysus*.
See *Bacus*
    Belloc   *In Praise of Wine* 8-13, 56 ff, 120-4
    Browning E. B.   *The Dead Pan* 14
        Wine of Cyprus i
    Browning R.   *Balaustion's Adventure* 161-3
    Byron   *Don Juan* ii 170, xvi 86
    Carew   *To My Friend G. N.* 63-4, 97 ff
    Chaucer   *Parliament of Fowls* 274-7
    Cowley   *Elegy on Anacreon* 91 ff
    Crabbe   *The Borough* x 27-8
    Diaper   *Dryades* 202-7
    Drayton   *Elinor Cobham to Duke Humphrey* 178
    Fletcher G.   *Christ's Victory on Earth* 51
    Fletcher P.   *Purple Island* i 49, vii 21
    Herrick   *The Vine* 10-3
    Hood   *Progress of Art* 6
    Jonson   *And must I sing?* 10-12
        Dedication of the King's New Cellar 13-15, 25-8
    Keats   *Endymion* iv 199 ff, 235 ff
        Lamia i 209-10
        Ode to a Nightingale
        Otho the Great V 5 120-5
        Sleep and Poetry 334-6
    Marlowe   *Hero and Leander* i 135-42
        Jew of Malta 1808-10
    Milton   *Comus* 46-7, 519-20
        L'Allegro 13-16
        Paradise Lost iv 275-9, vii 32-3
    Noyes   *The Burning Boughs* 13-16
    Praed   *Modern Nectar* 1-8
    Shakespeare   *Love's Labour's Lost* IV iii 335-41
    Shenstone   *The Judgment of Hercules* 188-9

    Skelton   *Garland of Laurel*
    Spenser   *Epithalamium* 255-7
        Faerie Queene I vi 15, II i 55, III ix 30, III xi 43, V i 2, viii 47
        Shepherd's Calendar, October 106-8
        Tears of the Muses 457-62
    Swift   *Vanbrugh's House* 119-20
    Swinburne   *Atalanta in Calydon* 105-6
    Tennyson   *Semele* 11 ff
    Wordsworth   *Ecclesiastical Sonnets* I xx 1-5
    Young   *Night Thoughts* ii

Bactra   Capital of the Persian province of Bactria (now Balkan Afghanistan), celebrated by the Greeks for its fertility.
        (Strabo XI xi; Virgil *Georgics* ii 138)
    Milton   *Paradise Regained* iii 284-8

Bacus
See *Bacchus*
    Chaucer   *Merchant's Tale* 1722-3
        Physician's Tale 58-60
        Legend of Good Women 2373-7
        Troilus and Criseyde v 206-10

Baiae   A former city on the Bay of Naples supposed to have been founded by Baius, helmsman of *Ulysses*. It was renowned as a temperate resort with hot springs, and several Roman Emperors had villas there.
        (Horace *Epistles* I i 83; Strabo V ii 9, IV v 1)
    Keats   *Ode to May* 1
    Shelley   *Ode to the West Wind* 29-32
        The Sensitive Plant iii 1-4

Baian
See *Baiae*
    Shelley   *Ode to Naples* 26-31

Bandusia, Bandusian   A fountain or spring near *Horace*'s Sabine farm, to which he addressed an ode.
        (Horace *Odes* III xiii)
    Wordsworth   *An Evening Walk* 72-3
        Memorials of a Tour in Italy 255-7
        River Duddon i 1-4

Those breathing tokens . . .
102-5

Barca, Barcaei   A city and people of Cyrenaica (Libya) famed for their warlike character.

(Virgil *Aeneid* iv 43)
Milton   *Paradise Lost* ii 902-3

Bassarid   A Bacchant or *Maenad*, being a priestess of *Bacchus*. Bassarids were named after Bassara, a Libyan town sacred to Bacchus.
Swinburne   *Atalanta in Calydon* 107-8
Prelude 101-4

Baucis   A Bithynian peasant married to *Philemon*. The elderly couple gave hospitality to *Zeus* and *Hermes* (disguised as mortals). Various miracles resulted, in one of which their hut became a temple, where Zeus allowed them to serve the rest of their lives as priest and priestess. They were allowed to die simultaneously, to save them sorrow. After death they were turned into an oak and a linden tree.
(Ovid *Metamorphoses* viii 618ff)
Lewis C. D.   *Baucis and Philemon*
Marlowe   *Dido Queen of Carthage* 288-9

Bavius   A dull Augustan poet, said to be equalled only by *Maevius*.
(Virgil *Eclogue* III 90)
Fletcher P.   *The Purple Island*
Pope   *To the Author of a Poem* 18-19

Belerium
See *Bellerus*
Pope   *Windsor-Forest* 316

Bellerophon   Hipponous (son of *Glaucus*) who was named Bellerophon (killer of monsters) for his exploits. He lived in the court of Proetus of *Argos*, where he may have fled after murdering his brother *Bellerus* (the other source of his name) and was accused of attempting the virtue of Queen Antaea (*Sthenoboea*), who had a passion for him. Proetus did not wish to offend hospitality and sent Bellerophon to Iobates, King of *Lycia*, with a letter asking Iobates to kill the miscreant. Iobates tried to arrange this honourably. He dispatched Bellerophon to deal with *Chimaera*, but he defeated the

monster with the help of his winged steed, *Pegasus*. Again, Iobates sent him to fight the *Amazons*, but he emerged the victor. In these adventures the innocent Bellerophon had the support of *Minerva*. He is then reputed to have tried to fly to heaven on Pegasus, but to have been thrown from the horse when *Jupiter* caused an insect to sting it. After this, Bellerophon spent a blind and vagrant life till death.
(Apollodorus II iii; Homer *Iliad* vi 156ff;
Pindar *Olympian Ode* XIII 84ff)
Dryden   *Aureng-Zebe* III i
Lewis C. D.   *Hero and Saint* 13-16
Pegasus 100-2
Marvell   *To That Renowned Man . . .* 1ff
Meredith   *Bellerophon*
Milton   *Paradise Lost* vi 16-19
Prior   *Carmen Seculare* 290-1
Wordsworth   *Sonnet, From the Dark Chambers* 2-7
Young   *Night Thoughts* vii

Bellerus   The Roman name for Land's End, possibly named after a giant.
(Diodorus Siculus V xxi 3)
See *Belerium*
Milton   *Lycidas* 159-60

Bellona   A goddess of war, the daughter or wife of *Mars*. She joined in battle, urging on the combatants with a whip and carrying a torch. She was worshipped by the Romans and her rites included self-mutilation.
Byron   *Don Juan* vii 1
Chaucer   *Anelida and Arcite* 1-6
Drayton   *The Owl* 267-8
Keats   *King Stephen* I iii 1-3
Marlowe   *Tamburlaine* II 3229-32
Milton   *Paradise Lost* ii 920-4
Prior   *Ode in Memory of George Villiers* 14
Shakespeare   *Macbeth* I ii 54-8
Shelley   *Oedipus Tyrannus* I i 413
Spenser   *Mutability Cantos* vi 3
Shepherd's Calendar, October 112-4
Faerie Queene IV xi 15

Belus   Son of *Neptune* and brother to *Agenor*. Belus was a Babylonian king who married Anchinoë, daughter of *Nilus*. Their children included Aegyptus and Danaus, and Belus was said to have been an ancestor of *Dido*. The temple of Belus, based on Babel, was legendary in wealth and had golden towers of great height. *Xerxes* was said to have destroyed it.

> (Apollodorus II i 4)
> Wordsworth   *The Excursion* iv 682ff

Berecynthia, Berecynthian   *Cybele*, goddess of fertility; the name is from Berecynthus, a mountain in Phrygia where she was worshipped.

> (Virgil *Aeneid* ix 82)
> Pope   *Dunciad* iii 123-6
> Southey   *Roderick* II 213-6

Berenice   The daughter of Ptolemy Philadelphus of Egypt, who had married his sister Arsinoë. Berenice in turn married her brother Euergetes. She loved him so extremely that she vowed to give all her hair to *Venus* if he came back safe from war. He did so, and so did she. The locks were subsequently missed from the Temple of Venus. It was said that *Jupiter* had taken them and made a constellation of them.

> (Catullus lxvi;
> Hyginus *Poetica Astronomica* ii 24)
> Drayton   *Eclogue* IX 216-22
> Lovelace   *On Sannazar* 101-2

Be-Rosciused
See *Roscius*

Biblis   A girl who fell in love with her twin brother (Caunus) and was turned into a fountain near *Miletus*.

> (Ovid *Metamorphoses* ix 454-665)
> Chaucer   *Parliament of Fowls* 288f
> Fletcher P.   *The Purple Island* V 19
> Spenser   *Faerie Queene* III ii 41

Bion   A Greek poet of Smyrna, whose dates are unknown. Bion gained a place in the history of pastoral elegy for a *Lament for Adonis* attributed to him (and formerly to *Theocritus*) since the Renaissance, but he was not principally a pastoral poet. As a result of this poem he in turn receives pastoral lament in a *Lament for Bion* attributed (now doubtfully) to *Moschus* of Syracuse, c.150BC, or even to Theocritus. From this we learn that he lived in Sicily and was killed by poison.

> Arnold   *Thyrsis* 82-90
> Browning E. B.   *Wine of Cyprus* 12

Bisalti, Bisaltes   The family of Theophane, with whom *Neptune* fell in love and whom he turned into a ewe to obstruct her other suitors. He himself changed into a ram and had by her a ram with a golden fleece. This was the ram which carried *Phryxus* to *Colchis*, but off which *Helle* fell into the sea thereafter called *Hellespont*. This fleece was the object of the *Argonauts'* quest.

> (Hyginus *Fabulae* clxxxviii;
> Ovid *Metamorphoses* vi 115-7)
> Spenser   *Faerie Queene* III xi 41

Boadiccea
See *Boudicca*

Boece
See *Boethius*
> Chaucer   *Wife of Bath's Tale* 1165-70
> *House of Fame* 972-8

Boethius   Anicius Manlius Boethius was a statesman of high birth and a consul intimate with Theodoric the Ostrogoth, ruler in Rome from 500AD. He was convicted of treason, imprisoned and executed. A man of stoical outlook, his most famous work, *De Consolatione Philosophiae*, was a dialogue between himself and true wisdom in a mixture of verse and prose. The book was greatly respected in the Middle Ages for its dealings in the fundamental problems of evil, fate and free will, predestination and fore-knowledge. Boethius wrote many translations and commentaries, but it is for this unique blend of stoicism, neo-Platonism and Christianity that he is known.

Bole
See *Taurus*
> Chaucer   *Troilus and Criseyde* II 54-6

Boreal
See *Boreas*
> Collins   *An Ode on the Popular Superstititions . . .* 37

Boreas   The North wind (blowing over the Hyperborean mountains), son of *Astraeus* and

Aurora. He was a deity represented with wings and white hair and surrounded by thick cloud. Boreas changed himself into a horse and produced twelve mares which crossed the sea so fast that their hooves remained dry.

(Hesiod *Theogony* 379;
Ovid *Metamorphoses* vi 682 ff)

Carew	*Upon Mr W. Montague* 25-6
Donne	*Elegy* xvi 19-23
Dryden	*The Hind and the Panther* iii 620-1
Keats	*Endymion* iii 529-31
Milton	*Paradise Lost* x 699-700
Pope	*Winter* 87
	A Winter Piece 1-4
Shakespeare	*Troilus and Cressida* I iii 37-40
Spenser	*Faerie Queene* I ii 33
	Shepherd's Calendar, February 226
Surrey	*In winter's just return* 1
Wordsworth	*Dion* 72-6
Young	*The Merchant* ii

Boudicca   The wife of a Roman tributary king of the East Anglians who, on his death in 60 BC, rebelled under her leadership against the absent governor, *Paulinus.* After sacking several cities, the rebels were defeated by Paulinus and their queen poisoned herself.

(Tacitus *Annals* xiv 31-7)
See also *Bunduca*

Brennus   A Gallic leader who invaded Rome in 347 BC, but whose assault on the *Capitol* was frustrated by the warning given by the geese kept there. The Capitol was commanded by *Manlius.* The invasion was subsequently defeated by the return of *Camillus* from exile.

(Livy v 46)

Browning R.	*Sordello* III 587-92
Byron	*The Deformed Transformed* II i 110
Thomson	*Liberty* iii 127-9
Vaughan	*To His Retired Friend* 11-14

Breseyda
See *Briseis*

Chaucer   *House of Fame* 397-404

Briareus, Briaros, Briarous   Briareus or Aegaeon was like a giant (though not one of

the true Giants), having a hundred hands and fifty heads. He was a son of *Poseidon* or *Uranus* and of *Ge.* For his part in the war against the Gods, in which he assisted the *Giants,* he was thrown under Mt *Aetna.* He was sometimes confused, as a *Titan,* with the Giant, *Typhon,* since Giants and Titans both revolted against *Zeus* and suffered similar fates. (Two other hundred-handed monsters were named *Gyges* and *Cottus.*)

(Hesiod *Theogony* 147-58, 617-735;
Homer *Iliad* i 400-406)

Johnson	*On the Famous Voyage* 81-4
Keats	*Hyperion* ii 19-22
Milton	*Paradise Lost* i 198-9
Pope	*Lines from Alcander* x 2-4
Shakespeare	*Troilus and Cressida* I ii 28-9
Southey	*Roderick* i 26-30

Briseis   When he killed her relations in the sacking of Lyrnessus (a town near *Troy*) *Achilles* took Briseis for his concubine as a prize of war. *Agamemnon* took as his mistress Chryseis, whom he then refused to return to her father for a ransom, but her prayers to *Apollo* (of whom her father, Chryses, was priest) brought a plague on the Greeks; Agamemnon then surrendered her but seized Briseis from Achilles, causing the latter to retire from the War. When Achilles was moved by the death of his friend *Patroclus* to return to battle, Agamemnon gave Briseis back to him. These Homeric events are elements in the largely non-Classical story of *Troilus* and *Cressida.*

(Homer *Iliad* i xix 246-302;
Ovid *Heroides* iii)

Britannicus   Tiberius Britannicus, son of *Claudius* Caesar. *Nero* displaced Britannicus and succeeded to the Empire in 54 AD by influence of *Agrippina* who was believed to have poisoned Claudius. Nero had Britannicus poisoned in 55 AD. He was so named after his father's invasion of Britain in 43 AD.

(Tacitus *Annals* xiii-xiv)
Gray   *Agrippina* 13-15

Brontes, Bronteus   One of the three *Cyclops* smiths employed by *Vulcan* in Mount *Aetna.* They forged *Aeneas'* shield from a thunderbolt.

The others were *Sterops* and *Pyracmon*.
(Virgil *Aeneid* viii 422-8)

Drayton	*Polyolbion* xx 165-6
Jonson	*Ode to James, Earl of Desmond* 40-6
Spenser	*Faerie Queene* IV v 37

Brut, Brutus (1) Legendary founder of the English people on *Albion*, Brutus was said to be son of *Sylvius* and great grandson of *Aeneas*. In flight after killing his father, he came upon Albion, inhabited then by giants, landed at Totnes and founded a line of kings and people with the stock of Trojans brought with him. The name probably arises from the similarity of Classical 'Brut' with 'Bryt' (Briton).

Blake	*King Edward* III vi 1ff
Drayton	*Polyolbion* i 309-14, i 335f, i 406ff
Prior	*Ode Inscribed to the Queen* 211-5
Spenser	*Faerie Queene* II x 9
Wyatt	*Tagus Farewell* 5

Brutus (2) Lucius Junius Brutus, a partly historical figure, seized the dagger from *Lucretia* as she committed suicide, and swore vengeance. He had the Roman people behind him, and the despotic *Tarquinius Superbus* and his line were banished. Thus Brutus was the reputed founder of the Republic in 510BC. He killed his own two sons because they conspired to restore Tarquin.

(Livy i 49)

Chaucer	*Legend of Good Women* 1861-5
Prior	*Carmen Seculare* 40-1
Shakespeare	*Coriolanus* I i 212-4
	Rape of Lucrece 1734-5, 1811-4
Southey	*Hymn to the Penates* 229-34
Tennyson	*The Princess* 262-8

Brutus (3) Marcus Junius Brutus, the assassin of *Caesar*. Brutus fought for *Pompey* in the Civil War but was pardoned by Caesar after *Pharsalus* in 48BC. He became Caesar's friend, but conspired against him in 44BC when it seemed to him that Caesar aimed to be a tyrant. Brutus was said to be an insomniac and at some time after the murder he saw a phantom which announced itself as his 'evil genius' which he would meet at *Philippi*.

Following the murder, he was obliged to leave home and had several administrative and military posts until, after gathering support in the East, he and *Cassius* met *Antony* and *Octavian* in 42BC at Philippi. After losing the second battle he committed suicide on his sword, held for him by a life-long friend, Strato. The 'honourable' Brutus was a friend of *Cicero* and was known for his interest in moral philosophy; he is traditionally the most intellectual and conscience-stricken of the assassins of Caesar.

(Plutarch *Brutus*)

See also *Porcia*

Byron	*Childe Harold* iv 82
	Consolatory Address to Sarah 9-12
	Don Juan XV 49
Campbell	*Pleasures of Hope* i
Chaucer	*Franklin's Tale* 1448-50
	Monk's Tale 3887-900
Coleridge	*Destiny of Nations* 9-10
Cowley	*Brutus* 3, 5
Dryden	*Don Sebastian* II i
Jonson	*Sejanus* I i
Pope	*Chorus to 'Brutus'* ii 7-8, 15-16
	Temple of Fame 177
Shakespeare	*Antony and Cleopatra* II v 16; III xi 35
	Julius Caesar I ii 28ff; III ii 181; V iv 47ff
	King Henry V II iii 36-8
	Merchant of Venice I i 165-6
Shelley	*Otho* 1-4
Swift	*To Stella Visiting Me* 39-41
Swinburne	*The Augurs*
Thomson	*Liberty* v 201-6
	Winter 524-6
Wordsworth	*The Prelude* x 198-92

Bunduca
See *Boudicca*

Spenser	*Faerie Queene* II x 54-5, III iii 54
	Ruins of Time 108-12

Burrhus
See *Burrus*

Gray	*Agrippina* 148-9

Burrus Sextus Afranius Burrus was praetor

under *Claudius* and, with *Seneca*, tutor and adviser to *Nero*, who probably arranged for his death by poison in 62 AD.

(Tacitus *Annals* xiv)

Busiris A legendary king of Egypt, notorious for his cruelty, who was defeated by *Hercules*. (Chaucer confused him with *Diomedes* after Ovid *Heroides* ix 67 ff.)

(Apollodorus II v)

See also *Busirus*

Crashaw	*Sospetto d'Herode* 45
Milton	*Paradise Lost* i 307

Busirus

See *Busiris*

Chaucer	*Monk's Tale* 3293-3300

Cacus A son of *Vulcan* and *Medusa*, Cacus was a three-headed monster vomiting smoke and flames. He stole cows from *Hercules* but was betrayed by the lowing of the remaining animals, which was answered by those that he had taken. Hercules then strangled Cacus, and a local festival was instituted to commemorate the victory.

(Ovid *Fasti* i 543-86;
Virgil *Aeneid* viii 184-270)

Butler S.	*Hudibras* II i 429-30
Chaucer	*Monk's Tale* 3293-300
Dryden	*Annus Mirabilis* 329-30
Milton	*Comus* 655
Shenstone	*The Ruined Abbey* 296-8

Cadmaean, Cadmeian

See *Cadmus*

Shelley	*Ode to Liberty* 91-4
	Prometheus Unbound iv 470-5
Swinburne	*Tiresias* 309-14
Tennyson	*Lucretius* 47-50

Cadmus The eponymous king of Cadmeia, later *Thebes*. Cadmus was son of *Agenor* of *Tyre*, and of Telepharsa, and he was ordered by his father to find his sister *Europa* when she was kidnapped by *Zeus*. He was accompanied on his voyage by the founders of several peoples, including *Phoenix* (Phoenicia) and Cilix (Cilicia). On the advice of the Delphic oracale, he abandoned the search for Europa

and settled where a distinctively-marked cow lay down; this was, in fact, the site of Cadmeia, where his men, seeking water, were killed by a dragon. He slew the dragon and, on *Athene*'s direction, sowed half its teeth in the ground, from which sprang up the Sparti or 'sown men'. The dragon had been guardian of a stream sacred to the god *Ares*, whose anger was appeased by Cadmus, serving him for eight years, after which Zeus rewarded him with *Harmonia* (daughter of Ares and *Aphrodite*). At their wedding the couple received a magic necklace and robe. Ares never forgave Cadmus, however, and his line was cursed with madness and violence; his daughters were *Ino*, *Semele*, *Agave* and *Autonoë*, and his grandchildren included *Actaeon*, *Pentheus* and *Melicerta*. Cadmus and his wife Harmonia were supposed to have lived to a great age and finally to have been transformed into serpents by Ares. Amongst Cadmus' miscellaneous achievements was said to be the introduction of the alphabet.

(Hesiod *Theogony* 937-40;
Apollodorus III iv-v; Euripides *The Bacchanals*; Ovid *Metamorphoses* iii)

See also *Tiresias*

Bridges	*Prometheus the Firegiver* 961
Byron	*The Isles of Greece* 10
Chaucer	*Knight's Tale* 1542-8
Daniel	*Civil Wars* vi 36
Diaper	*Dryades* 302-5
Drayton	*The Owl* 919-20
	Polyolbion xx 169-71
Herrick	*Women Useless* 1f
MacNeice	*The Island* iv
Shakespeare	*Midsummer Night's Dream* IV i 109-15
Spenser	*Faerie Queene* II ix 45
Swinburne	*Tiresias* 17-18
Tennyson	*Tiresias* 11-17, 108 ff

Caduceus

See *Hermes*

Keats	*Lamia* i 133
Spenser	*Faerie Queene* II xii 41, IV iii 42
	Mother Hubberd's Tale 1292-9
	Mutability Cantos vi 18

Caecilia

See *Cecilia*

Collins   *The Passions, an Ode for Music*
          114

Caeneus   One of the *Argonauts*, supposed
to have changed sex. Starting as a woman, he
had intercourse with Poseidon and asked to
become an invulnerable man. When his wish
was granted he distinguished himself fighting
centaurs, by whom he was eventually killed.
Later writers believed him to have become a
woman again after death, conforming to a
doctrine of transmigration of souls.
                    (Apollodorus *Epitome* i 22;
                    Apollonius Rhodius i 59 ff)
Davies Sir J.   *Orchestra* 560-3

Caesar Augustus
See *Augustus*
Shakespeare   *Antony and Cleopatra* II vi
              116-9

Caesar Gaius Julius   Julius Caesar (c.102-
44 BC) was the first Emperor of Rome and
supposedly descended from *Aeneas*'s son
Julus. Besides being a supreme general, he
initiated civic reforms in part directed towards
social equality, and is one of the greatest
military historians. As a young man he was
said (Plutarch *Caesar* xi 3) to have emulated
Alexander the Great and to have wept when
he fell short of him. *Suetonius* relates that
Caesar proposed to *Pompey*'s daughter, from
which it was widely, though wrongly, held
that they married. He married three times,
but had no sons. For a while he was infatuated
with *Cleopatra*, and he had several mistresses.
Cleopatra claimed that one of her children —
Ptolemy Caesar (*Caesarion*) — was his son.
Caesar suffered from Grand Mal epilepsy and
several writers contrast his secret sickness with
his outward strength. He invaded Britain in
54-5 BC before his battles with Pompey, and
the achievement of dictatorship. He was
murdered in 44 BC by a conspiracy led by
Brutus (3) and *Cassius*.
— *General*
Auden   *For the Time Being*
        Kairos and Logos 1ff
Blake   *Auguries of Innocence* 97-100
Butler   *Hudibras* I i 433-4
Byron   *Condolatory Address to Sarah*
        1-2

Don Juan xv 53
Manfred III iv 29-30
Vision of Judgment xliv
Campbell   *Pleasures of Hope* ii
Cowley   *Impossibilities* 1ff
Diaper   *Dryades* 610-1
Donne   *Second Anniversary* 283 ff
Dryden   *Upon the Death of Lord*
        Hastings 69-71
Herbert   *The Church* 121-3
Jonson   *To My Chose Friend* 1-2
Marlowe   *Tamburlaine* i 1250-3
Pope   *Epistle* i 213
        Essay on Man iv 145-8, 257-8
        Prologue to Addison's 'Cato' 33-6
        Temple of Fame 155-7
Rochester   *History of Insipids* 61-4
Shakespeare   *Antony and Cleopatra* I v
              70-2
              Hamlet V i 207-10
              Julius Caesar I ii 135-8;
              V iii 93-6
              King Henry IV pt 2 I i 20-3
              King Henry VI pt 1 I i
              55-6, ii 138-9
              King Richard II V i 1-2
              King Richard III III i 83-8
Spenser   *Faerie Queene* I v 49
Thomson   *Liberty* iii 475-6
Yeats   *Long-Legged Fly*
— *and Alexander*
Arnold   *Iseult of Brittany* 143 ff
— *Sickness and Murder*
Butler   *Hudibras* III iii 697-700
Chaucer   *Monk's Tale* 3869-3874,
          3887-900
Graves   *Rhea* 13-14
Marlowe   *Massacre at Paris* 1005
Masefield   *Rider at the Gate* 17 ff
Shakespeare   *Julius Caesar* I ii 100ff,
              115-8, 251-3; II ii 44-7;
              III ii 185-9
— *and Cleopatra*
Byron   *The Island* ii 318-21
Dryden   *All for Love* II i
Pope   *Epistle* i 81-4
Shakespeare   *Antony and Cleopatra* II ii
              230-2, vi 62-4, 69-70;
              III xiii 82-5
— *and Britain*
Shakespeare   *Cymbeline* II iv 17-23;
              III i 21-6, 47-9

Spenser   *Faerie Queene* II x 47, 49

Caesar Octavian
See *Augustus*

Caesarion   A name given to Ptolemy Caesar, the son of Cleopatra by (she claimed) Julius Caesar. He was executed by *Octavian*.
Shakespeare   *Antony and Cleopatra* III vi 3-6
Swinburne   *Song for the Centenary of Landor* 46

Caesar, Caesars   The surname of the Julian family, subsequently extended as a title. The Caesars and the dates of their lives were Julius 100-44BC; Augustus 63BC-14AD; Tiberius 42BC-37AD; Claudius 10BC-54AD; Nero 37-68AD; Galba 3BC-69AD; Otho 32-69AD; Vitellius 15-69AD; Vespasian 9-79AD; Titus 39-81AD; Domitian 51-96AD. Nero was in fact the last of the Julian line.
Auden   *New Year Letter*
Browning E. B.   *Casa Guidi Windows* ii 87-90
Burns   *The Fornicator* 43-7
Goldsmith   *The Traveller* 159
Keats   *To a Young Lady who Sent me a Laurel Crown* 12
Thomson   *Liberty* iii 490-7, v 201-6

Calabria, Calabrian   The 'heel!' of Italy, where the poet *Ennius* was born.
Keats   *Otho the Great* V 5 120-5
Macaulay   *Lake Regillus* 15
Milton   *Paradise Lost* ii 661-2

Calchas   A soothsayer from *Megara*, Corinth. As the Greeks set off for *Troy*, he advised that only the sacrifice of *Agamemnon*'s daughter *Iphigenia* would break the weather which becalmed them. Calchas died of a broken heart after losing a series of competitions with the diviner Mopsus, who was descended from *Tiresias*. Calchas's predictions were invariably unpleasant but proved to be correct, and he was greatly esteemed by the Greeks. He was associated with, and probably a priest of, *Artemis*.
(Aeschylus *Agamemnon* 104ff; Apollodorus *Epitome*; Homer *Iliad* i 68-100, ii 300ff)

See also *Calkas*
Henryson   *Testament of Cresseid* 106-9

Cales   A Campanian town near *Vesuvius*, famed for its wine.
(Horace *Odes* i 20, iv 12)
Milton   *Paradise Regained* iv 117-9

Caligula   The Emperor Gaius Germanicus, 12-41AD, called 'Caligula' because of his 'baby' military boots. From 33-8AD Caligula pursued a moderate rule, but thereafter he became a notorious monster. It is possible that some illness at the time produced the change. For the rest of his life he rejoiced in tyrannical, cruel and obscene behaviour which led to his eventual murder. He was suspected of incest with his sister Drusilla, fed humans to wild beasts, removed the statues of rivals to fame, and committed other atrocities. His sanity was probably precarious and he was said to have galloped along the French shore taking fish prisoner.
(Suetonius *Caligula*; Tacitus *Histories* V 9, *Annals* vi 45-51)
Browning R.   *The Ring and the Book* v 627-9
Butler S.   *Hudibras* III iii 359ff
Byron   *Marino Faliero* V i 440-1
Cleveland   *Smectymnuus* 65-7

Caliope
See *Calliope*
Chaucer   *Troilus and Criseyde* iii 45-8
Drayton   *The Muses' Elizium* iii 445-8
Henryson   *Orpheus and Eurydice* 36ff

Calistopee
See *Callisto*
Chaucer   *Knight's Tale* 2056-9

Calkas
See *Calchas*
Chaucer   *Troilus and Criseyde* iv 73-7, 330-2, v 897-8

Callimachus (1)   Greek sculptor of the 5th Century BC, supposed to have invented the Corinthian column and to have introduced acanthus leaves into sculpture. He was a noted perfectionist but from early times was criticised for over-elaboration of detail.

(Pliny xxv 167, xxxix 92)
Yeats *Lapis Lazuli*

Callimachus (2) Callimachus of *Cyrene*, a 3rd Century BC Greek poet who had a great vogue in his day and some influence on the Romans. He was the teacher of Apollonius Rhodius with whom he later engaged in a famous literary quarrel. He was versatile and fragments in all the main forms survive except for drama, which he possibly did not write.

Jonson *The Poetaster* I i
Prior *First Hymn of Callimachus* 7 ff

Calliope The Muse of heroic poetry, mother of *Orpheus* by *Apollo*, and possibly mother also of the mysterious *Linus*. Calliope appeared with a laurel crown, a book and a trumpet. Judging between *Aphrodite* and *Persephone* as to their claim to *Adonis*, she awarded to each half a year of his company.

(Apollodorus I iii; Hesiod *Theogony* 75-80; Hyginus *Poetica Astronomica* ii 7; Ovid *Metamorphoses* v 339 ff)
See also *Caliope, Muses*
Chaucer *House of Fame* 1399-1404
Fletcher P. *The Purple Island* v 61ff
Milton *Lycidas* 58-63
Paradise Lost vii 33-8
Spenser *Mutability Cantos* vi 37
Shepherd's Calendar, April 100-5, *June* 56-7
Tears of the Muses 13-19, 427-33, 457-62
Tennyson *Lucretius* 93-4

Calipsa
See *Calypso*
Chaucer *House of Fame* 1271-2

Calisto, Callisto Callisto or *Helice*, daughter of *Lycaon* King of *Arcadia*, was seduced by *Jupiter* in the guise of *Diana* (whom she served). *Juno*, in jealousy, turned her into a bear, but also made her a constellation.
See also *Arcas, Calyxte*
Milton *Paradise Regained* ii 181-8

Calydonian Boar Hunt
See *Meleager*
Chapman *Shadow of Night*
Chaucer *Troilus and Criseyde* v 1474-7

Marlowe *Tamburlaine* i 1571-6
Shakespeare *Antony and Cleopatra* IV xii 1-3
Swinburne *Atalanta in Calydon* 163 ff

Calypso A daughter of *Atlas* who received *Odysseus* on her land (*Ogygia*) and fell in love with him, keeping him there for seven years. He refused her offer of immortality in return for staying with her, and she released him at the command of *Hermes*. Some sources say she had children by Odysseus.

(Homer *Odyssey* v 55-268, vii 244-69)
See *Calipsa*
Byron *Childe Harold* ii 29
MacNeice *The Island* ii
Shelley *Hellas* 1076-7
Oedipus Tyrannus I i 169-72
Spenser *Faerie Queene* I iii 21

Calyxte
See *Callisto*
Chaucer *Parliament of Fowls* 286-7

Cam, Came, Camus The river Cam at Cambridge, personified in the Classical manner.
(cf. Virgil *Aeneid* viii 34ff)
Gray *Ode for Music* 29
Milton *Epitaph on the Marchioness of Winchester* 57-9
Lycidas 103-4

Cambyses The name borne by both father and son of *Cyrus* the Great of Persia. Of the father little is known. The son's reputation was that of a ruthless and manic despot who committed a serious crime, either the slaying of his brother, or the killing of *Apis*, a sacred bull, and was punished with madness. His father had conquered Asia, and Cambyses set about conquering Egypt. He succeeded, but he was usurped at home and was also defeated by Ethiopia and Carthage. He either committed suicide or was killed by gangrene from a wound in the thigh which exactly corresponded to that inflicted on Apis.

(Herodotus i-iii)
Byron *The Age of Bronze* 142-3
Prophecy of Dante ii 108-9
Summoner's Tale 2043-4
Shakespeare *King Henry IV pt 1* II iv 375-6

Camilla   A celebrated queen of the Volsci who was brought up in the woods and dedicated by her father to the service of *Diana*. She assisted *Turnus* against *Aeneas* and was noted for swiftness of running which amounted almost to aerial flight.

> (Virgil *Aeneid* vii 803-11, xi 636ff)
> Byron   *Don Juan* xiv 39
> Pope   *Essay on Criticism* 366ff
> Shenstone   *To the Virtuosi* 13-14
> Spenser   *Faerie Queene* III iv 2
> Swift   *Description of Mother Ludwell's Cave* 47

Camillus   Marcus Furius Camillus was a hero of Rome in the 4th Century BC. In 396 he captured Veii from the Etruscans after a long siege. It was alleged that he misappropriated some of the wealth won at Veii and exiled himself or was exiled. He then returned to save his country from the Gauls. He also led the Romans against the Aequi and the Volsci, was appointed dictator and was regarded as a second *Romulus*. In 367 he had a Temple to *Concord* built at Rome. Accounts of the career of Camillus are thought to have been fabulously embellished for political reasons, though the outlines are historical.

> (Livy v 1-22; Plutarch *Camillus*)
> Chapman   *Bussy d'Ambois* I i 65-70
> Dryden   *Threnodia Augustalis* 266-7
> Shelley   *Ode to Liberty* 97-8
> Thomson   *Winter* 509-10

Campaneus
See *Capaneus*
> Chaucer   *Anelida and Arcite* 57-63

Campania, Campanian   A country towards the south-west of Italy, of which Capua was the capital and Neapolis (Naples) a principal town. It was celebrated for its fertility (being volcanic) and scenic beauty.
> Goldsmith   *The Traveller* 5-6

Canace   The daughter of *Aeolus*, Canace had several children by *Neptune* in the form of a bull. She committed incest with her brother, Macareus, and then killed herself or was destroyed by Aeolus. Macareus became a priest or committed suicide.

> (Apollodorus I vii 3-4; Hyginus *Fabulae* ccxxxviii, ccxlii; Ovid *Heroides* xi)
> Chaucer   *Man of Law's Tale (Introduction)* 77-80
> *Legend of Good Women* 263-6
> Spenser   *Faerie Queene* IV ix 23

Canidia   A Neapolitan woman whom *Horace* called a sorceress.
> (Horace *Epodes* iii, xvii)
> Browning R.   *The Ring and the Book* ii 1269-70

Cannae   A village in Apulia where in 216 BC *Hannibal* inflicted a crushing defeat on the Romans.
> (Livy xxii 44ff)
See also *Varro*
> Shenstone   *Elegies* xix 37-40
> Thomson   *Liberty* iii 127-9
> Young   *The Last Day* ii

Canopus   An Egyptian city close to *Alexandria*.
> Tennyson   *A Dream of Fair Women* 145-6

Capaneus   The nephew of *Adrastus*, king of Argos, Capaneus was one of the *Seven Against Thebes*. He scaled the walls of Thebes, boasting that he would destroy the city even if *Zeus* were against him. For this impiety Zeus killed him with a thunderbolt. His wife, *Evadne*, leaped onto his funeral pyre.
> (Apollodorus iii 6)
See also *Campaneus*
> Browning E. B.   *Queen Anelida* 9
> Chaucer   *Knight's Tale* 931-3
> *Troilus and Criseyde* v 1502-5
> Prior   *On Fleet* 15-18

Capitol, Capitolian   A twin-peaked hill of Rome on which was built a huge temple dedicated to *Jupiter*, *Juno* and *Minerva*. The hill was a fortress as well as a religious centre. The original temple, which was approached by a hundred steps and was fitted out in gold and silver in fabulous luxury, was burnt down in 83 BC. It was supposed to have been named from the head (*caput*) of a dead man called Tolius, which was found when the foundations were laid. In a famous incident in 347 BC, the

Capitol was saved from being sacked by the Gauls when the cackling of the sacred geese of Juno betrayed the approaching forces and awakened Marcus *Manlius*, the consul.

(Livy v 47; Strabo v 3; Tacitus *Histories* iii 72)

See also *Brennus*

Arnold	*Alaric at Rome* 71-2
Butler S.	*Hudibras* II iii 799-802
Drayton	*The Owl* 899-903
Milton	*Paradise Regained* iv 47-50
Shelley	*Hellas* 142-4
	Ode to Liberty 100
Spenser	*Visions of the World's Vanity* 145-8
Wordsworth	*Memorials of a Tour in Italy* iii 1-4

Capreae   The island of Capri, where the Emperor *Tiberius* spent his last years in decline.

Milton	*Paradise Regained* iv 90-4
Moore	*Corruption* 115-8

Carausius   Sent by Maximian (assistant of the Emperor *Diocletian*) to control pirates in the Rhine estuary, Marcus Aurelius Carausias defected with his fleet. He came to Britain and there assumed power and the title 'Augustus', though he was in fact of humble origins. He established himself remarkably well and was eventually recognised by Diocletian and *Maximian*, but he was murdered after some five years by *Allectus*, his chief officer, in 293AD.

See *Constantine*

Spenser	*Faerie Queene* II x 57

Caria, Carian   A mountainous country south of the Macander River in what is now southern Turkey. It was absorbed by the Greeks in the 4th Century BC.

Keats	*Endymion* ii, iii, iv (passim)

Caribdis

See *Charybdis*

Chaucer	*Troilus and Criseyde* v 638ff

Caron

See *Charon*

Daniel	*Complaint of Rosamond* 8ff

Carpathian

See *Proteus*

Milton	*Comus* 872

Casca   An assassin of *Caesar* who dealt the first blow in the murder. His brother also was involved and both committed suicide at *Philippi*, 42BC.

Shakespeare	*Julius Caesar* III i 30

Cassandra, Cassandre   The daughter of *Priam* and *Hecuba* of *Troy*. Cassandra was a priestess of *Apollo*, who gave her the gift of prophecy as an unsuccessful bribe for her love. In his subsequent frustration he arranged that her word should not be taken seriously; or he spat in her mouth so that she would never be believed. She rightly foretold that calamity would follow *Paris*'s quest for *Helen*, and she rightly affirmed that the Trojan horse was filled with Greek soldiers — but she was not heeded on either occasion. At the sack of Troy she was violated by *Ajax* the Locrian in the Temple of *Athene*; Athene took revenge on the Greek fleet for the sacrilege. *Agamemnon* took Cassandra to Greece as his concubine, only to be murdered by his wife *Clytemnestra*, despite Cassandra's warnings. Finally, she herself was murdered, with two sons of Agamemnon, by Clytemnestra and her lover Aegisthus.

(Aeschylus *Agamemnon* 1050ff; Apollodorus *Epitome* V; Pausanias II xvi 7; Virgil *Aeneid* II 246-7)

Browning E. B.	*Wine of Cyprus* 18
Byron	*English Bards* 1007-8
Chaucer	*Book of the Duchess* 1244-9
	Troilus and Criseyde iii 409-11, v 1451ff
Lewis C. D.	*Transitional Poem* 7
Masefield	*Cassandra* 6ff
Meredith	*Cassandra*
Rosetti D. G.	*Cassandra* 2ff
Shakespeare	*Troilus and Cressida* II ii 110-12
Swinburne	*Athens* ep. i
	On the Cliffs 152ff
Tennyson	*Oenone* 257-71
Young	*Night Thoughts* ix

Cassiope, Cassiopeia   The wife of *Cepheus* of Ethiopia and mother of *Andromeda*. She boasted herself more beautiful than the

Nereids, who called *Neptune* (or *Ammon*) to their aid. Neptune sent a sea-monster against her which would be appeased only by the offer of Andromeda; she was then saved by Perseus. At her death she was placed among the stars as a constellation — but on her back and with her feet in the air as humiliation for her pride.

(Apollodorus II iv 3)

Chapman   *Andromeda Liberata*
Milton   *Il Penseroso* 16-21
Tennyson   *The Princess* iv 417-9

Cassius (1)   Cassius Longinus was Governor of Syria and — though blind — a famous lawyer in *Nero*'s reign. He was murdered on Nero's orders for having in his possession a picture of *Cassius*, murderer of *Caesar*.

(Juvenal *Satire* x; Tacitus *Annals* xii, xiv)

Gray   *Agrippina* 1234-5

Cassius (2)   Cassius Longinus, the assassin of *Caesar*, supported *Pompey* in the Civil War but, being absent on naval duties, withdrew on news of Pompey's defeat at *Pharsalus* in 48BC and soon afterwards obtained Caesar's pardon. After the murder of Caesar he was, like *Brutus* (to whose sister, *Junia*, he was married), obliged to leave Rome. He gathered support with Brutus in the East and met *Antony* and *Octavian* at *Philippi*, where he was captured in the first battle, in 42BC, and committed suicide. Cassius' motives for the murder of Caesar are less clearly of principle than are those of Brutus. He seems to have been a ruthless and irascible man, though not necessarily motivated by greed.

(Plutarch *Brutus*)

Chaucer   *Monk's Tale* 3887-900
Herrick   *The Welcome Sack* 61
Pope   *Chorus to 'Brutus'* ii 15-16
Shakespeare   *Antony and Cleopatra* III xi 35-9, II vi 15
   Julius Caesar I ii 31-4, 100ff
Shelley   *Otho* 1-4

Castalia
See *Castalian Spring*

Burns   *I am a Bard of No Regard* 5-8
   To Dr Blacklock 25-7
Drayton   *Polyolbion* v 83-8

Moore   *The Philosopher Aristippus* 38-42
Spenser   *Ruins of Time* 427-31
   Tears of the Muses 55-8
Young   *Night Thoughts* v

Castalian Spring   Fons Castalius, a spring rising in Mt *Parnassus* (near Castalia in Phocis). The fountain was sacred to the *Muses* and *Apollo*.

(Ovid *Amores* i 15, 16)

Chapman   *On Sejanus*
Herrick   *His Farewell to Sack* 29-30
Milton   *Paradise Lost* iv 272-5
Spenser   *Tears of the Muses* 271-5

Castor
See *Dioscuri*;

Chaucer   *House of Fame* 1004-8;
Davies Sir J.   *Orchestra* 484-7
Jonson   *On the Famous Voyage* 77-8

Cathegus   Cornelius Cathegus was a member of *Catiline*'s conspiracy.
See also *Cethegus*

Diaper   *Dryades* 439-42

Catiline   Lucius Sergius Catilina led a series of conspiracies in the 1st Century BC, ultimately against *Julius Caesar*. His motives were complex: he professed to champion the poor and was alleged to drink their blood; he resented his reputation for debauched extravagance; and he had been refused the position of consul on suspicion of extortion. His last plot, to turn the loyalty of Gallic envoys in Rome, was betrayed to *Cicero*, who was responsible for Catiline's eventual defeat, prosecution (in a series of famous orations) and death in 63BC. The other leaders were executed, but Cicero arranged for Catiline to die in battle, by provoking him to join an illicit force of disgruntled veterans in Etruria. Whilst he can hardly have been admirable, Catiline's character remains mysterious. Internal conflicts behind his behaviour emerge in the description by *Sallust* of his raving looks, irregular gait and his insomnia.

(Sallust *Catiline*; Plutarch *Cato* xxii, Cicero x-xii)

Byron   *Don Juan* vi 111
Diaper   *Dryades* 439-42

Jonson   *Catiline* I i, IV i, Vv
Pope   *Epistle* i 212
          Essay on Man i 155-6, ii 199-202
Prior   *To the Lord Bishop of Rochester*
          20-1
Thomson   *Liberty* v 425-8

Cato (1)   Dionysius Cato, the supposed author of a collection of maxims and proverbs of the 3rd or 4th Century AD. The work, *Disticha de Moribus ad Filium*, was translated by Caxton and was much used in the Middle Ages.
See also *Catoun*

Cato (2)   Marcus Porcius Cato — Cato the Elder, the Orator, the Censor, or the Lawgiver — of the 2nd Century BC. As a statesman he was celebrated for his austerity and declared impartiality. He affected a rustic manner to reflect his conservatism, which was particularly expressed in a dislike for customs from colonised Greece as they were absorbed into Roman life. He published his speeches, of which parts of eighty survive, and an influential *History*. His daughter, *Portia*, married *Brutus*, the assassin of *Caesar*. Cato the Elder died naturally, aged 85. One much cited incident of his political life recalled his introducing the idea of Africa into the Senate by dropping some figs there and remarking that their country of origin was a mere three days' sailing away. He attempted to inspire fear and hate for the defeated Carthage which he suspected to be re-arming; this was symbolised in the slogan 'Delenda est Carthago' (Carthage must be destroyed). His propaganda may well have hastened the Third Punic War which, however, his death preceded.
                (Plutarch *Marcus Cato*)
See also *Oppian*
Auden   *The Fall of Rome* 13-16
Crabbe   *Struggles of Conscience*
Daniel   *Civil Wars* viii 7
Dryden   *Annus Mirabilis* 689-92
          Upon the Death of Lord Hastings 69-71
Herrick   *Ultimus Heroum* 1-4
          When He would Have his Verses Read
Jonson   *Sejanus* I i
Pope   *Epistle to Henry Cromwell* 102-3

Shakespeare   *Merchant of Venice* I i
              165-6
Sidney   *Astrophel and Stella* iv 5
Southey   *History* 28-31
Swift   *To Stella Visiting Me* 39-41
Tennyson *The Princess* vii 107-11
Thomson   *Summer* 1491-3
          Winter 523

Cato (3)   Marcus Cato Uticensis (Cato the Younger), statesman and general, a supporter of *Pompey* and governor of Utica (near Carthage). *Plutarch* notes that Cato was 'unfortunate in the women of his household' and was obliged to shut his wife up for her frequent infidelities. He divorced *Marcia* so that she would marry his friend Hortensius, and took her back when Hortensius died. Cato was a stoic and is famous in literature chiefly for his curious manner of dying. When *Caesar* marched on Utica, Cato planned a carefully staged suicide, preparing his mind with a reading of *Plato*'s *Phaedo* on the immortality of the soul. His first attempt was a messy failure, but he was sewn up so that he could make a second attempt, which was successful.
                (Plutarch *Cato the Younger*)
Arnold   *Courage* 13-16
Byron   *Don Juan* vi 7
          Hints from Horace 823 ff
Dryden   *Don Sebastian* II i
Pope   *Epilogue to Jane Shore* 30-7
          Epilogue to the Satires 120
          Epistle to Dr Arbuthnot 209-10
          Prologue to Addison's 'Cato'
          23-4, 33-6
          Temple of Fame 176
Shakespeare   *Coriolanus* I iv 57 ff
              Julius Caesar V i 100-3

Catoun
See *Cato (1)*
Chaucer   *Merchant's Tale* 1377
          Miller's Tale 3227-8
          Nun's Priest's Tale 4130-1,
          4163-6

Catullus   Gaius Valerius Catullus, Roman poet c.84-54 BC. Catullus was a supreme technician and user of experimental metres. His work ranges from self-conscious rhetorical epigram to simple lyrical expressions of personal feeling. He had great influence, particularly on *Horace* and *Virgil*. His songs to *Lesbia* and her sparrow were especially noted.

Browning R.	*The Ring and the Book* VI 387-8
Byron	*Don Juan* i 42
	English Bards 287-8
Lewis C. D.	*A Letter from Rome*
Swinburne	*Dolores* 326 ff
	Song for the Centenary of Landor 47
Tennyson	*Hendecasyllabics* 9-12
	Poets and their Bibliographies 7-8
Yeats	*The Scholars*

Caucasus The range of mountains between the Caspian and Black Seas. It was thought to hold mineral wealth and gold was said to flow in its streams. The people were considered barbaric and the land remote. *Prometheus* was fastened to the top of Caucasus by *Jupiter*, his liver being continually devoured by vultures.

(Strabo XI ii 19, xi 8;
Virgil *Aeneid* iv 365-7)
Milton   *Paradise Regained* iii 317-8

Cecile
See *Cecilia*
Chaucer   *Second Nun's Prologue* 92-3, 99-101

Cecilia St Cecilia, the patron saint of music and the blind, was a Roman martyred in 176AD in Sicily. According to tradition, she married a nobleman, Valerius (*Valerian*), who agreed to take a vow of chastity on condition that he could see her guardian angel. In due course it appeared, decking them with garlands, and he was baptised. He was executed and she died in a boiling bath or vat of oil. The connection with music — that she attracted an angel by her singing, or that there was celestial music at her wedding — is late medieval.

Dryden	*Song for St Cecilia's Day* 51-4
Pope	*Ode for Music* 131-4
Tennyson	*Amy* 67-72
	Palace of Art 97-9
Wordsworth	*Ecclesiastical Sonnets* I xxiv 10-11

Cecrops An Egyptian leader who emigrated

to Attica with his people, or perhaps the first King of *Athens*. He established a colony known as Cecropia in very ancient times. He was reputed to have been a major civilising force, but is a mythical character, in effect the founder of Athenian civilisation.

MacNeice   *Autumn Journal* xxi

Cedasus
See *Scedasus*
Chaucer   *Franklin's Tale* 1422-30

Celaeno, Celeno Leader of the *Harpies*; daughter of *Neptune* and *Terra*.

(Virgil *Aeneid* iii 245;
Apollonius Rhodius ii 234 ff)
Fletcher G.   *Christ's Victory on Earth*
Spenser   *Faerie Queene* II vii 23-4
Swinburne   *Dirae-Celaeno*

Celeus A King of Eleusis. His son *Demophoon* (*Triptolemus*) was brought up by *Demeter*, who cured him of a severe illness and taught him agriculture. Demeter was supposed to have nourished him with her own milk and to have placed him to rest at night on hot coals to destroy his mortality and make him a god; but in this she was unsuccessful because she was interrrupted by the boy's mother, Metaneira.

(Homeric Hymn *To Demeter* ii)

Cenchrea, Cenchreas A port of Corinth in the Saronic Gulf between the mainland of Greece and the Peloponnesus.

Keats   *Lamia* 173-4, 223-5

Cenobia
See *Zenobia*
Chaucer   *Monk's Tale* 3437-41, 3501-9, 3541-8

Centaur, Centaurs The descendants, half man and half horse, of Centaurus, son of *Apollo* or *Ixion*. They were viewed either as monsters or as a primitive people of Magnesia. The Centaurs fought a famous battle with the Lapiths, another tribe of Thessaly who also claimed descent from Ixion and an equal share of the land. A peace was negotiated but at the feast the Centaurs took wine, to which they were unused, and assaulted the Lapith women. They were then defeated by the Lapiths and seem to have retired to *Arcadia*. When *Hercules* was seeking the wild boar of *Erymanthus*, he was refused wine by a Centaur, Pholus. He drank it, but killed many of the Centaurs attracted by its aroma. Pholus buried them but accidentally wounded himself with one of the *Hydra*'s arrows as he extracted it from a Centaur's body. Hercules was unable to save his life and called the place Pholoe. The Centaur constellation was represented with a bow aiming an arrow at *Scorpius*.

(Apollodorus II iv; Diodorus Siculus IV 69; Hesiod *Shield of Hercules* 178 ff; Ovid *Metamorphoses* xii 210 ff)

Arnold	*The Strayed Reveller* 143-50
Butler S.	*Hudibras* I ii 445-8
Chaucer	*Monk's Tale* 3288-92
Denham	*Progress of Learning* 161 ff
Hood	*Ode to Richard Martin* 78-9
Keats	*Endymion* iii 533-6, iv 597-9
Marlowe	*Hero and Leander* i 114
Shakespeare	*King Lear* IV vi 123-7
Shelley	*Witch of Atlas* 133-5
Spenser	*Faerie Queene* I xi 27, IV i 23, VI x 13
	Mutability Cantos vii 40

Cephalus   The grandson of *Aeolus* and son of Deioneus of Phocis. Cephalus married *Procris*, a princess of *Athens*, but was carried away by *Aurora*. When Aurora could not gain his love she persuaded him to try the fidelity of Procris by approaching her in disguise. In a different story Procris succumbed to bribery and was seduced by Pteleon; she fled to Euboea where she became a follower of *Diana* and received an infallible dart and dog for hunting — or she received these from *Minos* after an affair with him — and used them to regain Cephalus, whom she herself approached in disguise. They were reconciled, but whilst hunting Cephalus was heard to call out 'Aura' (a breeze) and this led Procris to believe he was seeing Aurora again. As she spied on him she made the leaves move; he thought this to be a wild animal and, hurling the dart, killed her.

(Apollodorus III 15; Ovid *Metamorphoses* vii 675 ff)

See also *Shafulus*

Chapman	*Ovid's Banquet of Sense*
Marlowe	*Tamburlaine* i 1571-6

Milton	*Il Penseroso* 121-5
Moore	*Cephalus and Procris* 17-22

Cepheus (1)   The Father of *Andromeda*. Cepheus was King of Aethiopia and was one of the *Argonauts*.

(Apollodorus II iv; Ovid *Metamorphoses* iv)

Chapman	*Andromeda Liberata*
Kingsley	*Andromeda* 53 ff

Cepheus (2)   Brother of *Ancaeus* and a hunter in the Calydonian Boar Hunt.

Swinburne	*Atalanta in Calydon* 452, 1250

Cephisus, Cephissus   The name of several rivers, of which one, the Boeotian, passes *Parnassus* and was a haunt of the *Graces*. The Attic Cephisus passes close to *Athens*. The god Cephissus (Boeotian) was father of *Narcissus*. The Attic Cephisus had beside it a shrine at which it was customary to offer a lock of hair in gratitude for any safe return.

(Homer *Iliad* xxiii 141; Pausanias I xxxvii 4; Sophocles *Oedipus at Colonus* 687)

Browning R.	*The Ring and the Book* VI 960-3
Byron	*The Corsair* III 41 ff
	The Curse of Minerva 42
Collins	*Ode to Simplicity* 18-21
Spenser	*Faerie Queene* III ii 44-5
Swinburne	*The Eve of Revolution* 685 ff
Wordsworth	*The Excursion* iv 745-9

Cerastes   A wandering snake with four horns on its head, which is shaped like that of a ram.

(Lucan ix 716)

Milton	*Paradise Lost* x 525

Cerberean

See *Cerberus*

Milton	*Paradise Lost* ii 653-5

Cerberus   Like the monsters *Hydra* and *Chimera*, Cerberus was the offspring of *Typhon* and *Echidna*. *Pluto*'s dog had many heads and guarded the entrance to *Hades*. According to Virgil, he lived in a cave on the bank of the *Styx*. *Orpheus* lulled him to sleep, and other heroes pacified him with a present of food when they visited *Hades*.

(Hesiod *Theogony* 310-12;

Pausanias III xxv; Virgil *Aeneid* vi 418)
See also *Tenarus*

Byron	*Vision of Judgment* lxxix
Chaucer	*Monk's Tale* 3258-92
	Troilus and Criseyde i 859-61
Cleveland	*Dialogue between the Two Zealots* 29-30
De La Mare	*I Wonder* 1-7
Fletcher P.	*Purple Island* v 66, xii 66
Graves	*The Utter Rim* 1
Henryson	*Orpheus and Eurydice* 254-8
Lovelace	*Cupid Far Gone* 25-30
	Painture 26-7
Marlowe	*Tamburlaine* i 333-6, ii 4207-10
Marvell	*Tom May's Death* 90-7
Milton	*L'Allegro* 1-3
Shakespeare	*Titus Andronicus* II iv 37ff
	Troilus and Cressida II i 31-4
Skelton	*Philip Sparrow*
Spenser	*Faerie Queene* I v 34, xi 41, IV x 58, VI i 7-8, xii 35
	Shepherd's Calendar, October 25-30
Swift	*A Quibbling Elegy on Judge Boat* 25-8
Young	*Night Thoughts* vii

Cereal
See *Ceres*

Wordsworth	*Memorials of a Tour 1820* xxxii 30-3

Ceres   The goddess (*Demeter*) of corn and harvest, daughter of *Saturn* and *Vesta*, mother of *Proserpina* by *Jupiter*. She demanded from Jupiter the restoration of Proserpina after she had been seized by *Pluto*, but Jupiter granted Proserpina only half the year on earth in response to her mother's entreaties. Ceres was closely associated with Sicily, where annual sacrifices to her were performed. The Romans held a festival, the Cerialia, each spring. She was represented with a plough, or with a torch searching for Proserpina, or with a cornucopia of fruit and flowers.

(Homeric Hymn *To Demeter* xiii; Ovid *Fasti* iv 417ff)

Byron	*Don Juan* ii 170, xvi 86
Carew	*To My Friend G.N.* 61-2, 97ff

Chaucer	*Parliament of Fowls* 274-7
	Troilus and Criseyde V 206-10
Drayton	*The Owl* 275-80, 286-90
Dryden	*To John Driden of Chesterton* 46
Gray	*Progress of Poesy* 9
Hopkins	*Escorial* 11
Keats	*Endymion* iii 34-40
	Fancy 79-83
	Lamia ii 186-8
Lawrence	*Purple Anemones* 62ff
Meredith	*Pastoral* ii
Milton	*Paradise Lost* iv 268-72, iv 979-82, ix 393-6
Pope	*Spring* 65-8
	Summer 65-6
	Windsor-Forest 37-40
Shakespeare	*King Henry VI pt 2* I ii 103
	Tempest IV i 60ff
Shelley	*Oedipus Tyrannus* I i 26-7
Spenser	*Faerie Queene* III i 51
Wordsworth	*Beguiled into Forgetfulness* 60-3

Cesar
See *Augustus*

Chaucer	*Legend of Good Women* 588ff

Cestius   Cestius Epulo, a tribune and praetor who died late in the 1st Century BC and is buried in a large pyramidal tomb in Rome, near the graves of Keats and Shelley.

Hardy	*At the Pyramid of Cestius* 5-8, 21-4

Cethegus   A tribune who joined *Catiline*'s conspiracy and was charged to murder *Cicero* in 62BC. He was discovered and put to death.
See also *Cathegus*

Jonson	*Catiline* III i, V i
Rochester	*Epilogue to 'Love in the Dark'* 38

Ceyx
See *Seys, Halcyon*

Chaerephon   A character in *Aristophanes'* *The Clouds*. He debates with *Socrates* how far a flea jumps from one beard to another.

Butler S.	*Hudibras* II iii 310-4

Chaerilus   A poet satirised by *Horace* as

having one or two good lines charming by their surprise.

(Horace *Ars Poetica* 357)
Pope   *To the Author of a Poem* 20

Chalbe, Chalbean   A people on the Black Sea coast of Northern Turkey. The country was rich in iron and the Chalybeans were famed for metalwork.

(Virgil *Aeneid* viii 421;
Xenophon *Anabasis* V v 1)
Milton   *Samson Agonistes* 133

Chaos   The void, or confused and shapeless matter existing before the formation of the world. *Erebus* (Dark) and *Nyx* (Night) were born of Chaos, from which came also *Ge* (Earth), *Tartarus* and *Eros*. Chaos varied according to current views of existence and creation. Sometimes it was considered part of the Underworld.

(Hesiod *Theogony* 116-23; Ovid *Metamorphoses* i 7-21, x 30; Virgil *Aeneid* iv 510)
Browning R.   *Sordello* v 555-6
Donne   *Elegy* viii 19-22
Keats   *Endymion* iii 40-3
Milton   *Comus* 331-5
Paradise Lost i 9-10, 543, ii 231-3, 894-6, 907ff, iii 17-18, 419ff, iv 665-7, v 577-9, vi 53-5, vii 90-3, 211-15ff, 269-72, x 230-3, 282-3, 316ff, 476-7, 635-7
Pope   *Windsor-Forest* 12-14
Shakespeare   *Othello* II iii 90
Shelley   *Adonais* 166-7
Epipsychidion 241-4
Hellas, Prologue 2-3
Ode to Naples 137-8
Daemon of the World 325-7
Revolt of Islam 352-60
Witch of Atlas 297-9
Spenser   *Faerie Queene* III vi 36-7, IV ii 47, ix 23
Hymn in Honour of Heavenly Love 57ff
Mutability Cantos vi 26
Wordsworth   *Memorials of a Tour in Scotland 1803* i 9-11
For 'The Recluse' 35-40

Chariclo   A nymph, mother of *Tiresias*. According to one version, Tiresias's blindness

was caused by his seeing *Pallas Athene* naked on Mt *Helicon*, at which she sealed his eyes. Chariclo interceded without success for restoration of his sight.

(Apollodorus III vi 7)
Swinburne   *Tiresias* 171ff

Charon   The ferryman who took the souls of the properly buried dead across the *Styx* or *Acheron*) for a fee of one *obol* — the dead were buried with this fare in their mouths. The unburied had to wait for a century.

(Euripides *Alcestis* 252-9;
Virgil *Aeneid* vi 298-330, 384ff)
Belloc   *To Dives* 10ff
Byron   *Don Juan* ii 101
Drayton   *Fourth Eclogue* 29-30
Dryden   *Albion and Albanius* II
Jonson   *Catiline* I i
Keats   *Endymion* iii 503-6
Lovelace   *Cupid Far Gone* 25-30
Marlowe   *Tamburlaine* i 2245-8
Noyes   *Drake* vii
Shakespeare   *King Richard III* I iv 44-7
Troilus and Cressida III ii
Shenstone   *The Charms of Precedence* 79-84
Skelton   *Philip Sparrow*
Swift   *A Quibbling Elegy on Judge Boat* 23-5
Tennyson   *Rifle Clubs* 5-8
Wordsworth   *The Prelude* iv 13-16

Charybdis   A whirlpool, opposite the cave of the monster *Scylla*, in the Straits of Messina on the coast of Sicily. It destroyed part of *Ulysses'* fleet.

(Homer *Odyssey* xii; Ovid *Metamorphoses* xiv 75; Virgil *Aeneid* III 420ff)
See also *Caribdis*
Jonson   *Catiline* III iii
Staple of News IV i
Milton   *Comus* 257-9
Paradise Lost ii 1019-20
Rochester   *Tunbridge Wells* 33-4
Shakespeare   *Merchant of Venice* III v 13-14

Chaeronea   A Boeotian city where the Athenians were defeated by the Boeotians in 447BC, and in 378BC by *Philip* of Macedon. It was the birthplace of *Plutarch*.

Milton   *Sonnet* x 6-8

Cheiron
See *Chiron*

Chersiphron, Cherisphrone   A Cretan architect, designer of a mighty Temple to *Artemis* in the 6th Century BC, for which *Croesus* was said to have provided most of the columns.
(Herodotus i 142; Strabo XIV i 22)
Chapman   *Shadow of Night*

Chersonese   The Gallipoli peninsular of *Thrace*, a land of great strategic importance guarding the Dardanelles route between Europe and Asia. Control of it was at various times in the hands of Sparta, Greece and Thrace.
Byron   *Isles of Greece* 12
Swinburne   *Atalanta in Calydon* 2133
Masque of Queen Besabe

Chimaera, Chimera   *Hydra*'s sister, a monster with three heads, parts of various animals (lion, goat, dragon), and breathing out fire. Chimera was held to occupy *Lycia* in Southern Turkey, where a volcano of the same name existed. The monster was defeated by *Bellerophon* mounted on the winged horse, *Pegasus*.
(Hesiod *Theogony* 321-5; Homer *Iliad* vi 178-82; Apollodorus II iii)
Browning R.   *Old Pictures in Florence* 270-2
Chapman   *Bussy d'Ambois* IV i 182-8
Cowley   *On Orinda's Poems* 4
Denham   *Progress of Learning* 161ff
Milton   *Comus* 515-7
Paradise Lost ii 626-8
Spenser   *Faerie Queene* VI i 7-8

Chios   An island off the Ionian coast between *Lesbos* and *Samos*. It was famous for expensive Chian wines.
(Horace *Odes* iii 19; Satires i 10)
Milton   *Paradise Regained* iv 117-9

Chiron   A *Centaur*, son of *Philyra* or *Nais* and *Saturn*. Unlike the other Centaurs, who were of different origin, he was wise, refined and immortal. He lived on Mt *Pelion*, where he educated many heroes, including *Jason*,

Aesculapius and *Achilles*, and instructed *Peleus* in the difficult wooing of *Thetis*. He was accidentally shot by *Hercules* in *Arcadia* and then regretted his immortality. *Prometheus* was said to have taken this burden from him and let Chiron die. Chiron became the constellation Centaur.
(Apollodorus I ii 4, II v 4, III xiii 5)
See also *Eacides*
Arnold   *Empedocles on Etna* I ii 57ff
Drayton   *Polyolbion* v 21-4
Southey   *Roderick* xvi 199-203
Spenser   *Mutability Cantos* vii 40
Stevenson   *Et Tu in Arcadia* 20-5

Choaspes   A Medean river whose waters were celebrated for sweetness, so that Persian kings carried some boiled with them on their campaigns.
(Herodotus I 188)
Milton   *Paradise Regained* iii 288-9

Chorasmian   Of the Chorasmi, a tribe on the lower waters of the Oxus.
Arnold   *The Strayed Reveller* 182-3

Chromius   Winner of a chariot race in the Nemean Games.
(Pindar *Nemean Ode* i)
Prior   *Carmen Seculare* 299-300

Chronos   Greek name for *Saturn*, Time, leader of the revolt of the *Titans* against *Uranus*.
Bridges   *Prometheus the Firegiver* 206-11, 632-6
Yeats   *Song of the Happy Shepherd*

Chrysaor   The name means 'golden sword'. Chrysaor was the monstrous offspring, with *Pegasus*, of *Medusa* and *Neptune* after *Perseus* beheaded Medusa. Chrysaor fathered *Geryon*.
(Hesiod *Theogony* 278-88)
Drayton   *Polyolbion* xx 164
Spenser   *Faerie Queene* IV xi 14, V i 9

Chryseis   The medieval *Cressida* -- the story of *Troilus* and Cressida is not developed in Classical Literature, though some of its basic elements are found there.
(Homer *Iliad* i 3334-56)
See also *Briseis, Cresseis, Criseyde*

Cicero, Ciceronian Marcus Tullius Cicero, Roman statesman and orator 106-43 BC. He was educated in philosophy and rhetoric in *Athens* and held as his first public position the post of quaestor or public prosecutor. He became consul in 63 and personally authorised execution of the Catilinian conspirators, publishing speeches and defences of the line he had taken. He was charged by Clodius (whom he had accused of incest) of executing a citizen without trial and Cicero fled, being pronounced an exile. Within a year he returned to popular acclaim and the support of *Pompey*, whom he had long favoured. He then gave outward support to *Caesar*, though had misgivings about his increasingly tyrannical behaviour. He was not a party to Caesar's assassination, but he approved it and was strongly opposed to *Mark Antony*. Antony included Cicero in his list of proscriptions inaugurating the Triumvirate in 43 BC, and Cicero was killed in attempting to escape. His head and hands were brought to Rome and displayed in the Forum, where *Fulvia*, Antony's wife, stabbed the tongue with a needle. In later life Cicero had occupied villas at Tusculum and Formiae, the former very near Rome, the latter on the coast to the South. He was the author of fifty-eight surviving speeches, of writings on rhetoric and philosophy, of verse (little survives) and of a great variety of letters. Much of his work was written in self-defence and is the main source of knowledge about him. His style was celebrated for its sonorous quality and periodic structure.

(Plutarch *Cicero*)

See also *Tully, Scithero*
— General
    Donne   *Second Anniversary* 283 ff
    Dryden   *Religio Laici* 78-84
    Rosetti D. G.   *Tiber, Nile and Thames* 1 ff
    Shakespeare   *Julius Caesar* I ii 185-8, IV iii 173-5
    Yeats   *Mad as Mist and Snow*
    Young   *Night Thoughts* ix
— Ciceronian Style
    Browning R.   *Ring and the Book* i 1156-7
    Cowley   *The Motto* 31-3
    Lamb   *The Female Orators* 14-16
    Pope   *Epilogue to Satires* 73

    Raleigh   *Epitaph on Sidney* 57-60
    Skelton   *Philip Sparrow, Commendation*

Cilenios
See *Cyllene*
    Chaucer   *Complaint of Mars* 113-4

Cimmerian, Cimmerians The Cimmerians of Asia Minor were regarded as living in a sunless land on the edge of the known world, and were reputed to be cave-dwelling. The extent of their invasions of Ionia and further West was debated by the Ancients. The supposed darkness of their habitat and their underground life-style led to their being associated poetically, from at least *Homer*'s time, with *Hades*.

(Herodotus I 6; Homer *Odyssey* xi 14 ff; Apollodorus II i; Ovid *Metamorphoses* xi 592 ff; Strabo III ii 12)

See also *Cymerie*
    Keats   *Endymion* iv 375
    Lovelace   *Ode, Calling Lucasta* 4-5
    Marlowe   *Tamburlaine* II 4400-1
    Milton   *L'Allegro* 1-10
    Pope   *The Dunciad* iii 2-4
    Shelley   *Ode to Naples* 77-82
    Spenser   *Tears of the Muses* 256-8
    Young   *Night Thoughts* iii

Cimon An Athenian leader, the son of *Miltiades*, in the 5th Century BC. Cimon was taken as an example of a debauched young man in youth who reformed and achieved eminence. As an officer he conducted battles against the Thracian and Persian forces and early in his career was associated with *Aristides*. He defeated the Persian fleet at *Salamis* in 480 BC. As a statesman he valued peace and his mercy and generosity were much praised. He negotiated several valuable treaties with *Sparta* and died on a campaign to recover Cyprus from the Persians.
    Thomson   *Winter* 464-70

Cincinnatus Lucius Quinctius Cincinnatus, a Roman summoned from the fields to defeat the Volsci in 458 BC and who, victorious, returned to his plough within three weeks. He had a similar brief spell as dictator in his old age.

(Livy iii 26; Pliny xviii 4)
    Thomson   *Summer* 1491-3
              Winter 512

Cinthia
See *Cynthia*
    Chaucer   *Troilus and Criseyde* iv 1601

Cipioun
See *Africanus (2)*
    Chaucer   *Nun's Priest's Tale* 4133-6

Cipride, Cipris
See *Venus*
    Chaucer   *Troilus and Criseyde* v 206-10,
        iii 724-5
        House of Fame 518-22

Circaean
See *Circe*
    Denham   *Progress of Learning* 2-3

Circe   The enchantress, daughter of the Sun (*Apollo* or *Helios*) and Perseis, an *Oceanid*. She lived on the island of *Aeaea*, said to be on the West coast of Italy, or on Cape Cicero (then an island) south of Rome. Circe was notorious for her seductiveness, which she furthered by changing men into animals. She turned *Picus*, son of *Saturn*, into a woodpecker for refusing her advances, and when *Glaucus* sought from her a love potion to woo *Scylla* she, out of jealousy, turned Scylla into a monster. She turned half of *Ulysses*'s men into stone, but Ulysses himself was protected by the herb *Moly* (provided by *Hermes*) and she could not harm him; when she fell in love with him, during his year on Aeaea, she restored his men and advised him to consult Tiresias on his fate. Ulysses had a son, Telegonus, by her who in due course accidentally killed his father. Circe was attended by river nymphs or *Naiads*.
        (Hesiod *Theogony* 956-7, 1011-4;
    Homer *Odyssey* x 133-574, xii 8-150;
        Ovid *Metamorphoses* xiii-xiv)
    Chaucer   *Knight's Tale* 1936-46
        House of Fame 1271-2
    Crabbe   *The Borough* xi
    Donne   *Satire* iv 129-31
    Dryden   *Conquest of Granada* I, III i
    Fletcher G.   *Christ's Victory on Earth*
        49
    Fletcher P.   *To E.C.* 59-61
    Keats   *Endymion* iii 411-4, 425-8,
        618-23

    Marlowe   *Edward II* 467-70
        Hero and Leander 59-65
    Meredith   *London by Lamplight*
    Milton   *Comus* 50-2, 252-5, 519-20
    Shakespeare   *King Henry VI pt 1* V ii
        34-5

Circean
See *Circe*
    Keats   *Lamia* i 115
    Young   *Night Thoughts* iii

Cirrea
See *Cirrha*
    Chaucer   *Anelida and Arcite* 15-20

Cirrha   A town at the foot of Mt *Parnassus*.
See *Cirrea*

Cirus
See *Cyrus*
    Chaucer   *Monk's Tale* 3917-24
        Summoner's Tale 2079-82

Cithaeron, Citheron   A mountain of Boeotia, named after a king. It was sacred to the *Muses* and was the site of the death of *Actaeon* and of a grove sacred to *Diana*. Here also the Dionysiac orgies occurred which resulted in the death of *Pentheus*.
        (Apollodorus III iv 4; Strabo IX ii 15;
        Virgil *Aeneid* iv 303)
    Byron   *The Curse of Minerva* 27-30
    Chaucer   *Knight's Tale* 1936-46, 2221-3
    Drayton   *Endymion and Phoebe* 295-6
    Swinburne   *Tiresias* 73-6

Cithe
See *Scythia*
    Chaucer   *Anelida and Arcite* 22ff

Citherea   The name given to *Venus Aphrodite* who, according to some accounts, landed on the island of Kythera, off the South Peloponnessus, after arising from the mutilated remains of *Uranus* when he was ousted by *Saturn*.
See also *Cytheraea*
        (Hesiod *Theogony* 190-8)
    Chaucer   *Knight's Tale* 2214-6
        Troilus and Criseyde iii 1254-8
    Wyatt   *Though this the Port . . .* 5-7

Clarius *Apollo* — named from Claros, a grove and oracle in Ionia. It was said to have been founded by Manto, daughter of *Tiresias*.

(Pausanias VII iii 1-4; Strabo XIV i 27)

Jonson   *An Ode to Himself* 9-10

Claudian Claudius Claudian, a Greek-speaking Alexandrian of the 4th Century AD who was court poet to the West Roman Emperor, *Honorius*. He wrote many political poems, which are of historical interest, and a great deal of occasional poetry. His work was widely used in the Middle Ages as source material.

Chaucer   *Merchant's Tale* 2232
           House of Fame 1509-12

Claudius (Marcus)
See *Verginius*

Claudius (Tiberius) Became Emperor in 41AD on the death of his nephew Gaius *Caligula*, who had been the preferred successor to Tiberius owing to Claudius' physical and mental handicaps. Claudius was born at Lyons and never fully identified himself with Rome. He preferred to speak Greek rather than his weak Latin. His reign was notable for moderation after the autocratic whims of Caligula. He was personally involved in the invasion of Britain in 43AD. He died in 54, probably poisoned by *Agrippina*, who had married him as a means of enlisting her son *Nero* (rather than his, *Britannicus*) into the succession.

Gray   *Agrippina* 169-71
Spenser   *Faerie Queene* II x 51

Clemency One of the *Virtues*, represented as carrying an olive branch.

Chaucer   *Knight's Tale* 928-30

Cleo
See *Clio*

Chaucer   *Troilus and Criseyde* II 8-10
Dunbar   *Ryght as the Stern of the Day* 77

Cleombrotus A youth from Ambrocia in Southern Epirus. He drowned himself in the sea after reading *Plato*'s *Phaedo* on the immortality of the soul.

(Callimachus *Epigrams* xxv; Ovid *Ibis* 493)

Milton   *Paradise Lost* iii 471-3

Cleone A village south of Corinth, on the way to *Argos*. It was near Cleone that *Hercules* was supposed to have performed his first labour, killing the *Nemean* lion.

(Apollodorus II v)

Keats   *Lamia* i 177-9

Cleopatra Queen of Egypt, daughter of Ptolemy XII. Of fabulous beauty, Cleopatra had an affair with *Julius Caesar* and claimed that her son, Ptolemy Caesar or *Caesarion*, was the result of this union. This matter was much debated. After the murder of Caesar, *Mark Antony* summoned her before him because she was known to have supported *Brutus* against Caesar; she beguiled him with her charms and they were married — despite the fact that Antony was party to an important political marriage with *Octavia*, sister of *Augustus Octavian*. In the ensuing battle of *Actium* (31BC) between Antony and Octavian, Antony mortally wounded himself, or attempted suicide in the false belief that Cleopatra was dead; Cleopatra then committed suicide by snake-bite to avoid falling into the hands of Augustus. In subsequent interpretations the affair of Antony and Cleopatra represents romantic love incompatible with worldly values.

(Plutarch *Antony* lxxviff)

See also *Apollodorus*, *Cleopatre*, *Cydnus*, *Fulvia*

— General

Brooke   *It's not Going to Happen Again* 11-14
Browning R.   *Fifine at the Fair* 218ff
Byron   *The Deformed Transformed* I i 198-200
Chaucer   *Legend of Good Women* 580-2, 614
Crabbe   *Villars*
Dryden   *All for Love* IV i
Keats   *Fragment of 'The Castle-Builder'* 48-50
Lawrence *The Universe Flows* 10-11
Shakespeare *Antony and Cleopatra* III xiii 117-20, IV xiv 38-41
          As You Like It III ii 135-9
Stevenson *After Reading 'Antony and Cleopatra'* 9-12

Clio   The *Muse* of History, daughter of *Zeus* and *Mnemosyne* (Memory). She particularly recorded the heroic and virtuous and is depicted bearing a book and a trumpet.

Clitermystra

Clitumnus, Clitumnian   A river of Campania which, if drunk by oxen, turned them white. It was noted for the sacrifice of cattle on its banks.

Cloacina   The goddess of sewage and all cloacal things, who presided over the huge cesspits of Rome.

Cloelia   A Roman hostage held by the Etruscans, Cloelia swam the *Tiber* with other hostages to escape *Porsenna* in 508BC.

See also *Horatius Cocles*
    Tennyson   *The Princess* ii 69-71

Clotho
See *Fates*
    Browning R.   *Apollo and the Fates* 11-13
    Lamb   *The Three Graves* 7-8
    Spenser   *Faerie Queene* IV i 48
                Hymn in Honour of Love 57ff

Clusium   An Etruscan town near Lake *Trasimene*.
See *Porsenna*

Clymene (1)   A *Nereid*, said by Ovid to be the mother of *Phaethon* by *Helios* or *Apollo*. She was married to *Merops*, king of Egypt.
          (Ovid *Metamorphoses* i 757ff)
See also *Heliades*
    Keats   *Hyperion* ii 75-6, 292-5
    Marlowe   *Tamburlaine* ii 4621ff
    Milton   *Paradise Regained* ii 181-8
    Spenser   *Faerie Queene* III xi 38

Clymene (2)
See *Prometheus*

Clytemnestra   The daughter of Tyndarus, King of *Sparta*, by *Leda*, and wife of *Agamemnon* king of Argos. She was seduced by Aegistheus (Agamemnon's cousin) when Agamemnon went to the Trojan War. The lovers murdered the king on his return, tying him in a net before killing him, either at a feast or as he left the bath. Clytemnestra then married Aegistheus, who ascended the throne. The son *Orestes*, having escaped murder by his mother with the help of his sister *Electra*, plotted revenge and arranged, on his return after seven years, for his own death to be announced. Then, with his friend Pylades, he killed the adulterers in the Temple of *Apollo*.
    Byron   *On Hearing that Lady Byron was Ill* 35-7
    Swinburne   *On the Cliffs* 152ff
                Atalanta in Calydon 426ff
    Thomas, Dylan   *Greek Play in a Garden* 23-4

Cnidos, Cnidus   A hill and Doric town sacred to *Venus* of whom a large monument was made there by *Praxiteles*.

          (Horace *Odes* i 30)
    Spenser   *Faerie Queene* III vi 29

Cocytus   A river of Epirus whose name means 'weeping'. Its name and its proximity to the river *Acheron* caused it to be regarded as a river of Hades.
        (Pausanias I xvii; Virgil *Aeneid* vi 295ff,
                       Georgics iv 479)
    Drayton   *The Barons' Wars* ii 6
    Marlowe   *Jew of Malta* 1400ff
               Tamburlaine i 1999-2001
    Milton   *Paradise Lost* ii 579-80
    Shakespeare   *Titus Andronicus* II iii 235-6
    Skelton   *Philip Sparrow*
    Spenser   *Faerie Queene* I i 37, II vii 56, III iv 55
    Wordsworth   *To the River Greta* 5-7

Codrus   A Roman poet of the 1st Century AD. He was celebrated for his poverty.
          (Juvenal *Satire* iii 203ff)
    Pope   *The Dunciad* ii 136
             To the Author of a Poem 20

Coelus
See *Uranus*
    Keats   *Hyperion* i 305-8

Coeus   A *Titan*, father of *Leto* (*Latona*) and *Asteria* by *Phoebe* (his sister).
        (Hesiod *Theogony* 134, 404-10)
    Keats   *Hyperion* ii 19-22

Collatina, Colina   A minor Roman goddess of hills.
    Drayton   *The Muses' Elizium* ix 41-2

Colchis, Colchos   A coastal country on the east of the Black Sea. It was the home of the *Golden Fleece* sought by the *Argonauts*.
See also *Aetes*, *Colcos*
    Marlowe   *Hero and Leander* 55-8

Colcos
See *Colchos*
    Chaucer   *Legend of Good Women* 1425ff

Colatyn
See *Collatinus*

Chaucer   *Legend of Good Women*
           1736-42

Coliseum
See *Colosseum*
    Byron   *Childe Harold* iv 145
             Manfred III iv 10-3
    Clough   *Amours de Voyage* i 45-7

Collatinus, Collatine   Husband of *Lucretia*
and nephew of *Tarquinius* Superbus.
    Shakespeare   *Rape of Lucrece* 1-7, 15-18,
                   254-9, 1291-3
    Tennyson   *Lucretius* 238-40

Collatia, Collatium   An early city close to
Rome and under her control from the earliest
times. Collatia was the legendary site of the
rape of *Lucretia* by *Tarquinius* Sextus; her
husband was Tarquinius *Collatinus*.
                            (Livy I lvii)
    Shakespeare   *Rape of Lucrece* 1-7

Colonos, Colonus   A hill only a short walk
from the *Acropolis* in *Athens*. It was the birthplace of *Sophocles* and celebrated in his
Oedipus at Colonus.
    Arnold   *To a Friend* 9-14
    Browning E. B.   *The Lost Bower* 56
    Swinburne   *Athens* str. i

Colosseum   A vast amphitheatre in Rome,
started in the 1st Century AD by *Vespasian*
and others on the site of the Golden House —
a huge landscaped palace built by *Nero* after
the fire of 64AD. The Colosseum held some
50000 people and was fully equipped for
displays of martial art, gladiatorial contests
and martyrdom. It was probably not completed before 217AD. The name is medieval
— to the Romans it was the Flavian Amphitheatre, named after Flavius Vespasian.
See *Coliseum*
    Lewis C. D.   *A Letter from Rome*

Colossus   Generally, a gigantic statue, so
called by *Herodotus*. In particular, a massive
bronze statue of *Helios* built somewhere near
the harbour of Rhodes in the 3rd Century BC.
It was later said to have straddled the harbour.
It was destroyed by an earthquake a century
later.

                            (Strabo VI iii 1)
    Browning R.   *Christmas Eve* 749-53
                   Consolatory Address to
                   Sarah 9-12
    Carew   *A Rapture* 6-9
    Chapman   *Bussy D'Ambois* I i 6-9
    Donne   *Elegy* iv 31-4
    Dryden   *All for Love* I i
    Jonson   *To Inigo* 13-14
    Shakespeare   *Julius Caesar* I ii 135-8
    Tennyson *Where is the Giant of the*
              Sun 1ff

Comatas, Comates   In *Theocritus*'s *Idyll* vii,
a musical goatherd imprisoned in a chest by a
tyrant but fed by honey-bees.
    Wordsworth   *The Prelude* xi 437ff

Cominius   A Roman consul who designated
the Volscian town of Corioli for attack by the
Romans. Coriolanus captured the town and
took his cognomen from it.
                    (Plutarch *Coriolanus* viii)
    Shakespeare   *Coriolanus* I i 234-5

Comus   A late Roman god of nocturnal
revelry and feasting, being originally a word
used of revellers at Bacchic orgies. He is described as a youth crowned with roses, bearing
a torch, and in a drunken stupor.
                    (Philostratus *Imagines* i 2)
    Jonson   *To Sir Robert Wroth* 47-50
    Keats   *Spirit Here that Reignest* 15-20
    Milton   *Comus* 54-8, 63-70, 519-20

Concord, Concordia   A Roman goddess of
peace, particularly civic and familiar harmony.
                            (Ovid *Fasti* vi 637-8)
See also *Pax*
    Collins   *Ode to Liberty* 131-4
    Spenser   *Faerie Queene* IV x 34

Constantine   Flavius Valerius — Constantine
the Great. Born c. 285AD in Serbia, the illegitimate son of *Constantius*, Emperor of the West.
Constantine spent his early years in the imperial court and then went with his father, who
was commanded to recover Britain from the
usurper *Carausius*. In 306AD, on his father's
death at York, Constantine was acclaimed by
the troops and Galerius (*Diocletian*'s successor
as Augustus Caesar) grudgingly recognised Con-

stantine as a Caesar. He married *Maximian*'s daughter and, after long disputes as to his hereditary right to the Empire, he emerged in sole command — Galerius having died and Maximian having committed suicide. He founded Constantinople on the site of Byzantium, and as an imperial centre for the East, and succeeded in reuniting the Empire. Also, by his personal support, he established Christianity as the religion of the Empire rather than that of a persecuted minority.

> Spenser   *Faerie Queene* II x 59

Constantius   Constantius, the father of *Constantine* the Great, was commissioned as *Diocletian*'s Caesar in the West to recover Britain from *Carausius*. This he did with the help of his prefect, *Asclepiodotus*, who defeated Carausius's murderer and successor, *Allectus*. He was succeeded by the future Constantine the Great in 306 AD, after years of very uncertain fighting in the south and east of England.

> Spenser   *Faerie Queene* II x 59

Corbulo   Domitius Corbulo governed Syria under *Nero*. He was a notable general who aroused Nero's jealousy and suspicion, probably unfounded, of conspiracy; he committed suicide after Nero had ordered his death.

> (Tacitus *Annals* xii-xv)
> Gray   *Agrippina* 110

Corcyra   The island of Corfu. It had varied political fortunes, being associated with Corinth until the 5th Century BC, when it joined *Athens* against Corinth. It was then claimed by various countries, but was a Roman naval station from the 3rd Century BC to the 2nd Century AD. At the time of *Thucydides* it was allied to Athens.

> MacNeice   *Hiatus* 9-11

Corinna (1)   A Boeotian lyric poetess of the 3rd Century BC of whom little is known. One fragment describes a contest between *Helicon* and *Cithaeron*. She was said to have competed in poetry with *Pindar (1)* and to have advised him that he should use mythology more sparingly.

> Donne   *A Valediction of the Book* 5-9

Marlowe   *Tamburlaine* ii 3059-63
Tennyson   *The Princess* iii 329-34

Corinna (2)
See *Ovid*

Coriolanus   Gnaeus Marcius Coriolanus, the eponymous hero of Corioli, a Volscian town which he captured. He was a soldier who rose from the ranks with acclaim but always, it seems, also with dislike for his pride and inflexibility. He was rejected by the people for consul in the 5th Century BC and was banished from Rome for his refusal to distribute corn gratis to the people. He then changed sides, joined forces with the Volsci and marched Rome. He was deaf to all entreaties for mercy until his wife, Volumnia, and mother, *Veturia*, intervened. He then withdrew, accusing some of the Volsci, by whom he was murdered in 488 BC.

> (Plutarch *Coriolanus*)
See *Amfidius, Marcius*
> Collins   *Epistle to Sir Thomas Hanmer* 121-4, 127-8
> Eliot T.S.   *A Cooking Egg* 10-12, 29-30
>   *The Waste Land* 415-6
> Shakespeare   *Coriolanus* I i 258-60, iv 57-62, ix 63-5; II i 18, 142, 153-6, ii 85 ff; III i 255-8, ii 1-6; V iv 20-1, 31 ff
>   *Titus Andronicus* IV iv 63 ff

Cornelia   A daughter of *Scipio Africanus (1)*. Her refusal to remarry (the suitors included Ptolemy VII), and her devotion to and education of her sons became exemplary. The sons were Tiberius and Gaius Gracchus, major statesmen of the 2nd Century BC.

> Shakespeare   *Titus Andronicus* IV i 12-14
> Tennyson   *The Princess* ii 69-71

Cornucopia
See *Amalthea, Ceres*
> Keats   *The Fall of Hyperion* i 35-7

Coronis   A daughter of Phlegyas and sister of *Ixion*. In the best known version of her story, she had an affair with *Apollo* and bore his son, *Aesculapius*, whom she exposed on a mountain. There he was suckled by goats, saved by Apollo, and reared by *Chiron*. Whilst pregnant with this son, she lay with Ischys, a young Thessalian, and was observed to do so by a crow placed on watch by Apollo. She and Ischys were then killed by Apollo or *Artemis*. The crow was thenceforth changed from white to black and deprived of its once beautiful song. Coronis was transformed into a sweet briar.

(Ovid *Metamorphoses* II 542 ff;
Hyginus *Fabulae* 202)

See also *Phoebus*
Spenser   *Faerie Queene* III xi 37

Corvus   The Raven or Crow Constellation.

Corybantes, Corybantian   Priests of *Cybele*. They secretly brought up *Jupiter* on Mt *Ida* in Crete. His mother (*Rhea*, Cybele, *Ops*) had saved him from destruction by his father *Saturn* (who had taken the throne on condition that he have no male heir and who consequently ate his babies). The Corybantian rituals were of abandoned fury with much beating of cymbals.

(Diodorus Siculus III l 9;
Ovid *Fasti* IV 201ff)

See also *Curetes*
Spenser   *Mutability Cantos* vi 27
Wordsworth   *Memorials of a Tour*
                1820 xxxii 33-6

Corydon   A shepherd's name in pastorals of *Theocritus* and *Virgil*. He competed in verse with *Thyrsis*, whom he defeated. In English poetry the name usually has no special significance.

(Theocritus *Idyll* iv;
Virgil *Eclogues* ii, vii)

Arnold   *Thyrsis* 77-80
Crabbe   *The Village* i 9-12
Milton   *L'Allegro* 83-5

Corynne
See *Corinna (1)*
Chaucer   *Anelida and Arcite* 21

Cottus   One of the three hundred-handed giants who helped *Zeus* in his war with the *Titans*, after which they were returned to *Tartarus* to guard the fallen Titans. The other hundred-handed giants were *Briareus* and *Gyges*.

(Hesiod *Theogony* 147-58, 617-35)
Keats   *Hyperion* ii 49-52

Cotys   A Thracian name for *Cotytto*.
Swinburne   *Prelude* 115-20

Cotytto   A Thracian fertility goddess whose rites (Cotyttia) were noted for their debauchery; they were held at night and there was penalty of death for anyone who revealed their nature.

(Horace *Epode* xvii 56-7;
Juvenal *Satires* ii 91-2)

See also *Cotys*
Hardy   *The Collector Cleans his Picture*
              29-30
Milton   *Comus* 128-36
Swinburne   *Dolores* 392-6

Cragus   A Lycian mountain sacred to *Apollo*.
(Strabo xiv 35)
Drayton   *The Muses' Elizium* 177-80

Crassus   Marcus Licinius Crassus, a very wealthy Roman of the 1st Century BC, who helped bring the dictator *Sulla (2)* to power. In a coalition with *Pompey* and *Caesar*, Crassus set out to conquer Parthia, where he sustained heavy losses and feigned surrender. He was beheaded and the head sent to *Orodes*, who had taken the Parthian throne from his brother *Mithridates*. Orodes had molten gold poured down the throat and the head put on display.

(Plutarch *Crassus*)

See *Metella*
Chaucer   *Troilus and Criseyde* i 1387-93
Shakespeare   *Antony and Cleopatra* III i
                1-3, 3-5

Cratis   An Arcadian river.
Prior   *First Hymn to Callimachus* 19 ff

Creet
See *Crete*
Milton   *Paradise Lost* i 514-5

Creon   The brother of *Jocasta*, who was mother and wife of *Oedipus*. Creon offered his Theban throne to whomever could rid him of the curse of the *Sphinx*. Oedipus did so and took the crown, in ignorance marrying his mother, by whom he had *Eteocles* and *Poly-*

neices. It was arranged that on the death of Oedipus his sons would rule alternately. Predictably, they fell out and Polyneices, aided by the Seven heroes, tried to wrest the throne from his unwilling brother. In the course of this struggle they killed each other. Creon resumed the throne until Eteocles' son should be of age, and he ordered that the aggressors remain unburied. This edict resulted in the deaths of *Antigone* and *Haemon* (Creon's son) and also of Creon himself at the hand of *Theseus*.

> (Apollodorus III; Sophocles *Antigone*;
> Statius *Thebaid*)

See also *Seven Against Thebes, Thebes*

Arnold	*Fragment of an 'Antigone'*
Browning E. B.	*Queen Anelida* 10
Chaucer	*Anelida and Arcite* 64-6
	Knight's Tale 938-47, 959-64

Cresseid

See *Chryseis*

Chaucer	*Troilus and Criseyde*
Henryson	*Testament of Cresseid* 71-4, 309ff, 371, 501-4

Cressida

See *Chryseis, Troilus*

Shakespeare	*Merchant of Venice* V i 3-6
	Troilus and Cressida I i 94ff, ii 276-7; III ii 180ff; IV ii 98ff

Cresus

See *Croesus*

Chaucer	*Knight's Tale* 1936-46
	Monk's Tale 3917-24, 3937-50
	Nun's Priest's Tale 4328-30
	House of Fame 103-6

Crete   The Mediterranean island regarded as the birthplace of *Zeus (Jupiter)*.

> (Ovid *Fasti* iii 443-4;
> Virgil *Aeneid* iii 104)

Keats	*Lamia* i 13-16

Creus/Crius   A *Titan*, father of *Astraeus*, *Pallas* and *Perses*.

> (Hesiod *Theogony* 134, 375-7)

Keats	*Hyperion* ii 41-3

Creusa (1)   Creusa (also named *Glauce*) was a daughter of Creon, king of Corinth (as opposed to *Creon of Thebes* in the *Oedipus* story). She put on a poisoned dress as she was about to marry *Jason*, was burned and died in agony. This occurred because the dress was a present from *Medea*, the enchantress and former wife of Jason, who had rejected her in favour of Creusa. Creon perished in the fire with his daughter.

> (Euripides *Medea*;
> Ovid *Ars Amatoriae* i 335)

Sidney	*A Shepherd's Tale* 409-12
Spenser	*Faerie Queene* II xii 45

Creusa (2)   The wife of *Aeneas* and mother of *Iulus*. Creusa was a daughter of *Priam* of *Troy*. She was lost in the flight from the sacked city but was repeatedly rescued by *Cybele* and became a priestess of her temple. She appeared to Aeneas in a dream and counselled flight from fallen Troy and pursuit of his destiny elsewhere.

> (Virgil *Aeneid* II 567ff, 771-89)

Chaucer	*House of Fame* 174-88
	Legend of Good Women 943-5

Critias   The extremist leader of the *Thirty Tyrants* who held Greece in a reign of terror after the Peloponnesian War, c.404 BC. A distant relative of *Plato* and a pupil and associate of *Socrates*, Critias was also a poet and tragedian honoured in Plato's *Critias Dialogue*. He arranged the death of Theramenes, leader of the moderates among the Thirty, who died by drinking hemlock. Critias was killed in battle in 403 BC.

> (Xenophon *Hellenica* II iii 50-6)

Spenser	*Faerie Queene* II vii 52, IV *Prologue* 3

Croesus   The last king of *Lydia*, Croesus was of fabulous wealth and was patron to *Aesop*. There was a legend that he met *Solon*, who distinguished the illusory happiness of being Croesus from the real happiness of being dead, but historically such a meeting could not have occurred. Croesus made war on *Cyrus* of Persia and was defeated in 546 BC. According to the legend, Cyrus ordered Croesus to be burned but, on hearing Croesus cry out Solon's distinction, Cyrus recanted and became friends with Croesus. In another version, Croesus was saved by the intervention of *Apollo*. There was also a tradition that he was hanged. He had prepared himself before the battle by consulting the Pythian priestess of the Delphic Oracle, where he received the message that if he embarked on conquest an empire would be overthrown. It proved to be his own empire.

(Herodotus I xxviff, liii; Plutarch *Solon*)
See also *Atys, Cresus*

Browning R.	*Sordello* v 81-4
Byron	*Manfred* II ii 140-1
De La Mare	*Kismet* 24-5
Henryson	*Orpheus and Eurydice* 329-30
Housman	*Atys* 8-15
Johnson	*Vanity of Human Wishes* 313-4
Skelton	*Philip Sparrow*
Spenser	*Faerie Queene* I v 47
Suckling	*Love and Debt* 9

Cronian Sea   The Arctic, called Mare Cronium by *Pliny* but better known as the Mare Concretum.

(Pliny iv 16)
Milton   *Paradise Lost* x 289-91

Croton, Crotona   An ancient south Italian town, with a temple to *Juno*. It had an academic reputation through the Pythagoreans, who established their school there in the 5th Century BC.

(Strabo VI i 11)
Moore   *To Lord Viscount Strangford* 1-4
Shelley   *Revolt of Islam* 3111-4

Crow   The crow, *Apollo*'s bird, was turned from white to black in the myth of *Coronis*. Alternatively, the greedy crow was slow to fetch water for Apollo, being diverted by waiting for some figs to ripen, and Apollo made it unable to drink. He set it in the heavens as the Corvus constellation, with water guarded by a snake.

(Ovid *Metamorphoses* ii 534-632)

Cteatus   *Eurytus* and Cteatus were the twin sons of *Neptune* (or Actor, one of Neptune's sons) and Molione, after whom they are called Molionides. They took part in the *Calydonian*

Boar Hunt and fought for Elis (ruled by their uncle, Augeias) against *Hercules*, whose half-brother, *Iphicles*, they killed. Hercules made peace, but later killed them in an ambush at Cleonae during a truce. They were sometimes said to have been deformed or to have been Siamese twins.

(Apollodorus II vii 2;
Homer *Iliad* xi 706-52, xxiii 638-42)
Spenser   *Faerie Queene* IV xi 14

Ctesiphon   A town developed by the Arsacid kings of Parthia as their winter seat. It was near *Seleucia* on the mainland, north of Cyprus.

(Strabo XVI i 16)
Milton   *Paradise Regained* iii 299-301

Cumae
See *Sibyl*

Cunaxa   A town north of *Babylon*, where *Cyrus* II of Persia was defeated and killed by the overwhelming forces of Artaxerxes II, his brother and the true ruler against whom Cyrus had rebelled.

(Plutarch *Artaxerxes* viii;
Xenophon *Anabasis* i 8)
Tennyson   *Persia* 47-50

Cupid, Cupids   The Greek *Eros*, God of Love. There are several versions of Cupid and his parentage — he may be born of *Mercury* and *Diana/Venus*, *Vulcan/Jupiter/Mars* and Venus, or *Nox* and *Erebus*. Whilst it is only with erotic love that he is associated, there are various interpretations according to whether love is seen as tragic, comic, desirable, fearful, frivolous, and so on. He is usually represented as a bright or purple winged infant with bow and quiver, but is also shown as a warrior hero with helmet and spear. *Hesiod* presents Eros as existing from the beginning of time, born with or out of Chaos. Cupid may be blind and invisible, reflecting the nature of the passion. His golden arrows are of love; his leaden ones are of disdain. He may be by himself or with Venus/*Aphrodite*. Eros becomes Erotes — Cupids, the Loves — diminutive versions of himself, usually seen accompanying a person rather than as protagonists.

(Apuleius iv-vi; Hesiod *Theogony* 116-22;
Moschus *The Runaway Love* (I);

Ovid *Remedies of Love* 701; Theocritus III
10-16; Virgil *Aeneid* i 683-90)
— *Select General Allusions*
Carew   *No more, blind God* 1-3
Chaucer   *Franklin's Tale* 765-6
    House of Fame 614-9, 666-8
    Legend of Good Women
    213-9, 226 ff
    Parliament of Fowls 652
    Troilus and Criseyde i 206-10,
    III 1807-10, v 206-10, 599-602
Donne   *Elegy* xviii 27-30
    Love's Exchange 15-18
Goldsmith   *Epilogue to 'The Sister'*
    17-18
    On a Beautiful Youth Struck
    Blind 1-4
    The Double Transformation
    9-10
Jonson   *To Mrs Philip Sidney* 3-8
Keats   *Endymion* i 888-9, ii 536-41, iii
    862 ff, 973-7, 983-7, iv 730, 979
    Lamia i 197-8
    You Say You Love 6-9
Marlowe   *Hero and Leander* 187-91,
    369-74
Milton   *Comus* 445
    Paradise Lost iv 763
Monro H.   *Children of Love* 15-18
Praed   *Lillian* ii 26-30
    Love at a Rout 1-7
Prior   *Cupid and Ganymede* 17-18
Shakespeare   *King Lear* IV vi 136-7
    Love's Labour's Lost I ii
    163; III i 169-76, 185;
    IV iii 53-4
    Merry Wives of Windsor
    II ii 121
    Midsummer Night's Dream
    I i 169 ff, 234-5; II i 157-65
    Much Ado About Nothing
    I i 32, 155, 233; III i 20-3,
    ii 7 ff
    Othello I iii 268-70
    Romeo and Juliet I i 206-9
    Sonnet 153, 154
    The Tempest IV i 92-4
Shelley   *Witch of Atlas* 297-9
Sidney   *Arcadia* VIII 11-2, 13-14,
    XX 9-10, LXII 77 ff
    Astrophel and Stella 13
Spenser   *Amoretti* 60

Faerie Queene II viii 6, ix 18;
    III i 39, ii 26, xi 29-30, 35, 38,
    xii 22
Hymn in Honour of Love
    156-7, 231-7, 280-7
Muiopotmos 97-101
Mutability Cantos vii 34
Shepherd's Calendar, March
    79-83
Suckling   *The Metamorphosis* 1-4
    Song 1-6
Tennyson   *The Burial of Love* 1ff
    The Talking Oak 66-8
Wordsworth   *Ode to Lycoris* 5-8
— *the Loves or Cupids*
Keats   *Endymion* ii 179-82, 385-6,
    418-27
Shakespeare   *Antony and Cleopatra* II ii
    202 ff
    Romeo and Juliet I iv 4-6
Spenser   *Faerie Queene* IV x 42, xii 13
— *and Psyche*
Keats   *Otho the Great* V v 28-30
Lewis C. D.   *Psyche* 71-80
Milton   *Comus* 1004-8
Moore   *Cupid and Psyche* 5 ff
Spenser   *Faerie Queene* III vi 50
    Muiopotmos 131-3
— *and Venus*
Browning R.   *The Ring and the Book*
    IX 527 ff
Campion   *The Peaceful Western Wind*
    17 ff
Chaucer   *Knight's Tale* 1963-66
    House of Fame 134-9
    Legend of Good Women 313,
    1140-4
Jonson   *Love is Blind* 1-8
Prior   *Alma* i 389-93
Shakespeare   *As You Like It* IV i 189 ff
    Love's Labour's Lost II i
    253-5
    The Tempest IV i 87-90,
    97-100
Spenser   *Colin Clout's Come Home*
    Again 765-70, 805-12
    Faerie Queene, Prologue 3;
    II vi 35; III vi 11-14; IV Pro-
    logue 4-5, vii 1, ix 2-3; VI vii
    37, viii 25
    Hymn in Honour of Beauty
    8-10, 57-63

Hymn in Honour of Love 22-7, 57ff
Tears of the Muses 396-402

Curetes   A people of *Crete*.
See *Corybantes*
Prior   *First Hymn to Callimachus* 59-62

Curius   Manius Dentatus Curius, a Roman general and consul who defeated the Samnites and *Pyrrhus* (I) in the 3rd Century BC. Like *Fabricius*, he was renowned for frugality and integrity.
(Plutarch *Cato Major*)
Milton   *Paradise Regained* ii 445-9

Curtius   In about 362BC a huge chasm appeared in the Forum in Rome. It was said to be due to an earthquake. The gods were consulted and a sacrifice was said to be required. Marcus Curtius offered himself as the sacrifice and then committed a spectacular suicide by plunging on horseback into the pit. *Livy*, writing early in the 1st Century AD, is exceedingly sceptical. There were other legendary explanations of the dried-up lake which was there in Livy's day.
(Livy VII 6)
Marvell   *The Loyal Scot* 67-8
Pope   *Essay on Man* ii 199-202

Cybele   The goddess of nature and fecundity, identified with *Rhea* (the Roman *Ops*, mother of *Jupiter* and other gods, including *Tellus*). She may appear with a turreted head and oak leaves, in a chariot drawn by tigers or lions and accompanied by *Attis*, a beautiful youth whom she loved and who, by self-mutilation, expiated his violation of a promise of perpetual celibacy. Among the lions drawing her chariot were *Hippomenes* and *Atalanta*, whom she had transformed into beasts when they profaned her temple. She was married to her brother *Saturn* and was reputed to be mother of a hundred gods. Feasts in her honour were noted for wildness and indecency.
(Homeric Hymn *To the Mother of the Gods* (XIV); Ovid *Fasti* vi 321-2, *Metamorphoses* x 560ff; Virgil *Aeneid* vi 785-7)
See also *Berecynthia*, *Corybantes*
Browning E. B.   *The Dead Pan* 19
Byron   *Childe Harold* iv 2

Keats   *Endymion* ii 4-5, 640-4
         The Fall of Hyperion i 425-6
Meredith   *The Empty Purse*
Milton   *Arcades* 20-3
Shelley   *Oedipus Tyrannus* II ii 1-5, 8-10
Spenser   *Faerie Queene* I vi 15; IV xi 28
Swinburne   *Dolores* 344ff
Wordsworth   *Memorials of a Tour 1820* xxxii 33-6

Cyclades   A group of islands in the Aegean, which surround *Delos* in a circle.
Byron   *Don Juan* iv 72
Eliot T. S.   *Sweeney Erect* 1-2
Keats   *Hyperion* iii 23-4
         To Homer 1-4
Milton   *Paradise Lost* v 264-5
Shelley   *Hellas* 1068-71
Wordsworth   *To the Clouds* 74-7

Cyclopean, Cyclopeian
See *Cyclops*
Burns   *Epistle to Robert Graham* 46-8
Marlowe   *Tamburlaine* i 616ff
Shelley   *Revolt of Islam* 4761-4

Cyclopes, Cyclops   Monsters, each with an eye in the middle of his head, born to *Coelus* and *Terra*. They were originally three in number and they lived in *Tartarus*, from which they were released by *Zeus* and the *Titans*. In the war between the Titans and Zeus, the Cyclopes made Zeus's thunderbolts for him, and they continued to do so until *Apollo* destroyed them in revenge for Zeus's killing of his son *Asclepios*. This semi-divine family of Cyclopes is probably distinct in origin from the race of shepherd giants of whom *Polyphemus* was one. However, they were substantially merged, so that the Cyclopes were said to forge thunderbolts beneath Mt *Aetna* and works of stupendous grandeur were said to be Cyclopean.
(Apollodorus I i; Apollonius Rhodius i 730-4; Hesiod *Theogony* 139-46; Homer *Odyssey* ix; Ovid *Metamorphoses* xiii 764ff; Virgil *Aeneid* viii 439-54)
Arnold   *Epilogue to Lacoon* 45-8
Bridges   *Septuagesima* 2-5
Browning R.   *Balaustion's Adventure* 372-6

Crashaw	*Sospetto d'Herode*
Drayton	*Fourth Eclogue* 97-100
	Astraea Redux 45-7
	The Medal 226-7
Keats	*Endymion* ii 26-7
MacNeice	*Day of Returning* iii
Marlowe	*Edward II* 609-10
Shakespeare	*Hamlet* II ii 483-6
	Titus Andronicus IV iii 45-6
Shelley	*The Witch of Atlas* 641-5
Wordsworth	*To the Same Flower (Daisy)* 25-6

Cycnus There are many versions of the 'swan' legend. In the commonest, Cycnus was a friend and relation of *Phaethon*, at whose falling from the sky Cycnus was so stricken with grief that Apollo turned him into a swan and constellation.

(Ovid *Metamorphoses* ii 367 ff)

See also *Swan*

| Jonson | *Ode Allegoric* 99-101 |

Cydippe
See *Acontius*

Cydnus A river in Cilicia which features in accounts of the infatuation of *Antony* for *Cleopatra*. Cleopatra displayed herself there in a fabulous barge before Antony and a great crowd early in their affair.

(Plutarch *Antony* xxvi)

Dryden	*All for Love* III i
Shakespeare	*Cymbeline* II iv 70-2
Shenstone	*Judgment of Hercules* 125-8
Tennyson	*Persia* 59-60

Cyeneae Two 'dark' or 'clashing' rocks in the Black Sea near the northern end of the Bosphorus. Between them lies the Asian boundary. With the sea breaking violently on them they were a notorious peril.

(Apollonius Rhodius ii 317, 600; Herodotus iv 85)

See also *Symplegades*

Cyllene An Arcadian mountain on which was a temple to *Hermes* (who was known as Cylleneius as it was his birthplace) and which was reputed to have white blackbirds. It was

said to be cold and snow-covered. A name for *Hermes/Mercury*.

(Pausanias viii 17; Virgil *Aeneid* viii 139)

| Milton | *Arcades* 98 |

Cymerie
See *Cimmerian*

| Chaucer | *House of Fame* 66-76 |

Cymo A *Nereid*.

| Spenser | *Faerie Queene* IV ii 51 |

Cymodoce
See *Cymothoe*

| Spenser | *Faerie Queene* IV ii 50 |
| Swinburne | *Garden of Cymodoce* |

Cymothoe A *Nereid* who assisted *Triton* to save the Trojan fleet from *Aeolus*'s storm.

(Virgil *Aeneid* i 148 ff)

Diaper	*Sea Eclogues* i 19-20
Marlowe	*Dido Queen of Carthage* 130-4
Spenser	*Faerie Queene* IV ii 50
Swinburne	*Thalassius* 18-20

Cynegirus *Aeschylus*'s brother, Cynegirus was at the Battle of *Marathon*, 490BC. He lost a hand in holding on to an escaping Persian ship and died apparently from loss of blood.

(Herodotus vi 114)

| Browning E. B. | *Battle of Marathon* 1437 ff |

Cynic The philosophy or set of attitudes in the 4th Century BC held by Antisthenes or *Diogenes* of *Sinope*. The latter was known as a 'dog' (cynic) and was said to live in a tub, because of his rejection of society, its decencies, conventions and comforts. Whilst the nature of the outlook was plain, there was no clear-cut school of Cynic philosophy and the name was freely used. The underlying principle was the development of self-knowledge, in the quest for which the pleasures of life were felt to be a distraction.

| Collins | *The Manners, an Ode* 75-6 |
| Milton | *Comus* 708-9 |

Cynosura, Cynosure A nymph of *Ida* who nursed *Jupiter* and was turned into the Lesser Bear (*Arcas*) constellation; the Phoenicians were said to sail by these stars.

(Ovid *Fasti* iii 107)

See *Arcas*

Milton   *Comus* 341-2

               L'Allegro 80

Cynthia, Cynthian A Roman name for *Artemis* (and, occasionally, *Apollo*) from the hill of *Cynthus* on the island of *Delos* where she and Apollo were born. Used of the moon, with which *Diana*/Artemis was identified.

See also *Cinthia, Cynthius, Luna, Hecate*

Chapman   *Shadow of Night*

Chaucer   *Troilus and Criseyde* V 1016-9

Donne   *Elegy* viii 19-22

Drayton   *Endymion and Phoebe* 331-2

Gray   *Ode for Music* 31-3

Henryson   *Testament of Cresseid* 253 ff

Jonson   *Cynthia's Revels* V iii

Keats   *Blue! 'Tis the Light of Heaven* 1-4

    Endymion ii 169-74, 179ff, iii 72-4, 97-9, iv 563-70, 827-33, 964-7

    I Stood Tiptoe Upon a Little Hill 201-4, 239

    To Charles Cowden Clarke 92-3

    To My Brother George 10-12

Marlowe   *Hero and Leander* 59-65

    Tamburlaine ii 3461-2

Milton   *Il Penseroso* 59-60

    On the Morning of Christ's Nativity 101-2

Pope   *Chorus to 'Brutus'* ii 21-4

    Dunciad iii 239-40

    Messiah 99-100

Prior   *Chloe Hunting* 17-18

Scott   *From 'Ivanhoe'*

Shakespeare   *Pericles* II v 8-12

    Romeo and Juliet III v 18-19

    Venus and Adonis 727-30

Spenser   *Epithalamium* 372ff

    Faerie Queene I i 39, vii 34; II i 53; III *Prologue*, i 43

    Mutability Cantos vi 9

    Prothalamion 119-22

    Shepherd's Calendar, April 86-90

Wordsworth   *Sonnet 'With How Sad Steps'* 13-14

Young   *Night Thoughts* ii

Cynthius Apollo, born on Mount *Cynthus*.
See also *Cynthia*

Drayton   *The Muses' Elizium* ix 15-17

Jonson   *Ode to James, Earl of Desmond* 8-10

Cynthus A mountain of *Delos* on which Apollo and *Artemis* were supposed to have been born and which was sacred to them.

(Ovid *Metamorphoses* vi 204-5; Virgil *Aeneid* i 498ff)

See also *Cynthia, Cynthius*

Drayton   *The Barons' Wars* vi 37

    The Muses' Elizium ix 73-7

Pope   *Spring* 65-8

    Windsor-Forest 165ff

Spenser   *Faerie Queene* II iii 31; VI ii 25

Cyparissus Son of *Telephus* and apparently affected by the misfortune which dogged his father's life. On accidentally killing a pet stag, he grieved so much that the gods turned him into a cypress tree. Alternatively, he was changed into the tree as he fled the attentions of *Apollo*, *Zephyrus* or *Silvanus*. The cypress has funereal associations from the earliest times.

(Ovid *Metamorphoses* x 106-142)

Marlowe   *Hero and Leander* 154-6

Spenser   *Faerie Queene* I vi 17

Cypress
See *Cyparissus*

Cowley   *On the Death of Mr Wm Hervey* 9

Milton   *Epitaph on the Marchioness of Winchester* 21-2

Cyprian
See *Venus*

Collins   *Written on a Paper* 9

Shenstone   *Elegies* viii 61-4

Spenser   *Faerie Queene* II xii 65

Swift   *A Love Song* 9-12

    Strephon and Chloe 47-52

Cypride Son of *Aphrodite* the Cypriot — that is, *Cupid*.

Chaucer   *Parliament of Fowls* 274-7

Cypris
See *Venus*
> Hopkins   *Escorial* 11

Cyrene   A great city of Libya, capital of Cyrenaica and one of the five cities making up Pentapolis. It was an important commercial centre and was at various times under Greek, Egyptian or Roman control. Legend ascribes its name to Cyrene, mother of *Aristaeus*.
See also *Euphemus*
> Cowper   *The Task* V 135-7
> Kipling   *The Bees and the Flies* 1-8
> Milton   *Paradise Lost* ii 903-4

Cyrus   Cyrus the Great, King of Persia in the 6th Century BC. Son of *Cambyses*, he was said to have been cast out by his family and brought up by a shepherdess. In due course he levied troops and in 559 BC defeated his grandfather, *Astyages* of Media. In 539 BC he captured *Babylon*, the Assyrian capital, by diverting the Euphrates and using the river-bed as an approach by night. (He had previously diminished the River Gyndes to a trickle by drawing its water off into 180 canals, after one of his horses had been lost in its torrent.) There are various stories of his death, one being that he was defeated and killed by *Tomyris*, a Scythian queen who soaked his head in a skin or pot full of his blood and insulted his body. He was regarded by the Greeks as an ideal ruler of mythic stature, holding an enormous empire with tolerance and good sense.
> (Herodotus i; Xenophon *Cyropaedia*)
See also *Cirus*
> Goldsmith   *The Captivity* 252 ff
> Marlowe   *Tamburlaine* i 137-8
> Milton   *Paradise Regained* iii 31-4, 280-4
> Pope   *Temple of Fame* 95-6
> Shakespeare   *King Henry VI pt 1* II ii 5-6
> Tennyson   *Babylon* 21-4
>   *Persia* 13-16
>   *The Princess* v 355-6

Cythaeron
See *Cithaeron*
> Pope   *Temple of Fame* 85-8
> Spenser   *Faerie Queene* VI x 9

Cythera, Cytheraea   The island (Kythera) south of the Peloponnesus, on which *Aphrodite* was said to have landed on being born from the remains of *Uranus*. Hence one of the several names for *Venus*.
> (Hesiod *Theogony* 195-8)
See also *Cypris*
> Browning E. B.   *The Battle of Marathon* 15-20
> Byron   *Childe Harold* iii 90
> Chaucer   *Parliament of Fowls* 113-6
> Coleridge   *On a Late Connubial Rupture* 6-8
> Collins   *Written on a Paper* 14
> Gray   *The Progress of Poesy* 28-9
> Keats   *Endymion* ii 492, iii 917-9, 973-7
> Pope   *Of a Lady Who Could Not Sleep* V
> Shakespeare   *Cymbeline* II ii 13-16
>   *Passionate Pilgrim* 4, 6, 9
>   *Taming of the Shrew, Induction* 47-51
>   *Winter's Tale* IV iv 115-24
> Shelley   *Prometheus Unbound* II v 20-8
> Spenser   *Hymn in Honour of Beauty* 253-61
>   *Tears of the Muses* 396-402
> Stevenson   *Madrigal* 5-8
> Swinburne   *Hymn to Proserpine* 75-6

Cytheron
See *Cithaeron*
> Spenser   *Faerie Queene* III vi 29

Daedale
See *Dedalus*
> Fletcher P.   *Purple Island* v 44-5
> Shelley   *Fragment, A Tale Untold* 3
>   *Hymn of Pan* 26-7
>   *Ode to Liberty* 18-19
>   *Prometheus Unbound* III i 25-6; IV 114-6, 415-7
> Spenser   *Faerie Queene* III Prologue 2

Daedalus
See *Dedalus*
> Cowley   *The Praise of Pindar* 1
> Cowper   *Anti-Thelyphthora* 52-5
> Praed   *The County Ball* 536-8
> Shakespeare   *King Henry VI pt 3* V vi 21-6

Swinburne   *Ballad against the Enemies*
                of France 10

Daemon
See *Genius*
Milton   *Il Penseroso* 93-6
            Comus 1-6
Shelley   *Prometheus Unbound* I 1-2;
            IV 529-32
            The Daemon of the World
            56-8

Dagon   A Semitic god associated with myths of fish, food and vegetation, and sometimes described as half man and half fish. *Azotus* (Ashdod) and Gaza were centres for his worship.
Milton   *Paradise Lost* i 462-3
            Samson Agonistes 12-13, 434-7,
            440-2, 461-5, 1150-1

Damocles   A court flatterer exposed by *Dionysius I* (2) of Syracuse who, to illustrate to him the falsity of the apparent pleasures of monarchy, at a banquet seated Damocles on the throne beneath a naked sword suspended by a hair. Damocles was duly terrified and lost all inclination to the life of kings.
                 (Horace *Odes* III i;
     Cicero *Tusculan Disputations* V 21)
Chaucer   *Knight's Tale* 2027-30
Lawrence   *Eagle in New Mexico* 32-4
Shelley   *Prometheus Unbound* i 396-400

Damoetas   A pipe-playing shepherd or goatherd of pastoral poetry.
                (Theocritus *Idylls* vi;
       Virgil *Eclogues* ii 37, iii, v 72)
Milton   *Lycidas* 36

Damon (1)   A typical goatherd of pastoral, and so also a pastoral poet.
          (Virgil *Eclogues* iii 17, 23, viii)
Collins   *No Longer Ask Me, Gentle*
            Friends 61-4
            Song from Shakespeare 1
MacNeice   *Eclogue by a Five-Barred*
            Gate 73-5
Marvell   *Damon the Mower*
Shenstone   *Elegies* vi 15ff

Damon (2)   A Pythagorean philosopher of Syracuse. He had a celebrated friendship with *Pythias* (1) (or Phintias) who was condemned to death by the tyrant *Dionysius*; he asked leave to settle his affairs and Damon stood pledge for him, ready to be killed in his place should he not return. Phintias duly came back and Dionysius was so struck by their friendship that he pardoned them.
                (Diodorus Siculus x 4)
Spenser   *Faerie Queene* IV x 27

Danae   Daughter of King *Acrisius* of *Argos*, and mother of *Perseus*. She was imprisoned in a tower by her father, who had been told that his grandson would kill him. *Zeus* however entered the tower as a shower of gold, and by him she had a son, Perseus, who later accidentally killed Acrisius with a quoit.
    (Ovid *Metamorphoses* iv 611, vi 103ff)
Browning E. B.   *A Vision of Poets* 204-7
Byron   *English Bards* 489ff
Carew   *Mediocrity in Love* 7-9
            A Rapture 81-4
Chapman   *Hero and Leander* i
Drayton   *Endymion and Phoebe* 137ff
Jonson   *The Alchemist* IV i
Keats   *Endymion* iv 606-7
Lawrence   *Tommies in the Train*
Marlowe   *Edward II* 852ff, 1574-8
            Hero and Leander 145-6
Marvell   *Mourning* 19-20
Moore   *Intolerance* 74
Prior   *Cupid and Ganymede* 11-2
            The Padlock 1-4
Rosetti D. G.   *Jenny*
Spenser   *Faerie Queene* III xi 31
Suckling   *The Metamorphosis* 1-4
Yeats   *The Herne's Egg*

Danaid, Danaides   The fifty daughters of Danaeus, King of *Argos* and rival of his brother, *Aegyptus*, whom he suspected of plotting, with his fifty sons, to take over his territory. In some accounts the girls were forced to marry their cousins, the sons of Aegyptus and, on instructions from Danaeus, killed their husbands. From this massacre *Lynceus* was spared; he was deeply loved by *Hypermnestra*, one of the daughters, and made war on, but was eventually reconciled to, Danaeus. The heads of the murdered men were cast into the marsh of *Lerna*, or their bodies were left there whilst their heads were buried at Argos. The murderous daughters were punished by having eternally to draw water into leaking pots in *Hades*. In another account Lynceus was said to kill Danaus.

> (Apollodorus II i 4-5; Horace *Odes* III 11)
> Spenser   *Faerie Queene* I v 35
> Tennyson   *The Princess* ii 318-21

Danao
See *Danaides*
> Chaucer   *Legend of Good Women* 2562 ff

Dane
See *Daphne (1)*
> Chaucer   *Knight's Tale* 2062-4
>   *Troilus and Criseyde* iii 726-8

Daphne (1)   A nymph with whom *Apollo* fell in love; he was provoked by *Cupid*, having disputed with him the power of his darts which Apollo, the recent conqueror of the *Python*, belittled. When he pursued Daphne on the banks of the River *Peneus* (her father) she was saved by being turned into a laurel by the gods. Apollo is therefore often represented crowned with laurel leaves.

> (Ovid *Metamorphoses* i 452 ff)
See also *Dane, Daphnis*
> Byron   *Childe Harold* i 63
> Carew   *A Rapture* 130-4
> Cowley   *On Dr Harvey*
> Fletcher P.   *Piscatory Eclogues* vii 20
> Herrick   *The Welcome to Sack* 92
> Jonson   *To His Lady, Then Mrs Cary* 3-8
> Lovelace   *Princess Louisa Drawing* 28-33
> Marvell   *The Garden* 27-9
> Meredith   *Daphne*
> Milton   *Comus* 661-3
>   *Paradise Regained* ii 181-8
> Pope   *Imitation of Cowley* 22-4
> Sassoon   *Solar Eclipse* 8 ff
> Shakespeare   *Midsummer Night's Dream* II i 230-2
>   *Taming of the Shrew, Induction* 55-7
> Skelton   *Garland of Laurel*
> Smart   *Apollo and Daphne*
> Spenser   *Faerie Queene* II xii 52,

>   III vii 26, III xi 36, IV vii 22
>   *Amoretti* 28
> Wordsworth   *The Russian Fugitive* 176-84

Daphne (2)
See *Daphnis*
> Pope   *Winter* 69 ff

Daphne (Grove of)   A grove near Antioch dedicated to *Apollo*. It was a pleasure resort of natural beauty, with temples and a stadium.
> (Strabo XVI 2)
> Milton   *Paradise Lost* iv 272-5

Daphnis   A Sicilian shepherd, son of *Mercury*. He was educated by the nymphs, *Muses* and *Pan*, and became a superb musician referred to as the first composer of pastoral poetry. He was fond of hunting and is sometimes confused with *Daphne (1)*. He is associated with the *Heraean* mountains in northern Sicily. *Theocritus* (i 66) has him smitten by an insatiable passion because he had scorned love. Daphnis became a symbol of the poet or singer, especially one who died young or was moved by unrequited love.

> (Diodorus Siculus iv 83-4;
> Theocritus *Eclogues*; Virgil *Eclogues*)
See also *Daphne (2)*
> Arnold   *Thyrsis* 182-5

Dardan, Dardania   The land (including *Troy*) named after *Dardanus*, of which the capital (Dardanus) was close to Mt *Ida*.
> Byron   *The Curse of Minerva* 75 ff
> Shakespeare   *Rape of Lucrece* 1437-8
>   *Troilus and Cressida, Prologue* 16-19

Dardanus   A son of *Jupiter* and *Electra* who, after a tempestuous youth, married Batia, daughter of Teucer, king of Teucria (*Phrygia*). He succeeded Teucer and in a very long reign built the city of Dardanus and was regarded as the founder of *Dardania* (*Troy* — Troas was one of his successors).
> (Apollodorus III xii;
> Homer *Iliad* xx 215 ff)
> Chaucer   *Troilus and Criseyde* ii 617-8

Dares Phrygius   Dares the Phrygian was the

supposed author of a Greek Troiad and is mentioned (though not as such) by *Homer*. A Latin work purporting to be a translation of this *Daretis Phrygii de excidio Troiae Historia* was widely read in the Middle Ages and was a main source of Trojan literary material. Neither its date nor its status is established.

(Homer *Iliad* v 9)

See also *Dictys*

Chaucer   *Book of the Duchess* 1067-70
                  House of Fame 1467
                  Troilus and Criseyde i 145-7

Darius I (1)   Darius murdered Gaumata, impersonating the dead Smerdis who had usurped the Persian throne on the death of *Cambyses* (522 BC), and was elected king. He quelled revolts in *Babylon* and the East, restored order, and laid down an administration by satraps or provincial governors responsible to him. He attacked the principal rival power, the Greeks, and was defeated at the Battle of *Marathon* in 490 BC. He was reputed to have had the word 'Athenians' repeated to him three times before every dinner to remind him who was his first enemy.

(Diodorus Siculus x-xii; Herodotus iii-vii, v 105)

Arnold   *The World and the Quietist* 28-32

Browning E. B.   *The Battle of Marathon* 962-4

Chaucer   *Monk's Tale* 3837-40

Darius III (2)   King of Persia during its invasion by *Alexander the Great*. His well-equipped army was defeated at Granicus and at Issus in 333 BC. At Issus, where the Persians sustained huge losses, Darius made an escape disguised at night. Alexander held Darius's family, but treated them with kindness, even giving them presents. Darius made a further attempt but was decisively defeated at Arbela and died in 331 BC, paying tribute to Alexander who granted him a state funeral. In some way by the death of Darius, Alexander acquired a celebrated jewel chest in which he then kept the works of *Homer*.

(Diodorus Siculus xvii 1-36; Plutarch *Alexander* xxvi)

Browning R.   *With Gerard de Lairesse* 33-5

Keats   *King Stephen* I iv 33-4

Shakespeare   *King Henry VI pt 1* I vi 21-6

Surrey   *The Great Macedon* 1-2

Datis   A general of *Darius I* who led the Persian troops at *Marathon*, where he was wounded. He was subsequently killed by the Spartans.

(Herodotus vi-vii)

Browning E. B.   *The Battle of Marathon* 1412 ff

Daulis   A nymph, and a town of Phocis named after her. This was where *Tereus* ate his son, Itys or *Itylus*.

Swinburne   *Itylus* 45-8

Decius   Decius Publius, a consul and general in the 4th Century BC, whose deeds may well be legendary. The most famous was a suicidal charge into the ranks of the Latin enemy in 340 BC, after dedicating himself to the Roman cause. His performance so terrified the opposition that Rome won the field.

(Livy viii 9)

Pope   *Essay on Man* ii 199-202

Dedal, Dedalian

See *Dedalus, Daedal*

Keats   *Sleep and Poetry* 302-4

Dedalus   A fabulous Grecian inventor and craftsman, Dedalus and his sister Perdix were descended from Erechtheus, a King of *Athens*. Dedalus killed his nephew Talus (or Calus or Perdix) when he showed signs of rivalling him, and as a result he was banished or fled from Athens and settled in Crete under *Minos*. Here, in response to *Pasiphae*, Minos's queen, he constructed a hollow cow, for Pasiphae was in love with a bull; she went to the fields in the cow, met the bull, and gave birth to the *Minotaur* monster, half man and half bull. Dedalus then constructed the labyrinth in which the Minotaur was kept and in which it was fed with Athenian boys and girls every nine years. It was at Dedalus's suggestion that *Ariadne* gave *Theseus* a ball of thread to help him find his way out of this maze, thus incurring the wrath of Minos who imprisoned Dedalus and his son *Icarus* in the labyrinth. They escaped on wings made of wax and feathers, but the wings of Icarus melted because he flew too near the sun, and he dropped into the Icarian sea. Dedalus reached Sicily and was received by King Cocalus. Minos, searching for Dedalus, publicised a problem requiring that a spiral sea-shell be threaded with cotton; Dedalus solved this by attaching the thread to an ant, but thereby revealed his identity. Cocalus refused to surrender him and Minos was killed either at war with Cocalus or by being deliberately scalded as he took a bath. Dedalus was credited with many architectural novelties and other inventions, including the saw and the compasses. Adjectives deriving from his name may refer merely to cunning contrivance.

> (Apollodorus *Epitome* i 8-15;
> Ovid *Metamorphoses* viii, 183-262;
> Diodorus Siculus i 61, 97)

See *Daedalus*

Chaucer	*Book of the Duchess* 568-73
	House of Fame 914-24

Dedaly
See *Dedalus*

Chaucer	*House of Fame* 1920-22

Deianira   A princess of Calydon, daughter of *Oeneus* of *Aetolia* (or of *Bacchus*) and Athaca. She became the wife of *Hercules*, who won her as the strongest of many contenders. Hercules permitted the centaur *Nessus* to carry her over the swollen River *Euenus*, and Nessus then attempted to violate her. Hercules shot him, but the centaur presented to Deianira his tunic, claiming that it would act as an aphrodisiac if given to her husband; in fact it was poisoned by the venom of Nessus's arrow and Hercules' donning it was one factor in his spectacular death on a pyre at Mt *Oeta*. Deianira killed herself in despair.

> (Apollodorus II vii;
> Ovid *Metamorphoses* ix 101ff)

See also *Dianyre, Dyanira*

Fletcher P.	*The Purple Island* xii 6
Graves	*To Ogmian Hercules* 4-8

Deipheobus, Deiphobus   The son of *Priam* and *Hecuba*, Deiphobus married *Helen* after the death of his brother *Paris*. Paris had taken Helen from her first husband *Menelaus*. When the Greeks sacked *Troy*, Menelaus sought her out and killed and mutilated Deiphobus (whom Helen may have betrayed). Deiphobus was brother also of *Troilus*, and this relationship was developed in medieval literature.

> (Homer *Iliad* xiii 402ff;
> Virgil *Aeneid* vi 494ff)

Chaucer	*House of Fame* 439-46
	Troilus and Criseyde ii 1396-8
Masefield	*The Spearman*

Delia   A name for *Diana/Artemis*, from her birthplace, *Delos*.

Milton	*Paradise Lost* ix 386-90

Delian
See *Delos*

Keats	*On Seeing a Lock of Milton's Hair* 17-18

Delius   *Apollo*, born on *Delos*.

Drayton	*The Muses' Elizium* ix 15-17
Tennyson	*Lucretius* 124-6

Delos   An island in the centre of *Cyclades*, in the Aegean. Accounts of its origin vary. According to one, *Neptune* raised it out of the water as a refuge for *Latona* (who was plagued by *Juno*, jealous as always of *Jupiter*'s amours). Delos floated until Jupiter bound it to the sea-bed with chains. The island was sacred to *Apollo* and *Diana*, who were born to Latona there. Delos was also called *Ortygia* (2) or *Asteria*.

> (Ovid *Metamorphoses* vi 184ff;
> Strabo viii 2)

Cowper	*On the Ice Islands* 49-56
Drayton	*The Muses' Elizium* xi 21-3
Fletcher P.	*Purple Island* i 47
Keats	*Endymion* i 965-6
	Hyperion iii 23-8
Lewis C. D.	*Elegy for a Woman Unknown* ii
Milton	*Paradise Lost* v 214-5, x 293-6
Spenser	*Faerie Queene* II xii 13
Swift	*Ode to Athenian Society* 44-7

Delphi   The site of the oracle and temple of *Apollo* — also known as Pytho, since Apollo killed the *Python* here. Delphi, which was close to a ravine, was believed to be the earth's centre or navel, because it was the meeting place of two doves, crows or eagles, released by *Jove* at the ends of the earth. The temple was said to be built or decorated with laurel boughs fetched by vestal virgins from *Tempe*.

(Ovid *Metamorphoses* x 168;
Pausanias xv; Strabo IX iii 6)

See also *Delphic, Delphos, Phoebus*

Byron	*Childe Harold* i 1, 64
	Hints from Horace 524-30
Gray	*Progess of Poesy* 66
Keats	*Endymion* ii 81-2
MacNeice	*Flowers in the Interval* i
Moore	*Hymn of a Virgin of Delphi*

Delphian

See *Delphi*

Campbell	*Pleasure of Hope*
Keats	*Hence Burgundy, Claret and Port* 7-10
Marlowe	*Dr Faustus* 170-2
Milton	*Paradise Lost* i 517-9

Delphic

See *Delphi*

Hood	*Hymn to the Sun* 5
Keats	*As Hermes Once* 3-4
	Endymion i 497-500
	Hyperion iii 10-12
	On Receiving a Laurel Crown 1-3
Milton	*On Shakespeare* 10-12

Delphicus

See *Delphi, Apollo*

Chaucer	*Troilus and Criseyde* i 70

Delphin, Delphinus   The Dolphin constellation, named after the dolphin which was alleged to have persuaded *Amphitrite* to marry *Poseidon*, or the dolphin rescuer of *Arion*. See also *Delphyn*

Delphyn

See *Delphin*

Chaucer	*House of Fame* 1004-8

Delphos

See *Delphi*

Chapman	*Ovid's Banquet of Sense*
Chaucer	*Franklin's Tale* 1077

Denham	*Panegyric on General George Monck* 34-8
Drayton	*The Muses' Elizium* ix 21-3
Keats	*Endymion* iv 713-4
Milton	*On the Morning of Christ's Nativity* 176-8
	Paradise Regained i 456-9
Shakespeare	*Winter's Tale* II i 182-4; III i 8-10, 143ff; V i 37-40
Young	*Night Thoughts* V i

Demeter   The Greek goddess of Earth and Fertility (Roman *Ceres*). She was daughter of *Saturn* and mother of *Persephone* (*Proserpina*).

Arnold	*Thyrsis* 175ff
Bridges	*Demeter* 28ff, 489-92, 563-5, 763ff, 873ff
Lawrence	*Bavarian Gentians* 3ff
Meredith	*The Appeasement of Demeter*
Swinburne	*At Eleusis* 26-7
Tennyson	*Demeter and Persephone* 13ff, 93-9, 114ff

Demetrius I   King of Macedonia, 294-283 BC, Demetrius was known as Poliorcetes (destroyer of cities) on account of his successful aggressive policies. He was notorious for gambling (because of which the Parthians were said to have sent him a symbolic set of golden dice to belittle his skill), and after his defeat of Seleucus in 285BC he turned to heavy drinking, which killed him in two years. Demetrius laid a spectacular but unsuccessful siege on Rhodes in 305BC employing ingenious war machines.

(Diodorus Siculus xx 85;
Plutarch *Demetrius*)

Byron	*Deformed Transformed* I i 245ff
Chaucer	*Pardoner's Tale* 621-6
	Franklin's Tale 1423-7

Democrates

See *Democritus*

Chapman	*Shadow of Night*

Democrite

See *Democritus*

Jonson	*The Famous Voyage* 111-4

Democritus   Greek philosopher of the 5th Century BC. Something of a polymath, Democritus was widely travelled and wrote on

ethics and mathematics as well as establishing a form of atomistic philosophy. His later life was that of a hermit who was said to be mad and on whose state of mind *Hippocrates* was called to pronounce. It was also said that he blinded himself in order to concentrate his mind inwardly. His work is not extant.
See also *Democrite*

Blake	*Mock on, mock on* 9-12
Byron	*Hints from Horace* 463-4
Dryden	*The Unhappy Favourite, Epilogue* 22-3
Johnson	*Vanity of Human Wishes* 49-52
Prior	*Democritus and Heraclitus* 1-4

Demodocus In *Homer*'s *Odyssey*, a musician at the court of King *Alcinous*, who entertained *Ulysses* and his crew.
(Homer *Odyssey* viii)
Milton   *At a Vacation Exercise* 47-9

Demogorgon A symbolic name, believed to be so terrible that it was mentioned only indirectly. It is a combination of the monster *Gorgons* and the neutral Chaos or benign Creator, Demiourgos, and represents a fundamental but indefinite power.
(Plato *Timaeus* 28-40; Statius *Thebaid* iv 513-6)

Drayton	*The Muses' Elizium* ix 45
Dryden	*Oedipus Song* III 41-4
Milton	*Paradise Lost* ii 964-5
Shelley	*Prometheus Unbound* II ii 42-7, iii 1-4; III i 17-22, 50-6
Spenser	*Faerie Queene* I i 37, v 22; IV ii 47

Demonesi A small island in the Sea of Marmara, off Istanbul.
Shelley   *Hellas* 162-5

Demophoon (1), Demophouon, Demophuon A king of *Athens*, the son of *Theseus* and *Phaedra* or *Antiope*. On his return from the Trojan War he stopped at *Thrace*, where the princess *Phyllis* fell in love with him. When he felt he must return to Athens or Cyprus, he abandoned her and she hanged herself or threw herself to her death from a precipice. It was believed that the trees growing over her tomb shed tears at certain times of the year.

(Apollodorus *Epitome* vi 16-17; Ovid *Heroides* ii)

Chaucer	*Book of the Duchess* 725-31
	Man of Law's Tale (*Introduction*) 65
	House of Fame 388-95
	Legend of Good Women 263-6, 2398-400, 2414ff, 2441-7, 2459-64ff
Herrick	*To the Maids* 13-14

Demophoon (2)
See *Triptolemus*
Bridges   *Demeter* 763ff

Demosthenes Athenian orator of the 4th Century BC, who concerned himself both with private legal cases and with major matters of state. In particular, he urged action against *Philip II* of Macedonia. After Philip's death he was banished for acceptance of a bribe, but he was recalled in splendour when Philip's successor, Antipater, declared war on Greece. It was said that, though he was a compelling speaker, he had triumphed over weak lungs by application, and had overcome a speech impediment by talking round pebbles in his mouth. He committed suicide when the surrender of the Greek orators was demanded by Antipater in 322 BC.
(Plutarch *Demosthenes*)

Burns	*The Author's Earnest Cry and Prayer* 79ff
Byron	*The Age of Bronze* 500-1
	Prophecy of Dante iii 96-7
Herrick	*His Farewell to Poetry* 71-4
Skelton	*Garland of Laurel*
Smart	*Epistle to John Sherratt* 11-2
Young	*Night Thoughts* viii

Demosthenic
See *Demosthenes*
Lamb   *Female Orators* 14-16

Destiny, Destinies
See *Necessity*, *Fates*

Herrick	*The Parcae* 5-8
Marlowe	*Hero and Leander* 447-8, 473-5
Shakespeare	*Pericles* I ii 106-8
Shelley	*Hellas* 711-6

Deucalion Son of *Prometheus* and married to *Epimetheus'* daughter *Pyrrha*, Deucalion was King of *Thessaly* when *Zeus*, in anger at men, flooded the earth. He saved himself and Pyrrha by making a ship, on Prometheus's advice, which grounded on Mt *Parnassus* when the floods subsided after nine days. In some accounts, there is no ship, and Deucalion finds refuge on either Parnassus or *Aetna*. After the flood, the couple were instructed by the oracle of *Themis* to throw behind them the bones of their mother *Pandora*, signifying earth. They rightly interpreted the 'bones' to mean 'stones', and from the stones which they threw there sprang up men and women to repeople the earth. Deucalion's stones produced men and Pyrrha's produced women.

(Apollodorus i 7;
Ovid *Metamorphoses* i 313-415)

Fletcher G.	*Christ's Triumph over Death* 7
Keats	*Endymion* ii 195-8
Lovelace	*Triumphs of Philamore* 35-8
Marlowe	*Dido Queen of Carthage* 1465-6
Milton	*Paradise Lost* xi 9-14
Shakespeare	*Coriolanus* II i 85
	Winter's Tale IV iv 421-2
Spenser	*Faerie Queene* III xi 42, V *Prologue* 2
Thomson	*Autumn* 770-2

Deva The English River Dee, which was supposed to change its channel to foretell the supremacy of English or Welsh people and so was held to be magical.

Milton   *Lycidas* 55

Deyscorides
See *Dioscorides*

Chaucer	*Canterbury Tales Prologue* 429-31

Diana, Diane
See *Artemis, Dyane*

Carew	*Upon the Sickness of E.S.* 17-22
Chaucer	*Knight's Tale* 1679-82, 1902-13, 2051ff, 2297-303
	Troilus and Criseyde iii 729-32, v 1464-8
Drayton	*Rosamond and Henry II* 139-42

	Polyolbion v 100-6
Fletcher P.	*Piscatory Eclogues* vi 11
Herrick	*The Vision* 12-15
Hood	*To the Moon* 20ff
	Progress of Art 6
Jonson	*To Mary, Lady Worth* 11-14
Keats	*Bards of Passion and of Mirth* 9-12
	Endymion i 511-13, 554-5, 613-9, 624-30, ii 260-2, 302-8, 692-4, 782-5, 983-5, 1005-7, iii 40-9, 277-9, iv 376-80, 429-31, 563-70, 701-3, 827-33, 996-7, 913-4
	Hyperion iii 31-2
	I Stood Tiptoe upon a Little Hill 192-204
	Sleep and Poetry 371-2
	To George Felton Matthew 78-83
	To Homer 13-14
Marlowe	*Edward II* 61ff
	Hero and Leander ii 260-3
	Tamburlaine i 2296
Milton	*Comus* 441-6
	Paradise Regained ii 353-6
Noyes	*Mount Ida* 138-44
Pope	*Spring* 65-8
	Summer 61-2
	Windsor-Forest 159-62, 165-6
Raleigh	*The Shepherd's Praise of Diana* 9-12
Shakespeare	*All's Well That Ends Well* I iii 107ff, iii 200-4; II iii 72-4
	As You Like It IV i 137-9
	Coriolanus V iii 64-7
	Cymbeline I vi 132-3; II iv 80-2; V v 179-81
	King Henry IV pt 1 I i 24
	King Henry VI pt 3 IV viii 19-22
	Merchant of Venice I ii 95-7
	Midsummer Night's Dream I i 89-90
	Much Ado About Nothing IV i 56-60
	Othello III iii 390-2
	Pericles II v 8-12; V iii 1-6, 70-1
	Romeo and Juliet I i 206-9
	Sonnet 153
	Taming of the Shrew II i 251-2

	Timon of Athens IV iii 381-4
	Titus Andronicus II i 55-9
	Venus and Adonis 742-6
Shelley	*Witch of Atlas* 587-90
Sidney	*Astrophel and Stella* 72
Spenser	*Faerie Queene* I v 39, vi 16, vii 4-5, xii 7, II ii 8-9, iii 31, vi 11, 17-18, IV vii 30, x 30
	Mutability Cantos vi 42
Swift	*To Lord Harley* 73-5
Tennyson	*On Sublimity*
Wordsworth	*Ode to Lycoris* 5-8
	Once I Could Hail 13-18
	River Duddon xxii 2-3
	Sonnet 'Lady I rifled . . .' 1-7

Dianira, Dianyre
See *Deianira*

Chaucer	*Wife of Bath's Prologue* 724-6
	Monk's Tale 3309-24

Dice
See *Dike*

Jonson	*A Panegyre* 20-7
Spenser	*Faerie Queene* V ix 31-42

Dictae, Dictaean, Dicte, Dictean Dictaeus Mons, a mountain in Crete. *Zeus* (*Jupiter*) was supposed to have been born in Crete and was often called 'Dictaean'.

(Strabo x 4; Virgil *Georgics* ii 536)
| Milton | *Paradise Lost* x 580-4 |
| Prior | *First Hymn to Callimachus* 7 ff |

Dictynna A nymph who attended *Diana* and was caught in a fisherman's net when escaping the attentions of *Minos*. She was therefore called Goddess of Nets and her name was used for Diana.

(Diodorus Siculus v 76)
| Shakespeare | *Love's Labour's Lost* IV ii 35-6 |

Dictys Dictis Cretensis wrote a diary of the Trojan War in about 250 AD, which in various versions was a main medieval source for the matter of *Troy*.
See also *Dares Phrygius, Dite*

Didius Didius Julianus, a wealthy senator who in 193 AD won a mock election to succeed the Emperor Pertinax, after his brief (three month) tenure. His victory was unpopular and he himself was assassinated after three months.
| Pope | *Epistle* iii 127-8 |

Dido Daughter of *Belus*, King of *Tyre*, and reputed founder of Carthage. Dido married *Sichaeus*, who was murdered by *Pygmalion* (Belus' successor) to obtain his wealth. She fled to Africa and bought as much land as could be covered by a bull's hide cut into strips. On this she built a citadel, Byrsa, which in course of time was enlarged to become Carthage. Dido was under pressure from her subjects to marry *Iarbas*, king of the menacing Gaetulia, but delayed the marriage for three months whilst she built a huge pyre, on which she was burnt after stabbing herself. According to *Virgil* and *Ovid*, the cause of her death was the departure of *Aeneas* (with whom she had fallen in love when he arrived at Carthage) on orders from the gods to fulfil his destiny. Ovid alone suggests that she was pregnant at the time. In Virgil's epic, Dido rejects Aeneas when he approaches her in *Hades* and excuses himself, claiming that he could not have known that his departure would kill her.

(Ovid *Heroides* xiv 80 ff;
Metamorphoses xiv 80 ff;
Virgil *Aeneid* iv, vi 467 ff)
See also *Anna*
— General
Chaucer	*Legend of Good Women* 263-6, 1004-7, 1168 ff, 1237-9, 1309 ff, 1346-51
	Parliament of Fowls 288 ff
Keats	*Imitation of Spenser* 19-21
MacNeice	*Autumn Sequel* iv
Shakespeare	*Taming of the Shrew* I i 147-9
	Tempest I ii 70-7
Tennyson	*To Virgil* i
— and Aeneas
Chatterton	*To Mrs Heywood* 1-4
Chaucer	*Man of Law's Tale, Introduction* 64
	House of Fame 234-44, 375-80, 427-32
	Legend of Good Women 1017-20, 1061-4
Cowley	*The Heart Fled Again* 2
Marlowe	*Dido Queen of Carthage* 719-

25, 1039ff, 1105ff, 1175-80,
1651ff
Pope   *Rape of the Lock* ii 92-5
Shakespeare   *Antony and Cleopatra* IV
xiv 51-4
Hamlet II ii 428ff
Merchant of Venice V i
9-12
Midsummer Night's Dream
I i 169ff
Titus Andronicus II iii
21-6; V iii 80-7
Swinburne   *Tristram of Lyonesse, Prel-
ude*
Wyatt   *Jopas' Song* 1-4
Young   *Letter to Mr Tickell*
— *and Ascanius*
Chaucer   *Legend of Good Women*
1140-4
Shakespeare   *King Henry VI pt 2* III
ii 114-7
— *in Hades*
Arnold   *The Scholar-Gipsy* 206-10
Chaucer   *House of Fame* 439-46
Keats   *Isabella* 99

Dike
See *Hours*

Dindymus   A Phrygian mountain sacred to
Cybele.
Swinburne   *Dolores* 344ff

Diocles, Diocletian   Gaeius Aurelius Diocletian,
the Roman Emperor of the 3rd Century AD.
He rose from an obscure background as a common soldier. In 293 Diocletian set up a unique
hierarchy, claiming for himself and respected
comrade, *Maximian*, the supreme name of
'Augustus', whilst creating in *Constantius* and
Galerius two subordinate 'Caesars', of the
East and West, who were bound to the Augusti
by marriage. Ten years later his health broke
down and he abdicated with Maximian, leaving
the Caesars (with two new ones under them)
in control. (Constantine was later to dismantle
this system and be sole Emperor again.) As a
general and administrator, Diocletian greatly
enlarged the Roman army and its defensive
works. His outlook was defensive and conservative though many of his administrative
changes lasted. He was notorious for his per-

secution of Christians, which he pursued in
defence of what he saw as traditional Roman
values.
Daniel   *Civil Wars* iii 68
Donne   *A Litany* 98-9
Spenser   *Faerie Queene* II x 8
Wordsworth   *Ecclesiastical Sonnets* i 6

Diogenes   Greek philosopher of the 4th Century BC, who established the *Cynic* frame of
thought. He became a legendary figure soon
after his death. Of his life little is known,
though he was famed for austere living,
choosing to live in the open. Among anecdotes
of Diogenes is one that he trampled on *Plato*'s
carpets, symbolising pride, to which Plato
commented that he thereby showed pride of
another sort. The source of such stories is a
compilation by Diogenes Laertius, *Lives of
Eminent Philosophers*, written probably in
the 3rd Century AD.
Butler S.   *Fragments of Satire on the
Imperfections of Human
Learning* 56-60
Byron   *Age of Bronze* 476-7
Childe Harold iii 61
Don Juan xv 73, xvi 43
Chaucer   *The Former Age* 33-5
Shelley   *Peter Bell the Third* 317-22

Diomedes (1)   King of *Thrace*, son of *Mars*
and *Cyrene*. It was the eighth labour of *Her-
cules* to capture the mares of Diomedes, which
ate human flesh. He did so and either fed
Diomedes to them or killed him himself.
(Apollodorus II v 8;
Diodorus Siculus IV xv 3-4)
Chaucer   *Monk's Tale* 3293-300
Crashaw   *Sospetto d'Herode* 45
Skelton   *Philip Sparrow*
Spenser   *Faerie Queene* viii 31

Diomedes (2)   Son of *Tydeus* and *Deipyle*.
With other sons of the *Seven Against Thebes*,
Diomedes took part in the return attack on
the city, where they successfully avenged their
fathers. He returned and expelled Agrius, his
uncle, who had usurped the throne of *Calydon*
from Tydeus's father, *Oeneus*. Diomedes, who
had earlier been a suitor of *Helen*, led a fleet
of eighty ships to *Troy* where he killed *Pandarus* and wounded *Aeneas* and *Aphrodite*

and, with *Odysseus*, stole the *Palladium*. On his return from Troy, the succession to the throne of Calydon was disputed and Diomedes went to Italy, where he founded the city of Argyrippa. He was tormented for the rest of his life by Aphrodite, who still rankled from her wound, and he was unable to help *Turnus* repel Aeneas's invasion.

(Apollodorus I viii 5-6; Homer *Iliad* v, x; Virgil *Aeneid* viii 9)

See also *Tydides*

Butler S.	*Hudibras* I iii 490-3
Chaucer	*Troilus and Criseyde* v 86-9, 799-804, 932-4
Shakespeare	*King Henry VI pt 3* IV ii 19-23
	Troilus and Cressida IV v 280-3; V ii 154-8, 169-74

Diomeid
See *Diomedes (2)*

Henryson	*Testament of Cresseid* 71-4

Dion   Dion, a general and tyrant of the 4th Century BC, was taught by *Plato* and related by marriage to Dionysius I of Syracuse. With this background, he attempted to influence *Dionysius II*, who held the ideal of being a philosopher-king, but was exiled in attempting to usurp him. In exile he achieved his object, freeing Syracuse from Dionysius with a small force, but he failed to achieve popular support and was murdered in 354BC by his associate Calippus.

(Diodorus Siculus xvi; Plutarch *Dion*)

Wordsworth	*Dion* 7-12
	The Prelude ix 408ff

Dione
See *Dyone*

Lovelace	*Advice to My Best Brother* 11-15

Dionysius (1)   Dionysius of Helicarnassus, a Greek historian of Rome in the 1st Century BC. Besides his *Roman Antiquities*, works on rhetoric and literature survive, including a commentary on *Homer*.

Pope	*Essay on Criticism* 665-6

Dionysius II (2)   Tyrant of Syracuse in the 4th Century BC. His court was frequented by philosophers, including *Plato* who (partly under the influence of *Dion*) instructed him in philosophy. While he was away in Italy in 357BC, his place was usurped by Dion who, after three years, was murdered. Dionysius lived out his life in exile in Corinth, where he became a schoolmaster.

Butler S.	*Fragment* 1-6
Dryden	*The Hind and the Panther* iii 1259-60
Wordsworth	*The Prelude* ix 408ff

Dionysus   The Greek God of wine and vegetation, son of *Zeus* and *Semele* (daughter of the king of *Thebes*); or of *Ammon* and *Amaltheia*; or of Zeus and *Persephone* in the guise of a snake. When *Hera*, wife of Zeus, discovered Semele's pregnancy, she persuaded Semele to ask her lover to reveal his true nature. This he did as a thunderbolt, which destroyed Semele. In the other parentage Ammon, to avoid discovery by *Rhea* his wife, hid Amaltheia and Dionysus on the island of *Nysa* (which was variously identified). Dionysus, however born, travelled many parts of the world with his followers (who are sometimes seen as an army). These were a troop of *Maenads*, *satyrs* and female votaries who conducted noctural rites and orgies on the mountains. At the climax they were granted visions of a bull or goat. It was at his interruption of such a festival that *Orpheus* was dismembered in *Thrace*. *Pentheus* suffered a somewhat similar disaster. According to one legend, Dionysus himself was eventually dismembered by *Titans*, but his heart was rescued by *Athena*. Dionysus, who possibly originated in the Egyptian god *Osiris*, is represented with a crown of ivy leaves and a distinctive thyrsus or wand; or he may ride naked on the shoulders of *Pan* or of *Silenus* his attendant or foster-father. He may be young, having eternal youth, or old, incorporating a warning against depravity. The fir, yew, fig, ivy and vine were all sacred to him and he is also associated with the ram (in which form his father had appeared to him). His chariot may be drawn by leopards, tigers or other wild beasts.

(Apollodorus iii 4-5; Diodorus Siculus iii 67-70; Herodotus ii 48-9; Hesiod *Theogony* 940-2; Ovid *Metamorphoses* iii 259ff)

See also *Ariadne, Bacchanalia, Bacchus,*
Iacchus, Tyrrhene

Browning R.	*Apollo and the Fates* 156-7
Lawrence	*Medlars and Sorb-apples* 53-5
	Middle of the World 4-5
	They Say the Sea is Loveless 5ff
Shelley	*Adonais* 289-94
Tennyson	*The Coach of Death* 181-4
	Pierced through with Knotted Thorns 36-8
Yeats	*Two Songs from a Play* i

Dioscorides A Roman physician of the 1st
Century AD, author of *Materia Medica*, for
long a standard pharmacopoeia.

Dioscuri *Castor* and *Pollux*, the twin sons
of *Jupiter* (*Zeus*) as a swan, and *Leda*. From
the same eggs were born also *Helen* and
Clytemnestra. The twins accompanied the
Argonauts, clearing the Hellespont of pirates
and calming storms. When invited to celebrate
the marriages of Lyncaeus and *Idas* to Phoebe
and Talaira (daughters of their uncle Leucippus), they attempted to seduce the ladies. In
the ensuing battle Castor, having killed Lynceus, was killed by Idas, whom Pollux then
slew. Pollux was immortal and implored
Jupiter that he might either become mortal
and die with his brother or that Castor be
restored to life. The latter happened, but the
twins were separated, each spending half a
day or year on earth and in *Hades*. They were
placed in heaven as the Gemini who never
appear together.

	(Apollodorus III xi)
Spenser	*Faerie Queene* V *Prologue* 6
	Mutability Cantos vii 34
	Prothalamion 168-74
	Ruins of Time 386-9
Swinburne	*Atalanta in Calydon* 411ff
	Athens ep. ii

Diotima A priestess and teacher of *Socrates*.
She is his spokesman at the feast in *Plato's*
Symposium. The feast is for *Agathon*, winner
of a poetic competition.

	(Plato *Symposium* 201-12)
Shelley	*Fragment Connected with Epipsychidion*
	Prince Athanase 224-9

Tennyson   *The Princess* iii 284-6

Dipsas A fish whose bite caused raging
thirst.

(Lucan ix 718)

See also *Amphisbaena*

Dircaean, Dircean
See *Dirce*

Jonson	*Ode Allegoric* 19-20
Swinburne	*Tiresias* 67-70

Dirce A spring near *Thebes* where *Cadmus*
killed the dragon sacred to *Ares* and brought
about the curse of Thebes. Dirce was also the
birthplace of the poet *Pindar*. The name derives from Dirce, wife of *Lycus*, King of
Thebes; she hated her niece *Antiope*, and she
and Lycus mistreated her. Antiope's sons took
revenge by tying Dirce to a bull, which killed
her. They also killed Lycus. At the spot where
Dirce died, *Dionysus* (of whom she was a
follower) caused a spring to come forth.

(Apollodorus I v 5)

See also *Dircean, Tiresias*

Tennyson   *Tiresias* 11-17, 134-7

Dis
See *Pluto, Plutus*

Marlowe	*Hero and Leander* ii 322-5
Milton	*Paradise Lost* iv 268-71
Shakespeare	*King Richard III* I iv 44-7
	Tempest IV i 87-90
	Winter's Tale IV iv 115-24

Discordia The Roman version of *Eris*, the
Greek goddess of Discord, who was instrumental in causing the Trojan War. Pictured as having
bloodstained, snake-like locks, fiery eyes and
a dagger, she is often accompanied by *Bellona*.
She was sometimes identified with *Ate*.

(Virgil *Aeneid* VI 280)

Dite
See *Dictys*

Chaucer   *Troilus and Criseyde* i 145-7

Dittany A Cretan herb, associated with
Diana and supposed to repel weapons.

Dodona The site, in Epirus (north-west
Greece), of an oracle of *Zeus*, whose procla-

mations were made by oak trees or the doves inhabiting them. Before Epirus was sacked by the Romans in 167BC, Dodona was widely consulted as an alternative to *Delphi*. Consultation was by written message on strips of lead.

(Herodotus II 53-7; Homer *Iliad* xvi 233; Strabo VII vii 10)

Browning E. B.	*The Dead Pan* 29	
Byron	*Childe Harold* ii 53	
Cowper	*Yardley Oak* 40-4	
Milton	*Paradise Lost* i 517-9	
Shelley	*Hellas* 793-5	
Wordsworth	*Oak of Guernica* 1-5	

Dog-Star
See *Sirius*

Dolabella   A young man specially trusted by *Augustus* and sent to reason with *Antony* — already dead — and *Cleopatra* when she had decided on suicide.

(Plutarch *Antony* lxxxiv)

Dryden   *All for Love* III i
Shakespeare   *Antony and Cleopatra* V i 1

Dolon   A Trojan boy, a fast runner, who was sent ahead by *Hector* to spy on the Greek fleet. He was intercepted by *Ulysses* and *Diomedes*, to whom he revealed all about the Trojan army. Diomedes then killed him for his treachery. Ulysses whistled soon after this, to show Diomedes that he wanted to return to the ship.

(Homer *Iliad* x 314ff)

Byron   *Don Juan* xiii 105
Keats   *Hyperion* ii 19-22

Dolphin
See *Delphin*, *Delphinus*

Domiduca, Domiducus   A minor Roman god of marriage, and a name for *Juno*, who presided over marriages.

Herrick   *An Epithalamie* 41-50

Domitian   Titus Domitian, son of *Vespasian*, and Roman Emperor from 81AD. He was the instigator of a reign of terror in the latter part of his rule, which ended in 96, when he was murdered. Domitian twice banished philosophers from Rome and disbanded their influential schools c.90AD.

(Suetonius *Domitian*)

Arnold	*To a Friend* 6-8
Jonson	*To the Ghost of Martial* 1-2
Shenstone	*To the Virtuosi* 33-6
Vaughan	*To his Retired Friend* 37

Dorian
See *Doric*

Keats   *Hyperion* iii 10-12
Milton   *Paradise Lost* i 549-51
    Paradise Regained iv 256

Doric   Strictly, from Doris, an area of central Greece called Tetrapolis (having the four towns Pindus, Erineum, Cytinium and Borium), and close to *Parnassus*. Frequently used of rustic dialect in general and as a description of Greek pastoral by *Theocritus*, *Bion* and *Moschus*. The type of column called Doric (which it may not strictly be) is short, fluted and tapered upwards; its purpose is to support an architrave or beam.

Collins	*Ode on the Popular Superstitions* 18
Hopkins	*Escorial* 7
Keats	*Lines Rhymed in a Letter from Oxford* 2
Milton	*Lycidas* 189
	Paradise Lost i 517-9, 713-5
Thomson	*Autumn* 1-4
Yeats	*Two Songs from a Play* ii

Doris (1)   Sister and wife of *Nereus*. A sea-goddess, daughter of *Oceanus*, she was the mother of the *Nereids*.

(Hesiod *Theogony* 240-64, 350; Virgil *Eclogues* x 5)

Keats	*Endymion* iii 999-1000
Shelley	*Fragments Written for 'Hellas'* 8-9
Spenser	*Faerie Queene* IV xi 48
Swinburne	*Garden of Cymodoce*

Doris (2)   A *Nereid*, daughter of *Doris (1)*.
Spenser   *Faerie Queene* IV ii 49

Doto   A *Nereid*.
(Virgil *Aeneid* ix 102)
Spenser   *Faerie Queene* IV ii 48

Draco, Draconic   A legendary Athenian lawgiver, probably of the 7th Century BC. Draco was held responsible for the first written constitution and legal code of the Greeks. He was supposed to have advocated death as the penalty for both minor and major crimes on the grounds that it was appropriate to the minor ones. He was also said to have written in blood. Nothing is known of his life and his historicity is doubtful.

(Plutarch *Solon*)
Byron   *Childe Harold* iii 64
Marlowe   *Jew of Malta* 20-1

Drusus (1)   Julius Drusus was son of the Emperor *Tiberius* and married *Livia Livilla (2)*. He was a consul and prospective successor to the Emperor but was poisoned, allegedly by *Sejanus* and Livia, in 21 AD.
Jonson   *Sejanus* II i

Drusus (2)   The son of Tiberius Nero, a general of *Julius Caesar* who, however, proposed rewards for the murderers of Caesar. Drusus was brought up by his mother *Livia (1)* and *Octavian* (who had just married her). Octavian persuaded Tiberius to divorce Livia. Drusus Nero became a general highly regarded by *Augustus* (as Octavian was later called).

Dryad, Dryads   Wood nymphs, each of whom presided over a tree as its genius, living and dying with it.
See also *Hamadryads, Wood-Nymphs*
Browning E. B.   *The Dead Pan* 7
                 The Lost Bower 33
                 A Vision of Poets 40-3
Cowper   *Conversation* 537-40
De La Mare   *Mournst Thou Now* 5-6
Drayton   *Eurydice and Phoebe* 793-5
Hood   *Bianca's Dream* 5
             The Elm Tree 7-8
Keats   *I Stood Tiptoe Upon a Little Hill* 153-4
             Lamia i 1-5
             Ode to a Nightingale 7
             Ode to Psyche 56-7
Milton   *Comus* 962-5
             Paradise Lost ix 386-7
Pope   *Winter* 11-12
Shelley   *Woodman and the Nightingale* 68-70
Shenstone   *The Progress of Taste* iii 11ff
Skelton   *Garland of Laurel*

Southey   *Hymn to the Penates* 80-1
             Roderick xvi 212-4
Tennyson   *The Talking Oak* 286-8
Wordsworth   *The Triad* 8-14

Dryas   A son of *Ares*, present at the *Calydonian Boar Hunt*.
(Apollodorus I viii 2)
Swinburne   *Atalanta in Calydon* 1263

Dryope (1)   One of the claimed mothers of Pan, by *Mercury* in *Arcady*.
(Homeric Hymn *To Pan* XIX)
Keats   *Endymion* i 290

Dryope (2)   Daughter of *Eurytus (2)* of *Oechalia*, Dryope married Andraemon, but was seduced by *Apollo* and bore him a son, Amphissus. Shortly afterwards, she was slowly turned into a lotus tree, protesting her innocence and nursing the baby as long as she could.
(Ovid *Metamorphoses* ix 324-93)
Keats   *Endymion* i 493-5

Dryope (3)   A nymph, mother of Tarquitus (who assisted *Turnus* against *Aeneas*) by *Faunus*.
(Virgil *Aeneid* x 551)
Shelley   *Witch of Atlas* 105-9
Spenser   *Faerie Queene* I vi 15

Dyane
See *Diana*
Chaucer   *Parliament of Fowls* 281-4
Dunbar   *Ryght as the Stern of Day* 76

Dyanira
See *Deianira*
Chaucer   *House of Fame* 397-404

Dydo
See *Dido*
Chaucer   *Book of the Duchess* 731-6

Dynamene   A *Nereid*.
(Apollodorus I ii 6)
Spenser   *Faerie Queene* IV xi 49

Dyone   Dione, an obscure *Titan* or *Oceanid*, called the mother of *Venus Aphrodite* by *Homer* and *Virgil*.

(Homer *Iliad* v 370; Hesiod *Theogony* 17;
Virgil *Aeneid* iii 19)
Chaucer   *Troilus and Criseyde* iii
1807-10

Eacide
See *Aeacides*

Eacides Chiron   *Chiron* the centaur, so described by *Ovid*; *Achilles* (the centaur's pupil)
was grandson of *Aeacus*.
(Ovid *Ars Amatoriae* i 17)
Chaucer   *House of Fame* 1201-7

Earth
See *Ge, Tellus, Terra*
Milton   *Paradise Lost* v 338
Shelley   *Prometheus Unbound* i 152-3,
iv 470-5
Song of Proserpine
Spenser   *Mutability Cantos* vi 26

Ebon   A name for *Bacchus*.

Ecbatana   The capital of Media, and of
Parthia under the Arsacid dynasty, Ecbatana
was captured in 559 BC by *Cyrus* from his
grandfather *Astyages*. It had seven walls of
ascending heights and different colours, and
the palace was within the inmost, golden, wall.
(Herodotus i 98; see also, in Biblical
Apocrypha, Judith i 2-4)
Milton   *Paradise Regained* iii 286-8

Echetlaeos, Echetlos   A humble ploughman,
hero of the Battle of *Marathon*. Nothing is
known of him and he vanished after the battle.
Perhaps a classical 'unknown soldier'.
(Pausanias i 32)
Browning R.   *Echetlos* 25-7

Echidna   A monster, half nymph and half
serpent, who lived in a cave, into which she
attracted visitors. She was mother by *Typhon*
of a brood of ogres including *Geryon*, *Cerberus*,
Hydra, *Orthrus* and the *Nemean* lion, and was
killed by *Argus*.
(Apollodorus II i 2;
Hesiod *Theogony* 295-332)
Chapman   *Epicedium*

Spenser   *Faerie Queene* V x 10, 23,
VI vi 10-11

Echo, Echoes   Echo was the daughter of
Air and *Earth* and the confidante of *Zeus*. She
talked too much and was deprived of speech
save to reply to questions put to her; this was
arranged by *Hera*, who found that she was
distracted by Echo's chatter whilst Zeus went
courting other nymphs. She was pursued by
Pan, but her own love was for *Narcissus*, who
despised her; as a result, she pined away and
hid in woods. When she died, she remained a
voice, whilst her bones were turned to stone.
(Ovid *Metamorphoses* III 358 ff)
See also *Ekko, Ecquo*
Collins   *Ode to Pity* 17-18
Jonson   *Cynthia's Revels* I i
Keats   *Endymion* i 947-59, 966-9, iii
232-3
Isabella 435-6
I Stood Tiptoe Upon a Little Hill
172-8
Lovelace   *Princess Louisa Drawing* 1ff
Milton   *Comus* 230-7, 241
Pope   *Winter* 41-4
Shakespeare   *Romeo and Juliet* II ii
159-63
Shelley   *Adonais* 127-32, 195-8
The Retrospect 106-7
Wordsworth   *Advance, come forth . . .*
6-9

Ecquo
See *Echo*
Chaucer   *Book of the Duchess* 731-6

Ector
See *Hector*
Chaucer   *Book of the Duchess* 326-34,
1055-75
Knight's Tale 2830-3
Man of Law's Tale 197-9
Nun's Priest's Tale 4331-8
Troilus and Criseyde i 113,
ii 152-3, 158, 176-80,
V 1553 ff

Edippe, Edippus
See *Oedipus*
Chaucer   *Troilus and Criseyde* ii 101-2,
iv 300-1

Edon, Edonian   A mountainous part of *Thrace*.
Swinburne   *Prelude* 115-20

Egeria
See *Numa*
Byron   *Childe Harold* iv 115
Tennyson   *Palace of Art* 110-2
The Princess ii 64-5

Egeus
See *Aegeus*
Chaucer   *Knight's Tale* 2905-6
Legend of Good Women 1943-7
Marlowe   *Tamburlaine* ii 3991-5

Egiste
See *Aegyptus*
Chaucer   *Legend of Good Women* 2562ff

Egyptian Thebes
See *Heliopolis*
Milton   *Paradise Lost* v 272-4

Eione   A *Nereid*.
(Apollodorus I ii 6)
Spenser   *Faerie Queene* IV xi 50

Eirene
See *Hours*, *Irene*
Fletcher G.   *Christ's Victory in Heaven* 68
Spenser   *Faerie Queene* V ix 31-2

Ekko
See *Echo*
Chaucer   *Clerk's Tale* 1189-90
Franklin's Tale 944-52

Electo
See *Alecto*
Henryson   *Orpheus and Eurydice* 261ff, 475-8

Electra   The daughter of *Agamemnon* King of *Argos*. Electra urged her brother, *Orestes*, to kill their mother, *Clytemnestra* — who with her lover Aegisthus had killed Agamemnon. Electra married *Pylades*, a close friend of Orestes and a cousin, who assisted them in avenging their father's murder. In these events, Electra is a main character in plays of *Sophocles* and *Euripides*. It was also said that she nearly blinded her sister, *Iphigenia*, because she had been falsely told that Iphigenia, a priestess, had sacrificed Orestes to *Artemis*.
(Euripides *Electra*, *Orestes*; Sophocles *Electra*; Hyginus *Fabulae* 122)
Browning E. B.   *Crowned and Buried* 19-20
Portuguese Sonnets 5
Collins   *Ode to Simplicity* 18
Milton   *Sonnet* 8
Thomas, Dylan   *Greek Play in a Garden* 4-8, 17-20, 25-8

Elephantis   A licentious Greek poet, of whose works *Tiberius* was said to have a copy in his retirement villa at Capreae.
Jonson   *The Alchemist* II i

Eleusi, Eleusis, Eleusinian   The third town of *Attica*, which long remained independent of *Athens*. It was the seat of the mysteries in honour of *Demeter* and *Persephone*, to whom many temples were built.
(Pausanias I xxxvii 4, VIII xv)
Moore   *Fall of Hebe* 97-100
Evening in Greece 551-2
Shelley   *Oedipus Tyrannus* I i 26-7

Eleyne
See *Helen*
Chaucer   *Troilus and Criseyde* i 61-3, 453-5, ii 1667-8, iii 409-11, iv 1345-8, v 890-6

Elicon
See *Helicon*
Chaucer   *House of Fame* 518-22

Elisa, Elissa   A name for *Dido*.
Dryden   *To the Duchess of Ormond* 160-2

Elisian, Elisium
See *Elysium*
Marlowe   *Edward II* 10-11
Milton   *Paradise Lost* iii 358-9
Spenser   *The Ruins of Time* 330-6
Shepherd's Calendar 178-9

Elisos

Elisos
See _Elysium_
    Chaucer   _Troilus and Criseyde_ iv 789-91

Eliza   _Elissa_, a name for _Dido_.
    Pope   _Temple of Fame_ 206

Ellops   A swordfish or serpent.

Elycon
See _Helicon_
    Chaucer   _Anelida and Arcite_ 15-20

Elysian
See _Elysium_
    Keats   _Bards of Passion and of Mirth_ 10-12
    Marvell   _Upon Appleton House_ 753ff
    Milton   _Comus_ 977-1011
    On the Death of a Fair Infant 38-40
    Paradise Lost v 292-4
    Pope   _Letter to Cromwell_ 2-4
    Ode for Music 72-5
    Shelley   _Epipsychidion_ 424-8
    Fiordispina 78-82
    Prometheus Unbound iv 529-32
    Revolt of Islam 4726-7
    Stevenson   _To H. F. Brown_ 1ff
    Tennyson   _The Lotos-Eaters_ 169-70
    The Princess iii 323-7
    Wordsworth   _Memorials of a Tour 1820_ xxxiv 9-10

Elysium   The idyllic world where the souls of those honoured by the gods (or, later, of the virtuous) spent an after-life of revelry, feasting or pleasant martial exercise. The Elysian Fields were located by writers variously in the Atlantic off Africa, on Leuce (an island south of _Lesbos_), in Italy, close to the moon, or at the earth's centre; or they were regarded as a select part of _Hades_.
    (Homer _Odyssey_ iv 561ff;
    Pindar _Olympian Ode_ ii 61ff;
    Virgil _Aeneid_ vi 638ff)
See also _Elisian_
    Keats   _Endymion_ i 371-3, iii 425-8
    Lamia i 205-8
    Marvell   _Thyrsis and Dorinda_ 31-7
    Milton   _Comus_ 253-9

    Shakespeare   _Cymbeline_ V iv 97-8
    King Henry VI pt 3 I ii 29-31
    Twelfth Night I ii 4
    Shenstone   _Charms of Precedence_ 79-84

Emathia, Emathian   A name for Macedonia, of which strictly it was a district. _Alexander the Great_'s father was king of Emathia and the adjective is sometimes applied to Alexander.
    Milton   _Paradise Regained_ iii 289-91
    Sonnet viii
    Wordsworth   _Sonnet, When Haughty Expectations . . ._

Empedocles   Sicilian philosopher, poet and leader of the 5th Century BC. He held that life is ruled by the four elements alternately in strife and harmony, which gives rise to cycles in history. He was supposed to have died in _Aetna_, either being led too close by curiosity, or suicidally attempting to gain the intervention of the gods.
    (Horace _Ars Poetica_ 464ff)
    Arnold   _Empedocles on Aetna_ II i 327-30
    Butler S.   _Hudibras_ III iii 871-6
    Fragments of a Satire on the Imperfections of Learning 49-52, 56-60
    Meredith   _Empedocles_
    Milton   _Paradise Lost_ iii 469-71
    Tennyson   _Lucretius_ 93-4

Enceladus   A _Giant_ who, in the war of the Giants and the Gods, fought against _Athena_ but was crushed, by either Athena or _Zeus_, with Mount _Aetna_ or the whole island of Sicily. Aetna's eruptions represent him continuing to breathe forth flames. His story is partly that of _Typhon_, who in the war of Gods and Giants drove the Gods to take refuge in the forms of birds and animals.
    (Apollodorus I vi 2; Euripides _Ion_ 239ff;
    Ovid _Metamorphoses_ v 325-31;
    Virgil _Aeneid_ iii 578ff)
    Keats   _Hyperion_ ii 65-72, 105-10, 303-4
    Shakespeare   _Titus Andronicus_ IV ii 93-7
    Spenser   _Faerie Queene_ III ix 22

Endymion   A shepherd King of Elis who asked _Jupiter_ to make him ever young. Diana saw him sleeping naked on Mt *Latmus* and fell in love with him, bearing him fifty daughters. It was also said that he was an astronomer who fell in love with *Cynthia/Diana*, the moon, and that she stayed in a cave for a long period to enjoy his company.

(Apollodorus I vii 5-6; Pausanias V ii 8)

Arnold	*Isolation* 19-24
Drayton	*Endymion and Phoebe* 9-14, 89ff, 137ff, 803-6
Hood	*To the Moon* 20ff
Keats	*Endymion* i 35-7, 190-2, 525-6, ii 299-300, iii 712-3, iv 376ff, 426-8, 860-4, 986-93
	I Stood Tiptoe Upon a Little Hill 190-204, 239-41
Shakespeare	*Merchant of Venice* V i 109 10
Shelley	*Witch of Atlas* 587-90
Spenser	*Epithalamium* 377-81
	Shepherd's Calendar, July 63-4
Swift	*To Lord Harley* 73-5
Tennyson	*Lucretius* 85ff
Vaughan	*Monsieur Gombauld* 51-2
Wordsworth	*Written in a Grotto* 10-15

Eneas
See *Aeneas*

Chaucer	*House of Fame* 162-9, 174-88, 212-8, 234-44, 293-9, 427-32, 439-46, 451-8, 1481-5
	Legend of Good Women 940-7, 1017ff, 1061-4, 1140-4, 1237-9, 1285-9

Eneydos
See *Aeneid*

Chaucer	*Nun's Priest's Tale* 4545-51
	House of Fame 375-80
	Legend of Good Women 928-9

Enna A town in the middle of Sicily surrounded by a plain often regarded as an earthly paradise, from which *Persephone* was taken by *Pluto* whilst gathering flowers.
See also *Ethna*

Bridges	*Demeter* 28ff
Goldsmith	*Translation of a South American Ode* 1-2
Lawrence	*Purple Anemones* 23ff
Meredith	*Day of the Daughter of Hades*

Milton	*Paradise Lost* iv 268-71
Shelley	*Arethusa* 73-8
	Prometheus Unbound III iii 40-5
	Song of Proserpine
Tennyson	*Demeter and Persephone* 35-9

Ennius Quintus Ennius, Roman epic poet and playwright, 239-169 BC. He was closely associated with *Scipio* and it was claimed that their tombs were together. *Cato (2)* was his patron. Ennius claimed the title of (and was often regarded as) the *Homer* of the Romans. He combined a roughness and energy of style with a dedication to the patriotic work of the epic poet. His *Annales*, of which only fragments survive, set out the matter of Rome from the flight from Troy, through the founding of Rome and Punic Wars. He established the hexameter as the metrical form for Roman epic.

Skelton	*The Garland of Laurel*
Spenser	*Sonnet, 'Those prudent heads . . .*

Ennopye *Oenopia* or *Aegina*, ruled by *Aeacus*. An island off the Peloponnesus.

Chaucer	*Legend of Good Women* 2144-8, 2155-60

Envy The classical depiction of Invidia is provided by *Ovid* — an old woman in a dark and filthy cave.

(Ovid *Metamorphoses* ii 760-4)

Shakespeare	*King Henry VI pt 2* III ii 314

Enyo A sister of *Ares* (*Mars*) and the Greek equivalent of Roman *Bellona*.

Chapman	*Adromeda Liberata*

Eoan
See *Eos*

Shelley	*Ode to Liberty* 256-9

Eolus
See *Aeolus*

Chaucer	*House of Fame* 198-209, 1571ff, 1586-90, 1636ff, 2117-20
Dunbar	*Quhen Merche Wes* 33, 64-7

Eos   The Greek goddess (Roman *Aurora*) of the dawn, and so of the East. She was daughter of *Hyperion* and *Thea*, and drove across the sky in a chariot drawn by colts, Lampos and *Phaethon* (her son). She was supposed to be the mistress of *Ares* and so to have incurred the jealousy of his partner, *Aphrodite*. *Cephalus*, *Orion* and *Tithonus* were among her famous lovers and she married *Astraeus*, her brother.

(Hesiod *Theogony* 372;
Homer *Odyssey* xxiii 246)
Spenser   *Faerie Queene* IV xi 13

Eos, Eous   A horse of the sun driving *Apollo*'s chariot.

(Ovid *Metamorphoses* ii 153)
Drayton   *The Muses' Elizium* ix 32-7

Epaminondas   A Theban commander in the 4th Century BC, who defeated the Spartans at Leuctra in 371 BC. After spending some time pursuing relations with the defeated Spartans, he was accused of treason on his return, but pardoned on explaining his motives. He went on to fight a reassembled Spartan army at Mantinea where he died in 363 BC. He was said to have been buried at public expense because he had only an iron coin at death.

(Plutarch *Pelopidas*, *Fabius Maximus* xxvii)
Byron   *Childe Harold* ii 84
Don Juan ix 8
Chapman   *Bussy d'Ambois* I i 70-5

Epeirot
See *Pyrrhus*

Epeios, Epeus   Maker of the Wooden Horse by which the Greeks entered Troy at the end of the Trojan War.

(Homer *Iliad* xxiii 664 ff)
Marlowe   *Dido Queen of Carthage* 66-7,
438-44
Masefield   *The Horse*

Ephestion
See *Hephaestion*
Marlowe   *Edward II* 689-94

Epictetus   The Stoic philosopher was born a slave in 55 AD but was freed as a young man. He taught philosophy in Rome until *Domitian*

banished philosophers, when he settled in Nicopolis (Epirus). He was a believer in divine order, self-awareness and self-control, and held misfortunes to be temporary aspects of a general working for good. His work was collected and summarised by Flavius Arrianus (*Arrian*), and greatly influenced Marcus *Aurelius*. Epictetus died in 135 AD.

Arnold   *To a Friend* 6-8

Epicurean
See *Epicurus*
Milton   *Paradise Regained* iv 276-80
Tennyson   *Lucretius* 217-8
Wordsworth   *The Excursion* iii 347 ff

Epicurus   The Greek philosopher, born at *Samos* in 341 BC. Of humble origin, he travelled widely as a young man, setting up groups of followers. He settled in *Athens* c. 307 and bought property which became his school. Here he remained until his death in 270 BC. The school was in the nature of a communal retreat, including slaves and women and, notwithstanding the philosophy's later reputation, was in fact run on austere lines. Basic to this philosophy was a conviction of human limitation and mortality; the belief that pleasure was a goal of life carried with it the insistence that apparent pleasure might be false. Epicurus held atomist views with regard to the origin and nature of life. His followers attempted to distinguish degrees of pleasure and to distinguish pleasure of the soul from that of the body. Epicurus was famed for a prolific output but little has survived.

Byron   *Don Juan* ii 207
Chaucer   *Canterbury Tales, Prologue*
336-8
Dryden   *Religio Laici* 14 ff
Moore   *A Dream of Antiquity*
Grecian Girl's Dream 41-2
The Sceptic 26-7
The Summer Fete 77-82
Shakespeare   *Julius Caesar* V i 76-8
Swift   *Pethox the Great* 27-30
Tennyson   *Lucretius* 116-20
Thomson   *Liberty* ii 241-2
Young   *Night Thoughts* viii

Epimetheus   Son of *Iapetus* and *Clymene* (an *Oceanid*) or *Asia*, and the brother of

Prometheus. Epimetheus unwisely married *Pandora*, who brought forth the evils of the world.

> (Hesiod *Theogony* 507-14, *Works and Days* 47-105; Apollodorus i 2)

Milton *Paradise Lost* iv 714-19

Epistrophus A prince of Phocis who joined the Greeks in the Trojan War and was among the many suitors of *Helen*.

> (Apollodorus III x 8; Homer *Iliad* II 517)

Shakespeare *Troilus and Cressida* V v 6-11

Erato (1) The *Muse* of lyric and love poetry, bearing lute and lyre and crowned with roses and myrtle. She was daughter of *Zeus* and *Mnemosyne*.

> (Apollodorus I iii 2)

Drayton *The Muses' Elizium* iii 433-6
Spenser *Tears of the Muses* 379-84

Erato (2) A *Nereid*.

> (Apollodorus I ii 6)

Spenser *Faerie Queene* IV xi 49

Eratostratus
See *Herostratus*
Byron *Curse of Minerva* 201-4

Ercules
See *Hercules*
Chaucer *Book of the Duchess* 1055-75
Man of Law's Tale 197-202
Wife of Bath's Prologue 724-6
House of Fame 397-404
Legend of Good Women 510-5, 1453-7, 1542-7

Erebus Son of *Chaos*. The god Erebus (Darkness) married Night to produce Day and Upper Light (Aether). He is associated particularly with that part of *Hades* reserved for the virtuous destined for the Elysian Fields, but is also used as a name for Hades generally.

> (Hesiod *Theogony* 123-5)

Keats *Endymion* iv 120-2
Marlowe *Tamburlaine* i 1417-8
Milton *Comus* 802-5
Paradise Lost ii 879-83
Noyes *Drake* ii

Shakespeare *Julius Caesar* II i 83-5
King Henry IV pt 2 II iv 147
Merchant of Venice V i 83ff
Shelley *The Daemon of the World* 311-5
Shenstone *The Ruined Abbey* 264-5
Southey *Waterloo*
The Sacred Mountain 3
Wordsworth *Laodamia* 70-2
For 'The Recluse' 35-40

Eridan, Eridanus The modern River Po in Italy, whose majesty is widely celebrated by Classical poets. It was particularly known for amber, and as the receiver of the fallen *Phaethon*, whose sisters' tears were changed into amber.

> (Virgil *Georgics* i 482)

See also *Padus*
Denham *Cooper's Hill* 193-5
Fletcher G. *Christ's Triumph Over Death* 1

Erigone A daughter of Icarius, a wealthy Athenian who gave wine to peasants who were unaware of its effects and killed them in their drunkenness. She hanged herself on the death of her father. She was courted by *Bacchus* in the form of a grape. (Note: Spenser *Faerie Queene* III xi 43 — a possible error for *Philyra*.)

> (Ovid *Metamorphoses* vi 125)

Swinburne *Masque of Bersobe*

Erinna A poetess, long associated with *Sappho* and *Lesbos*, but in fact Doric and probably of the 4th Century BC.

Swinburne *Anactoria* 17ff

Erinnyes, Erinnys
See *Eumenides*, *Herines*
Cowley *Pindaric Ode* 5
Crashaw *Sospetto d'Herode* 50
Fletcher P. *The Locusts* i 23
Lawrence *Eloi Eloi* 90-2
Spenser *Faerie Queene* II ii 29
Swinburne *On the Cliffs* 48-9

Eriphyle The sister of *Adrastus*, King of *Argos*, and wife of *Amphiareus*. Amphiareus refused to join in the expedition of the *Seven Against Thebes*, but Eriphyle revealed his whereabouts in return for a bribe from *Polyneices*, a golden necklace which had once been given to Hermione by *Venus*. Amphiareus duly went to war, but ordered his son Alcmeon to murder his mother Eriphyle as soon as it was known that he (Amphiareus) had been killed. This Alcmeon did and went mad.

> (Apollodorus III vii 2-5;
> Virgil *Aeneid* vi 44-5)

Eris   The goddess of Discord and Strife, daughter of Night and mother of Toil, Oblivion, Famine and other disagreeable things. Eris was refused admission to the wedding of *Peleus* and *Thetis* and threw among the guests a golden apple inscribed 'for the fairest'. She thus brought about the conflict of *Juno*, *Athene* and *Venus* — Hera, Athena and *Aphrodite* — which issued in the Trojan War. She was sister of *Ares* (*Mars*), god of War.

> (Hesiod *Theogony* 225-32; *Works and*
> *Days* 11-19; Hyginus *Fabulae* 92)

See also *Discordia*
Tennyson   *Oenone* 217 ff

Erisicthon   A Thessalian who offended *Ceres* by cutting down her sacred trees. As a result, she made him insatiably hungry. To obtain funds for food, he repeatedly sold his daughter, Mistra, who could change herself into any shape (a gift from *Neptune*, her lover); but was eventually driven to eat his own flesh.

> (Ovid *Metamorphoses* viii 741ff)

Crashaw   *Sospetto d'Herode* 42
Fletcher P.   *Purple Island* ii 38

Eros
See *Cupid*
Auden   *In Memory of Sigmund Freud*
111-2
Swinburne   *Eros*

Erro
See *Hero*
Chaucer   *Man of Law's Tale, Intro-*
duction

Erudice
See *Eurydice*
Chaucer *Troilus and Criseyde* iv 789-91

Erycine   *Venus*, who had a temple on Mount Eryx in Sicily.
Marlowe   *Hero and Leander* ii 303-7

Erymanth, Erymanthus   A wooded mountain (also a river and a town) in *Arcadia*, where *Hercules* killed a mighty boar. Seeing this, *Eurystheus* — who had commanded the deed — was so terrified that he hid in a brass vessel which he kept prepared as a refuge.

> (Ovid *Metamorphoses* ii 499;
> Virgil *Aeneid* vi 802)

Milton   *Arcades* 100
Shelley   *Arethusa* 14-20

Erymanthian
See *Erymanth*
Chaucer   *Monk's Tale* 3293-300

Eryx   Son of *Aphrodite* by *Neptune* or the *Argonaut* Butes. Eryx challenged all comers to fight with him for his kingdom in northwest Sicily. Hercules accepted, and killed him. A city and mountain were named after him.

> (Apollodorus II v 10;
> Diodorus Siculus IV 23)

Spenser   *Faerie Queene* IV xi 14

Escaphilo
See *Ascalaphus*

Eschylus
See *Aeschylus*
Burns   *Sketch* 13-18

Esculapius
See *Aesculapius*
Chaucer   *Canterbury Tales, Prologue*
429-31
Young   *Night Thoughts* ii

Eson
See *Aeson*
Chaucer   *Legend of Good Women*
1396-1402

Esperian
See *Hesperian*
Sidney   *Astrophel and Stella* 82

Esquiline   The name of the eastern plateau of Rome, the Mons Esquilinus. It was at one time used as a place of execution and also a cemetery. It was bounded by the city wall, in which was the Porta Esquilina, the Esquiline Gate.

See also *Port Esquiline*

Eteocles

See *Antigone, Polyneices*
    Browning E. B.   *Queen Anelida* 9
    Chaucer *Anelida and Arcite* 57-63

Ethiocles

See *Eteocles*
    Chaucer   *Troilus and Criseyde* v 185-91,
                      1506-8

Ethna

See *Enna*
    Chaucer   *Merchant's Tale* 2229-31

Ethon

See *Aethon*
    Drayton   *The Muses' Elizium* 1x 32-7

Etna

See *Aetna*
    Arnold   *Empedocles on Etna* II i 37ff
    Byron   *Age of Bronze* 179-84
    Swinburne   *A Nympholet* 134-6

Etruria, Etrurian   A country with the coastline north-west of Rome and from which much of Roman belief, superstition and ceremony was derived. Once the centre of a sizable empire, Etruria was largely in Roman possession by the 3rd Century BC.

See also *Tuscan*
    Milton   *Paradise Lost* i 302-4
    Shelley   *Marenghi* 9-12

Euboea, Euboic   A large island in the Aegean off the Greek coast, whose capital was Chalcis.
    Milton   *Paradise Lost* ii 542-6

Euclid   The Alexandrian mathematician of the 4th Century BC, who numbered *Ptolemy* among his famous pupils. His thought extended over astronomy, optics, and music as well as mathematics, but the works which have survived are concerned mainly with geometry and the theory of numbers.
    Milton   *Sonnet* 21

Eucrate   A *Nereid*.
                  (Apollodorus I ii 6)
    Spenser   *Faerie Queene* IV xi 48

Eudemus   A Cyprian who urged *Dion* to free Sicily from *Dionysius II*, and on whose account *Aristotle* wrote *On the Soul*.
                  (Plutarch *Dion* xxii)
    Wordsworth   *The Prelude* viii 408ff

Eudore   A *Nereid*.
                  (Apollodorus I ii 6)
    Spenser   *Faerie Queene* IV xi 48

Evenus   An Aetolian river flowing through *Calydon*.
        (Ovid *Metamorphoses* viii 527, ix 104)
    Swinburne   *Atalanta in Calydon* 36

Eulimene   A *Nereid*.
                  (Apollodorus I ii 6)
    Spenser   *Faerie Queene* IV xi 49

Eumenides   The name ('kindly ones') is thought to be a euphemism (for they were the cruel avenging agents of the gods) taken over from different fertility gods. The Eumenides were usually three in number and called *Tisiphone, Megaera* and *Alecto*, but *Nemesis* and Adrasta were sometimes included. Their parentage is variously attributed to *Pluto* and *Proserpina, Acheron* and *Night*, or *Chaos* and *Terra*; or they are said to have sprung from the blood of *Uranus* after he was mutilated by *Saturn* for his ill-treatment of the *Titans*. They were portrayed in terrible form, with black clothes, whips, scorpions, torches and with snakes in their hair. They were honoured in a temple in Achaia. They were, perhaps, originally the *Erinnyes*, spirits of the earth whose curse was implacable and who were confused with originally benign Eumenides.
           (Ovid *Metamorphoses* iv 451ff)
See also *Erynnyes, Furies, Herynes*

Eunica   A *Nereid*, Eunice.
                  (Apollodorus I ii 6)
    Spenser   *Faerie Queene* IV xi 49

Eunomia

See *Hours*

| Jonson | *A Panegyre* 20-7 |
| Spenser | *Faerie Queene* V ix 31-2 |

Euphemus, Euphoemus A son of *Neptune* and *Europa*, who was so fleet of foot that he could run over water with his feet dry. He took part in the *Calydonian Boar Hunt* and urged his comrade *Argonauts* to row faster as the *Argo* approached the Clashing Rocks. He accepted from *Eurypylus* (a disguised *Triton*) a clod of earth as a sign of welcome when the Argonauts were stranded in Libya, and he dreamed that this was a beautiful lady who told him she was a daughter of Triton. *Jason* advised him to throw the earth into the sea, where an island (Calliste) later emerged. Here descendants of Euphemus subsequently founded the city of *Cyrene*.

> (Apollonius Rhodius i 179-84,
> ii 549-90, iv 1464ff)

| Spenser | *Faerie Queene* IV xi 14 |

Euphrosyne One of the *Graces*, representing Mirth.

> (Hesiod *Theogony* 909;
> Pausanias IX i 35)

Byron	*Hints from Horace* 347-8
Milton	*L'Allegro* 11-13
Spenser	*Faerie Queene* VI x 22
Wordsworth	*The Triad* 98ff, 112-14, 121-2

Eupompe A *Nereid*.

| Spenser | *Faerie Queene* IV xi 51 |

Euripides The Greek tragedian was born at Phlya, near *Athens*. His life is obscure, though it is known that he went as ambassador to Syracuse; he was said to be of a dour disposition and was associated with the *Sophists*. Much of his writing was supposed to have been done in a solitary sea-cave in *Salamis*, where he lived for some time. He was apparently a rival of *Sophocles* and his plays were sometimes ridiculed. In later life, Euripides retired at the invitation of King Archelaus to the Macedonian court, where he wrote his last play, *Iphigenia at Aulis*. He died at *Pella* in Macedonia in 406BC — legend has it that he was torn to pieces by the royal hounds. There was a tradition that he was born on the day of the battle of Salamis in 480BC, but his birth is now usually dated as 485BC.

Browning E. B.	*A Vision of Poets* 301-9
	Wine of Cyprus 12
Browning R.	*Aristophanes' Apology* 120-2, 283-6, 301-3, 316, 428-30, 1677-8
	Balaustion's Adventure 37-9, 132-6, 291-4, 2670
	Bishop Bloughram's Apology 182-8
Jonson	*To Shakespeare* 31-7
Milton	*Sonnet* 8

Euripus The strait separating *Euboeia* and Boeotia near Chalcis.

| Arnold | *Fragment of 'Antigone'* 54ff |
| Chapman | *Tears of Peace* |

Europa, Europe The daughter of King *Agenor* of Phoenicia or of his son *Phoenix*. *Jupiter* assumed the form of a bull among Agenor's herds in order to seduce her while she was gathering flowers. She caressed the animal and mounted it, whereupon it carried her to Crete; Jupiter in his own form declared his love, and Europa became mother of *Minos* and *Rhadamanthus*. She subsequently married Asterius, King of Crete, who adopted the children. Gifts from Jupiter were a bronze guardsman, and a hound and javelin which never missed their quarries.

> (Apollodorus III i 1;
> Ovid *Metamorphoses* II 836ff)

Chaucer	*Legend of Good Women* 110-4
	Troilus and Criseyde iii 722-4
Lovelace	*Amarantha* 105-10
Marlowe	*Hero and Leander* i 149-50
Shakespeare	*King Henry IV pt 2* II ii 167-70
	Merry Wives of Windsor V v 1ff
	Much Ado About Nothing V iv 43-7
	Taming of the Shrew I i 163-5
Shelley	*Oedipus Tyrannus* II i 65-70, ii 103-4
Spenser	*Muiopotmos* 277-80
	Faerie Queene III xi 30, V *Prologue* 5
	Mutability Cantos vii 33
Tennyson	*Palace of Art* 117-20

Yeats   *Crazy Jane Reproved* ii

Eurotas   The river of Laconia by which *Sparta* stood. It was worshipped locally as a god, and is also noted as a haunt of *Diana* and her nymphs.

(Virgil *Aeneid* i 498ff)
Davis Sir J.   *Orchestra* 484-7
Milton   *On the Death of a Fair Infant* 25-6
Spenser   *Faerie Queene* II iii 31
Swinburne   *Atalanta in Calydon* 424
Eve of Revolution 85ff
Vaughan   *Olor Iscanus* 1-2
Yeats   *Lullaby*

Eurus   The east wind, brother of *Zephyrus*, represented as an impetuous young man.
(Ovid *Tristia* I ii 27)
Burns   *To Miss C.* 6
Milton   *Paradise Lost* x 704-5
Young   *The Merchant* ii

Eurydice   The wife of *Orpheus*, Eurydice was said to be a daughter of *Zeus* and *Ge* (*Tellus*). As a nymph, she was pursued by *Aristaeus*, a son of *Apollo*, but was bitten by a snake as she fled. Orpheus her husband followed her into *Hades* to regain her and *Pluto* agreed to restore her on condition that Orpheus did not look back before he was out of Hades. He broke the condition and Eurydice vanished from him. Eurydice had two sons, *Musaeus* and Dres, by Orpheus. See also *Erudice*
Fletcher P.   *Purple Island* v 61ff
Henryson   *Orpheus and Eurydice* 365ff
Herrick   *His Farewell to Poetry* 67-70
Keats   *Endymion* ii 164-70
Lamia i 246-50
Lovelace   *Orpheus to Beasts* 1ff
Milton   *L'Allegro* 145-50
Pope   *Ode for Musick* 71ff, 110ff
Shelley   *Orpheus* 55, 58
Spenser   *Daphnaida* 463-6
Epithalamion 16-17
Faerie Queene IV x 58
Ruins of Time 390-2
Shepherd's Calendar, October 25-30
Swinburne   *Eurydice* 1ff

Eurynome (1)
See *Ophion*
Milton   *Paradise Lost* x 580-4

Eurynome (2)   An *Oceanid*, mother of the *Graces* by *Zeus*.
(Hesiod *Theogony* 907-11)
Spenser   *Faerie Queene* VI x 22

Eurypulus, Eurypylus   *Triton* in the form of a Libyan king who welcomed the *Argonauts* to his country by giving them a symbolic clod of earth.
(Apollonius Rhodius iv 1552ff)
Spenser   *Faerie Queene* IV xi 14

Eurystheus   The son of *Sthenelus* and rival of *Hercules* — *Zeus* had been tricked by *Hera* into giving him power over Hercules. To demonstrate his superiority (on the command of the Delphic Oracle) he imposed the twelve labours on Hercules. After Hercules' death, Eurystheus persecuted the children, one of whom (Hyllus) killed him and sent his head to Hercules' mother; she gorged out the eyes.
(Apollodorus II viii)
Owen   *Antaeus* 1ff

Eurythion   With the fabulous dog *Orthus*, the guardian of *Geryon*'s purple cattle which *Hercules* stole as his tenth labour.
Spenser   *Faerie Queene* V x 10

Eurytion   A king of Phithia, accidentally killed by *Peleus* in the *Calydonian Boar Hunt*.
(Apollodorus III xiii 2)
Swinburne   *Atalanta in Calydon* 1259, 1312

Eurytus (1)   Eurytus and *Cteatus* were the twin sons of *Neptune* or Axtor and Molione, after whom they are called Molionides.
Spenser   *Faerie Queene* IV xi 14

Eurytus (2)
See *Dryope (2)*, *Iole*, *Oechalia*

Euterpe   The *Muse* of Music, a daughter of *Zeus* and *Mnemosyne*. She is depicted as holding a flute (which she was supposed to have invented) and wearing a crown of flowers.
Drayton   *The Muses' Elizium* iii 409-12

Henryson   *Orpheus and Eurydice* 36 ff
Noyes   *Euterpe* 1-4
Spenser   *Tears of the Muses* 289-92

Evadne   The wife of *Capaneus*, one of the *Seven Against Thebes*.
Chaucer   *Knight's Tale* 931-3

Evan, Evander   A minor Arcadian god associated with *Pan* and *Faunus*, and having a human role in myths of *Hercules*, *Dardanus* and *Aeneas*, whom he guided round the future site of Rome. Shelley identified him with *Bacchus/Dionysus*.
(Virgil *Aeneid* viii 52 ff)
Shelley   *Witch of Atlas* 316 ff

Evarna   A *Nereid*.
Spenser   *Faerie Queene* IV ii 51

Evening Star
See *Vesper*
Milton   *Paradise Lost* vii 104-6, viii 518-20, xi 587-8
Shelley   *Charles the First* iv 8-10
Spenser   *Epithalamium* 285-92

Fabius Maximus   Fabius Maximus Cunctator (the Delayer) was a consul in 233 BC, who urged a policy of deliberate delay and attrition against the continuing assaults of *Hannibal* — a policy at first received with contempt, but subsequently approved. It probably had an effect in wearing down Hannibal before the more aggressive tactics of *Scipio* in Africa.
(Plutarch *Fabius Maximus*)
Denham   *Panegyric on General George Monck* 13-14
Dryden   *Threnodia Augustalis* 389-90
    To My Dear Friend (Congreve) 35-8
Johnson   *Festina Lente* 17-20
Prior   *Carmen Seculare* 42-3
Swift   *Ode to William Temple* 70-1

Fabricius   Gaius Luscinus Fabricius, a Roman consul and hero in the Pyrrhic Wars of the 3rd Century BC. He was celebrated for his integrity in refusing bribes from *Pyrrhus*.
(Plutarch *Pyrrhus*)

Milton   *Paradise Regained* ii 445-9
Thomson   *Winter* 511

Falerne   A fertile part of Campania, celebrated for its wine.
(Horace *Odes* i 20, *Satire* i 10;
Virgil *Georgics* ii 96)
Milton   *Paradise Regained* iv 117-9

Fama, Fame   The goddess of Rumour and Reputation, often shown as blowing a trumpet or as a winged monster with many mouths.
(Ovid *Metamorphoses* xii 43 ff;
Virgil *Aeneid* iv 173 ff)
Chaucer   *Troilus and Criseyde* iv 659-61
Milton   *Lycidas* 78-82
Pope   *Temple of Fame* 265 ff
Spenser   *Ruins of Time* 421-7

Fasces   A bundle of elm or birch rods (*virgae*) tied round an axe with red thongs and carried before a Roman magistrate as a symbol of authority.
Shelley   *Ode to Liberty* 217-21

Fates   The three sisters (*Parcae*) — *Atropos*, *Clotho* and *Lachesis* — two of whom wove man's destiny and the other (Atropos) of whom cut the thread with scissors at death.
See also *Destinies*, *Necessity*
Bridges   *Prometheus the Firegiver* 562-6
Browning R.   *Apollo and the Fates* 52-4
Chapman   *Hero and Leander* vi
Herrick   *The Dream* 1-6
Keats   *Endymion* iii 251-2
Milton   *Arcades* 63-70
Shakespeare   *Midsummer Night's Dream* V i 276-9
Spenser   *Daphnaida* 14-21
    Faerie Queene IV ii 48
    Ruins of Time 18-20
    Shepherd's Calendar, November 148-9
    Tears of the Muses 13-18
Swinburne   *Atalanta in Calydon* 257-9, 290-3
Tennyson   *Demeter and Persephone* 80-6

Fauns, Fawns   Countryside deities deriving from *Faunus*. They are represented as having legs and ears of goats and are little different from *Satyrs*, whose brothers they were said to be.

(Ovid *Metamorphoses* vi 392-3)
Brooke   *The Old Vicarage, Grantchester* 38-42
Browning R.   *Balaustion's Adventure* 1269-72
Cowper   *Anti-Thelyphthera* 199-202
Denham   *Cooper's Hill* 236-7
Keats   *Bards of Passion and Mirth* 9-12
Endymion i 263-4, iii 533-6
I Stood Tiptoe Upon a Little Hill 153-4
Lamia i 1-5, 101-3
Sleep and Poetry 360-3
Milton   *Lycidas* 34-5
Paradise Regained ii 188-91
Praed   *Love at a Rout* 1-7
Shelley   *Hymn of Pan* 18-24
Spenser   *Faerie Queene* I vi 7, 11, 15
Shepherd's Calendar, July 77-80
Tennyson   *In Memoriam* cxviii 25-8
Wordsworth   *On the Power of Sound* 145ff

Faunus   Son of *Picus* (son of *Saturn*) or of *Mars*, Faunus was a god of the country, and especially of agriculture. With Picus, he was caught by *Numa* and obliged to show how *Jove*'s lightning could be averted, a secret which is, however, withheld from the reader. (The attribution of the *Arethusa* story to Faunus by Spenser seems to be his own invention.)   (Ovid *Fasti* iii 285ff; Virgil *Aeneid* vii 45-103)
See also *Phanus*
Browning E. B.   *Flush or Faunus* 5ff
The Lost Bower 37
Herrick   *The Country Life* 51-2
Upon Faunus 1-2
Milton   *Paradise Lost* iv 705-8
Shelley   *Witch of Atlas* 105-9
Spenser   *Faerie Queene* II ii 7
Mutability Cantos vi 42
Tennyson   *Lucretius* 181-3

Favonius, Favonian
See *Zephyr*
Keats   *Ah, Woe is Me, Poor Silver-Wing* 10-11

Milton   *Sonnet* 20
Shelley   *To a Star* 8-11
Shenstone   *Judgment of Hercules* 278-81
Young   *Night Thoughts* ii

Fenix
See *Phoenix*
Chaucer   *Book of the Duchess* 981-4

Feretrian   A name given to *Jupiter*, 'subduer of enemies', by *Romulus* after one of his victories.   (Livy i 10)
Dryden   *Heroic Stanzas (Cromwell)* 77-8

Flaccus
See *Horace*
Auden   *The Horatians* 53ff
MacNeice   *Memoranda to Horace* ii, iii

Flamininus   Titus Flamininus, as consul gained the support in 198 BC of Greece against Philip V, in the Second Macedonian War. He soundly defeated Philip at Cynoscephalae in Thessaly, 197 BC. He declared Greece free in 196 BC at the Isthmian Games and subsequently aided defence of her autonomy.
(Livy xxxii-vi; Plutarch *Flamininus*)
Thomson   *Liberty* iii 257ff
Wordsworth   *A Roman Master Stands . . .* 1-4
When Far and Wide . . . 9-14

Flaminius   Gaius Flaminius, a general and consul who, in his legal measures, was an early challenger of the power of the senate. He and his forces were trapped at *Thrasymene* by *Hannibal* in 217 BC and sustained massive losses. He died heroically but remained a controversial figure; the loss of battle and his own death were attributed by some to his improper observance of religious formalities beforehand.   (Livy xii)
Johnson   *Festina Lente* 9ff
Wordsworth   *Memorials of a Tour in Italy* xiii 6-10

Flegetoun
See *Phlegethon*
Chaucer   *Troilus and Criseyde* iii 1599-1600

Flora   The Greek *Chloris*, goddess of flowers and gardens. She married *Zephyrus*, who made her queen of flowers, and lived an eternal spring. Many allusions are routine and barely Classical

	(Ovid *Fasti* v 195 ff)
Chaucer	*Book of the Duchess* 402-9
	Legend of Good Women 171-4
Cowper	*The Winter Nosegay* 9-12
Donne	*Eclogue 1613* 7-8
Keats	*Endymion* iv 565-70
	Sleep and Poetry 101-2
	To Leigh Hunt Esq. 5-8
Meredith	*The Rape of Aurora*
Milton	*Paradise Lost* v 15-17
Pope	*Windsor-Forest* 37-40
Spenser	*Faerie Queene* I i 48
	Shepherd's Calendar, May 27-33
Swift	*Description of Mother Ludwell's Cave* 11-12
Vaughan	*An Elegy* 7-11
Wordsworth	*Rural Illusions* 13-17

Fortuna, Fortune   The Roman goddess of Luck or Good Fortune, later of Chance in any aspect. She is sometimes shown as a blind-fold figure holding a horn of plenty or a wheel or rudder. Though possibly in origin a fertility goddess, she was identified with the Greek *Tyche*. Fortuna was greatly developed in medieval times with only remote Classical reference.

	(Ovid *Fasti* vi 569; Livy *passim*)
Carew	*Coelum Britannicum* 687-90
Chaucer	*Book of the Duchess* 618-23, 628-34
	Knight's Tale 925-6
	Franklin's Tale 1355-6
	Troilus and Criseyde i 848-52, iii 617-8, iv 1ff
Marlowe	*Edward II* 2627-31
Pope	*Temple of Fame* 296-7
Shakespeare	*As You Like It* I ii 27-30
	King Henry V III vi 25-7
	Rape of Lucrece 939 ff

Fulvia   The third wife of *Mark Antony*. She was the widow of Clodius, by whom she had a son, and a daughter named Claudia, who married *Octavian*. She was a dominating personality who did not hesitate to involve herself in her husband's politics and the power-struggle with Octavian, and this seems to have adversely affected the marriage. According to *Plutarch*, she died of a sickness in 41 BC whilst on her way to attempt a reconciliation with Antony. She was succeeded, as his wife, by *Octavia*, sister of Octavian; this was a political marriage, attempting to avoid conflict between Antony and Octavian, agreed at Brundisium, 40 BC.

	(Plutarch *Antony*)
Dryden	*All for Love* II i
Rosetti D. G.	*Tiber, Nile and Thames* 1ff
Shakespeare	*Antony and Cleopatra* I i 31-2, 41, ii 123-5, iii 27-9, 64-5; II i 40, ii 98

Furies, Fury
See *Eumenides*

Byron	*Childe Harold* iv 132
	Curse of Minerva 279-82
Chaucer	*Legend of Good Women* 2252
	Troilus and Criseyde ii 435-6
Collins	*Ode to Fear*
Fletcher P.	*Purple Island* v 65
Milton	*Paradise Lost* ii 671
Pope	*Ode for Musick* 66-70
Shakespeare	*Antony and Cleopatra* II v 38-41
	King Richard III I iv 55-7
	Midsummer Night's Dream V i 276-9
Shelley	*Prometheus Unbound* i 326-32, 458, 470-2
Spenser	*Faerie Queene* I iii 36, v 31, vii 13, II v 37, xii 41
	Amoretti 86
Tennyson	*Lucretius* 259-64

Gaditane   A name for *Hercules* from Gades (Cadiz), where the monster *Geryon* was killed by Hercules and worship of the hero was instituted.
Swinburne   *St Dorothy*

Galataea, Galathaea   A *Nereid* vainly loved by the giant *Polyphemus*, who sang uncouth songs which she detested. Meanwhile, she conducted an affair with the Sicilian shepherd Acis, who was crushed by Polyphemus with a boulder. Acis was later changed into a fountain.

(*Lament for Bion* 58-63; Ovid *Metamorphoses* xiii 789 ff; Virgil *Aeneid* ix 102)
Arnold   *Epilogue to Laocoon* 45-8
Spenser   *Faerie Queene* IV xi 49

Galba (1)   Servius Galba rose from the ranks to hold several provincial governorships in the reign of *Nero*, whom he was invited to succeed in 68 AD when he marched on Rome from Spain. The army did not support him and he soon became unpopular for his meanness and perhaps as being an administrator rather than a leader. He was assassinated early in 69 AD by conspirators prompted by *Otho*, whom he had passed over as his successor, preferring the senator *Piso*.

                    (Tacitus *Histories*)
Dryden   *Astraea Redux* 67-70
Tennyson   *The Druid's Prophecies* 29-32

Galba (2)   A character in a Satire of *Horace*. In a discussion of terrible penalties and mutilation for adultery, Galba alone dissents from such extreme law.

                  (Horace *Satires* II ii 46)
Browning R.   *The Ring and the Book* viii 1227-31

Galen   A celebrated physician of the 2nd Century AD who, born in Pergamum, became doctor to Marcus *Aurelius* in Rome. Galen's aim in his many writings was to comprehend the whole field of medicine and medical theory, and he drew on *Aristotle*, *Plato* and *Hippocrates*. This and his relation of all matters to God made him, with Hippocrates, the ideal physician of the Middle Ages.
See *Galyen*
Browning R.   *Paracelsus* v 177-80
Chaucer   *Book of the Duchess* 568-73
Kipling   *Our Fathers of Old* 41-4
Shakespeare   *Coriolanus* II i 107-10
                Merry Wives of Windsor II iii 27; III i 60-2
Tennyson   *The Princess* i 19

Galene   A *Nereid*.
Spenser   *Faerie Queene* IV xi 48

Galgopheye
See *Gargaphia*

Chaucer   *Knight's Tale* 2626-33

Galyen
See *Galen*
Chaucer   *Canterbury Tales, Prologue* 429-31

Ganymede, Ganymedes   A Phrygian youth who was taken up to heaven by *Jupiter* while tending his father's flock on Trojan Mt *Ida*, and appointed cupbearer to the gods (after the disgrace of *Hebe* in this office). It was also said that an eagle carried him to heaven because Jupiter desired him. The bereaved father (Tros) of Ganymede received either horses or a golden vine made by *Hephaestus*, as consolation.

                (Homer *Iliad* xx 231 ff;
       Ovid *Metamorphoses* x 155-161;
                Pausanias X xxiv)
Browning R.   *Filippo Baldinucci* 397-400
Chaucer   *House of Fame* 589-91
Fletcher G.   *Christ's Victory after Death*
Keats   *Endymion* i 169-70
Marlowe   *Dido Queen of Carthage* 12-15
                Edward II 474-7
                Hero and Leander i 147-8, ii 157 ff
Milton   *Paradise Regained* ii 350-3
Noyes   *Mount Ida* 85-8
Shakespeare   *As You Like It* I iii 120-1
                Comedy of Errors V i 331-3
Shelley   *Prometheus Unbound* III i 25-6
Spenser   *Faerie Queene* III xi 34, xii 7
Tennyson   *Palace of Art* 121-4
                The Princess iii 55-6
Wordsworth   *Memorials of a Tour 1820* xxv 10

Garamantes   A people in the north of modern Libya. They were polygamous and lived naked.
              (Lucan iv 334; Pliny V viii)
Shelley   *Oedipus Tyrannus* I i 171-2
              Witch of Atlas 130

Gardens of Adonis
See *Adonis*

Gargaphia   A valley and fountain near

Plataea in southern Boeotia, where *Actaeon* was torn by his hounds.

(Pausanias IX iv 3)

Gargarus   A town and highest peak in the *Ida* mountains near Troy.

(Virgil *Georgics* i 103)

See also *Ida (2)*

Tennyson   *Oenone* 10-11

Ge
See *Terra, Tellus*

Gemonies   Scalae Gemoniae, steps down to the *Tiber* in Rome, onto which the bodies of criminals were thrown.

(Tacitus *Histories* III lxxiv)

Jonson   *Sejanus* IV v

Genii
See *Genius*

Collins	*Ye Genii Who in Secret State . . .* 1-4
Diaper	*Dryades* 85-6
Shelley	*Prometheus Unbound* iv 539-41
	Daemon of the World 53-5
Vaughan	*Olor Iscanus* 15-18
Wordsworth	*Descriptive Sketches* 340ff

Genius   A spirit presiding over the birth and life of every man as a guardian angel. The daemon or genius gave evidence at the moment of death which determined the mode of the individual's after-life. Some held that there was for every person a good and a bad genius. Genii were held to live on the moon, just outside the earth's shadow, awaiting the separation of soul and mind, when mind would return to the sun. They were reckoned to be subordinates of the gods and were worshipped in appropriate shrines, whence arises the genius of the place, the 'genius loci' — for some believed that genii attended places and apparently inanimate objects.

Donne	*A Valediction, of my Name in the Window* 43ff
Milton	*Arcades* 43
	Il Penseroso 154
	Lycidas 182-5
	On the Morning of Christ's Nativity 184-6

Shakespeare	*Julius Caesar* II i 63-9
	Macbeth III i 53-6
Spenser	*Faerie Queene* II xii 47
	Ruins of Time 18-20
Wordsworth	*Sonnet, Dogmatic Teachers* 7-9
	The Wishing-Gate 40-2

Gerania, Gerenia   A mountain near Corinth.
Swinburne   *Atalanta in Calydon* 1249

Germanicus   Germanicus Julius Caesar was adopted and promoted by his uncle *Tiberius* to be Emperor of the East after a series of victories in Germany. He was poisoned in 19 AD, after his success and acclaim had aroused growing envy from Tiberius. He was married to *Agrippina (2)* the Elder, who was granddaughter of Augustus and was to be grandmother of *Nero*. He was a popular hero and his death caused much suspicion and ill-feeling, as his murderer was not identified.

Gray	*Agrippina* 5-6
Jonson	*Sejanus* I i, II ii

Gerontion   A transliteration of the Greek word for 'old man'.
Eliot T. S.   *Gerontion*

Geryon   A three-headed, or three-bodied, monster of Erythrea, Geryon was son of *Medusa*. He kept a herd of purple cattle which were guarded by *Eurytion* and a two-headed dog named *Orthus*. It was the tenth labour of Hercules to capture this herd, and in so doing he killed Geryon, Eurytion and Orthus.

(Apollodorus II v 10;
Hesiod *Theogony* 287-94)

Browning R.	*Pietro of Albano* 434-5
Crashaw	*Sospetto d'Herode* 46
Fletcher P.	*The Locusts* v 32
Milton	*Paradise Lost* xi 410-1
Skelton	*Philip Sparrow, Addition*
Spenser	*Faerie Queene* V x 9-10

Giants, Gigantes   Sons of *Uranus* (heaven) and *Ge* (earth), the enormous Giants sprang from the blood of Uranus when he was mutilated by *Saturn* in the war of the *Titans*. As the successors of the Titans, they again tried to oust *Zeus* but were defeated by Zeus's son *Heracles*, with help from *Minerva*. The Giants were said to have a hundred arms each and serpents as legs, to cover a huge area when laid on the ground, to regard a human as a small snack and to carry a staff the size of a ship's mast, and so on. Later they were associated with the Biblical giant offspring of the mingling of the sons of God and daughters of men (*Genesis* VI).

(Apollodorus I vi;
Hesiod *Theogony* 183-7;
Ovid *Metamorphoses* i 151-62)

Jonson   *If Men and Times were Now*
       37-41
Milton   *On the Death of a Fair Infant*
       47-9
       Paradise Lost i 197-8, 777-9,
       iii 464-5, vii 604-5

Glauce   A *Nereid*.
Spenser   *Faerie Queene* IV xi 48

Glauconome   A *Nereid*.
(Apollodorus I ii 6)
Spenser   *Faerie Queene* IV xi 50

Glaucus   A fisherman of Anthedon in Euboea, Glaucus was transformed by eating a herb so that he became part-fish and was accepted as a minor prophetic sea-god. He fell in love with Scylla and sought advice from *Circe*. Circe was angry at his rejection of her own charms and changed Scylla into a monster. Glaucus may be seen as an old man emerging from the sea and was said to be related to *Nereus*.

(Apollonius Rhodius i 1310ff;
Ovid *Metamorphoses* xiii 898ff)

Diaper   *Seal Eclogues* i 1-2
Keats   *Endymion* iii 193-200, 310,
       352-5, 399ff, 590-9, 775-82,
       807-10
Milton   *Comus* 874
Spenser   *Faerie Queene* IV xi 13
Swinburne   *Ballad Against the Enemies*
       of France 35

Gnidus
See *Cnidus*

Golden Age   The first age of man, under *Chronos* (*Saturn*), an age of peace and freedom, followed by ages of silver, brass, heroism

and (the present) iron. It was commonly held, perhaps following traditional interpretation of *Virgil*'s fourth *Eclogue*, that the birth of Christ reinstated at least the possibility of another Golden Age.

(Hesiod *Works and Days* 109-201;
Ovid *Metamorphoses* i 89ff;
Virgil *Eclogue* iv)

See also *Astraea*

Carew   *Upon My Lord Chief Justice*
       15ff
Chaucer   *The Former Age* 56-8
Henryson   *The Want of Wise Men* 9-10
Keats   *Endymion* ii 895-7
Marlowe   *Hero and Leander* i 456
Prior   *A Pindaric* 65-7
Shakespeare   *Tempest* II i 161
Shelley   *Prometheus Unbound* II iv
       36-43
       Epipsychidion 422-8
       Hellas 1060-3
Spenser   *Faerie Queene* V Prologue 2, 9
       Mother Hubberd's Tale 146-
       51
Wordsworth   *The Excursion* iii 756-9
       Vernal Ode 127-30

Golden Fleece   *Aeetes*, King of *Colchis*, had obtained the Golden Fleece by murdering *Phrixus*, who had escaped the hatred of his step-mother *Ino*, with his sister *Helle*, by riding away on a ram. Helle fell off into a sea which was thereafter called the Hellespont, whilst Phrixus went on to Colchis; here the ram was sacrificed, and its fleece was hung up in the grove of *Ares*, where it was guarded by a dragon. *Jason* was set the task of recapturing the Golden Fleece.
See also *Argo*, *Colchos*

Gordian
See *Gordius*

Browning R.   *The Ring and the Book*
       ii 1167-8
Byron   *Don Juan* xvi 74
Drayton   *Endymion and Phoebe* 165-6
Fletcher P.   *To My Ever-Honoured*
       Cousin 1-2
Herrick   *Description of a Woman* 59-62
Keats   *Lamia* i 47
Milton   *At a Vacation Exercise* 89-90
       Paradise Lost iv 347-9

Gordius

Shakespeare   *Cymbeline* II iii 35
               King Henry V I i 45-7
Shelley   *Ode to Liberty* 217-21

Gordius   On consulting an oracle during a
revolution, the Phrygians were told to select
as king the first man going in a chariot to the
Temple of *Jupiter*. Gordius, a peasant, was
the first man, but when his chariot was to be
consecrated in the Temple it could not be
unfastened. A search was instituted for someone to undo the 'Gordian knot'. *Alexander
the Great* was crossing Phrygia and cut the
knot with his sword, an act taken to predict
a wide empire for him.
See also *Gordian*

Gorgon   The three Gorgons were sisters,
Stheno, Euryale and *Medusa*. Either Medusa
alone or all three Gorgons had serpents in
their hair, and they had scaly bodies. They
were able to turn to stone those on whom
they looked. The Gorgons were reputed to
live in Scythia or Libya or westwards beyond
the seas. Of the three, Medusa alone was mortal
and she was killed by *Perseus*; *Aeschylus*
states that they had one eye between them
and that it was as they changed the eye that
Medusa was killed. From her neck sprang the
winged horse *Pegasus*, her child by *Poseidon*.
Athene/Minerva was Perseus's support in this
encounter — he gave Medusa's head to her,
and they both wore it in their shields, where
it petrified all who looked directly on it. The
Gorgons were also held to be a race of *Amazons* conquered by Perseus.

(Aeschylus *Prometheus* 793 ff;
Apollodorus II iv; Hesiod *Theogony* 276 ff,
Shield of Heracles 219 ff;
Ovid *Metamorphoses* iv 614 ff)
Browning R.   *Ring and the Book* xi 507
Byron   *Curse of Minerva* 75 ff
         The Giaour 895-8
Chapman   *Shadow of Night*
Dryden   *Don Sebastian* III i
Graves   *The Naked and the Nude* 21-4
Gray   *Ode to Adversity* 34-5
Hopkins   *Andromeda* 14
Keats   *Endymion* iv 128-9, 754
         Hyperion ii 73-4
Milton   *Comus* 447-9
          Paradise Lost ii 626-8, x 526-8

Pope   *Epistle* iii 295
Rosetti D. G.   *Aspecta Medusa* 1-5
Shakespeare   *Macbeth* II ii 69-70
Tennyson   *Death of Oenone* 70-5

Gorgonian
See *Gorgon*, *Pegasean*
Chapman   *Shadow of Night*
Milton   *Paradise Lost* ii 610-13, x 293-7
Shelley   *On the Death of Leonardo
           da Vinci*   25-6
Spenser   *Faerie Queene* III ix 22

Gracchus   Gaius Gracchus was the brother
of Tiberius Gracchus, whose reforms — aimed
principally at a more even distribution of
landed property — he supported and whose
murder he set out to avenge. He was able to
pass a series of reforms, similar in spirit to
those of Tiberius, but was eventually killed
by a mob in the backwash of an unsuccessful
attempt to enlarge qualification for Roman
Citizenship. His head was conveyed through
the streets by a former friend, *Septimuleius*,
to Gracchus's arch-enemy Opimius. The
achievements of the Gracchi in the 2nd
Century BC were both symbolic and real;
Gracchus developed his brother's inspiration
to bring about real social, administrative and
economic change, but finally his breadth of
vision lost him the support necessary to
convert many of his ideals into reality.
Byron   *Marino Faliero* III ii 454-5
Donne   *Satire* iii 65-8
Pope   *Epistle to Henry Cromwell* 70-4

Grace, Graces   The *Charites* (Greek) or
Gratiae (Roman) attended *Venus Aphrodite*.
They were usually held to be daughters of
Zeus and *Hera* or *Eurynome*, but there was
also a tradition that they were offspring of
Bacchus and Venus. Their number varied, as
did their individual names, which included
Aglaia, *Thalia*, *Euphrosyne*, Charis, Pasithea,
Cleta and Phaënna. They are often shown as
naked maidens, holding hands and dancing
in a circle. They presided over gentleness,
loveliness and charm.
(Hesiod *Theogony* 907-11;
Pausanias vi 24, ix 35;
Servius *Aeneid* i 720)
See also *Loves*

102

Collins   *Epistle to Sir Thomas Hanmer*
15-16, 63
Stanzas on a Female Painter
29-30
To Simplicity 28-9
Gray   *Epitaph on Sir William Williams* 3
Progress of Poesy 37
Herrick   *Epithalamie* 41-50
Keats   *Apollo to the Graces* 1-3
To Georgina Augusta Wylie 11-14
To Mary Frogley 39-40
Milton   *Comus* 986-7
L'Allegro 13-16
Paradise Lost iv 266-7, viii 60-1
Shenstone   *Elegies* i 40-4
Spenser   *Epithalamion* 103-9, 255-7
Faerie Queene I i 48, II viii 6,
III vi 2, IV v 5, VI x 9, 22, 115
Hymn in Honour of Beauty
253-61
*Sonnet, 'Receive, most noble
Lord . . .'*
Tears of the Muses 175-80,
403-6
Tennyson   *The Princess* 13-14
Thomson   *To Amanda* 18-20
Wordsworth   *On the Power of Sound*
76-80

Greece
Byron   *Childe Harold* ii 73
Don Juan iii 55
Fletcher P.   *The Locusts* iii 13
Shelley   *To William Shelley* 46
Thomson   *Liberty* ii 85-9

Greek, Greke
Chaucer   *Troilus and Criseyde* i 56-63
Rochester   *Grecian Kindness* 1-6

Griffin, Gryfon   A legendary monster, half eagle, half lion (representing respectively watchfulness and courage) which was said to guard the Amiraspian gold of *Scythia*.
Milton   *Paradise Lost* ii 943-5

Gyes, Gyges (1)   One of the hundred-handed giants (the others being *Briareus* and *Cottus*) born, like the *Titans*, of *Uranus* and *Ge*. They were imprisoned in the earth by Uranus along with the *Cyclopes*, in consequence of which cruelty Ge persuaded the Titans, led by

Chronos (*Saturn*) to castrate Uranus. Ge also persuaded Chronos' son *Zeus* to free these giants so that they could help him in his war with the Titans. They were then imprisoned again in *Tartarus* and placed in charge of the defeated Titans there.

(Apollodorus I i 4-5;
Hesiod *Theogony* 147-58, 617-735)
Keats   *Hyperion* ii 19-22

Gyges (2)   A Lydian, to whom the king Candaules showed his queen naked. She was enraged and ordered Gyges either to be killed or to murder Candaules. He murdered Candaules, took the queen for himself and ascended the throne. These feats were performed with the help of a ring, found on the remains of a giant mounted on a horse and buried deep in the earth. This ring made its wearer invisible.

(Plato *Republic* ii)
Swift   *Ode to Athenian Society* 154-8

Habradate
See *Abradates*
Chaucer   *Franklin's Tale* 1414-8

Hades   'Hades' stood for 'House of Hades'; it was the name of one of the sons of *Chronos* (*Saturn*), who carried off and married Kore, in a myth cognate with that of *Pluto* and *Persephone*. 'Hades' was perhaps an unmentionable person and Pluto (or *Dis*) was substituted; however, the meaning of 'Pluto' (wealth) and his association with *Demeter* and her daughter Persephone also suggests a fertility myth, with the source of riches lying underground. Hades or Pluto guarded the spirits of the dead with the help of *Cerberus*, and he supervised the punishment of malefactors. The punitive aspect of Hades was, however, developed in relatively late times by the Romans – originally, Hades was a neutral resting place, of which indeed part (the Elysian Fields) was sometimes regarded as set aside for the blest or good. The kingdom is, in *Homer*, bounded by *Ocean*, but thereafter by the *Styx*. Its rivers (*Acheron*, Styx, *Lethe*, *Cocytus*, *Avernus*, *Phlegethon*) contribute to its atmosphere. New entrants crossed the Styx or Acheron in

Charon's ferry, were allowed to enter, but not to return, by Cerberus, and then were purged of earthly memories in Lethe. *Chaos* was sometimes said to be part of Hades, and *Tartarus* was reserved for the fallen *Titans*. Various geographical locations were suggested, depending on the date and background of the writer.

(Homeric Hymn *To Demeter* (2) 74ff;
Homer *Iliad* xv 187-93, *Odyssey* xxiv 11-14;
Ovid *Metamorphoses* iv 432ff;
Virgil *Aeneid* vi)

Marlowe   *Tamburlaine* ii 3202-4
Shelley   *Prometheus Unbound* i 195-9, 209-14
Swinburne *By the North Sea* iii 8
Tennyson   *Demeter and Persephone* 26-8
Thomas E. *The Sun used to Shine* 15-17

Haemon   The disowned son of *Creon* and lover of *Antigone*.
Arnold   *Fragment of an 'Antigone'* 39-42

Haemus   Mountains separating *Thrace* and Thessaly, the Balkans. Their name, meaning 'blood', was said to derive from *Typhon*'s loss of blood here when *Zeus* struck him with thunderbolts. Alternatively, it was from Haemus (son of *Boreas*) who was changed into the mountain for rebelling against *Jove*. In one version, Haemus and *Rhodope*, begotten by one father and in love with each other, called themselves *Juno* and *Jupiter*; for this pride they were turned into mountains. Rhodope was also said to be the daughter of Haemus and to have had a giant baby, called Athos, by *Neptune*.
(Apollodorus I vi, II v, III v;
Ovid *Metamorphoses* vi 87-9, x 86ff;
Strabo VI v)
See also *Hemus*
Pope   *Ode for Musick* 111
Spenser   *Mutability Cantos* vii 12
Thomson   *Autumn* 1316-9

Halcion
See *Halcyon*
Carew   *Upon Mr W. Montague* 20-2

Halcyon, Halcyone   Halcyone, the daughter

of *Aeolus*, married *Ceyx*, and was warned in a dream of his being drowned. When she found his body on the shore, she cast herself into the sea, and the two were changed into halcyons (kingfishers) who keep the waters calm for seven to fourteen days in midwinter whilst they build their floating nests.
(Ovid *Metamorphoses* xi 410ff;
Pliny x 47)

See also *Alcyon*, *Halcion*
Coleridge *Domestic Peace* 3-8
Diaper   *Sea Eclogues* ii 11-12
Dryden   *Astraea Redux* 236-7
           Heroic Stanzas (Cromwell) 143-4
Fletcher P. *Piscatory Eclogues* I i
Milton   *On the Morning of Christ's Nativity* 68
Shelley   *Fragment* 1-4

Hamadryads
See *Dryads*
Bridges   *A Water-Party* 7ff
Drayton   *Endymion and Phoebe* 787-9
Keats   *Endymion* i 236-7
Shelley   *Witch of Atlas* 217-9
Spenser   *Faerie Queene* I vi 18
Wordsworth *Haunted Tree* 21-7

Hammon
See *Ammon*
Milton   *On the Morning of Christ's Nativity* 203

Hannibal   The Carthaginian general, son of Hamilcar, to whom he pledged continued enmity to Rome. After a period of training with his father against Spain (where he married a Spanish princess) Hannibal began his career by subduing that country. When he took Saguntum, a Roman ally, by siege (219BC), he decided to leave his Spanish base and to march on Rome, recruiting as he crossed the Alps (which had been deemed impassable and cost his army dearly). After a series of victories, he imposed a crushing defeat in 216BC at *Cannae*; but central and northern Italy remained loyal to Rome and the Romans took steps to avoid another pitched battle. Hannibal marched on Rome but withdrew to Capua, where it has been said that his army's morale suffered. He won over major towns, including

Tarentum (213) which was later recaptured, but for sixteen years he was a threat to Rome without being able to deliver a decisive blow. In 202 he was defeated by *Scipio* the Great at Zama — the Romans having decided to take the war away from Rome to Carthage, to whose defence Hannibal returned. In Carthage he instituted social and political reforms but was thought to be in league with Antiochus of Syria, to whom he did indeed flee and whom he possibly urged to invade Italy. Antiochus was defeated by the Romans at Magnesia (190) and Hannibal then became a fugitive, finally committing suicide to avoid extradition to Rome c.183 BC. His crossing of the Alps particularly inspired later writers, including the vivid detail of causing rocks to crumble by heating them and pouring vinegar on them.

(Livy xxi, xxii; Polybius *passim*)

See also *Hanybal*

Cowley	*The Motto* 17-18
	To Dr Scarborough 2
Drayton	*Polyolbion* xxv 31ff
Dryden	*MacFlecknoe* 112-5
	To John Driden of Chesterton 164-6
	To My Dear Friend (Congreve) 35-8
Jonson	*To the Immortal Memory of That Noble Pair* 1-8
Milton	*Sonnet* 17
Prior	*Satire on Modern Translators* 111-3
Raleigh	*Epitaph on Sidney* 57-60
Shakespeare	*Measure for Measure* II i 165
Shenstone	*Elegies* xix 37-40
Sidney	*My Mistress Lovers* 44-5
Skelton	*Philip Sparrow*
Spenser	*Faerie Queene* I v 49
Swinburne	*Song for the Centenary of Landor* 40

Hanybal

See *Hannibal*

Chaucer	*Man of Law's Tale* 288-93

Harmodius

See *Aristogeton*

Byron	*Age of Bronze* 276
	Childe Harold iii 20
Moore	*Evenings in Greece* 451-5

Swinburne	*Athens* ep. i
Wordsworth	*The Prelude* x 198-202

Harmonia A daughter of *Mars* and *Venus* for whose wedding, to *Cadmus*, *Vulcan* provided a dress and bracelet (or necklace) foretelling the misfortunes of the Cadmian line.

(Apollodorus III iv)

Campbell	*Pleasures of Hope*
Chaucer	*Complaint of Mars* 245 ff
Swinburne	*Tiresias* 17-18

Harpies, Harpy Monsters with women's faces and vultures' bodies. They were two or three in number and most often named Aello, Ocypete and *Celeno*, the leader. The Harpies were sent by *Juno* to punish *Phineus*, King of *Thrace*, who blinded his children because of a false accusation that they aspired to his throne. Phineus was himself made blind, and the Harpies tried to take his food and fouled everything with their smell and excrement. They were driven away to the Strophades Islands, west of the Peloponnesus, by Phineus's brothers-in-law, Zetes and Calais. They were sometimes closely associated with the *Furies*.

(Apollodorus I ix 21; Apollonius Rhodius ii 188ff; Hesiod *Theogony* 265-9; Homer *Odyssey* xx 61ff; Virgil *Aeneid* iii 209-57, vii 289)

See also *Arpies*

Crashaw	*Sospetto d'Herode* 42
Marlowe	*Tamburlaine* i 899-901
Milton	*Comus* 602-4
Shakespeare	*Pericles* IV i 47-9
Swinburne	*Dirae-Celaeno*
Tennyson	*Lucretius* 159-60

Hasdrubal A Carthaginian general, son of Gisco, who was defeated by *Scipio Africanus* (2) in the Third Punic War, 146 BC. At the last moment he changed sides and begged for his life, at which his wife and children threw themselves on the flames of Carthage which they had set alight.

(Livy li; Polybius xxxviii 20)

Chaucer	*Franklin's Tale* 1399-1404
	Nun's Priest's Tale 4552-5

Hebe Hebe Juventas, the goddess of Youth, was daughter of *Jupiter* and *Juno*. She performed small services for the gods, which included cup-bearing (until superseded by *Ganymede* when she fell over and exposed herself), and married *Hercules* when he became a god. She is regarded as a personification of youthful beauty.

(Apollodorus II vii 7;
Ovid *Metamorphoses* ix 400-1)

Arnold	*Empedocles on Etna* II i 84-8
Collins	*Ode to Liberty* 108
Crashaw	*Music's Duel* 126-7
Davies Sir J.	*Orchestra* 552-3
Drayton	*Barons' Wars* vi 36
	The Shepherds Sirena 13-16
Goldsmith	*Epilogue to 'The Sister'* 17-18
Graves	*To Ogmian Hercules* 4-8
Hardy	*In St Paul's a While Ago* 17-18
Keats	*Endymion* iv 415-7, 436-8
	Fancy 81-8
Marlowe	*Hero and Leander* i 386 ff
Milton	*At a Vacation Exercise* 38-9
	Comus 290
	L'Allegro 28-30
Moore	*Fall of Hebe* 70-4
Praed	*The Modern Nectar* 59-60
Spenser	*Hymn in Honour of Love* 280-7
	Ruins of Time 379-86
Tennyson	*The Gardener's Daughter* 135-6
Wordsworth	*Lines Written as a School Exercise* 20

Hebon
See *Ebon*, *Bacchus*, *Dionysus*
Marlowe *Jew of Malta* 1400 ff

Hebrus A Thracian river flowing over sand into the Aegean. It was into the swiftly flowing Hebrus that the head of the dismembered *Orpheus* was thrown by Bacchic revellers.

(Ovid *Metamorphoses* xi 50; Virgil
Aeneid i 317, *Georgics* iv 524)

Cowper	*On the Death of Mrs Throckmorton's Bullfinch* 61-6
Drayton	*Tom Himself and the Harp* 36-42
Milton	*Lycidas* 62-3
Spenser	*Faerie Queene* I xi 30
Vaughan	*Olor Iscanus* 3-4

Hecate
See *Artemis*, *Persephone*

Byron	*Curse of Minerva* 65-9
	A Sketch 50-4
Chapman	*Shadow of the Night*
Herrick	*The New Charon* 31-4
Keats	*On the Sea* 1-4
Milton	*Comus* 134-6, 535-6
	Paradise Lost ii 662-6
Noyes	*Drake* iii
Shakespeare	*Hamlet* III ii 251-2
	King Lear I i 108 ff
	Macbeth II i 50-1, ii 40-3; III v 14 ff
Spenser	*Faerie Queene* I i 43
	Mutability Cantos xi 3

Hecatompylos The 'city of a hundred gates', in Parthia. Its site remains uncertain.

(Strabo XI viii 9)
Milton *Paradise Regained* iii 286-8

Hector The eldest son of *Priam* and *Hecuba*, and leader of the Trojans in the War — a tragedy which, in his blunt way, Hector regarded as irresponsibly caused and unnecessary. He performed many heroic exploits, and fought *Ajax* in a drawn duel, before he was killed by *Achilles* (in revenge for Hector's killing of *Patroclus*) and dragged round the city by chariot. Achilles refused to surrender Hector's body until persuaded by his mother *Thetis*, when the Trojans were allowed to ransom it and to have a period of peace for mourning. Hector married *Andromache*, from whom he had a son Astyanax who, saved by his mother from the burning Troy, was thrown to his death from the battlements by the Greeks or by *Ulysses* in particular.

(Apollodorus *Epitome* v 23; Homer *Iliad*;
Ovid *Metamorphoses* xiii 415)

Auden	*Moon Landing* 22-4
Belloc	*But O Not Lovely Helen* 1 ff
Bridges	*Growth of Love* 53
Brooke	*Fragment*
Browning E. B.	*Battle of Marathon* 890-5
Byron	*Deformed Transformed* I i 267 ff
Chapman	*Bussy d'Ambois* II i 54-9
Diaper	*Dryades* 625-6
Dryden	*All For Love* 21-2
Hopkins	*Vision of Mermaids*

Marlowe	*Dido Queen of Carthage* 104-8, 496ff
	Tamburlaine ii 3566-70
Marvell	*Elegy on the Death of Lord Villiers* 97-104
Milton	*Paradise Lost* ix 13-16
Pope	*Temple of Fame* 188ff
Rosetti D. G.	*Cassandra* 9-11
Shakespeare	*Coriolanus* I iii 39-43
	King Henry VI pt 1 II iii 18-21
	Much Ado About Nothing II iii 171-2
	Troilus and Cressida I ii 4-5, V iii 83-6, ix 4-6, x 3-5, 17-19
Skelton	*Philip Sparrow*
Spenser	*Faerie Queene* II ix 45
Yeats	*A Man Young and Old* vi

Hecuba The wife of King *Priam* of *Troy* and mother of *Paris*, the cause of the Trojan War in which most of her children were killed. After the War she was taken by *Ulysses* with the Greeks and her daughter Polyxena was sacrificed on *Achilles'* grave to ensure the Greeks' safe return. When they landed on a Thracian island (*Chersonese*) she found in a dream that its king, *Polymnestor*, had murdered her son Polydorus for his money. She savagely blinded him and killed his sons. She was subsequently transformed into a dog with flaming eyes and threw herself into the sea.

(Ovid *Metamorphoses* xiii 536-75; Virgil *Aeneid* III 22ff)

Shakespeare	*Coriolanus* I iii 39-43
	Cymbeline IV ii 314-5
	Hamlet II ii 551-5
	Rape of Lucrece 1366-72, 1447-9
	Titus Andronicus I i 136-8, IV i 20-1
	Troilus and Cressida V iii 51-5, 83-6

Helen The daughter of *Nemesis* by *Zeus*, or of *Leda* and Zeus (as a swan). Claimed to be the most beautiful woman in the world, she chose as husband *Menelaus*, King of *Sparta*, but was seduced by *Paris*, son of King *Priam* of *Troy*. Menelaus joined with her previous suitors (who had sworn to defend her) to make war on Troy. Late in the war, Paris was killed, and Helen married his brother *Deiphobus*, whom Menelaus killed. Menelaus was then reconciled to Helen and they lived in Sparta until he died, when she was driven out by his illegitimate sons and went to Rhodes. Here she was murdered at the instigation of a widow, Polyxo, who held it against Helen for causing the war that had killed her husband. In another legend, it was a ghost of Helen that went to Troy, whilst she herself stayed in Egypt. There are other versions, particularly of the later life of Helen.

(Euripides *Helen*; Homer *Iliad* ii, *Odyssey* iv, xv; Pausanias iii 19)

See also *Eleyne*

— *General*

Brooke	*It's Not Going to Happen Again* 11-14
Browning E. B.	*Battle of Marathon* 890-5
Browning R.	*Fifine at the Fair* 210-1, 305-12
	Ring and the Book ii 1003-4
Byron	*Siege of Corinth* 225-8
Lewis C. D.	*Transitional Poem* 7, 18, 19
Masefield	*Clytemnestra* 4
	A King's Daughter
Pope	*To Belinda* 5-8
Shakespeare	*As You Like It* III ii 135-9
	Taming of the Shrew I ii 240-1
Sidney	*Astrophel and Stella* 33
Spenser	*Faerie Queene* III x 12-13
Swinburne	*Atalanta in Calydon* 426ff
Yeats	*Long-Legged Fly*
	Prayer for My Daughter
	When Helen Lived

— *and the Trojan War*

Browning E. B.	*The Fourfold Aspect* 37-46
Browning R.	*With Charles Avison* 224-6
Denham	*Friendship and Single Life* 93-5
Marlowe	*Tamburlaine* ii 3054-8
Masefield	*The Tale of Nireus* 32-9
Rosetti D. G.	*Troy Town* 1-7
Shakespeare	*All's Well That Ends Well* I iii 66-9
	Troilus and Cressida, Prologue 7-10, IV i 70-4

Heliads, Heliades Daughters of the *Sun* who were so grieved by the death of their brother *Phaethon* that they were changed into poplars shedding amber tears. *Clymene*, their mother, wandered the earth in search of his bones.

Helice

Helicon The highest mountain of a range in West Boeotia, north-west of *Athens*. Helicon was superseded as the Seat of the *Muses* by *Olympus* and *Parnassus*. At its foot was the fountain of inspiration, *Aganippe*, after which the Muses were sometimes called Aganippedes. Nearer the peak was the similar spring, *Hippocrene*, supposed to have been created by *Pegasus* with a stamp of his hoof.

(Pausanias ix 28-9)

See also *Aonia, Elicon, Elycon, Heliconian*

Heliconian
See *Helicon*

Chatterton   *Fragment* 3-4
               Elegy for Mr Phillips 69-70
Donne   *To Mr S. B.* 5-8
Keats   *To B. R. Haydon*
Spenser   *Sonnet 'Receive, Most Noble*
           Lord . . .'
Tennyson   *Lucretius* 224

Heliopolis   The City of the *Sun* (with a
temple thereto) close to the root of the Nile
Delta in Egypt. Also known in glosses as
Egyptian Thebes.
                              (Herodotus ii;
               Ovid *Metamorphoses* xv 391-407)

Helios, Helius   Helios (*Sol*), son of *Hyperion*,
was the god of the *Sun*. He witnessed the rape
of *Proserpina* and was father of *Circe* and of
Phaethon. Helios is represented in a golden
helmet driving a golden chariot across the sky
daily until it sinks into Ocean at *Tartessus*
near Cadiz. The chariot has four horses, named
Pyrois, *Eous*, *Aethon* and *Phlegon*. The chariot
and other accoutrements of Helios are found
also with *Apollo* as the sun.
               (Hesiod *Theogony* 371; Homeric
               Hymns *To Helios* (xxxi) and *Demeter*
               (xiii); Ovid *Metamorphoses* ii, 107-10,
                                           153-5)
Milton   *Comus* 95-7

Hellas   A name for *Greece*, variously defined.
The name was possibly from Hellene, a son of
Deucalion and *Pyrrha*.
                              (Pliny iv 7; Strabo ix 5)
Browning E. B.   *The Dead Pan* 1
                   An Island 25
Browning R.   *Aristophanes' Apology*
               115-7
Butler S.   *Life After Death*
Shelley   *Hellas: The World's Great Age*
               Begins Anew 1066

Helle   Daughter of *Athamas*, King of *Thebes*,
from whose house she escaped to avoid the
cruelty of her mother-in-law *Ino* (whom he
had married under pretence that his first wife
Nephele was mad). In the flight, in which she
was borne by a golden ram provided by
Hermes or *Neptune*, she fell into the sea, which
was then called *Hellespont*.
               (Apollodorus i 9; Hyginus

Fabulae 3; Ovid *Fasti* iii 853 ff)
See also *Phrixus*
Marlowe   *Hero and Leander* ii 179-80
Moore   *Evenings in Greece* 451-5
Spenser   *Faerie Queene* III xi 30,
           V *Prologue* 5

Hellespont, Hellespontus   The modern Dar-
danelles, named after *Helle*. The Hellespont,
with the towns *Abydos* and *Sestos* on either
side, was the setting for the story of *Hero* and
Leander and also the site of *Xerxes'* bridge of
boats into Greece.
               (Apollodorus i 9; Herodotus vii 36;
                              Ovid *Heroides* xviii)
Byron   *Written After Swimming from*
           Sestos 1ff
Donne   *Elegy* xviii 60-3
Hood   *Hero and Leander* 18
MacNeice   *Suite for Recorders* 9-12
Marlowe   *Hero and Leander* 1-5
Meredith   *Milton*
Milton   *Paradise Lost* x 306-10
Shakespeare   *Othello* III iii 457-62
               Two Gentlemen of Verona
               I i 21-5
Spenser   *Mutability Cantos* vii 32
Wordsworth   *Laodamia* 167-73

Hemera   Sister of *Memnon*, King of Ethiopia.
Milton   *Il Penseroso* 11-18

Hemonydes
See *Maeon*
Chaucer   *Troilus and Criseyde* V 1492-3

Hemus
See *Haemus*
Spenser   *Faerie Queene* III ix 22

Hephaestion   The close friend from child-
hood and follower of *Alexander the Great*. He
was a distinguished general but valued principally as a confidant and, as favourite, was not
popular with the Macedonians. He died two
years before Alexander, whose grief was in-
consolable and who accused the doctors of
negligence. An extravagant funeral was held.
               (Plutarch *Alexander*)

Hephaestus
See *Vulcan*

Auden   *Shield of Achilles* 65-72
Bridges   *Demeter* 489-92
Jonson   *And Must I Sing?* 13-15
Kingsley   *Andromeda* 37-40, 440-2

Hera
See *Juno*
Browning R.   *Artemis Prologizes* 1ff
               Ring and the Book viii
               897-8

Heracles, Herakles   The Greek name for
Hercules.
Meredith   *The Labourer*
Owen   *Antaeus* 1ff

Heracleitus, Heraclitus   The Greek philosopher of c. 500 BC who conceived the universe
to be an eternal flux and conflict of opposites;
wisdom lay in the comprehension of this
whole rather than of the parts, and so in self-
knowledge. For Heracleitus the prime force
was fire. He did not believe in a creation in
time. Because this view of things was prone to
sombre interpretations, Heracleitus was sometimes known as the 'weeping philosopher'. He
was also said to be a misanthrope who resided
on a dunghill so that its warmth might cure
him of his melancholy.
Browning R.   *Try our Hyson* 3
Donne   *Satire* iv 197-8
Dryden   *The Unhappy Favourite, Epi-*
             logue 22-3
Prior   *Democritus and Heraclitus* 1-4
         The Dove 19-20

Heraen   The Heraen mountains, a Sicilian
range where *Daphnis* was supposed to have
lived.
                    (Diodorus Siculus iv 84)
Moore   *To Joseph Atkinson* 31ff

Herculean
See *Hercules*
Milton   *Paradise Lost* ix 1060

Hercules   The Greek *Herakles*, son of *Jupiter*
(in the form of *Amphitryon*) and *Alcmena*.
He was also known as *Alcides* after his grandfather, *Alcaeus*, and 'the Theban', having been
brought up at *Thebes*. Hercules was intended
by Jupiter to be the greatest hero ever known

and this, and the circumstances of his birth
to Alcmena, inspired the jealousy of *Juno*,
Jupiter's wife. Almost at his birth she sent
venomous snakes to kill him, which the infant
warded off with his bare hands, and after his
marriage to *Megara (2)* she deceived him into
killing his own children. Hercules was subser-
vient to the will of his brother *Eurystheus*
since Jupiter had decreed before their birth
that the younger of the two should submit to
the elder, and Juno had influenced the outcome. Eurystheus impressed the fact by im-
posing on Hercules the feats known as the
twelve labours of Hercules (listed below).
Hercules achieved these labours by the support
of the gods, being armed with a sword by
Mercury, a horse by *Neptune*, a shield by
Jupiter, bow and arrows by *Apollo*, and a
bronze club by *Vulcan*. After completing
these and many further heroic deeds, Hercules
was put in agony by assuming the tunic of
Nessus and finally was elevated to the gods,
making a spectacular charioted ascent from
a burning pyre — a scene in which the suicidal,
sacrificial and funeral aspects are strangely
mingled. Among other feats ascribed to him
were his freeing himself from his bonds when
about to be sacrificed by *Busiris* of Egypt,
and the freeing of the King of *Troy*'s daughter
(*Hesione*) from a sea-monster, to whom she
was subjected because *Laomedon* in building
Troy had broken a bargain agreed with Apollo.
The labours of Hercules were:
1. Killing the *Nemean* Lion
2. Killing the *Hydra*
3. Capturing the Cerynitian hind
4. Capturing the *Erymanthean* boar
5. Cleaning the *Augean* stables
6. Banishing the Stymphalian birds
7. Capturing the *Cretan* bull
8. Fetching the Mares of *Diomedes*
9. Obtaining *Hippolite*'s belt
10. Capturing the cattle of *Geryon*
11. Fetching the Apples of the *Hesperides* —
    during which he temporarily took the
    world from *Atlas*'s shoulders whilst Atlas
    sought apples
12. Bringing *Cerberus* out of *Hades*, from
    which the hero emerged with a garland of
    poplar whose leaves, being light and dark,
    signified conquest of all worlds.
                (Apollodorus II iv-vii; Hesiod

Shield of Herakles; Ovid *Metamorphoses*
ix 134ff, xi 199ff; Sophocles *Trachiniae*;
Theocritus *Eclogue* xxiv;
Virgil *Eclogue* vii 61)
See also *Deianira, Ercules, Herculean, Hylas,*
Iole, Iphiclus, Oechalia, Oeta, Omphale,
Tenarus, Tirynthian
— General
Browning R.   *Aristophanes' Apology*
511-3, 534-8, 540-4
Balaustion's Adventure
1054-9
Sordello III 939-42
Butler S.   *Hudibras* II i 351-6
Byron   *The Island* iii 47-50
On the Death of Mr Fox 12-16
Chapman   *Shadow of Night*
Chaucer   *Monk's Tale* 3288-92,
3309-24
House of Fame 1412-4
Parliament of Fowls 288ff
Troilus and Criseyde IV 31-2
Drayton   *Fourth Eclogue* 25-9
Aureng-Zebe II i
To My Honoured Friend
(Howard) 39-40
Graves   *To Ogmian Hercules* 1-3
Jonson   *And Must I Sing?* 4-6
Keats   *Endymion* iii 405-6
Lewis C. D.   *Hero and Saint* 13-16
Marlowe   *Dido Queen of Carthage* 12-15
Milton   *Sonnet* 23
Shakespeare   *All's Well That Ends Well*
IV iii 233-4
Coriolanus IV i 15-18
Cymbeline IV ii 115-6,
309-12
King Henry VI pt 1 II iii
18-21; *pt 3* II i 50
Love's Labour's Lost I ii
163; IV iii 162ff
Merchant of Venice II i
32-4; III ii 82-4
Midsummer Night's Dream
IV i 109-15
Much Ado About Nothing
II i 221ff, 329; IV i 315
Sidney   *Espilus and Therion* 7-12
Southey   *Roderick* i 26-30
Spenser   *Faerie Queene* I xi 27, IV x 27,
xi 16, V i 2, v 24, viii 2 [Iole =
Omphale]

Hymn in Honour of Love
280-7
Ruins of Time 379-86
Tears of the Muses 457-62
Swinburne   *Atalanta in Calydon* 53ff
Wordsworth   *Laodamia* 79-84
— Augean Stables
Butler S.   *Hudibras* I ii 457-8
Skelton   *Philip Sparrow*
— Geryon
Skelton   *Philip Sparrow, Addition*
Spenser   *Faerie Queene* V x 10
— Hesperides and Atlas
Browning R.   *Prince Hohenstiel-*
Schwangau 715-8
Ring and the Book iii
382-6
Marlowe   *Hero and Leander* ii 297-300
Marvell   *Letter to Dr Ingelo* 49-50
Shakespeare   *Coriolanus* IV vi 99-100
Love's Labour's Lost IV iii
335-41
Skelton   *Philip Sparrow, Addition*
Spenser   *Amoretti* 77
Faerie Queene II vii 54
— Cerberus
Browning R.   *Aristophanes' Apology*
511-3

Here
See *Hera*
Kingsley   *Andromeda* 37-40

Herebus
See *Erebus*
Spenser   *Faerie Queene* II iv 41, III iv 55

Herenus   A doubtful reading, possibly for
Erinnyes.
Chaucer   *Complaint to Pity* 92

Hermes
See *Mercury, Calypso*
Auden   *Under Which Lyre* 67-72
Bridges   *Demeter* 575
Browning E. B.   *The Dead Pan* 18
Browning R.   *Pauline* 333-5
Jonson   *To My Chosen Friend* 17
Keats   *As Hermes Once* 1-5
Endymion ii 875-7, iv 66-7,
827-8
Lamia i 7-11, 22-6, 70-5, 81, 89

*Welcome Joy and Welcome
  Sorrow* 1-2
MacNeice   *The Island* ii
Marlowe   *Hero and Leander* i 473-5
  Tamburlaine ii 3899-900
Milton   *Paradise Lost* iii 600-3, iv 714-
  19, ix 129-33
Pope   *Dunciad* iii 343-5
Swift   *The Virtues of Sid Hamet* 35-8
Wordsworth   *Laodamia* 19-24

Herminius   A Roman who, according to
Livy, shared some of the heroism of *Horatius*
in defending the Roman bridge against the
Etruscans in 508 BC.
Macaulay   *Horatius* 30, 54 ff
  Lake Regulus 26, 28

Hermus   A large river in Asia Minor, of
which *Pactolus* is a tributary. Both rivers were
said to have beds lined with gold.
Housman   *Atys* 1-2
Pope   *Windsor-Forest* 355 ff

Hero   The priestess of *Venus* at *Sestos* who
was loved by *Leander* of *Abydos*. Leander
escaped his family's watch at night and swam
across the *Hellespont*, as Hero guided him
from a tower, holding a torch. After many
nocturnal meetings, Leander was drowned
while crossing in a storm which put out the
torch, and Hero flung herself to her death in
the sea. (*Musaeus (2)* is the usual source for
English poets.)
  (Musaeus Grammaticus *Hero and
  Leander* (5th Century AD);
  Ovid *Heroides* xviii, xix;
  Virgil *Georgics* iii 258 ff)
Browning R.   *The Dance of Death* 47-50
Byron   *Bride of Abydos* ii 1ff
  *Written After Swimming from
  Sestos* 1ff
Chaucer   *Legend of Good Women*
  263-6
Donne   *Epigram, Hero and Leander*
Hood   *Hero and Leander* 36, 42,
  116
  Love's Champion 6 ff
Housman   *Terry, Delight, So Seldom
  Meet* 4-7
Keats   *On a Leander Gem*
Kipling   *A Song of Travel* 1-4

Marlowe   *Hero and Leander* i 5-8, 11-
  15, 37-40, 45, 187-91, 209-
  14, 299 ff, ii 45-8, 74-6, 260-
  3, 322-5
Moore   *Hero and Leander* 7-12
Rosetti D. G.   *Hero's Lamp* 1ff
Shakespeare   *As You Like It* IV i 90ff
  Two Gentlemen of Verona
  III i 117-20
Stevenson   *Madrigal* 5-8, 9-12
Swinburne   *Tristram of Lyonesse, Pre-
  lude*
Tennyson   *Hero and Leander* 38-41

Herod   Herod the Great rose to a high position in Judaea and fled to Rome to avoid
Parthian invaders. Here he may first have supported *Brutus* and *Cassius*, but subsequently
gained and kept the favour of *Mark Antony*.
After *Actium* he secured the support of *Augustus* but disorder (including the killing of one
of his wives and children) led eventually to
intervention by Rome. He mingled flattery of
the Romans with brutality in his administration, but he seems to have been torn between the need for Roman support and a wish
for independence for his people.

Herostratus   An Ephesian who was so bent
on eternal fame that he set alight the fabulous
temple of *Diana* at Ephesus on the night that
Alexander the Great was born in 356 BC.
  (Strabo XIV i 22)
See also *Erostratus*
Chapman   *Shadow of Night*
Chaucer   *House of Fame* 1843-5

Herse   The daughter of *Cecrops*, King of
Athens, and *Agraulus*. She was loved by *Mer-
cury* and bore him a son, Cephalos, despite
the efforts of her envious sister, also named
Agraulus, to prevent the lovers from meeting.
  (Ovid *Metamorphoses* ii 708 ff)
See also *Hierse*

Herynes
See *Eumenides*, *Erinnyes*
Chaucer   *Troilus and Criseyde* IV 22-4

Hesiod   A Greek poet, probably of the 8th
Century BC and born in Asera in Boeotia. He
was notable for the *Theogony* (an ancient

history of the deities of Greece) and the *Works and Days*, a poem of worldly and moral advice by way of proverbs and illustrative myths. The Hesiodic canon is disputed; fragments survive but much certainly is lost.

Browning E. B.	*A Vision of Poets*
	310-21
Chapman	*Shadow of Night*
Drayton	*The Muses' Elizium* iii
	116-20
Jonson	*To George Chapman* 1-2

Hesione   Hesione, daughter of *Laomedon* of *Troy*, was in early life rescued from a sea-monster by *Hercules*. After defeating Laomedon and killing many of the family, Hercules gave Hesione to his friend *Telamon* in marriage and he set *Priam* on the Trojan throne. Priam, however, did not forget that his sister had been given away without his choice to Telamon of Greece, and he sent his son *Paris* to reclaim her and her possessions, or perhaps to carry away Helen as an act of revenge. Thus the fate of Hesione was among the causes of the Trojan War.

(Apollodorus ii 5-6)

Browning R.	*Ring and the Book* IX
	966-70
Shakespeare	*Troilus and Cressida* II ii
	76-80
Swinburne	*Masque of Queen Bersabe*

Hesper   The planet Venus when visible in the West after sunset, and so a name for evening. Hesper, shown as a boy carrying a torch, was regarded as the son of *Astraeus* or of *Atlas*. Hesper and its opposite, *Phosphor*, being morning and evening aspects of the same planet, were convenient metaphors for resurrection, life in death. *Vesper*, sometimes found in this group of images, derives from Hesper.
See also *Evening Star, Hesperides, Hesperus*

Donne	*Second Anniversary* 197-8
Noyes	*At Dawn* 1-2, 49
Shelley	*Epipsychidion* 220-4
Spenser	*Prothalamion* 163-6
Tennyson	*Hesperides* 82
	In Memoriam cxxi 1-2, 9-12, 17-18
	Leonine Elegiacs 11-13
	Mariana in the South 89-90

Hesperian
See *Hesperides*

Browning R.	*Aeschylus' Soliloquy* 76-8
	Ring and the Book iii 382-6
Cleveland	*Upon a Miser* 54
Clough	*Trunks the Forest Yielded* 1ff
Jonson	*The New Inn* III ii
Milton	*Comus* 393-7
	Paradise Lost i 519-20, iii 567-9, iv 248-51, viii 630-2
Noyes	*Memories of the Pacific Coast* 5-8
	Mount Ida 138-44
Pope	*Temple of Fame* 81-2
Shelley	*Revolt of Islam* 2940-4
Tennyson	*Oenone* 65ff

Hesperides   *Nymphs*, numbering from three to seven, variously said to be daughters of *Atlas* and Hesperis, or of *Night* and *Erebus*, and named *Aegle*, Erythia, *Vesta* and *Arethusa*. They guarded the golden apples given by *Juno* to *Jupiter* at their wedding. These apples were in a garden also protected by a dragon (*Ladon*) and which, being in the evening West, was thought to be in Africa near Mt Atlas. It was the eleventh labour of *Hercules* to obtain the apples, in some accounts with the help of Atlas. After he had done so, they were returned to the Gardens by *Athene*. 'Hesperian Fields' was sometimes used as a term for Italy, being west of Greece. The Hesperides were also called *Atlantides*.

(Apollodorus II xi)

Auden	*New Year Letter*
Chaucer	*Monk's Tale* 3258-92
Crabbe	*The Candidate*
De La Mare	*Winged Chariot*
Drayton	*Endymion and Phoebe* 40-2
Herrick	*Description of a Woman* 69-73
Keats	*Endymion* ii 452-3, iv 411-2
	Otho the Great IV i 81-7
Kipling	*The Second Voyage* 28
Lawrence	*We Have Gone Too Far* 35-6
Marlowe	*Hero and Leander* ii 297-300
Milton	*Comus* 981-3
	Paradise Regained ii 355-7
Shakespeare	*Love's Labour's Lost* IV iii 335-41
	Pericles I i 27-9
Skelton	*Philip Sparrow, Addition*

Spenser   *Faerie Queene* II vii 54
           Amoretti 77
Tennyson   *The Hesperides* 24-8

Hesperus
See *Hesper*
Keats   *Blue, 'tis the light of heaven* . . .
         1-4
         Calidore 161-2
         Endymion i 684-6, iv 565-70
         On the Story of Rimini 5-6
Marlowe   *Hero and Leander* ii 327-33
Milton   *Comus* 93-4, 981-3
          Lycidas 30-1
          Paradise Lost iv 605-6, ix
          48-50
Shelley   *Hellas* 1036-41
           Queen Mab i 232-8
           Daemon of the World 169-70
Spenser   *Epithalamion* 92-3
           Faerie Queene I ii 6, vii 29-30,
           III iv 51
Wordsworth   *It Is No Spirit* 4 ff

Hierocles   Neoplatonist Alexandrian philosopher of the 5th Century AD. He wrote a commentary on *Pythagoras* which is extant, but the rest of his canon is disputed.
Lovelace   *To the Genius of Mr John Hall*
            45-50

Hierse
See *Herse*
Chaucer   *Troilus and Criseyde* iii
           729-32

Hilas
See *Hylas*
Marlowe   *Edward II* 143-5, 689-94

Himera   The modern River Salso, which nearly bisects Sicily.
Shelley   *Prometheus Unbound* III iii
           40-5

Himera, Himeros   An ancient Sicilian city on one of the two rivers of that name. It was destroyed by *Hannibal* in 408 BC. The name means 'love' or 'yearning'.
                                    (Strabo vi 2)
Shelley   *Letter to Maria Gisborne*
           316-7

Hipolyte, Hipolytus, Hippolyte
See *Hippolytus*
Cleveland   *Parting with a Friend* 1-2
Graves   *To Ogmian Hercules* 4-8

Hipparchus   The first of *Mark Antony's* freedmen to go over to *Augustus* after the Battle of *Actium*.
                        (Plutarch *Antony* lxvii)
Shakespeare   *Antony and Cleopatra* III
               xiii 148-50

Hippasus   The father of Actor, an *Argonaut*.
                        (Apollodorus I ix 16)
Swinburne   *Atalanta in Calydon* 1267

Hippias   The son of *Pisistratus*, Hippias succeeded in 527 BC as Tyrant of *Athens*, with his brother Hipparchus. When Hipparchus was assassinated, Hippias took refuge with *Darius I* of Persia, after winning a short-lived victory against the Spartans. He then fought with the Persians against Athens and was killed at *Marathon* in 490 BC.
            (Herodotus V-VI; Thucydides VI)
See also *Aristogiton*
Browning E. B.   *Battle of Marathon*
                  15-20, 1412 ff
Byron   *Childe Harold* iii 20

Hippocrates   The Greek physician, a contemporary of *Socrates*. Little is known of his life, which was at the turn of the 5th and 4th Centuries BC. Although *Plato* attributed to him a certain theory of medicine, in practice his many works approach medicine from various viewpoints and are inconsistent with each other.
See also *Ipocras, Ypocras*
Bridges   *Wintry Delights* 254
Graves   *The Naked and the Nude* 9-10
Kipling   *Our Fathers of Old* 41-4
Meredith   *Bellerophon*
Shakespeare   *Merry Wives of Windsor*
               III i 60-2

Hippocrene   A fountain of Mt *Helicon*, sacred to the *Muses*. It was named 'the horse's fount' because it had burst forth from the ground when struck by the hooves of *Pegasus*.
            (Ovid *Metamorphoses* v 256 ff)
Coleridge   *A Tombless Epitaph* 21-5

Jonson   *Dedication of the King's New*
           Cellar 25-8
Keats   *Ode to a Nightingale* 15-17
Moore   *The Garden Fete* 785-90
Vaughan   *In Amicum Foeneratorem*
           30-2

Hippolita, Hippolite The mother of Hippolitus.
See also *Ypolita, Antiope (2)*
  Browning R.   *Artemis Prologizes* 22-8
  Fletcher P.   *Purple Island* v 39
  Shakespeare   *Midsummer Night's Dream*
                 II i 75-80
  Swinburne   *Phaedra*

Hippolytus The son of *Theseus* by a mistress, *Hippolyta* or *Antiope*. Although Theseus was married to *Phaedra*, she fell in love with Hippolytus, with disastrous consequences. As a follower of *Artemis*, goddess of Chastity, Hippolytus rejected Phaedra's course of love. She then informed Theseus that Hippolytus had raped her. Theseus banished his son and cursed him, so that *Neptune* raised from the sea a bull which terrified Hippolytus' horses, and he was dragged to his death among the rocks. Phaedra committed suicide. In some accounts, Hippolytus was brought back to life by *Aesculapius* and, protected by Artemis, instituted rites in her honour. There were centres of his cult (as Virbius) at Troezen and *Sparta*.
            (Apollodorus *Epitome* i 18-19;
                  Euripides *Hippolytus*;
            Ovid *Metamorphoses* xv 417ff;
                  Virgil *Aeneid* vii 761-82)
  Browning E. B.   *Queen Anelida* 6
  Browning R.   *Artemis Prologizes* 13-14,
                 22-8, 35-8, 51ff, 101ff
  Marlowe   *Hero and Leander* i 77-8
             Tamburlaine ii 4631-4
  Spenser   *Faerie Queene* I v 36-9, V viii
             43
  Swinburne   *Phaedra*

Hippomanes, Hippomenes
See *Atalanta*
  Moore   *Rhymes on the Road* iii 1-4

Hippomedon One of the *Seven Against Thebes*. He was killed either by Ismarus or in

a Theban valley as he nearly drowned in the supernaturally enlarged River *Ismenus*.
            (Apollodorus III vi 8;
            Statius *Thebaid* ix 446ff)
  Browning E. B.   *Queen Anelida* 9

Hippotades
See *Aeolus*
  Milton   *Lycidas* 93-7

Hippothoe A *Nereid*.
            (Apollodorus I ii 6)
  Spenser   *Faerie Queene* IV xi 50

Hirtius An officer of *Caesar*, and consul-designate, with *Pansa*, at the time of Caesar's murder. He opposed *Antony* and was with *Octavian* in raising the siege of *Mutina* (Modena) by Antony in 43BC. Here he died and with Pansa received a public funeral.
  Shakespeare   *Antony and Cleopatra* I iv
                 56-9

Homer The Greek poet, perhaps of the 8th Century BC. He was thought to have been born in Maeonia (*Lydia*) and so was called Maeonides. By long tradition Homer (in company with many seers) was blind, and lived on the island of *Chios* (south of *Lesbos*) or at Smyrna. He was also said to have been born and lived by the river *Meles* (near Smyrna). Other rivers also claimed him. A single authorship of the *Odyssey* and *Iliad*, generally ascribed to Homer, has for long been disputed but until there is firmer evidence the single name and its traditions are convenient and indicative. His poetry was held to be envied by *Apollo*. The much-used phrase 'Homer nods' derives from Horace, *Ars Poetica* 359.
            (Homeric Hymn *To Apollo* (3))
See also *Omer, Phantasia*
— General
  Arnold   *To a Friend* 2-4
  Browning E. B.   *An Island* 26-7
                    Vision of Poets 295-7
  Browning R.   *Cleon* 138-45
                 Development 54-8
                 Prince Hohenstiel-
                 Schwangau 2080-1
                 Ring and the Book ix
                 1389-91
  Byron   *Don Juan* iii 98, vii 79

— *and the Iliad*

— *and the Odyssey*

— *as Writer of Epic, and Model*

Honorius   Flavius Honorius, Roman Emperor from 395 AD till 423 AD (his guardian, Stilicho, ruled until 409). Honorius had a hand in the partition of the Empire (which proved to be a mistake) between centres at Rome and Constantinople, and he saw the loss of Britain by the Romans. He is regarded as a particularly ineffectual Emperor.

Horace   Quintus Horatius Flaccus (65-8 BC) was introduced to the patronage of Maecenas, and so to a relationship with *Augustus*, by *Virgil*. He speaks of a humble origin from a freedman, but he was educated in Athens. Through the circle of Maecenas he acquired status and influence, of which the bestowal of a country estate — the *Sabine* farm which was his great delight — is some evidence. He was reputed to have been short, fat and unprepossessing in appearance, and his works contain a good deal of personal material, probably unreliable. The keynote of his work is informal discourse, noted for its relaxed manner and urbanity.   (Horace *Epistles* xx)

See *Flaccus*

— *General*

90-5, 102-5

— *as Writer*

Denham	*On Abraham Cowley* 34-40
Dryden	*To My Ingenious Friend Mr Henry Higden* 12-15
Pope	*Epilogue to Satires* 11ff
	Essay on Criticism 653-6
	Temple of Fame 202-5
Prior	*Alma* i 398-404
	Ode Inscribed to the Queen 1ff
	Satire on Modern Translators 159-62
Tennyson	*Poets and their Bibliographies* 5-6

Horatius Cocles A possibly legendary one-eyed Roman hero who in 508 BC single-handedly held a wooden bridge against the Etruscan army under *Porsenna*, as it besieged Rome. The Romans cut the bridge away behind him so that the *Tiber* could not be crossed. According to various accounts, he either perished or swam the Tiber with severe wounds. Again, he may have been accompanied by two others, named as *Spurius Larcius* and Titus Harminius. An ancient statue (possibly of *Vulcan*) was said to commemorate his heroism.

(Livy II x 8-11; Polybius vi 55; Virgil *Culex* 361)

See also *Cloelia*

Macaulay *Horatius* 27 ff, 65-8

Hortensia A Roman lady who, when all women had to provide inventories of their possessions and to limit their wealth with a view to covering expenses of war, refused and led others with her in protest. These events occurred when Rome was threatened by the approaching *Hannibal*, in 215 BC. The 'Oppian Law' was in force for twenty years.

(Livy xxxiv 7)

Tennyson *The Princess* vii 112

Horus Horus, a son of *Isis* and *Osiris*, helped Isis defeat Osiris' brother, *Typhon*.

Hostilius Tullus Hostilius, King of Rome from 673 BC, captured the city of *Alba* Longa from the Latians.

Shakespeare *Coriolanus* II iii 235-42

Hours The Horae were three daughters of *Jupiter* representing spring, summer and winter. They were identified as *Eirene* (peace), *Eunomia* (order) and Dike (justice). They are often shown accompanying *Venus* and the *Graces*, and they were appointed by Jupiter as porters at the gates of heaven.

(Hesiod *Theogony* 902; Homer *Iliad* v 749)

See also *Irene*

Collins	*Ode to Evening* 23
Gray	*Ode on the Spring* 1-2
Keats	*Endymion* iv 422-4
	Hyperion i 213-7
	Fall of Hyperion ii 57-61
Milton	*Comus* 986-7
	Paradise Lost iv 266-7, vi 2-4
Noyes	*At Dawn*
Shelley	*Dirge for the Year*
	Hellas 901-5
	Hymn of Apollo 5-6
	Prometheus Unbound I 48-51, II iv 130-40
	Song of Proserpine 7-12
	Pine Forest of the Cascine 9-11
Spenser	*Faerie Queene* V ix 31-2
	Mutability Cantos vii 45
	Epithalamium 98-102
Thomson	*To Amanda* 18-20
Wordsworth	*Memorials of a Tour in Scotland 1803* xi 1-4

Hyacinth, Hyacinthus A Spartan youth loved by *Apollo* and *Zephyrus*, and also by *Thamyris*, a Thracian bard. Thamyris was first, and apparently the love was mutual and attended by no disaster. Hyacinthus rejected the love of Zephyrus. Apollo brought the youth up and, as they were playing with the discus, the wind Zephyrus blew Apollo's discus so that it hit and killed Hyacinthus. (Alternatively, Apollo himself killed him by accident.) Apollo changed the blood of Hyacinthus into a light blue flower (not the modern hyacinth), bearing on its petals the lament *ai ai!* He also decreed an annual festival, the Hyacinthia, to be held at the tomb in Laconia.

(Ovid *Metamorphoses* x 162-219; Apollodorus I iii 3; Pausanias iii 19; Theocritus *Idylls* x 28)

Drayton   *The Barons' Wars* vi 33
           The Muses' Elizium ix 57-60
Fletcher P.   *Piscatory Eclogues* vii 20
Hopkins   *Escorial* 11
Housman   *Look Not in My Eyes* 9-15
Keats   *Endymion* i 327-9, iv 68-72
Milton   *Comus* 996-9
          Lycidas 106
          On the Death of a Fair Infant
          23-8
Shelley   *Adonais* 140-4
           Prometheus Unbound II i
           138-41
Sidney   *Arcadia* lxxv 29
Spenser   *Faerie Queene* III vi 45, xi 37

Hyacinthin, Hyacinthine
See *Hyacinth*
    Milton   *Paradise Lost* iv 301-3

Hyades   Daughters of *Atlas* and sisters of
Hyas, who, from an excessive enthusiasm for
hunting, was killed by a wild boar. His sisters
sorrowed to death and *Jupiter* turned them
into stars, which were associated with rain.
Further sisters so mourned the Hyades that
they, in turn, became the *Pleiades*.
    Tennyson   *Ulysses* 10-11

Hybla   A Sicilian mountain near Syracuse,
which had a town of the same name at its
foot. Hybla, famous for honey and herbs,
was also known as *Megara (1)* and Megara
Hyblaea.
        (Pausanias v 23; Virgil *Eclogues* vii 37)
See also *Hyblean*
    Campbell   *Pleasure of Hope*
    Carew   *Upon a Mole* 2-4
    Collins   *Ode to Fear* 34-5
             Ode to Simplicity 13-14, 16
    Crashaw   *John XV* 1-2
    Dryden   *Absalom and Achitophel* ii
             1123
    Fletcher G.   *Christ's Victory on Earth*
                  40
    Keats   *Had I a man's fair form* 9-11
    Marlowe   *Dido Queen of Carthage*
             1419-24
    Pope   *Spring* 65-8

Hyblean
See *Hybla*

Young   *Night Thoughts* ii

Hydaspes   A tributary of the Indus, now
called the Jhehum. It was famed for its size
(450 miles long) and for its association with
the Indian campaign of *Alexander* the Great
in 327-5BC.
                    (Horace *Odes* I xxii 8;
                    Virgil *Georgics* iv 211)
    Goldsmith   *The Traveller* 320
    Keats   *The Cap and Bells* 1-3
    Milton   *Paradise Lost* iii 431-6
    Shelley   *Witch of Atlas* 450-3

Hydra, Hydras   The offspring of *Echidna*
and *Typhon*, the Hydra was a many-headed
monster, each of whose heads would be replaced by two more if cut off. It was the terror
of the *Lerna* area of the Peloponnesus and
was defeated by *Hercules* (his second labour)
and Iolaus, who cauterised the wound to
prevent further heads from growing.
        (Apollodorus ii 5; Hesiod *Theogony* 312-8)
    Byron   *Curse of Minerva* 7ff
             Marino Faliero III ii 327-8
    Chaucer   *Monk's Tale* 3293-300
    Crashaw   *Sospetto d'Herode* 6, 44
    Daniel   *Civil Wars* iv 15
             Happy in Sleep 9-10
    Diaper   *Dryades* 593-4
    Dryden   *Annus Mirabilis* 993-4
             Don Sebastian I i
    Herrick   *A Dream on a Snow* 23-4
    Jonson   *On the Famous Voyage* 81-4
    Lewis C. D.   *The Antique Heroes* 25-8
    Lovelace   *Painture* 26-7
    Marlowe   *Jew of Malta* 1400ff
             Tamburlaine i 1238-9
    Marvell   *Character of Holland* 137-8
    Milton   *Comus* 602-6
             Paradise Lost ii 626-8
             Sonnet 15
    Noyes   *Mount Ida* 113-6
    Shakespeare   *Coriolanus* III i 91-7
                  King Henry IV pt 1 V iii
                  25
                  King Henry V I i 35-7
                  Othello II iii 293-4
    Shelley   *Prometheus Unbound* I 326-8
             Queen Mab iv 194-6
             Revolt of Islam 417-20,
             4288-92

Spenser   *Faerie Queene* I vii 17, II xii
           23, VI xii 32

Hydrus   A water-snake whose venom causes
dropsy.

Hylas   A beautiful youth taken onto the
Argo by *Hercules* (who loved him) who
drowned while fetching water. The water-
nymphs were said to have desired him and
stolen him from Hercules, who abandoned the
Argonauts' expedition to search for him.
                (Apollodorus I ix 19; Theocritus
                Idyll xiii; Virgil *Eclogue* vi 43-4)
See also *Hilas*
    Milton   *Paradise Regained* ii 350-3
    Pope   *Autumn* 5-6, 15-16
    Spenser   *Faerie Queene* III xii 7, IV x 27

Hyleus   A hunter killed by the Calydonian
Boar.
                        (Apollodorus I viii 2)
    Swinburne   *Atalanta in Calydon* 1267

Hymen, Hymenaeus   The god of Marriage,
son of *Bacchus* and *Venus* or of *Apollo*. One
story· is that Hymen fell in love above his
station, disguised himself as a woman in a
female procession in order to accompany his
beloved, and killed pirates who assaulted the
women. The women were enslaved but in
Athens he promised to restore their freedom
in return for the privilege of marrying whom
he liked, a plea which was granted. Hymen
may be described as having flowers, a nuptial
torch and a purple gown. He was invoked at
weddings as his presence was felt to confer
success on the marriage. The Hymenean in-
vocation was *Hymen, Io Hymen*, found in
several epithalamia. Where the marriage was
ill-omened or to be followed by early death,
Hymen's torch was unlit or guttered.
            (Ovid *Metamorphoses* x 6-7, xii 213-7;
                            Catullus *Epithalamion*)
See also *Ismeneus*
    Burns   *To R.G. of F.* 29-30
    Chapman   *Hymn to Hymen*
              Hero and Leander v
    Collins   *On the Use and Abuse of*
              Poetry 14
              Written on a Paper 9
    Cowper   *Anti-Thelyphthera* 199-202

Herrick   *Epithalamie* 41-50
Housman   *Epithalamium* 1-4
Keats   *Otho the Great* I i 132-4
Marlowe   *Edward II* 467-70
           Massacre at Paris 58-9
Milton   *Epitaph on the Marchioness*
           of Winchester 17-22
           L'Allegro 125-6
           Paradise Lost xi 589-91
Pope   *Chorus to Brutus* ii 21-4
Prior   *To the Earl of Dorset* 41-4
Shakespeare   *As You Like It* V iv 135-8
           Tempest IV i 22-3, 92-4
Shelley   *Oedipus Tyrannus* I i 282-6
Spenser   *Epithalamion* 25-9, 140, 146,
           255-7
           Faerie Queene I i 48
Swift   *Strephon and Chloe* 47-52

Hymenean, Hymeneus
See *Hymen*
    Marvell   *Upon the Death of Lord*
               Hastings 43-6
    Milton   *Paradise Lost* iv 709-11

Hymettus, Hymettian   A mountain two
miles south east of Athens, known for its
honey.
    Browning E. B.   *Wine of Cyprus* 7
    Browning R.   *Aeschylus' Soliloquy*
                   84-90
    Byron   *Curse of Minerva* 33-4
               Don Juan xv 73
    Coleridge *To Sheridan* 4
    MacNeice   *Flowers in the Interval* i
    Milton   *Paradise Regained* iv 247-9
    Moore   *Evenings in Greece* 451-5
    Swinburne *Song for the Centenary of*
               Landor 15
    Thomson   *Liberty* ii 138-40

Hyperbolus   An Athenian tyrant of the 5th
Century BC. He ostracised (banished for ten
years) *Alcibiades* and Nicias, but was himself
ostracised by them when they united against
him.
    Cleveland   *The Rebel Scot* 115-6

Hyperion   The *Titan* Hyperion, son of
Uranus (*Coelus*) and *Ge* (*Terra*), married his
sister *Thea* (or Euryphaëssa) to produce *Eos*
(*Aurora* — dawn), *Helios* (*Sol* — sun) and

Selene (*Luna* — moon). Hyperion is often regarded as the sun personified. He was among the Titans expelled by *Zeus* and imprisoned in *Tartarus* for usurping and castrating their father Uranus. The Titans were led by *Chronos* (*Saturn*).

          (Hesiod *Theogony* 371-4;
          Homeric Hymn *To Helios* (31))

Bridges	*Prometheus the Firegiver* 234-9, 632-6
Chapman	*Shadow of Night*
Gray	*Hymn to Ignorance* 11
	Progress of Poesy 53
Keats	*Hyperion*
	The Fall of Hyperion
Shakespeare	*Hamlet* III iv 55-63
	King Henry V IV i 263-73
	Titus Andronicus V ii 54-7
Spenser	*Faerie Queene* I ii 7, I xi 31, II iii 1, vi 31, xi 9, III iv 60
	Muiopotmos 49-52
Tennyson	*Lucretius* 124-6

Hypermnestra A daughter of Danaus, an early king of *Argos* who came from Egypt. He had fifty daughters, and his brother *Aegyptus*, with whom he constantly quarrelled, had fifty sons. They intermarried, Hypermnestra marrying *Lynceus*. Danaus disapproved of the arrangement and ordered the daughters to kill their husbands. Hypermnestra helped Lynceus escape and they were eventually reconciled to Danaus and inherited his kingdom; or, alternatively, Lynceus killed Danaus.

    (Apollodorus ii 1-2; Ovid *Heroides* xiv)
See also *Hypermystra*, Danaides, *Ypermestre*

Hyponeo A *Nereid*.
    Spenser   *Faerie Queene* IV xi 51

Hypsiphil
See *Hypsipyle*
    Spenser   *Faerie Queene* II x 57

Hypsipyle The Queen of *Lemnos*, during whose reign *Venus* commanded that the Lemnian women should kill all the menfolk, because her altar had been neglected. Hypsipyle spared her father, *Thoas*, by setting him afloat to sea or hiding him in a chest (or both). *Jason* and the *Argonauts* arrived at Lemnos and Jason fell in love with Hypsipyle, but was obliged to leave her in his quest for the Fleece. She had twin sons by him. It then became known that Hypsipyle had spared her father and the jealous women reacted in fury and sold her as a slave, or pirates captured her and sold her. She was bought by King *Lycurgus* of Nemea.

          (Apollodorus I ix 17, III vi 4)
See also *Archemorus, Hypsiphil, Isiphile, Ysiphele*

Hyrcania, Hyrcanian A Parthian country in the region of modern Turkmen, U.S.S.R. It was traditionally associated with the mountainous wildness of the Caucasus on the opposite side of the Caspian Sea (Hyrcanum Mare); but it began to be known during the Roman Empire as being in fact fertile, temperate in climate, and not notably hilly. Poetically, it was known for bears and a strange breed of luminous bird.

        (Pliny x 47; Strabo I ii, II i, XI vii;
        Virgil *Aeneid* IV 365ff)

Daniel	*Restore thy Tresses* 12-13
Marlowe	*Tamburlaine* ii 4101-2
Milton	*Paradise Regained* iii 317-8
Moore	*Dream of Antiquity* 52-6
Noyes	*Black Bill's Honeymoon* i
Scott	*From 'Waverley'*
Shakespeare	*King Henry VI pt 3* I iv 154-5
	Macbeth III iv 100-3
Shelley	*Ode to Liberty* 106-9

Hyrcanus II High Priest of the Jews, 78-40BC. Hyrcanus was in and out of office several times, according to how the political wind blew from Rome. When in his seventies, he was captured by the Parthians and his ears were cut off to prevent him from holding priestly office again. After a time in exile in Babylon, he was allowed to return to Jerusalem, but was executed for treason in 30BC.
    Milton   *Paradise Regained* iii 363-7

Iaccho, Iacchus A name for *Bacchus* (*Dionysus*) suggesting the noisy shouts of the Bacchanals.
    Arnold   *Bacchanalia* 28-31

The Strayed Reveller 276-80
Herrick   Hymn to Bacchus 1-2
Lawrence   Late at Night 21ff

Iapetus
See *Japetus*
Bridges   *Prometheus the Firegiver*
           632-6
Keats   *Hyperion* ii 44-8

Iarbas, Iarbus   A king of Gaetulia who sold *Dido* the land on which to build Carthage, and was displaced as her lover by *Aeneas*. His being loved by Dido's sister, Anna, is a non-Classical addition.
(Virgil *Aeneid* iv)
Marlowe   *Dido Queen of Carthage*
           1077-9, 1105ff, 1137ff

Iberia, Iberian   A country between *Colchis* and *Albania*, within which was much of the Caucasus range of mountains. It was thickly wooded and is often referred to as dark. It was invaded by *Pompey* in 65BC but never became part of the Roman Empire.
Keats   *Otho the Great* V 5 120-5
Milton   *Paradise Regained* iii 317-8

Icarus   The son of *Dedalus* who, escaping from King *Minos* of *Crete* on wings of wax and feathers, flew too near the sun and caused his wings to melt, when he fell into the Aegean Sea.
See also *Daedalus, Ycarus*
Keats   *Endymion* iv 441-4
Marlowe   *Dido Queen of Carthage*
           1651ff
Shakespeare *King Henry VI pt 1* IV vi
           54-6, *pt 3* V vi 21-6

Ida (1)   A mountain in *Crete* where *Jupiter* was said to have been brought up in secret by the *Corybantes* to save him from death at the hand of *Saturn*, who reigned there in a prior golden age.
(Virgil *Aeneid* iii 104;
Propertius III 13, 25ff)
Arnold   *The Youth of Nature* 75-8
Bridges   *Prometheus the Firegiver*
           206-11
Keats   *A Hermes Once* 7-12
           Endymion ii 761

Meredith   *Swathed in Mist*
Milton   *Il Penseroso* 28-30
           Paradise Lost i 514-5
Wordsworth *The Triad* 8-14

Ida (2)   A range of mountains in *Mysia*, near *Troy*. Here was held the Judgment of *Paris* between the beauty of *Juno, Minerva* and *Venus*, the winner receiving the golden apple thrown in by *Eris*, Goddess of Discord. It was famed also as the birthplace of *Aeneas*, as one of the homes of the *Muses*, as a centre for worship of *Cybele*, and for the many rivers flowing into it. In poetry it may be confused with Mt *Ida (1)* in *Crete*, after which it may have been named and which was associated with *Rhea* (sometimes identified with Cybele).
(Euripides *Andromache* 274ff;
Strabo xiii i 43)
Arnold   *Youth of Nature* 75-8
Byron   *Age of Bronze* 13-18
Fletcher G. *Christ's Victory on Earth* 40
Milton   *Paradise Lost* v 380-2
Noyes   *Mount Ida* 2-3, 85-8
Spenser   *Faerie Queene* II xii 52, III ix
           36
           Shepherd's Calendar, July
           57-60, 145-8
Swinburne *Athens* ep. ii
Tennyson   *Ilion, Ilion* 3-6
           Oenone 1-2
Thomson   *Summer* 1305-6

Idaean
See *Ida (2)*
Shelley   *Prometheus Unbound* III i 25-6
Spenser   *Faerie Queene* II vii 55, viii 6

Idalia, Idalian   Of Idalium or Idalus; Idalium was a town at the foot of Mount Idalus in Cyprus. The mountain was sacred to *Venus*.
(Virgil *Aeneid* i 680-2, x 86)
Gray   *Progress of Poetry* 27-8
Jonson   *To Mary, Lady Worth* 11-14
Marvell   *Upon Appleton House* 753ff
Pope   *Spring* 65-8
Tennyson   *Oenone* 170-1
Wordsworth *The Triad* 112-4

Idas   An *Argonaut* and Calydonian Boar hunter, who in later life killed *Castor*.
(Apollodorus I viii, III iii)

See also *Dioscuri*
   Swinburne   *Atalanta in Calydon* 1265

Ide
See *Ida (2)*
   Donne   *Elegy* viii 15-16

Ides
See *Idus*
   Shakespeare   *Julius Caesar* I ii 17; III i 1;
                   IV iii 7; V i 114

Idomeneus   Successor to *Deucalion* on the
Cretan throne, and a doughty hero for the
Greeks in the Trojan War. Vowing to *Neptune*
that he would offer up the first human who
crossed his path on a successful return from
Troy, he committed himself to sacrifice his
own son, a vow which he carried out and
which appalled his people, who sent him to
exile.
                   (Apollodorus *Epitome* vi 10;
         Homer *Iliad*; Virgil *Aeneid* iii 122 ff)
   Jonson   *Epistle to Elizabeth* 51ff
   Meredith   *Idomeneus*

Idus   The 15th day of March, May, July or
October, and the 13th of other months. The
word probably refers to moonlight. *Caesar*
was murdered on the Ides of March, 44 BC.
See also *Ides*
   Chaucer   *Squire's Tale* 47

Ierne   Ireland, regarded by the ancient
Greeks as remote and uninhabitable.
                   (Strabo i 2)
   Shelley   *Adonais* 268-9
   Swift   *Ode to the King* 99-100
            *Verses on the Drying Up of
            St Patrick's Well* 5-6

Iliad, Iliades   With the *Odyssey*, the major
works attributed to *Homer*, and dating perhaps
from the 8th Century BC. The *Iliad* treats of
the Trojan War, principally as it concerns the
Greek hero *Achilles*. The title refers to *Ilium*,
the name of *Troy* or its fortress, after an early
king Ilus.
   Daniel   *Civil Wars* v 5
            Read in My Face 1-2
   Drayton   *The Owl* 969-74

Ilion
See *Ilium*
   Byron   *Childe Harold* i 45
   Chaucer   *Man of Law's Tale* 288-93
            House of Fame 158-61
   Drayton   *The Barons' Wars* vi 69
   Keats   *King Stephen* I ii 20-2
   Marlowe   *Tamburlaine* ii 4090-2
   Shakespeare   *Rape of Lucrece* 1366-72
   Spenser   *Faerie Queene* III ix 34, IV i 22
   Tennyson   *Ilion, Ilion* 3-6
            Tithon 53
            To Virgil i

Ilissus   A river near *Athens*, close to which
was a temple to the *Muses*.
See also *Ilyssus*
   Browning R.   *Aeschylus' Soliloquy*
                   84-90
   Burns   *To W. S. . . . . n*
   Collins   *Epistle to Thomas Hanmer*
            33-4
            Ode to Pity 13-15
   Gray   *Progress of Poesy* 68
   Milton   *Paradise Regained* iv 249-50
   Wordsworth   *Dion* 42-3

Ilium   A fortress in *Troy*, or the town in a
country called Troy, built by Ilus, king of
Troy (which was named after his father, Tros).
Ilium is usually taken to mean the city of Troy.
                   (Strabo xiii 24-7)
See also *Ilion*, *Ylion*
   Marlowe   *Doctor Faustus* 1328-31
   Milton   *Paradise Lost* i 577-9
   Shenstone   *Economy* iii 123-8

Imaus   Part of Mount *Taurus (2)*, a mountain
range stretching from Asia Minor to Iran (the
Himalayas) and seen as the backbone of Asia.
   Milton   *Paradise Lost* iii 431-2

Imeneus
See *Hymen*
   Chaucer   *Legend of Good Women*
            2244-50
            Troilus and Criseyde iii
            1254-8

Inachus   Son of *Oceanus* and *Tethys*, and
father of *Io*, Inachus was a river god and legendary founder of *Argos*.

	(Apollodorus II i 3)
Bridges	*Prometheus the Firegiver* 90-7
Drayton	*Polyolbion* xx 173-6
Spenser	*Faerie Queene* II ix 56-7, IV xi 15
	Tears of the Muses 447-8

Inarime
See *Ischia*

| Shelley | *Ode to Naples* 43-6 |

Ino
See *Leucothea*

Bridges	*Prometheus the Firegiver* 931-6
Cowley	*Pindaric Ode* 3
Spenser	*Faerie Queene* IV xi 13, V *Prologue* 5, viii 47

Io   A priestess of *Hera* (*Juno*) at *Argos*, Io was courted in her dreams by *Zeus*. In obedience to the Delphic Oracle, which had been consulted as to the import of the dreams, her father *Inachus* exiled her. She was then either changed into a cow by Hera to save her from Zeus, or she was so changed by Zeus to conceal her from Hera. Hera received the cow as a present from Zeus, and put it under the guard of many-eyed *Argus*, from which it was released by *Hermes*, for Zeus. Further to frustrate Zeus, Hera arranged for a fly to sting the cow. Under this stimulus it began protracted wanderings until it reached *Memphis*, on the Nile, where Zeus restored it to human form. Io then gave birth to a son, Epaphus. She subsequently married King Telegonus and was concerned with the early worship of Demeter.
(Aeschylus *Suppliant Women*, *Prometheus Bound* 561ff; Apollodorus II i 3; Ovid *Metamorphoses* i 583ff)

Browning E. B.	*Aurora Leigh* vii 827ff
Daniel	*Complaint of Rosalind* 409-13
Drayton	*The Barons' Wars* vi 35 *Rosamond and Henry IInd* 163-6
Keats	*As Hermes Once* 7-12
Lovelace	*Amarantha* 105-10
Marlowe	*Hero and Leander* i 386ff *Tamburlaine* ii 2527-30
Shakespeare	*Taming of the Shrew, Induction* 52-3
Shelley	*Oedipus Tyrannus* I i 152-3

| Sidney | *Arcadia* viii 13-14 |
| Suckling | *The Metamorphosis* 1-4 |

Iola, Iole   Daughter of *Eurytus* of Oechalia, who promised her to anyone who could beat him at archery. *Hercules* beat him, but he refused to honour the bargain. Hercules later killed Eurytus and took Iole as his mistress. It was this that caused Hercules's wife, *Deianeira*, to send him the poisoned robe which killed him.
(Apollodorus II vi 1, vii 7)
See also *Nessus*, *Yole*

| Spenser | *Faerie Queene* V v 24 (mistaken for 'Omphale') |

Ione   One of the *Nereids*.
(Apollodorus I ii 6)

| Shelley | *Prometheus Unbound* I 221-5, II i 43-7, III iii 26-7 |

Ionia, Ionian   A country of Asia Minor, between *Caria* and *Lydia* on the Aegean. It was held to have been colonised by Greek refugees. By the 8th Century BC the Ionians were a powerful and cultured people, identified in the East as 'Greek' (though according to Genesis they were descended from Noah). In the 5th Century they were overcome by Lydia and Persia, after which they were freed but in due course subjugated by the Greeks.
(Herodotus i 145-8)

Drayton	*Endymion and Phoebe* 1ff
Eliot T. S.	*The Waste Land* 263-5
Keats	*Endymion* i 308-11, ii 358-63
Milton	*Paradise Lost* i 508-10
Shelley	*Epipsychidion* 422-8, 541-2 *Ode to Liberty* 103-5 *Oedipus Tyrannus* II ii 103-7
Tennyson	*Palace of Art* 137-40

Iopas   One of the suitors of *Dido* when *Aeneas* arrives at Carthage, Iopas entertains the company with philosophic songs. He had been taught his art by *Atlas*.
(Virgil *Aeneid* i 740ff)
See *Jopas*

| Skelton | *Garland of Laurel* |

Iphicles, Iphiclus   Iphiclus was the first-born half-brother of *Hercules*; *Alcmena* was his mother and *Amphitryon* was his father (whilst the father of Hercules was *Zeus* disguised as Amphitryon). He was terrified by the snakes (which Hercules strangled) sent to visit their crib by *Juno*, who was jealous of Hercules as an illegitimate child of her husband. By this fear Iphiclus revealed that he was of less than divine parentage, and it was also said that Amphitryon had put the snakes there to discover which boy was his. Iphiclus was at enmity with Hercules and took part in the *Calydonian Boar Hunt*, but little is recorded of him.

(Apollodorus II iv 8-9)
Herrick *The Welcome to Sack* 49-50
Swinburne *Atalanta in Calydon* 1258

Iphigenia Daughter of *Agamemnon* and *Clytemnestra*, or of *Theseus* and *Helen*. Agamemnon offended *Artemis/Diana* by killing her favourite stag. Therefore the Greeks, heading for *Troy* and becalmed by Diana, were not released until Iphigenia had been sacrificed to the goddess. Agamemnon was persuaded by *Ulysses* and others to comply with this condition, and the scene was set for the sacrifice, but Iphigenia miraculously vanished as *Calchas* raised the sacrificial knife; a remarkable stag appeared and was slaughtered instead, ending the calm. It was said that Iphigenia's innocence had moved Diana, and Iphigenia became a priestess of Artemis, in which role she came very close to killing her brother *Orestes*. A trilogy on the story of Iphigenia was the last work of *Euripides*.

(Euripides *Iphigenia at Aulis*;
Ovid *Metamorphoses* xii 31)
Browning E. B. *Aurora Leigh* ii 779-82
Browning R. *Aristophanes' Apology* 314-6
Marlowe *Jew of Malta* 174-6
Masefield *Clytemnestra* 31ff
Surrey *When Raging Love* 7-12
Tennyson *Dream of Fair Women* 105-12

Iphimedia A daughter of Triops, King of *Argos*. Iphimedia fell in love with *Neptune*, by whom she had two giant sons, Otus and Ephialtes, known as the Aloides (since their supposed father was Aloeus, who married Iphimedia). The Aloides piled up the hills to assault heaven but were killed by *Apollo*.

(Apollodorus I vii 4;
Diodorus Siculus v 50f)
See also *Pelion*
Spenser *Faerie Queene* III xi 42

Iphis A lowly-born youth of *Salamis* who fell deeply in love with *Anaxarete*, a type of the hard-hearted beloved. When she refused him and mocked him, he hanged himself from her doorpost and she was turned to stone as she watched his funeral procession.

(Ovid *Metamorphoses* xiv 698ff)
Lovelace *Princess Louisa Drawing* 22-5

Ipocras
See *Hippocrates*
Chaucer *The Book of the Duchess* 568-73

Ipolita
See *Hippolyta*
Chaucer *Anelida and Arcite* 36-42

Ipomedon
See *Hippomedon*
Chaucer *Anelida and Arcite* 57-63

Ipsithilla The subject of some of *Catullus*'s most seductive verses.

(Catullus, Carmina xxxii)
Swinburne *Dolores* 326ff

Irassa A Libyan town near Lake *Tritonis* (modern Nefta).

(Pindar *Pythian Ode* ix 106)
Milton *Paradise Regained* iv 562-6

Irene
See *Eirene, Hours*
Jonson *A Panegyre* 20-7

Iris An *Oceanid*, messenger to *Juno*. Her job was to sever at death the thread holding the soul and body together. She was identified with the rainbow and is depicted with many-coloured wings. She was also said to provide the clouds with water.

(Ovid *Metamorphoses* i 271ff;
Virgil *Aeneid* iv 694)
Keats *Endymion* iii 850-4
Marlowe *Hero and Leander* i 149-50

Milton   *Comus* 82-4, 992-9
           Paradise Lost xi 240-4
Shakespeare   *All's Well That Ends Well*
           I iii 141-3
           Tempest IV i 76-81
Shelley   *Orpheus* 80
           Triumph of Life 356-9, 440
Spenser   *Faerie Queene* III xi 47
           Muiopotmos 88-96
Tennyson   *The Princess* iii 10-11
Young   *Night Thoughts* ii

Irus   An Ithacan beggar, also known as Ar-
naeus, who begged of the suitors of *Penelope*,
and threatened *Odysseus* when he came home
disguised as a beggar. In the ensuing contest
Irus was felled and disgraced by Odysseus.
           (Homer *Odyssey* xviii 1-116)
Spenser   *Tears of the Muses* 447-8

Ischia   An island in the Bay of Naples, a
centre of trade with Etruria and a source of
clay for pottery. It was also called *Inarime*,
and under it *Zeus* imprisoned *Typhoeus*. A
third name for island and city was *Pithecusa*.
           (Virgil *Aeneid* ix 715-6)

Isiphile
See *Hypsipyle*
Chaucer   *House of Fame* 397-404

Isis   Isis — Egyptian Goddess of the Earth
and wife (in some versions also sister) of
Osiris — assembled the dead king's mutilated
body and initiated his worship. Being comp-
lementary to Osiris, who was represented by
an ox, Isis is associated with cows, and was a
goddess of agriculture and fertility. She is also
seen as moon to Osiris's sun, and aspects of
her wide significance correspond with that of
Venus, *Minerva*, *Demeter* and *Cybele* in other,
partly derivative, Classical mythology.
See also *Yside*
Herrick   *Love Perfumes* 5-8
           Song to the Maskers
Lawrence   *Don Juan* 1-2
Milton   *Paradise Lost* i 477-9
Shakespeare   *Antony and Cleopatra* I v
           70-2; III vi 16-18
Spenser   *Faerie Queene* V vii 2-3

Ismena, Ismene   Daughter of *Oedipus* and

sister of *Antigone*. When Antigone was condemned to death by *Creon* for burying *Polyneices*, Ismena offered to link her lot with her.
           (Sophocles *Antigone*)
Prior   *Epilogue to Phaedra* 11-13

Ismenian   'Theban' — named after the River
Ismenus near *Thebes*.
Milton   *Paradise Regained* iv 572-6

Ismenus   A river in Boeotia, near *Thebes*.
Cowley   *Complaint* 1

Isocrates   Athenian orator (436-338BC)
whose political comment on his age (in written
speeches) and system of rhetoric (taught at
his school in Athens) were both influential,
though as a public speaker he was noted for
his ineffectiveness. His training had been partly
abroad, for he was of a rich family and his
associates included critics of Athenian society.
He was a friend of Philip of Macedon, but distrusted his ambition. When Philip conquered
Athens (at Cheronea, 338BC) Isocrates was
said to have starved himself in protest and to
have died within the week. The style of Isocrates is famed for studied smoothness and
intricate sentences. His *Panegyricus*, a speech
advocating invasion of Persia in 380BC, was
reputed to have taken ten years to compose.
Browning R.   *Ring and the Book* IX
           1570-2
Milton   *Sonnet* 10

Isse   A shepherdess beloved by *Apollo*, who
changed himself into a shepherd to court her.
           (Ovid *Metamorphoses* vi 124)
Spenser   *Faerie Queene* III xi 38-9

Ister   The modern River Danube.
Spenser   *Faerie Queene* IV xi 20

Ithaca   An island in the Ionian Sea, south-
west of Greece. It was the home of *Ulysses*
(*Odysseus*) and *Penelope*, but has no other
Classical association.
Herrick   *Welcome to Sack* 15-17

Ithacensian   Of *Ithaca*.
Tennyson   *The Princess* iv 99-101

Itylus   Itylus or Itys was the son of *Procne*

and Tereus, and *Tereus* was made by Procne
to eat Itylus.
See also *Daulis, Philomela*

   Swinburne   *Itylus* 45-8
                 Atalanta in Calydon 70

Iulo
See *Iulus*

   Chaucer   *The House of Fame* 174-88

Iulus   The son (also known as *Ascanius*) of
Aeneas by *Creusa (2)*. He was saved from the
flames of Troy by Aeneas and accompanied
him to Latium, where he distinguished himself in the War. He succeeded Aeneas as king
and built *Alba* Longa, leaving his name for the
Julian line of Roman Emperors.

              (Livy I iii; Virgil *Aeneid*)
   Spenser   *Faerie Queene* III ix 43

Ivy
See *Dionysus*

Ixion   A King of *Thessaly*. He married Dia,
but did not produce to her father, Eioneus,
the present he had promised. Eioneus took
some of Ixion's horses as security, at which
Ixion swore to satisfy him if he paid a personal
call; Eioneus did so and was murdered in a
burning pit. Ixion could find no one to purify
him of this crime and *Zeus* (who perhaps loved
Ixion's wife) compassionately invited him to
Olympus. True to form, Ixion tried to seduce
Hera, but was tricked by Zeus who arranged
for a cloud to appear as substitute; from this
cloud was born *Centaurus*. Ixion was banished
from heaven and sentenced to be tied to a
burning and spinning wheel in *Hades*.

         (Apollodorus *Epitome* i 20;
            Diodorus Siculus iv 69;
          Pindar *Pythian Ode* ii 21-48)
See also *Centaurs*

   Browning R.   *Ixion* 1-4
   Chaucer   *Troilus and Criseyde* v 211-2
   Denham   *Progress of Learning* 161ff
   Fletcher P.   *Purple Island* v 64
   Henryson   *Orpheus and Eurydice* 496ff
   Herrick   *To Electra* 9-10
   Keats   *Hyperion* i 28-30
   Kinglsey   *Frank Leigh's Song* 11-12
   Lovelace   *Advice to My Best Brother*
              25-6

              Against the love of Great Ones
                10-14
   Marlowe   *Hero and Leander* i 114
   Marvell   *Tom May's Death* 90-7
   Pope   *Ode for Musick* 66-70
   Shelley   *Letter to Maria Gisborne* 22-4
   Skelton   *Garland of Laurel*
   Spenser   *Faerie Queene* I v 35
              Mutability Cantos VI 29
   Tennyson   *Lucretius* 259-64
              The Two Voices 194-5

Janus   The Roman god of doors, gates and
the beginnings of things, supposed to have
introduced agriculture to Italy. He was thought
to be a son of *Apollo* or of *Coelus* and *Hecate*,
and is shown with two or four faces looking
in different directions and often holding a key.
His temple was open in times of war and closed
(very seldom) in times of peace. Janus has an
analogue in Noah, who was regarded sometimes as the first priest and looked two ways,
to before and after the Flood.

     (Ovid *Fasti* i 65; Virgil *Aeneid* 607-10)
   Byron   *On Hearing that Lady Byron*
              was Ill 52-3
   Chaucer   *Troilus and Criseyde* ii 77
   Cowley   *To the New Year* 1
   Donne   *Progress of the Soul* 21-2
   Dryden   *To My Dear Friend (Congreve)*
              6-8
   Fletcher G.   *Christ's Triumph after*
              Death 23
   Herbert   *Church Militant* 205-7
   Jonson   *A New Year's Gift* 9-10
   Marlowe   *Tamburlaine* ii 3080-3
   Marvell   *Upon the Death of the Lord*
              Protector 232-7
   Milton   *Paradise Lost* xi 127-9
   Prior   *Carmen Seculare* 1, 318-9
              To the Earl of Dorset 38-40
   Shakespeare   *Merchant of Venice* I i 50-1
              Othello I ii 33
   Shelley   *Triumph of Life* 93-5
   Spenser   *Amoretti* 4
   Swift   *Stella's Birthday (1726-7)* 73-6
              To Janus on New Year's Day 1
   Wordsworth   *Excursion* ii 251

Japet, Japetus   A *Titan*, son of *Chronos* and

Ge, and father of *Atlas*, *Prometheus* and *Epimetheus*, whose mothers vary according to different accounts. For the Greeks he was the father of mankind by Prometheus. Iapetus was imprisoned in *Tartarus* when *Zeus* defeated the Titans.

(Hesiod *Theogony* 132-6, 507-14;
Apollodorus i 2)

Japhet A traditional identification of the Son of Noah with *Japetus*.

Milton *Paradise Lost* iv 714-9

Jarre
See *Eris*

Spenser *Faerie Queene* II iv 41

Jason The leader of the *Argonauts*, great-grandson of *Aeolus*, Jason was brought up in secret. He was the son of *Aeson*, who lived powerless in Iolchus, *Thessaly*, where the throne had been usurped by his half-brother *Pelias*. Pelias had been warned that he would eventually be overthrown by a man with only one sandal. When he was twenty-one, Jason attended an annual festival of Pelias, thinking to declare his own right to the throne. On the way he had to carry an old woman (*Hera*, who had scorned Pelias and was about to punish him) over a river and lost a sandal in doing so; Pelias recognised the omen and sought to dispose of Jason, so he accepted Jason's boast that he would bring back the *Golden Fleece*, from *Colchis*, an apparently impossible task. *Medea*, the sorceress, was princess of Colchis and Jason believed that her assistance was necessary to overthrow Pelias. He and she fell in love, the Fleece was captured after various fanciful trials (set by its guardian *Aetes*) had been performed with the help of Medea's magic, and Jason and Medea returned to Iolchus. (Meanwhile Jason had enjoyed an affair with *Hypsiphile*, who bore him twin sons.) In Iolchus Aeson had either been poisoned by Pelias or become very decrepit, and he was restored to youth by Medea; Iolchus, because Jason's men were too few, was captured with the help of Medea, who persuaded the daughters of Pelias to kill him. Perhaps because of this deed, Jason did not rule here — the throne passed to Pelias's son Acastus, and Jason and Medea settled in Corinth. Jason possibly left

Medea for *Creusa (1)*, *Creon* of Corinth's daughter. Medea killed Creusa by means of a robe that caught fire when worn. She also killed Creon and her own children by Jason.

(Apollonius Rhodius; Apollodorus i 9;
Euripides *Medea*;
Ovid *Metamorphoses* vii 1ff)

See also *Absyrtus*, *Argo*, *Bisaltes*, *Phrixus*
— *General*

Chaucer *Book of the Duchess* 326-34
Squire's Tale 547-54
Legend of Good Women
1368-70, 1396-402
— *the Fleece and the Argonauts*
Browning E. B. *The Claim* 3
Chaucer *Legend of Good Women*
1425ff, 1453-7, 1542-7,
1589ff, 1598ff
Cowley *On Dr Harvey* 5
Denham *On Abraham Cowley* 34-40
Progress of Learning 20-1
Jonson *Alchemist* I i
Keats *Fragment of 'The Castle-Builder'*
62-3
Marlowe *Hero and Leander* i 55-8
Jew of Malta 1808-11
Tamburlaine i 1646-7
Prior *Down Hall* 1-4
On Beauty 10ff
Shakespeare *Merchant of Venice* I i
169-72
Spenser *Faerie Queene* II xii 44-5
Swift *A Motto* 1-4
*Verses on the Drying Up of
St Patrick's Well* 7-8
Swinburne *Atalanta in Calydon* 1263
*Ballad Against the Enemies
of France* 1-2
— *Medea and the Children*
Chaucer *Book of the Duchess* 725-31
*Man of Law's Tale, Intro-
duction* 72-4
MacNeice *Autumn Sequel* xi
Spenser *Faerie Queene* II xii 44-5
— *and Hypsipyle*
Chaucer *Legend of Good Women*
263-6, 1559-63, 1598ff,
1634ff
House of Fame 397-404

Jocasta
See *Oedipus*

Collins *Ode to Fear* 38-9
Herrick *To Myrrha Hard-Hearted* 3-4
Swinburne *Athens* ep. ii

Jopas
See *Iopas*
Wyatt *Jopas' Song* 1-4

Jove The English and Latin words (Jove, Iovis) are related to Yaweh (Jehovah), the Hebrew name for omnipotent God; so also are *Jupiter* (*Iovis pater*), *Zeus* and *Ju-* or *Jo-* (*Dieu*). Whilst original distinctions between these various names for an Almighty have always been defended, the English 'Jove', Latin 'Iove' or 'Jupiter' and Greek 'Zeus' are for most purposes the same, and 'Jove' means the Classical Almighty. Its use is very wide and in most cases of no special significance. Therefore only a selection of examples in English Poetry is given; to most of these the principal Classical myths associated with Zeus apply.
Jupiter (Zeus) was son of *Saturn* (*Chronos*) and *Ops* (*Rhea*). Chronos swallowed his male children, because he held the throne of the world on the condition of not having a son. Rhea, however, preserved Zeus (and possibly others — accounts vary) when born by substituting a dressed-up stone, which Chronos swallowed instead. She hid Zeus in a cave on Mt *Dicte* or Mt *Ida* in Crete, where he was nourished on goats' milk by *Amalthea*, and brought up by the *Corybantes*. Later, the other children similarly saved, or all the children then spewed forth by Chronos, rose up with Zeus and fought Chronos and the other *Titans* (who had in fact previously usurped the throne from *Uranus*). Zeus and his party won control of *Olympus* and the world was divided between him (earth), *Poseidon* (sea) and *Hades* (Underworld). This kingdom was soon attacked by *Giants*, offspring of *Ge* and Uranus, but they were eventually put down. *Typhoeus*, the most formidable, was crushed under Sicily. Zeus was never able to resist an attractive goddess or nymph, and the list of his conquests, some by bizarre means, is very long. It includes *Themis*, *Leto*, *Erynome*, *Hera* (his sister, *Juno*), *Io*, *Danae*, *Leda* and *Europa*. Zeus's instrument of war was the thunderbolt and his symbols were the eagle and the oak.

— *General*
Chaucer *Troilus and Criseyde* iii 1016, v 1-4, 206-10
Donne *Elegy* viii 23-4
  Love's Deity 15-16
Fletcher P. *Piscatory Eclogues* vii 20
Goldsmith *On Seeing Mrs . . . Perform the Character of . . .* 9-10, 13-14
Gray *Progress of Poetry* 20-1, 46-7
Hardy *Rome — On the Palatine* 1-2
Jonson *Sejanus* IV v
Keats *Endymion* iv 376-80, 606-8, 991-4
  Lamia i 7-11
  To Homer 5-8
Marlowe *Doctor Faustus* 104-5
  Hero and Leander i 59-65
Milton *Arcades* 43-4
  Comus 1-2, 17-21
  Il Penseroso 28-30, 47-8
  Lycidas 82-3
  Paradise Lost i 487-9, 741-2, iv 714-19, ix 395-6
Pope *Dunciad* ii 79-83, 165
  Essay on Man i 41-2
  Rape of the Lock 126-7
Shakespeare *Hamlet* III iv 55-63
  King Henry VI pt 3 V ii 11-15
  Othello III iii 358-60
  Love's Labour's Lost 111-6
  Passionate Pilgrim 16
  Pericles I i 6-9, ii 104
Shelley *Hellas* 230-4
  Letter to Maria Gisborne 22-4
  Prometheus Unbound i 448, II iv 49-52, 59-60
Southey *Thalaba* i 12
Spenser *Faerie Queene* II v 31, vi 2, 50, V i 9
  Mother Hubberd's Tale 1225-31
Tennyson *Coach of Death* 191-2
— *Chronos, Titans, Giants*
Dryden *Astraea Redux* 37-42
Keats *Hyperion* i 248-50, ii 44-8
Marlowe *Hero and Leander* i 456-8
  Tamburlaine i 2291-2
Milton *Paradise Lost* i 198, 512-4
Spenser *Mutability Cantos* vi 27

— *Birth and Upbringing*
Davies, Sir J.   *Orchestra* 523-5
Spenser   *Mutability Cantos* vii 41, 53
— *and Eagle*
Arnold   *Empedocles on Etna* II i 74-83
Browning E. B.   *The Dead Pan* 10
Keats   *Endymion* ii 473-6, 657-8, 911
Shakespeare   *Cymbeline* IV ii 349-52
Spenser   *Faerie Queene* II xi 43
          Visions of the World's Vanity
          43
— *and Thunder*
Keats   *Endymion* ii 472-6, iii 872
Milton   *Comus* 802-4
          Paradise Lost i 386-7, xi 185
Pope   *Dunciad* i 7-8
Shakespeare   *Coriolanus* III i 255-8
          Cymbeline V iv 30-4, 94-6
          King Lear II iv 225-7
          Measure for Measure II ii
          110-3
          Tempest I ii 200-5
Spenser   *Faerie Queene* I iv 11, 17, v 19,
          20, viii 9, II vi 10, IV vi 14
          Visons of the World's Vanity
          43
— *his Loves*
Browning E. B.   *Aurora Leigh* vii 827f
Chaucer   *Troilus and Criseyde* iii 722-4
Drayton   *Endymion and Phoebe* 648ff
          Fourth Eclogue 65-6
Herrick   *To Electra* 1-6
Keats   *As Hermes Once* 7-12
Marlowe   *Edward II* 474-7
          Hero and Leander i 147-8,
          149-50
Milton   *Paradise Regained* ii 213-5
Shakespeare   *Merry Wives of Windsor*
          V v 1ff
          Much Ado About Nothing
          V iv 43-7
Spenser   *Epithalamion* 305-10
          Faerie Queene III xi 30-5,
          V ix 31
          Prothalamion 37-42

Jovial, Jovian
Keats   *Endymion* iv 413-5
Shakespeare   *Cymbeline* IV ii 309-12

Julian   The Julian line of Caesars, said to
derive from *Aeneas*' son, *Iulus*.

Gray   *Agrippina* 50

Julius
See *Caesar (Gaius Julius)*
Chaucer   *Knight's Tale* 2031-5
          Man of Law's Tale 197-9,
          400-3
          Monk's Tale 3887-900
          House of Fame 1497-1502
Milton   *Paradise Regained* iii 39-42
Prior   *Carmen Seculare* 52-3
Shakespeare   *Hamlet* I i 113-6

Junia   Sister of *Brutus (3)* and wife of *Cassius*, the assassins of *Caesar*. At the funeral of
Junia, *Tiberius* refused to allow the presence
of statues of Brutus and Cassius, because of
their part in Caesar's death.
(Tacitus *Annals* iii 76)
Byron   *Don Juan* xv 49
Pope   *Chorus to 'Brutus'* ii 15-16

Juno   *Juno (Hera)* was the sister and wife
of *Jupiter (Zeus)*, being the daughter of *Saturn*
(Chronos) and *Ops (Rhea)*. Jupiter gained her
favours by taking the form of a cuckoo in cold
weather, when he was pitied by Juno and taken
in as her lover; he then revealed his true self.
In most accounts Juno had *Mars* and *Hebe* by
Jupiter, but she was much occupied by his
numerous extra-marital affairs and devoted
herself to hounding their products (such as
Hercules). She was jealous of her own beauty,
and the Judgment of *Paris* in favour of *Venus*
provoked the Trojan War and her enmity to
Aeneas and the Trojans. This hatred was intense. Jove told her that it could be satisfied
only by eating *Priam* and his offspring raw.
Juno was nonetheless widely worshipped as
the sovereign goddess, with a particular interest
in femininity, childbirth and marriage. She is
frequently accompanied by peacocks; this is
in memory of *Argus*, who was killed by *Mercury* — she had his hundred eyes set in her
peacock's tail.
(Hesiod *Theogony* 453ff, 921ff;
Homeric Hymn *To Delian Apollo (3)*
305-54; Homer *Iliad* iv 35ff;
Ovid *Metamorphoses* iii 255ff, ix 280ff;
Pausanias ii 17)
— *General*
Browning E. B.   *The Dead Pan* 11

Centuries AD. Little is known of his life, although it is likely that he was exiled, probably by *Domitian*, and he seems to have a strong sense of failure and lack of preferment. His satires are bitter and specific, though he was wary of using living targets. His work mingles the conversational and the lofty styles and he is a skilled epigrammatist.

Byron   *Don Juan* i 43
Chaucer   *Wife of Bath's Tale* 1192-4
        Troilus and Criseyde iv 197-201

Keleus
See *Celeus*
Bridges   *Demeter* 763 ff

Kronos
See *Saturn*
Southey   *Roderick* i 26-30

Labienus   Quintus Labienus after the death of *Julius Caesar* supported *Cassius* against the Triumvirate. He subsequently led a Parthian army against *Mark Antony*, overrunning Syria as far as *Lydia* and *Ionia*, and called himself the 'Parthian Emperor'. He was finally defeated by *Augustus'* general, *Ventidius*.

(Plutarch *Antony* xxxiii)
Shakespeare   *Antony and Cleopatra* I ii 97-100

Lacedaemon
See *Sparta*, *Lacedomye*
Shakespeare   *Timon of Athens* II ii 152
Spenser   *Faerie Queene* III ix 34

Lacedomye
See *Lacedaemon*
Chaucer   *Franklin's Tale* 1379-85

Lachesis
See *Fates*
Butler S.   *Upon Philip Nye* 97-100
Chapman   *Hero and Leander* vi
Chaucer   *Troilus and Criseyde* v 4-5
Spenser   *Faerie Queene* IV i 48

Ladon   A tributary of the River *Alpheus* in *Arcadia*, near which occurred the changing of *Syrinx* into a reed.

(Ovid *Metamorphoses* i 702)
Milton   *Arcades* 97
Shenstone   *Elegies* xiv 39-40
Swinburne   *Atalanta in Calydon* 46
        Song for the Centenary of Landor 29

Laertes   King of *Ithaca* and (adopted) father of *Ulysses*; Ulysses was by some accounts son of *Sisyphus* from Anticlea, whom Laertes married when she was pregnant. Laertes ceded his crown to Ulysses and retired to country gardening. In some versions he was an *Argonaut* and at the *Calydonian Boar Hunt*.

(Apollodorus I ix 16)
Milton   *Paradise Lost* ix 439-41
Swinburne   *Atalanta in Calydon* 1248
        Song for the Centenary of Landor 49

Laian, Laians   A name of *Oedipus*, after his father *Laius*, King of *Thebes*. After the usurpation of *Amphion* and Zethus, Laius was reinstated and married *Jocasta*, daughter of *Creon*. In a tragic contretemps, he was killed by his son Oedipus.
See also *Sphinx*
Shelley   *Hellas* 1080-3

Lais   A prostitute, born in Sicily but living mainly in Greece in the 4th Century BC. She charged enormous sums and was widely sought, being particularly successful in Corinth. She was eventually murdered by jealous wives in *Thessaly*.

(Ovid *Amores* I v; Plutarch *Nicias* xv)
Browning R.   *Prince Hohenstiel-Schwangau* 9 ff
Byron   *Curse of Minerva* 185 ff
Carew   *A Rapture* 115-8
Noyes   *Tales from the Mermaid* vii
Prior   *On Beauty* 10 ff

Laius   King of *Thebes* and married to *Jocasta*, who bore *Oedipus*, despite a warning to Laius that a child of his would kill him. In later life, travelling to the oracle at *Delphi*, Laius met a stranger who would not allow him passage; in the ensuing scuffle Laius was killed by the young man — Oedipus. The tragedy was variously attributed to ignoring the warning, and to his having kidnapped the young man Chrysippus, by whom he was infatuated, whilst taking refuge years before at the court of *Pelops* of Pisa.

(Apollodorus V v 5-7)

See also *Laian*

Swinburne   *Tiresias* 85-90

Lameadoun
See *Laomedon*
Chaucer   *Troilus and Criseyde* iv 120-4

Lamia, Lamiae   Monsters, half woman and half serpent, who were said to live in Africa and to devour strangers, particularly children, whom they enticed with pleasant sounds. They represented the destructive potential of female seductiveness.

(Flavius Philostratus *Life of Apollonius* iv;
Horace *Art of Poetry* 340)

See also *Lycius (Mennipus)*
Keats   *Lamia* i 146-9, 185-90, 216-9,
304-6, 324-7, ii 296-300

Laocoon   A Trojan priest of *Apollo* or *Poseidon*, who attempted to dissuade the Trojans from bringing the fateful wooden horse, which they worshipped, into *Troy*, and flung a spear at it. For this, or for some offence to Apollo or Poseidon, his two sons were killed by sea-serpents which appeared as he sacrificed a bullock to Poseidon, and Laocoon died in extreme agony as he tried to save them. It was Laocoon who 'feared the Greeks even when bearers of gifts', a now proverbial line from the *Aeneid*. Laocoon's story is enshrined in marble statuary in the Vatican.

(Virgil *Aeneid* ii 49, 201ff;
Hyginus *Fabulae* 135)

Byron   *Childe Harold* iv 160
Hood   *The Elm Tree* 41-2
Noyes   *Drake* iii

Laodamia   A daughter of Acastus, King of Iolchus. She married *Protesilaus*, a Thessalian king, who was the first of the invading Greeks to land at *Troy* and was immediately killed by *Hector*. Laodamia so missed him that *Hermes* restored him to her for three hours, after which

Laodamia stabbed herself. Alternatively, she had a statue of him in her bed and a servant told her father that a strange man visited her; discovering the truth, Acastus burned the statue, whereupon Laodamia threw herself on the fire and died. The tomb of Protesilaus was within a long sight of Troy and some trees close by were said to grow until visible from the city, when they withered and grew up once more.

(Apollodorus *Epitome* iii 30;
Homer *Iliad* xiii 681, xv 705;
Hyginus *Fabulae* 103-4; Ovid
Metamorphoses xii 68; Pliny xvi 88)

See also *Laodomya, Laudomia*
Clough   *Amours de Voyage* iii 85-90
Wordsworth   *Laodamia* 19-24, 140-2,
155-7, 167-73

Laodomya
See *Laodamia*
Chaucer   *Franklin's Tale* 1445-7

Laomedia   A *Nereid*.
Spenser   *Faerie Queene* IV xi 51

Laomedon   The son of King Ilus of *Troy* and father of Podarces, later known as *Priam*. Laomedon built the walls of Troy with help from *Apollo* and *Neptune* but, on refusing to reward them, brought a flood and plague onto the city, for which the only appeasement was the annual sacrifice of a Trojan virgin to a sea-monster. When Laomedon's daughter, *Hesione*, was next in line for this fate, Hercules agreed to free the city of the scourge in return for a gift of fine horses, but the horses were not forthcoming. Hercules returned with an army, took the city and killed Laomedon, who was succeeded by the future Priam.

(Apollodorus II v 9; Homer *Iliad* xxi
441-60; Ovid *Metamorphoses* xi 200-30)

See also *Lameadoun*
Chaucer   *Book of the Duchess* 326-34

Lapithae   A People of *Thessaly* descended from Lapithus, a son of *Apollo* and the brother of Centaurus. At a feast to celebrate the marriage of *Pirithous* (their king, a friend of *Theseus*) they met with the *Centaurs* who, unaccustomed to wine, became drunk and assaulted the bride, Hippodamia. The Centaurs were defeated and retired to *Arcadia*. Theseus and *Nestor* were among the Lapith heroes. The true origin of the quarrel was said to be that the Lapiths omitted to invite *Mars* to the feast, and this was his revenge.

(Diodorus Siculus iv 69; Hesiod *Shield of Achilles* 178ff; Ovid *Metamorphoses* xii 210ff)
Spenser   *Faerie Queene* IV i 23, VI x 13

Lares, Lars   Roman deities presiding over private households, who were perhaps originally spirits of ancestors or local fertility spirits. They may be presented with horn and cup, symbols of fertility. The corresponding evil spirits were *Lemures*. The *Penates*, though associated more with the innermost privacy of the house, were similar to the Lares.

Marlowe   *Dido Queen of Carthage* 258-9
Milton   *On the Morning of Christ's Nativity* 191

Lartius   Titus Lartius, a Roman officer to whose charge *Cominius* entrusted the siege of Corioli in the 5th Century BC.

Shakespeare   *Coriolanus* I i 237-8, vi 36-8

Latian
See *Latium, Campania*
Gray   *Progress of Poesy* 77-8
Pope   *Temple of Fame* 205
Prior   *Carmen Seculare* 557-8
        Ode Inscribed to the Queen 281-3
Wordsworth   *River Duddon* i 1-4

Latinus   The eponymous King of *Latium*, son of *Faunus* and a nymph, Marica, and a great grandson of *Saturn*. Latinus married Amata and had a daughter, *Lavinia*, who was secretly promised by her mother to *Turnus*, king of the neighbouring Rutuli, though the oracles said that she would marry a foreign prince. They seemed on the verge of fulfilment when *Aeneas* arrived in Italy and Latinus offered him Lavinia, but Turnus disputed his claim and war broke out. Aeneas won and married Lavinia, Latinus dying soon after.

(Virgil *Aeneid*; Livy I ii)
See also *Latyne*
Dryden   *The Hind and the Panther* iii 766ff

Spenser   *Faerie Queene* III ix 42-3

Latium   Originally the land round the Alban mountain, but amalgamated with *Campania* in 292AD, Latium became the land south-west of Rome. Though naturally fertile, it became waste and depopulated owing to war and nearby Rome and was often regarded as desolate. Its capitals were, in succession, Laurentium, Lavinium and *Alba*. From the 4th Century BC Latium was regarded as an autonomous state, though it supplied manpower to Rome, but it lost this autonomy in the 1st Century BC. As the destination of *Aeneas*, and the site of Alba Longa the city built by his son, Latium was the legendary foundation of the Roman civilisation.

(Strabo V 3, VI 4; Virgil *Aeneid* vii 38f)
See also *Lavyne*
Pope   *Essay on Criticism* 709-11
Prior   *Carmen Seculare* 26-7
Spenser   *Faerie Queene* III ix 42

Latmian
See *Latmus*
Hood   *To the Moon* 20ff
Keats   *Endymion* ii 429, 1010, iii 663, iv 457

Latmus   A mountain in *Caria*, southern Turkey, famous as the site of the amours of *Diana* and *Endymion*.

Drayton   *Endymion and Phoebe* 9-14
Keats   *Endymion* i 64-5, iv 805-6, iii 449
        I Stood Tiptoe upon a Little Hill 193-204

Latona   Daughter of the *Titans Coeus* and *Phoebe*, and mother of *Apollo* and *Artemis*, Latona (*Leto*) was loved by *Zeus*. When pregnant, she wandered the country in search of a place to bear Apollo but no one would have her; they were either put off by the idea of so important a birth or unwilling to attract the hatred of *Hera*, offended as ever by her husband's love affairs. In some accounts, *Poseidon* took her to the island of *Ortygia (2)* and flooded it so that, being no longer land, it would be exempt from Hera's wrath. Leto then rather curiously gave birth up an olive tree; possibly only Artemis was born in this way, and she proceeded to help with the birth of Apollo on *Delos*. Alternatively, both children were born on Delos, which was identified with Ortygia, while Leto clung to an olive tree. Leto went on to have miscellaneous adventures, in some of which the jealous hand of Hera played its part. When Lycian peasants would not let her drink from a well, Latona turned them into frogs. She was saved from rape near *Delphi* by her children, when the Giant *Tityus* attacked her. She and Artemis supported the Trojans in the Trojan War, and healed the wounds of *Aeneas*. The name 'Latona' is sometimes used for Artemis/*Diana*.

(Apollodorus I iv 1, III x 4; Homeric Hymn
To Delian Apollo (3); Hesiod *Theogony*
404-10, 918-20; Homer *Iliad* v 447-8,
Odyssey xi 576-81; Ovid *Metamorphoses*
vi 157-381)

Chaucer	*Troilus and Criseyde* v 652ff
Fletcher P.	*Purple Island* i 47
Keats	*Endymion* i 862
	Hyperion iii 31-2
Marlowe	*Tamburlaine* i 2296
Milton	*Arcades* 20-3
	Sonnet 12
Sidney	*Arcadia* xxvi 5ff
Spenser	*Faerie Queene* II xii 13, IV vii 30, V x 7, VI ii 25
	Shepherd's Calendar, April 86-90
Swift	*To Lord Harley* 31-2

Latumyus   A name, invented or corrupted by Chaucer, for the husband whose wife or wives (accounts vary) committed suicide by hanging from a tree in the garden, so unsatisfactory was the marriage. The Arrius to whom the tale is told was a friend of *Cicero*, who seems to have originated it. Later versions use various names.

(Cicero *De Oratore* ii 69)

Chaucer	*Wife of Bath's Prologue* 757-61

Latyne
See *Latinus*
Chaucer	*House of Fame* 451-8

Laudomia
See *Laodamia*
Chaucer	*Legend of Good Women* 263-6

Lavinia   A daughter of *Latinus*, King of Latium, who was engaged to *Turnus*, King of the Rutuli, although oracles said that she would marry a foreign prince. Turnus was killed by *Aeneas* in single combat and Lavinia married the newly-arrived Aeneas. On Aeneas' death she was pregnant and retired into the woods (where she produced Aeneas Sylvius) rather than face conflict with *Ascanius*, her son-in-law. Ascanius did in fact succeed Aeneas and was himself followed by Sylvius.

(Ovid *Fasti* iv 879-80, *Metamorphoses*
xiv 451ff; Virgil *Aeneid* vii 56ff, xii)

Chaucer	*House of Fame* 451-8
Dryden	*The Hind and the Panther* iii 766ff
Marlowe	*Tamburlaine* i 2174ff
Milton	*Paradise Lost* ix 13-17

Lavyne
See *Lavinia*, *Latium*
Chaucer	*House of Fame* 143-8
	Legend of Good Women 256-60

Layus
See *Laius*
Chaucer	*Troilus and Criseyde* ii 101-2

Leander, Leandre
See *Hero*
Browning R.	*Dance of Death* 47-50
Byron	*Bride of Abydos* ii 1ff
	Written after Swimming from Sestos 1ff
Chaucer	*Man of Law's Tale, Introduction*
Cowley	*Impossibilities* 5-6
Daniel	*Most Fair and Lovely Maid* 1-2
Donne	*Epigram, Hero and Leander*
Herrick	*Leander's Obsequies* 1-4
Hood	*Hero and Leander* 45
	Love's Champion 6ff
Housman	*Tarry, Delight, So Seldom Met* 4-7
Keats	*Endymion* iii 97
	On a Leander Gem 9-11
	Woman, When I Behold Thee . . . 13-14
Kipling	*Song of Travel* 1-4
Marlowe	*Edward II* 6-9

Hero and Leander i 51-3, 55-8ff,
73-6, ii 153-8, 297-300
Moore   *Hero and Leander* vii 12
Rosetti D. G.   *Hero's Lamp* 1ff
Shakespeare   *As You Like It* IV i 90ff
Much Ado About Nothing
V ii 27ff
Two Gentlemen of Verona
I i 21-5; III i 117-20
Spenser   *Hymn in Honour of Love*
231-7
Tennyson   *Hero to Leander* 38-41

Learchus   The son, with *Melicerta*, of *Ino*.
She threw herself into the sea with Melicerta
in a bid to save him from her maddened husband *Athamas*, King of *Thebes*, who had
dashed Learchus against a wall because he
took Ino to be a lioness and her sons whelps;
this delusion had been implanted by the jealous
Juno – for Ino was descended from her rival,
Venus.
See also *Leucothea*

Leda   The daughter of King *Thestius* of
Aetolia. She married the exiled King Tyndareus of *Sparta* and bore *Helen*, *Clytemnestra*, the *Dioscuri*, Polydeuces and others.
Jupiter saw her bathing in the River *Eurotas*
when she was already pregnant; he changed
himself into a swan, who was pursued by
Venus in the form of an eagle, and was embraced by Leda. Leda in due course produced
two eggs, one of which contained *Pollux* and
Helen, children of Jupiter, and the other of
which contained *Castor* and Clytemnestra,
children of Tyndareus. Leda – because of the
fateful nature of these births – was sometimes
identified with *Nemesis*.

(Apollodorus III x 7;
Homeric Hymn *To the Dioscuri* (17))
Browning R.   *Filippo Baldinucci*
97-400
Carew   *The Comparison* 19
Davies, Sir J.   *Orchestra* 484-7
Graves   *Leda* 2-4, 9-10
Keats   *Endymion* i 157-8
*Fragment from 'The Castle-
Builder'* 65-6
Lawrence   *Leda* 1ff
Shakespeare   *Merry Wives of Windsor*
V v 1ff

Taming of the Shrew I ii 240-1
Spenser   *Faerie Queene* III xi 32
Mutability Cantos vii 34
Prothalamion 37-42
Ruins of Time 386-9
Swinburne   *Atalanta in Calydon* 411ff,
1583-7
Athens ep. ii
Thomas, Dylan   *The Morning, Space for
Leda* 1-4, 29-33
Yeats   *The Herne's Egg*
Leda and the Swan
Lullaby

Ledaen
See *Leda*
Yeats   *Among School Children* ii, iv

Lemnian
See *Lemnos*
Spenser   *Muiopotmos* 369-74
Wordsworth   *Sonnet 'When Philoctetes
. . .'* 1-4

Lemnos   An island in the north Aegean. It
was sacred to *Vulcan*, who was held to have
fallen there after his expulsion by *Jupiter*.
Milton   *Paradise Lost* i 745-6
Spenser   *Faerie Queene* IV v 4

Lemures   The evil spirits of Roman ancestors.
They were appeased or driven away in the May-
time Lemuria festival, during which temples
were closed and it was the custom to burn
black beans onto graves or to burn them with
an exorcism.

(Ovid *Fasti* v 429 f)
See also *Lares*
Milton   *On the Morning of Christ's
Nativity* 191

Lenaeus, Lenaean   A name – meaning 'wine
press' – for *Bacchus* and his festival, Lenaea.
Belloc   *In Praise of Wine* 135-8

Lentulus   Publius Cornelius Lentulus (Sura)
was a member of an important and wealthy
Roman family and became Governor of Sicily
in 74BC and consul in 71. He was expelled
from the Senate for immorality and then
joined *Catiline*'s conspiracy, with others
plotting to murder *Cicero*. He was betrayed

and executed in 63 BC. Earlier, accused by *Sulla (2)* of fraud, he refused to provide accounts and insolently extended the calf (*sura*) of his leg, on which boys were punished.

> (Plutarch *Cicero* xvii)

Diaper	*Dryades* 439-42
Jonson	*Catiline* V v
Spenser	*Faerie Queene* I v 49

Leonidas   Leader of the Spartans against *Xerxes* at *Thermopylae* in 480 BC. After initial success the Spartans were annihilated by a Persian detachment attacking from the rear. Leonidas either disbanded his troops or was deserted. Beheaded on Xerxes' orders, he was celebrated as a martyr. A stone lion was erected by the Greeks in his honour, and temples and festivals were set up in his name.

> (Herodotus vii)

Byron	*Don Juan* vii 82
Coleridge	*Destiny of Nations* 9-10
MacNeice	*Cock o' the North* i
Swinburne	*Song for the Centenary of Landor* 24
Thomson	*Winter* 453-8
Wordsworth	*Memorials of a Tour in Scotland 1814* ii 37-42

Leontium   A famous Athenian prostitute and mistress of *Epicurus*, of whom she was also a serious student.

| Moore | *The Grecian Girl's Dream* 41-2 |

Leoun
See *Nemean Lion*

| Chaucer | *Troilus and Criseyde* v 1016-9 |

Lepidus   Marcus Aemilius Lepidus was *Julius Caesar*'s chief of cavalry and, on Caesar's assassination, a consul. Thereafter he gave military support to *Antony* and was one of the Triumvirate with *Octavian* and Antony. Deposed from this office in 36 BC, he supported Octavian in a number of governorships, but was deposed by him on a (possibly trumped-up) rumour of conspiracy. Lepidus, who seems to have had a somewhat wooden personality, retired to private life and died naturally.

| Shakespeare | *Antony and Cleopatra* II i 70-2; III ii 15 |
| | *Julius Caesar* IV i 35-40 |

Leprion, Leprium   A town of Elis.

| Prior | *First Hymn to Callimachus* 39 ff |

Lerna, Lernaean   A river and marshy area of *Argolis* in the Peloponnesus. Here *Hercules* killed the *Hydra* and into Lerna swamps were thrown the murdered cousins of the *Danaides*.

> (Strabo viii 6)

Browning R.	*The Ring and the Book* ix 399-402
Drayton	*Polyolbion* xxv 44
Marlowe	*Tamburlaine* i 1656-61
Spenser	*Faerie Queene* I vii 17, V xi 22

Lesbia
See *Catullus*

| Marlowe | *Tamburlaine* ii 3059-63 |

Lesbian
See *Lesbos*

| Milton | *Lycidas* 62-3 |
| Shelley | *Oedipus Tyrannus* I i 120-1 |

Lesbos   The Aegean island, whose capital was Mytilene. It was an important commercial and cultural centre in the 6th and 7th Centuries BC and was celebrated for its wine and music; it was known also for depravity and indulgence and was a centre for the worship of *Bacchus*. *Sappho* was born on Lesbos and this gave the island its association with homosexual women.

> (Strabo X iii 7; Virgil *Georgics* ii 90)

| Swinburne | *On the Cliffs* 380-3 |
| | *The Interpreters* |

Lestrygonians   A gigantic cannibal people usually said to have inhabited Sicily and spread to Italy. They ate one of *Ulysses*' men and stoned his fleet with boulders.

> (Homer *Odyssey* x 115 ff; Ovid *Metamorphoses* xiv 233 ff)

| Crashaw | *Sospetto d'Herode* 45 |

Lethaean
See *Lethe*

| Arnold | *To a Gipsy Child* 54 |

Lethe   The River of Forgetfulness in *Hades*, where souls drank and forgot their previous existence.

> (Virgil *Aeneid* vi 714)

See also *Lethean*

Byron *The Adieu* 88-90
      Hints from Horace 35
Chaucer *House of Fame* 66-76
Coleridge *The Snow-Drop* 39-40
De La Mare *I Wonder* 1-7
      Lethe 1-2
Donne *Second Anniversary* 27-9
Goldsmith *Song from 'She Stoops to Conquer'* 1ff
Hood *Hero and Leander* 10
Housman *Crossing Alone the Nighted Ferry* 1-4
Keats *Fill for Me a Living Bowl* 7-11
      Ode on Melancholy 1-4
      Ode to a Nightingale 1-4
      Welcome Joy and Welcome Sorrow 1-2
MacNeice *Autumn Journal* xviii, xxiv
Milton *Paradise Lost* i 266, ii 73-4, 582-6
Owen *To a Comrade in Flanders* 1-4
Pope *Dunciad* ii 314-9
Shakespeare *Antony and Cleopatra* II i 26-7
      Hamlet I v 32-4
      King Henry IV pt 2 V ii 72
      King Richard III IV iv 248-52
Shelley *On Leaving London for Wales* 12-13
Spenser *Faerie Queene* I iii 36
      Ruins of Time 427-31
      Shepherd's Calendar, May 23
Swinburne *Anactoria*
      In The Bay 32
Tennyson *The Two Voices* 349-51
Vaughan *To My Ingenious Friend R. W.* 39-42
Wordsworth *Sonnet 'Lady, I rifled . . .'* 1-7

Lethean
See *Lethe*
Brooke *Hauntings* 9-11
Dryden *Don Sebastian* III i
Gray *Hymn to Ignorance* 17
Keats *Hush, Hush! Tread Softly* 10-11
      Isabella 435-6
Milton *Paradise Lost* ii 604-8
Shelley *Rosalind and Helen* 402-9
      Revolt of Islam 2089-91
      Triumph of Life 463

Swinburne *Hymn to Proserpine* 37
      Memorial 17
Tennyson *In Memoriam* xliv 9-12
Yeats *Vacillation* iii

Leto
See *Latona*
Bridges *Prometheus the Firegiver* 962-5

Leucadia, Leucadian, Leucas An island and cliff (Santa Maura) in the Ionian Sea, from which *Sappho* committed suicide when her passion for *Phaon* was unrequited.
Byron *Childe Harold* ii 41
Moore *Evenings in Greece* 131-8
Swinburne *Ave Atque Vale* ii
      On the Cliffs 315-6

Leucothea A Roman goddess of Dawn (*Mater Matuta*). It was a curiosity of her worship that suppliants prayed for the children of others, not of themselves. This arose from her being the divine form of *Ino*, who in a Bacchic frenzy helped *Agave* (her sister) to dismember her son *Pentheus* of *Thebes*. Ino hated the children of *Athamas'* first wife, *Phrixus* and *Helle* (whom she would have destroyed if they had not escaped on a golden ram), because they were preferred for the throne before her own children. These were two sons, *Learchus* and *Melicerta*, the latter of whom she tried to save from Athamas' madness by jumping into the sea with him from a cliff, where they both perished.

(Ovid *Fasti* vi 479 ff)
Milton *Comus* 875-6
      Paradise Lost xi 133-6

Leucothe, Leucothoe The daughter of Orchamus, a king of Syria, and Eurynome. *Apollo* fell in love with Leucothoe and courted her by assuming the form of her mother. His deception was betrayed by Clytie — who had been deserted by Apollo for Leucothoe — and Orchamus had his daughter buried alive. Apollo sprinkled perfumes on the site and a frankincense-bearing tree grew there.
(Ovid *Metamorphoses* iv 196 ff)
Chapman *Hero and Leander* vi
Lovelace *Princess Louisa Drawing* 26-8

Liagore   A nymph, daughter of *Nereus*.
(Hesiod *Theogony* 257)
Spenser   *Faerie Queene* IV 11 51

Liber   A name for Bacchus.
Kipling   *Samuel Pepys* 16-19

Liberty   A goddess represented as a woman holding a rod and a cap, symbols of the slavery from which she conferred release. Her temple was on the Aventine Hill of Rome.
(Ovid *Tristia* III i 72)
Thomson   *Liberty* i 26-30

Lichas   The young messenger of *Hercules* who brought him the poisoned tunic from *Deianeira*. Hercules threw him into the sea, in the agony of wearing the tunic, and Lichas became a rock.
(Ovid *Metamorphoses* ix 211ff)
See also *Oechalia*
Milton   *Paradise Lost* ii 542-6
Shakespeare   *Merchant of Venice* II i 32-4

Ligea   A name of one of the *Sirens*.
(Virgil *Georgics* iv 336)
Milton   *Comus* 878-82

Ligurges
See *Demophoon*
Chaucer   *Legend of Good Women* 3424-6

Liguria   A country of north-west Italy whose capital was Genoa.
Collins   *Ode to Liberty* 49

Linus   A legendary poet-musician whose parentage was variously assigned to *Urania*, *Apollo*, *Calliope* and others. In one version, he was a son of Urania and was killed by Apollo, who envied his skill in music. Alternatively, he was a teacher of music to *Hercules*, who killed him when he punished him in a lesson. He was also said to be the brother and teacher of *Orpheus*. He was the subject of a ritual dirge, or was the name of a dirge, and seems to be associated with ritual lament for dying vegetation.
(Hesiod *Contest of Homer and Hesiod* 311-4; *Fragment* attributed to Hesiod i; Apollodorus I iii 2, II iv 9; Diodorus Siculus III 67; Homer *Iliad* xviii 569-72)
See also *Lityerses*

Fletcher P.   *Purple Island* i 17
Spenser   *Ruins of Time* 330-6

Lion   See *Nemean Lion*

Lipare, Lipari   An island on the coast of Sicily. In this region, and under *Aetna*, *Vulcan* forged *Jove*'s thunderbolts.
(Virgil *Aeneid* viii 416-28)
Spenser   *Faerie Queene* IV v 37

Lisianassa   A *Nereid*.
Spenser   *Faerie Queene* IV 11 50

Lisippus
See *Lysippus*
Spenser   *Ruins of Time* 414-20

Litae   Homer refers to prayers as the daughters of *Zeus*, depicting them as old ladies.
(*Iliad* ix 502ff)
Spenser   *Faerie Queene* V ix 31

Lityerses   A Phrygian king, possibly a son of *Midas*. He was reputed to have enlisted strangers in his harvest work-force and then to have killed them. One such was *Hercules*, who killed him. His harvest song is generic, like the song of *Linus*, and is associated with death and rebirth.
(Theocritus *Idyll* x 42ff)
Arnold   *Thyrsis* 182-5

Livia (1)   Livia Drusilla married Tiberius Nero and was by him mother of *Tiberius*, the future Roman Emperor. Divorced from him in 39BC, she married *Octavian* (*Augustus*) and was renamed *Augusta (2)*. Accounts of her vary between admiration of her intelligence and beauty, and accusations of intrigue in the deaths of *Marcellus (2)* and *Germanicus*, and in gaining power for Tiberius.
Hardy   *Rome — On the Palatine* 1-2

Livia (2), Livia Livilla   Livia was sister to *Germanicus*, married to Caius Caesar (the adopted son of *Augustus*) and subsequently to *Drusus (1)*, son of the Emperor *Tiberius*. *Sejanus* asked Tiberius for her hand and Tiberius later believed that she had been Sejanus' mistress and had aided and possibly effected the poisoning of Drusus.
Jonson   *Sejanus* II i, III i

Livius   Titus Livius, the Roman historian, was born in Padua in about 60BC and spent most of his life in Rome or Padua, where he died in about 12AD. His *History of Rome*, which comprised 142 books of which 35 are extant, had the support of *Augustus* and was clearly written with patriotic purpose, warning against a decline from earlier virtues. It is annalistic in form, and episodic, built up from an eclectic use of sources. It is noted for pictorial vividness and lucidity of style.

Chaucer	*Book of the Duchess* 1082-4
	Physician's Tale 1-4
	Legend of Good Women 1680-3
Jonson	*Sejanus* III i

Livy
See *Livius*

Longinus (1) Gaius Cassius
See *Cassius*

Longinus (2)   The supposed author (Dionysius Longinus) of an influential Greek treatise of 1st Century AD, *Peri Pathos* or *On the Sublime*. It elevates individual genius above rules and stresses the moral value of literature.

Byron	*Don Juan* i 42
Pope	*Essay on Criticism* 675-80

Lotos-Eaters   Eaters of the sweet lotos fruit, whose attractions were so powerful that anyone eating it lost the will and the knowledge to return home. They were encountered by *Odysseus*, who had to carry his men away, weeping, to the ships.

	(Homer *Odyssey* ix 82 ff)
Browning R.	*Pauline* 919-21
Fletcher P.	*To E. C.* 59-61
Swinburne	*Anactoria*
	In Harbour 8
Tennyson	*The Lotos-Eaters* 28 ff, 153-5

Love, Loves
See *Cupid*

Browning E. B.	*The Dead Pan* 17
Coleridge	*Songs of the Pixies* 57
Donne	*Elegy* xviii 60-3
Gray	*Progress of Poesy* 28-9
Keats	*To Mary Frogley* 26-30
Moore	*The Sale of Loves* 1-4

Pope	*Elegy to the Memory of an Unfortunate Lady* 59-60
	Winter 21-4
Shenstone	*Elegies* i 40-4
	Song vi 9-10
Spenser	*Amoretti* 16
	Hymn in Honour of Beauty 239-42
Swift	*Strephon and Chloe* 49-50
Swinburne	*Sapphics* 9 ff
Wordsworth	*River Duddon* x 1304

Lucan   Marcus Annaeus Lucan, Roman poet, wrote *Pharsalia*, an epic of the war between *Caesar* and *Pompey* and the defeat of the latter at *Pharsalus* in 48BC. He fell out of favour with *Nero* and was obliged to commit suicide in 65AD when aged only twenty-six. Lucan was said to have been helped in his versification by his wife, *Polla*.

	(Statius *Sylvae* II vii;
	Tacitus *Annals* XV, XVI)
Chaucer	*Man of Law's Tale* 400-3
	Monk's Tale 3909-11
	House of Fame 1497-1502
	Troilus and Criseyde v 1786 ff
Collins	*Epistle to Sir Thomas Hanmer* 71-2
Donne	*A Valediction, of the Book* 5-9
Jonson	*To My Chosen Friend . . .* 14-16
Lovelace	*On Sannazar* 35-6
Young	*Night Thoughts* ix

Lucian   Greek rhetorician and sophist of the 2nd Century AD, who specialised in satirical dialogues. Lucian was notorious for his impiety and was said to have been torn to pieces by a pack of dogs because of it.

Shenstone	*Charms of Precedence* 79-84
Vaughan	*The Charnel House* 16-17

Lucifer   The daystar, the planet *Venus* when it appears in the morning before the sun. The name was applied to Satan by reference to Isaiah xiv 12 and Luke x 18, but there was an established non-satanic use (e.g. Ovid *Tristia* I iii 72).
See also *Morning Star*, *Phosphorus*

Keats	*Endymion* i 529-31
Milton	*On the Morning of Christ's Nativity* 72-4

Lucifera

Shakespeare   *Merry Wives of Windsor*
              I iii 72-3
Shelley   *Triumph of Life* 413-20

Lucifera   A name for *Artemis/Cynthia/ Diana.*
Chapman   *Shadow of Night*

Lucina   A Roman goddess of childbirth and also of chastity. She was daughter of *Jupiter* and either *Juno* or *Latona*. She shared her sphere of influence with *Diana* and Juno, who were also called Lucina. The name is thus applied also to the moon and to *Proserpina*.
              (Ovid *Fasti* ii 449-52)
Chaucer   *Franklin's Tale* 1065-76,
          1045-8
          Knight's Tale 2083-5
Crabbe   *Inebriety*
Herrick   *Conubii Flores* 36-7
Milton   *Epitaph on the Marchioness of Winchester* 25-30
Shakespeare   *Pericles* I i 6-9; III i 10-14
Spenser   *Faerie Queene* II i 53, III vi 27
Swift   *Cadenus and Vanessa*

Lucos
See *Lycus*
Browning R.   *Aristophanes' Apology*
              540-4

Lucrece
See *Lucretia*
Carew   *A Rapture* 115-8
Macaulay   *Virginia*
Pope   *Essay on Man* iv 207-8
       To Belinda 19-22
Prior   *On Beauty* 10ff
Shakespeare   *Cymbeline* II ii 11-12
              Rape of Lucrece 1-7,
              254-9, 316-21, 477-82,
              673ff, 1070-80, 1127ff,
              1291-3, 1723-9, 1850-5
              Taming of the Shrew II i
              206-7
              Titus Andronicus II i
              108-9; IV i 64-5
              Twelfth Night II v 86ff
Wyatt   *Love with Unkindness* 31-5

Lucresse
See *Lucretia*

Chaucer   *Anelida and Arcite* 81-2
          Book of the Duchess 1080-4
          Franklin's Tale 1405-8
          Legend of Good Women
          256-60, 1686, 1736-42,
          1789-93, 1853ff

Lucretia   A celebrated Roman beauty of the 5th Century BC, who won a contest between soldiers as to the best representative of womanly virtues. She married *Tarquinius Collatinus*, but was raped by *Tarquinius Sextus*. Telling her husband and her father of this by letter, she then committed suicide with a dagger. According to the legend, this outrage resulted in a popular uprising and the expulsion of the Tarquins from Rome. The story is similar in type to that of *Virginia*.
              (Livy I lvii-lviii)
See also *Lucrece*, *Lucresse*, *Tarquinius Superbus*, *Verginius*
Browning E. B.   *Queen Anelida* 12
Browning R.   *Ring and the Book* ix
              187-90
Shakespeare   *As You Like It* III ii 135-9
Tennyson   *Lucretius* 235-40

Lucretian
See *Lucretius (2)*
Dryden   *Prologue to the University of Oxon* 32-5

Lucretilis   A mountain near *Horace*'s Sabine farm.
              (Horace *Odes* I 17)
Wordsworth   *The Prelude* viii 181-4

Lucretius (1)   Tricipitinus Spurius Lucretius, the father of *Lucretia*. He seems to be almost entirely a literary creation.
See also *Lucretia*, *Tarquinius*
Shakespeare   *Rape of Lucrece* 1732ff

Lucretius (2)   Titus Lucretius, poet and philosopher of the 1st Century BC. There is little certain known of the life of Lucretius; Jerome (4th Century AD) is not thought to have had a factual basis for his notions that Lucretius was poisoned by an aphrodisiac, wrote his great work whilst so suffering, and eventually committed suicide. *De Rerum Natura*, his sole work, assumes an atomistic

140

view of the universe and is in some respects Epicurean; the mortality of the soul and pointlessness of the fear of death are among major themes. He approached his work with technical assurance, acute observation and linguistic virtuosity; it is a literary, as much as a philosophical masterpiece.

See also *Lucretian*

Browning E. B.   *A Vision of Poets* 334-42
Byron   *Don Juan* i 43
Prior   *Alma* i 136ff
         Satire on Modern Translators 53-4
Tennyson   *Lucretius* 14-19, 37-9, 116-20, 259ff

Lucrine Bay
See *Lucrinus*
Milton   *Paradise Regained* ii 344-7

Lucrinus   A former lake near Naples, famed for its fish and particularly its oysters.

(Horace *Satires* II iv 32, *Epode* ii 49)

Lucullus   Lucius Licinius Lucullus, a consul, general and envoy of *Sulla*. After a career of statesmanship he retired to a life of studied luxury in which he eventually became insane. Among his passions was good food, and it is noted that he introduced cherry trees to Italy.

(Pliny xv 30)

Byron   *Don Juan* xv 66
Cowper   *The Task* ii 596-9
Pope   *Epistle* i 218-9

Lucumo   An Etruscan name meaning 'chief' – an adherent of *Porsenna* or *Tarquinius Superbus*, who bore the name in its Romanised form of 'Lucius'.
Macaulay   *Horatius* 23, 47

Lucyfer
See *Lucifer*
Chaucer   *Troilus and Criseyde* iii 1417-8

Luna   Goddess of the moon and sometimes identified with *Diana*, Luna was daughter of *Hyperion* and *Terra*. She may be represented with a chariot drawn by black and white horses signifying night and day, or the chariot may be drawn by dragons.

(Ovid *Metamorphoses* vii 220-1, xv 790)
See also *Cynthia, Lucina*
Arnold   *Isolation* 19-24
Browning R.   *Pan and Luna* 48, 65-9, 81-3, 89
Chaucer   *Canon Yeoman's Tale* 826-7

Lupercalia   A Roman festival in the spring, the origin of which was propitiation of a wolf god. The Lupercal Cave, its centre, was at the foot of the *Palatine* Hill in Rome.
Shakespeare   *Julius Caesar* I i 68-70

Lyaeus   A name for *Bacchus*, signifying freedom from care.

(Horace *Epode* ix 37-8)
Jonson   *Swell Me a Bowl* 1-3
Moore   *The Fall of Hebe* 16ff
Spenser   *Faerie Queene* III i 51

Lyagore
See *Liagore*
Spenser   *Faerie Queene* III iv 41

Lycaeus, Lycaean   An Arcadian mountain named after *Lycaon*, the first king of *Arcadia*, who built on it a temple to *Jupiter*. It was held to be a haunt of *Pan*.

(Ovid *Metamorphoses* i 698; Virgil *Georgics* i 16-17)
Keats   *Endymion* i 305-6
Milton   *Arcades* 98
Prior   *First Hymn to Callimachus* 13-15

Lycaon   The first Arcadian king, turned into a wolf by *Jupiter* for offering human sacrifices. Lycaon had fifty sons and a daughter, *Callisto*.

(Ovid *Metamorphoses* i 221ff; Pausanias viii 2ff)
Bridges   *Prometheus the Firegiver* 954-8
Crashaw   *Sospetto d'Herode* 42

Lyceum   A park east of Athens, near the *Ilissus*, originally a sanctuary of Apollo Lyceius. *Aristotle* did his peripatetic teaching there.

(Pausanias I xix 3)
Milton   *Paradise Regained* iv 251-3

Lycia, Lycian   Mountainous country north of Rhodes. The origins of its peoples and their names (Solymi, Milyades, Termili, Lycians) were disputed, but they were noted for military prowess and archery in particular. They appear in the Trojan War with their heroes Sarpedon and *Glaucus*. Apollo was the country's principal god and was said to spend the winter there in the temple at Patara. According to Herodotus, Lycians took their names from their mothers, not their fathers.

> (Herodotus i 173; Strabo xii, xiv;
> Virgil *Aeneid* iv 143-4, vii 816)
> Prior   *Carmen Seculare* 290-1
> Tennyson   *The Princess* ii 108 ff

Lycid, Lycidas   The name of a shepherd or goatherd famous for his piping.

> (Bion ii, vi; Theocritus *Idylls* vii, xxvii;
> Virgil *Eclogues* vii ix)
> See also *Daphnis*
> Keats   *Keen Fitful Gusts* 11-12
>   *Not Aladdin magian* 23-8
> Milton   *Lycidas* 8-11

Lycius   A young man who, travelling between Cenchreas and Corinth, was seduced by a beautiful lady. He stayed in her house and married her. One of the wedding guests was the mystic philosopher *Apollonius*, who realised that the lady was a *Lamia* or serpent. When he refused to keep this knowledge to himself, the house and everything in it vanished. The story was told as a tribute to the perception of Apollonius and as a caution against the passion of love.

> (Flavius Philostratus *Life of Apollonius*
> iv, via Burton *Anatomy of Melancholy*)
> Keats   *Lamia* 216-9, 305-8

Lycomedes   The King of Scyros, who brought up *Achilles* when his mother (*Thetis*) disguised him as a girl to avoid the Trojan War. He was also held responsible for the death of *Theseus*, who inherited land on Scyros and may also have been banished there by Menistheus and the Athenians; possibly in league with Menistheus, Lycomedes led Theseus up a cliff to display his kingdom, which he feared Theseus might usurp, then pushed him over the edge to his death.

> (Apollodorus III xiii 8, *Epitome* c 11)
> Cleveland   *Upon a Hermaphrodite*
>   49-53

Lycophron
See *Periander*
> Meredith   *Periander*

Lycurgus (1)   A King of *Thrace*. He was a noted teetotaller who drove himself mad, banishing *Bacchus* from his kingdom, killing his own son, Dryas, and cutting off his own legs in the belief that they were vines.

> (Apollodorus III v 1;
> Homer *Iliad* vi 130ff)
> Chaucer   *Knight's Tale* 2129-47

Lycurgus (2)
See *Demophoon*

Lycurgus (3)   Ruler of *Sparta* and founder of the country's constitution, law and society. Lycurgus dates probably from the 8th Century BC, but is also legendary. He was thought to have been an ideal philosopher-king, with an austere but also moderate disposition, who made early Sparta something of a commonwealth, where personal possessions and interests had to serve the common good, where money was outlawed as temptation and where equality was a guiding principle. He was thought to have committed suicide in Stoic fashion and to have first exacted a general oath that what he had done could not be undone.

> (Plutarch *Lycurgus and Numa*)
> Thomson   *Liberty* ii 111-9
>   *Winter* 453-8

Lycus   A son of *Neptune* and King of *Mysia*, by gift of *Hercules*. He threatened Hercules's family and wife, *Megara (2)*, whilst Hercules was in *Hades*, and he usurped the throne of *Thebes*. He did, however, offer hospitality to the *Argonauts*. Hercules killed Lycus on his return, but as a result the implacable *Juno* made him mad so that he killed Megara and burnt her children.

> (Apollodorus I 9, II 4-5;
> Euripides *Herakles*)

Lydia, Lydian   A country of East Turkey between *Caria* and *Mysia*, with much mineral wealth. The Lydians were a powerful and warlike nation between the 8th and 6th Centuries BC. They were the first to use coinage and were celebrated for their music. This was thought to be of a soft and effeminate character, to which they declined under the Persians after their era of power.

(Plato *Republic* iii 398-9)

Collins   *Ode to Liberty* 47
Keats   *To George Felton Mathew* 17-23
     Written in Disgust of Vulgar
     Superstition 5-7
Milton   *L'Allegro* 135-6
Spenser   *Faerie Queene* III i 40
Wordsworth   *On the Power of Sound*
     76-80

Lynceus, Lyno (1)   One of the sons of *Aegyptus*, saved by *Hypermnestra* from the slaughter of the sons of Aegyptus.
See also *Danaides*

Chaucer   *Legend of Good Women*
     2562 ff, 2656 ff

Lynceus (2)   The brother of *Idas*.
Swinburne   *Atalanta in Calydon* 1266

Lynus
See *Linus*
Drayton   *The Muses' Elizium* iii 116-20

Lysander   A Spartan general who opposed, and in 404 BC slew, *Alcibiades* in the Peloponnesian War. He was generally disliked — by his commentators not least — for his cool arrogance and ambition. With the support of *Cyrus*, Lysander routed the Athenians in 405 BC and forced them to come to terms with him and his plan for *Thirty Tyrants*. He did not have wholehearted support from *Sparta* and his position vis à vis the Greeks was weakened. He was surprised and killed in the Corinthian War of 395 BC, in which Corinth, Athens and others united against Sparta.

Browning R.   *Aristophanes' Apology*
     70 ff

Lysimachus   A general of *Alexander* the Great and afterwards ruler of *Thrace*. He made war on the Getae in 291 BC and was taken prisoner, reputedly on the offer of cold water to slake his and his army's thirst.

(Plutarch *Moralia* 126)

Carew   *Coelum Britannicum* 797-800

Lysippus   A 4th Century BC sculptor of

Sicyon in the north-east Peloponnesus. *Alexander* the Great commissioned a statue from him because he was particularly adept at facial realism. He made several hundred statues, including one of *Socrates*, noted for their fidelity to detailed likeness.

(Horace *Epistles* II i 240;
Plutarch *Alexander* IV i)

See also *Lisippus*

Macedon
See *Alexander*
Surrey   *The great Macedon* 1-2

Macedonian Philip
See *Philip II*

Macrobius   Ambrosius Theodosius Macrobius is a Latin writer of the 5th Century AD of whom little is known, save that he was not Roman (he may have been African) and was not a Christian. His principal works are the *Saturnalia* (a miscellany centred on Virgilian criticism) and the *Commentarii in Somnium Scipionis* which, when *Cicero*'s original was presumed lost, was the means by which the influential Ciceronian *Somnium* became known to the Middle Ages.
See also *Africanus (2)*, *Macrobye*

Chaucer   *Book of the Duchess* 278-88
     Nun's Priest's Tale 4133-6
Skelton   *Garland of Laurel*

Macrobye
See *Macrobius*
Chaucer   *Parliament of Fowls* 110-1

Maeander   A river celebrated for its devious course ('meander'), flowing across Turkey into the Aegean south of Priene. It was said to have given *Daedalus* the idea for the labyrinth in which he was confined by *Minos* and out of which he flew on wings of waxed feathers.

(Ovid *Metamorphoses* viii 162-8)

Arnold   *Empedocles on Etna* II i 132-6
Gray   *Progress of Poesy* 69-70
Prior   *To Charles Montague* 2
Spenser   *Faerie Queene* IX xi 21

Maecenas (Gaius)   Roman literary patron of

the Augustan age. He was the statesman and close friend of the Emperor *Augustus* and was patron to *Virgil*, Propertius and *Horace*, among others. He never held formal office and was well known for his apparently luxurious and indolent life; but he did in fact write in prose, though little remains, and his indirect influence by way of providing security in a great age of classical verse was very great. Virgil and Horace dedicated works to him.

(Plutarch *Augustus*)

Auden	*The Horatians* 31-3
Coleridge	*To a Friend (Charles Lamb)* 20-4
MacNeice	*Memoranda to Horace* ii
Spenser	*Sonnet, 'That Mantuan's Poet's Incomparable Spirit' Shepherd's Calendar, October* 55 ff

Maenad, Maenade, Maenads   A name for the wild female followers of *Bacchus* (*Dionysus*), the Bacchae. They wore skins and wreaths of leaves and carried snakes, following the god in his travels. The Maenads accompanied Dionysus from *Lydia* to *Thrace* and Greece, and there were also Maenads in *Thebes*. *Orpheus* and *Pentheus* were killed by the maddened devotees of Dionysus, who roamed the country giving suck to wolf cubs. Their characteristic cry was *Euhue* or *evoe*, meaning 'hurrah' or 'joy'.
See also *Bacchanals*

Arnold	*Bacchanalia* 24-31
Browning E. B.	*The Dead Pan* 14
Shelley	*Ode to Liberty* 91-4
	Ode to the West Wind 15-23
	Orpheus 52-5
	Prometheus Unbound II iii 7-10, III iii 154, IV 472-5
	The Sensitive Plant i 33-4
Spenser	*Faerie Queene* V viii 47
Swinburne	*Atalanta in Calydon* 107-8
	Tiresias 306-8

Maenalus, Maenaliani   An Arcadian mountain sacred to *Pan* and named after the son of *Lycaon*, first king of *Arcadia*. It was wooded with pines, the haunt of wild animals.

(Pausanias VIII 36)

Milton	*Arcades* 102
Shelley	*Hymn of Pan* 30-1

Swinburne	*Atalanta in Calydon* 46
Wordsworth	*Dion* 72-6
	On the Power of Sound 145 ff

Maeon   Son of *Haemon*, and a Theban warrior. *Eteocles*, the usurper of *Thebes*, sent fifty men, including Maeon, to kill *Tydeus*. Tydeus killed all but Maeon, for certain mysterious religious reasons, or to bear the news back from *Argos* to Thebes.

(Homer *Iliad* iv 391 ff)

Maeonian
See *Homer*

Cowper	*Yardley Oak* 156 ff
Pope	*Essay on Criticism* 645-8
Spenser	*Faerie Queene* II x 3

Maeonides
See *Homer*

Milton	*Paradise Lost* iii 34-6
Wordsworth	*Written in a Blank Leaf of Ossian* 79-82
Young	*Night Thoughts* i

Maeotis   The Sea of Azor in the north-east of the Black Sea.

Drayton	*Polyolbion* xxv 39-43
Milton	*Paradise Lost* ix 762-8

Maevius
See *Bavius*

Fletcher P.	*Purple Island* i 18

Maia   The month of May, daughter of *Atlas* and mother of *Mercury* by *Jupiter*. One of the *Pleiades*, Maia was a shy goddess who lived apart in a cave of *Cyllene*.

(Apollodorus III 10; Homeric Hymn *To Hermes* (18))

Bridges	*Demeter* 575
Drayton	*To Himself and the Harp* 36-42
Jonson	*Cynthia's Revels* V ii
Keats	*Ode to May* 1-3
Milton	*Paradise Lost* v 285-6
Spenser	*Epithalamion* 305-10
	Faerie Queene IV iii 42
	Mother Hubberd's Tale 1256-63
	Mutability Cantos vi 15-16

Shepherd's Calendar, May 16-17
Thomson   *Autumn* 516-7

Maian
See *Maia*
    Keats   *Fall of Hyperion* ii 102-3

Maids
See *Graces, Muses*
    Collins   *The Manners* 45
        Epistle to Sir Thomas Hanmer
        37

Maevius   A minor Augustan poet. He attacked *Horace* and *Virgil*, who replied.
        (Horace *Epode* x; Virgil *Eclogue* iii 90)
See also *Bavius*
    Pope   *To the Author of a Poem* 18-19
        Essay on Criticism 34-5
    Swift   *To Stella, Who Collected His*
        Poems 71-8

Mamilius   Octavius Mamilius was a general of Tusculum in the 6th Century BC, and a son-in-law of *Tarquinius Superbus*, whom he supported in an attempt to return as king of Rome. As commander of the Latin League, he was defeated and killed at Lake *Regillus*, c. 496 BC.
        (Livy ii 20)
See also *Horatius Cocles, Porsenna*
    Macaulay   *Horatius* 12, 24
        Lake Regillus 11, 28

Manes   Indefinite local gods or spirits of a place, or more impressive deities from *Hades*. They are conceived very variously but are clearly associated with the spirits of past resident heroes and other personalities having tutelary deities.
    Chaucer   *Troilus and Criseyde* v 890-6

Manlius   A Roman officer who held the *Capitol* (and so was named Capitolinus) against the Gauls under *Brennus* in 347 BC.
    Browning R.   *Sordello* iii 587-92

Mantoan
See *Mantua*
    Chaucer   *Legend of Good Women* 924-7

Mantua, Mantuan   The birthplace of *Virgil*,

near Cremona in north Italy.
    Crabbe   *The Village* i 14-16
    Davies, Sir J.   *Orchestra* 883-4
    Diaper   *Dryades* 388-93
    Eliot T. S.   *Difficulties of a Statesman*
    Pope   *Autumn* 5-6
        Essay on Criticism 129
        Temple of Fame 200-3
    Prior   *Satire on Modern Translators*
        53-4
    Shakespeare   *Love's Labour's Lost* IV ii
        89 ff
    Thomson   *Spring* 456-7

Marathon, Marathonian   A town some twenty miles north-east of Athens, where the Persians were defeated in 490 BC. *Aeschylus* fought in the battle. The news of Greek victory was conveyed to Athens by a runner; hence the modern English use of 'Marathon'.
        (Herodotus vi 102 ff)
See also *Pheidippides*
    Browning E. B.   *The Battle of Marathon*
        962-4
    Browning R.   *Echetlos* 1-3
        Sordello i 65-8, iii 950-4
    Byron   *Childe Harold* ii 89
        Isles of Greece 3-4
    Collins   *Ode to Fear* 30-1
    Shelley   *Hellas* 52-7
    Swinburne   *Eve of Revolution* 85 ff
        Athens ant. ii
    Thomson   *Liberty* ii 183-5
    Wordsworth   *Descriptive Sketches*
        387-8
        Memorials of a Tour in
        Scotland 1814 ii 37-42
        When far and wide . . .
        9-14

Marcellus (1)   Marcus Claudius Marcellus, a Roman general who first came to notice in an expedition against the Gauls after the First Punic War, and then commanded the Roman forces against *Hannibal* in 216 BC. He was the first to achieve any success against the Carthaginian leader. He continued to oppose him until 208 when he was killed in Venusia, southern Italy. He had built several temples in gratitude for his victories and the story goes that one of them was struck by lightning as he was dedicating it. He had also brought back treasures of art to Rome, having taken them in 211 at Syracuse, which he captured despite the ordnance and other instruments of *Archimedes*. He was a great and popular general and had a funeral of famous splendour. A descendant of his married *Augustus'* daughter, Julia, but died in 23 BC, aged 20. This young Marcellus had been regarded as a possible successor to Augustus and his death profoundly shocked Rome and was noted by several poets of the day (in particular, *Virgil*).

(Livy xxix 24, 28 ff;
Virgil *Aeneid* vi 855 ff)

Chapman	*Epicedium*
Dryden	*To the Memory of Mr Oldham* 22-3
Spenser	*Ruins of Time* 414-20

Marcellus (2)   A supporter of *Pompey* who, after the Battle of *Pharsalus* (in which *Caesar* defeated Pompey in 48 BC), retired to Mytilene to devote himself to literature and philosophy. He was murdered in 45 BC and some suspected that Caesar was involved. *Cicero* wrote a speech in honour of Marcus Claudius Marcellus.

Pope   *Essay on Man* iv 257-8

Marcia
See *Marsyas*
Chaucer   *House of Fame* 1229-32

Marcia Cato   The wife of *Cato (3)*, who lent her to *Hortensius* so that his friend could have children. After Hortensius' death, Cato had her back; the affair was a notable scandal in Rome.

(Plutarch *Cato the Younger* 25)
Chaucer   *Legend of Good Women* (252-3)

Marcius Gnaeus (1)
See *Coriolanus*
Shakespeare   *Coriolanus* I i 6, ix 63-5, II i 153-6, III i 211-3, IV vi 66-7

Marcius Ancus (2)   Ancus Martius was an ancient king of Rome (7th Century BC) and a supposed ancestor of Gnaeus Marcius (*Coriolanus*). He was succeeded by Tarquinius Priscus (*Lucumo*).

(Livy I 32 ff)

Shakespeare   *Coriolanus* II iii 235-42

Marcus Antonius
See *Antony (Mark)*
Pope   *Chorus to 'Brutus'* ii 7-8

Marcus Claudius
See *Verginius*
Chaucer   *Physician's Tale* 140-1, 178-85, 267-73

Mareotid Lake, Mareotis   A lake near *Alexandria*, close to the Nile Delta. It was said to be relieved of baneful qualities or stagnation by overflow from the Nile. The area was famed for wine.

(Horace *Odes* i 37; Strabo V i 7;
Virgil *Georgics* ii 91)
Drayton   *Polyolbion* xxv 39-43
Shelley   *Witch of Atlas* 505-11

Marius   Caius Marius was a Roman hero of the 2nd Century BC whose bravery was legendary. From a humble background he raised himself, through military posts and by marriage to Julia (who was to be an aunt of *Caesar*), to become consul. In this he displaced his rival *Metellus* by special law, and he supported himself with a privately raised army. After a series of victories against invaders he came into conflict with *Sulla (2)*, at whose invasion of Rome he was lucky to escape with his life, being found hidden in a marsh up to his neck. Taken to *Minturnae*, which sided with Sulla and sentenced him to death, he made such an authoritative impression that he was released, and he then sailed to Carthage. He gathered an army en route and returned to Rome, to join Cinna again as consul; he treated the opposition with despotic brutality, but died of pleurisy within a short time. Apparently illiterate and even boorish in behaviour, Marius was known for his commanding and inflexible sternness, which he applied no less to himself. In a well known anecdote, he had a leg amputated without showing expression, and then proceeded to offer the surgeon the other leg as well.

(Plutarch *Caius Marius*)
Byron   *Don Juan* xii 78
Prophecy of Dante i 104-6
Daniel   *Civil Wars* iii 73

Mars   God of War and Hunting, Mars was son of *Juno* alone, and was identified with Ares, the Greek God of War, who was son of *Hera* and *Zeus*. (Some writers make Mars son of *Jupiter* as well as of Juno.) Mars fell in love with *Venus* but the two were trapped, at the instigation of *Apollo*, by Venus' husband *Vulcan* (*Hephaestus*), who surrounded their bed with a net and made their amours the object of ridicule among the gods. Mars is often associated with *Thrace*, where there was a temple to him on Mount *Haemus*. He is drawn in a chariot by the steeds Flight and Terror.

(Hesiod *Theogony* 922, 934;
Homer *Odyssey* viii 266ff; Ovid *Fasti*
229ff, *Art of Love* ii 561-92)

See also *Mart*, *Martes*, *Salii*

Marsyas   A *Satyr* who, on finding a cursed flute discarded by *Athena*, developed great skill and challenged *Apollo* in the art. Apollo accepted on condition that the loser be entirely at the winner's mercy. Apollo won and flayed Marsyas to death; when he was mourned by the *Fauns*, Satyrs and *Dryads*, and a river of

tears, named after him, sprang forth in *Phrygia*.
(Ovid *Metamorphoses* vi 382 ff)
See also *Marcia*
> Arnold   *Empedocles on Etna* II i 141 ff

Mart, Marte
See *Mars*
> Chaucer   *House of Fame* 1446-7
> *Legend of Good Women*
> 2244-50
> *Troilus and Criseyde* ii 435-6
> Spenser   *Faerie Queene, Prologue* 3

Martial (1)   Marcus Valerius Martial, Roman
poet of the 1st Century AD, an epigrammatic
realist depicting Roman life at all levels. His
quest for realism and bent for satire at times
led him into obscenity, as was often noted by
later poets and critics.
> Byron   *Don Juan* i 43
> Jonson   *To the Ghost of Martial*

Martial (2)
See *Mars*
> Shakespeare   *Cymbeline* IV ii 309-12

Massinissa   King of *Numidia* in the 2nd
Century BC, Massinissa was visited by *Scipio
Africanus (2)*, who discussed his father with
him; *Africanus (1)* had shown generous kindness in the treatment of one of Massinissa's
subjects and as a result the king became a
staunch ally of Rome. The son's dream of the
father is in the *Sonium Scipionis* of *Cicero*
and *Macrobius*.
> Chaucer   *Parliament of Fowls* 29 ff

Mausolus
See *Artemisia*
> Marlowe   *Tamburlaine* ii 3100-4
> Spenser   *Ruins of Time* 414-20

Maximian   Marcus Aurelius Maximian was
one of the Caesars of *Diocletian*'s tetrarchic
system and was promoted to Augustus in
286 AD. He received *Constantius* as his Caesar
and gave him his step-daughter, Theodora, in
marriage. In 305 he abdicated with Diocletian
and subsequently formed a close alliance with
Constantine, to whom he gave his own daughter, Fausta. Repeatedly involved in the power
struggles following Diocletian's abdication, in

310 he led an unsuccessful revolt against Constantine in the south of France. Being given
the choice of manner of death, he strangled
himself. (Spenser's reference to a daughter of
Constantine is an error.)
> Spenser   *Faerie Queene* II x 61

Meander
See *Maeander*
> Crashaw   *On a Foul Morning*
> Keats   *Endymion* ii 116-9
> *Sleep and Poetry* 71-5
> Milton   *Comus* 230-3
> Swift   *A Love Song* 25-6
> Young   *Night Thoughts* iv

Mecene
See *Messenia*
> Chaucer   *Franklin's Tale* 1379-85

Medea   Enchantress and princess of *Colchis*,
Medea (like *Circe*, her aunt) was a priestess of
the Underworld goddess *Hecate*. She was led
to visit Greece by *Hera*, in order to destroy
Pelias, King of Iolchos, who refused to sacrifice to Hera; the voyage of the *Argonauts* was
the device for bringing her to Greece, since it
was contrived that she fall in love with *Jason*,
leader of the expedition. Jason was a son of
Aeson, whose throne had been usurped by
Pelias. On arriving at Iolchos, Medea charmed
her way in and carried out an elaborate ritual
to restore Aeson to youthful vigour, which
involved chopping him into pieces. Under the
influence of Hera, Medea then persuaded
Pelias' daughters to assist in a similar murder
of their father, who was not, of course, restored to life. The Argonauts then entered
and captured the city. Versions of this story
vary, as, still more, do accounts of Medea's
later life. In some versions Jason and Medea
retired to Corinth, where they separated and
where she killed his mistress *Creusa (1)*. She
and their children fled the wrath of the Corin-
thians and made for Athens, where she married
Aegeus. She was banished by him for attempting to poison *Theseus*, his first son, as a potential rival to her own son (Medus) by Aegeus.
Other sorts of magic and misfortune are related
to her life. Sometimes Jason and Medea are
simply reconciled. Whether she died or was
regarded as immortal is not stated.

(Apollodorus I ix; Apollonius Rhodius;
Euripides *Medea*)

See also *Argo*

Byron	*Don Juan* i 86
Chaucer	*Book of the Duchess* 326-34, 725-31
	Knight's Tale 1936-46
	Man of Law's Tale 72-4
	House of Fame 397-404, 1271-2
	Legend of Good Women 1598-601, 1634 ff, 1678-9
Davies, Sir J.	*Nosce Teipsum* v 21-4
Drayton	*The Barons' Wars* iii 8
	Henry to Rosamond 85-9
MacNeice	*Autumn Sequel* xi
Shakespeare	*King Henry VI pt 2* V ii 56-9
	Merchant of Venice V i 12-14
Shelley	*Alastor* 672-5
Sidney	*A Shepherd's Tale* 409-12
Skelton	*Philip Sparrow*
Spenser	*Faerie Queene* II xii 44-5, V viii 47
Swinburne	*Atalanta in Calydon* 630
	Song for the Centenary of Landor 23
Wordsworth	*Laodamia* 79-84

Medusa   The mortal sister in the three *Gorgons*. She was strikingly beautiful and *Neptune*, who assaulted her in the Temple of *Minerva*, loved her. For the sacrilege Minerva changed Medusa's hair into serpents. Medusa was killed by *Perseus*, who then set her head on his shield where it petrified all who crossed him. From Medusa's blood were held to have come forth *Pegasus* and the serpents of Africa.

Chapman	*Andromeda Liberata*
Crashaw	*Sospetto d'Herode* 42
	Polyolbion xx 164
Jonson	*If Men and Times Were Now* 37-41
Kingsley	*Andromeda* 358 ff
Milton	*Paradise Lost* ii 610-13
Shelley	*The Medusa of Leonardo da Vinci* 17-19, 25-9
Skelton	*Philip Sparrow*
Spenser	*Faerie Queene* III xi 42
	Ruins of Time 645-9

Megara (1)
See *Hybla*

Megara (2)   The daughter of *Creon*, King of *Thebes*, Megara was given in marriage to *Hercules* in reward for his saving Thebes from the Orchomenians. She was assaulted by *Lycus*, who was then killed by Hercules. *Juno* — who hounded Hercules in jealousy because he was the son of *Jupiter* from *Alcmena* — made Hercules mad so that he then killed both Megara and their children.

(Apollodorus II iv)

Browning R.	*Aristophanes' Apology* 540-4
Graves	*To Ogmian Hercules* 4-8

Megera, Megaera   One of the *Eumenides*.
(Virgil *Aeneid* xii 845-8)

See also *Mygra*

Chaucer	*Troilus and Criseyde* IV 22-4
Kingsley	*Frank Leigh's Song* 1
Marvell	*Tom May's Death* 90 ff
Milton	*Paradise Lost* x 558-60
Spenser	*Tears of the Muses* 163-8

Melampus   A seer of *Argos* who claimed to understand the speech of animals (which he had learnt from tame snakes) and who was instructed in healing by *Apollo*. When the tyrant *Neleus* promised his daughter Pero to whomever could catch the oxen of Phylacus, Melampus undertook to help her suitor. This was Bias, Melampus' brother. For his scheming, Melampus was imprisoned for a year in a chest or cell, but he secured his release and the cattle by demonstrating his magical powers — more particularly by enabling the impotent *Iphiclus* (Phylacus' son) to have children. Melampus accomplished other feats and eventually became King of Argos.

(Homer *Odyssey* xv 223 ff;
Apollodorus I ix 11 ff)

Stevenson	*As One Who Having Wandered* 17-22

Melanchaetes   A black-haired dog of *Actaeon*, the first to sink its fangs into its owner.
(Ovid *Metamorphoses* iii 232)

Skelton	*Philip Sparrow*

Melanion
See *Atalanta*
    Spenser   *Faerie Queene* II vii 54

Melanthius   A minor Greek tragic poet of the 5th Century BC, known mainly for ridicule of his effeminacy and gluttony.
    Browning R.   *Aristophanes' Apology* 948-9

Melantho   A daughter of *Deucalion*, raped by *Neptune* in the form of a dolphin.
                 (Ovid *Metamorphoses* vi 120ff)
    Spenser   *Faerie Queene* III xi 42

Melas   An Arcadian river.
    Prior   *First Hymn to Callimachus* 19ff

Meleager   A prince of Calydon for whom *Clotho* and *Lachesis* predicted at his birth a great future, but for whom the third *Fate*, *Atropos*, foretold disaster. She said he would survive as long as a stick in the fire was unburnt, so *Althaea*, his mother, extinguished the fire and hid the brand. Meleager was one of the *Argonauts* and, on his return, killed the Calydonian Boar (inflicted on his father *Oeneus* by *Diana* for omitting to sacrifice to her) and fell in love with *Atalanta*, who was among the illustrious hunters present. He gave the boar's skin to her, but the gift was disputed by his uncles, whom he then killed. In revenge, Althaea drew the hidden stick out and threw it into the fire, whereupon Meleager died and she committed suicide. Alternatively, the dispute was between the Calydonians and their neighbouring enemies the Cretans, who had also taken part in the hunt; in the battle Meleager killed his uncles and was himself slain. The story of the *Calydonian Boar Hunt* was often illuminated in art and may have appeared on ancient weaponry.
                 (Apollodorus I vii 10, viii 2-3;
                 Diodorus Siculus iv 34;
                 Ovid *Metamorphoses* viii)
    Chaucer   *Knight's Tale* 2069-72
               Troilus and Criseyde v 1474-7
    Cowley   *Elegy on Anacreon* 35-6
    MacNeice   *Cock o' the North* i, ii
    Swinburne   *Atalanta in Calydon* 247-302, 1257ff, 1338-54, 1900-5, 1991-7, 2286

Meles, Melesegines   The River Meles near Smyrna. A reputed birthplace of *Homer* and a name for him.
    Browning E. B.   *An Island* 26-7
    Milton   *Paradise Regained* iv 259-60

Meliboea, Meliboean   A town at the foot of Mount Ossa in Magnesia. It was famous for its dyeing of wool and as the birthplace of *Philoctetes*.
    Milton   *Paradise Lost* xi 241-2

Meliboeus   The name of a shepherd in *Virgil*'s pastorals.
                 (Virgil *Eclogues* i, iii, v, vii)
    Milton   *Comus* 821-3

Melicerta, Melicertes   A son of *Ino*, who jumped from a cliff into the sea with him to save him from the frenzy of his father *Athamas*. *Juno* (opposed to Ino as descended from *Venus*) had driven the mad Athamas to dash his other son, *Learchus*, against a rock, or to shoot him with an arrow. Ino was then created the goddess *Leucothea* by *Neptune*. Melicerta, renamed Palaemon, was the recipient of prayers from sailors who arrived safely home.
           (Apollodorus i 9; Ovid *Metamorphoses*
            iv 512-42; Virgil *Georgics* i 436-7)
    Milton   *Comus* 875-6
    Spenser   *Faerie Queene* IV xi 13, V viii 47

Melissa
See *Periander*
    Meredith   *Periander*

Melita, Melite   The island of Malta which was under Carthage until 218BC, after which it was administered by the Romans from Sicily.
    Shelley   *Oedipus Tyrannus* I i 169-72

Melite   A *Nereid*.
                 (Apollodorus I ii 6)
    Spenser   *Faerie Queene* IV xi 49

Melos   The island of Milos in the Cyclades, east of the Peloponnesus. It was neutral and independent until 416BC, when it was brutally subjugated by the Athenians, though it was later reinstated by *Lysander*. It is likely that

Alcbiades had a hand in the repression of Melos.

(Strabo X v 1; Thucydides V 84-96)
MacNeice   *Autumn Sequel* xix

Melpomene   The Muse of Tragedy, sometimes represented with buskins and a dagger. She was the daughter of *Zeus* and *Mnemosyne* and was said to be mother of the *Sirens*.

(Apollodorus *Epitome* vii 18;
Hesiod *Theogony* 77)

See also *Muses*
Byron   *Hints from Horace* 130-1
Henryson   *Orpheus and Eurydice*
Keats   *Isabella* 441-2
Meredith   *The Two Masks*
Milton   *Il Penseroso* 97ff
Spenser   *Muiopotmos* 10-15
           Tears of the Muses 151-7, 163-8
           Shepherd's Calendar, November 53
Tennyson   *In Memoriam* xxx

Memmius   Caius Memmius, dedicatee of *Lucretius (2)*'s *De Rerum Natura*, was married to the daughter of *Sulla (2)* and was a politician, of whom little is known, in the 1st Century BC. He was apparently a man of culture and a patron.
Tennyson   *Lucretius* 116-20

Memnon   Son of *Thithonus* and *Aurora*, and King of Ethiopia. Leading a large army to support the Trojans, he distinguished himself in the Trojan War and was killed by *Achilles*. Aurora implored *Zeus* to show her son some special honour, and this he did by causing birds to come from the smoke of the funeral pyre. These birds, known as Memnonides, returned annually to sprinkle water on his grave and the water was said to be Aurora's tears of grief. Memnon was believed to have conquered Egypt and much of Persia before his intervention at Troy. The palace at *Susa*, the Persian capital, was named Memnonia after him. A celebrated Ethiopian statue of him produced music as it was affected by the rays of the rising and setting sun.

(Hesiod *Theogony* 984; Homer *Odyssey* iv 184; Ovid *Metamorphoses* xiii 576-622; Pindar *Pythian Odes* vi 27ff)

Keats   *Hyperion* ii 373-6
Milton   *Il Penseroso* 11-18
Swinburne *John Ford* 1-6
Tennyson   *Palace of Art* 169-72
           Where is the Giant of the Sun 22-7
Wordsworth *Descriptive Sketches* 31-2

Memnonian
See *Memnon*
Milton   *Paradise Lost* x 306-10

Memnonides
See *Memnon*

Memphian
See *Memphis*
Milton   *On the Morning of Christ's Nativity* 213-14
           Paradise Lost i 307

Memphis   The former capital of Egypt on the west bank of the Nile south of the Delta. It was among a chain of pyramids and was noted for its temples to the Egyptian god *Apis (Osiris)* and the cult of the ox.
Keats   *Endymion* iii 847-9
Shelley   *Witch of Atlas* 646-8

Menalcas   The name of a shepherd in pastorals of *Theocritus* and *Virgil*.
Spenser   *Shepherd's Calendar, June* 102-4

Menander   Greek comic writer, c.300BC, who specialised in domestic comedy and was extensively drawn on by *Plautus* and *Terence*.
Collins   *Epistle to Sir Thomas Hanmer* 30
Jonson   *The Poetaster* I i
MacNeice   *Autumn Journal* ix
Pope   *Autumn* 7-8

Menas   A pirate under *Pompeius Sextus* in the 1st Century BC.
(Plutarch *Antony* xxxii)
Shakespeare *Antony and Cleopatra* I iv 48-51

Menecrates   A pirate or small naval commander with *Menas*.

Shakespeare *Antony and Cleopatra* I iv
48-51

Menelaus Generally said to be the son of
Atreus, Menelaus was brother of *Agamemnon*
and King of *Sparta*. Banished with his brother
by *Thyestes* (Atreus' brother) he sought the
hand of *Helen* and was successful. When
Menelaus was absent at Crete for the funeral
of his mother's father (Catreus), *Paris* of *Troy*
claimed Helen and carried her off. As *Aphrodite* had promised Helen to Paris and was at
enmity with *Athena* and *Hera*, the scene was
set in heaven and on earth for the Trojan War.
Late in the War, Paris was nearly killed in
single combat with Menelaus, but was rescued
by Aphrodite, though subsequently killed by
an arrow of *Philoctetes* — another suitor of
Helen. When the War ended, Menelaus found
Helen living with *Deiphobus* (Paris' brother)
to whom she was then married. He killed
Deiphobus and carried Helen home in disgrace,
declaring he would kill her; but he was molli-
fied by the passage of time. They then resumed
life as king and queen and were immortalised
at death; there are other accounts, however,
of what happened to Helen in later life, and
of what occurred when Menelaus fatefully left
home for Crete.

(Apollodorus III x-xi, *Epitome* iii, v, vi)
Brooke *Menelaus and Helen* 1ff
Byron *Don Juan* xiv 72
Drayton *The Owl* 969-74
Graves *Judgment of Paris* 5-6
Masefield *A King's Daughter
Tale of Nireus* 32-9
Shakespeare *King Henry VI pt 3* II ii
146-9
*Troilus and Cressida, Pro-
logue* 7-10, I i 110-11

Menenius Agrippa A consul, in 503 BC, of
plebeian origin and sympathies. He was reputed
to have recited to the people the parable of
the belly (the Senate) and limbs (the plebs) in
which the limbs rebel against slavery to the
belly and try to starve it, whereupon the whole
body atrophies. The particular audience was a
gathering of disenchanted plebeians who fled
Rome and set up a vocal, but peaceful, camp
of dissent outside.

(Livy ii 32; Plutarch *Coriolanus* vi)

Shakespeare *Coriolanus* I i 50, 94-5

Menippe A *Nereid*.
Spenser *Faerie Queene* IV xi 51

Menon A Trojan soldier killed by Leonteus
in the War.
(Homer *Iliad* xii 193)
Shakespeare *Troilus and Cressida* V v
6-11

Mercurial
See *Mercury*
Shakespeare *Cymbeline* IV ii 309-12

Mercurie
See *Mercury*
Chaucer *Canon Yeoman's Tale* 826-7
Knight's Tale 1385-90
House of Fame 427-32
Spenser *Mother Hubberd's Tale* 1247-9,
1279-82, 1289-98
Ruins of Time 666-70

Mercurius
See *Mercury*
Blake *Imitation of Spenser* 19 ff
Dunbar *Ryght as the Stern of Day* 112-7
Goldsmith *A New Simile*
Henryson *Testament of Cresseid* 239 ff

Mercury Mercury (*Hermes*) was the son of
Jupiter (*Zeus*) and *Maia* and was born in Arcadia. He was messenger of Jupiter and the
gods and so also god of travellers. As his fugitive role (and power to make himself invisible)
associated him with dishonesty, he was also
god of thieves (and merchants) — he robbed
Neptune of his trident and *Mars* of his sword.
He may appear with winged sandals, a large
hat and a short sword. Sometimes he holds a
purse (related to commerce) and has a cock
(vigilance) on his arm, or he may be without
arms (representing the power of speech over
action). He was credited with the invention
of the lyre, in return for which he received
Apollo's *caduceus* — an olive staff or wand
sometimes wound about with snakes and
credited with bringing sleep — and he was
made keeper of herds. He was also known as
a god of sports and games and was thought to
have pioneered astronomical discovery. The

invention of the harp was attributed to him. One of Mercury's duties was to guide the souls of the dead to *Hades*. His main love was for *Aphrodite*, mother of his child Hermaphroditus.

(Homeric Hymn *To Hermes* (18); Horace *Odes* i 10; Ovid *Fasti* v 663 ff, *Metamorphoses* i 671 ff, ii 708 ff; Virgil *Aeneid* viii 138 ff)

See also *Mercurie*, *Mercurius*

— *General*

Donne	*Second Anniversary* 199-200
Drayton	*Barons' Wars* vi 36
	To Himself and the Harp 36-42
Keats	*Endymion* i 378-84
Marlowe	*Hero and Leander* i 386 ff
Milton	*Comus* 962-5
Shakespeare	*Hamlet* III iv 55-63
	King Richard III IV iii 54-5
	Love's Labour's Lost V ii 917
	Merry Wives of Windsor II ii 71
Spenser	*Mother Hubberd's Tale* 1247-9, 1256-63, 1266-70
Swift	*Answer to a Scandalous Poem* 99
Tennyson	*The Lover's Tale* i 294-7

— *as Thief*

Donne	*Epigram — Mercurius* 7-8
Keats	*Cap and Bells* 618-21
Marlowe	*Hero and Leander* i 386 ff
Shakespeare	*Winter's Tale* IV iii 24-5

— *Appearance and Accoutrements*

Chapman	*Andromeda Liberata*
Keats	*Calidore* 113-15
	Endymion i 554-63, iv 331-6
	I Stood Tiptoe upon a Little Hill 23-5
Shakespeare	*King John* IV ii 4-5
Shelley	*Prometheus Unbound* I 318 ff, 325, 437-8
Spenser	*Faerie Queene* II xii 41, IV iii 42
	Mother Hubberd's Tale 1279 ff, 1292-9

Meroe An Ethiopian island in the Nile, named after the sister of *Cambyses*. *Pliny* notes that there the sun makes no shadow twice a year.

(Pliny ii 75)

Milton *Paradise Regained* iv 70-1 (error by Milton)

Merope One of the *Pleiades*. She was supposed to shine the least brightly because she was the only one to marry a mortal (*Sisyphus*).

(Apollodorus I ix 3; Ovid *Fasti* iv 175)

Tennyson *Did Not Thy Roseate Lips . . .* 15-16

Merops An Asian king, father of *Adrastus* and Amphius and the cause of the catastrophic driving of *Phaethon*'s sun-chariot.

Shakespeare *Two Gentlemen of Verona* III i 153-5

Messalina The wife of a consul murdered by *Nero*. Messalina proceeded to marry the murderer, but took up a literary life after Nero's death.

(Tacitus *Annals* XV 68 ff)

Swinburne *Masque of Bersabe*

Messenia The south-west of the Peloponnesus, half bleak and mountainous, half a fertile plain. Messenia was one party to the three Messenian Wars which occurred from the 8th to the 5th Centuries BC, concerning the independence of the Messenians from the Spartans (who were assisted by the Athenians). The immediate cause of the First War was the Messenian violation of Spartan women who had come to a religious ritual at Limnae on the border; it was claimed that the 'women' were in fact disguised soldiers.

Messenus

See *Misenus*

Chaucer *House of Fame* 1243-4

Metamorphoses The principal work of *Ovid*, a source-book for mythologising later poets.

Carew	*Elegy on the Death of John Donne* 65-7
Chaucer	*Man of Law's Tale, Introduction* 91-3

Metella Metella is known only from her tomb near Rome, where the stone names her as the wife of *Crassus*. This puts her in the prodigiously wealthy and influential family of Marcus Licinius Crassus, the associate in the

Metellius

1st Century BC of *Sulla (2)*, *Pompey* and *Cicero*. Her husband may have been his son.

Metellius   A Roman alleged to have beaten his wife to death for drinking. It is told also of one Egnatius Maetennus by *Pliny*.

(Valerius Maximus *Factorum . . . Libri*
VI 3; Pliny xix 13)
  Chaucer   *Wife of Bath's Prologue*
460-3

Mezentius   An Etruscan king who joined *Turnus* against *Aeneas*. Aeneas eventually killed him and his son Lausus.
(Virgil *Aeneid* vii-x)
See also *Latinus*
  Crashaw   *Sospetto d'Herode* 46

Mida, Midas   A King of *Phrygia* renowned for his wealth and generosity. He was rewarded by *Bacchus* with an open choice for having taken *Silenus* into his hospitality; he asked that whatever he touched be turned to gold. When his food turned to gold he discovered his mistake, but he was cured by bathing in the River *Pactolus*. Later, he contended that the music of *Pan* was superior to that of *Apollo*, for which opinion Apollo changed his ears into those of an ass. A servant or barber, unable to keep this metamorphosis secret, whispered it to a hole in the ground, from which grew a clump of reeds whispering the secret to all who listened.
(Ovid *Metemorphoses* xi 89 ff)
See also *Myda*
— *Asses' Ears*
  Blake   *In Imitation of Spenser* 15-18
  Byron   *Hints from Horace* 734-6
  Campion   *To His Sweet Lute Apollo*
1ff
  Coleridge   *Talleyrand to Lord Grenville*
47-8
  Fletcher P.   *Purple Island* i 17ff
  Marlowe   *Hero and Leander* i 473-5
  Milton   *Sonnet 13*
  Pope   *Epistle to Dr Arbuthnot* 69-72
— *Gold*
  Byron   *Age of Bronze* 659-61
  Chaucer   *Troilus and Criseyde* 1387-93
  Cowper   *The Task* iv 506
  Donne   *Elegy* xix 17-18
  Jonson   *Cynthia's Revels* V iii

    That Love's a Bitter Sweet
19-23
  Keats   *If by Dull Rhymes* 10-12
  Shakespeare   *Merchant of Venice* III ii
101-2
  Swift   *Fable of Midas* 1ff, 33-40

Mighty Mother   A name for *Cybele* or Nature.
(Ovid *Ars Amatoria* i 507;
Virgil *Georgics* IV 64)
  Gray   *Progress of Poesy* 85-6

Milesie
See *Miletus*
  Chaucer   *Franklin's Tale* 1409-11

Miletus   The capital of *Ionia* and a notable sea-power with many colonies until its fall to the Persians in 494BC and then the Gauls in the 3rd Century BC. A collection of Milesian Tales, perhaps pastoral romances, is referred to by *Ovid* and others as proverbially frivolous, but has not survived.
(Ovid *Tristia* ii 409-20; Strabo xiv 1)
See also *Milesie*

Milky Way   The Milky Way was viewed mythologically as milk — for example, as spurted when *Hera* tore her breast away on discovering that she was suckling *Hercules*, the son of her husband's mistress. It was also held to have been caused by the wild driving of *Phaethon* and the sun's chariot. It might be seen as a highway in and out of heaven to *Zeus*, lined by palaces of lesser gods.
(Ovid *Metamorphoses* i 168-76)
  Chaucer   *House of Fame* 936ff
  Drayton   *The Shepherd's Sirena* 13-16
  Keats   *Endymion* i 579-80
  Milton   *Paradise Lost* iv 974ff, vii 574-84

Milo   An Italian athlete of fabulous strength. He was said to have saved the life of *Pythagoras* (of whom he was a disciple) by holding up the collapsing building where he lectured. He died eaten by wild animals when his hands became trapped in a tree which he tried to uproot.
(Pausanias VI xiv 5-9)
  Shakespeare   *Troilus and Cressida* II iii
239-42

Miltiades II   The Athenian ruler of Thracian

Chersonese (Gallipoli) in the 6th Century BC. He won one of the victories against the Persians at *Marathon* in 490BC, but died in prison (where he had gone following accusations of treason) of wounds received in besieging *Paros* (one of the *Cyclades*) in 489.

(Herodotus vi)

Browning E. B.	*Battle of Marathon* i 142-6
Browning R.	*Aristophanes' Apology* 457-51
	Echetlos 28-9
Byron	*Isles of Greece* 12

Mincius A tributary of the River Po in North Italy. By it is *Mantua*, the birthplace of *Virgil*, who describes it as slow-flowing and edged with reeds.

(Virgil *Eclogues* vii 12-13, *Georgics* iii 14-15)

Milton   *Lycidas* 85-7

Minerva Minerva (*Pallas*, *Athene*, *Athena*) was daughter of *Zeus*, without a mother. She sprang fully armed from his head when it was split by the axe of *Prometheus* or *Vulcan/ Hephaestus*. She was goddess of war, wisdom, chastity, the arts and justice — a diverse sphere reflecting her pre-Hellenic origin. ('Both Minervas' refers to her main responsibilities — war and wisdom.) As the patron goddess of Athens and *Attica*, she led her chosen people to battle; in this she is distinct from *Mars*, whom she superseded to a degree. Her origin is reflected in her curious association, though a virgin warrior, with fertility. Probably at an early stage she was already goddess of crafts — spinning, weaving, metalwork, pottery. Later, she was identified with Athens and an explanation evolved for this: Minerva quarrelled with *Neptune* as to who should name Cecropia (Attica) and contested with him to produce the most useful article for the people; Neptune offered a horse, and Minerva an olive. As it represented peace, this was preferred by the gods; it also became a symbol for Minerva. Athens was then named after her and she represented this local triumph in her tapestry competition with *Arachne*. According to these many roles, Minerva may appear as a warrior with sword and helmet, sometimes with a cock on it, or in a flowing robe and with winged

shoes. Her shield has *Medusa*'s head on it, because she helped her half-brother *Perseus* kill that Gorgon. The owl and cock were associated with her and she may bear an olive bough — the owl represents wisdom and the cock, war.

(Apollodorus iii 14; Hesiod *Theogony* 938ff; Homeric Hymns *To Athena and Hephaestus* (20, 28); Homer *Iliad* v 738-41; Ovid *Fasti* iii 5-8, 809-22, *Metamorphoses* vi 70-102)

See also *Paris*, *Triton*

— *General*

Byron	*Curse of Minerva* 75ff
	Don Juan xv 97
Chaucer	*Book of the Duchess* 1055-75
	Troilus and Criseyde ii 1062
Daniel	*Civil Wars* ii 100
Drayton	*The Owl*
Jonson	*Charis* v 45ff
	Vision of Ben Jonson 31-2
Keats	*Endymion* ii 790-1
Marlowe	*Tamburlaine* i 1035-7
Pope	*Temple of Fame* 155-7
Spenser	*Faerie Queene* IV i 22
Swift	*Description of Mother Ludwell's Cave* 11-12
Wordsworth	*Evening Voluntaries* vii 26ff
Young	*Sea Piece* i

— *Birth*

Daniel	*Go, Wailing Verse* 1-2
Dryden	*Britannia Rediviva* 208-13
Herbert, Lord	*To His Mistress for Her True Picture* 113-15
Keats	*Otho the Great* I i 93-5
Lovelace	*To My Friend, Mr E. R.* 40-4
Milton	*Paradise Lost* ii 75-8
Wordsworth	*The Prelude* vii 538-9

— *and War*

Blake	*Imitation of Spenser* 44ff
Spenser	*Faerie Queene* III ix 22

— *Arachne, Arts and Crafts*

Jonson	*To Sir Henry Savile* 13-16
Lovelace	*Paris's Second Judgment* 5-6, 9-10
Spenser	*Muiopotmos* 272ff
Wordsworth	*On Seeing a Needlecase in the Form of a Harp* 5ff

— *and Medusa*

Browning	*Ring and the Book* xi 507
Chapman	*Andromeda Liberata*

Jonson	*If Men and Times Were Now* 37-41
Milton	*Comus* 447-9
Prior M.	*Prologue, Spoken at Court* 33-6

Minos   A King of *Crete*, son of *Zeus* and *Europa*, and brother of *Rhadamanthus* and Sarpedon. Minos was adopted by Asterius of Crete, whom he claimed the right to succeed. In a test of his own powers he challenged *Poseidon* to produce a bull from the sea, which could then be sacrificed; Poseidon obliged, but the beast seemed too handsome for such a fate and Minos substituted another, so incurring Poseidon's enmity. After Minos had married *Pasiphaë*, Poseidon made her fall in love with the bull, with which she had intercourse; she then gave birth to the *Minotaur* monster for which *Daedalus* constructed a labyrinth, where he was imprisoned but from which he managed to escape. Minos pursued Daedalus to Sicily but was killed there by a trick of King Cocalus. Minos was celebrated so widely that it has been supposed that there were several of that name, or that the name signified some title. Thus he had an unrelated reputation as a law-giver, having been given some insight into justice by Zeus, and was said to have established a legal system in Crete. This role he carried on after death, being a judge in *Hades* with his brother, Rhadamanthus.

See also *Mynos*

Auden	*Letter to Lord Byron* 792-3
Keats	*Visiting the Tomb of Burns* 8-10
Shakespeare	*King Henry VI pt 3* V vi 21-6
Shelley	*Oedipus Tyrannus* I i 136-40
Yeats	*Delphic Oracle Upon Plotinus*

Minotaur   The 'bull of Minos' (literally) was the product of the union of *Pasiphaë* and the Cretan Bull. It was kept in a maze, the Labyrinth (a Greek word of unknown meaning), which was designed and made by *Daedalus*, and it was fed on an annual tribute of youths and maidens extracted from the conquered Athens by *Minos* of Crete. *Theseus* ended this horror when, with *Ariadne*, Minos' daughter, he escaped from the Labyrinth and beat the monster to death. Daedalus suggested the clue

of thread by which Theseus was able to escape, and Daedalus and his son, *Icarus*, perhaps imprisoned for being accessories, made their escape on waxed wings.

(Ovid *Metamorphoses* viii 152ff; Apollodorus iii 15, *Epitome* i)

See also *Androgeus*

Auden	*New Year Letter*
Byron	*Don Juan* ii 155
Chaucer	*Knight's Tale* 975-80
	Legend of Good Women 1928ff, 2144-8
Crashaw	*Sospetto d'Herode* 44
Lewis C. D.	*Ariadne on Naxos*
Rosetti D. G.	*Burden of Nineveh* 10-14
Shelley	*Oedipus Tyrannus* I i 115-16, II i 136-40, ii 103-7

Minturnae   A town in central Italy near which Caius *Marius* hid from *Sulla (2)* in the marshes and where he was first sentenced to death and then released.

Byron   *Prophecy of Dante* i 104-6

Mirra

See *Myrrha*

Chaucer   *Troilus and Criseyde* iv 1138-9

Misenus   The trumpeter of *Hector* and *Aeneas*. He met his death from an envious *Triton* whom he had challenged, and Aeneas buried him on the promontory of Misenum, named after him.

(Virgil *Aeneid* vi 162ff)

See also *Messenus*

Mithridates VI (Eupator)   A King of Persia in the 1st Century BC. He was notorious for his ruthlessness, both in personal relationships (he imprisoned his mother, murdered his brother and married his sister), and in his conduct of the Mithridatic Wars with Rome. He began his career by sampling antidotes for all poisons that his enemies used or might use. He occupied most of Asia Minor and the Aegean islands, and much of Greece, from which *Sulla (2)* expelled him. He was defeated finally by *Pompey* at Nicopolis in 66BC and attempted to poison himself. Ironically, his lifelong study of prophylactics made this form of suicide unavailable to him and he had to be stabbed by a guard.

(Plutarch *Pompey*, *Lucullus*)
Shelley   *Oedipus Tyrannus* I i 354-6

Mnemosyne   Mnemosyne the Titaness was a daughter of *Uranus* and *Ge* (*Coelus* and *Terra*). As Goddess of Memory, she is largely an abstraction but has the important role of Mother of the *Muses* (to whom *Zeus* was Father), who may accompany them in the role of a shepherdess.

(Hesiod *Theogony* 53-74;
Ovid *Metamorphoses* vi 103 ff;
Aeschylus *Prometheus Bound* 459-61)
See also *Moneta*
Keats   *Hyperion* ii 29-30, iii 61-8, 72 ff
Spenser   *Faerie Queene* I xi 5-6, III iii 4, xi 35
Ruins of Time 363-9
Swinburne   *On the Cliffs* 423
Wordsworth   *Memorials of a Tour in Italy* vi 7-14

Modena
See *Mutina*
Shakespeare   *Antony and Cleopatra* I iv 56-9

Moeneceus
See *Tiresias*
Tennyson   *Tiresias* 134-7, 158-9

Moeris   A man-made lake supplied by flood-waters of the Nile. It contained two half-sunken pyramids, and there was a large horse-shoe shaped group of buildings regarded as a labyrinth. Its crocodiles were held to be sacred.

(Herodotus ii 148)
Shelley   *Witch of Atlas* 505-11

Moly   A herb with a black root and white or yellow flower. It was given to *Ulysses* by *Hermes*, to make him proof against the charms of *Circe*.

(Homer *Odyssey* x 302-6;
Pliny xxi 180)
Milton   *Comus* 636-7
Shelley   *Prometheus Unbound* II iv 59-63
Spenser   *Amoretti* 26

Momus, Momos   The god of ridicule or criticism, a son of *Nox*. Momus was expelled

from *Olympus* for ridiculing *Venus*, *Minerva* and other deities.

(Hesiod *Theogony* 214)
Coleridge   *Lines to a Comic Author* 4 ff
Keats   *Spirit Her that Reignest* 15-20
Welcome Joy and Welcome Sorrow 21
Pope   *Epistle* iii 3-4

Mona   Either Anglesey or the Isle of Man, which were once thought to have been peopled by elves and fairies. As centres of Druidism they were reduced by the Romans in the 1st Century AD.

(Caesar *Gallic War* v 13)
Collins   *Ode to Liberty* 81-2
Milton   *Lycidas* 52-4
Tennyson   *The Druid's Prophecies* 1-4

Moneta   A name occasionally given to *Mnemosyne* as *Titan* and Mother of the *Muses*. It was also used of *Juno* when she was regarded as the Mother. The name was explained as that of a temple from which was issued a warning or admonition, specifically an order to sacrifice in order to avert an earthquake. The matter remains obscure.

(Cicero *De Divinatione* i 45;
Hyginus *Praefatio* 3, 27; Livy vii 28)
Keats   *The Fall of Hyperion* i 224-7, 256 ff

Morn, Morning
See *Aurora*
Milton   *Comus* 753
Paradise Lost vi 2-4
Shelley   *Adonais* 120-3
Spenser   *Faerie Queene* I ii 7
Epithalamion 74-7

Morphean
See *Morpheus*
Keats   *Eve of St Agnes* 257

Morpheus   The son and minister of *Somnus*, God of *Sleep*, Morpheus has been depicted as a fat winged child holding poppies. He had the gift of being able perfectly to imitate people and this he employed in appearing in dreams. He may appear with his brothers *Phobetor* (animal forms) and Phantasos (inanimate natural forms).

(Ovid *Metamorphoses* xi 635 ff)

Byron   *To M.S.G.* 5-6
Chaucer   *Book of the Duchess* 136-46, 155-77
        House of Fame 66-76
Donne   *To Mr R.W.* 1-5
Drayton   *The Barons' Wars* vi 47
Keats   *Endymion* i 554-60, iii 121-2
Marlowe   *Hero and Leander* i 347-50
        Jew of Malta 674-7
Milton   *Il Penseroso* 9-10
Pope   *Ode for Musick* 25 ff
Sidney   *Astrophel and Stella* 32
Spenser   *Faerie Queene* I i 36, 39, iv 44, VI viii 34
Swift   *A Love Song* 23-4

Moschus   A Syracusian poet of the 2nd Century BC, author of pastorals and at one time accredited author of the *Lament for Bion*, an important poem in the development of pastoral elegy. His *First Idyll* concerns the loss of *Cupid* by *Venus*.

Browning R.   *Ring and the Book* ix 527 ff

Mulciber   A name for *Vulcan*, representing his occupation as 'softener' or blacksmith.

(Ovid *Metamorphoses* ii 5, ix 423, *Ars Amatoria* ii 567)

Milton   *Paradise Lost* i 740 ff
Spenser   *Faerie Queene* II vii 5, III xi 26

Musaeus (1)   A legendary Greek poet, son or pupil of *Orpheus* and founder of *Attic* poetry. He is placed in the Elysian Fields by *Virgil*, towering over a crowd of worshippers.

(Aristophanes *Frogs* 1032-3; Plato *Republic* 364E; Virgil *Aeneid* vi 667)

Denham   *Progress of Learning* 23-4
Drayton   *Endymion and Phoebe* 997-8
Marlowe   *Doctor Faustus* 142-5
Milton   *Il Penseroso* 103-4
Wordsworth   *Written in a Blank Leaf of Ossian* 37-44

Musaeus (2)   A Greek poet of the late 5th Century AD, known as Musaeus Grammaticus. He was the author of *Hero and Leander*, which was influential on English versions.

Herrick   *Apparition of His Mistress* 26-7
Marlowe   *Hero and Leander* i 51-3

Muse   The goddess, inspiration or essence of an art; one of the *Muses*. References are so numerous that only a selection is given here.

Byron   *Childe Harold* i 1
Chaucer   *Troilus and Criseyde* ii 8-10
Collins   *Ode on the Popular Superstitions* 32, 139, 191
        Epistle to Sir Thomas Hanmer 31-2
        Ode to Fear 26-7
        Ode to Pity 34
Gray   *Elegy Written in a Country Churchyard* 71-2
        Epitaph on Sir William Williams 3
Keats   *To George Felton Matthew* 31-4, 53-6
Milton   *Lycidas* 66, 132-3
        Paradise Lost ix 20-4
Spenser   *Faerie Queene* I vi 5
Wordsworth   *Epistle to George Beaumont* 38-43
        Vernal Ode 75-80

Muses   The Muses were daughters of *Zeus* (or *Phoebus*) and *Mnemosyne* (or *Antiope*). They are the patron spirits of the arts. In most accounts they are nine in number and their names are *Clio* (history), *Euterpe* (music), *Thalia (1)* (pastoral and comedy), *Melpomene* (tragedy), *Terpsichore* (dancing), *Erato (1)* (lyric poetry), *Polyhymnia* (singing and rhetoric), *Calliope* (heroic poetry) and *Urania (1)* (astronomy) — though the assignment of arts to individual Muses is not always consistent. They had their seat on Mount *Helicon*, or, with the gods, on *Olympus*, or on *Pierus*, and they were said to dance round the thrones of *Saturn* and *Jupiter*. They were variously imagined — *Pindar* gives them both fair hair and violet (bright) tresses, and the latter are sometimes recalled in English poetry. Only a few of he many references are given here.

(Hesiod *Theogony* 1-10, 36-85; Pausanias ix 29; Pindar *Pythian Ode* i 2, *Isthmian Ode* vii 23)

See also *Muse*, *Parnassus*, *Pierian*, *Nine*

Browning E. B.   *Portuguese Sonnets* 19
Chaucer   *Man of Law's Tale, Introduction* 91-3

	House of Fame 1399-404
	Troilus and Criseyde iii 1807-10
Collins	*Lines on the Music of the*
	Grecian Theatre 9-11
Cowley	*On Orinda's Poems* 4
Herrick	*His Farewell to Poetry* 83-8
Keats	*Lamia* i 70-5
Marlowe	*Tamburlaine* i 1035-7
Milton	*Il Penseroso* 47-8
	Paradise Lost iii 26-9
Noyes	*Mount Ida* 2-3
Pope	*Spring* 3-4
	Winter 21-4
Skelton	*Garland of Laurel*
Spenser	*Epithalamion* 1-3, 14
	Faerie Queene II xii 71,
	VI *Prologue* 2-3
	Ruins of Time 365-77
	Shepherd's Calendar, April
	41-5, 100-5, *June* 28ff,
	November 146-7
	Tears of the Muses 1-12,
	55-8, 271-5, 403-6
Tennyson	*The Princess* 13-14

Music
See *Euterpe*

Collins	*The Passions* 95ff

Music of the Spheres *Plato* — directly or indirectly the source for most writing on this theme — describes a spindle of Necessity on which the systems of the universe, eight concentric whorls, revolve, each emitting a different note; these notes combine into a single harmony. This was readily adapted to the Ptolemaic system of fixed stars and planets — spheres. The music represents that which keeps Nature on her course, imperceptible to man. It was a very popular idea with poets and moralists despite the fact that *Aristotle* dismissed it as fanciful. There were several explanations as to why this celestial music, betokening a concord in the scheme of things, should be inaudible to mortals. One was that habit made them immune to it; others were that only angels, the supremely virtuous, and the unfallen or the regenerate soul could hear such things.

(Plato *Republic* x 617ff;
Plotinus *Enneads* II iii 9)
See also *Necessity (Platonic)*

Chaucer	*Parliament of Fowls* 59-63
	Troilus and Criseyde i 1812-3
Crashaw	*Music's Duel* 116-20
Davies, Sir J.	*Orchestra* 123-6
Donne	*A Litany* 200-1
Henryson	*Orpheus and Eurydice* 219ff
Keats	*Endymion* ii 674-5
	Lamia i 265-70
	Sleep and Poetry 171-7
	To Kosciusko 1-4
	To My Brother George 4-5
	On Leaving Some Friends 11-12
Milton	*Arcades* 63-73
	Comus 111-4, 1019-21
	On the Morning of Christ's
	Nativity 125-35
Pope	*Essay on Man* i 201-6
Shakespeare	*As You Like It* II vii 5-6
	Merchant of Venice V i
	58-65
	Pericles V i 225-8
Shelley	*Daemon of the World* 244-50
	Prometheus Unbound IV 186ff,
	246ff
	Queen Mab ii 76-82, vi 40-1,
	vii 18
Tennyson	*The Lover's Dream* i 463-7
	Parnassus 8

Mutina Modern *Modena*, the site of a siege in 43BC, in which *Pansa* and *Hirtius* were killed on *Augustus*'s side, and *Mark Antony* was defeated.

Mycerinus An ancient Egyptian king. Told by an oracle that he had but six years to live, Mycerinus chose to double the allotted span by making the nights into days of revelry. The reason for his sentence was that his justness and kindness on the throne were contrary to a destiny of 150 years of misery due to Egypt.

(Herodotus ii 129-33)

Arnold	*Mycerinus* 7-12, 122

Myda
See *Midas*

Chaucer	*Wife of Bath's Tale* 952-77

Mygra
See *Megaera*

Henryson	*Orpheus and Eurydice* 261ff,
	475-8

Mylae A north Sicilian town, site of an important coastal naval battle in 260 BC, when the increased and refitted Roman navy defeated the Carthaginians.

> Eliot T. S. *The Waste Land* 69-72

Mynerve
See *Minerva*

> Chaucer *Legend of Good Women* 930-3

Mynos
See *Minos*

> Chaucer *Legend of Good Women* 1886-90, 1894-8, 1907-16, 1928 ff
> *Troilus and Criseyde* IV 1187-8

Myrmidons The people of Phthia, whose King was Peleus, whose son was *Achilles*; the Myrmidons were Achilles and the men he took to the Trojan War.
See also *Aegina*

> Marlowe *Dido Queen of Carthage* 418-19
> Shakespeare *Troilus and Criseyde* I iii 378-9; V v 30-4

Myrrh, Myrrha A daughter of Cinyras, King of Cyprus. She was punished by *Aphrodite* for not honouring her, or because her mother boasted excessively of the girl's beauty. The punishment was an incestuous passion for her father; aided by her nurse, Myrrha slept with him for twelve nights and became pregnant. He pursued her when he discovered that he had been duped, but the gods made her invisible, changing her into a myrrh tree, whose precious gum her tears were said to be. After nine months, the tree split open and revealed the baby *Adonis* inside. Cinyras committed suicide. Myrrha was also known as Smyrna.

> (Apollodorus III xiv 4; Ovid *Metamorphoses* x 298 ff)
> Spenser *Faerie Queene* III vii 26, IV vii 22

Myrtle, Myrtles
See *Venus*

> Keats *Sleep and Poetry* 248-51
> Milton *Paradise Lost* iv 260-3, 692-4, ix 217-19, 428-32, 626-7

Mysia A country north of *Lydia*, now northern Turkey.
See also *Atys*

Nabis A Spartan general and tyrant of the 2nd Century BC. He was known particularly for the instrument of torture named after his wife, *Apega*.

> (Livy xxix, Polybius xiii)

Naiad, Naiades A class of nymph presiding over springs, rivers and wells. Naiads haunted the locale of their particular water and were depicted as beautiful maidens, sometimes with an urn from which flowed water. Many references to them are general and of no particular interest. There follows a selection.

> Arnold *Lines Written on the Seashore* 1 ff
> Brook *The Old Vicarage, Grantchester* 38-42
> Browning E. B. *The Dead Pan* 6
> *The Lost Bower* 36
> Collins *Ode on the Popular Superstitions . . .* 1-2
> Drayton *Endymion and Phoebe* 798-801
> *Polyolbion* vi 7-10
> Hood *Hero and Leander* 36
> Keats *Endymion* i 271-2, ii 98-100, iv 701-9
> *How fevered is the man* 7-8
> *Fall of Hyperion* i 317-8
> *To George Felton Mathew* 20-3
> Milton *Paradise Regained* ii 353-6
> Noyes *At Dawn* 58-61
> Scott *Saint Cloud* 10-11
> Shakespeare *The Tempest* IV i 127-33
> Shelley *Ode to Liberty* 110-3
> *Witch of Atlas* 217-9, 226-7
> Shenstone *Progress of Taste* iii 11 ff
> Spenser *Faerie Queene* I vi 6
> Tennyson *Adeline* 15-16
> Wordsworth *River Duddon* xii 6
> *The Triad* 8-14

Nais An *Oceanid*, the mother of *Glaucus* (by *Neptune* or by Magnes, son of *Aeolus*); and, by some accounts, of *Chiron*.

> (Apollodorus i)

Keats   *Endymion* iii 898-902
Spenser   *Mutability Cantos* vii 40

Narcissus   A beautiful youth born at Thespis in Boeotia, son of the river god *Cephissus*. Seeing his image reflected in water, he mistook it for the nymph of the place and fell in love with it. Eventually he committed suicide, and his blood was changed into a flower. Earlier, his self-love had caused the death of *Echo*, who had fallen in love with him.

(Ovid *Metamorphoses* iii 346, 370ff; Hyginus *Fabulae* 271)

Auden   *Death's Echo* 27
Bridges   *A Water-Party* 7ff
Chaucer   *Book of the Duchess* 731-6
    Franklin's Tale 944-52
    Knight's Tale 1936-46
Cowley   *Platonick Love* 3
    Weeping 2
Crashaw   *Sospetto d'Herode* 10
De La Mare   *Winged Chariot*
Goldsmith   *On a Beautiful Youth Struck Blind with Lightning* 1-4
Jonson   *Cynthia's Revels* 1 i
Keats   *I Stood Tiptoe Upon a Little Hill* 172-8
Lawrence   *Narcissus* 4ff
Marlowe   *Hero and Leander* i 73-6
Milton   *Comus* 230-7
    Paradise Lost iv 460-8
Pope   *Of a Lady Who Could Not Sleep* II
Shakespeare   *Antony and Cleopatra* II v 95-6
    Rape of Lucrece 264-6
    Venus and Adonis 161-2
Shelley   *Adonais* 140-4
    Lines to a Reviewer 11-13
Sidney   *Astrophel and Stella* 82
Spenser   *Amoretti* 35, 83
    Faerie Queene III ii 44-5, vi 45
Suckling   *The Metamorphosis* 1-4

Naso
See *Ovid*
Chaucer   *Legend of Good Women* 724ff, 928-9, 2218-20
Shakespeare   *Love's Labour's Lost* IV ii 115ff

Nautilus   A Mediterranean mollusc, called Nautilus by the Greeks. The paper nautilus, *Argonautica argo*, has some resemblance to a ship. Shelley uses the name for himself in punning reference to 'shell'.

Shelley   *Revolt of Islam* 3060-3

Naxos   The largest of the Cyclades islands in the Aegean Sea. Naxos was where *Ariadne* was reputed to have been abandoned by *Theseus*. It was fertile and famous for its wines, and *Bacchus* was its principal god.

Chaucer   *Man of Law's Tale, Introduction* 68-9
Moore   *Evenings in Greece* ii 79-80

Neaera   A nymph famed for her chestnut-coloured hair.

(Horace *Odes* iii 14; Tibullus *Lygdamus* iii 2; Virgil *Eclogues* iii 3)

Browning R.   *Ring and the Book* v 669-72
Milton   *Lycidas* 68-9

Necessity (Platonic)   As described by *Plato*, Necessity supports a steel shaft on which turn the eight concentric whorls of the universe, giving out music. The spindle rests on the knees of Necessity and round her are her daughters, the *Fates*, who rotate it, singing and spinning with the harmony. *Atropos*, the oldest of the three, cuts the spun thread at the moment of death. In versions of Christian times there are said to be nine spheres, matching nine orders of angels. In an analogous description, Plato likened the stellar systems to a choric dance.

(Plato *Republic* 617-21, *Timaeus* 40; Plotinus *Enneads* II iii 9)

See also *Destiny, Music of the Spheres*
Milton   *Arcades* 63-70
Shelley   *Daemon of the World* 288-91
Yeats   *His Bargain*

Nectar   The drink, or blood, of the gods.
See also *Ambrosia*
Keats   *Endymion* iii 924-6
Milton   *At a Vacation Exercise* 38-9
    Comus 478-80, 837-40
    Lycidas 172-5
    Paradise Lost iv 237-40, v 632-5
Shelley   *Prometheus Unbound* III i 30

Spenser	*Hymn in Honour of Beauty* 248-9
	Hymn in Honour of Love 280-7
	Ruins of Time 398-9
	Shepherd's Calendar, November 193-6

Nectarin, Nectarous
See *Nectar*

Keats	*Endymion* iii 891-2
Milton	*Paradise Lost* iv 331-2, v 303-7, vi 331-3

Neda   A river of Elis in *Arcadia*.

Prior	*First Hymn to Callimachus* 39 ff

Neleus   Children of *Tyro* by *Neptune*, Neleus and *Pelias* were left out in the wilds by their mother. Tyro wished to conceal them from her future husband Cretheus, King of Iolchus. Reared by horse-herders, they usurped the throne from *Aeson*, who was Tyro's son by Cretheus. They subsequently parted and Neleus founded the city of *Pylos*. He married Chloris, daughter of *Amphion* — she was the sole surviving child of Amphion and *Niobe* whose children died because Niobe boasted her superiority to *Latona*. *Hercules* killed all of Neleus' family except for *Nestor*; their enmity arose because Hercules had murdered Iphitus and Neleus was a friend of Iphitus' father. The equally fraught story of Pelias, and his death at the hands of his daughters at the instigation of *Medea*, is the tragic background to the epic of *Jason* and the *Argonauts*.

(Apollodorus I ix 8-9, 16; Apollonius Rhodius)

Drayton	*Polyolbion* xx 167-8
Spenser	*Faerie Queene* IV xi 14

Nemea, Nemean (Lion)   A town of *Argolis* in the Peloponnesus. This was where *Hercules* performed his first labour, slaying the fabulous offspring of *Typhon* or of Orthus and *Echidna*. The animal was invulnerable to weapons, so Hercules strangled it. Thereafter he wore its skin. The lion was set in the sky as the constellation Leo.

(Apollodorus ii 5)

Chaucer	*Monk's Tale* 3258-92
Marvell	*Letter to Dr Ingelo* 49-50

Shakespeare	*Hamlet* I v 81-3
	Love's Labour's Lost IV i 81-6
Spenser	*Daphnaida* 162-6
	Faerie Queene II v 31, V Prologue 6
	Muiopotmos 65-72
	Mutability Cantos vii 36

Nemertea   A *Nereid*.

Spenser	*Faerie Queene* IV 11 51

Nemesis   Goddess of Fate and Retribution, daughter of *Nox* (Nyx). In one myth, *Zeus* was at enmity with her because she rejected him. In another, Nemesis is brought into the story of Zeus and *Leda*. Here Nemesis takes the place of Leda and produces the eggs, which are then given to Leda, who hatches them. Nemesis represented vengeance, vengeance usually believed by someone to be just, and so her relationship with Zeus the Almighty — another supreme avenger — was bound to be problematic. She might be depicted with a ship's wheel and wings — control and speed — and was worshipped in a Greek festival (Nemesia) of the departed, whose interests she was held to look after.

(Hesiod *Theogony* 223-4; Apollodorus III x 7)

Byron	*Childe Harold* iv 132
Daniel	*Civil Wars* vi 30 ff
Keats	*Endymion* iv 478-80
Shakespeare	*King Henry VI pt 1* IV vii 77-8
Spenser	*Muiopotmos* 1-3

Neoptolemus
See *Pyrrhus (2)*

Shakespeare	*Troilus and Cressida* IV v 142-5

Nepenthe   A pain- and grief-killing drug, perhaps opium, put into *Menelaus'* wine by *Helen*. She had been given it by an Egyptian woman, *Polydamna*, for Egypt was said to be the land richest in herbs. Her purpose was to quell the general lament which followed recollections of the apparently lost *Odysseus* in the presence of his son, *Telemachus*.

(Homer *Odyssey* iv 219-32)

Milton	*Comus* 675-7

Pope   *Epilogue to the Satires* 98
Shelley   *Prometheus Unbound* II iv
       59-63
       Triumph of Life 356-9
Spenser *Faerie Queene* IV iii 43-4
Thomson *Castle of Indolence* i xxvii

Neptune, Neptunus Originally a minor water-deity, Neptune was identified with the Greek *Poseidon*, God of the Sea, who was a son of *Chronos* (*Saturn*) and *Rhea* (*Ops*). When Chronos and the *Titans* were defeated by *Zeus*, Poseidon and other gods, the kingdom was divided between Zeus, Poseidon and *Pluto*; these three had (by the devices of Rhea) survived their father's habit of swallowing his children at birth lest they supersede him. Poseidon conspired to dethrone his brother Zeus for having an unfair share, but he was defeated; his mythology is full of such territorial disputes. He was god of all water, as well as the sea, and had the power to cause earthquakes. Neptune/Poseidon fathered numerous children, the mothers of whom included *Amphitrite*, *Tyro*, *Antiope*, *Eurynome*, *Alcyone*, *Arethusa* and *Oenone*. These mothers were visited by him in many forms – a ram, a bird, a bull, a dolphin. His affair, as a ram, with Theophane produced the *Golden Fleece*. He was indeed among the most promiscuous of Classical deities and the poets have vied in listing his affairs and their offspring. He usually carries a trident and may ride in a chariot drawn by dolphins.

    (Hesiod *Theogony* 453-67; Homer
      Iliad xv 187-93; Apollodorus I i;
         Virgil *Aeneid* v 816-26)

See also *Triton*
– *General*
Chaucer *Franklin's Tale* 1045-8
       Legend of Good Women
       2414ff
       Troilus and Criseyde IV 120-4
Crabbe *To the Monthly Review* 5-9
Crashaw *Mark IV* 7-8
Drayton *Polyolbion* xx 165-6
Dunbar *Quben Merche Wes* 64-70
Keats *Endymion* i 347-8, 592-3, 880-4,
    iii 81-2, 210-2, 238-48, 352-5,
    718-27, 807-10, 833-43, 944ff,
    1010-5
    To Homer 5-8

Marlowe *Tamburlaine* i 1035-7
Milton *At a Vacation Exercise* 43-4
    Comus 17-21, 67-70, 89-90
    Paradise Lost ix 13-19
    Paradise Regained ii 188-91
Shakespeare *Antony and Cleopatra* IV
    xiv 57-60
    Hamlet I i 117-20
    King Henry IV pt 2 III i
    49-51
    King John V ii 33-6
    King Richard II II i 61-3
    Macbeth II ii 60-3
    Midsummer Night's Dream
    III ii 370-3
    Pericles III i 35-7; V i 16-17
    The Tempest I ii 200-5;
    V i 33-6
    Troilus and Cressida V ii
    169-74
    Winter's Tale V i 153-4
Spenser *Faerie Queene* I iii 32, xi 54,
    II vi 10, xii 22, III iv 10, 32,
    42, vii 30, xi 40-1
    Muiopotmos 272ff
    Mutability Cantos vii 26
Wordsworth *Memorials of a Tour 1820*
    xxxii 30-3
– *Appearance and Accoutrements*
Browning E. B. *The Dead Pan* 15
Byron *The Island* ii 466ff
Keats *Endymion* iii 862-5, 886-92
Marvell *Last Instructions to a Painter*
    543ff
Shakespeare *Coriolanus* III i 255-8
Spenser *Faerie Queene* III xi 40,
    IV xi 11
– *His Loves*
Drayton *Rosamond and Henry II*
    153-8
Lovelace *Triumphs of Philamore* 123
Marlowe *Hero and Leander* ii 153ff
Shakespeare *Winter's Tale* IV iv 25-30
Spenser *Faerie Queene* III xi 42,
    IV ix 23
– *Origin and Birth*
Drayton *Polyolbion* xx 156-9
Keats *Hyperion* i 142-7, ii 232-5
– *Children*
Drayton *Polyolbion* xx 167-76
Spenser *Faerie Queene* IV xi 15-16

Nereid, Nereids Fifty (or, in some accounts, thirty) sea-nymphs, daughters of *Nereus* (the son of *Oceanus* and a predecessor to *Poseidon*) and *Doris (1)*. They were minor gods in service to *Neptune*/Poseidon, having the moods of the sea in their control, and being the recipients of prayers from seafarers. They lived in caves, where they had altars, and are portrayed as sportive and beautiful maidens with an abundance of fine tresses. Many names are listed for the fifty, but accounts vary. *Thetis, Galatea, Psamathe* and *Ione* occur most often.

(Apollodorus I ii 6; Hesiod *Theogony* 1003-7; Homer *Iliad* xviii 37 ff)

Bridges   *Demeter* 328-35
Browning E. B.   *The Soul's Travelling* 159-60
Cowper   *Conversation* 537-40
Diaper   *Sea Eclogues* i 10-12
Dryden   *Prologue to the Duchess* 14-15
Gray   *On the Death of a Favourite Cat* 34
Hood   *Hero and Leander* 36
Keats   *Endymion* iii 888-91, 1010-5
   Lamia i 205-8
Milton   *Il Penseroso* 19-21
Shakespeare   *Antony and Cleopatra* II ii 202 ff
Shelley   *Prometheus Unbound* II v 20-8, III ii 44-8
Spenser   *Faerie Queene* IV xi 48-52
Swinburne   *Atalanta in Calydon* 607
Wordsworth   *Memorials of a Tour 1820* 3 ff
Young   *Ocean*

Nereus Father of the *Nereid* sea-nymphs, a son of *Oceanus* and *Terra* and married to his sister, *Doris (1)*. He was a prophet who, when pressed, told *Hercules* how to obtain the golden apples of the *Hesperides*, and warned *Paris* of the great risk of taking *Helen*. He was able to change his shape at will and was regarded as one of the oldest of the gods. He lived with the Nereids in the Aegean, and was represented as a beneficent old man with a flowing beard.

(Hesiod *Theogony* 233-64; Apollodorus I ii 6, II v 2; Homer *Iliad* xviii 38 ff; Horace *Odes* i 15)

Drayton   *Barons' Wars* iii 47
   Polyolbion v 21-4

Kingsley   *Andromeda* 136-8
Milton   *Comus* 835, 871
   Endymion iii 997-1000
Spenser   *Faerie Queene* I iii 31, III iv 19, IV xi 18

Nero The son of *Agrippina The Younger (2)*. Adopted by *Claudius* Caesar in 50AD (whom he succeeded in 54) by the influence of Agrippina, Nero started his reign in an acceptable and virtuous manner. *Suetonius* records that, aged seventeen, Nero wished he could not write so that he might be unable to sign a death warrant. With the murder of Agrippina, however, whom he came to regard as an obstacle to his power, he began a career of bloodshed which has become a byword for barbarity. Having had Rome set on fire in imitation of the sacking of Troy, and contemplated the scene from a tower, he rebuilt parts of the city at his own expense, including a palace (the Golden House) of celebrated extravagance for himself to occupy. This was one expression of his passion for art. A less estimable one was his insistence that no one, even mortally ill or about to give birth, might leave an audience whilst he himself was singing or reciting. Neither did the creations of *Lucan* or *Seneca* save them from death at his instigation, despite earlier favours. As the army eventually turned against him, Nero committed suicide in 68AD. His personality was one of unstable and tortured contradictions and on his death the people reacted appropriately with mingled grief and delight.

(Tacitus *Histories* i, ii; Suetonius vi)

— *General*
Lewis C. D.   *Letter from Rome*
Browning R.   *Ring and the Book* 1x 830-3
Byron   *The Island* ii 191
   Don Juan iii 109
Chaucer   *Knight's Tale* 2031-5
   Monk's Tale 3653-7
Crashaw   *Sospetto d'Herode* 46
Herbert   *Church Militant* 141-2
Marvell   *Flecknoe* 117 ff
Pope   *Essay on Man* ii 195-8
Shakespeare   *Hamlet* III ii 383-6
   King Henry VI pt 3 III i 38-41
   King John V ii 152-3

Swinburne *Birthday Ode* 340-4
Young *Night Thoughts* vi
— *Burning and Rebuilding of Rome*
  Chaucer *Nun's Priest's Tale* 4559-63
  Pope *Epistle* iv 69ff
  Shakespeare *King Henry VI pt 1* I iv
        93-5
  Shelley *Queen Mab* iii 176-88
— *Some Victims*
  Chaucer *Monk's Tale* 3705-10
  Cowley *Brutus* 3
  Gray *Agrippina* 64-7

Nervii A Flemish tribe defeated by Caesar in 57BC, in a battle where Caesar's personal role was regarded as critical.
          (Caesar *Gallic War* II v 10;
           Plutarch *Caesar* xx 3-5)
  Shakespeare *Julius Caesar* III ii
        169-74

Neso A *Nereid*.
  Spenser *Faerie Queene* IV 11 50

Nessus A centaur killed by *Hercules* in the final phase of his career. Nessus' job was to ferry people over the River *Euenus* in Calydon (the south-eastern Greek mainland), and he claimed divine right for it. He assaulted Hercules' bride Deianira, a princess of Calydon, and was shot in the heart by Hercules. As he died, Nessus pretended contrition to Deianira. He suggested that she give his bloody tunic (or blood from it) to Hercules, on whom it would act as an aphrodisiac, whereas in fact the blood was tainted with venom. She had cause to try the charm when Hercules took a new mistress, and its effects amply demonstrated the vindictiveness of Nessus; when Hercules put the tunic on, his skin burned, and when he took it off, flesh came off also. When she heard of the results, Deianira committed suicide. The poisoned Shirt of Nessus was a major factor in the rather obscure events surrounding Hercules' death soon afterwards.
          (Apollodorus ii 7; Diodorus Siculus iv 36;
           Ovid *Metamorphoses* ix 101ff;
           Sophocles *Trachiniae* 555ff)
See also *Oechalia*
  Byron *Don Juan* xvi 11
  Chaucer *Monk's Tale* 3309-24

Drayton *Elinor Cobham to Duke
        Humphrey* 117-20
Dryden *Aureng-Zebe* II i
Eliot T. S. *Little Gidding* iv
Jonson *The Poetaster* III i
Shakespeare *All's Well that Ends Well*
        IV iii 233-4
Spenser *Faerie Queene* I xi 27

Nestor Nestor, an *Argonaut*, was the sole survivor of the sons of *Neleus* when *Hercules* destroyed that family. After a heroic life, which he delighted to recount, he became the respected, if somewhat ineffective, elder statesman of the Trojans — he was in fact King of *Pylos* and brought ninety ships to help Troy — in the War. His longevity (three generations) was celebrated by Greek and Roman poets.
  Browning E. B. *Battle of Marathon*
        425-6
  Drayton *Polyolbion* xx 167-8
  Gray *Extempore on Dr Keene* 1-2
  Hood *Progress of Art* 5
  Jonson *Volpone* III iv
  Keats *King Stephen* I iii 11-12
  Rochester *On Drinking in a Bowl* 1-4
  Shakespeare *King Henry VI pt 1* II v
        5-7; *pt 3* III ii 188-93
        Love's Labour's Lost iii
        162ff
        Rape of Lucrece 1401ff
        Troilus and Cressida I iii
        61, 291-2, IV v 203
  Sidney *Arcadia* lxxiv 19-20
        Astrophel and Stella 35
  Spenser *Faerie Queene* II ix 56-7
  Swinburne *Atalanta in Calydon* 1249
        *Song for the Centenary of
        Landor* 12

Nicanor An officer of *Alexander* the Great in the capture of *Thebes* 336BC. (The story of the Theban girl who sacrificed herself for his life — as of the other girl with her — is told by Jerome *Contra Jovinianum*.)
See also *Nichanore*

Niceratе The wife of Niceratus who killed herself when her husband was slain by the *Thirty Tyrants* imposed on Athens by *Lysander* in 404BC.
          (Diodorus Siculus XIV v 5)

Nichanore
See *Nicanor*
    Chaucer   *Franklin's Tale* 1431-3

Nicias
See *Nikias*

Night
See *Nox.*   The references below are to the
goddess.
— *Mourner*
    Collins   *Persian Eclogues* ii 53-4
— *and Chaos*
    Milton   *Paradise Lost* i 543, ii 894-6,
                961-3, 969-70, iii 17-18, 424-6,
                iv 665-7, x 476-7
    Spenser   *Faerie Queene* v 22, III iv 55
— *and Chariot*
    Keats   *Otho the Great* IV ii 30-5
    Milton   *Comus* 552-4
                *On the Morning of Christ's
                Nativity* 235-6
    Spenser   *Faerie Queene* I v 28

Nightingale
See *Philomel*, *Philomela*
    Milton   *Comus* 233-5
    Spenser   *Shepherd's Calendar, August*
                183-6
    Wordsworth   *To Enterprise* 144-6

Nikias   An Athenian general (470-413 BC)
and rival of Cleon after the death of *Pericles.*
He disagreed with the aggressive policy of *Alcibiades* towards Sicily, but was nonetheless appointed to lead an expedition against Syracuse
during the Peloponnesian War. By then he was
a sick man and made several misjudgments;
his troops were defeated at Assinarus and he
was captured and executed.
                      (Plutarch *Nicias*;
                      Thucydides vii 86)
    Browning R.   *Balaustion's Adventure*
                7-10

Nine
See *Muses*
    Arnold   *Empedocles on Etna* ii 445 ff
    Blake   *To the Muses* 1 ff
    Burns   *Epistle to Davie* 143-6
                Epistle to J. L . . . k 92-4
    Byron   *The First Kiss of Love* 9-12

    Campbell   *Pleasures of Hope*
                  Song of the Greeks 43-4
    Drayton   *To Himself and the Harp* 11-15
    Goldsmith   *On Seeing Mrs . . . Perform
                  in the Character of . . .* 1
    Gray   *Progress of Poesy* 77-8
    Keats   *Acrostic* 15
                Endymion iv 11-12
                To Apollo 1-6, 42-3
    Kipling   *Samuel Pepys* 23-7
    Moore   *The Philosopher Aristippus*
                38-42
    Noyes   *Helicon* 1-4
    Pope   *Temple of Fame* 265 ff

Nineveh   The capital of Assyria, built by
Belus and *Semiramis*, father and wife of *Ninus.*
It was of prodigious size and surrounded by
high walls whose thickness was the width of
three chariots. It was also known as Ninus. The
city was destroyed by the Medes in 612 BC,
but rebuilt by Nebuchadnezzar, when it was
regarded as one of the Wonders of the World,
though as capital it was superseded by *Babylon*,
which Nebuchadnezzar also rebuilt.
                (Diodorus Siculus ii 7, iii 1-4;
                      Herodotus i 178)
    Chaucer   *Canon Yeoman's Tale* 972-5
    Keats   *Endymion* iii 847-9
    Milton   *Paradise Regained* iii 275-8

Ninus   The first king of Assyria and founder
of the capital Ninus, or *Nineveh*, of *Babylon.*
He married *Semiramis*, wife of one of his offi-
cers, and she may have had a hand in his
death. His reputation was war-like, but he is
a largely legendary figure, deified after his
death. *Pyramus* and *Thisbe* arranged to meet
at Ninus' tomb.
                      (Diodorus Siculus ii;
                    Ovid *Metamorphoses* iv 88)
    Milton   *Paradise Regained* iii 275-8
    Pope   *Temple of Fame* 95-6
    Shakespeare   *Midsummer Night's Dream*
                V i 136-7
    Spenser   *Faerie Queene* I v 48, II ix 21,
                56-7
                Ruins of Time 509-11

Niobe, Niobean   Daughter of *Tantalus* and
married to *Amphion*, Niobe boasted in the
number of her children from Amphion — seven,

ten or twelve sons and daughters according to various accounts. She presumed to rival *Latona*, who had only *Apollo* and *Diana*, and she ridiculed worship of the goddess. Latona sought help from her children, and Apollo destroyed with darts all of Niobe's offspring except Chloris. Niobe herself was changed into a stone on Mount *Sipylus*, where she wept incessantly.

(Homer *Iliad* xxiv 605-17;
Ovid *Metamorphoses* vi, 146-312)
See also *Nyobe*

Bridges	*Prometheus the Firegiver* 962-5
Browning E. B.	*The Dead Pan* 12
Byron	*Bride of Abydos* ii 491-6
	Childe Harold iv 78-9
Chapman	*Ovid's Banquet of Sense*
Donne	*Epigram — Niobe*
Dryden	*Threnodia Augustalis* 7-8
Graves	*New Legends* 16-18
Hood	*Hero and Leander* i
	Love and Lunacy 37
Jonson	*Cynthia's Revels* I i, V iii
Keats	*Endymion* i 337-43
Marlowe	*Dido Queen of Carthage* 298-301
Noyes	*Niobe* 11-15
Shakespeare	*Hamlet* I ii 149
	Troilus and Cressida V x 17-19
Spenser	*Faerie Queene* IV vii 30, V x 7
	Shepherd's Calendar, April 86-90
Swinburne	*Ave Atque Vale* xviii
Tennyson	*Princess* iv 352-3

Nireus A King of *Naxos* who was a Greek leader in the Trojan War.

(Homer *Iliad* ii 671)
Masefield   *Tale of Nireus* 7-9, 32-9

Nisibis A town on a tributary of the Euphrates in Mesopotamia; it was regarded as the boundary between Roman and Persian empires.
Milton   *Paradise Regained* iii 289-91

Nisus (1) Nisus was King of Megara (Corinth), a son of *Pandion* and half-brother of *Aegeus*, whom he helped to regain the throne of Athens. When Megara was attacked by *Minos* of Crete, Nisus' daughter, *Scylla (2)*, betrayed her father,

whose secret was that his life and throne depended on the retention of a bright or purple lock among his grey hair. She had unfortunately fallen in love with Minos, but she had also misjudged her man; when she cut off the lock of hair and gave it to Minos he drowned her (or rejected her, at which she drowned herself), so appalled was he at her treachery. The scene of this drama was a lofty tower on which *Apollo* was reputed to have once laid his lyre. Nisus had two other daughters, *Eurynome (2)* and Iphinoe.

(Apollodorus III xv 5-8;
Ovid *Metamorphoses* viii 8ff)
Chapman   *Ovid's Banquet of Sense*
Fletcher G.   *Christ's Triumph over Death* 7

Nisus (2) Born on Mount *Ida* of *Troy*, Nisus was a comrade of *Aeneas* and close friend of Euryalus. These two distinguished themselves against the Rutulians, but Nisus was killed in trying to rescue Euryalus, and the deaths of the celebrated friends were mourned by the Trojans. Earlier, Nisus and others engaged in a race, in which Nisus slipped on some sacrificial blood but, from the ground, obstructed the rival Salius so that Euryalus could win.

(Virgil *Aeneid* v 315ff, ix)
Dryden   *To the Memory of Mr Oldham* 7-10

Nonacrian Of Nonacris, an Arcadian town which had a fountain supposed to feed the River *Styx*.

(Pausanias VIII xvii 6)
Dryden   *Don Sebastian* III i

Notus The south wind, also called *Auster*. It was associated with rain and said to be bad for both plants and health.

(Hesiod *Theogony* 380;
Ovid *Tristia* I ii 30)
Milton   *Paradise Lost* x 701-2
Young   *The Merchant* ii

Nox (Nyx) The goddess of *Night*, daughter of *Chaos*, who produced Day from her union with her brother *Erebus*; she was mother also of the *Fates* (*Parcae*). Night progresses in a chariot accompanied by constellations, sometimes with black and white children representing night and day, or she may appear as a mourner or dark-winged bird. By association with *Sleep*, she may live in a cave.

(Hesiod *Theogony* 125, 212, 512;
Virgil *Aeneid* v 721, viii 369, xii 846 ff)
Keats   *Endymion* iii 131-3
Spenser   *Faerie Queene* VI viii 44

Numa   Marcus Pompilius Numa was King of Rome from 715 BC. A number of reforms to civil and religious practices were ascribed to him but there is little historical fact. Numa courted and possibly married a nymph, *Egeria* who, he said, inspired his laws and who was changed into a weeping fountain by *Diana* on his death. Another legend was his catching *Faunus* and *Picus*, from whom he learnt how to avert *Jove*'s lightning.

(Livy i 19; Ovid *Metamorphoses* xv
479 ff, *Fasti* iii 285 ff)
Diaper   *Dryades* 326-9
Dryden   *Threnodia Augustalis* 465-71
              Upon the Death of Lord
              Hastings 69-71
Moore   *To the Invisible Girl* 39-42
Prior   *Carmen Seculare* 35-6
Shakespeare   *Coriolanus* II iii 235-42
Tennyson   *Lucretius* 181-3
              Palace of Art 110-2
Young   *Epistle to Lord Lansdowne*

Numidia, Numidian   The country of African Nomads, in the region of modern Tunisia. It was colonised by the Romans as Africa Nova in the 1st Century AD. The Numidians were famed particularly for their cavalry. During the 2nd Century BC they settled into townships and developed an agriculture based on cereals and olives, and they reared cattle and sheep on their hills.

(Strabo II v 33, XVII iii 15)
Keats   *Fragment of 'The Castle-Builder'*
              62-3
              Hyperion ii 371
Shelley   *Prometheus Unbound* III iii
              39-41

Nyctimene   Daughter of Nycteus, a son of *Neptune*. She had incestuous relations with her father. When he discovered the fact, Nycteus tried to kill her, but she was transformed by *Minerva* into an owl. She was sister to *Antiope (1)*.   (Ovid *Metamorphoses* ii 590 ff)
Drayton   *The Owl* 298 ff

Nymphs   Local female divinities including Napaeae and *Oreads* of the hills, *Naiads* of fresh water, *Oceanids* and *Nereids* of the sea and *Dryads* and *Hamadryads* who belonged to oaks (or trees generally). They are girls of maddening beauty and are either very long-lived or immortal. Often they seem to represent little more than the spirit of a place and its associations. In pastoral elegy they were supposed to guard the life of the poet of their haunts. The word 'nymph' was sometimes also used of the *Muses*. Many references to Nymphs are general and of no particular interest. There follows a selection.

(Theocritus *Idylls* i 66-9;
Virgil *Eclogues* x 9-12)
— *General*
Byron   *To Romance* 49-54
Collins   *Ode to Evening* 5, 25
              Ode to Fear 47
Drayton   *Polyolbion* v 83-8
Keats   *Endymion* iii 533-6
              Sleep and Poetry 63-7
Milton   *Arcades* 32-3
              Comus 421-3
              Il Penseroso 136-8
              L'Allegro 25-6
              Lycidas 50-1
              Paradise Lost iv 705-8
Noyes   *At Dawn* 58-61
Pope   *Winter* 21-4
Shelley   *Hymn of Pan* 18-24
Spenser   *Epithalamion* 37-40
              Faerie Queene II iii 31,
              IV vii 22
              Mutability Cantos vii 26
              Prothalamion 20-6
— *Not Available to Modern Poets*
Cowper   *The Task* IV 513-9
Eliot T. S.   *Waste Land* 174 ff
Hood   *The Elm Tree* 6-8
Keats   *Lamia* i 1-5
              To Leigh Hunt Esq. 5-8
Milton   *Lycidas* 50-1
Praed   *Love at a Rout* 1-7

Nynus
See *Ninus*

Chaucer   *Legend of Good Women*
           778 ff

Nysus
See *Nisus*
Chaucer   *Legend of Good Women*
           1907-16

Nyobe
See *Niobe*
Chaucer   *Troilus and Criseyde* 699-700

Nysa   An island in the River Triton (Tunisia).
Dionysus (Bacchus) was reputedly born there
from *Ammon* (King of Libya) and *Amaltheia*.
There were other places of the same name
connected with Dionysus.
                (Diodorus Siculus iii 67-70)
Shelley   *Prometheus Unbound* III iii
           154-5

Nyseian
See *Nysa*
Milton   *Paradise Lost* iv 275-9

Nysus
See *Nisus, Scylla (2)*
Chaucer   *Troilus and Criseyde* v 1110

Oceanides   The sea-nymph daughters of
Oceanus and *Tethys*, said to be three thousand
in number. There are several (apparently
abridged) lists of names. Among the best
known Oceanides were *Amphitrite* (who may
be said to be a *Nereid*), *Doris (1)*, Metis,
Calypso, *Europa*, *Asia*, *Clymene*, *Eurynome*
and *Styx*. The distinction from Nereids is
somewhat vague.
                        (Apollodorus I ii)
Bridges   *Demeter* 328-35
Noyes   *At Dawn* 58-61

Oceanus   A *Titan*, God of the Sea, who
married *Thetys*: he had many rivers and
Oceanides from her. Oceanus was regarded as
one of the oldest of the gods and was not
among the rebel Titans; he was in fact rearing
Hera, the daughter of his sister *Rhea*, away
from the troubles. He was taken to surround
Earth, being symbolised by a snake with its

tail in its mouth, or as a very broad river
stemming from *Hades*.
                (Hesiod *Theogony* 133, 337, 787;
           Herodotus II xxi 23; Homer *Iliad* xiv)
Browning E. B.   *Man and Nature* 12-13
Keats   *Endymion* iii 993-7
           Hyperion ii 75-6, 163-6, 232-5
           Not Aladdin magian 23-8
Milton   *Comus* 867-70
Shelley   *Lines Written Among the*
           Euganean Hills 94-9, 115-8
           Prometheus Unbound II i 44,
           II i 203-6, III ii 21-5
           Witch of Atlas 121-6
Spenser   *Faerie Queene* IV xi 18

Ochus   A name of Artaxerzes III of Persia
in the 4th Century BC. He was notorious for
his brutality both in winning and retaining the
throne, and was poisoned by his chief minister
after twenty years of rule.
Crashaw   *Sospetto d'Herode* 46

Octavia   In 40 BC Octavia, sister of *Octavian*,
was married to *Mark Antony* to seal the pact
of Brundisium between the Triumvirate of
Octavian, Antony and *Lepidus*. Her first
husband — Gaius Marcellus, a consul — had
died shortly before. To what was apparently
a marriage of convenience Octavia brought
remarkable fidelity. Even after her divorce
from Antony (in favour of *Cleopatra*) she
brought up his children by both *Fulvia* and
Cleopatra. She herself had two daughters by
Antony.
                        (Plutarch *Antony*)
Chaucer   *Legend of Good Women* 588 ff
Dryden   *All for Love* II i
Shakespeare   *Antony and Cleopatra* II ii
           130-2, iii 39-41, vi 116-9;
           III ii 18-21, v 12-14; IV
           xiii 37-8

Octavian
See *Augustus*
Chaucer   *Book of the Duchess* 365-8
Graves   *Troublesome Fame* 11-14

Octavius
See *Augustus*
Browning R.   *Imperante Augusto Natus*
               Est 28-32, 44-6

Cowley   *Brutus* 5
Diaper   *Dryades* 388-93
Dryden   *All for Love* III i
Marlowe   *Edward II* 689-94
Shakespeare   *Julius Caesar* IV iii 166-9

Octovyan
See *Octavian*
    Chaucer   *Legend of Good Women*
                     624-5

Odaenathus   A Prince of Palmyra in the 3rd
Century AD. Supporting the Emperor Gal-
lienus, he became recognised as his partner
and effective Emperor of the East. He married
Zenobia who, after his death, pursued an ag-
gressive policy until defeated by the new
Emperor *Aurelian* in 273 AD.
See also *Odenake*

Odenake
See *Odaenathus*
    Chaucer   *Monk's Tale* 3501-9

Odysseus
See *Ulysses*
    Belloc   *In Praise of Wine — Homer*
                     15-17
    Lewis C. D.   *The Antique Heroes* 25-8

Oechalia   A country generally thought to
have been in south Peloponnesus adjacent
to Laconia, but also placed on the island of
Euboea. It was ruled by *Eurytus (2)* at one
time. He offered his daughter *Iole* to the best
archer but refused to give her to the winner of
the contest, *Hercules*, on the grounds that Hercules had killed his own children. Later,
Hercules recalled this broken promise and as
his final heroic act destroyed Oechalia and
took Iole as his mistress. There followed
agony and death from the poisoned robe
given by *Deianira* and sent by Hercules' herald
Lichas. In his pain, Hercules uprooted trees
and hurled Lichas into the sea, where he
became a rock.
    (Apollodorus ii 7; Ovid *Metamorphoses*
ix 136 ff; Sophocles *Trachiniae* 756 ff)
See also *Nessus*
    Milton   *Paradise Lost* ii 542-4

Oedipus   Son of *Laius* and *Jocasta* of *Thebes*,

Oedipus, as a descendant of *Venus*, inherited
the enmity of *Juno* (who had been passed over
in favour of Venus in the Judgment of *Paris*).
Laius lived with the oracle's information that
he would be killed by his son, and he ordered
Jocasta to destroy her offspring at birth.
Instead, she arranged for Oedipus to be reared
apart from men. He was named 'Oedipus'
('Swellfoot') from wounds incurred in this
episode, of which there are various versions;
in one account, Laius pierced the baby's
feet before giving it to shepherds. Oedipus
was found, and brought up in Corinth. When
he was a grown man, Oedipus was told by the
Delphic Oracle not to return home because he
would kill his father; but he took 'home' to
be Corinth, journeyed towards Phocis, and
killed his father Laius after refusing to make
way for his chariot as it passed by. Laius had
left *Creon*, Jocasta's brother, in charge whilst
he was away. On Laius' death, Creon offered
the throne to anyone who could answer the
riddle of the *Sphinx*, which Oedipus proceeded
to do; he came to the throne and married
Jocasta, his mother, by whom he is usually
said to have had four children, including
Eteocles and *Polyneices*. When Thebes was
later stricken with plague, the oracle declared
that it could be freed only by the banishment
of the killer of Laius. After extensive enquiry,
Oedipus discovered his own parricide and
incest, and blinded and banished himself.
    (Apollodorus III v 7-9; Homer *Odyssey*
        xi 271-8; Sophocles *Oedipus the King*,
            Oedipus at Colonus, Antigone)
See also *Edippe*
    Browning E. B.   *The Lost Bower* 56
    Byron   *Don Juan* xiii 12
    Collins   *Ode to Fear* 41
    Jonson   *Sejanus* III i
    Swinburne   *Athens* ep. 2
                     Tiresias 67-70, 85-90

Oeneus   The King of Calydon, husband of
Althaea and father of (among others) *Meleager*,
Tydeus and *Deianira*. His country was visited
by the scourge of a wild boar because of
his neglect of the worship of *Diana*. The
Calydonian Boar Hunt followed. Though the
beast was killed, there were many losses to
the family and Oeneus abdicated and spent
his days in sad retirement. Earlier he had given

Deianira to *Hercules* as wife, although the hero had killed one of Oeneus' servants at his court for some trifling fault.

(Apollodorus i 7-8;
Homer *Iliad* ix 533-83)

See also *Atalanta*

Fletcher P.	*Purple Island* xii 6
Swinburne	*Atalanta in Calydon*

Oenone A nymph of Mt *Ida* in *Troy*. Oenone married *Paris* and, when about to be supplanted by *Helen*, predicted that his voyage to Greece would meet with disaster — she had gifts of prophecy and healing. Paris abandoned her but, when wounded by *Philoctetes*, gave orders to be carried into her presence; she refused to heal him and he died. She stabbed herself to death. Oenone was the mother, by Paris, of Corythus who was killed by Paris for trying to persuade him to leave Helen and return to Oenone.

(Apollodorus III xii 6; Ovid *Heroides* v)

Chaucer	*House of Fame* 397-404
	Troilus and Criseyde i 651-5
Drayton	*Fourth Eclogue* 67-8
Spenser	*Faerie Queene* III ix 36,
	VI ix 36
Swinburne	*Song for the Centenary of*
	Landor 18
Tennyson	*Oenone* 65ff, 217ff
	Death of Oenone 14-18,
	25-9, 70-5, 102-6, 257-71

Oeta, Oetan, Oetea Modern Katavothra, the mountain on which *Hercules* burnt himself after casting *Lichas* into the Euboean sea, 'Oetan' is used to refer to Hercules. The sun, moon and stars were thought to rise behind its great height.

(Apollodorus II vii 1;
Ovid *Metamorphoses* ix 211ff)

See also *Oechalia*

Housman	*Epithalamium* 13-14
Keats	*Endymion* iii 405-6
Milton	*Paradise Lost* ii 542-6
Spenser	*Faerie Queene* V viii 2
	Ruins of Time 379-86

Oetes

See *Aetes*

Chaucer	*Legend of Good Women*
	1425ff, 1589ff, 1598-601

Ogmian, Ogmi A non-Roman name for *Hercules*.

Ogyges One of the first kings of *Thebes*, a son of *Terra* or *Neptune*, and married to Thebe, daughter of *Jupiter*. His reign was met with various portents and disasters, including a plague and a flood, and many towns were named after him. 'Ogygian' was used for 'Theban'.

(Pausanias IX v 1)

Spenser	*Faerie Queene* IV xi 15

Ogygia The island of *Calypso*, whose location is disputed.

(Pliny iii 10)

Shelley	*Oedipus Tyrannus* I i 169-72

Olympia The seat of *Zeus*, in the Elis valley close to *Alpheus* in the west Peloponnesus. Olympia was the site of the Olympic Games, held every four years, which were said to have been founded by *Hercules* in honour of *Jupiter*. They were held in 776BC, but their first date has not been established.

(Pindar *Olympian Odes* ii 3, vi 68ff;
Strabo viii 3)

See also *Olympic*

Spenser	*Faerie Queene* III vii 41

Olympian

See *Olympia, Olympus*

Keats	*Endymion* ii 911
	Extracts from an Opera 1
	Ode to Psyche 41-3
Milton	*Paradise Lost* ii 529-30, vii 3-4

Olympic

See *Olympia, Olympus*

Spenser	*Faerie Queene* II v 31

Olympus A mythological mountain supposed to be the seat of some twelve gods, and of *Jupiter*, from which his thunderbolts were sent. It is probably the modern Mt Olimbus in Thessaly, with the Vale of *Tempe* at its foot. (*Olympia*, also known as the seat of Jupiter and having at one time an immense temple, is on the Peloponnesus, some 180 miles to the south-west of Olympus.) Olympus was believed to touch the sky and its summit to be blessed with eternal spring. Besides being the seat of the gods, it was the home and birthplace of the *Muses*, as also were *Helicon* and *Parnassus*. When heaven was assailed by the *Giants*, piling mountain on mountain, Zeus defeated them with thunderbolts and Olympus was said to have rocked or been shattered.

> (Apollodorus I vii 4; Hesiod *Theogony* 841-2; Ovid *Metamorphoses* i 151-62)

— *General*

Milton	*On The Death of a Fair Infant* 43-4
Shakespeare	*Coriolanus* V iii 29-31
	Hamlet V i 245-8
	Othello II i 185-6

— *Olympic Games*

| Drayton | *To My Noble Friend Roger Dover* 5-8 |

— *as Home of the Gods*

Keats	*Endymion* i 604-5, ii 782-5
	Lamia i 70-5
	Ode to Psyche 24-5
Lovelace	*Cupid Far Gone* 25-30
Marlowe	*Doctor Faustus* 791-5
Meredith	*Swathed in Mist*
Milton	*Paradise Lost* i 514-7, vi 5-7, x 580-4
Pope	*Windsor-Forest* 33-6
Shelley	*Prometheus Unbound* III i 49-51
Spenser	*Faerie Queene* III vii 41
Wordsworth	*Epistle to George Beaumont* 38-43
	Sonnet — Pelion and Ossa

Omer
See *Homer*

Chaucer	*House of Fame* 1464-6, 1475-80
	Troilus and Criseyde i 145-7, v 1786 ff
Dunbar	*Ryght as the Stern of Day* 66-9

Omphale The Queen of *Lydia* who bought *Hercules*, when he permitted himself to be sold into slavery believing that it would cure him of disease at the end of his career. She was said to have made him dress up as a woman and to spin, but freed him and possibly married him after three years' servitude. In one incident *Pan* fell in love with her and sought her bed, but entered that of Hercules by mistake and was injured as a result.

> (Apollodorus II vi 3; Diodorus Siculus IV xxxi 5-8; Ovid *Fasti* II 303 ff)

Browning R.	*Ring and the Book* ix 987-8
Butler S.	*Hudibras* II i 351-6
	Sardanapalus III i 218 ff
Prior	*On Beauty* 10 ff
Sidney	*Espilus and Therion* 7-12
Spenser	*Faerie Queene* V v 24

Ophion An obscure deity who, with the Oceanid *Eurynome* (2) ('wide-ruling') took over *Olympus*. They were defeated by *Chronos* (*Saturn*) and *Rhea* (*Ops*) and fell into Ocean. The association of the Fall of Ophion with that of Satan was traditional. *Claudian* describes Ophion as one of the deadly serpents which enemies of the gods have become.

> (Apollonius Rhodius i 503-9; Claudian *De Raptu Proserpine* iii 348)

| Milton | *Paradise Lost* x 580-4 |

Ophiusa An island in the Propontis or Sea of Marmara notorious for its snakes. The name means 'abounding in serpents'.

| Milton | *Paradise Lost* x 526-8 |

Oppian The 'Oppian Law' was a war-time measure during the Second Punic War against *Hannibal*. It was named after its author, Gaius Oppius, and it limited the amount of gold that might be worn by a woman as well as laying down other puritanical provisions. It lasted for some twenty years and was repealed in 195 BC, against the protestations of *Cato* (2).

> (Livy xxxiv 2-4)

| Tennyson | *Princess* vii 107-11 |

Ops
See *Cybele*, *Rhea*

Drayton	*Polyolbion* xx 152-4
Keats	*Hyperion* ii 77-80, 115-7
Marlowe	*Hero and Leander* i 456-8
Milton	*Paradise Lost* x 580-4
Spenser	*Mutability Cantos* vii 26

Orcas, Orcades The Orkney Islands or the promontory of Caithness facing them.

| Collins | *Ode to Liberty* 72 |

Orcus A Roman name for *Hades* and hence also for *Pluto* (*Dis*), King of the Underworld.

Donne   *Elegy* xiii 23 ff
Lamb   *The Ballad-Singers* 30-3
Marlowe   *Tamburlaine* i 983-4, ii 2944-7
Milton   *Paradise Lost* ii 963-4
Spenser   *Faerie Queene* II xii 41

Oread, Oreades   *Nymphs* of mountains and hills, daughters of *Hecate*, who accompanied *Artemis* when hunting.

         (Virgil *Aeneid* i 499-500)
Browning E. B.   *The Dead Pan* 8
Drayton   *Endymion and Phoebe* 772 ff
Keats   *Endymion* i 670-1, ii 961
Milton   *L'Allegro* 36
         Paradise Lost ix 386-7
Noyes   *The Burning Boughs* 13-16
Shelley   *Witch of Atlas* 217-9
Shenstone   *Progress of Taste* iii 11 ff
Southey   *Hymn to the Penates* 82
         Roderick xvi 212-4
Swinburne   *The Last Oracle* 12-15
Tennyson   *Lucretius* 188-91
         Oenone 65 ff
Wordsworth   *Excursion* iv 872-6

Orestes   Details and characterisation in the story of Orestes vary in the many versions. The following is a general outline. Orestes was the son of *Agamemnon* and *Clytemnestra*. He was saved from being killed by his mother (who had killed Agamemnon when he discovered her affair with Aegisthus) by the intervention of his sister, *Electra*. He was brought up by Strophius, king of the neighbouring Phocis, with whose son *Pylades* he formed a deep friendship. When grown up, he avenged his father by killing Clytemnestra and Aegisthus, for which murder he was hounded by the *Furies* in the form of madness. To a degree, Pylades and Electra assisted him. He then learned from *Apollo* at *Delphi* that he would be rid of the Furies if he stole a statue of *Diana* from the Taurians and took it to *Attica*; he set out on this mission with Pylades accompanying him. The Taurians made a practice of sacrificing strangers in their land and the two men were captured and prepared for the altar; the priestess, however, turned out to be *Iphigenia*, the eldest sister of Orestes, and she arranged a devious escape for them. Orestes subsequently became king of Mycenae and *Argos*, as had been Agamemnon. In a related tradition, *Menelaus* (Agamemnon's brother) had early promised his daughter, Hermione, to Orestes, but subsequently gave her to *Pyrrhus (2)* (Neoptolemus) son of *Achilles*; Orestes, and possibly Pylades, killed Pyrrhus on their mission to Delphi and eventually there were two marriages – of Hermione to Orestes and of Pylades to Electra.

     (Aeschylus, Sophocles, Euripides;
     Apollodorus *Epitome* vi 14, 24-8;
         Hyginus *Fabulae* 119-20)
Browning E. B.   *Crowned and Buried* 19-20
Byron   *Childe Harold* iv 132
Fletcher G.   *Christ's Triumph over Death* 47
Johnson   *Festina Lente* 9 ff
Marlowe   *Tamburlaine* i 436-40
Spenser   *Faerie Queene* IV x 27
Swinburne   *Ave Atque Vale* xi
Thomas, Dylan   *Greek Play in a Garden* 4-8

Orion (1)   A giant hunter fabulously said to have sprung from the urine of *Jupiter, Neptune* and *Mercury*. Orion wished to marry *Merope*, daughter of Oenopion, King of *Chios*. The King disliked the giant and imposed on him the condition that he free the land of wild beasts, which was thought to be impossible. Orion succeeded and the enraged Oenopion blinded him. Orion recovered his sight by facing directly into the sun. He was an attendant, and perhaps a lover, of *Diana* and she eventually killed him when he assaulted her, or because, through the influence of *Venus*, he fell in love with *Aurora*. Other stories of his death were that Diana accidentally shot him with an arrow or that he was killed by a scorpion for boasting he was invulnerable. He was celebrated for ironwork, for hunting, and for building the promontory of *Pelorus* as a defence against the sea. At his death he was made a constellation. (References simply to the constellation are omitted.)

     (Apollodorus I iv; Diodorus Siculus iv 85;
         Homer *Odyssey* v 121-4;
         Ovid *Fasti* v 493-544)
Arnold   *Fragment of an 'Antigone'* 54 ff
Keats   *Endymion* ii 195-8
Spenser   *Faerie Queene* II ii 46
         Mutability Cantos vii 39

Orion (2)
See *Arion*
    Chaucer   *House of Fame* 1201-7
    Marlowe   *Dido Queen of Carthage*
                1651ff

Orithia, Orithya   The daughter of King
Erechtheus of Athens. Orithyia was carried
off by *Boreas* when neither she nor her father
would yield to his words.
             (Ovid *Metamorphoses* vi 682-710)
    Donne   *Elegy* xvi 19-23
    Milton   *On the Death of a Fair Infant*
             8-9

Orodes   Orodes II, a Parthian leader and
eventually king, of the 1st Century BC. He
led the Parthian resistance to Roman invasion
which ended in massive defeat for the Romans
and the death of *Crassus* in 53 BC. The war
continued under Orodes' son *Pacorus*, who
was defeated by *Ventidius*, Mark *Antony*'s
general, in 38 BC. Orodes was murdered by
another son, Phraates, who had more success
in holding off Antony and in time came to an
agreement with *Augustus*.
    Shakespeare   *Antony and Cleopatra* III
             i 3-5

Orontes   A river of Syria (modern Asi)
flowing into the Mediterranean near Antioch.
             (Strabo vi 2, xvi 2)
    Milton   *Paradise Lost* iv 272-5, ix 80-3

Orphean
See *Orpheus*
    Keats   *Endymion* ii 164-70
             Otho the Great V 5 23-6
    Milton   *Paradise Lost* iii 17-18
    Wordsworth   *Memorials of a Tour 1820*
             xi 7-14

Orpheus   The son of *Apollo* (or possibly of
Oeagrus, a Thracian King) and the Muse *Calliope*. He was taught the lyre by *Apollo* or
Mercury and reached such perfection that he
could influence nature, animate and inanimate,
by his playing. He fell in love with *Eurydice*,
but she was pursued by another suitor, *Aristaeus*, and received a lethal snake-bite as she
fled. Orpheus' music charmed his way into
Hades where he implored *Pluto* to restore

Eurydice to life. Pluto agreed, on condition
that Orpheus did not look back till he had
left the Underworld; the agreement was
broken and Eurydice vanished. Having once
looked back, Orpheus could not regain entry
to meet Eurydice again, and he lamented his
loss in his music. When he returned to *Thrace*,
he offended the women by his coldness or un-
naturalness, and they tore him to pieces during
a Bacchic revel; they threw his head into the
River *Hebrus*, where it continued to cry out
for Eurydice as it floated south to *Lesbos*.
Some accounts make Orpheus a notable musician, lawgiver and leader who was killed by a
thunderbolt. It is also said that he accompanied
the *Argonauts* and saved them from the *Sirens*
by providing a rival song. Whether or not he
corresponds to an actual person, Orpheus is
the original symbol of the cult of Orphism, a
developed religious system from the 7th Century BC, and his myths have parallels in other
established religions.
    (Apollodorus I ix 25; Apollonius
    Rhodius i 23 ff; Ovid *Metamorphoses* x, xi;
    Pausanias ix 30; Virgil *Georgics* ix 520-8;
             Hyginus *Fabulae* xiv, *Poetica*
                      Astronomica ii 7)
See also *Amphion*
— *General*
    Auden   *Orpheus* 1-4
    Belloc   *Of Meadows Drowsy* 1ff
    Byron   *Hints from Horace* 662-6
    Carew   *Elegy on the Death of John
             Donne* 37ff
    Chaucer   *Book of the Duchess* 568-73
    Drayton   *The Muses' Elizium* iii 116-20
    Fletcher G.   *Christ's Triumph over Death* 7
    Graves   *Food of the Dead* 1-3
    Keats   *Endymion* i 793-4, iii 98
    Lawrence   *Medlars and Sorb-Apples*
             40-2
    Moore   *Genius of Harmony* 60-2
             Vision of Philosophy 25-8
    Pope   *Ode for Music* 37-41, 131-4
    Rosetti D. G.   *The Kiss* 5-8
    Shelley   *Hellas* 1074-5
             Orpheus 114-8, 120-5
    Southey   *Thalaba* vi 21
    Spenser   *Epithalamion* 16-17
             Ruins of Time 330-6
    Tennyson   *Idylls, The Last Tournament*
             320-4

Orphic
See *Orpheus*

Orphne   A nymph of *Hades*, mother of *Aesculapius* and Ascalaphus by *Acheron*.

Orsilochus   A Trojan killed by *Camilla*.
(Virgil *Aeneid* xi 690)

Orthrus, Orthus   A two-headed dog of *Geryon* which guarded his purple cattle. It was born of *Typhon* and *Echidna* and fathered the *Sphinx* and *Nemean* lion. Orthrus was destroyed by *Hercules* when he stole the cattle as his tenth labour.
(Apollodorus II v 10;
Hesiod *Shield of Heracles* 290-4)

Ortygia, Ortygian (1)   The Sicilian island, once part of the city of Syracuse, to which *Alpheus* pursued *Arethusa*.

Ortygia, Ortygian (2)   A name for the island of *Delos*.

See also *Asteria*

Orus
See *Horus*
    Milton   *Paradise Lost* i 477-9

Osirian
See *Osiris*
    Keats   *Endymion* iv 257-8
    Shelley   *Witch of Atlas* 510-12

Osiris   An Egyptian God, son of *Jupiter* and *Niobe*, brother to *Typhon*, *Apollo* and *Pan*, and husband of *Isis*. He was regarded as an Egyptian king who, having brought great reforms, travelled abroad spreading principles of government and religion. On his return he found that Typhon had usurped his throne and Osiris, not being basically war-like, tried to persuade him of the error of his ways. In this he was unsuccessful and Typhon killed him; but Isis, with her son *Horus*, recovered the dismembered body and set up images containing parts of Osiris, thus initiating his cult. This was associated with the ox, and Osiris may be represented with horns, though he was also the sun, as Isis was the moon.
    (Herodotus ii 144, iii 27-9)

See also *Apis*
    Milton   *On the Morning of Christ's Nativity* 213-20
               Paradise Lost i 477-9
    Spenser   *Faerie Queene* V vii 2-3

Ossa
See *Pelion*
    Marvell   *Epigram on Two Mountains* 11-12
    Spenser   *Faerie Queene* II x 3
    Wordsworth   *Sonnet, Pelion and Ossa*

Otho   Marcus Otho succeeded *Galba (1)* as Emperor in 69 AD, having arranged Galba's assassination. Like Galba, he had held provincial administrative posts during *Nero*'s chaotic rule, and in due course supported Galba, who however, offended him by not naming him as successor. Like Galba, he could not fully win over the troops, and he was defeated by the armies of *Vitellius*. He committed suicide after only four months in office.
    (Tacitus *Histories*)

Dryden   *Astraea Redux* 67-70
Tennyson   *The Druid's Prophecies* 29-32

Ovid, Ovidian (Publius Ovidius Naso)   The Roman poet (43 BC - 17 AD) studied at Rome and Athens and became one of the leading poets of Rome. He was then mysteriously banished by *Augustus* to the Black Sea, at Tomis, which he found dangerous and isolated. The woman referred to in his poetry as 'Corinna' might or might not have been a cause of the expulsion. There has always been speculation as to the offence, but there is no certainty. As a poet, he was an outstanding technician, giving an appearance of ease in the most complex imaginative subject, and keeping his narratives moving. His work, particularly the *Metamorphoses*, has provided one of the most fruitful sources for later poets.
    (Ovid *Tristia* IV x 60;
    Art of Love iii 538)

See also *Naso*, *Ovyde*
— *General and Poetry*
    Auden   *Lakes* 25-8
    Browning R.   *Ring and the Book* i 1156-7
    Byron   *Don Juan* i 42
    Chaucer   *Man of Law's Tale, Introduction* 53-5
               House of Fame 1486-9
               Troilus and Criseyde v 1786 ff
    Drayton   *To Henry Reynolds* 157-8
    Noyes   *The Tramp Transformed* 152-5
    Prior   *Satire on Modern Translators* 79-80
            Written in an Ovid 1-4
    Shakespeare   *As You Like It* III iii 5-6
               Titus Andronicus IV i 42 ff
    Suckling   *Love and Debt* 11-12
    Yeats   *The Herne's Egg*
— *Banishment*
    Browning R.   *Ring and the Book* ii 1221-2, viii 970-1
    Diaper   *Brent* 122-5
    Jonson   *Helen, Did Homer Never See* 17-20
    Masefield   *Letter from Pontus*
    Shakespeare   *Taming of the Shrew* I i 31-3

Ovyde
See *Ovid*

Chaucer	*Book of the Duchess* 568-73
	House of Fame 375-80
	Merchant's Tale 2125-31
	Wife of Bath's Tale 952-77, 981-2
	Legend of Good Women 305-6, 1465-8, 1678-9, 1680-3

Owl
See *Minerva*

Drayton	*The Owl*
Wordsworth	*Evening Voluntaries* vii 26 ff

Pacorus
See *Orodes*

Shakespeare	*Antony and Cleopatra* III i 3-5

Pactolus A Lydian river in which *Midas* washed himself after having perceived the disadvantages of the golden touch. It was supposed to have golden sands.

(Ovid *Metamorphoses* xi 142-5; Virgil *Aeneid* x 142)

Byron	*Age of Bronze* 662-5
	The Deformed Transformed I i 267-9
Drayton	*The Shepherd's Sirena* 182-5
MacNeice	*Autumn Sequel* xx
Pope	*Spring* 61
Praed	*The Modern Nectar* 51-4
Spenser	*Faerie Queene* IV vi 20
Swift	*The Fable of Midas* 33-40
	Upon the South Sea Project 109-12
Tennyson	*The Pallid Thunderstricken* 1-6
	Persia 41-2

Pacuvius A Roman tragedian born in 220BC, who made considerable use of the great Greek dramatists.

(Horace *Epistles* II i 56)

Jonson	*To Shakespeare* 31-7

Padus The River Po, into which *Phaethon*

was held to have fallen from the sky. It was also known as the *Eridanus*.

(Diodorus Siculus V xxiii 3)

Drayton	*The Barons' Wars* vi 40

Paean, Paian Originally a hymn or prayer to a god, *paean* was apparently mythologised into the name of a god of healing, who cured the wounds of gods in the Trojan War. He was variously identified later with *Asclepius* and *Apollo*, whilst the word continued to be used also to indicate a hymn of praise for victory. As healer, Paean was said to be a son of Apollo. Spenser's account of him is fictitious.

(Hesiod *Fragments* 2; Homer *Iliad* v 401, 899-901; Virgil *Aeneid* vii 769; Ovid *Metamorphoses* xv 534 ff)

See *Paeon (1)*, *Pean*

Shenstone	*Elegies* xxii 69
Swinburne	*The Last Oracle* 23-4
Young	*Ocean*

Paeon (1)
See *Paean*

Jonson	*Cynthia's Revels* V ii
Spenser	*Faerie Queene* III iv 41

Paeon (2) The founder of Paeonia, a country now in Yugoslavia. He was a son of *Endymion* and, losing to his brother Epeius in a race held by Endymion to settle succession to the throne of Elis, he exiled himself to this remote land.

(Pausanias V i 4)

Palamedes A Greek leader, son of Nauplius, renowned for his cunning. He detected Odysseus' playing the madman to avoid going to the Trojan War, by forcing him to defend his son *Telemachus* in a perfectly sane manner. Odysseus gained revenge by arranging for temporary moving of the Greek camp and burying some gold where Palamedes' tent had been. He then had written a forged letter from *Priam* to Palamedes seeking betrayal of the Greeks in return for a large amount of gold. Palamedes denied all knowledge of the plot when accused, but the gold was found where arranged and he was incriminated and stoned to death.

(Apollodorus *Epitome* iii 7-8, vi 8-9; Ovid *Metamorphoses* xiii)

Marvell   *To That Renowned Man . . .*
            Graphologist 42-4
Shakespeare   *Troilus and Cressida* V v
            11-15

Palatine, Palatinus   The principal and first occupied hill of Rome. It was the site of temples to *Apollo*, Victoria and *Jupiter* Victor. Apollo, called Palatinus, became worshipped there. *Tiberius* built a large palace there which was progressively extended by later Emperors and which was possibly the origin of the word 'palace'. There was also a famous House of *Livia (1)*.
            (Livy VIII xix 4, XX viii;
            Tacitus *Histories* i 27)
Hardy   *Rome – On the Palatine* 1-2
Milton   *Paradise Regained* iv 50-4
Shelley   *Ode to Liberty* 103-5

Palaemon, Palemon
See *Melicertes*
  Spenser   *Faerie Queene* IV xi 13

Pales   The Roman goddess of pastures and folds. She was worshipped at a festival called the Romaea, supposed to correspond to the laying of the foundation stone of the City. The ceremony was also called Palalilia.
            (Ovid *Fasti* iv 721ff;
            Virgil *Georgics* iii 1, 194)
Jonson   *A New Year's Gift* 28-30
Milton   *Paradise Lost* ix 393-5

Palici   Twin gods of a lake in Sicily, the sons of *Jupiter* by a Sicilian maid, Thaleia, or Aetna. When she became pregnant she asked to be buried, to prevent discovery by *Juno*, and in due course the newly born twins made their way up through the lake. The lake was noxious and dipping in it was supposed to result in death for a liar.
            (Aeschylus *Fragment* 3;
            Diodorus Siculus xi 88-9;
            Ovid *Metamorphoses* v 406-8)
Spenser   *Tears of the Muses* 13-18

Palinurus   The pilot of *Aeneas'* ship, Palinurus fell overboard and was cast ashore, where he was buried without funeral rites. In *Hades* Aeneas assured him of a proper burial and lasting monument.

            (Virgil *Aeneid* vi 341)
Chaucer   *House of Fame* 439-46

Palladion, Palladium   The Palladium was an animated statue of *Pallas* supposed to have fallen from the sky to Ilus, founder of *Ilium*. Whatever its origin – there were several legends – it was kept as a precious talisman by the Trojans, and the Greeks tried to steal it. *Ulysses* was possibly successful in this but the Romans chose to think that he stole only one of several reproductions, the real statue being preserved and eventually transmitted by *Aeneas* to Rome. The capture of the Palladium was one of the conditions for the fall of Troy which were named by Helenus, the Trojan soothsayer captured by Ulysses.
            (Apollodorus III xii 3, *Epitome* v 10;
            Ovid *Metamorphoses* xiii 333ff;
            Virgil *Aeneid* ii 166ff)
Arnold   *Palladium* 1ff
Chaucer   *Troilus and Criseyde* i 153-4
Denham   *Panegyric on General George Monck*

Pallas   A name for *Minerva*, *Athene*, possibly originally meaning 'girl'.
– *General*
Byron   *The Curse of Minerva* 65-9
Chaucer   *Physician's Tale* 49-51
            Troilus and Criseyde ii 425-7,
            iii 729-32
Fletcher P.   *Purple Island* vii 21
Hood   *Progress of Art* 6
Keats   *Endymion* ii 788-803, iv 413-5
            King Stephen I ii 20-2
Marlowe   *Hero and Leander* i 321-2
Southey   *Hymn to the Penates* 12-13
Yeats   *Beautiful Lofty Things*
– *Her Birth*
Cowper   *On Mrs Montagu's Feather-Hangings* 24-7
Dryden   *To My Lord Chancellor* 100-4
Jonson   *And Must I Sing?* 13-15
Pope   *Dunciad* i 7-8
            Upon a Girl of Seven Years Old 3-6
– *and War*
Blake   *Imitation of Spenser* 44ff
Chaucer   *Anelida and Arcite* 1-6
– *and Medusa*
Byron   *Curse of Minerva* 215ff

Palmyra　　An oasis, and its capital, between Syria and *Babylon*. According to *Pliny*, it flourished from its lonely position between Roman and Parthian Empires and it captured trade across the desert between them in the 1st Century BC. It was later the capital of an empire under *Odaenathus* and *Zenobia* but was sacked by *Aurelian* in 273 AD and never recovered prosperity.　　　　(Pliny v 21)

Chaucer　　*Monk's Tale* 3437-41
Moore　　*Rhymes on the Road* xiii 55-8
Shelley　　*Queen Mab* ii 110-13

Palmyrene
See *Palmyra*
Tennyson　　*Princess* ii 69-71

Pan　　The god of shepherds, huntsmen and the country and perhaps originally an Egyptian fertility god. Pan was son of either *Mercury* or *Jupiter* and in appearance resembled an elongated upright goat. He was abandoned by his nurse, Sinoe, an Arcadian nymph, and brought up in heaven, where he was named by *Bacchus*. Pan was well known for transient affairs and his ladies included *Echo*, *Diana*, *Omphale* and *Syrinx*; he invented the Syrinx flute for the latter, and she was changed into a reed when he offered violence. On one occasion he or *Faunus* sought Omphale but entered the bed of *Hercules* in error and as a result was injured. There are accounts of his entering into rivalry in music with *Apollo*, the contest being wrongly judged by King *Midas*. Pan is often found in the company of *Satyrs* and is occasionally himself in the plural, Panes. The festivals to him, in Greek Lycaea, were taken over by the Romans as *Lupercalia*. In later poetry he and Christ are brought into relation — they may be identified through the common association with shepherds. *Plutarch* relates what became a well known story, that a voice was heard announcing Pan's death at the time of the Crucifixion.

(Herodotus ii 145; Homeric Hymn *To Pan* (19); Ovid *Metamorphoses*, i 689 ff, xi 153 ff, Fasti ii 303 ff; Plutarch *De Defectu Oraculorum* 418)

— *General*
Blake　　*Imitation of Spenser* 1ff
Browning E. B.　　*Battle of Marathon* 668-71

　　　　The Dead Pan 1
　　　　Flush or Faunus 5ff
　　　　The Lost Bower 37
　　　　A Musical Instrument 4
Browning R.　　*Pan and Luna* 48, 65-9, 81-3, 89
　　　　Peidippides 65-9
Chaucer　　*Book of the Duchess* 511-3
De La Mare　　*Sorcery* 1-5, 13-15
　　　　They Told Me 1-4
Fletcher P.　　*Piscatory Eclogues* vii 20
Hood　　*The Elm Tree* 23
Jonson　　*A New Year's Gift* 28-30
Keats　　*Endymion* i 77-8, 232-5, 243-6, 271-2, 278, 290, ii 895-7, iv 634-6, 815
　　　　Fall of Hyperion i 410-11
　　　　Sleep and Poetry 101-2
　　　　To Homer 5-8
　　　　To Leigh Hunt Esq. 11-12
Milton　　*Comus* 173-6
　　　　Paradise Lost iv 266-7, 705-8
Pope　　*Dunciad* iii 102-4
　　　　Summer 50
　　　　Windsor-Forest 37-40
Shelley　　*Hymn of Pan* 10-12, 18-24
　　　　Witch of Atlas 113-18
Sidney　　*Espilius and Therion* 7-12
　　　　Arcadia lxiii 37
Spenser　　*Shepherd's Calendar, January* 17ff, *April* 50-1, *May* 109-14, *June* 28-32
Stevenson　　*Et Tu in Arcadia* 20-5
Swinburne　　*Atalanta in Calydon* 105-6
　　　　Pan and Thalassius
Tennyson　　*In Memoriam* xxiii 10-13
Thomson　　*Summer* 853-5
Wordsworth　　*Excursion* iv 886-7
　　　　On the Power of Sound 145ff
　　　　Prelude viii 181-4
— *and Syrinx*
Keats　　*Endymion* i 243-6
　　　　I Stood Tiptoe Upon a Little Hill 156-62
Lovelace　　*Princess Louisa Drawing* 14-17
Shelley　　*Hymn of Pan* 26-31
　　　　Orpheus 15-17
Spenser　　*Shepherd's Calendar, April* 50-1

— *and Christ*
Browning R. *Ring and the Book* xi
1973-4
Milton *On the Morning of Christ's
Nativity* 85-90
Shelley *Hellas* 230-4
Spenser *Shepherd's Calendar, May*
51-4, 109-14, *July* 49-52,
143-4, *December* 5
— *Midas and Apollo*
Campion *To His Sweet Lute Apollo* 1ff
Milton *Paradise Regained* ii 188-91
Spenser *Shepherd's Calendar, June*
65-72

Pandarus A Trojan hero, son of *Lycaon*,
killed by *Diomedes*. The go-between of the
Troilus and *Cressida* story is almost entirely
a medieval invention.
(Homer *Iliad* iv 88ff, v 168ff)
Shakespeare *All's Well That Ends Well*
II i 96-7
Merry Wives of Windsor I
iii 72-3
Troilus and Cressida I i 94
Twelfth Night III i 48-50

Pandion King of Athens having, from
Zeuxippe, twin sons and the daughters *Procne*
and *Philomela*. Pandion received some help in
solving a boundary dispute from *Tereus* of
Thrace, to whom he gave Procne in marriage,
with tragic consequences.
(Apollodorus iii 14)
Chaucer *Legend of Good Women*
2244-50
Shakespeare *Passionate Pilgrim* 20

Pandora Pandora, the first woman, was
made by *Vulcan*, at *Jupiter*'s request, out of
clay to be a wife for *Prometheus*; it was an act
of spite in return for Prometheus' theft of fire
from heaven. She was given all female charac-
teristics and so, it was said, called *Pandora* —
'all the gifts'. Prometheus mistrusted Jupiter's
present, which was handed to him by *Mercury*,
and she married his brother, *Epimetheus*,
instead. She bore a box of gifts — *Pandora*
again — which, when opened, released all the
evils of the world, leaving Hope alone inside.
(Hesiod *Theogony* 570-612,
Works and Days 47-105)

Byron *Fill the Goblet Again* 25-7
Daniel *Civil Wars* vi 31
Dryden *Upon the Death of Lord
Hastings* 53-4
Jonson *Execration upon Vulcan* 213-5
Milton *Paradise Lost* iv 714-19
Rosetti D. G. *Pandora* 1-4
Spenser *Amoretti* 24
Tears of the Muses 577-9

Pandorian
See *Pandora*
Wordsworth *Protest Against the Ballot*
11-14

Pangaeus, Pangean The Thracian mountain
on which *Orpheus* sang and where *Lycurgus*
was dismembered.
(Apollodorus iii 5;
Virgil *Georgics* iv 462)
Moore *The Genius of Harmony* 60-2

Panope, Panopea A *Nereid* invoked by sea-
men during storms and on return from a safe
voyage.
(Hesiod *Theogony* 251; Virgil *Aeneid*
v 239-40, 821, *Georgics* i 436-7)
Milton *Lycidas* 98-9
Spenser *Faerie Queene* III viii 37,
IV ii 49

Pansa A tribune and, later, consul designate,
who joined with *Hirtius* to support *Augustus*
against *Antony*. He was wounded and subsequently died, possibly poisoned by Augustus,
at *Mutina*.
Shakespeare *Antony and Cleopatra* I iv
56-9

Pantheon A lavishly-fitted temple in Rome,
built by *Agrippa* in 25BC, and dedicated to
'all the gods'.
Shakespeare *Titus Andronicus* I i 335
Wordsworth *Power of Music* 1-4

Paphian
See *Paphos*
Bridges *Ode* iv 3
Browning E. B. *Wine of Cyprus* 7
Collins *Written on a Paper* 14
Goldsmith *On seeing Mrs . . . Perform
in the Character of . . .* 9-10

Keats   *Endymion* i 510, iii 850-4
Moore   *Sale of Loves* 1-4
Tennyson   *Oenone* 170-1

Paphos A city of south-west Greece supposed
to have been colonised from *Arcadia*. It was
known for prostitution and licentiousness and
had a temple to *Aphrodite*. *Venus* was often
called 'Paphian'.
See also *Pygmalion*
      Byron   *Childe Harold* i 66
      Graves   *Purification* 23-5
      Keats   *Sleep and Poetry* 248-51
      Kipling   *Second Voyage* 17-18
      Shakespeare *Tempest* IV i 52-3
                 Venus and Adonis 1189-94
      Spenser   *Faerie Queene* III vi 29, IV x 5

Parcae
See *Fates*, *Parcas*
      Byron   *Don Juan* v 6
      Chaucer   *Troilus and Criseyde* iii 733-5
      Crashaw   *Sospetto d'Herode* 43
      Shakespeare *King Henry IV pt 2* II iv
                 188-9
                 King Henry V V i 18-19
      Wordsworth *Laodoamia* 65-7

Parcas
See *Parcae*
      Chaucer   *Troilus and Criseyde* V 1-4

Parian
See *Paros*
      Browning R. *Ring and the Book* vi
                 1168-70
      Pope   *Temple of Fame* 27-30
      Praed   *Bridal of Belmont* 252-8
      Shelley   *Epipsychidion* 502-7
                 Ode to Liberty 56-8

Paris The son of *Priam*, King of *Troy*, by
Hecuba. Paris was isolated and was cared for
first by a she-bear and then by shepherds on
Mt *Ida* (2), because of prophecies that he
would destroy the house of Troy. He married
Oenone, a nymph of Ida, and was readmitted
into the royal family after achieving distinction
in games and contests. At the marriage of
Peleus and the goddess *Thetis*, the uninvited
guest *Eris* (Strife) threw into the party a
golden apple inscribed 'for the fairest'. This

was claimed by *Hera* (*Juno*), *Athena* (*Minerva*)
and *Aphrodite* (*Venus*). *Zeus* commanded that
the judgment between them be made by the
handsomest man, Paris, who was then keeping
his sheep on Ida. In return for the offer of the
most beautiful woman in the world, the judgment of Paris went to Aphrodite. The judgment
caused the Trojan War, with its sequel in the
hatred of rejected Juno for *Aeneas*: because
Paris proceeded to seduce Helen – as the most
beautiful woman – and her husband, Menelaus,
joined with her previous suitors to make war
on Troy. Late in the War, mortally wounded
by one of the charmed arrows of *Philoctetes*,
Paris was carried at his wish before Oenone on
Ida. She alone could heal him, but she refused;
though when he died she stabbed herself over
the body or hanged herself. Paris was also
known as Alexander ('Defender') for his
prowess as a shepherd.
      (Apollodorus III xii, *Epitome* III i-v;
            Euripides *Trojan Women* 920-32;
      Homer *Iliad* iii 15-382; Ovid *Heroides* V)
See also *Hesione*
– *General*
      Browning R. *Ring and the Book* ii
                 1005-7
      Byron   *Childe Harold* iv 51
      Chaucer   *Book of the Duchess* 326-34
                 Squire's Tale 547-54
                 Parliament of Fowls 290-5
      Hopkins   *Escorial* 11
      Pope   *Dunciad* ii 209-10
      Prior   *On Beauty* 10ff
      Shakespeare *Troilus and Cressida* I i
                 110-11
– *Helen and the Trojan War*
      Brooke   *It's Not Going to Happen Again*
                 11-14
                 Menelaus and Helen 1ff
      Byron   *Don Juan* xiv 72
      Chaucer   *Troilus and Criseyde* i 61-3
      Daniel   *Civil Wars* V 62
      Marlowe   *Tamburlaine* I 73-4
      Masefield *Clytemnestra* 4ff
                 The Spear Man
                 Tale of Nireus 32-9
      Prior   *Alma* ii 91ff
      Rosetti D. G. *Troy Town* 92-9
      Shakespeare *Rape of Lucrece* 1473-5
                 Troilus and Cressida Pro-
                 logue 7-10; II ii 76-80

181

Parnassus, Parnasse   A mountain of Phocis (north-west of Athens). It was sacred to the *Muses*, *Apollo* and *Bacchus*. *Delphi* was on one of its summits.

Parnes   A Greek mountain forming a boundary between Boeotia and *Attica*.
   Arnold   *Fragment of an 'Antigone'* 61-4

Paros   One of the Cyclades Islands between Greece and Turkey, known as Minoa and by other names. It was a rich and powerful centre said to have been founded by Paros, a son of *Jason*. It was particularly noted for work in marble and for marble quarries of great depth.
   (Diodorus Siculus II 52-9; Strabo X v 7;
            Virgil *Aeneid* i 393)
See also *Parian*
   Spenser   *Faerie Queene* III ix 36-7

Parrhasia   An Arcadian town supposed to have been founded by a son of *Jupiter*.

Prior   *First Hymn to Callimachus* 13-15

Parthenopaus   One of the *Seven Against Thebes*, coming from *Parthenope (2)*.
   Browning E. B.   *Queen Anelida* 9

Parthenope (1)   One of the *Sirens*.
                                    (Strabo i 2)
   Milton   *Comus* 878-80

Parthenope (2)   The city of Naples, named after the *Siren*. It was *Neapolis*, the new city, colonised from Athens on the site of the ancient Parthenope. It became a favourite resort of the Roman Emperors, and *Virgil* wrote much of the *Georgics* there.
                              (Strabo I ii 13, 18)
   Shelley   *Oedipus Tyrannus* I i 172-3
   Shenstone   *Elegies* v 37-40
   Wordsworth   *Memorials of a Tour in Italy* 263-9

Parthes
See *Parthia*
   Chaucer   *Pardoner's Tale* 621-6

Parthia, Parthian   A country — now in Iran — which reached the peak of its power in the 2nd Century BC. Defeated by *Alexander* the Great c. 330BC, it rose into prominence under *Arsaces*, the first of a line of Arsacides. In this new empire the Parthians were renowned for originality in war and were undefeated by the Romans, though subdued by Persia in the 3rd Century AD. It was their proverbial custom to let off their arrows whilst retreating at full speed. They were reputed to be incestuous and debauched but in reality were perhaps more tolerant and easy-going than the Romans.
                     (Ovid *Fasti* v 580; Strabo xi 9)
See also *Parthes*
   Chatterton   *Resignation* 1-2
   Milton   *Paradise Regained* iii 289 ff, 363-7
   Shakespeare   *Antony and Cleopatra* III i 33
                           Cymbeline I v 19-20
   Shelley   *Alastor* 242-3
                     Fragment of a Satire on Satire 29-30
   Young   *Night Thoughts* ii

Parthonope
See *Parthenopaus*
   Chaucer   *Anelida and Arcite* 57-63
                     Troilus and Criseyde v 1502-5

Pasipha, Pasiphae   A daughter of *Helios*, Pasiphae was happily married to *Minos*, King of Crete and had children including *Ariadne*, *Phaedra* and Deucalion. However, *Poseidon* made her fall in love with a bull when Minos offended him by refusing to sacrifice the special bull called forth by Poseidon, and she was satisfied with a hollow wooden cow made for her by *Daedalus*. From this union was born the *Minotaur*, which was kept in the Labyrinth, another creation of Daedalus.
                              (Apollodorus III i)
   Bridges   *Prometheus the Fire-Giver* 941-3
   Byron   *Don Juan* ii 155
   Chaucer   *Wife of Bath's Prologue* 733-6
   Graves   *Lament for Pasiphae* 9-13
   Lewis C. D.   *Ariadne on Naxos*
   Shelley   *Oedipus Tyrannus* I i 136-40, II i 65-70
   Spenser   *Faerie Queene* III ii 41
   Swinburne   *Masque of Queen Bersaba Phaedra*

Pasithee   A *Nereid*.
   Spenser   *Faerie Queene* IV xi 49

Patroclus   Patroclus was born in Opus (Phocis) but fled northwards with his father to the court of *Peleus* in Phthia (Magnisia) because he had accidentally killed a boy (Clitonymus) during a game of dice. In Phthia he became the constant companion of *Achilles*, younger son of Peleus, and went with him to the Trojan War. Here he made a great impression by fighting in Achilles' armour, but was eventually killed by *Hector*; there followed a long skirmish before the Greeks could regain the body. In revenge, Achilles killed twelve Trojans at the funeral. Patroclus and he were often regarded as lovers.
                     (Homer *Iliad* xi 599 ff, xvi-xviii)
   Dryden   *Annus Mirabilis* 253-6
   Marlowe   *Edward II* 689-94
   Pope   *Temple of Fame* 188 ff
   Shakespeare   *Troilus and Cressida* I iii 146-50; V v 30-4

Paulinus
See *Boudicca*
>   Spenser   *Faerie Queene* II x 55

Pausanias   The much-travelled author of a *Description of Greece* in the 2nd Century AD. This is particularly given to religious and historical remains, and to statues and memorials of legend, and has been found to be generally reliable.
>   Arnold   *Epilogue to Laocoon* 15-19

Pax, Peace   The goddess of peace, seen holding *Plutus* (Wealth) or a horn of plenty, and a branch of olive or of myrtle (representing love).
>   (Pausanias ix 16)
>   Collins   *Ode to Peace* 1-3
>   Milton   *On the Morning of Christ's Nativity* 46-52
>   Pope   *Windsor-Forest* 429-30

Peacock   The bird associated with *Hera* (*Juno*). According to *Ovid*, the peacock displays its plumes when praised and hides them if denied compliment.
>   (Ovid *Art of Love* i 627)
>   Milton   *Paradise Regained* ii 220-4

Pean, Paean   An unknown healing god, or *Apollo*. The name was closely associated with a hymn of praise in honour of Apollo (a healer).
>   (Homer *Iliad* v 401, 900 ff)
See also *Paeon (1)*, *Paean*
>   Marlowe   *Dido Queen of Carthage* 1013-5
>   Sidney   *Astrophel and Stella* 63

Pegasean   Of *Pegasus* or the nymphs sprung from him and his fountain.
See also *Gorgonian*
>   Drayton   *Polyolbion* v 83-8
>   Milton   *Paradise Lost* vii 3-4
>   Pope   *A Rhapsody*

Pegasee
See *Pegasus*
>   Chaucer   *Squire's Tale* 204-9

Pegasus   A winged horse tamed by *Neptune* or *Minerva* and used by *Bellerophon* to defeat *Chimaera*. Pegasus sprang from *Medusa*'s blood by the sea after *Perseus* decapitated her. He

lived on Mt *Helicon*, where he created a fountain called *Hippocrene*, with his hoof, at which nymphs and *Muses* were born. (There were also other accounts of the birth of the Muses.) After the defeat of Chimaera, he jettisoned Bellerophon when stung by a gadfly sent as a punishment by Jupiter, for attempting to fly to the gods. Pegasus himself flew onward to heaven. Poets have used Pegasus as a symbol for Inspiration.
>   (Apollodorus II iii;
>   Hesiod *Theogony* 282 ff;
> Ovid *Metamorphoses* iv 785, v 259 ff, vi 119)
See also *Pegasean*, *Pegasee*
>   Burns   *Epistle to Davie* 147-50
>   Fletcher P. *The Locusts* v 34
>   Keats   *The Cap and Bells* 634-9
>   *Sleep and Poetry* 185-7
>   Lewis C. D. *Pegasus* 13-18, 79-84, 100-2
>   Marlowe   *Tamburlaine* i 289-90
>   Marvell   *The Loyal Scot* 63-4
>   Milton   *Paradise Lost* vi 3-4
>   Prior   *Carmen Seculare* 212-3
>   Shakespeare *King Henry IV pt 1* IV i 107-10
>   Spenser   *Ruins of Time* 421-7, 645-9
>   *Faerie Queene* I ix 21, III xi 42

Peiraius   The port of Athens.
>   Browning R. *Aristophanes' Apology* 75 ff

Peisistratus
See *Pisistratus*

Pelasgian, Pelasgus   The eponymous founder of the Pelasgi, who occupied parts of the Peloponnesus, Epirus and Thessaly, and may have been Greek in origin. He had various parentages assigned to him, including those of *Zeus* and *Neptune*, and he was father of *Lycaon*. 'Pelasgian' generally means 'Greek'.
>   (Apollodorus II i 1; III viii 1)
>   Belloc   *In Praise of Wine* 37-44
>   Drayton   *Polyolbion* xx 173-6
>   Spenser   *Faerie Queene* IV xi 15
>   *Mutability Cantos* vii 9

Pelethroni   A tribe (also known as *Lapithae*) occupying the foothills of Mt *Pelion*. *Chiron* lived in a cave here and educated a succession of Greek heroes, including *Jason* and *Achilles*.

Stevenson   *Et Tu In Arcadia* 20-5

Peleus   King of Thessaly, the son of *Aeacus* (a son of *Jupiter*). Peleus was brought up in the court of Eurytus or *Eurytion*, whose daughter *Antigone* he married and whom he accidentally killed in the *Calydonian Boar Hunt*. He was purified of this crime by Acastus, King of Iolchos, but incurred Acastus' enmity when the king's wife, Astydamia, having failed to seduce him, accused him of violating her. Acastus arranged for Peleus to be left, perhaps tied to a tree, as a prey to wild animals and centaurs on Mt *Pelion*. When rescued from this fate by *Jupiter* and *Vulcan*, he took Iolchos and killed Astydamia with notable brutality, and perhaps also Acastus. After the death of Antigone, Peleus courted *Thetis* who eventually married him; it was into their wedding feast that *Eris* provocatively threw the apple inscribed 'for the fairest' which caused the Trojan War. Peleus had a daughter, Polydora, from Antigone, and *Achilles* was his son from Thetis.

(Apollodorus III xii 6 ff;
Ovid *Metamorphoses* xi 217 ff)

Arnold   *Empedocles on Etna* I ii 57 ff
Byron   *Deformed Transformed* I i 267 ff
Chapman   *Bussy d'Ambois* IV i 182-8
Fletcher P. *Purple Island* i 9
Swinburne   *Atalanta in Calydon* 405-9, 1306
Yeats   *News for the Delphic Oracle*

Pelias   The aggressive Pelias, twin to *Neleus*, murdered his mother *Tyro*, who had deserted him as a baby, and usurped the throne of Iolchos from his half-brother *Aeson*. In this he was accompanied by Neleus, whom, however, he soon expelled. Because Aeson's son, *Jason*, was reared in secret by the *Centaurs*, Pelias was ignorant of the threat to him from this quarter. When he did find out, he sent Jason off in quest of the *Golden Fleece*, and destroyed several relatives meanwhile. On Jason's eventual return with the enchantress *Medea*, she persuaded Pelias' daughters to kill Pelias (in the belief that she would restore his youth), cutting him into pieces and eating him. Jason surrendered the throne to Pelias' son, Acastus,

either voluntarily or under duress. These appalling events were ascribed to Pelias' life-long contempt for the goddess *Hera*, in whose sanctuary he had killed Tyro.

(Apollodorus I ix)

See also *Peleus*

Spenser   *Faerie Queene* IV xi 14

Pelides   *Achilles*, son of *Peleus*.

Browning E. B.   *Battle of Marathon* 890-5
Byron   *Deformed Transformed* II ii 21-2

Pelion   A mountain in Magnesia, Thessaly, which was supposed to be the home of *Chiron* and the *Centaurs*. It was part of the same range as *Ossa*. The giants Otus and Ephialtes, after capturing *Ares*, God of War, piled up Pelion, Ossa and neighbouring *Olympus* in order to assail heaven. They were defeated by *Apollo*.

(Apollodorus I vii 4;
Diodorus Siculus iv 70;
Homer *Odyssey* xi 305-20)

See also *Iphimedia*

Arnold   *Empedocles on Etna* I ii 57 ff
            Strayed Reveller 143-7
Marvell   *Epigram on Two Mountains* 11-12
Pope   *Ode for Music* 37-41
Shakespeare *Hamlet* V i 245-8
Shelley   *Hymn of Pan* 13-15
Wordsworth *Sonnet, Pelion and Ossa When far and wide . . .* 9-14

Pella   The site of the death of *Euripides* in 406 BC, and of the birth of *Alexander* the Great in 356 BC. Pella was capital of Macedonia, now in north-west Greece.

Collins   *Ode to Pity* 7

Pellaean
See *Pellean*

Cowley   *Leaving Me, Then Loving Many* 17 ff
            On the Death of Sir H. Wooton

Pellean   Of *Pella* — usually referring to *Alexander* the Great, who was born there.
See also *Pellaean*

Milton   *Paradise Regained* ii 196-200

Pelleus
See *Pelias*
    Chaucer   *Legend of Good Women*
              1396-1402, 1425 ff

Pelops   Pelops was son of *Tantalus*, a king of *Phrygia*, who tried the omniscience of the gods by attempting to make them cannibal in giving them the body of his murdered son to eat. *Ceres*, possibly intoxicated, was taken in and ate some of Pelops' shoulder. *Jupiter* restored Pelops to life, but gave him an ivory shoulder which had magical healing powers. Pelops later entered into a contest for Hippodamia, whose father (Oenomaus) had promised her to whoever could beat him in a chariot race. Pelops won, with the help of *Neptune* or by bribing Myrtilus (his opponent's charioteer). With Hippodamia as his queen, Pelops became ruler of a huge kingdom, including the Peloponnesus (named after him), and was subsequently worshipped as a god at *Olympia*. He was father of (among others) *Atreus* and *Thyestes*, conspicuous for their tragic destinies. In another tradition, Pelops was loved by *Poseidon* and elevated to be cup-bearer to the gods, a predecessor of *Ganymede*, but was banished when his father Tantalus aspired to heaven.
            (Apollodorus *Epitome* ii 3-9;
                    Hyginus *Fables* lxxxviii;
                Ovid *Metamorphoses* vi 404 ff;
                    Pindar *Olympian Ode* i;
                        Strabo VII vii 1)
Cleveland   *To Julia* 41-2
Marlowe   *Hero and Leander* i 59-65
Milton   *Il Penseroso* 97-100

Pelorus   The north-east promontory of Sicily. The story goes that it was named after a pilot whom *Hannibal* killed for vaguely calling it a cape of Sicily. Hannibal subsequently realised Pelorus was right and named the headland after him. It was also held to have been built as a defence against *Babylon*.
            (Strabo I i 17)
See also *Orion (1)*
    Milton   *Paradise Lost* i 230-3
    Shelley   *Ode to Liberty* 183-7

Penalopee
See *Penelope*
    Chaucer   *Legend of Good Women*
              252-3

Penates   'Gods of the store-cupboard or larder', and so guardian spirits of each individual Roman household and hearth. There are various conflicting accounts of this celebrated Roman institution.
See also *Lares*
    Byron   *Deformed Transformed* II i
              103-4
    Southey   *Hymn to the Penates* 7-13

Peneian
See *Peneus*
    Meredith   *Daphne*

Penelope   The wife of *Ulysses*, by whom she had a son, *Telemachus*, and whom she accompanied to *Ithaca* from her native *Sparta*. When Ulysses was at the Trojan War, suitors occupied the house and lived off his estate. She kept them at bay by pretending to be weaving a shroud for *Laertes* (her father-in-law), secretly unravelling it at night. She managed to hold off the suitors until Ulysses' return, when he killed them. The couple then had a second son, Acusilaus.
            (Apollodorus *Epitome* vii 31-9;
                    Homer *Odyssey*)
See also *Penalopee*
    Browning E. B.   *Queen Anelida* 12
    Byron   *Childe Harold* ii 39
    Carew   *A Rapture* 125-30
    Chaucer   *Anelida and Arcite* 81-2
              Book of the Duchess 1080-2
              Franklin's Tale 1442-4
    Davies Sir J.   *Orchestra* 1-4
    Herrick   *The Parting Verse* 29-32
    Jonson   *Epigram to the Honoured
              Countess* 19-25
    MacNeice   *Day of Returning* ii
    Marlowe   *Dr Faustus* 587-8
    Noyes   *Drake* i
    Prior   *Down Hall* 6-10
    Shakespeare   *Coriolanus* I iii 82-3
    Skelton   *Garland of Laurel*
              Philip Sparrow
    Spenser   *Amoretti* 23
              Faerie Queene V vii 39

Peneus   A Thessalian river bordering *Olympus* and flowing through *Tempe*. It was said to be the father of *Daphne*, who was changed into a laurel on the river's banks.

(Ovid *Metamorphoses* i 452ff;
Diodorus Siculus iv 69)

See also *Peneian*

Moore   *Evenings in Greece* 331-4
Shelley   *Hellas* 1068-71
           Hymn of Pan 13-15
Spenser   *Faerie Queene* IV xi 21
           Prothalamion 73-80

Penthesilea   A queen of the *Amazons* who became an ally of *Troy* after King *Priam* purged her of the (accidental) bloodshed of another Amazonian queen — *Hippolyte*, or Glauce, or Melanippe. She killed many Greeks but was slain by *Achilles* (or by his son, *Pyrrhus (2)*) who, when mocked for falling in love with her corpse, killed *Thersites* the scoffer.

(Apollodorus *Epitome* V 1-11;
Diodorus Siculus II xlvi 5)

Graves   *Penthesilea* 1-5
Spenser   *Faerie Queene* II iii 31, III iv 2

Pentheus   Pentheus, King of *Thebes*, was son of *Agave (1)* and Echion. He refused to recognise the divinity of the new god *Dionysus/Bacchus* and forbade the Theban women to join in his festivals, but Dionysus instilled in him a deep wish to witness Bacchic orgies. He was dismembered and killed by the mad Agave whilst spying on a Bacchic feast on Mt *Cithaeron*, either because he was mistaken for a wild animal or because he was an intruder. Bacchus may or may not have been present on the occasion — it was he who had maddened the women of Thebes. *Tiresias* the seer witnessed the event and was converted by these frenzied scenes.

(Ovid *Metamorphoses* iii 531ff)

Fletcher G.   *Christ's Triumph over Death* 47
Spenser   *Faerie Queene* V viii 47
Swinburne   *Tiresias* 73-6

Peracmon
See *Pyracmon*
Jonson   *Ode to James, Earl of Desmond* 40-6

Periander   A tyrant of Corinth c.600BC. He killed all possible enemies and murdered his wife, *Melissa*. He was said to have committed incest with his mother and to have banished his son, *Lycophron*, for mourning Melissa. He illustrated his principle of survival — killing those who stood highest — by levelling a field of corn, also destroying the best of the crop.

(Herodotus v 92)

Daniel   *Civil Wars* vii 56
Meredith   *Periander*

Pericles   The Athenian statesman of the 5th Century BC, who planned Greek strategy for the Peloponnesian War. This was the culmination of an eminent career in which he had lessened the power of the Areopagus and dedicated himself to making Athens an imperial city. In 430 he was driven from office and was tried for embezzlement — this coincided with a virulent plague which killed all his family, and himself in the following year. In character he was haughty and patrician. He was the friend of important philosophers and artists of the day, including *Anaxagoras*, *Sophocles* and *Phidias*. From the latter he commissioned work on the Parthenon, including the statue of *Athene*.

(Plutarch *Pericles*; Thucydides i, ii)

Spenser   *Faerie Queene* IV x 40
Swinburne   *Song for the Centenary of Landor* 37

Perigouna, Perigune   The mother of Theseus' son, Melanippus. Theseus killed her father, Sinis, an outlaw whose custom it was to tear travellers apart by making them bend springy pine-trees, and Perigune, who was terrified of Sinis, accepted Theseus' offer of help.

(Plutarch *Theseus* viii)

Shakespeare   *Midsummer Night's Dream* II i 75-80

Perillus
See *Phalaris*
Marvell   *Flecknoe* 151-2

Peripatetics   Philosophers, followers of *Aristotle*, who used to teach whilst walking up and down in Athens. A school was set up by Theophrastus after Aristotle's death, though it in fact devoted itself to criticism and biography rather than to philosophy.

Milton   *Paradise Regained* iv 276-80

Pernaso
See *Parnassus*
    Chaucer   *Franklin's Prologue* 721-2
                    Troilus and Criseyde III
                    1807-10

Perotheus
See *Pirithous*
    Chaucer   *Knight's Tale* 1192-1200

Persean
See *Perseus*
    Keats   *Isabella* 393-6

Persephone   The queen of *Hades* and wife of *Pluto*. She was called *Luna* in heaven, *Diana* on earth, and *Hecate*, Persephone or *Proserpina* in Hades — hence the title *Triceps* or *Diva Triformis*. The daughter of *Zeus* and *Demeter* (*Jove* and *Ceres*), she was carried off to Hades by Pluto who found her gathering flowers in the plain of *Enna*. Zeus favoured the match with Pluto but Demeter implored him against it. In a compromise solution, Zeus arranged for Persephone to spend half the year with Pluto in Hades and half the year with Demeter on earth. We hear little of her activities in the latter period, but evidently the pattern has its origin in fertility mysteries. In another story, she was courted by Zeus in the form of a snake. Persephone presided over the death of Man, in conjunction with *Atropos*, and required an offering of human hair as a rite of passage for all who died. She had a grove close to the entrance of Hades. As goddess of the Underworld, Hecate became associated with sorcery and darkness and was said to travel in the company of a pack of hell-hounds. She was represented with the heads of dog, horse and boar, and her rites were celebrated at crossroads. She was also identified with *Artemis*, sharing the name of Diana.

(Apollodorus I iv 5;
Hesiod *Theogony* 411ff, 767;
Homer *Odyssey* x 509; Ovid
Metamorphoses v 385ff, vi 103ff, vii 94,
194, *Fasti* iv 420ff; Pausanias viii
37-9; Virgil *Aeneid* iv 511, 698)
    Belloc   *Of Meadows Drowsy* 1ff

Bridges   *Demeter* 28ff, 328-35, 873ff
Lawrence   *Bavarian Gentians* 3ff
                    Autumn Sunshine 1ff
Meredith   *Youth in Memory*
Spenser   *Faerie Queene* III xi 35
                    Tears of the Muses 163-8
Swinburne   *At Eleusis* 46-50, 178-80
                    Memorial Verses 4-9
Tennyson   *Demeter and Persephone*
                    13ff, 35-9, 93-9, 114ff
                    Princess iv 417-9

Persepolis   The summer seat of *Cyrus* of Persia, captured by *Alexander* the Great in 331BC and burned down shortly afterwards (possibly by accident). It was of legendary wealth and prosperity.

(Diodorus Siculus xvii 71)
Marlowe   *Tamburlaine* i 44-5
Milton   *Paradise Regained* iii 284-9
Moore   *Rhymes on the Road* xiii 55-8
Southey   *Thalaba* i 12
Tennyson   *Persia* 26-32
Wordsworth   *Yarrow Revisited* xxvi
                      6-9

Perseus   Perseus was the son of *Jupiter* and *Danae*, who conceived him in a shower of gold, a form chosen by Jupiter. Danae's father, *Acrisius*, learnt from an oracle that a son of Danae would kill him, and he therefore set mother and son adrift in a chest. They were rescued by Dictys, whose brother, King Polydectes, lusted for Danae. Perseus opposed him and Polydectes then pretended he was to marry Hippodameia, and asked for wedding gifts. Perseus promised him the head of *Medusa* and Polydectes accepted, believing this would be the death of Perseus. But Perseus slew the *Gorgon* and captured the head, with *Athene*'s help and with a magic helmet (conferring invisibility), winged sandals and a sword of adamant, supplied by *Hermes*. On his way back he transformed *Atlas* into a mountain by means of Medusa's head, because Atlas opposed him on the grounds that *Themis* had warned him that a son of Jupiter would steal the Hesperidean apples from him. Perseus also released *Andromeda* from the rock where she was chained and then, by using Medusa's head to petrify the opposition, wrested Andromeda from her betrothed, *Phineus (2)*. Returning to

Seriphus (the Aegean island where he had been discovered in the chest), Perseus found that Polydectes had pursued and perhaps married Danae in his absence. Producing the Gorgon's head as the promised gift, he turned king and court to stone. Subsequently, he returned to *Argos* and accidentally killed Acrisius with a discus, thus fulfilling the prophecy. He would not succeed to Argos with blood on his head, and settled rather in nearby Tinyns, founding the city of Maecenae.

(Apollodorus ii 4;
Ovid *Metamorphoses* iv, v)

See also *Pegasus*

Browning R.	*Sordello* ii 210-11
Chapman	*Andromeda Liberata*
Cleveland	*To Prince Rupert* 161-2
Fletcher P.	*Purple Island* xii 42
Hopkins	*Andromeda* I 9
Keats	*Endymion* iv 602-6
Kingsley	*Andromeda* 238-41, 262-4, 358ff
Pope	*Temple of Fame* 80
Prior	*Prologue, Spoken at Court* 33-6
Rosetti D. G.	*Aspecta Medusa* 1-5
Shakespeare	*King Henry V* III vii 21-4 *Troilus and Cressida* IV v 185-6
Spenser	*Ruins of Time* 645-9

Petronius Petronius Arbiter, a Roman romancer, writing mainly in prose. It remains obscure how far the indifferent nature of his work is due to an intention to parody writers of the time. He has often been thought to be identical with Petronius, a favourite official of *Nero*, and to have translated that court's taste for indulgence into his work.

Byron	*English Bards* 642-3
Pope	*Essay on Criticism* 667-8
Yeats	*Upon a Dying Lady*

Phaedra, Phedra, Phidra The daughter of *Minos*, Phaedra married *Theseus* after his desertion of *Ariadne*, her sister. As a descendant of *Apollo* she was envied by *Venus* (because Apollo had discovered Venus' affair with *Mars*) and was inspired by Venus with a passion for *Hippolytus*, the son of Theseus by *Hippolyte*. When he was unresponsive, she accused him before Theseus of making advances to her, and Theseus exiled him, enlisting *Neptune*'s

help. Neptune had Hippolytus' horses terrified by sea-monsters so that he was smashed to death on the rocks. Phaedra then admitted her guilt and hanged herself.

(Euripides *Hippolytus*;
Ovid *Heroides* iv)

Browning R.	*Aristophanes' Apology* 419-24
	Artemis Prologises 22-8
Collins	*Epistle to Sir Thomas Hanmer* 21-2
Spenser	*Faerie Queene* I v 37, 39, V viii 43
Swinburne	*Phaedra*

Phaethon The son of *Clymene* (or *Aurora*) and either *Helios* (*Apollo*) or the Egyptian king, *Merops*. Mocked by his friend, Epaphus (son of *Io* and *Zeus*), for not knowing who his father was, Phaethon set out to prove that it was Helios, and visited the sun-god's palace in the East. Here he was accepted as son, and his request was granted to be allowed to drive the sun-chariot across the sky. His mishandling of this important vehicle caused the burning of the coloured races and a scar (the *Milky Way*) in the sky. *Zeus* intervened with a thunderbolt to prevent Phaethon from doing more damage and Phaethon fell into the River *Eridanus* (Po). Here his sisters (the *Heliades* or *Phaetontiades*) mourned him along its banks until they were turned into poplars and their tears became amber. Phaethon was transformed into a purple cyclamen.

(Apollonius Rhodius IV 597ff;
Diodorus Siculus v 23;
Lucretius V 396ff;
Ovid *Metamorphoses* ii 31ff)

See also *Pheton*

Browning R.	*Paracelsus* v 126-8
Byron	*Don Juan* x 78
Carew	*A Fly that Flew* 13-16
Chapman	*Ovid's Banquet of Sense*
Crashaw	*Sospetto d'Herode* 10
Donne	*Eclogue 1613 (Epithalamion)* 142-5
Drayton	*Barons' Wars* vi 40
Fletcher G.	*Christ's Triumph over Death* 7
Lovelace	*Triumphs of Philamore* 97-8
Marlowe	*Hero and Leander* i 96-102 *Tamburlaine* ii 4621ff

Meredith *Phaethon*
Pope *Weeping* 13-18
Prior *To the Lord Bishop of Rochester* 4-6
Rochester *Could I But Make My Wishes* 9-10
Shakespeare *King Henry VI pt 3* I iv 33-4; II vi 11-13
King Richard II III iii 178-80
Romeo and Juliet III ii 1-4
Two Gentlemen of Verona III i 153-5
Spenser *Faerie Queene* I iv 9, III xi 38, V viii 40
Tears of the Muses 1-12
Swinburne *Tristram of Lyonesse, Prelude*

Phaethontiades The sisters of *Phaethon*, who were transformed by *Jupiter* into poplars shedding amber tears when Phaethon lost control of the sun's chariot and fell into the river *Padus* or Po.
Drayton *Barons' Wars* vi 40

Phalaris A Sicilian tyrant of the 6th Century BC whose barbarity — particularly the habit of roasting victims alive in a hollow brazen bull made by *Perillus* — was legendary. He eventually suffered this torment himself when the people overthrew him. Letters in his name appeared in the 2nd Century AD, but were proven spurious c.1700.
(Diodorus Siculus ix 18)
Byron *Age of Bronze* 356-7
Cowley *The Dissembler* 5
Crashaw *Sospetto d'Herode* 46
Marlowe *Jew of Malta* 22-6
Meredith *The Empty Purse*

Phantasia An Egyptian poetess who was sometimes said to be the authoress of *Homer*'s epics.
Donne *A Valediction, Of the Book* 5-9

Phanus
See *Faunus*

Phao A *Nereid*.
Spenser *Faerie Queene* IV xi 49

Phao, Phaon The legendary boatman lover of *Sappho*. Phaon was beautified by the gift of some ointment from *Venus*, but after a long affair lost his love for the poetess, who (in some versions) cast herself from a cliff in despair and drowned.
(Ovid *Heroides* xv)
Donne *Elegy* xx 25-6
Prior *Epilogue to Lucius* 9 ff

Pharos An Alexandrian island (Faro) celebrated for a huge tower, built by *Ptolemy I* in the 4th Century BC as a lighthouse. The flames were said to be visible for a hundred miles, and the word *pharos* was thereafter used for 'lighthouse'.
Butler S. *Hudibras* I i 713-9
Stevenson *To My Father* 7-8

Pharsalia, Pharsalus A city in Thessaly with a plain, Pharsalia, below. This was the site of several important battles including that in which *Julius Caesar* defeated *Pompey (1)* the Great in 48 BC.
Daniel *Civil Wars* viii 3
Marlowe *Tamburlaine* i 1250-3
Shakespeare *Antony and Cleopatra* III vi 31-2

Phasides Tributaries of the River *Phasis*.
Spenser *Faerie Queene* IV xi 21

Phasis The modern Rion, a large Armenian river flowing into the Black Sea. Into it the *Argonauts* sailed after a dangerous voyage.
(Apollonius Rhodius II; Strabo XI ii 17)
See also *Phasides*

Phebus
See *Phoebus*

Phedra
See *Phaedra*
Chaucer *House of Fame* 405-20
Legend of Good Women 1968-72, 1985, 2170-6

Pheidias
See *Phidias*
MacNeice *Autumn Sequel* xix

Pheidippides
See *Phidippides*
Browning R.   *Pheidippides* 16-17, 63-9,
72-3, 107ff

Pheidon, Phidon   King of *Argos* and one of
the *Thirty Tyrants*. (Chaucer's macabre study
of him derives from Jerome, *Contra Jovinianum*.)
(Pausanias VI xxii 2)
Chaucer   *Franklin's Tale* 1368-78

Phemius   A musician unwillingly among
Penelope's suitors; in reality a trusty retainer
of *Ulysses* left at home during Ulysses' absence.
(Homer *Odyssey* xvii 264)
Davies Sir J.   *Orchestra* 59-60

Pherusa   A *Nereid*.
(Apollodorus I ii 6)
Spenser   *Faerie Queene* IV xi 49

Pheton
See *Phaethon*
Chaucer   *House of Fame* 936ff
Troilus and Criseyde V 664-5

Phidian
See *Phidias*
Bridges   *The Growth of Love* 31
Byron   *English Bards* 1027-30
Keats   *Ode on Indolence* 9-10
Shelley   *Prometheus Unbound* III iv
112-3

Phidias   A Greek sculptor of the 5th Century BC, famed for huge statues of *Pallas* at
the Parthenon and of Zeus at Olympia, but
also for painting and engraving. He was responsible for carving some of the decorative
work at the Parthenon, some of which was
bought by Lord Elgin and placed in the
British Museum in 1801-2 (the 'Elgin Marbles'),
but none of his certain work is extant.
(Plutarch *Pericles* xiii)
See also *Phidian, Phedias*
Browning R.   *Aristophanes' Apology*
111-2
Cleon 138-45
Byron   *Curse of Minerva* 75ff
Prophecy of Dante iv 41-3
Pope   *Dunciad* iii 102-4

Praed   *Bridal of Belmont* 252-8
Spenser   *Faerie Queene* IV x 40
Swinburne   *Statue of Victor Hugo* 22
Yeats   *Nineteen Hundred and Nineteen* i
Statues
Under Ben Bulben iv

Phidippides   The runner who ran from
Athens to *Lacedaemon*, some 150 miles (and
back), to ask *Sparta* for help against the
Persians at *Marathon*. During the run, which
took two days and nights, he was said to have
met *Pan*, who accused the Greeks of neglecting
him. The tradition that the subsequent run
from Marathon to Athens (some 20 miles)
with news of victory, delivered by an expiring
athlete, was also made by Phidippides was
apparently started by *Lucian* in the 2nd Century AD, some seven centuries after the event.
(Herodotus VI 105-6)
See also *Pheidippides*

Philemon
See *Baucis*

Philip II   King of Macedonia and father of
Alexander the Great. In civil and commercial
life he brought Macedonia together and by a
series of victories extended her economic and
mineral resources in the 4th Century BC, so
that for a while he was effectively king of
Greece. He also developed the strength and
morale of the army to provide a unit on which
Alexander was subsequently able to build.
Milton   *Paradise Regained* iii 31-4

Philippi   A Macedonian city, probably named
after *Philip II*, which was the site of two battles
in which *Mark Antony* defeated *Brutus* and
Cassius in 42 BC.
Diaper   *Dryades* 610-1
Shelley   *Hellas* 52-7
Ode to Naples

Phillira
See *Erigone*. In his poem Spenser refers to the
two passages in Ovid.
(Ovid *Metamorphoses* ii 632ff, vi 125)
Spenser   *Faerie Queene* III xi 43

Phillis
See *Phyllis, Demophon*

Philoctetes

Chaucer	*Legend of Good Women* 262-6, 2414ff, 2465ff, 3424-6

Philoctetes   A close friend of *Hercules*, Philoctetes erected the pyre for Hercules' miraculous death and was given by him the arrows which Hercules had dipped in the *Hydra*'s blood and which could not fail to kill. He was one of the suitors of *Helen* and, in some versions, an *Argonaut*. Wishing to join the Greeks for the Trojan War, he was refused because of the nauseous smell of a wounded foot and he was isolated on *Lemnos* almost thoughout the War. After ten years he initially refused invitations to rejoin the Greeks with a view to clinching the War, but was persuaded by a vision of Hercules; he was cured of his gangrene by *Aesculapius*. The wound had allegedly been caused by the enmity of *Juno* towards his love of Hercules, or by an accident with one of the charmed arrows.

(Apollodorus iii 27; Homer *Iliad* ii 716ff)

Wordsworth   *Sonnet, When Philoctetes* 1-4

Philomel, Philomela   The beloved of *Tereus*, King of *Thrace*, who was married to her sister *Procne* (*Progne*). He seduced Philomela, whose companionship Procne was missing, whilst fetching her to join the marital home. He then cut out Philomela's tongue so that she could not recount the facts. But Philomela wove her story into some fabric and Procne learned the truth. Procne cut up her and Tereus' son and served the remains to Tereus at a banquet. When Tereus pursued them, Philomel was turned into a nightingale and Procne into a swallow. The nightingale's sad song was also said to be caused by a thorn in its breast.

(Ovid *Metamorphoses* vi 455ff; Pausanias I xli)

Arnold	*Philomela* 5ff
Browning R.	*Ring and the Book* vi 582
Chapman	*Amorous Contention of Phillis and Flora* 83
Chaucer	*Legend of Good Women* 2288ff, 2360-4, 2373-7
Coleridge	*The Nightingale* 32ff

Eliot T. S.	*The Waste Land* 97-103
Fletcher G.	*Christ's Triumph over Death* 66
Fletcher P.	*To my Beloved Cousin* 6-10 *Verses of Mourning and Joy* 6-9
Goldsmith	*Haunch of Venison* 115
Hood	*Hero and Leander* i
Keats	*Calidore* 154 *To One who Has Been Long in City Pent* 9-10
Milton	*Il Penseroso* 56-62
Shakespeare	*Cymbeline* II ii 43-5 *Passionate Pilgrim* 20 *Rape of Lucrece* 1079-80, 1127ff *Titus Andronicus* II iii 42-3, iv 37ff; IV i 42ff; V ii 195-6
Shenstone	*Elegies* vi 15ff
Sidney	*The Nightingale* iff
Spenser	*Shepherd's Calendar, November* 141
Swinburne	*Athens* ant. iii

Philomene, Philumene
See *Philomela*

Spenser   *Daphnaida* 474-6

Philopoemen   Leader of the Confederacies and Megalopolis in the 3rd Century BC. His main achievements were as a general in reform of the army, his subsequent victory over *Sparta*, and then the integration of that once powerful country. He was poisoned in 182BC by the Messenians in revolt against the Confederacy.

Thomson   *Winter* 493-7

Philyra, Philyrea   One of the *Oceanides* who was courted by *Chronos* (*Saturn*) in the guise of a horse (to deceive his wife, *Rhea*). The product of this union was the horse-man *Chiron*, and its mother was mercifully changed into a lime-tree to hide her shame.

(Apollodorus I ii 4; Apollonius Rhodius I 1232; Ovid *Metamorphoses* ii 676, vi 176)

Cowper   *Anti-Thelyphtera* 82-3

Phineus (1)   A King of *Thrace* or Bithynia who was blinded because his gift of prophecy led him to reveal the ways of the gods, or as a punishment for wrongfully accusing his children of designs on his throne and blinding them — other causes are also given. He assisted the *Argonauts* in their journey to *Colchis* and his sight was then restored.

(Apollodorus III 15;
Diodorus Siculus iv 43)

See also *Harpies*
Milton   *Paradise Lost* iii 34-6

Phineus (2)   The brother of *Cepheus* and uncle of *Andromeda*, to whom he was engaged. When Cepheus, her father, held a feast to celebrate the rescue of Andromeda by *Perseus*, Cepheus created havoc by accusing Perseus of having taken her away in the first place. He then objected to her proposed marriage to Perseus, who turned him into a stone. Several different versions of the story exist.

(Ovid *Metamorphoses* v 12ff)
Fletcher P.   *Purple Island* xii 42

Phisiologus
See *Physiologus*
Chaucer   *Nun's Priest's Tale* 4459-62

Phitoun
See *Python*
Chaucer   *Manciple's Tale* 105-10

Phlegethon   A burning river which formed one of the boundaries of *Hades*.
(Ovid *Metamorphoses* xv 532;
Virgil *Aeneid* vi 551)
See also *Flegetoun*
Byron   *Childe Harold* iv 69
Coleridge   *The Nose* 10
Fletcher G.   *Christ's Victory on Earth*
Marvell   *Tom May's Death* 90-7
Milton   *Paradise Lost* ii 580-1
Pope   *Ode for Music* 49-50
Spenser   *Faerie Queene* I v 33, II iv 41, vi 50, IV ii 1
Tennyson   *Demeter and Persephone* 26-8

Phlegon   A horse of the sun drawing *Apollo's* chariot.
(Ovid *Metamorphoses* ii 154)
Drayton   *Muses' Elizium* lx 32-7

Phlegra, Phlegraean   The Macedonian site (now Pallene) where the *Giants* attacked the Gods and were defeated by *Hercules*.
(Ovid *Metamorphoses* x 150-1)
See also *Jove*
Milton   *Paradise Lost* i 576-9
Spenser   *Faerie Queene* II x 3

Phobetor   Brother of *Morpheus*, Phobetor also was associated with sleep and dreams, and could assume the forms of birds and animals.
(Ovid *Metamorphoses* xi 638-40)
Donne   *To Mr R.W.* 1-5

Phocion   An Athenian statesman of the 4th Century BC, noted for moderation and peace-seeking, as for austere self-discipline which helped to make him an outstanding general. He was condemned to death by poison, which he reputedly took as he prayed for Athens. He refused burial. His death followed an accusation of treachery to the Macedonians which was more probably a misjudgment of the traitor *Nicanor*.
(Plutarch *Phocion* xxxvi-vii)
Drayton   *Tom Himself and Harp* 21-5
Dryden   *The Medal* 95-8
Pope   *Temple of Fame* 176
Thomson   *Winter* 478-84

Phoebe   *Diana*, the moon, named (as was her brother, *Phoebus Apollo*) for her brightness. Select allusions.
Drayton   *Endymion and Phoebe* 181ff, 559-60, 648ff, 823-8
Keats   *Endymion* iv 54-7, 301-3, 436-8, 985-8
          Hyperion ii 29-32
          Ode to Psyche 26-7
Shakespeare   *Love's Labour's Lost* IV ii 35-6
          Midsummer Night's Dream I i 208-10
          Titus Andronicus I i 315-7
Spenser   *Epithalamion* 148-50
          Faerie Queene I vii 4-5
          Shepherd's Calendar, June 28-32, *July* 63-4

Phoebus   The epithet 'bright' of *Apollo*, connecting him with the sun. Select allusions.
See also *Helios*

Phoenix (1)   The myth of the phoenix is probably Eastern in origin, but was developed by the Greeks and Romans. There are of course many references which are barely Classical or mythological, and these are omitted here. The accounts are of a fabulous solitary bird which, after living to a great age (as much as 500 years) consumed itself in fire in a nest of spices on a palm tree, and was then reborn from its own ashes. When the new bird could fly, it transported the nest and other spiced remains to *Heliopolis* (the City of the Sun, now Baalbek in the Lebanon) and laid them in the temple there. At any one time there was supposed to be only one live phoenix in existence. The myth was widely used to represent rebirth and concepts of immortality.

(Herodotus ii 73;
Ovid *Metamorphoses* xv 391-407;
Tacitus *Annals* vi 28)

See also *Fenix*

Phoenix (2)   A son of *Agenor*, King of *Tyre* (himself a son of *Neptune*); he was brother of *Cadmus* and *Europa* and was the eponymous founder of Phoenicia. When Europa was kidnapped by *Zeus* in the form of a bull, the brothers sought her, but were unsuccessful, since Zeus transported her to Crete. Phoenix then settled in the area. As he is sometimes said to be Europa's father, it is likely that Agenor and Phoenix were one and the same or were very soon confused.

(Apollodorus III i 1)

Spenser   *Faerie Queene* IV xi 15

Pholoe   A variant of *Phoebe*.

Phorcus, Phorcys   A god of the sea who from his sister, Ceto, fathered monsters, notably the *Gorgons*, the dragon guarding the apples of the *Hesperides*, and possibly also *Scylla*.

            (Apollodorus i 2, *Epitome* vii 20;
            Hesiod *Theogony* 237-9)

Drayton   *Polyolbion* xx 156-9
Keats   *Hyperion* ii 73-4
Spenser   *Faerie Queene* IV xi 13

Phosphorus   The planet Venus when visible in the East ahead of the morning sun. At epithalamia, the rising of Venus was the occasion for lighting the bridal lamp and leading bride to bridegroom. Only references to the Morning Star which have some apparent Classical element are included here.
See also *Hesperus*

Milton   *Paradise Lost* v 166-9
Tennyson   *Hesperides* 82
            In Memoriam cxxi

Phrixus   Phrixus was the son of *Athamas* of *Thebes*, and brother of *Helle*, with whom he fled the hatred of his mother-in-law *Ino* on a golden ram. Helle fell off into the sea thereafter called the *Hellespont*, but Phrixus arrived at *Colchis*, where he sacrificed the ram to *Mars* and where he married Chalciope, daughter of King *Aeetes*. However, he was later murdered by Aeetes, who believed Phrixus to be a threat to his throne and sought possession of the *Golden Fleece*. Recapturing the Fleece was the purpose of *Jason*'s expedition with the *Argonauts*.

            (Apollodorus I ix;
         Ovid *Metamorphoses* vii 1ff)
Spenser   *Faerie Queene* V *Prologue* 5

Phrygia   The area of Phrygia varied over the ages but it was a mountainous region of modern Turkey, conquered by the Phryges some 2000 years before Christ. The Lydians invaded it and founded a kingdom, famous for associations with Greek mythology, which eventually became part of the Roman province of Asia. In poetry, Phrygia is known for the reed pipe, supposed to have been invented there. It was a pastoral land of small villages and had its own composite religion, in which the worship of *Cybele* played an important part.
See also *Maeander, Marsyas*

Arnold   *Empedocles on Etna* II i 129-33

Phrynichus   An Athenian tragic poet of the 5th Century BC. He produced a play about the taking of *Miletus* by the Persians (494 BC) and was fined for bringing his audience to tears at the misfortunes of their friends. He was much admired by *Aristophanes* and was also held to be the first dramatist to introduce (masked) female characters.

Browning R.   *Aristophanes' Apology*
            176-80

Phryne, Phrynean   A celebrated Greek prostitute in the 4th Century BC. She won a law suit by exposing her body to the judges.

Browning R.   *Ring and the Book* ix
            187-90

Phyllis
See *Phillis, Demophon*

Chaucer   *Book of the Duchess* 725-31
            House of Fame 388-95
            Man of Law's Tale, Intro-
            duction 65
Herrick   *To the Maids* 13-14

Physiologus   *Physiologus de Natura Animalium*, a collection of Latin fables which is a sort of bestiary of Christian allegory. Neither its date nor its provenance is firmly established. It was much used as source material in the Middle Ages and was certainly known by the 4th Century AD.
See also *Phisiologus*

Pictagoras
See *Pythagoras*
Chaucer   *Book of the Duchess* 1167-9

Picus   A man transformed into a woodpecker for ignoring the attentions of *Circe*, who fell in love with him. Picus, son of *Saturn*, was made father of *Faunus* and grandfather of *Latinus*, founder of *Latium*. The woodpecker was supposed to be prophetic and was sacred to *Mars*. Picus and Faunus were caught by *Numa*, who obliged them to reveal how to avert *Jove*'s lightning (a secret withheld from the reader).

(Ovid *Fasti* iii 285ff,
Metamorphoses xiv 310ff)
Tennyson　*Lucretius* 181-3

Pierian
See *Pierus*
Coleridge　*Lines to a Beautiful Spring* 4-6
Drayton　*Fourth Eclogue* 9-10
Pope　*Essay on Criticism* 215-6
Shenstone　*Anacreontic* 29
Spenser　*Ruins of Time* 393-7
Swinburne　*Memorial Verses* 30
Tennyson　*Parnassus* 17-18
Wordsworth　*Ode 1814* 111ff

Pierides　The *Muses*, or their rivals.
See also *Pierus*
Chaucer　*Man of Law's Tale, Introduction* 91-3
Marlowe　*Tamburlaine* i 1035-7
Skelton　*Garland of Laurel*

Pierus　A mountain in Thessaly sacred to the *Muses*. It was close to *Olympus* and was named after a King Pierus, held to have been father of *Hyacinth* from *Clio*. His nine daughters rivalled the Muses proper and were turned into magpies for their presumption. The real and would-be were alike known as *Pierides*.

(Apollodorus I iii 3;
Ovid *Metamorphoses* v 302ff)
See also *Pierian*
Drayton　*Polyolbion* v 83-8

Pigmalion
See *Pygmalion*
Cowley　*The Gazers* 2
Daniel　*Behold What Hap* 1-4

Pigmean
See *Pygmies*
Milton　*Paradise Lost* i 777-81

Pigmies
See *Pygmies*
Shelley　*Witch of Atlas* 133-5

Pimpla, Pimplaea　A *Muse* of the Mount Pimpla in Macedonia, with a fountain. *Catullus*

represents Pimpla as defended by Muses with pitch-forks.

(Catullus 105; Horace *Odes* i 26;
Strabo X iii 17)
Drayton　*Polyolbion* v 83-8
Tennyson　*I Dare not Write an Ode . . .* 1-2

Pindar, Pindaric (1)　Greek lyric poet (518-438BC) who was born near *Thebes*. His manner was partly — and was later taken wholly to be — grand and effusive, celebrating victories by effusions in which the events became religious occasions and the heroes often deified. His form was, in fact, conservative and disciplined, but his manner led him to seem for many English poets the prototype of the 'enthusiast' whose urgent need for expression dominates formal considerations. It was noted by *Plutarch* and *Pliny* that *Alexander* the Great respected Pindar, sparing his former house and his descendants in the sack of Thebes in 335BC.　(Pliny vii 19)
See also *Corinna*
Auden　*The Horatians* 53ff
Browning E. B.　*Portuguese Sonnets* 19
An Island 26-7
A Vision of Poets 310-21
Wine of Cyprus 12
Byron　*Curse of Minerva* 149-50
Collins　*Lines Addressed to James Harris* 27ff
Cowley　*Praise of Pindar* 1, 2
The Resurrection 4
Denham　*On Abraham Cowley* 47-8
Donne　*A Valediction of the Book* 5-9
Milton　*Sonnet* 8
Jonson　*Ode Allegoric* 19-20
Pope　*Temple of Fame* 202-5, 212-5
Prior　*Carmen Seculare* 205-6
Satire on Modern Translators 159-62
Swinburne　*Statue of Victor Hugo* 12
Tennyson　*Princess* iii 329-34
Young　*The Merchant* iii

Pindar, Pindarus (2)　A prisoner and slave of *Cassius*. On Cassius' suicidal order, he killed his master at *Philippi*, when Cassius mistakenly believed that *Brutus* had lost the first battle.

(Plutarch *Antony* xxii)

Shakespeare   *Julius Caesar* V iii 47-50

Pindus   A mountain range in northern Greece between Thessaly and Epirus. It was sacred to the *Muses* and *Apollo*, and from its foot flowed the River *Peneus* on through the Vale of *Tempe*.
(Ovid *Metamorphoses* i 568-70;
Virgil *Eclogue* x 11)
Drayton   *Polyolbion* v 83-8
Marvell   *Epigram on Two Mountains* 11-12
Meredith   *Daphne*
Pope   *Messiah* 3-6
Smart   *Prologue to 'A Trip to Cambridge'*
Spenser   *Faerie Queene* III iv 41
             Prothalamion 37-42

Piramus
See *Pyramus*
Chaucer   *Legend of Good Women* 724ff, 778ff, 823ff
             Parliament of Fowls 288ff

Pirithous
See *Perotheus, Theseus*
Spenser   *Faerie Queene* IV x 27
Swinburne   *Atalanta in Calydon* 1258

Pirois
See *Pyrois*
Drayton   *The Muses' Elizium* ix 32-7

Pirous
See *Pyrois*
Chaucer   *Troilus and Criseyde* iii 1702-6

Pirrus (1)
See *Pyrrhus (1)*
Chaucer   *Nun's Priest's Tale* 4545-51

Pirrus (2)
See *Pyrrhus (2) (Neoptolemus)*
Chaucer   *Man of Law's Tale* 288-93
             House of Fame 158-61

Pisistratus   An Athenian tyrant of the 6th Century BC who was related to *Solon*. As a despot, Pisistratus was apparently benevolent, but his rule significantly contrasted with the preceding era of Solon, who had believed in the dispersal of power among the people.

Browning E. B.   *Battle of Marathon* 15-20
Meredith   *Solon*

Piso
See *Galba*
Dryden   *Astraea Redux* 67-70

Pithagores
See *Pythagoras*
Chaucer   *Book of the Duchess* 666-9

Pithecusa
See *Ischia*
Shelley   *Ode to Liberty* 183-7

Plataea   A city of Boeotia, at the foot of Mount *Cithaeron*. It was protected by Athens and shared its mixed fortunes in the wars with the Persians in the 5th Century BC. The Athenian and Plataean forces defeated the Persians at *Marathon* in 490BC. In the next ten years, the Greeks seem to have been somewhat complacent, but in the Battle at Plataea in 479BC they inflicted a crushing defeat on *Xerxes*.
(Herodotus vi-viii)
Browning R.   *Sordello* iii 950-4
Tennyson   *Exhortation to the Greeks* 17-18

Plato   The Athenian philosopher (c.429-347BC), a pupil of *Socrates*. Plato is popularly known for 'idealism' as *Aristotle* is for 'materialism'. Plato associates virtue with knowledge of a supraphysical world of 'form' and 'idea', imitated by the phenomenal world, for all the latter's imperfections. He believed also in a close interaction of politics and philosophy and furthered the notion of a philosophic statesman or king. He worked just outside Athens, in *Academia*, a park planted with olive trees, although in later life he retired from the city and travelled widely. As a stylist he is very comprehensive, ranging from the racy to the rich and even lavish, as required.
See also *Platonic*
— *General*
Browning E. B.   *An Island* 26-7
Browning R.   *Pauline* 435-6
             Ring and the Book vi 960-3

Byron   *Don Juan* i 116
Campbell   *Pleasures of Hope*
Chaucer   *Canterbury Tales, Prologue*
741-2
Manciple's Tale 207-10
House of Fame 929-31, 753-9
Denham   *Progress of Learning* 35-9
Fletcher G.   *Christ's Victory on Earth*
40
Keats   *Where's the Poet?*
Milton   *Paradise Regained* iv 244-5
Moore   *Nature's Labels* 5-8
Shelley   *Hellas, Prologue* 94-5
Prince Athanase 224-9
Tennyson   *Lucretius* 146-9
Palace of Art 164
Wordsworth   *Dion* 7-12
Wyatt   *Farewell Love*
Yeats   *The Delphic Oracle Upon Plotinus*
Young   *Night Thoughts* vix
— and Philosophy
Auden   *New Year Letter*
Graves   *Cry Faugh!* 4-6
MacNeice   *Autumn Journal* xii
Milton   *Il Penseroso* 48-92
Pope   *Essay on Man* 23-6
Spenser   *Hymn of Heavenly Beauty*
78-83
Yeats   *Among School Children* ii, vi
His Bargain
The Tower i, iii
— as Writer
Collins   *Lines Addressed to James Harris*
13
Smart   *Epistle to John Sherratt* 4, 12
Thomson   *Liberty* ii 236-7

Platonic
See *Plato*
Wordsworth   *Ecclesiastical Sonnets*
III iv
Yeats   *Two Songs from a Play*

Plautus Titus Maccius Plautus was a Roman writer of comedies in the 3rd Century BC. He concentrated in extracting maximum effect from individual scenes rather than on developing plot. He was considerably indebted to *Menander*.
Jonson   *To Shakespeare* 51-4
Pope   *Autumn* 7-8

Pleiades, Pleiads The seven daughters of *Atlas* from Pleione, an *Oceanid*, who became a constellation after death. Their names were *Alcyone*, Celeno, *Electra*, *Maia*, *Merope*, Sterope and Taygeta. The constellation showed the time most favourable for important activities such as harvest and navigation — the name is derived from 'sail'. An alternative name (Vergiliae) means 'spring'. They were also called *Hesperides* (from Atlas' gardens) and *Atlantides*, and they died of grief for the *Hyades*. One of the stars is dimmer than the others. This is either Merope — dim from having alone married a mortal (*Sisyphus*), or Electra — mourning the death of her son *Dardanus* and the ruin of *Troy*.
(Apollodorus III x; Hesiod *Works and Days*
303-7, 571ff, *Astronomy* i)
Chaucer   *House of Fame* 1004-8
Keats   *Lamia* i 265-70
To Apollo 25-6
Milton   *Paradise Lost* vii 373-5
Pope   *Spring* 102
Spenser   *Faerie Queene* III i 57

Plexippus A brother of *Althaea*, Plexippus was killed by *Meleager* in the *Calydonian Boar Hunt*, for insulting *Atalanta*.
(Ovid *Metamorphoses* viii 440)
Spenser   *Faerie Queene* VI ix 36
Swinburne   *Atalanta in Calydon* 460,
1274, 1553

Pliny Gaius Plinius (Pliny the Elder), 24-79 AD, spent many years as a cavalry officer (when he wrote a history of campaigns in Germany) before beginning the *Natural History* which is his main work. He also returned to the forces in later life as a naval commander. In this capacity, while sailing in 79 AD to observe the eruption of *Vesuvius*, he was overcome by fumes from the volcano and died. Pliny claimed some credit for the eclectic encyclopaedic nature of the facts gathered in the *Natural History*, and it is of value as a curious miscellany of personal observation and inference together with facts, rather than as an ordered scientific work.
Coleridge   *The Nose* 39-40
Lovelace   *Painture* 1-2
Swift   *Description of a Salamander*
45-6

Plistus   A Phocian river.
Moore   *Hymn of a Virgin of Delphi*
49-52

Plotinus   A philosopher of the 3rd Century
AD. His nationality is not known, but he spent
much of his time in Rome, where he was the
centre of an intellectual circle. His *Enneads*
were collected and edited by his disciple,
Porphyry, shortly after 300AD, in Greek.
They stress the importance of subconscious
mental activity and are of a mystical nature,
hinting at the possibility of an ecstatic union
of the one with the One — such a union is
subliminal, the result neither of human effort
nor of divine grace. Plotinus has been thought
to have been a leper, and was well known for
excesses of abstinence and self-mortification.
Yeats   *The Delphic Oracle upon Plotinus*
News for the Delphic Oracle
The Tower i, iii

Plutarch   The prolific Roman writer of the
1st Century AD. He taught in Rome and
Greece, whose cultures he tried to relate, and
ended his long life as a priest at *Delphi*. His
output included rhetorical and antiquarian
works, and philosophical dialogues, but his
greatest influence on later literature was his
Lives, of which twenty-three pairs survive.
They are very readable and a source of incident
and analogue, though their historical reliability
has often been questioned. The Elizabethans,
particularly Shakespeare, were heavily indebted
to Plutarch in their historical drama and
Thomas North's translation of 1595 was a
major source.
Byron   *Don Juan* xii 19
Dryden   *Religio Laici* 78-84
Pope   *Epilogue to Jane Shore*

Pluto   Known also as *Dis* and *Orcus*, Pluto
was King of the Underworld and brother of
Zeus (*Jupiter*), who ruled earth, and of *Poseidon* (*Neptune*), who ruled the sea. His
wife was *Persephone*, whom he carried off
from earth as she was picking flowers in the
vale of *Enna*. *Ploutos* means 'wealth' (in
effect, mineral wealth from below ground)
and Dis is a contraction of *dives*, of similar
meaning. *Plutus* (God of Wealth) and Pluto
may well have been the same.

(Apollodorus I iv; Homer *Iliad* xv 187 ff)
See also *Aidoneus, Hades*
— *General and Hades*
Browning E. B.   *Battle of Marathon*
670-1
Dead Pan 15
Chapman   *Andromeda Liberata*
Chaucer   *Knight's Tale* 2081-2
Merchant's Tale 2034-41,
2225-36
House of Fame 1509-12
Donne   *Elegy* xviii 27-30
Dunbar   *Ryght as the Stern of Day*
125-6
Gray   *Lines Spoken by the Ghost of*
John Dennis 38-9, 44
Herrick   *The New Charon* 27-30
Keats   *Endymion* iii 99, 473-4
Fancy 79-83
Hyperion i 142-7
Lamia i 211-2
Lawrence   *Purple Anemones* 1ff
Milton   *Comus* 17-21
Shakespeare   *King Henry IV pt 2* II iv
147
Titus Andronicus IV iii
11-16, 37-41
Spenser   *Faerie Queene* II vii 20-1,
23-4, VI xii 35
Tennyson   *Demeter and Persephone* 13 ff
— *and Persephone*
Bridges   *Demeter* 28ff, 873 ff
Chaucer   *Franklin's Tale* 1072-6
Marlowe   *Tamburlaine* ii 4011ff
Meredith   *The Day of the Daughter*
of Hades
Spenser   *Faerie Queene* I iv 11, v 32
Tennyson   *Demeter and Persephone*
93-9, 114ff
— *and Orpheus*
Henryson   *Orpheus and Eurydice* 365 ff
Milton   *Il Penseroso* 103-8
L'Allegro 145-50
Shakespeare   *Rape of Lucrece* 552-3
Shenstone   *Love and Music* 7-9
Spenser   *Faerie Queene* IV x 58
Shepherd's Calendar, October
25-30

Plutonian
See *Pluto*
Milton   *Paradise Lost* x 443-5

Plutus The God of Wealth, a son of *Ceres*, was reared by *Pax*: Peace and Wealth are often shown together as a general picture of prosperity. Plutus was blind (indiscriminate in his largesse) and lame (slow to produce it). *Aristophanes' Plutus* shows the curing of his blindness so that he visits only honest people. The name *Dis* (*dives* – rich) was used of him and *Pluto*, king of *Hades*, and the two were sometimes regarded as the same god.

(Hesiod *Theogony* 969 ff)
Browning R.   *Ring and the Book* ii
442
Shakespeare   *All's Well That Ends Well*
V iii 101-4
Julius Caesar IV iii 100-3
Timon of Athens I i 276 ff
Troilus and Cressida III iii
196-200

Pnyx An Athenian hall used for assemblies.
MacNeice   *Autumn Sequel* i

Po The river in North Italy, which in Classical times was known as *Eridanus*, the name of a mythical 'winding' river. Into the Eridanus the unskilled charioteer *Phaethon* plunged, and for *Virgil* it was 'king of rivers'.
(Virgil *Georgics* i 482, iv 372)
See also *Padus*
Pope   *Windsor-Forest* 227-9

Podaleirius, Podalirius The son of *Aesculapius*, Podalirius learnt his arts from the *Centaur Chiron*, and led thirty ships to *Troy*, where his role was soldier/physician. He was sometimes said to have cured the running sore of *Philoctetes*, and he subsequently married Syrna, daughter of Damoetas of *Caria*. He was worshipped by the Carians after his death.
(Apollodorus *Epitome* v 8, vi 18;
Homer *Iliad* ii 729)

Podalyrius
See *Podaleirius*
Spenser   *Faerie Queene* VI vi 1

Poilleys
See *Apulia*
Chaucer   *Squire's Tale* 189-95

Polimio
See *Polyhymnia*
Henryson   *Orpheus and Eurydice* 46 ff

Polites A son of *Priam* and *Hecuba* of *Troy*. He was killed by *Pyrrhus (2)* (Neoptolemus) in Priam's presence.
(Virgil *Aeneid* ii 528)
Chaucer   *House of Fame* 158-61

Polixena, Polixene, Polyxena, Polyxene
Daughter of *Priam* and *Hecuba* of *Troy*. *Achilles* (a Grecian) and she fell in love, but a marriage was opposed by her brother, *Hector*. She was said to have accompanied Priam on order to retrieve the body of Hector from Achilles after he had killed him. By this killing, marriage became out of the question. When, later, Achilles visited the temple of *Apollo*, or *Minerva*, with one Archilocus, in a final marriage bid, they were killed there by *Paris*, and Polyxena sacrificed herself on Achilles' grave. In another version, Polyxena was sacrificed by Achilles' son *Neoptolemus* at the demand of the Greeks, prompted by the spirit of the dead Achilles. The idea seems to have been that Achilles and Polyxena should be united in death.
(Hyginus *Fabulae* 110;
Ovid *Metamorphoses* xiii 448 ff)
Byron   *Deformed Transformed* I i 267 ff
Chaucer   *Book of the Duchess* 1055-75
Troilus and Criseyde i 453-5,
iii 409-11

Polixenes/Us A Greek leader, son of Agasthenes, in the Trojan War.
(Homer *Iliad* ii 624)
Shakespeare   *Troilus and Cressida* V v
11-15

Polla Polla Argentaria, wife of the poet *Lucan*, who was said to have helped him with his versification.
(Statius *Sylvae* II vii)
Donne   *A Valediction, of the Book* 8

Pollio Gaius Assinius Pollio is the addressee of *Virgil's Eclogue* IV, the 'Messianic', which prophesies a new Golden Age. After a military career, Pollio devoted himself to literature and was the friend of *Catullus*, *Horace* and

Virgil. His own work was in several genres, though his reputation rested mainly on his historical writing, which was used as a source by *Plutarch*.

| Goldsmith | *On the Death of the Right Honourable . . .* 1-2 |
| Tennyson | *To Virgil* v |

Pollux
See *Dioscuri*

Chaucer	*House of Fame* 1004-8
Davies Sir J.	*Orchestra* 484-7
Jonson	*On the Famous Voyage* 77-8

Poltis   King of *Thrace* during the Trojan War.
    Prior   *Alma* ii 91ff

Polycrates   A tyrant of *Samos* in the 6th Century BC, which he made into a great naval power. In 522BC he was tricked to visit Magnesia on the mainland by Oroctes, the Persian governor, and was crucified there.
(Herodotus iii 125)
    Byron   *Isles of Greece* 11

Polydamna   The Egyptian woman, wife of Thon, who gave *Helen* the anodyne *Nepenthe* to put into *Menelaus'* wine.
    Milton   *Comus* 675-7

Polydamas, Polydamus   A bold Trojan leader who was killed by *Ajax* in the War.
(Homer *Iliad* xii 60-90)
    Shakespeare   *Troilus and Cressida* V v 6-11

Polyhymnia   The Muse of singing, rhetoric and harmony; dressed in white, she has a jewelled crown, and often holds one arm upraised.
See also *Muses, Polimio, Polymya*

| Drayton | *The Muses' Elizium* III 457-60 |
| Spenser | *Tears of the Muses* 547-55 |

Polymnestor
See *Hecuba*
    Shakespeare   *Titus Andronicus* I i 136-8

Polymya
See *Polyhymnia*
    Chaucer   *Anelida and Arcite* 15-20

Polymytes
See *Polyneices*
    Chaucer   *Troilus and Criseyde* v 1485-91, 1506-8

Polyneices   The younger brother of *Eteocles*, sons of *Oedipus* and *Jocasta* of *Thebes*. The brothers inherited the throne and agreed to share it year and year about. Eteocles by seniority took it first and refused to deliver it in a year, banishing his brother. Polyneices fled to *Argos* and married *Argia*, daughter of King *Adrastus*. Adrastus and Polyneices then attacked Thebes in the episode known as the *Seven Against Thebes*. The war ended in a duel between the brothers, who killed each other.
(Apollodorus III v 6)
See also *Antigone*

Arnold	*Fragment of an 'Antigone'*
Browning E. B.	*Queen Anelida* 9
Chaucer	*Anelida and Arcite* 57-63
Meredith	*Antigone*

Polynoe, Polynome   A *Nereid*.
(Apollodorus I ii 6)
    Spenser   *Faerie Queene* IV xi 50

Polypheme
See *Polyphemus*

Drayton	*Polyolbion* xx 156-9
Jonson	*On the Famous Voyage* 111-4
Keats	*Sleep and Poetry* 231-5
Marlowe	*Tamburlaine* ii 2351-3
Pope	*Acis and Galatea, Chorus* 4-8
Shelley	*Witch of Atlas* 133-5

Polyphemus   A one-eyed giant, the son of *Poseidon*, Polyphemus, King of the *Cyclopes* in Sicily, lived on human flesh. He loved the sea-nymph *Galatea*, but she would not have him and loved *Acis* the son of *Faunus*. Polyphemus, coming upon Galatea in the arms of Acis, crushed his rival with a rock taken from *Aetna* — an act which brought the giant no nearer to Galatea. Polyphemus lived with the prophecy that he would lose his single eye to a man called *Odysseus*. When *Ulysses'* party came to the cave in their wanderings, he started to eat them, two a day; Ulysses, under the pseudonymn 'nobody', managed to make the giant drunk on wine, and drove a hot pointed stake into his eye. Although Polyphemus stopped up the cave with a rock, Ulysses and his men escaped him in his blindness, being fastened below rams as they were taken to pasture. Polyphemus was sometimes grotesquely represented, for example combing his hair with a rake and trimming his beard with a sickle.

(Homer *Odyssey* ix 105-566;
Ovid *Metamorphoses* xiii 738-897;
Virgil *Aeneid* iii 616)

Auden   *The Age of Anxiety*
Noyes   *Forty Singing Seamen*

Pomona   A Roman goddess of fruit and gardens. She received advances from many admirers but rejected them with coldness until *Vertumnus*, a god of Spring, won a way into her presence disguised as an old woman. She was represented sitting on a basket of fruit and flowers and holding a bough or pruning tool.

(Ovid *Metamorphoses* xiv 623-771)

Carew   *To My Friend G.N.* 93-4
Coleridge   *To the Author of Poems* 41-2
Fletcher P.   *Purple Island* vii 21
Keats   *Endymion* ii 444-6
Milton   *Paradise Lost* v 377-9, ix 393-5
Pope   *Windsor-Forest* 37-40
Swift   *Description of Mother Ludwell's Cave* 11-12
Thomson   *Summer* 663-6

Pompe
See *Pompey (1)*
Chaucer   *House of Fame* 1497-1502

Pompeii   The Campanian town engulfed, with Herculaneum, by the eruption of *Vesuvius* in 79 AD. Its remains were first excavated in 1748.
Shelley   *Ode to Naples* 1-2

Pompei
See *Pompey*
Chaucer   *Man of Law's Tale* 197-9

Pompeius Sextus   The younger son of *Pompey the Great*. He occupied Sicily and parts of Italy against *Octavian* and *Antony* in the aftermath of *Julius Caesar*'s assassination. Octavian defeated him, and it was one of

Antony's quarells with Octavian that the latter did not share Sicily with him. Sextus fled to Asia, where he was defeated and killed by Titius.

(Plutarch *Antony* lv)
Shakespeare   *Antony and Cleopatra* I ii 177-9, 179-84, iii 49-52; II vii 65-7; III vi 23-6

Pompeus
See *Pompey (1)*
Chaucer   *Monk's Tale* 3869-3874

Pompey, The Great (1)   The great general lived from 106-48BC. His first claim to fame was in the defeat of Sicily and Africa. He then had the dictator *Sulla*'s support, but they rapidly became rivals. When in 81 Sulla created him *Magnus*, Pompey was said to have observed that the sun is brighter in rising than in setting and, holding no public office, he marched in triumph through Rome. On the death of Sulla, he defeated *Lepidus* and became consul; he went on to defeat *Mithridates* of *Pontus* and Tigranes of Armenia, in effect creating a large empire to the East. As a tactical move, he returned to Rome as an ordinary citizen and set about relating to the leaders there. *Caesar* he feared, and he arranged to marry Caesar's daughter Julia. *Crassus*, the remaining obstacle to Pompey's ambitions, was defeated in Syria (where Caesar had arranged to send him, playing on Crassus' thirst for military glory). The struggle between Caesar and Pompey became open, and when Pompey secured further powers, Caesar felt obliged to march on Rome in 49/48BC. In 48 he finally defeated Pompey at *Pharsalus*, and Pompey stabbed himself in Egypt soon afterwards. Caesar respected, as he feared, Pompey and he built a monumental column to his memory.

(Plutarch *Pompey*)
See also *Pompe*, *Pompeius*
Byron   *The Age of Bronze* 109-10
         Childe Harold IV 87
Dryden   *Heroic Stanzas (Cromwell)* 31-2
Jonson   *To my Chosen Friend . . .*
Milton   *Paradise Regained* iii 31-6
Praed   *To Susan Praed* 113-6
Rochester   *History of the Insipids* 61-4

Shakespeare *Antony and Cleopatra* I ii
179-84
Julius Caesar I i 37ff;
III ii 185-9
King Henry V IV i 70ff
Measure for Measure II ii
206-7, 232-3
Spenser *Faerie Queene* I v 49

Pompey (2) Gnaeus Pompey, a Roman general and son of *Pompey the Great*. He was believed to have had an affair with *Cleopatra*.
(Plutarch *Antony* xxv)
Shakespeare *Antony and Cleopatra* III
xiii 117-20

Pontic King/Tyrant
See *Mithridates VI*

Pontic Sea The Euxine or Black Sea, through the Bosphorus to the Propontic or Sea of Marmora, and the *Hellespont* or Dardanelles.
Shakespeare *Othello* III iii 457-62

Pontifex Maximus Head of the Roman *Pontifices* — the state priesthood. The head pontiff kept discipline among the priests and could flog lax Vestal Virgins of the temples.
Browning R. *Ring and the Book* II 1245

Pontus (1) Countries, now in Northern Turkey, on the South coast of the Black Sea.
Milton *Paradise Lost* v 338-41

Pontus (Euxinus) (2) The Black Sea.
Milton *Paradise Lost* ix 76-8
Paradise Regained ii 344-7

Poplar This tree is particularly associated with *Hercules* and the *Phaethoniades*.
Spenser *Faerie Queene* II v 31

Porch
See *Stoics*
Collins *The Manners, an Ode* 13-14

Porcia (1) The wife and cousin of *Brutus*, the assassin of *Caesar*. On the suicide of Brutus, his wife was arrested but eluded her guard and killed herself by holding burning coals in her mouth.
(Plutarch *Brutus* lii-liii)

See also *Portia*
Chaucer *Franklin's Tale* 1448-50

Porcia (2) The sister of Cato the Younger.
(Plutarch *Cato the Younger* i, xl)

Poris A *Nereid*.
Spenser *Faerie Queene* IV xi 49

Porphyrion A giant of exceptional might whom *Zeus* defeated by instilling in him a love for *Hera* and then, with *Heracles* or *Apollo*, attacked him as he tried to rape her.
(Apollodorus I vi;
Pindar *Pythian Ode* viii)
Keats *Hyperion* ii 19-22

Porsenna Lars Porsenna was an Etruscan general from Clusium, near Lake Trasimene. He was perhaps simply an early conqueror and harsh ruler of Rome or, as more specific legend has it, was summoned by the exiled *Tarquinius Superbus* in the 6th Century BC to reinstate the Tarquinian line.
(Livy ii-viii)
See also *Tarquinius Superbus*
Macaulay *Horatius* i, xxiv

Porta Esquilina
See *Esquiline*
Spenser *Faerie Queene* II ix 32

Portia The daughter of Cato the Younger and wife of *Brutus*, Caesar's assassin — her second marriage. She was rightly believed to be involved in the conspiracy, and committed suicide on hearing of Brutus' death.
See also *Porcia (1)*
Pope *Chorus to 'Brutus'* ii 15-16
Shakespeare *Julius Caesar* II i 295;
IV iii 150-4
Merchant of Venice I i
165-6

Portunus A minor Roman god of Harbours.
(Virgil *Aeneid* v 241-3)
Dryden *Astraea Redux* 120-2
To the Duchess of Ormond
48-50

Poseidon
See *Neptune*

Praxitelean

Auden   *Lakes* 25-7
Bridges   *Prometheus the Firegiver* 941-3
Browning R.   *Artemis Prologises* 35-8,
                51ff
Fletcher P.   *The Locusts* i 2

Praxitelean
See *Praxiteles*
Shelley   *Prometheus Unbound* III iii
            161-6

Praxiteles   Greek sculptor of the 4th Century BC, known particularly for expressive marble statues of *Artemis*, *Aphrodite* and others of the Greek pantheon. His work included a famous statue of *Venus* at *Cnidos*, and the apparent expression of feeling was regarded as his forte.

(Horace *Odes* I 30)
Spenser   *Faerie Queene* III, *Prologue* 2

Priam, Priamus   Priam, King of *Troy*, was married to *Hecuba* and father of *Hector*, *Paris* and some fifteen other children, possibly including *Troilus*. When Paris had been promised the most beautiful woman in the world by *Venus* and had captured *Helen* (contrary to his father's orders to rescue *Hesione*, Priam's sister, from *Hercules*) he initiated ten years of war between Greece and Troy. The war was a personal tragedy for Priam. Most of his children were killed and he himself, an old man, was unceremoniously stabbed by *Neoptolemus*, son of *Achilles*, as he clung to the altar of *Zeus*. *Hera* was opposed to Priam and Troy because Paris had preferred *Aphrodite* to her in the beauty contest prompted by the apple of *Eris*; Zeus summed up her attitude by saying she would like to eat Priam and his offspring raw.

(Homer *Iliad* iii 146ff, iv 35ff, vii 345ff,
            xxii 408ff, xxiv)
See also *Laomedon*
Belloc   *But O Not Lovely Helen* 1ff
Brooke   *Fragment*
Browning E. B.   *Battle of Marathon*
                15-20, 900-4
Chaucer   *Book of the Duchess* 326-34
            Nun's Priest's Tale 4545-51
            House of Fame 158-61
            Troilus and Criseyde i 1-2
Goldsmith   *Haunch of Venison* 109-10

Masefield   *Clytemnestra* 4ff
Shakespeare   *All's Well That Ends Well*
                I iii 66-9
                Hamlet II ii 428ff, 483-6
                King Henry IV pt 2 I i 70-4
                King Henry VI pt 3 II v
                118-9
                Rape of Lucrece 1366-72,
                1447-9, 1490-1, 1520-2
                Titus Andronicus I i 79-80;
                V iii 80-7
                Troilus and Cressida V iii
                51-5, x 17-19
Spenser   *Faerie Queene* II iii 31, IV xi
            19
Surrey   *So Cruel Prison* 1-4

Priapus   A monstrous fertility god first worshipped around the *Hellespont* and sometimes said to be the son of *Dionysus*. Asses, symbols of lust, were sacrificed to him and he was represented with grotesquely enlarged genitals. For the Greeks, who met him at a relatively sophisticated stage of religious development, he seems to have been partly an object of fun. Besides presiding over lust, he was god of goats, bees, sheep and gardens. He offered violence to the nymph Lotos, daughter of *Neptune*, who was rescued by the gods and turned into a lotos tree.

(Diodorus Siculus i 88; Ovid *Fasti*
            i 415, vi 304ff; Pausanias I xxxi 2)
Chaucer   *Merchant's Tale* 2034-41
            Parliament of Fowls 253-9
Eliot T. S.   *Mr Apollinax*
Lawrence   *Name the Gods* 10-11
Lewis C. D.   *Transitional Poem* 12
Rosetti D. G.   *Jenny*
Shakespeare   *Pericles* IV vi 2-4
Shelley   *Witch of Atlas* 124-6

Priscian, Priscianus   A grammarian of the 6th Century AD whose extensive works, interlaced with quotations and commentaries on Classical authors, were much used in the Middle Ages.
Butler S.   *Hudibras* II ii 221-5
Swift   *The Pardon* 5-6

Procne   The daughter of *Pandion* of Athens and wife of *Tereus* of *Thrace*. Procne loved her sister *Philomela* dearly and grieved when separated by marriage to Tereus. It was arranged for Tereus to go to fetch Philomela from Athens to Thrace, but Tereus became infatuated by Philomela, whose tongue he cut out when he had raped her. He then hid her away, returning to tell Procne that her sister was dead. After a year's mourning Procne learned that this was not so, since she received from Philomela an account of her misfortunes woven into a tapestry. In revenge, Procne then killed and served to Tereus the remains of their son *Itylus*, at a Bacchic feast. After the moment of revelation the three principal characters were turned into birds — Philomela into a nightingale and Procne into a swallow (both died of grief); there are several versions of Tereus' demise, but he is said to have been turned into a hoopoe.

> (Ovid *Metamorphoses* vi 455 ff;
> Pausanias i 41)

See also *Progne*
> Chaucer   *Legend of Good Women*
>   2244-50, 2342-7, 2373-7
> Davies Sir J.   *Orchestra* 691-3

Procris
See *Cephalus, Procrus*
> Moore   *Cephalus and Procris* 17-22

Procrus
See *Cephalus, Procris*
> Shakespeare   *Midsummer Night's Dream*
>   V i 197

Procrustes   A son of *Neptune* who captured travellers and tailored them to fit a notorious bed, stretching them if too short and truncating them if too long. It was one of the labours of *Theseus* to give Procrustes (whose name means 'stretcher' and whose real name was Damastes or Polupemon) his own treatment, and he killed him.

> (Hyginus *Fabulae* 38)
> Crashaw   *Sospetto d'Herode* 45
> Spenser   *Mutability Cantos* vi 29

Proculeius   A Roman soldier specially trusted by *Augustus* and sent by him to bring *Cleopatra* to him as she was about to commit suicide. The dying *Antony* advised Cleopatra to rely on Proculeius but, as they conversed inside and outside her monument, she refused and

committed suicide despite his attempts to dissuade her.

> (Plutarch *Antony* lxxviii-ix)
> Shakespeare   *Antony and Cleopatra* IV
>   xv 47-8; V i 61-3

Proculus   Julius Proculus claimed to have seen his friend *Romulus* after death, that sacrifices should be offered to the dead hero and that Rome would be the capital of the world.

> (Livy I xvi; Plutarch *Romulus* xxviii 1)
> Butler S.   *Hudibras* III ii 226-7
> Pope   *Rape of the Lock* 168-71

Proigne, Progne
See *Procne*
> Chaucer   *Troilus and Criseyde* ii 63-6
> Crashaw   *Sospetto d'Herode* 42
> Fletcher P.   *To my Beloved Cousin*
>   6-10
> Shakespeare   *Titus Andronicus* V ii
>   195-6

Promethean
See *Prometheus*
> Chapman   *Shadow of Night*
> Keats   *Endymion* iv 955
> Noyes   *Niobe* 11-15
> Shakespeare   *Love's Labour's Lost* IV
>   iii 346-9
>   *Othello* V i 10-3
> Shelley   *Prometheus Unbound* IV 156-8
> Swinburne   *Song of Italy*

Prometheus   The son of *Iapetus* and Clymene (an *Oceanid*) or *Asia*. He was renowned for his cunning, which led to his theft of fire from heaven for the benefit of man. Testing divinity, he filled skins with flesh and with bones and asked *Jupiter* which he would prefer as a sacrifice. Jupiter, deceived, chose the bag of bones, leaving man with the meat as food. As a result Jupiter took fire from earth as punishment. With *Minerva*'s help, Prometheus stole replacement fire from the chariot of the sun. Enraged, Jupiter forced newly-created woman onto him, but Prometheus disposed of her (*Pandora*) to his brother *Epimetheus*. Jupiter's patience was exhausted, and he had Prometheus nailed to a rock (the *Caucasus*) for thirty thousand years, with an eagle incessantly devouring his liver. He was eventually freed, and the bird killed, by *Hercules*; it was disputed whether Jupiter permitted this because Prometheus possessed a secret (that consummation of marriage between Jupiter and *Thetis* would lead to Jupiter's downfall by a son) which could be used as a bargain, or for the greater glory of his son, Hercules. Some ascribed to Prometheus the creation of men and women from clay animated with fire. By writer after writer he has been taken to embody the noble and intellectual in man, sometimes with what is seen as a concomitant suffering, and has been portrayed as the just rebel supporting the dignity of freedom.

(Aeschylus *Prometheus Bound*; Apollodorus I ii; Hesiod *Theogony* 507-616, *Works and Days* 47-105)

— *General and as Symbolic Hero*

Bridges   *Prometheus the Firegiver* 507-8

Byron   *Age of Bronze* 227-32
Prometheus 35, 45-7
Prophecy of Dante IV 11-16

Davies Sir J.   *Orchestra* 449-51

Shelley   *Prometheus Unbound* I 117ff, 179-84, 209-14

Spenser   *Mutability Cantos* vi 29

Swinburne   *Athens* ep. i

— *his Punishment*

Bridges   *Prometheus the Firegiver* 1163-9

Browning E. B.   *Wine of Cyprus* 18

Browning R.   *With Gerard to Lairesse* 188-94

Byron   *Prometheus* 1-7, 26-30

Shakespeare   *Titus Andronicus* II i 15-17

Shelley   *Prometheus Unbound* I 12ff, 285ff, 492-3

Swift   *Prometheus* 31ff

Wordsworth   *The Excursion* vi 539-45

— *his Theft of Fire for Men*

Bridges   *Prometheus the Firegiver* 90-7

Browning R.   *Death in the Desert* 279-86
With Bernard de Mandeville 301-7

Byron   *Childe Harold* iv 163
Don Juan i 127

Coleridge   *The Nose* 5-8

Daniel   *Civil Wars* vi 26ff

Denham   *To His Mistress* 7-8

Milton   *Paradise Lost* iv 714-19

Swift   *Apollo to the Dean* 93-4

— *his Creation or Animation of Man*

Diaper   *Callipaedia* 27-30

Drayton   *Idea* viii 5-8

Shelley   *Prometheus Unbound* II iv 72

Spenser   *Faerie Queene* II x 70

— *his Secret over Jupiter*

Shelley   *Prometheus Unbound* I 371-6

Promethii

See *Prometheus*

Drayton   *The Owl* 672

Pronaea   A *Nereid.*

Spenser   *Faerie Queene* IV xi 50

Proserpene, Prosperpina, Proserpine

See *Persephone, Proserpyne*

Arnold   *Thyrsis* 82-90, 91-100

Browning E. B.   *Calls on the Heart* 4

Browning R.   *Pauline* 333-5

Chaucer   *Franklin's Tale* 1072-6
Merchant's Tale 2034-41, 2225-36

Donne   *Elegy* viii 23-4

Drayton   *Idea* xix 7-8
The Owl 286-90

Gray   *Lines Spoken by the Ghost of John Dennis* 38-9

Henryson   *Orpheus and Eurydice* 365ff

Hood   *Autumn* 19-20

Keats   *Endymion* i 443-6
Fancy 81-8
Lamia i 61-3
Ode on Melancholy 1-4
Fall of Hyperion i 35-7

Lamb   *The Ballad-Singers* 30-3

Lawrence   *Purple Anemones* 18-21, 23ff

Marlowe   *Tamburlaine* i 4011ff

Meredith   *Appeasement of Demeter*
Day of the Daughter of Hades
Pastoral II

Milton   *Paradise Lost* iv 268-71, 393-6

Pope   *Ode for Music* 83-6

Prior   *Ode in Memory of George Villiers* 55-9

Shakespeare   *Tempest* IV i 87-91
Troilus and Cressida II i 31-4
Winter's Tale IV iv 115-24

Shelley	*Song of Proserpine*
	Witch of Atlas 578-83
Spenser	*Daphnaida* 14-21, 463-6
	Faerie Queene I i 37, ii 2,
	II vii 53-6, III xi 1
	Ruins of Time 372-7
Swinburne	*Gardens of Proserpine* 16-20
	Hymn to Proserpine 4-8
Wordsworth	*Once Could I Hail* 13-18

Proserpyne
See *Proserpina, Proserpine*
Chaucer   *House of Fame* 1509-12

Protagoras   A Greek *Sophist* philosopher of the 5th Century BC. He was a sceptic and agnostic and laid a stress on the relativity of opinions to their holders and the notion that a question embraced contrarieties. His death came by drowning, though he had previously been exiled following the common trials for impiety.
Browning R.   *Aristophanes' Apology* 2039-44

Protean
See *Proteus*
Wordsworth   *To the Clouds* 74-7

Proteselaus
See *Laodamia*
Chaucer   *Franklin's Tale* 1445-7
Clough   *Amours de Voyage* iii 85-90
Wordsworth   *Laodamia* 19-24, 43-7, 155ff

Proteus   The elusive and prophetic sea-god, son of *Neptune* or *Oceanus*. He had the ability to change his shape in a fluid manner and had to be bound before he would give consultation. He was supposed to live in the Carpathian Sea. As the shepherd of seals, Proteus may be depicted carrying a crook.
(Homer *Odyssey* iv 363ff; Ovid *Metamorphoses* viii 731ff; Virgil *Georgics* iv 386ff)
See also *Protean*
Cowper   *On the Ice Islands* 3-4
Diaper   *Sea Eclogues* ii 73-6, viii 5-6
Dryden   *Annus Mirabilis* 57-70
    Hind and the Panther iii 818
Fletcher P.   *The Locusts* ii 5

Graves	*New Legends* 12-15
Gray	*The Character of the Christ-Cross Row* 43
Keats	*Not Aladdin magian* 42
Kipling	*The Bees and the Flies* 1-8
Marlowe	*Hero and Leander* i 135-42
Milton	*Paradise Lost* iii 603-5
Noyes	*The Tramp Transformed* 152-5
Shakespeare	*King Henry VI pt 3* III ii 191-3
Shelley	*Letter to Maria Gisborne* 45-6
	Prometheus Unbound III iii 21-5, 65-6
	Triumph of Life 270-2
Spenser	*Colin Clouts Come Home Again* 245-51
	Faerie Queene I ii 10, III iv 25, 37, III viii 37, 41
Swift	*Ode to Athenian Society* 189-93
	Pethox the Great 81-2
Wordsworth	*Sonnet, The World is Too Much With Us*

Proto   A *Nereid*.
(Apollodorus I ii 6; Hesiod *Theogony* 243)
Spenser   *Faerie Queene* IV xi 48

Protogenes   A sculptor from *Caria* in the 4th Century BC. He was associated with *Apelles*.
Prior   *Protogenes and Apelles* 17-18

Protomedaea, Protomedlaea   A *Nereid*, known also as Protomedusa or Protomelia.
(Hesiod *Theogony* 249)
Spenser   *Faerie Queene* IV xi 49

Psamanthe, Psamathe   A *Nereid*, mother of Phocus, the founder of Phocis, by King *Aeacus* of *Aegina*.
(Apollodorus III xii 6)
Spenser   *Faerie Queene* IV xi 51

Psyche   The daughter of unknown parents, Psyche's beauty was so great that she distracted from the worship of *Venus*. Venus therefore had *Cupid* make Psyche fall in love with a man of no station by whom she was duly visited. Her mysterious lover promised she would bear a divine child if she never looked at him or sought his identity. Her sisters persuaded her she was sleeping with a monster and urged her to kill him forthwith. Holding a lamp with this in mind, she discovered her lover to be Cupid, but unhappily he was awakened by a drop of oil or wax from the lamp and deserted her. The enraged Venus upbraided Cupid and set Psyche a series of hard and worthless labours, such as sorting grain, which she accomplished but of which she died. Cupid revived her and sought *Jupiter's* approval to their marriage, from which was born a daughter, Volupta. Psyche represented the soul. As a goddess she appeared late and had no cult or temple. She was associated with moths and butterflies as representing the airy incorporeal spirit.

(Apuleius iv 28 - vi 26)

Byron   *Don Juan* iii 74
Keats   *I Stood Tiptoe Upon a Little Hill*
     141-50
     Ode on Melancholy 6-7
     Ode to Psyche 24-9, 40-3
     Otho the Great V v 28-30
Lewis C. D.   *Psyche* 28-30, 71-80
Milton   *Comus* 1004-8
Moore   *Cupid and Psyche* 5 ff
     To Mrs Henry Tighe 29-32
Spenser   *Faerie Queene* III vi 50
     Muiopotmos 131-3

Ptolemy (1)   Ptolemy I (c. 337-283 BC) was founder of the Macedonian dynasty of Egypt. He laid down many of the administrative systems of Alexandria and, a patron of the arts, himself wrote a history of it. Ptolemy II was joint ruler with his father from 285 BC to 283 BC. He developed commerce and finance and continued to patronise the arts, building a great Library and Museum. Ptolemy XII, c.115-53 BC, preceded his daughter Cleopatra VII — the *Cleopatra* for whom *Mark Antony* counted the world well lost.
See also *Ptholomee*, *Tholome*
Collins   *Lines on the Music of the*
     Grecian Theatre 1-7

Ptolemy (2)   Claudius Ptolemaeus, astronomer and mathematician of the 2nd Century AD, whose chief work is an astronomical textbook known in the Middle Ages by its Arabic title of *Almageste*. This set out the system of astronomy by which sun, stars and planets revolve round the earth, a system only

gradually superseded by the heliocentric view of things advocated by Copernicus in the 16th Century. Ptolemy's work was based on fresh observation and mathematical argument, though it acknowledged debts to earlier authorities. He lived and worked in Alexandria but very little is known of his life.

Ptolomee
See *Ptolemy (2)*
Chaucer   *Wife of Bath's Prologue*
     180 ff, 324-7

Publicola   Valerius Publicola was reputedly one of the first Roman consuls and in power at the time of *Coriolanus*. His life and claims to fame are uncertain and sources of them unreliable. Nothing is known of his sister, *Valeria*.
Shakespeare   *Coriolanus* V iii 64-7

Punic Wars   Three wars between Rome and Carthage in the 3rd and 2nd Centuries BC, by means of which Rome gradually achieved supremacy in the western Mediterranean.
(Livy *Polybius*)
Dryden   *Annus Mirabilis* 17-20

Pygmalion   A legendary king of Cyprus who, finding all women fell short of his requirements, sculpted a marble statue with which he fell in love. In reply to his prayer, *Aphrodite* gave life to the statue, whom Pygmalion married and who bore him a daughter, Paphos (or in later versions, Galatea), eponym of a land sacred to Aphrodite.
(Ovid *Metamorphoses* x 243-97)
See also *Pigmalion*
Browning E. B.   *Aurora Leigh* v
     399-406
Browning R.   *The Dance of Death*
     88-91
Carew   *To the Painter* 39-42
Chaucer   *Physician's Tale* 14-18
Cowley   *Answer to the Platonics* 29-30
Crabbe   *Resentment*
Lewis C. D.   *The Perverse* 9-12
Marlowe   *Dido Queen of Carthage*
     311-2
     Tamburlaine II 2527-30
Shakespeare   *Measure for Measure* III ii
     41 ff

Pygmies   The Pygmaei, a miniature people located in India and reputed to build houses with egg-shells, to live in holes in the ground, and to be engaged in constant combat with attacking birds, particularly cranes.

(Homer Iliad iii 1-6;
Ovid Metamorphoses vi 90;
Strabo I ii 28, XVII ii 1)

   Milton   *Paradise Lost* i 575-6

Pylades
See *Orestes*
   Byron   *To Romance* 19-20
   Marlowe   *Tamburlaine* i 436-40
   Spenser   *Faerie Queene* IV x 27

Pyle
See *Thrasybulus*
   Byron   *Childe Harold* ii 74

Pylos, Pylian   A town, variously identified, of which *Nestor*, Greek leader in the Trojan war, was King.

(Homer Iliad ii 591ff; Pausanias iv 36)

   Browning E. B.   *Battle of Marathon* 425-6
   Keats   *King Stephen* I iii 11-12

Pyracmon   One of the *Cyclopes* employed by *Vulcan* in Mount *Aetna* to make *Aeneas'* shield from a thunderbolt.

(Virgil Aeneid viii 422-8)

See also *Brontes, Peracmon, Steropes*
   Lamb   *The Ballad-Singers* 24-5
   Spenser   *Faerie Queene* IV v 37

Pyramus   A Babylonian youth who fell in love with *Thisbe*. The parents objected to a marriage and the couple communicated by nods and signs through a chink in the party-wall of their adjacent houses. They eventually eluded watch and met by the tomb of *Ninus*, but Thisbe, arriving first, was terrified by a lion and, fleeing, dropped her veil, which the beast marked with blood. On arriving, Pyramus feared the worst and stabbed himself. The returning Thisbe found him dying and fell on his sword. There was a white-berried mulberry tree nearby and its berries were changed to red by the spurting blood of Pyramus, and they have remained that colour ever since.

(Ovid Metamorphoses iv 55ff)

See also *Piramus*
   Chaucer   *Merchant's Tale* 2125-31
   Donne   *Epigram, Pyramus and Thisbe*
   Shakespeare   *Midsummer Night's Dream* II i 18-19, 75-6; III i 43ff; V i 56-7, 127ff, 136ff
        Titus Andronicus II iii 226ff
   Surrey   *Divers Thy Death (Wyatt)* 11-14

Pyreneus   A King of Phocis who sheltered the *Muses* in a shower but offered them violence. The Muses flew away and Pyreneus, trying to follow them by taking flight from a tower, fell and broke his neck.

(Ovid Metamorphoses v 274-93)

   Drayton   *To Himself and the Harp* 21-5

Pyrois   One of the four horses of the sun, with *Eous, Aethon* and *Phlegon*.

(Ovid Metamorphoses ii 153ff)

See also *Pirois, Pirous*

Pyrrha   The daughter of *Epimetheus* and *Pandora*, and wife of *Deucalion*.
   Keats   *Lamia* i 329-33
   Milton   *Paradise Lost* xi 9-14
   Spenser   *Faerie Queene* V Prologue 2

Pyrrhus (1)   A King of Epirus, living from c. 318-272 BC and reputedly descended from *Achilles* and *Hercules*. He attempted to assert the independence of Epirus against Macedonia, though he came to the throne when only twelve years old, with the support of *Demetrius* of Macedonia. He married Antigone, the step-daughter of *Ptolemy II*, at whose court he was a hostage, but in due course regained his throne, with Demetrius' help. However, he sought independence and made war on Demetrius and gained half Macedonia before being driven out by *Lysimachus* in 283. He defeated the Romans in 280 at Heraclea and again at Asculum in 279, but was unable to achieve a lasting victory and was forced to withdraw from Sicily in 275, sustaining heavy losses. After a further attempt on Macedonia and an attempted siege of *Sparta*, he was killed in a street fight at *Argos*. He was, from the first, commended for gallantry and tactics, but his victories amounted to no coherent achievement and that at Heraclea was achieved with

209

such losses as to be the archetype of the 'Pyrrhic victory'.

(Livy viii, xiv; Plutarch *Pyrrhus*)

See also *Pirrus (1)*

| Milton | *Sonnet* xvii |
| Young | *Night Thoughts* vii |

Pyrrhus (2) Neoptolemus Pyrrhus entered the Trojan War young and late in the day; he was born of a youthful affair between *Achilles* and Deidameia and joined the Greeks after a prophecy that his doing so was a condition of their victory once Achilles had been killed by Paris. He proved a valiant fighter, being with the Greeks inside the Wooden Horse, sacrificing *Priam*'s daughter (*Polyxena*) according to the gods' command, and possibly killing *Hector*'s son, Astyanax, by casting him from the ramparts. It was he who slew Priam, holding him by the hair as he stabbed him in the side, as the old man made an infirm attack on him for the murder of yet another of his sons, *Polites*. He was sometimes said also to have added to these triumphs the killing of *Penthesilea*.

(Apollodorus xi 504-40;
Homer *Odyssey* xi 504-40;
Virgil *Aeneid* II 469-558)

See also *Pirrus (2)*

Shakespeare	*Hamlet* II ii 483-6
	Rape of Lucrece 1447-9
	Troilus and Cressida III iii 209-13
Spenser	*Faerie Queene* II iii 31

Pythagoras, Pythagorean Greek (Samian) philosopher and mathematician of the 6th Century BC. He is a legendary figure and no writings survive. There were two main attributions to him; a philosophy based on the belief that the soul is a fallen divinity imprisoned in an earthly body, and obliged to undergo a series of transmigrations or reincarnations from which a rigorous asceticism is the chief way out; and the discovery of the mathematical relations determing the musical scale, on which was based a numerical symbolism applied also to philosophy. Pythagoras lived and taught at Crotona, Italy and a religious house, reputedly based on his ideas, developed there. There were many curious legends as to his appearance and powers: he had a golden leg, could convey reflections from a mirror to the moon, or could appear in two places at the same time.

(Ovid *Metamorphoses* xv 60ff;
Plato *Republic* VII xii, X iv;
Plutarch *Numa* VIII 7, XI 2, *Dion* XI i)

See also *Pictagoras, Pithagores, Theano*

Cowley	*Upon the Chaie* 3-6
Denham	*On Abraham Cowley* 67-8
	Progress of Learning 35-9
Jonson	*The Alchemist* IV iii
	To Sir Henry Davile 1-4
Lawrence	*Tortoise Shell* 19-21
Moore	*Grecian Girl's Dream* 48-51
	To Lord Viscount Strangford 1-4
Prior M.	*Ode in Memory of George Villiers* 15-18
Shakespeare	*Merchant of Venice* IV i 130-3
	Twelfth Night IV ii 49-50
Thomson	*Liberty* iii 37ff
Yeats	*Among School Children* vi
	The Delphic Oracle Upon Plotinus
	Full Moon in March (Song)
	Statues

Pythia The name given to the priestess of the oracle at *Delphi* on the same site as the Pythian Games; the name was held to derive from *Apollo*'s defeat of the *Python* on this spot. These Games, which in some accounts were a musical competition, and in which the gods were participants, were held in the third year of each Olympiad and were next in importance to the *Olympics*. The Pythia gave utterance in a state of frenzy and sat on a tripod or form of three-legged stool. The word 'Pythoness' is occasionally used to mean 'Pythian'.

(Ovid *Metamorphoses* i 437ff;
Pausanias x 5, 7; Strabo ix 5, 10)

Browning E. B.	*The Dead Pan* 30
Campbell	*Pleasures of Hope*
Keats	*Fall of Hyperion* i 202-4

Pythian

See *Pythia*

Browning R.	*Sordello* v 81-4
Byron	*Childe Harold* i 64, iii 81
Milton	*Paradise Lost* ii 529-30, x 529-31
Shelley	*Adonais* 240-51

Pythias (1)   A stereotyped pastoral lad usually found with *Damon*.
Spenser   *Faerie Queene* IV x 27

Pythias (2)   The niece of Hermias, a tyrant of *Mysia*. Hermias gathered round him a circle of *Platonic* philosophers, joined by *Aristotle*, who married Pythias shortly after 348BC.
Moore   *The Grecian Girl's Dream* 44-5

Python   A serpent monster left in the mud after the flood of *Deucalion* — or produced by *Juno* to persecute *Latona, Jupiter's* mistress. Python was killed by *Apollo*, son of Latona, who instituted the Pythian Games and, in some accounts, also the oracle at *Delphi*, site of the conquest.
(Ovid *Metamorphoses* i 434ff; Strabo ix 3)
See also *Phitoun, Pythia*
Arnold   *Empedocles on Etna* II i 201-7
Coleridge   *Destiny of Nations* 435-7
Drayton   *The Muses' Elizium* ix 65-8
Hood   *Hymn to the Sun* 3
Hopkins   *Escorial* II
Keats   *Endymion* iii 529-31
Lamia ii 78-81
Milton   *Paradise Lost* x 529-31
Shelley   *Rosalind and Helen* 701-3
Sidney   *Arcadia* xxvi 5ff
Thomson   *Liberty* iv 163-7

Queen of Love
See *Venus*
Goldsmith   *On Seeing Mrs . . . Perform the Character of . . .* 9-11

Quinctius, Quintius
See *Cincinnatus*
Milton   *Paradise Regained* ii 445-9

Quintilian   A Spanish rhetorician who opened a school of rhetoric in the 1st Century AD. He became a leading advocate, teacher of the Younger Pliny and tutor to the heirs of the Emperor *Domitian*. His standard work, *Institutio Oratoria* — a popular book of the Renaissance in England — set rhetoric into a broad theory of education in which the sound orator becomes a good citizen and admirable example.
Milton   *Sonnet* xi
Pope   *Essay on Criticism* 669-70

Raven
See *Corvus*
Chaucer   *House of Fame* 1004-8

Regillus, Lake   The site, now uncertain, of a battle c.496BC, where Mamilius, a Tuscan commanding the Latin armies, was defeated by the Romans under Posthumius, their Dictator.
(Livy ii 20)
Macaulay   *Lake Regillus* 2, 3

Regulus   Marcus Atilius Regulus was consul during the First Punic War in the 3rd Century BC. After outstanding successes in Africa, he offered peace on unacceptable terms and was then defeated. On being taken prisoner and sent with terms to Rome, he advised against accepting them and returned to Carthage, a voluntary exile. Here, however, he was tortured to death for not securing peace. It is now difficult to distinguish gallantry from stupidity in his behaviour, but his became a very popular and much-embroidered story. He was a popular hero and is twice (*Odes* I xii and III v) praised with *Augustus* by *Horace*.
(Diodorus Siculus xxiii 12, 15; Livy xxviii 42)
Auden   *The Horatians* 70-1
Belloc   *The Modern Traveller* xiv
Cleveland   *Upon a Hermaphrodite* 24-6
Lovelace   *Triumphs of Philamore* 212
MacNeice   *Memoranda to Horace* iii
Milton   *Paradise Regained* 445-9
Swift   *Pethox the Great* 53ff
Thomson   *Liberty* iii 166-75

Remus
See *Romulus*
Byron   *Childe Harold* iv 88
Deformed Transformed I ii 80-4
Diaper   *Callipaedia* 203-7
Macaulay   *Prophecy of Capys* 6

Rhadamanthus   The son of *Zeus* and *Europa*, born in Crete, where he was supposed to have established a legal system. He competed with his brothers, *Minos* and Sarpedon, for the affection of a youth, *Miletus*. When Miletus declared his preference for Sarpedon, Minos drove out his brothers and assumed the throne of Crete, but left a part to Rhadamanthus, whom he feared; alternatively, Rhadamanthus fled to Boeotia where he married *Alcmene* after the death of her husband *Amphitryon*. After his death, Rhadamanthus (like Minos) was made a judge in *Hades* and *Elysium*.

> (Apollodorus III i 1-2;
> Diodorus Siculus v 79;
> Homer *Iliad* iv 531-9)

Cowley	*Pindaric Ode* 8
Jonson	*Sejanus* I i
Keats	*Endymion* iv 953
Yeats	*The Delphic Oracle Upon Plotinus*

Rhea

See *Cybele*

Bridges	*Demeter* 563-5
	Prometheus the Firegiver 206-11, 632-6
Browning E. B.	*Wine of Cyprus* 7
Fletcher G.	*Description of Enculpius* 9-10
Graves	*Rhea* 17-18
Milton	*Paradise Lost* i 512-3, iv 275-9
Prior	*First Hymn to Callimachus* 13-14, 19 ff, 39 ff
	To the Countess Dowager of Devonshire 43-4

Rhea Silvia Daughter of Numitor, King of *Alba* Longa, Rhea was committed by her uncle *Amulius*, who had usurped the throne, to be a Vestal Virgin, with the object of denying the possibility of inconvenient heirs. From this secluded life, however, she was seduced by *Mars* and gave birth to *Romulus* and *Remus*, who ousted Amulius.

> (Livy i 3-4)

Chaucer	*Parliament of Fowls* 290-5
Marlowe	*Dido Queen of Carthage* 104-8

Rhesus A Thracian king who came to help the Trojans, who had previously supported his throne. Shortly after his arrival, a Trojan spy, *Dolon*, tried to save his own life by telling the Greeks *Diomedes* and *Odysseus* of Rhesus,

his men and his horses. The two Greeks then killed Dolon and completed the episode by killing Rhesus and some of his men by night, driving off the horses.

> (Homer *Iliad* x 432 ff)

Shakespeare	*King Henry VI pt 3* IV ii 19-23

Rhodanus The modern River Rhone.

Spenser	*Faerie Queene* IV xi 20

Rhodope (1) A mountain range in *Thrace*, now Southern Bulgaria, where *Orpheus* was dismembered by the Bacchic revellers. The mountain was supposedly named after the wife of *Haemus*, King of Thrace, and was sacred to *Dionysus/Bacchus*. There are various accounts of the link between Haemus and Rhodope. In one, Rhodope was said to have been the daughter of Haemus and to have had a giant baby, called *Athos*, by *Neptune*.

> (Ovid *Metamorphoses* vi 87;
> Plutarch *De Fluviis*;
> Virgil *Eclogues* vi 30, viii 44)

Fletcher G.	*Christ's Victory on Earth* 40
Lamb	*The Ballad-Singers* 30-3
Marlowe	*Tamburlaine* i 283-5
Milton	*Paradise Lost* vii 33-5
Spenser	*Faerie Queene* II xii 52

Rhodope (2) A Greek prostitute who was freed by — and married to — Charaxes, brother of *Sappho*. She was held to have made so much money from her trade that she had a pyramid built in Egypt. Her removal to Egypt was accomplished by means of an eagle, which flew there with one of her slippers as she bathed, and brought her to the attention of King Psammetichus. The few rather inchoate stories may well be compilations of myths about more than one person.

> (Herodotus II 134-5)

Shakespeare	*King Henry VI pt 1* I vi 21-6
Tennyson	*The Princess* ii 68

Rimmon A Syrian God of the sky and of thunder, the centre of whose worship was at Damascus.

Milton	*Paradise Lost* i 467-8

Riphean, Riphoean The Riphaean hills, north of the Black Sea, were the legendary abode of the *Gorgons* and were notorious for their coldness.

(Virgil *Georgics* iv 518)

Herrick	*Description of a Woman* 59-62
Spenser	*Faerie Queene* III viii 6

Rome, Romans Select allusions.

Burns	*A Fragment* 47-8
Byron	*Childe Harold* iv 78-9
Chaucer	*Canon Yeoman's Tale* 972-5
Collins	*Ode to Liberty* 7-20
Dryden	*To Sir Godfrey Kneller*
Jonson	*Catiline* I i
Marlowe	*Dido Queen of Carthage* 96-9, 104-8
Milton	*Paradise Lost* ix 670-2
	Paradise Regained iii 383-5, iv 45-7
Shakespeare	*Titus Andronicus* III i 54-5
Shelley	*Hellas* 142-4, 992-5
	Ode to Liberty 91-4
	Queen Mab ii 162-72
Spenser	*Faerie Queene* i 22
	Sonnet, 'Those prudent heads . . .'
Tennyson	*The Druid's Prophecy* 73-6

Romulus Born with *Remus*, the sons of *Mars* and *Rhea Silvia* (known also as Ilia). The two were thrown into the *Tiber* by their usurping uncle *Amulius* (Numitor being the true king), but were saved and suckled by a she-wolf when the Tiber stopped flowing. They were discovered by a shepherd, Faustulus, and in due course, when acquainted with their origin, put down and killed Amulius, reinstating Numitor. After a competition to see which could see most birds from the Aventine and *Palatine* Hills, Romulus, the winner, started foundations for a city, to become Rome. Remus was killed either by his brother, after mocking him by jumping the small new walls, or at Romulus' agency, in a dispute as to which of them had in fact seen the greater number of birds. Romulus was held to have been taken up to heaven in 714BC, after a reign notable for savagery, but also for the establishment of a rudimentary legal state, which included punishments for adultery. A temple was raised to him, with a priest to conduct regular sacri-

fices. He reputedly lived in a tiny thatched cottage which was compared to a cell in a honeycomb.

(Livy i 4-7; Ovid *Fasti*)

See also *Proculus*

Auden	*Secondary Epic* 47ff
Browning R.	*Ring and the Book* i 219-23
Butler S.	*Hudibras* III ii 226-7
Byron	*Childe Harold* iv 88
	Deformed Transformed I ii 80-4
Chaucer	*House of Fame* 589-91
	Parliament of Fowls 290-5
Diaper	*Callipaedia* 203-7
Dryden	*MacFlecknoe* 130-3
Kipling	*Romulus and Remus* 9-12
Macaulay	*Prophecy of Capys* 6
Marvell	*Upon Appleton House* 37-40
Milton	*Paradise Regained* iii 82-7
Pope	*Rape of the Lock* 168-71
Prior	*Carmen Seculare* 31-4
Spenser	*Faerie Queene* I v 49, III ix 43

Roscius A celebrated Roman comic actor of the 1st Century BC. He was defended by *Cicero* against charges of dishonesty.

See also *Be-Rosciused*

Byron	*An Occasional Prologue* 11-13
	English Bards 564-5
Goldsmith	*Retaliation* 118
Herrick	*Good Friday — Rex Tragicus* 17-20
Jonson	*To Edward Alleyn*
Shakespeare	*King Henry VI pt 3* V vi 10

Roses

See *Venus*

Milton	*Paradise Lost* ix 217-9, 426-32

Rubellius Plautus The great-grandson of *Tiberius*, murdered by *Nero* on suspicion of inciting revolt against him.

(Tacitus *Annals* xiii)

Gray	*Agrippina* 99-100

Rubicon A small reddish river, the boundary between Italy and Cisalpine Gaul. By crossing it, after some deliberation, in 49BC, Caesar transgressed the Roman frontier and precipitated Civil War, effectively declaring against

Pompey and the Senate. *Lucan* gravely depicts the act.

(Lucan *Civil War* i 185 ff)
Browning E. B.   *Casa Guidi Windows*
    ii 87-90
Byron   *Age of Bronze* 137-9
Drayton   *Polyolbion* xv 247-8
MacNeice   *Autumn Journal* xxiv
Pope   *Essay on Man* iv 244-6
Wordsworth   *The Wagoner* 81-2

Rufus (1)   Rufus of Ephesus was physician to the Roman Emperor *Trajan* at the beginning of the 2nd Century AD. His approach was through dietetics and pathology, and he preferred the symptomatic study of specific illness to general theory.

Chaucer   *Canterbury Tales, Prologue*
    429-31

Rufus (2)   Verginius Rufus, a Roman officer in Gaul who rebuffed attempts to make him emperor and composed his epitaph, saying that it was better to serve the country's interest than to rule the world. This morality was formulated in the 1st Century AD.

(Pliny *Epistles* vi 10)
Dryden   *To My Honoured Friend*
    (Howard) 96-8

Rumor, Rumour
See *Fama*
Gray   *A Long Story* 73
Milton   *Paradise Lost* ii 965-7
Shakespeare   *King Henry IV pt 2* Induction 3 ff

Sabean   Of Sheba (Sabe) in modern Yemen, famed for gold and spices.

Dryden   *Aureng-Zebe* IV i
Milton   *Paradise Lost* iv 162-3
Tennyson   *Adeline* 51-4

Sabellus   The name of a Roman soldier killed, in the Civil War of 49-45 BC, by a small poisonous African snake, *seps*. His death and the dissolution of his body are horribly described by *Lucan*.

(Lucan *Civil War* ix 764 ff)
Shelley   *Prometheus Unbound* III i 39-41

Sabini, Sabine   A tribe living just north of Rome. *Numa* was possibly Sabine. The Sabini, once absorbed, provided several Patrician families of early Rome, and they were associated with good living. The Rape of the Sabine Women is a much-illustrated episode in which the Sabini rise up against the Romans for raping their women, at what was meant to be a hospitable entertainment. It has analogues and little to support it as historical fact, but it is recorded by *Livy* as one of the earliest attacks on Rome by her neighbours. *Horace* received a Sabine farm from Augustus' patronage, and he makes many references to the comfortable Sabine way of life.

(Horace *Epistles* I vii 77, *Satires* II vii 118;
    Livy i 9-10)
Byron   *Childe Harold* iv 174
Clough   *Amours de Voyage* iii 229
Noyes   *A Spring Hat* 1-6
Prior   *Carmen Seculare* 31-4
Tennyson   *Princess* ii 64-5
Wordsworth   *An Evening Walk* 72-3
    Memorials of a Tour in
    Italy 255-7
    River Duddon i 1-4
    Those Breathing
    Tokens . . . 102-5

Saguntum   Sagunto, a Spanish city allied to Rome, and besieged and sacked by *Hannibal* in 219 BC. According to *Pliny*, a newly-born child returned to the womb there in the year of the siege; it is among his catalogue of prodigious births.

(Pliny V II iii 39; Livy xxi 7)
Jonson   *To the Immortal Memory of*
    that Noble Pair

Salaminian
See *Salamis*
Arnold   *Sonnet to the Hungarian*
    Nation 12-14

Salamis   An Ionian island, site of a major naval battle in which the Greeks, heavily outnumbered, defeated the Persians under *Xerxes I* in 480 BC. *Aeschylus* may have fought there. *Euripides* wrote there.   See also *Cimon*

Browning R.   *Balaustion's Adventure*
    75-7, 132-6
    Sordello iii 950-4

Byron   *Age of Bronze* 282 ff
          Isles of Greece 3-4
Swinburne *Athens* str. i, ant. ii
          Eve of Revolution 85 ff

Salii   A body of priests of *Mars* set up by Numa in the 8th Century BC. They performed many rituals, but their main function was to guard the shields of Mars or *Ancilia*. These were supposed to have fallen from heaven and their possession was the guarantee of security for Rome. The March festival, lasting three days, entailed carrying the shields round the City amid song and dance.
                              (Livy i 20)
Wordsworth *Memorials of a Tour 1820*
            xxxii 30-3

Sallust   Gaius Sallust, Roman historian of the 1st Century BC. Sallust's political future ended when, as governor in Africa, he was charged with extortion, though saved by *Caesar*'s intervention. He spent the rest of his life, some ten years, writing his history of mainly very recent events. He is not a very reliable historian, but a readable writer with a liking for incident and for first-hand material like letters.
Byron   *Don Juan* vi 111
Jonson   *To Sir Henry Savile* 22-3

Salmacis   A nymph who pursued the youth Hermaphroditus, who for his part ignored her when he came to bathe in her spring. She hugged him and prayed for lasting union, at which the gods transformed them into a hermaphrodite. The fountain of Salmacis, near Helicarnassus, was held to have similar effects on those who drank from it.
                  (Ovid *Metamorphoses* iv 285 ff)
Fletcher P. *Purple Island* v 19
Marlowe   *Hero and Leander* ii 45-9
Swinburne   *Hermaphroditus* 51-5

Salmanassar   A King of Assyria who captured Samaria and Israel c. 720 BC.
                              (2 Kings xvii 6)
Milton   *Paradise Regained* iii 275-8

Salmoneus   Son of *Aeolus* and brother of *Sisyphus* (whom he hated), Salmoneus aspired to be a god and drove his flashing chariot

decked out in such a way as to imitate lightning. *Jupiter* had short shrift with him, struck him with a thunderbolt and sent him to join his brother in *Hades*.
                      (Apollodorus I ix 7;
                       Hyginus *Fabulae* 63)
Bridges   *Prometheus the Firegiver* 922-7

Samos   An island, and town of the same name, in the Aegean. It was reputed to be the site of the birth and marriage of *Juno*, who was venerated there. It was claimed as the birthplace also of *Pythagoras*.
        (Ovid *Metamorphoses* viii 221, xv 60 ff;
                          Strabo xiv 15-19)
Milton   *Paradise Lost* v 214-5

Samothrace, Samothracia   An Aegean island off the coast of *Thrace* and north of *Lesbos*. It was famous for reputedly having been overwhelmed by a flood, thought to be due to the overflowing of the Black Sea, during prehistory. The island — which was also known as (Thracian) Samos and *Melite* — was held sacred, being the centre of the cult of the Two Cabiri, who were non-Hellenic gods of the 5th and 6th Centuries BC and were later confused with the *Dioscuri*.
              (Strabo x; Virgil *Aeneid* vii 208)
Shelley   *Revolt of Islam* 2101-4

Sao   A *Nereid*.
                        (Apollodorus I ii 6)
Spenser   *Faerie Queene* IV xi 48

Sapphic, Sapphick
See *Sappho*
Pope   *Temple of Fame* 202-5

Sappho   The poetess of *Lesbos*, born c.612 BC. After an unexplained period of exile in Italy, Sappho became the centre of a young female cult which was dedicated to *Aphrodite* and the *Muses*, in Mytilene, the chief city of Lesbos. The cult was run on intimate lines. Its members wrote poems to each other and celebrated their marriages. Sappho herself married Cercylas and had a child. Her deepest passions were, however, reserved for *Phaon*, who did not reciprocate them, and for whom she committed suicide from a cliff (*Leucadia*). Whether or not this story had any substance, it was the

Sarra

one about Sappho which most appealed to later poets. Fragments of Sapphic poetry survive; it was direct, personal and lyrical in character, with sharp observation.

(Horace *Odes* II 13; Ovid *Heroides* xv)
See also *Alcaeus*, *Anactoria*

Browning E. B.	*A Vision of Poets* 310-21
Burns	*Sketch* 13-18
Byron	*Childe Harold* ii 39
	Don Juan i 42, ii 205
	Isles of Greece I
Coleridge	*The Picture* 170-1
Cowley	*On Corinda's Poems* 4
Donne	*Elegy* xx 25-6
Dryden	*To the Pious Memory of Mrs Killigrew* 29-33
Hood	*Hero and Leander* I
	Love's Champion 6 ff
Jonson	*Helen, Did Homer Never See . . .?* 3-5
Keats	*After Dark Vapours* 9-12
	Sleep and Poetry 381-4
Kingsley	*Sappho* 16-19
Moore	*Evenings in Greece* 131-9
	The Summer Fete 659 ff
Prior	*Epilogue to Lucius* 9 ff
Swinburne	*Anactoria* 1-4
	Ave Atque Vale ii
	The Interpreters
	Masque of Queen Bersabe
	On the Cliffs 279-83, 315-6, 380-3
	Sapphics 23-7
	Satia Te Sanguine
Tennyson	*Leonine Elegiacs* 13
Wordsworth	*Departing Summer Hath Assumed* 46-8

Sarra   Tyre, named Sarra after the shellfish from which its famous dye was made.

Milton   *Paradise Lost* xi 240-4

Saturn, Saturnus   The God of Time (and also of Winter), son of *Coelus* and *Terra* (or, as *Chronos*, of *Uranus* and *Ge*) and leader of the *Titans*. Armed with a scythe provided by his mother, he mutilated his father in revenge for Uranus' cruelty to his offspring (he imprisoned most of them in the bowels of the earth). Saturn married his own sister, *Rhea*, and they produced *Jupiter, Juno, Pluto, Neptune, Ceres*

and others. He was held to have reigned on Mt *Ida* in Crete, monarch of a *Golden Age* prior to the birth of Jupiter (*Zeus*), who supplanted him by the use of thunderbolts, banishing his followers to Tartarus. On the victory of Jupiter, the universe was split between the brothers Jupiter, Neptune and Pluto — all of whom, by the help of Rhea, survived their father's partiality for devouring his male babes.

(Apollodorus i I; Hesiod *Theogony* 74, 126-38, 459-68; Ovid *Metamorphoses* i 113-4)

Browning R.	*Imperante Augusto Natus Est* 154-6
	Sordello V 555-6
Byron	*Don Juan* xiv 1
Campion	*Peaceful Western Wind* 17 ff
Chapman	*Shadow of Night*
Chaucer	*Canon Yeoman's Tale* 828-9
	Knight's Tale 2443, 2454-69
	House of Fame 1448-50
	Troilus and Criseyde iii 715-20
Drayton	*Polyolbion* xx 152-4
Dryden	*Annus Mirabilis* 629-32
Dunbar	*Ryght as the Stern of the Day* 112-7
Henryson	*Testament of Cresseid* 156 ff, 309 ff
	Want of Wise Men 9-10
Jonson	*To Benjamin Rudyerd* 1-4
	To Sir Robert Wroth 47-50
Keats	*Endymion* ii 993-4, 126-9, iv 956-7
	Hyperion i 3 ff, 55-9, 89-91, 142 ff, ii 105-10, 132-8, 188-90, 352-5
	Fall of Hyperion i 224-7
	Welcome Joy and Welcome Sorrow 21
Marlowe	*Hero and Leander* i 435-8
Masefield	*Arthur and His Ring*
Milton	*Comus* 802-5
	Il Penseroso 27-30
	Paradise Lost i 510-12, 519-20, x 580-4
Prior	*First Hymn to Callimachus* 59-62
Shakespeare	*Much Ado About Nothing* I iii 8-9
Shelley	*Hellas* 1090-4
	Prometheus Unbound II iv 32-3, 36 ff, III i 54

Shenstone   *Elegies* xvi 69-70
Spenser   *Faerie Queene* III xi 43,
             V *Prologue* 9
             Mutability Cantos vi 27, vii 40
Tennyson   *Coach of Death* 191-2

Saturnalia   An ancient winter feast of
Saturn, notorious for its debauchery. Slaves
were given temporary freedom and presents
were exchanged.
    Auden   *Many Happy Returns* 53-6
    Byron   *The Island* i 83-4

Saturnia   *Juno*, daughter of *Saturn*.
    Chapman   *Ovid's Banquet of Sense*

Saturnian
See *Saturn*
    Prior   *A Pindaric*
    Shelley   *Witch of Atlas* 185-9
    Yeats   *On a Picture of a Black Centaur*

Satyrs   Spirits of wild nature, shown as half
animal and half man. Satyrs (not entirely distinct from *Fauns* and *Sylvans*) represent un-
controlled fertility and may be depicted with
large genitals, horses' or goats' legs and often
with horns. Their character varies from the
tender to the brutish, the graceful to the monstrous. A particular Satyr had an unrequited
passion for the nymph Lyda, but mainly the
Satyrs are not individualised.
    Brook   *The Old Vicarage, Granchester*
             38-42
    Browning E. B.   *Flush or Faunus* 5 ff
    Browning R.   *With Gerard de Lairesse*
             283 ff
    Collins   *The Manners, an Ode* 46
             The Passions, an Ode for Music
             76-7
    Cowper   *Anti-Thelyphthera* 199-202
    Keats   *Endymion* i 263-4, 278, iii
             533-6, iv 228-35
             Lamia i 1-5, 13-16, 101-3
             Sleep and Poetry 360-7
    Milton   *Lycidas* 34-5
             Paradise Regained ii 188-91
    Pope   *Summer* 50
    Praed   *Love at a Rout* 1-7
    Shelley   *Witch of Atlas* 133-5
    Spenser   *Faerie Queene* I vi 7, 11, 15 ff,
             III x 44, 48

Tennyson   *Lucretius* 192 ff
Wordsworth   *On the Power of Sound*
              145 ff
              Prelude ix 456-61

Scaevola   Gaius Mucius, nicknamed Scaevola
('left handed') from his story. During the
attacks of the Etruscans under *Porsenna* in
the 6th Century BC, Mucius entered Porsenna's
tent in disguise and stabbed his attendant in
mistake for the Etruscan leader. He was in-
terrogated and held his right hand in the fire
to display Roman bravery as he told Porsenna
he was a Roman and that three hundred men
were involved in the plot. Porsenna was so
struck by Scaevola's audacity or impudence
that he released him and came to terms with
Rome. Various explanations of what is, evidently, a legend have been offered.
                              (Livy ii 12)
    Macaulay   *Virginia*

Scamander   A Trojan river, known also as
Xanthus, which had the property of beautifying
the hair of all who bathed therein. *Minerva*,
Juno and *Venus* bathed there before submitting to the Judgment of *Paris*. Scamander or
Xanthus was father of Teucer, first King of
Troy. As a river-god, he favoured the Trojans
and was opposed by *Hephaestus* (*Vulcan*).
When *Achilles* filled the river with Trojan
corpses after the death of *Patroclus*, Scamander went into flood, and Achilles was saved
from drowning by the intervention of Hephaestus, whose fire dried up the water.
                    (Apollodorus iii 12;
                     Homer *Iliad* xxi 120 ff)
    Jonson   *The Sad Shepherd* I i
    Lewis C. D.   *Transitional Poem* 18
    Spenser   *Faerie Queene* III ix 35,
             IV xi 20
    Swift   *Pethox the Great* 17-18
    Tennyson   *Ilion, Ilion* 3-6

Scedasus   A Boeotian who, in the Spartan
wars led by the King Cleombrotus, had two
daughters, Molpia and Hippo, who were raped
by Spartan soldiers and hanged themselves in
shame. Scedasus committed suicide.
                          (Pausanias ix 13)
See also *Cedasus*

Sceptic, Scepticism A school of Greek philosophy established by Pyrrhon (c. 360-270 BC). In its development, one of its ends was the proof of the impossibility of knowledge (which was taken to be the basis of a calm of mind similar to that sought by the *Epicureans*), and the assertion, in place of knowledge, of a certain empirical common sense.

Milton *Paradise Regained* iv 296

Schinis, Shinis A robber who tore his victims assunder by springing them between the boughs of pine trees.

(Ovid *Metamorphoses* vii 440-2)
Crashaw *Sospetto d'Herode* 45

Scipio (1)
See *Africanus (1)*
Campbell *Pleasures of Hope* i
Dryden *Annus Mirabilis* 197-8
  To my Dear Friend (Congreve) 35-8
Milton *Paradise Regained* iii 31-6, 100-4
Pope *Epistle* I, 216-7
  Windsor-Forest 257-8
  Temple of Fame 163-4
Raleigh *Epitaph on Sidney* 57-60
Skelton *Philip Sparrow*
Spenser *Faerie Queene* I v 49
Swinburne *Song for the Centenary of Landor* 40
Thomson *Castle of Indolence* I xvii
  Liberty V 419-21
  Winter 517-20

Scipio (2) (Somnium Scipionis)
See *Africanus (2)*
Chaucer *House of Fame* 914-20

Scipioun
See *Africanus (2)*
Chaucer *Book of the Duchess* 278-88
  Parliament of Fowls 29 ff
  House of Fame 514-7

Scithero
See *Cicero*
Chaucer *Franklin's Tale and Prologue* 721-2

Scylla (1) The daughter of *Typhon*, beloved of *Glaucus*, who invoked the aid of *Circe* in his courting of the indifferent Scylla. However, Circe fell in love with Glaucus herself, and she changed the unresponsive Scylla into a monstrous amalgam of animals, being dog below the waist and having many heads. In despair, Scylla cast herself into the sea between Italy and Sicily and was changed into a dangerous rock opposite the whirlpool, *Charybdis*. Poetically, she is not always distinct from *Scylla (2)*.

(Ovid *Metamorphoses* xiv 12-74)
See also *Silla*
Hood *Hero and Leander* 42
Jonson *On the Famous Voyage* 81-4
Keats *Endymion* iii 399-404, 460-2, 618-23, 775-82, 807-10, 893-6
Milton *Comus* 257-9
  Paradise Lost ii 659-61
Shakespeare *Merchant of Venice* III v 13-14

Scylla (2) The daughter of *Nisus*, King of Megara. Scylla fell in love with *Minos* of Crete when he attacked Megara and her passion led her into an act of abominable treachery towards her father. In some way the safety of Megara depended on the hair of Nisus, and this she cut off whilst he slept, offering it to Minos. Minos, on this occasion, behaved honourably: he was so outraged by Scylla's treachery that either he changed her into a lark or cast her into the sea from a high tower. She was not a hazard to shipping, but is often confused with *Scylla (1)*, who was.

(Apollodorus iii 15;
Ovid *Metamorphoses* viii;
Virgil *Georgics* i 405)
Chaucer *Legend of Good Women* 1907-16
  Troilus and Criseyde v 1110
Jonson *On the Famous Voyage* 81-4

Scyron A rocky Aegean island to which *Achilles* was taken to avoid joining the Trojan War and where he had a son, *Neoptolemus* (*Pyrrhus (2)*).

(Homer *Iliad* xix 326, *Odyssey* vi 509)
See also *Lycomedes*
Crashaw *Sospetto d'Herode* 45

Scithia, Scythia A large part of modern Russia and Scandinavia — lands which to the ancients were partly unexplored. The Scythians were noted for their barbarity during their incursions into Asia Minor and Europe, but there was also a stoical quality in their character which seems to have led to their being admired. They had monarchs but were a nomadic people famed for their skill at horse, and particularly for their use of mounted archers in battle.

See also *Cithe*

Chaucer	*The Knight's Tale* 860-8
Campbell	*Pleasures of Hope*
Chatterton	*English Metamorphosis* 1-4
Cowley	*Hymn to Light* 8
Dryden	*Aureng-Zebe* V i
Goldsmith	*Prologue to 'Zobeide'* 9-11
Gray	*Alliance of Education and Government* 476-7
Lovelace	*The Snail* 43-4
Milton	*Paradise Regained* iii 299-301
Pope	*Temple of Fame* 125-6
Shakespeare	*King Lear* I i 115-8
	Titus Andronicus I i 131-2
Shelley	*Revolt of Islam* 3160-2, 3650-2

Sea Nymphs

See *Oceanids, Nereids, Nymphs*

Keats	*On the Sea* 13-14
	Endymion iii 210-12
Shakespeare	*Tempest* I ii 396ff
Spenser	*Faerie Queene* IV xi 48, 52
Wordsworth	*Isle of Man* 6-9
	The Triad 8-14

Sejanus Lucius Sejanus was a confidant of the Emperor *Tiberius* and commander of the Praetorian guards. By his plausible manner and cunning exploitation of personal relationships, he pursued a course of total self-interest and made himself the *de facto* power of Rome in the later days of Tiberius. Leaving a trail of murders in his path, Sejanus probably played a part in Tiberius' retirement to the island of *Capreae*, leaving himself in sole command in Rome. But Tiberius became suspicious (warned by Antonia, widow of Tiberius' brother, Drusus) and had Sejanus impeached before the Senate, after which he was strangled in prison in 31AD.

(Tacitus *Annals* iii)

| Jonson | *Sejanus* I i, II i, ii, III i, V i, x |
| Milton | *Paradise Regained* iv 95-7 |

Selene The moon, as daughter of *Hyperion*. Selene is probably the oldest of the various names for goddesses of the moon.

| Bridges | *Prometheus the Firegiver* 234-9 |
| Chapman | *Shadow of Night* |

Seleucia A city in Syria fitted out by *Alexander the Great*'s general, Seleucus Nicator, as a seat of government in the 4th Century BC. It was named 'The Great' (Pieria) to distinguish it from the many other centres named after the Seleucid line, and it was near modern Baghdad. With *Alexandria* and *Antioch* it was one of the major cities of the East.

(Pliny vi 30; Strabo xvi 1)

| Milton | *Paradise Regained* iii 289-91 |

Semele Daughter of *Cadmus* and *Harmonia/Hermione* and descended from *Mars* and *Venus*. She was the mother of *Dionysus* by *Jupiter/Zeus*, but was destroyed by him with lightning when she wished to see her lover in his real nature.

(Ovid *Metamorphoses* iii 253 ff)

Browning R.	*Apollo and the Fates* 156-7
Cowley	*Pindaric Ode* I 3
Herrick	*To Electra* 1-6
Keats	*Endymion* iv 536-7
Lovelace	*Against the Love of Great Ones* 21-4
Marlowe	*Doctor Faustus* 1341-7
Milton	*Paradise Regained* ii 181-8
Spenser	*Faerie Queene* III xi 33
Swift	*Strephon and Chloe* 105-8
	Vanbrugh's House 119-20
Swinburne	*Tiresias* 313-4
Tennyson	*Semele* 11ff

Semiramis A fabulous queen of Assyria, wife of *Ninus*, whose seduction and marriage of her brought about the suicide of her first husband, an officer of Ninus called Menones. Semiramis, famed for her beauty, was daughter of the goddess Derceto and was at birth exposed in the desert, where she was cared for by doves until found by shepherds of Ninus. Semiramis outlived Ninus — indeed, she may have killed him for his power — and continued the reign, reputedly building *Babylon*. She had, however, an incestuous love for her son, Ninyas, and he killed her. At death she was transformed into a dove, which was held sacred. She was famed as a military leader and also for her promiscuity — *Pliny* asserts that she fell in love with and married a horse.

(Diodorus Siculus II; Herodotus i 184; Pliny viii 64)

See also *Semyrame, Semyramis*

Burns	*A Fragment* 39-42
Butler S.	*Hudibras* II i 700-13
Byron	*Don Juan* v 61
	Sardanapulus I ii 181
Chaucer	*Legend of Good Women* 706-8
Marlowe	*Tamburlaine* ii 3537-9
Spenser	*Faerie Queene* I v 50, II x 56
Swinburne	*Laus Veneris* 200
	Masque of Queen Bersabe
	Song for the Centenary of Landor 42
Tennyson	*The Princess* ii 66

Semyrame
See *Semiramis*
Chaucer   *Man of Law's Tale* 368-9

Semyramis
See *Semiramis*
Chaucer   *Parliament of Fowls* 288 ff

Seneca   Lucius Annaeus Seneca (born in Cordova, Spain c.1 AD) was a Stoic philosopher, tutor and admirer of *Nero*, and author of rhetorical tragedies. Under pressure from Nero, who found his virtuous counsels tedious, Seneca was impelled to commit a famous and excruciating suicide in 65 AD, severing his arteries and bringing about the end by taking a hot bath. His work has a strangely hyperbolic, operatic appeal, particularly in horror scenes, and had considerable influence on English Elizabethan and Jacobean tragedy.

(Tacitus *Annals* xiiff, xv 64)

See also *Senek*

Chaucer	*Man of Law's Tale, Introduction* 25-8
	Monk's Tale 3705-10
	Pardoner's Tale 292-5
	Wife of Bath's Tale 1183-4
Dryden	*Religio Laici* 78-84
	Upon the Death of Lord Hastings 69-71
Gray	*Agrippina* 146-7
Jonson	*To Shakespeare* 31-7

Wyatt   *Farewell Love*

Senek
See *Seneca*
Chaucer   *Merchant's Tale* 1375-6
         Wife of Bath's Tale 1165-70

Septentrion, Septentrionalis   The seven stars near the North Pole, the Great Bear and, from this derivation, northern winds and regions.

(Pliny xi 14)
Milton   *Paradise Regained* iv 31

Septimuleius   A former friend of Caius *Gracchus*, who conveyed to Gracchus' despotic enemy, Opimius, the head of Gracchus weighted with lead in place of the brain — since Opimius had offered as reward a weight equal in gold.

(Plutarch *Caius Gracchus* xvii)
Pope   *Epistle to Henry Cromwell* 70-8

Serbonis, Serbonian   A lake on the Egyptian coast bounded by quick-sands, in which *Typhon* was said to have been caught after his unsuccessful revolt against *Zeus*.

(Diodorus Siculus i 30)
Milton   *Paradise Lost* ii 592-9

Sertorius   A Roman general who was accepted by Lusitanian tribes and adopted an ambiguous stance in Spain towards Rome in the 1st Century BC, even setting up a senate with himself as consul. Roman generals, including *Pompey* and *Metellus*, made little impression on his hold over Spain, but he was betrayed by Perpenna, one of several jealous subordinates, all of whom stabbed him. Sertorius was something of a charismatic; he liked to be accompanied everywhere by a white hind and he laid very great, possibly expedient, stress on religious observance.

(Plutarch *Sertorius*)
Wordsworth   *Prelude* i 190-4
             They Seek, and Are Sought . . . 10-14

Servilia   Married to Marcus Junius Brutus, a tribune, and mother of *Brutus (3)*, the assassin. Servilia was a mistress of *Julius Caesar* and a sister of *Cato*.

(Plutarch *Cato* xxiv)

Byron   *Deformed Transformed* I i
         198-200
Pope   *Epistle* i 213

Sesiphus
See *Sisyphus*
    Chaucer   *Book of the Duchess* 587-90

Sesostris   A fabulous Egyptian king who was
brought up with his future subjects to ensure
their allegiance. He followed many military
victories by a period of peace in which he
devoted himself to the arts and to building.
He appears to have oscillated between mild-
ness and brutality in his conquests, and liked
to have his chariot drawn by defeated kings.
                    (Herodotus ii 102-3;
                Lucan *Pharsalia* x 276-7;
                    Strabo xv 1, xvi 4)
Byron   *Age of Bronze* 45-7
         Werner III i 288-9
Gray   *Hymn to Ignorance* 36-7

Sestos   A town on the *Hellespont*, facing
Abydos. It was *Hero*'s birthplace.
See also *Leander*
    Donne   *Elegy* xviii 60-3
    Hood   *Hero and Leander* 3
    Housman   *Tarry, Delight, So Seldom
               Met* 4-7
    Marlowe   *Hero and Leander* i 1-5, 91-3,
               135-42

Setia   Modern Sezza, near Rome, famous for
its wine.
                (Martial viii 12; Pliny xiv 5-6)
    Milton   *Paradise Regained* iv 117-9

Seven Against Thebes   Seven *Argive* heroes
who attempted to wrest *Thebes* from *Eteocles*,
who had refused to yield the throne to his
brother *Polyneices* after the agreed term of one
year. The Seven — corresponding to the city's
seven gates — were variously listed from Mecis-
teus, *Capaneus*, *Amphiareus*, *Hippomedon*,
Parthenopaus, to *Tydeus* and Polyneices himself. They were led by *Adrastus*. The versions
of events befalling them and acts of individuals
are many and various. In the outcome, Polyneices met Eteocles in single combat and they
killed each other. As Polyneices' cause was by
no means upheld by this tragedy, a sequel was

required, and in this the sons of the Seven,
sometimes known as the Epigoni, subsequently
attacked and destroyed Thebes.
            (Aeschylus *Seven Against Thebes*;
                    Apollodorus III 5-6;
            Sophocles *Oedipus at Colonus* 1313ff;
                    Statius *Thebaid*)
Browning E. B.   *Queen Anelida* 9
Swinburne   *Athens* ant. ii
             Tiresias 67-70

Severus (1) Julius   A Roman governor of
Britain under the Emperor Hadrian. He built
the Wall between the Tyne and the Solway.
Whether he engaged with *Boudicca*'s rebels,
and where, is unknown.
                (Tacitus *Annals* xiv 31-7)
    Spenser   *Faerie Queene* II x 57

Severus (2) Septimus   A distinguished soldier
(145-211 AD) who succeeded *Pertinax* as Emperor in 193. Severus conducted many successful provincial campaigns, finishing with Britain,
where he died at York. He rebuilt Hadrian's
Wall and made an unsuccessful attempt to invade Scotland. He had a reputation as a ruthless
disciplinarian but also showed some interest
in bringing about civil reforms. Gibbon may,
however, have been perceptive in his view that
the simple-minded militarism of Severus made
a considerable contribution to the decline and
fall of the Empire.
    Tennyson   *The Druid's Prophecies* 53-6

Sextus
See *Tarquinius (Sextus)*
    Macaulay   *Lake Regillus* 12
                Horatius 24

Seys
See *Ceyx*
    Chaucer   *Book of the Duchess* 70-5,
               136ff, 203-14

Shafulus
See *Cephalus, Procris*
    Shakespeare   *Midsummer Night's Dream*
                   V i 197

Sibille
See *Sibyl, Cassandra*
    Chaucer   *Troilus and Criseyde* v 1451ff

Sibyl, Sibylla, Sibylline   The first Sibylla gave prophecies near *Troy* under the inspiration of *Apollo*. He gave her long life, but failed to provide comparable good health and youth, so that Sibylla lived over seven hundred years in a state of decrepitude. Of singular and wandering origin, the prophetic Sibylla multiplied into several Sibyls, each active in a particular place, so that the word had the general meaning of 'prophetess'. Perhaps the best known is Virgil's Sibyl of Cumae, near Naples; with characteristic frenzy she wrote her inspired prophecies on leaves which were spread abroad by the winds, an effective but random means of distribution. Varro (116-27 BC) listed ten Sibyls at work in different countries, and other lists were made.

(Virgil *Aeneid* iii 445-51, vi 71-6, 98-102)
See also *Cassandra*, *Sibille*

Collins	*Epistle to Sir Thomas Hanmer* 137-8
Crabbe	*The Newspaper* 116-7
Crashaw	*Sospetto d'Herode* 12
Donne	*Upon Mr Thomas Coryat's Crudities* 71ff
	A Valediction, of the Book 5-9
Shakespeare	*King Henry VI pt 1* I ii 51ff
	Merchant of Venice I ii 95-7
	Othello III iv 70-2
	Taming of the Shrew I ii 66-8
	Titus Andronicus IV i 105-6
Tennyson	*Did Not thy Roseate Lips* 21-30

Sicanian   A word for 'Sicilian' — named after the Sicani who settled there after leaving Spain in pre-historic times.

Cowley   *Coldness* 4

Sichaeus   The wealthy husband of *Dido*. Sichaeus was murdered by *Pygmalion*, her jealous brother, and her husband's ghost warned Dido to flee from Tyre. She landed in Libya and founded Carthage. In some versions, Sichaeus is Dido's uncle.

(Virgil i 347ff)

Sicinius   Sicinius Velutus, with *Brutus (2)*, a tribune who fought in the struggles with *Coriolanus* and was one of his accusers, constantly urging execution.

(Plutarch *Coriolanus* xviii)
Shakespeare   *Coriolanus* I i 212-4

Sidon, Sidonian   Sidon was the capital of Phoenicia, west of Syria, on the Mediterranean coast. It was an important harbour and was known for commerce, arithmetic and astronomy. Special claims to fame were the invention of glass-blowing, and the purple dye which it made from fish (as did *Tyre*, some twenty-five miles to the north). It was the site of a temple of *Astarte*.

Milton   *Paradise Lost* i 439-41

Silanus   Torquatus and Lucius Silanus were brothers descended from *Augustus*. Lucius, engaged to Octavia Claudia in his youth, was forced by *Agrippina (2)* to commit suicide so that *Nero* could marry Octavia. Torquatus was poisoned to prevent him from taking revenge.

(Tacitus *Annals* xii, xiii)

See also *Syllani*

Silenus, Sileni   *Satyr* companions of *Bacchus*, noted for their music and for a gift of prophecy. Silenus was the foster-father of Bacchus. He is shown as a jovial, carefree old man, sometimes riding on an ass.

(Ovid *Metamorphoses* iv 26, xi 89ff; Virgil *Eclogues* vi)

Arnold	*The Strayed Reveller* 261ff
Chapman	*Amorous Contention of Phillis and Flora* 87
Graves	*The Procession* 15
Keats	*Endymion* iv 215-7
	Lamia i 101-3
	The Fall of Hyperion i 55-6
Lovelace	*Ode, To Lucasta* 13-16
Shelley	*Prometheus Unbound* II ii 89-95
	Hymn of Pan 18-24
	Witch of Atlas 105-8
Wordsworth	*On the Power of Sound* 150-2

Sileucia, Sileucian
See *Seleucia*
Milton   *Paradise Lost* iv 211-2

Silla
See *Scyllas (1)*
Chaucer   *Parliament of Fowls* 290-5

Silurian   Of Siluria, a Roman town in South Wales.

    Diaper   *Dryades* 6 4-70

Silvans   Countryside deities akin to *Satyrs* and derived from *Silvanus*.

    Milton   *Paradise Regained* i 478-80,
             ii 188-91

Silvanus   A god of the country, originally of woodland, being born of a shepherd and a goat and represented as half man and half goat. He was also said to be son of *Mars* or *Picus* (a son of *Saturn*) and was confused with *Faunus*, a son of Picus. He loved a youth called *Cyparrissus*, who was changed into the cypress tree, of which Silvanus may be seen carrying a bough.

    (Ovid *Metamorphoses* x 106ff;
    Virgil *Eclogue* x 24-5, *Georgics* i, 20)
    Drayton   *Endymion and Phoebe* 9-14
             The Muses' Elizium x 57
    Milton   *Paradise Lost* iv 705-8

Simois   A Trojan river rising in Mount *Ida*. A tributary of *Xanthus*, Simois tried to drown *Achilles* and was attacked by *Hephaestus*, who burnt its banks.

    (Homer *Iliad* xxi 305ff)
See also *Scamander*, *Symois*
    Dryden   *Annus Mirabilis* 925-6
    Shakespeare   *Rape of Lucrece* 1437-8
    Tennyson   *Ilion, Ilion* 3-6

Simonides   Greek poet of the 5th to 6th Centuries BC. He was especially famed for his elegies and among them is a hymn of memorial for *Thermopylae*. Little of his poetry remains, but it evinces a distinctively harmonious manner. Of his life nothing is known save for the traditional belief that he was at one time saved from shipwreck by a ghost.

    (Cicero *De Divinatione* i)
    Swinburne   *Song for the Centenary of
             Landor* 15
    Wordsworth   *I find It Written of
             Simonides* 12-14

Sinon   A young friend of *Ulysses*, Sinon provided the means by which the Greeks entered *Troy* in the Wooden Horse. He went to *Priam*, pretending that he had been elected by the Greeks as a sacrifice but had escaped, the Greeks having fled. Priam believed him and was persuaded to have the horse brought into the city to consecrate it to *Minerva*. Sinon subsequently released the Greek soldiers from inside the horse. He was also said to have lighted a beacon to signal the opening of the horse or to guide the Greek fleet back to Troy. In medieval times his name was almost synonymous with treachery.

    (Apollodorus *Epitome* v 15-19;
    Homer *Odyssey* viii 492ff;
    Virgil *Aeneid* ii 13ff)
See also *Synon*
    Jonson   *Sejanus* V i
    Marlowe   *Dido Queen of Carthage*
             403-6, 438-44
    Shakespeare   *Cymbeline* III iv 55-9
             King Henry VI pt 3 III ii
             188-93
             Rape of Lucrece 1520ff
             Titus Andronicus V iii 80-7

Sinope   A city of *Pontus* on the Euxine Sea, where *Diogenes*, the *Cynic* philosopher, was born. It was a natural fortress surrounded by mountains and was the site of many battles. Sinope was named after a daughter of Asopus whom *Apollo* loved and abducted there.

    Byron   *Age of Bronze* 480-1

Sipylus   A Lydian mountain.

    Bridges   *Prometheus the Firegiver*
             968-72

Siren, Sirens   Two, or three, *Sea-Nymphs* whose singing was so seductive that all who listened forgot to eat and died. Some said they were bird-women, daughters of *Achelous* (a river-god) by a Muse (either *Melpomene* or *Terpsichore*); their wings were to help in the search for the lost *Persephone*, or were a punishment for failing in such a quest. All this is late accretion; *Homer* tells us little of the Sirens. They were also said to live on an island white with the bones of those who had succumbed to them, though its location was debated. The *Argonauts* passed them safely because *Orpheus* drowned their song with the music of his lyre. *Odysseus* was less comfortable; he had to be tied to the mast whilst his companions stopped their ears with wax. The Sirens were sometimes said to have perished in a contest with the

Muses, or for permitting the passage of the Argonauts and Odysseus. The name of their un-identified island was held to be Anthemoessa.

(Apollodorus I ix 25, *Epitome* vii 18;
Homer *Odyssey* xii 39-54, 158-200;
Apollonius Rhodius iv;
Ovid *Metamorphoses* v 552-63)

See also *Syren*

Arnold	*The New Sirens* 41-4
Coleridge	*On a Late Connubial Rupture* 17-18
Davies, Sir J.	*Nosce Teipsum* v 26-9
Dryden	*Annus Mirabilis* 81-4
	Conquest of Granada pt 1 III i
Keats	*Endymion* iii 241-2, 888-91
	On Sitting Down to Read 'King Lear' 1-2
Lewis C. D.	*Magnetic Mountain* 6
Milton	*At a Solemn Music* 1-2
	Comus 252-3, 878-80
	Arcades 61-4
Rosetti D. G.	*Death's Songsters* 9-12
Shakespeare	*Sonnet* 119
Spenser	*Faerie Queene* II xii 31

Sirius   The Dog-Star — *Canis Major* or *Canicula* — associated with heat or drought on earth and regarded as presaging destruction. Sirius was sometimes identified with *Isis* or regarded as the Dog of the hunter *Orion*.

(Diodorus Siculus iv 82;
Homer *Iliad* xxii 25 ff;
Virgil *Aeneid* III 141, x 273)

Milton	*Lycidas* 138
Spenser	*Faerie Queene* I iii 31

Sisters (1)   The *Muses*.

Collins	*The Passions, an Ode for Music* 107-8
	Epistle to Sir Thomas Hanmer 27-8
Milton	*Lycidas* 15-16
Scott	*From Ann of Grierstein*

Sisters (2)   *Naiads*.

Collins	*Ode Occasioned by the Death of Mr Thomson* 30

Sisyphus   Sisyphus, the son of *Aeolus*, was a confirmed rival of the trickster Autolycus, but his main fame was for being condemned in hell to roll uphill a huge stone which per-petually rolled down again. His crime was variously said to be: telling Asopus that it was *Jupiter* who had raped his daughter (*Aegina*); or failing to return to *Hades* after being granted parole, ostensibly to arrange a proper burial for himself (a matter which his wife, *Merope*, had — on his instruction — neglected). There were other explanations also. An unspecified crime would be appropriate to so wily an in-dividual.

(Apollodorus i 9, iii 12; Homer
Iliad iv 154-5, *Odyssey* xi 592-600;
Ovid *Metamorphoses* iv 460 ff, xiii 26, 32)

See also *Sesiphus*, *Sysiphus*

Browning R.	*Ixion* 28-9
Byron	*English Bards* 410-14
Cowley	*To Dr Scarborough* 2
Dryden	*Conquest of Granada* 2, III ii
Fletcher P.	*Purple Island* 64
Lamb	*The Ballad-Singers* 30-3
Marlowe	*Hero and Leander* ii 277
Spenser	*Faerie Queene* I v 35
Swift	*Ode to the King* 97-8

Sithon, Sithonian   A King of *Thrace* whose name is also used for Thrace.

(Ovid *Heroides* ii 6)

See also *Sytho*

Sleep   Selected allusions only.

(Ovid *Metamorphoses* xi 635 ff)

See also *Somnus*, *Morpheus*

Keats	*Endymion* iv 370-3, 375, 386
	Sleep and Poetry 11-15, 348
Milton	*Il Penseroso* 146

Sleep — Gates of   Two gates to the cave of *Somnus* and *Morpheus*, said to be of horn (true vision) and polished ivory (false dreams).

(Homer *Odyssey* xix 562-7;
Virgil *Aeneid* vi 893-8)

Smyrna   Mother of *Adonis*.
See *Myrrha*

Socrates   The Greek philosopher, 469-399 BC, who was the son of an Athenian sculptor. Socrates served with distinction in the army but his later life was poverty-stricken, and ap-parently marred by his wife, *Xantippa*, a lady whose supposed bad temper has become legendary — and from whom he perhaps found relief in the charms of *Aspasia*. In 399 BC Socrates was tried for corrupting youth and introducing false gods. The true nature of the accusations against him is hard to assess, but, whatever the real matter, he condemned himself to death and poisoned himself with hemlock rather than attempt lawless escape. Socrates is famous for his inquisitorial way of developing an argument, his reliance on question and answer. His lasting contribution to philosophy is uncertain. He was perhaps more a teacher of unique intelligence than a systematic thinker on a large scale. His large circle included notable disciples, including *Plato*, and it seems clear that questions of conduct and morality were his serious concern. He seems to have had a very unremarkable appearance for one of such influence.

— *General and Historical*

Browning R.	*Balaustion's Adventure* 291-4
Byron	*Don Juan* xv 85
Chaucer	*Fortune* 17-19
Crabbe	*The Borough* xvii
Denham	*Progress of Learning* 35-9
Diaper	*Callipaedia* 228-33
Dryden	*Oedipus, Prologue* 1-4
Keats	*To J. H. Reynolds Esq.* 5-9
MacNeice	*Autumn Journal* xx
	Autumn Sequel xix
	The Stygian Banks vii
Milton	*Paradise Regained* iv 273-80, 293-4
Moore	*To the Invisible Girl* 39-42
Pope	*Temple of Fame* 170-1
Shelley	*Fragment Connected with Epipsychidion*
Spenser	*Faerie Queene* IV *Prologue* 3
Thomson	*Liberty* ii 223 ff
Young	*Night Thoughts* iv

— *Appearance*

Byron	*Deformed Transformed* I i 217-22

— *and Plato*

Campbell	*Pleasures of Hope*
Graves	*Cry Faugh!* 4-6

— *his Death*

Chaucer	*Book of the Duchess* 715-9
	Man of Law's Tale 197-202
Dryden	*The Medal* 95-8
Milton	*Paradise Regained* iii 96-9
Pope	*Essay on Man* iv 233-6

Spenser	*Faerie Queene* II vii 52
Tennyson	*The Princess* iii 284-6
Young	*Night Thoughts* ix

— *Xantippa, Aspasia*

Chaucer	*Wife of Bath's Prologue*
Moore	*The Grecian Girl's Dream* 46-7

Sogdiana   A province of the Roman Empire, in modern Kazakhstan. Bounded to the North by *Scythia*, it was subject to frequent attack from that direction.

(Herodotus iii 93)

Milton	*Paradise Regained* iii 299-382

Sol

See *Apollo*, *Helios*, *Sun*

Select Allusions:

Drayton	*The Muses' Elizium* ix 15-17
Keats	*Endymion* ii 101-4

Solon   A descendant of *Cadmus*, Solon was a Greek statesman, poet and seer of the 6th Century BC. He solved social and economic crises in Athens by cancelling the many debts for which lives or freedom were the only security, and for which some people were selling themselves into slavery. He made other far-reaching reforms. He introduced a four-class system, apparently related to production, into society and delegated political power accordingly, replacing the harsh legal code of *Draco*, though retaining severe punishment for adultery and other offences. He was said to have arranged that his laws be kept until repealed and then to have left the capital for ten years to ensure that the system had a good start. As a thinker, he was a sombre realist and incurred the displeasure of *Croesus* by telling him that the quality of dying was of more importance than earthly prosperity. He is often cited as an exemplary statesman and legislator.

(Plutarch *Solon*; Herodotus i 29 ff)

Browning R.	*Fifine at the Fair* 483
	Ring and the Book i 219-23
Crabbe	*The Borough* xvii
Johnson	*Vanity of Human Wishes* 313-4
Jonson	*Epigram on Sir Edward Coke* 15-17
Meredith	*Solon*

Shakespeare   *Titus Andronicus* I i 176-8
Shelley   *Oedipus Tyrannus* I i 64

Solyma   An ancient and much disputed name for *Lycia* and its warriors, with whom *Bellerophon* did battle.
(Herodotus i 173; Homer *Iliad* vi 184, 204;
     Strabo XII vii 5; XIV iii 10)
Shelley   *Oedipus Tyrannus* I i 169-72

Somnium Scipionis
See *Africanus (2)*, *Aemilianus Numantinus*

Somnus   The Roman God of Sleep (Greek Hymnos), son of *Erebus* and *Nox*. He lived in a dark *Cimmerian* cave surrounded by poppies, and he slept on a bed of feathers with black curtains. *Morpheus*, his son and minister, prevented him from being awakened.
(Hesiod *Theogony* 211-2;
     Ovid *Metamorphoses* 592 ff)
Chapman   *Shadow of Night*

Sophist, Sophists   Itinerant teachers from the 5th Century BC who propounded ways of thinking and behaviour which they thought conducive to material success — they were of no serious or consistent philosophical persuasion but proverbially reliant on subtle arguments for the situation in hand. Some did perform a worthwhile function in teaching oratory and memory. In Roman society the term meant more often a teacher of rhetoric, which was regarded as a key to advancement.
See also *Protagoras*
Browning R.   *Aristophanes' Apology*
     2102-4
Herbert   *Church Militant* 51-2

Sophocles   The important Greek tragedian lived from c.496-406 BC, holding various Athenian State appointments. He was a rival of *Euripides* and wrote about one hundred tragedies, of which seven survive. Whilst their dating and the nature of his development are not clear, Sophocles certainly extended the techniques and experience of tragedy and brought to it a range and variety unsurpassed by *Aeschylus* or Euripides.
Arnold   *Dover Beach* 9 ff
     To a Friend 9-14
Browning E. B.   *A Vision of Poets* 301-9

Browning R.   *Aristophanes' Apology*
     120-2, 3500-6
     Balaustion's Adventure
     37-9
Dryden   *Oedipus, Prologue* 1-4
Jonson   *To Shakespeare* 31-7

Soranus   Marcius Barea Soranus was murdered by Nero for suspected intimacy with Rubellius Plautus, an ambitious and dangerous enemy.
(Tacitus *Annals* xvi)
Gray   *Agrippina* 122-5

Sossius   Gaius Sossius, a general who supported *Mark Antony* in the struggle which followed *Caesar*'s assassination, and was active in Syria. He was a commander of Antony's forces at *Actium* in 31 BC, but was pardoned by *Augustus* when the latter defeated Antony.
(Plutarch *Antony* IV 34)
Shakespeare   *Antony and Cleopatra* III i
     17-20

Sparta   Also known as *Lacedaemon*, the capital of Laconia on the Peloponnesus. The Spartans had a precarious relationship with their neighbours, especially the Messenians, with whom they were often at war, and with *Athens*, notably at the Peloponnesian War (in which Athens conceded defeat in 404 BC). They were famous for the fierceness of their army and the austerity of their way of life. A 'Spartan regime' was well known from earliest times.
See also *Messenia*
Browning R.   *Aristophanes' Apology*
     115-7
Shelley   *Queen Mab* ii 162-72
Thomson   *Liberty* ii 111-9

Spartan
See *Sparta*
Collins   *Ode to Liberty* 1
Milton   *On the Death of a Fair Infant*
     25-6

Spercheius, Sperchius   A river and river god of Thessaly. *Peleus* promised Sperchius the hair of his son *Achilles'* head, and a copious sacrifice, if Achilles returned safely from the Trojan War, as he failed to do.

(Homer *Iliad* xxiii 144 ff)
Byron   *Deformed Transformed* I i
             270-2

Sphinx   A monster of which various parts
were those of a woman, a dog, a serpent, a
bird and a lion. It was born of *Typhon* and
Echidna, or of others with the *Chimaera*. Sent
by *Juno* to plague the family of *Cadmus* (who
had married *Harmonia*, daughter of her rival,
Venus), it settled on Mount Phicium outside
Thebes and demanded answers to riddles,
devouring those unable to answer them. When
the son of *Creon*, *Haemon*, was eaten, Creon
offered the throne and his sister *Jocasta* to
whoever could answer the special riddle —
what walked on four legs in the morning, two
at noon and three in the evening. (An oracle had
predicted that the Sphinx would be satisfied
once this conundrum had been resolved.) This
fell to *Oedipus*, son of Jocasta, whom he
therefore married; he perceived that the riddle
was a summary of the ages of man from infancy
to old age. The Sphinx thereupon flung itself
to its death.

(Apollodorus III v 8;
Euripides *Phoenician Maidens*;
Hesiod *Theogony* 326-9)
Auden   *The Sphinx* 1-4
Browning R.   *Prince Hohenstiel-*
                  Schwangau 9 ff
Byron   *Don Juan* xiii 12
Crashaw   *Sospetto d'Herode* 44
Jonson   *Sejanus* III i
Masefield   *Roses are Beauty* 6-7
Milton   *Paradise Regained* iv 572-6
Shakespeare   *Love's Labour's Lost* IV
                  iii 225-41
Shelley   *Hellas* 1080-3
Swinburne   *Tiresias* 309-14

Spio   A *Nereid*.
(Apollodorus I ii 6)
Spenser   *Faerie Queene* IV xi 48

Sporus   An effeminate favourite of *Nero*.
Little is known of him. The name was used by
Pope for Lord Hervey, in a famous passage of
the *Epistle to Dr Arbuthnot*.
(Plutarch *Galba* ix;
Suetonius *Nero* xxviii)
Byron   *Don Juan* xi 58

Pope   *Epistle to Dr Arbuthnot* 117 ff

Spurius Lartius   According to *Livy*, Spurius
Lartius shared some of *Horatius'* courage in
defending the Roman bridge against the Etruscans.
Macaulay   *Horatius* 30

Stace
See *Statius*
Chaucer   *Anelida and Arcite* 21
             Knight's Tale 2393-4
             House of Fame 1456-63
             Troilus and Criseyde v 1786 ff

Stagirite, Stagyrite   A native of Stagira or
Stagirus, a town on the west of Macedonia,
and a metrically convenient term for Aristotle,
who was born there.
Browning R.   *Paracelsus* I 417-8
Butler S.   *Fragments of Satire on the*
             Imperfections of Human
             Learning 43-4
Cleveland   *Upon the Death of M. King*
             26-7
Cowley   *The Motto* 27-8
             To Mr Hobbs 2
Dryden   *Religio Laici* 14 ff
             To My Honoured Friend 1-4
Lamb   *Written at Cambridge* 12-13
Moore   *Nature's Labels* 5-8
Pope   *Dunciad* 349-51
             Essay on Criticism 645-8
             Temple of Fame 232-7
Young   *Night Thoughts* ix

Statius   Publius Statius, Roman poet of the
1st Century AD. He was born and died at
Naples but spent most of his life at Rome,
where he enjoyed the favour of the Emperor
Domitian. His main works are the epic *Thebaid*
and five books of occasional poems, the *Silvae*.
He was admired in the Middle Ages, particularly
for descriptive and pathetic episodes, but has
generally been found weak in point of epic
structure.
See also *Stace*

Steropes   One of the three *Cyclopes* who
forged *Aeneas'* shield from a thunderbolt, the
others being *Brontes* and *Peracmon*.
(Virgil *Aeneid* viii 424-53)

Jonson   *Ode to James, Earl of Desmond*
40-6

Stesichorus   A Greek lyric poet of the 6th Century BC. Only titles and a few fragments of apparently copious works remain. He is known particularly for a curious legend: he was first blinded, for holding that *Helen* married *Menelaus* — the usual assumption — and then his sight was restored when, in a recantation, he held that, contrary to *Homer*, Helen did not go to *Troy*.

(Plato *Phaedrus* 243)

Spenser   *Colin Clout's Come Home
Again* 919-23

Sthenelus   Son of *Capaneus*, Sthenelus was one of the Epigoni — sons of the *Seven Against Thebes*. He was also a suitor of *Helen* and was among those in the Trojan horse.

(Apollodorus III vii 2, x 7;
Virgil *Aeneid* ii 261)

Browning E. B.   *Battle of Marathon*
865-71

Stheneoboea   Daughter of Iobates, king of *Lydia*. She married Proetus but was infatuated with *Bellerophon* and, when he rejected her, accused him before Proetus of assaulting her. Bellerophon married her sister, once Iobates had been convinced by a series of strenuous adventures that he must indeed be an innocent young knight. At this marriage to Philinoe (the sister), Stheneoboea committed suicide. Another version was that Bellerophon arranged her murder in revenge by placing her on *Pegasus* at a great height. She was also known as Antaea.

(Apollodorus ii 2-3; Homer
Iliad vi 162 ff; Hyginus lvii)

Spenser   *Faerie Queene* I v 50

Stix
See *Styx*

Stoa
See *Stoicism*

Milton   *Paradise Regained* iv 251-3

Stoicism   A sect or school of philosophy, developed from the *Cynics*. It was founded by *Zeno* c. 300 BC and named after the *Stoa*

Poikile, a painted or cloistered ambulatory in Athens in which members of the sect taught. The Stoic goal was a certain union of the Self, based on a view of things corresponding with experienced reality, on harmony with nature, and on reason (being the rational faculty, but also being identified with God and Providence). Neither pain nor fear could affect a person so organised and he would be prepared to commit suicide rather than compromise principle. (The *Stoa* or 'porch' was often used to refer to Greek philosophy more generally.)

(Pausanias I iii, XIV vi)

Milton   *Comus* 706-9
            Paradise Regained iv 276-80,
            300-6

Shakespeare   *Julius Caesar* V i 100-2
            Taming of the Shrew I i
            31-3

Stygian
See *Styx*
Select allusions only.

Keats   *Endymion* iii 503-6
MacNeice   *Stygian Banks* vii
Marlowe   *Tamburlaine* i 2036-9
Milton   *L'Allegro* 1-3
            Paradise Lost i 239-40
Shakespeare   *Troilus and Cressida* III ii
            7-12
Shenstone   *The Ruined Abbey* 264-5
Spenser   *Daphnaida* 19-20
            Faerie Queene II xii 41, V xi
            22, VI i 7-8
Swift   *A Quibbling Elegy on Judge Boat*
            23-5

Stymphalides, Stymphalis
See *Aristoclides*

Chaucer   *Franklin's Tale* 1387-94

Styx   A river of Elis, *Arcadia*. It was supposed to surround *Hades* nine times and to flow from a rock into silver-pillared caves. Stygian waters imposed senselessness for a year and a draught was decreed by *Zeus* for gods who had perjured themselves. Those entering Hades were ferried across the Styx by *Charon*. Select allusions only.

(Hesiod *Theogony* 775-806;
Virgil *Aeneid* ci 349)

Byron   *Don Juan* xiii 99

Brooke   *It's Not Going to Happen Again*
          9-10
Goldsmith   *Song from 'She Stoops to
          Conquer'* 1ff
Hood   *Hero and Leander* 18
MacNeice   *Autumn Journal* xviii
Marlowe   *Tamburlaine* i 2245-8
Milton   *Paradise Lost* ii 577
Owen   *To a Comrade in Flanders* 1-4
Pope   *Dunciad* ii 314-19
Prior M.   *First Hymn to Callimachus*
          39 ff
Shakespeare   *King Richard III* I iv 44-7
          Titus Andronicus I i 86-9
Spenser   *Faerie Queene* I i 37, II viii 70,
          IV xi 4
Stevenson   *To H. F. Brown* 1ff
Young   *Resignation*

Suetonius   Tranquillus Gaius Suetonius, the
Roman writer of the 1st Century AD, held
positions in the Roman administrative service
and seems to have been of a quiet and scholarly
nature. Surviving works are biographical,
notably the twelve lives of the Caesars, which
follow a somewhat uneasy blend of topical
and chronological arrangement.
See also *Swetoun*
Chaucer   *Monk's Tale* 3653-7

Sulla (1) Cornelius   Cornelius Sulla, son-in-
law of *Claudius*. He was believed to be plotting
against *Nero* and was murdered on his orders.
                    (Tacitus *Annals* xiii)

Sulla (2) Lucius   Lucius Cornelius Felix Sulla
came of an old but impoverished family and
raised himself, during his life (138-78 BC), by
ruthless ambition. In 82 BC, having lost power
whilst away in battle against *Mithridates*, he
advanced on Rome (and his rival, *Marius*, who
escaped) and took the city by force; he was
obliged, however, to allow the election of
Cinna rather than his own candidate to consul.
On Cinna's death in 84 he assembled his own
men, with those of *Metellus*, *Crassus* and
Pompey, and invaded Italy, crushing all opposition. He was elected Dictator and during a
reign notorious for its daily lists of proscriptions and executions, carried out a programme
of some constitutional reform; eventually he
resigned the Dictatorship and became in due

course consul and private citizen. He assumed
the name 'Felix' out of extreme belief in his
luck, which may now be seen to have gone
hand in hand with his arrogant ruthlessness.
                    (Livy lxxxix; Plutarch *Sulla*)
See also *Sylla*
Spenser   *Faerie Queene* I v 49

Sulpicia   A minor Roman poetess of the 1st
Century AD.
Skelton   *Philip Sparrow*

Sun
See *Apollo, Helios, Hyperion, Phoebus, Titan*
Selected examples.
Keats   *Endymion* i 589-52
          Song of the Four Fairies 46-7
Milton   *L'Allegro* 59-62
          *On the Morning of Christ's
          Nativity* 18-19
          Paradise Lost v 139-40
Spenser   *Daphnaida* 22-5
          Faerie Queene I i 32, V viii 40

Sunium   Cape Colonni at the southern tip
of *Attica*, site of a Temple of *Minerva*.
Byron   *Don Juan* xv 73

Susa   The Persian capital and winter seat of
Darius and *Xerxes*, his successor. It was also
called Memnonia, the palace of *Memnon*,
because Memnon had ruled there; his fabulous
palace was said to have been built by his father
Tithonus.   (Strabo xv 3)
Milton   *Paradise Lost* x 306-10
          Paradise Regained iii 288-9

Swan
See *Cycnus, Apollo*
Wordsworth   *Sonnet, I Heard (alas . . .)*

Swetoun
See *Suetonius*
Chaucer   *Monk's Tale* 3909-11

Sybil
See *Sibyl*
Auden   *Under Sirius* 8-9
Chaucer   *House of Fame* 439-46
Drayton   *Fourth Eclogue* 45-6
Herrick   *Not Every Day Fit for Verse* 1ff
          To the Rt Hon. Mildmay 3-4

Swift   *Description of Mother Ludwell's Cave* 55-6

Syene   Syene (Assonan) was on the Nile at the extreme south of the Roman Empire and at one time was regarded as its boundary.
         (Tacitus *Annals* ii 61)
Milton   *Paradise Regained* iv 67-71

Sylla
See *Sulla (2)*
    Byron   *Childe Harold* iv 83
                 Don Juan viii 61
    Chapman   *Epicedium*
    Crashaw   *Sospetto d'Herode* 45
    Gray   *Agrippina* 99-101
    Herrick   *The Invitation* 5-6
    Jonson   *Catiline* I i
    Rochester   *Tunbridge Wells* 33-4
    Shakespeare   *King Henry VI pt 2* IV i 83-5
    Tennyson   *Lucretius* 47-50
    Thomson   *Liberty* iii 430-1

Syllani
See *Silanus*
    Gray   *Agrippina* 170-1

Sylvan, Sylvans, Sylvanus
See *Silvan*
    Denham   *Cooper's Hill* 236-7
    Marlowe   *Hero and Leander* i 154-6
    Milton   *Il Penseroso* 134-5
    Pope   *Winter* 21-4
    Shelley   *Hymn of Pan* 18-24
    Spenser   *Faerie Queene* I vi 7, 14, 15, 17, 33
                 Shepherd's Calendar, July 77-80

Symois
See *Simois*
    Chaucer   *Troilus and Criseyde* i 1548-9

Symplegades   The Symplegades or Planctae, with sisters Cyaneae, were rocks through which the *Argonauts* had to pass into the *Hellespont*, or through which *Odysseus'* men, as related by *Circe*, had to pass. No particular group of obstructions may always have been had in mind by the various writers.
         (Homer *Odyssey* xii 59 ff;

         Apollonius Rhodius iv 860 ff)
Fletcher P.   *Purple Island* iii 28
Shelley   *Revolt of Islam* 2905-7
Swinburne   *Atalanta in Calydon* 613, 2150

Synon
See *Sinon*
    Chaucer   *Nun's Priest's Tale* 4418-9
                 Squire's Tale 204-9
                 House of Fame 151-6
                 Legend of Good Women 930-3

Syren
See *Sirens*
    Campbell   *Pleasures of Hope* ii
    Drayton   *The Owl* 1229-32

Syrinx   An Arcadian nymph pursued by *Pan* but, at the River *Ladon*, changed into a reed by the gods. Pan made his pipe from such reeds.
         (Ovid *Metamorphoses* i 690 ff)
    Crabbe   *The Wish* 7-8
    Keats   *Endymion* i 243-4, iv 686
               I Stood Tiptoe Upon a Little Hill 156-62
    Lovelace   *Princess Louisa Drawing* 14-17
    Marvell   *The Garden* 27 ff
    Milton   *Arcades* 106
               Paradise Regained ii 181-8
    Shelley   *Hymn of Pan* 25-31
               Orpheus 15-17
    Spenser   *Shepherd's Calendar* 50-1

Syrtes, Syrtis   Two notorious and proverbially shifting sandbanks off the North African coast near Carthage.
         (Lucan ix 303; Virgil *Aeneid* iv 41)
Milton   *Paradise Lost* ii 939-40

Sysiphus
See *Sisyphus*
    Pope   *Ode for Music* 66-70

Sytheo
See *Sichaeus*
    Chaucer   *Legend of Good Women* 1004-7

Sytho
See *Sitho*

Chaucer   *Legend of Good Women*
           2508-9

Tacitus   Cornelius Tacitus, Roman historian
of the 1st Century AD (dates uncertain). Little
is known of his life, save that he married
Agricola's daughter and pronounced several
important orations. His principal works, the
Histories and *Annals* (probably incomplete),
date from the end of the century. As an historian, mainly of quite recent events, Tacitus
is a deliberate artist with a vision of the consequence of human affairs, and a highly com-
pressed personal style.
Browning R.   *Ring and the Book* ix
               884-6
Jonson   *To Sir Henry Savile* 1-4

Taenaros
See *Tenaros*

Tagus   The Spanish River Tajo, whose sands
were supposedly full of gold.
               (Ovid *Metamorphoses* ii 251)
Byron   *Childe Harold* I 14
Crashaw   *The Weeper* 14
Drayton   *Polyolbion* xv 267-9
           The Shepherd's Sirena 182-5
Skelton   *Philip Sparrow, Commendation*
Wyatt   *Tagus, Farewell* 1-2

Talia
See *Thalia (1)*
Henryson   *Orpheus and Eurydice* 46ff

Tanagra, Tanagraean   A Boeotian town near
the *Euripus* strait and the *Asopus* River.
Arnold   *Fragment of an 'Antigone'*
          61-4

Tantale
See *Tantalus*
Chaucer   *Book of the Duchess* 709

Tantalus   Son of *Jupiter* and King of *Lydia*,
Tantalus either stole Jupiter's dog, gave the
nectar and ambrosia of the gods to mortals, or
was punished for killing his son *Pelops* and
offering his body to the gods to eat, as a trial
of their divinity. For some such crime he became an exemplar of the tortures of *Tartarus*,

being condemned to stand up to his neck in
water which he could never drink, to be for
ever tempted by a bunch of grapes which
vanished as he tried to grasp it, or to sit under
a huge rock in continuous fear of its falling
on him.
               (Homer *Odyssey* xi 581ff;
               Pindar *Olympian Ode* i 36ff)
See also *Tantale, Niobe*
Browning R.   *Ixion* 28-9
               Pietro of Abano 259-60
Crashaw   *Sospetto d'Herode* 42
Fletcher P.   *Purple Island* v 64
Henryson   *Orpheus and Eurydice* 281-8,
            521-6
Marlowe   *Hero and Leander* ii 74-6
Milton   *Paradise Lost* ii 612-4
Shakespeare   *Venus and Adonis*
               599-600
               Rape of Lucrece 855-61
Sidney   *Astrophel and Stella* 24
Spenser   *Faerie Queene* I v 35, II vii 58
           Hymn in Honour of Love
           200-3
Swinburne   *Atalanta in Calydon* 980
Wordsworth   *Excursion* vi 539-45

Tarpeian (Rock)   A cliff thought to have
been close to the *Capitol* in Rome. It was the
custom to cast murderers from it in execution.
The name was said to derive from Tarpeia,
daughter of a governor of the Capitol, who
was bribed to let in the Sabine enemy in ex-
change for their gold. The Sabines entered,
but cast their shields as well as their gold onto
Tarpeia, who was crushed by their weight.
               (Ovid *Fasti* ii 261ff)
Byron   *Childe Harold* iv 112
Macaulay   *Horatius* 16
Milton   *Paradise Regained* iv 47-9
Shakespeare   *Coriolanus* III i 211-3,
               ii 1-6, 102-4
Wordsworth   *Memorials of a Tour in
              Italy* iii 1-4

Tarquin Collatinus, Tarquinius Collatinus
The husband of the violated *Lucretia* and, by
the association of her rape with the expulsion
of the monarchy, one of the earliest consuls.
He was a cousin of *Tarquinius Superbus* and
found himself in a difficult position, assisting
in expelling the Tarquins but belonging to

their family. As a result he voluntarily exiled himself.

See also *Collatinus*

Tarquin, Tarquinius Sextius, Sextus The son of *Tarquinius Superbus*, he has two claims to fame or notoriety. The first was his trick played on the Galbii as his family pursued war against rebel townships near Rome: pretending to desert to the people of the town, he was appointed their general and then destroyed them from within, the plan having been devised between himself and his father. The second was the rape of *Lucretia*, which led to the banishment of his family from Rome. He was killed at Gabii.

See also *Sextus*

        (Livy I liii-iv, lvii-viii)
Auden   *Plains* 64
Browning R.   *Ring and the Book* ix 187-90
Chaucer   *Legend of Good Women* 1694-1702, 1789-93, 1861-5
Shakespeare   *Cymbeline* II ii 11-12
      Rape of Lucrece 1-7, 155-8, 316-21, 477ff, 673ff, 1850-5

Tarquin Superbus, Tarquinius Superbus The last King of Rome (539-510BC). There is some historical base to accounts of his reign and longevity, but much legendary accretion. He gained the throne by murdering Servius Tullius, his father-in-law, and pursued a dictatorial reign untroubled by consultation with the people or senate. Lucretia committed suicide when raped by Tarquin's son *Sextus*, and at this culmination of extravagance and depravity the people rebelled and under *Brutus (2)* banished Tarquin in 510BC. In exile with the Etruscans he made unsuccessful attempts to gain support for a return, but eventually died at Cumae at a great age.

See also *Porsenna*

    (Ovid *Fasti* ii 6-7; Plutarch *Publicola*; Livy i 57-8, i-ii 7)
Chaucer   *Legend of Good Women* 1680-3
Macaulay   *Horatius* I
Shakespeare   *Coriolanus* II i 142, ii 85ff
    Julius Caesar II i 52-4
    Macbeth II i 52-6

Spenser   *Faerie Queene* I v 49
Wyatt   *Love with Unkindness* 31-5

Tarquyn
See *Tarquinius Sextus*
   Chaucer   *Franklin's Tale* 1405-8

Tarsus The capital of Cilicia, reputedly founded by *Hercules*. Tarsus, on the River *Cydnus*, was a cultural centre rivalling *Alexandria* and *Athens*, and had its own school of philosophy. It was also the birthplace of Saint Paul. (A confusion with *Tartessus* is possible in Milton's reference.)
   Milton   *Samson Agonistes* 711-9
   Shakespeare   *Pericles* I iv 22-4

Tartarean, Tartarian
See *Tartarus*
   Gray   *Lines Spoken by the Ghost of John Dennis* 9-10
   Milton   *Paradise Lost* ii 68-70
   Shelley   *Revolt of Islam* 2499, 2714-6
   Wordsworth   *Prelude* vii 83-4
     Vernal Ode 127-30

Tartar, Tartare, Tartarus The walled and dark underground prison reserved for the *Titans*, and later for more general torment of the wicked. It was said to be as far below earth or *Hades* as Heaven was above.
    (Hesiod *Theogony* 119, 713-35; Apollodorus I i 3; Homer *Iliad* viii 13-16; Ovid *Metamorphoses* iv 447ff; Virgil *Aeneid* vi 295ff)
Goldsmith   *A New Simile* 51-2
Keats   *Endymion* iii 269-71
Milton   *Paradise Lost* i 72-3, ii 858, vi 52-4
Spenser   *Faerie Queene* I vii 44, II xii 6
    Mother Hubberd's Tale 1292-4

Tartessus A Spanish port on the Mediterranean near Cadiz. In mythology it was regarded as the extreme West, where the Sun unharnessed horses from his chariot at the end of the day. *Hercules* captured the cattle of *Geryon* near Tartessus.
    (Ovid *Metamorphoses* xix 416)
Chapman   *Shadow of Night*
Milton   *Samson Agonistes* 711-16

Taurus (1) The constellation supposed to be named after *Jupiter* in the form of the white bull which bore *Europa* to *Crete*; here, through Jupiter, she became the mother of *Minos* and *Rhadamanthus*. The sun appears to pass through the area of Taurus in Spring.
See also *Bole*

    Chaucer   *Legend of Good Women* 2223-4
    Milton   *Paradise Lost* i 769

Taurus (2) A large mountain in Asia Minor, and the range to which it belongs, in modern Turkey. It was regarded as the spine of Asia.
    Shakespeare   *Midsummer Night's Dream* III ii 141-2

Tegea The birthplace of *Atalanta* and burial site of *Orestes*. A town in *Arcadia*, founded by Tegeates, son of *Lycaon*.
    (Ovid *Metamorphoses* viii 317, 380)
    Swinburne   *Atalanta in Calydon* 1039

Teian From *Teos*, in Ionia, north of Ephesus. Teos was the birthplace of *Anacreon*.
    Browning R.   *Ring and the Book* ix 225-7
    Moore   *A Dream of Antiquity* 65-6
    Spenser   *Hymn of Heavenly Beauty* 210-1

Teos, Teios An Ionian city on the north coast of Ephesus, site of a temple of *Dionysus*, and the birthplace of *Anacreon* (who called it Athamantis).
    (Strabo xiv i 3)

Telamon Brother of *Peleus* and with him banished from *Aegina* by their father *Aeacus*, because they had killed their half-brother, Phocus. Telamon went to nearby *Salamis* and married the princess Glauce there, inheriting the throne on her father's death. He sailed with the *Argonauts* and stormed *Troy* with his friend *Hercules*. Telamon was first in, which irritated Hercules; but Hercules presented him with *Hesione* — it was the refusal of her father, *Laomedon*, to pay for her rescue from a sea-monster that had led the two men to launch their attack. Hercules also prayed to his father *Zeus* that Telamon might be blessed with a brave son, and *Ajax* and *Teucer* were the results.

Ajax is sometimes referred to as Telamon or Ajax Telamon.
    (Apollodorus II vi 3, II vii 69)
    Shakespeare   *Antony and Cleopatra* IV xii 1-3
    Swinburne   *Atalanta in Calydon* 443 ff, 1260

Telemachus The son of *Ulysses* and *Penelope*. A baby when Ulysses left for the Trojan War, Telemachus went in quest of his father after the War, found him eventually just arrived home, and extricated Penelope from her suitors. According to later legend, he subsequently married *Circe* or her daughter Cassiphone.
    (Apollodorus *Epitome* vii;
    Homer *Odyssey* xvii, xxii, xxiv etc.)
    Tennyson   *Ulysses* 33-5

Telephus A son of *Hercules* and *Auge* who was abandoned on a hill (saved by a goat), or to the sea. This was because Aleus, Auge's father, disapproved of her affair with Hercules. Telephus was taken in and offered a crown and the princess by King Teuthras of *Mysia*; unhappily, this princess was none other than Auge, whom Teuthras had adopted as his daughter after taking her on as a slave. The lovers were providentially separated by an intervening serpent, and Hercules revealed to Auge that Telephus was her own son. Telephus went on to marry a Trojan princess and to join the Trojan cause. Here he was obstructed by *Bacchus*, who supported the Greeks and caused Telephus to be tripped up by a vine, whereupon *Achilles* seriously wounded him. This wound, the oracle asserted, had to be cured by Achilles himself, and he was persuaded to assist by *Ulysses* (who believed that a son of Hercules was necessary on the Greek side if the Trojans were to be defeated, and cast Telephus in this role). The wound was healed with a salve of rust from the spear which had inflicted it, and Telephus joined the Greek forces in gratitude.
    (Apollodorus II vii 4, III ix 1, *Epitome* III xvi-xix; Hyginus *Fabulae* 99-101;
    Ovid *Metamorphoses* xiii 171-2)
See also *Thelophus*

Tellus
See *Terra, Ge, Cybele*

Keats   *Endymion* iii 70-1
           Hyperion i 246, ii 53-5, 391
Shakespeare   *Pericles* IV i 14-18

Tempe A valley between *Olympus* and *Ossa* in Thessaly, down which the River *Peneus* flows into the Aegean. It was regarded as a rural paradise and the name 'Tempe' was applied to other such valleys. Tempe in Thessaly was the home of *Io*.

             (Ovid *Metamorphoses* i 568-76;
              Virgil *Georgics* ii 469)
Collins   *The Passions, an Ode for Music* 86
Drayton   *Idea* xxviii 13-14
Fletcher G.   *Christ's Victory on Earth* 40
Keats   *As Hermes Once* 7-12
        Ode on a Grecian Urn 5-7
Marvell   *Upon Appleton House* 753 ff
Meredith   *Daphne*
Moore   *Hymn of a Virgin of Delphi*
Shelley   *Hymn of Pan* 13-15
        Hellas 1068-71
Sidney   *Astrophel and Stella* 74
Spenser   *Epithalamion* 305-10
        Faerie Queene II xii 52
        Prothalamion 73-80
Thomson   *Autumn* 1316-9
Vaughan   *In Amicum Foeneratorem* 30-2

Tenaros A mountain on the south coast of Laconica, with a large cave supposed to be an entrance to *Hades*. *Hercules* dragged *Cerberus* up through the cave and, when the dog spat, its saliva produced a plant, *aconitum*, with a lethal juice (used by *Helen* in an attempt to poison *Theseus*).

            (Ovid *Metamorphoses* vii 408 ff)
Donne   *Elegy* xiii 19-20

Tenedos An island in the Aegean some six miles west of *Troy* on the west coast of modern Turkey. The Greeks landed here first before attacking Troy, and also withdrew to Tenedos to deceive the Trojans as they speculated what the Wooden Horse might be.

            (Apollodorus *Epitome* iii 23, v 15 ff)
Drayton   *The Owl* 969-74
Marlowe   *Tamburlaine* ii 3054-8
Meredith   *Swathed in Mist*

Shakespeare   *Troilus and Cressida Prologue* 11-13

Terence Publius Terentius Afer, Roman writer of comedies in the 2nd Century BC. Some of his plays were skilfully adapted and translated from *Menander*. Terence is known for technical skill with plot and for realistic dialogue.

Jonson   *To Shakespeare* 51-4
Pope   *Autumn* 7-8
Wyatt   *Love with Unkindness* 24-7

Tereus King of *Thrace* and son of *Mars*, Tereus assisted *Pandion* of Athens against the incursions of Labdacus, King of *Thebes*. Pandion rewarded him with the hand of his daughter, *Procne* (by whom he had a son, Itys). On a visit to Athens, because Procne pined in the absence of her sister *Philomela*, Tereus fell in love with Philomela and seduced her, offering the argument that Procne (whom he had sent away in hiding) was dead. Eventually Philomela learned that Procne was alive, and Tereus cut out her tongue to silence her. She then wove the events into a tapestry which she had conveyed to Procne. On learning the truth, Procne cut up their son, Itys, and served him to Tereus in a dish. When the enraged Tereus pursued them, the sisters were turned into a swallow and a nightingale, and he into a hoopoe.

            (Apollodorus iii 14;
            Ovid *Metamorphoses* vi 424 ff)
Chaucer   *Legend of Good Women* 2228 ff, 2309 ff, 2360 ff
Davies, Sir J.   *Orchestra* 691-3
Eliot T. S.   *Waste Land* 97-103, 203-6
Fletcher P.   *Verses of Mourning and Joy* 6-9
Shakespeare   *Cymbeline* II ii 43-5
            Passionate Pilgrim 20
            Titus Andronicus II iv 22-7, 37 ff; IV i 42 ff
Shenstone   *Elegies* vi 15 ff
Sidney   *The Nightingale* 1 ff

Terminus A late Roman god, whose rule was over land and its limits, and more generally over limitations. He was a peculiarly static god, represented without limbs and having

an immovable shrine on the *Tarpeian Rock*.
(Livy i 55)
    Auden   *Ode to Terminus* 47 ff

Terpander The father of ancient Greek music, who lived on *Lesbos* and in *Sparta* in the 7th Century BC. His life and works are matter of legend. The nightingale is associated with him.
    Browning R. *Christmas Eve* 673-6
        Cleon 138-45

Terpsichore The Muse of dancing, daughter of *Zeus* and *Mnemosyne*.
See also *Muses, Thersychore*
    Byron *The Waltz* 1-6
    Davies, Sir J. *Orchestra* 36-40
    Drayton *The Muses' Elizium* iii 421-2
    Wordsworth *The Triad* 105-6

Terra One of the first goddesses, known to the Greeks as *Ge* (*Gaea*) and to the Romans also as *Tellus* (sometimes identified with *Cybele*). She was the offspring of *Chaos* and, without a mate, produced *Uranus*; by *Coelus* she bore *Saturn, Hyperion, Themis, Oceanus* and others. In another account, she married Uranus and produced the *Titans* and *Cyclopes*: because Uranus hated his monstrous progeny, Ge urged revenge, and there occurred a series of upheavals and revolts among the gods, *Giants* and Titans. She was depicted with many breasts (fecundity), a turreted crown (Cybele), a sceptre, and sometimes a key and a tamed lion.

Tesbee
See *Thisbe*
    Chaucer *Merchant's Tale* 2125-31

Tessalie
See *Thessalia*
    Chaucer *Legend of Good Women*
        1396-1402

Tethys A Titaness, sister to *Oceanus*, for whom she is a sort of regal female counterpart.
(Hesiod *Theogony* 337-40; Homer *Iliad* xiv 201-4)
    Davies, Sir J. *Orchestra* 43-5
    Keats *Hyperion* ii 75-6
    Milton *Comus* 867-70

    Spenser *Faerie Queene* I i 39, iii 31,
        II xii 26, IV xi 18

Teuta A queen of Illyria from 231 BC. A headstrong and arrogant character as shown by Polybius, but for Jerome she is an example of chastity.
(Jerome *Contra Jovinianum*;
Polybius *Histories* II ivff)
    Chaucer *Franklin's Tale* 1453-4

Thais A Greek consort of *Alexander the Great*. Her power over him was said to be such that she persuaded him to burn *Persepolis*.
(Plutarch *Alexander* xxxviii 3)
    Tennyson *Persia* 26-32

Thalassian Of the sea – the reference is usually to *Venus*, who sprang from the sea into which Saturn had cast the mutilated body of *Uranus*.
    Swinburne *Dolores* 221-4

Thalestria, Thalestris A Queen of the *Amazons*, reputed to have had intercourse with *Alexander the Great*.
(Strabo xi 5)
    Prior *Henry and Emma* 343-4

Thalia (1) The Muse of pastoral and comic poetry, and one of the *Graces*. She may be depicted with a shepherd's crook and with her face concealed by a mask held by one of her sisters.
(Hesiod *Theogony* 907-11; Horace *Odes* iv 6; Virgil *Eclogues* vi 2)
See also *Talia*
    Byron *English Bards* 516-7
        Hints from Horace 130-1
    Drayton *The Muses' Elizium* 396-402
    Keats *To Mary Frogley* 37-8
    Meredith *The Two Masks*
    Shenstone *Elegies* xix 17-18
    Spenser *Faerie Queene* VI x 22
        Tears of the Muses 175-80
    Young *Resignation*

Thalia (2) A *Nereid*. May be the same as above.
(Apollodorus I iii 1;
Hesiod *Theogony* 909)

Thamer
See *Timarete*
    Skelton   *Garland of Laurel*

Thammuz   The lover of *Astarte*, Thammuz was son of a Syrian king. A parallel to the Greek *Adonis*, he represents a vegetation myth in which the year's dying is lamented in annual ritual. Thammuz was killed by a boar and, at Astarte's instance, permitted to spend half the year on earth and half the year in the underworld.
    Milton   *On the Morning of Christ's Nativity* 204
                Paradise Lost i 446-52

Thamyris (1)   A Thracian poet-musician who loved *Hyacinthus*. He challenged the *Muses* in song and lost, being then blinded and having his lyre destroyed.
          (Apollodorus i 3;
          Homer *Iliad* ii 594-600)
    Milton   *Paradise Lost* iii 34-6

Thamyris (2) (Tomyris)   A queen of the Massagetae, a *Scythian* tribe, who defeated *Cyrus* the Great of Persia in the 6th Century BC. She had his head cut off and thrown into a pot of blood for which, she said, he had thirsted.   (Herodotus i 205 ff)
See also *Thomyris*
    Skelton   *Garland of Laurel*

Thanatos   Greek for 'Death', which was regarded as a son of *Nix* (night) and brother of *Hypnos* (sleep).
          Hesiod *Theogony* 758-60)
    MacNeice   *Eclogue by a Five-Barred Gate* 21-3

Thea, Theia   A Titaness, sister and wife of *Hyperion*, by whom she bore *Eos*, *Helios* and *Selene*. She was also known as Euryphaessa.
        (Hesiod *Theogony* 371-4;
    Homeric Hymn *To Helios* (31) 4-8)
    Bridges   *Prometheus the Firegiver* 632-6
    Keats   *Hyperion* i 27ff, 95-6
             Fall of Hyperion 335-8

Theano   The wife of *Pythagoras*.
    Moore   *Grecian Girl's Dream* 48-51

Theban
See *Thebes*, *Oedipus*
    Collins   *Epistle to Sir Thomas Hanmer* 23-4
    Wordsworth   *Sonnet, When Haughty Expectations . . .*

Thebes   The capital of Boeotia (north-west of Athens) whose monarchy included such tragic figures as *Cadmus*, *Laius*, *Oedipus* and his son, *Eteocles*. The woes of Thebes were attributed to *Juno*'s jealousy of *Jupiter*'s relations with *Semele*, the daughter of King Cadmus. Late in the sad tale, it was agreed that after Oedipus' death his sons would reign alternately, but Eteocles refused to give up at the end of his year. His brother, *Polyneices*, and the *Argive* army headed by seven heroes, marched against Eteocles, entering the city by its seven gates; the brothers slew each other in single combat and all the heroes were killed, save for *Adrastus* of *Argos*. This attack was known as the *Seven Against Thebes*. In view of its indecisiveness, the sons of the leaders (the Epigoni) returned and sacked the city later. In the 4th Century BC Thebes was almost wholly destroyed by *Alexander the Great*.
See also *Amphion*, *Capaneus*, *Creon*
    Browning E. B.   *Queen Anelida* 8, 10
    Chaucer   *Anelida and Arcite* 50-3
             Knight's Tale 1329-31, 1542-8
             Man of Law's Tale 197-202, 288-93
             Troilus and Criseyde ii 101-2, v 599-602, 1485-91
    Milton   *Il Penseroso* 97-100
             Paradise Lost i 577-9
    Shelley   *Hellas* 1080-4
    Spenser   *Faerie Queene* II ix 45, IV i 22
    Swinburne   *Tiresias* 67-70
    Wordsworth   *Excursion* vi 539-45

Thelophus
See *Telephus*
    Chaucer   *Squire's Tale* 236-40

Themis   A goddess and oracle, the daughter of *Uranus* and *Ge*, who was devoted to order, justice and assembly. She was sometimes said to be the mother of *Prometheus* and it was she who told *Deucalion* and *Pyrrha* to re-people Earth after the flood by throwing soil over their shoulders. She also warned *Atlas* that a descendant of *Zeus* (*Hercules*) would steal golden apples from his garden tended by the *Hesperides*. Her daughters were the Hours — *Dice*, *Eirene* and *Eunomia*.

(Hesiod *Theogony* 135;
Ovid *Metamorphoses* i 377 ff, iv 643-5)

Chapman	*Shadow of Night*
Jonson	*A Panegyre* 20-7
Keats	*Hyperion* ii 77-80
Marlowe	*Tamburlaine* i 1571-6
Milton	*Paradise Lost* xi 9-14
	Sonnet xxi
Spenser	*Faerie Queene* V ix 31

Themistocles   Themistocles (c. 528-462 BC) was a Greek statesman and founder of the Greek naval power. He commanded the Greek fleet against the Persians, winning the important battle of *Salamis* in 480 BC. His stress on naval power was not always supported by colleagues or men. *Plutarch* gives instances of Themistocles' rhetorical art and reliance on augury in changing a man's mind. It seems that he was a man of the moment with such a man's persuasive powers. He fell into some disgrace after Salamis, though whether this indicates victory for the military forces or some fault of his own is not known. However, when he retired to *Argos*, he was in due course accused of conspiracy with Persia and was under sentence of death in Athens. When and how he died are not known.

(Herodotus vii-viii;
Plutarch *Themistocles*;
Thucydides i)

Browning R.	*Echetlos* 28-9
Chapman	*Bussy D'Ambois* I i 65-70
Keats	*Endymion* ii 22-3

Theocritean
See *Theocritus*

MacNeice	*Eclogue by a Five-Barred Gate* 15-16

Theocritus   Greek pastoral poet of the 3rd Century BC, born in Syracuse, but living mainly outside Sicily; much of his poetry is nostalgic of that area and of southern Italy. His work shows great variety of form and is highly wrought. It had enormous influence on subsequent pastoral poetry — partly by way of

Virgil, who borrowed extensively from the Greek.
See also *Comates*

Browning E. B.	*Portuguese Sonnet* i
	A Vision of Poets 322-34
	Wine of Cyprus 12
Burns	*Sketch* 19
Noyes	*Mount Ida* 121-2
Skelton J.	*The Garland of Laurel*
Swinburne	*Song for the Centenary of Landor* 47
Wordsworth	*Prelude* xi 437 ff

Theodamus   The *Theban* priest and augur in the war of the *Seven Against Thebes*.

(Statius *Thebaid* viii 279 ff)

Chaucer	*Merchant's Tale* 1718-21
	House of Fame 1243 ff

Thermae   A Persian river near *Thermopylae*.

Shelley	*Hellas* 688-91

Thermiste   A *Nereid*, Themisto.

(Hesiod *Theogony* 261)

Spenser	*Faerie Queene* IV xi 51

Thermopylae   A narrow pass, named 'hot gates' after its sulphur springs, between Thessaly and Locris. It was the site of a great battle fought between the Persians, under *Xerxes*, and the Spartans, under *Leonidas*, in 480 BC. Three hundred Spartans held the massive Persian army till taken from the rear by a secret passage, when they were massacred.
See also *Thermae*

Byron	*Childe Harold* ii 73
	The Island iv 259-60
	Isles of Greece 7
Eliot T. S.	*Gerontion*
Keats	*Endymion* i 317-9
Shelley	*Hellas* 52-7
Swinburne	*Athens* ep. i
	The Eve of Revolution 85 ff
	Song for the Centenary of Landor 24
Tennyson	*Third of February 1852* 45-8
Thomson	*Winter* 453-9

Therodamas   A Scythian king who threw

strangers to notoriously ferocious lions.

(Ovid *Ibis* 383)
  Crashaw   *Sospetto d'Herode* 45

Theron   Winner of a chariot race in Olympic Games.

(Pindar *Olympics* ii)
  Prior   *Carmen Seculare* 299-300
  Young   *The Merchant*

Thersander   A legendary brave Greek, son of *Polyneices*. He was among the sons of the *Seven Against Thebes* (Epigoni) who sacked Thebes, and he emerged as king.
  Cowley   *Pindaric Ode* 5

Thersites   A sadly deformed Greek soldier in the Trojan War who had a reputation for raillery at the expense of his leaders. He was killed by *Achilles* for mocking his falling in love with *Penthesilea*.

(Apollodorus *Epitome* V i; Homer *Iliad* ii 211ff)
  Graves   *Penthesilea* 7-10
  Shakespeare   *Cymbeline* IV ii 253-4
            Troilus and Cressida I iii 73, 193-5

Thersycore
See *Terpsichore*
  Henryson   *Orpheus and Eurydice* 36 ff

Thesaphone, Thesaphany
See *Tisiphone*
  Henryson   *Orpheus and Eurydice* 261ff, 475-8

Theseus   Theseus, King of *Athens*, was son of *Aegeus*, or of *Poseidon*, but grew up with his mother Aethra. When he was of age she sent him to Aegeus with a sword by which he would be recognised. There *Medea*, who was living with Aegeus, tried unsuccessfully to have Theseus poisoned by his then unwitting father, but Aegeus recognised the sword and Theseus was accepted by father and people. Many later feats of prowess were attributed to him. They included the capture of the Bull of *Marathon* and delivery from the *Minotaur* which was, by edict of the inimical *Minos* of Crete, exacting from Athens an annual meal of seven youths. When Theseus was chosen or volunteered to

join the yearly party, he fell in love with *Ariadne* Minos' daughter (whom he later abandoned) and on the instructions of *Daedalus* she helped him to escape from the Labyrinth by a clue of thread. Theseus then succeeded to Aegeus' throne, since Aegeus drowned himself when the hero by error returned from his quest with black sails, signifying failure. Theseus accompanied *Hercules* against the *Amazons* and brought back one of their Queens, *Antiope (2)*, by whom he had a son *Hippolytus*. He then married, apparently as a political arrangement, *Phaedra*, another daughter of Minos; by her false accusations (inspired by *Venus*) the tragedy of Hippolytus and Phaedra ensued. In later life, Theseus struck a celebrated friendship with *Pirithous*, king of the Lapithae — who had been at the *Calydonian Boar Hunt*. As both men were widowers (Phaedra having committed suicide), they determined to pursue daughters of the gods, of which the first (*Helen*) fell to Theseus. The friends were said then to have invaded *Hades* in search of *Persephone*, and there, in some accounts, they remained in eternal torture (Theseus being condemned to motionless sitting). In other versions they eventually returned to earth, but were rejected by their peoples; or, again, 'Persephone' was merely the name of some earthly princess. The manner of their ends thus remains obscure, though Theseus was sometimes said to have been killed by *Lycomedes*. Theseus had a son, *Demophon*, by either Antiope or Phaedra, in addition to Hippolytus.

(Ovid *Metamorphoses* vii 404-52, viii 152ff, 40307; Virgil *Aeneid* vi 617-8;
Apollodorus III xv 7-9, *Epitome* i 15-16)
— *General*
  Byron   *The Corsair* III 41ff
  Chaucer   *Anelida and Arcite* 22ff
            Knight's Tale 860-8, 959-64, 975-80
            Legend of Good Women 1886-90, 2441-7
  Goldsmith   *Theseus did see . . .* 1-4
  Shakespeare   *Midsummer Night's Dream* II i 75-80
  Spenser   *Faerie Queene* I v 35, IV x 27
— *Minotaur and Desertion of Ariadne*
  Chaucer   *House of Fame* 405-20
            Legend of Good Women

1943-7, 1968ff, 2074ff, 2170ff,
2544-8, 2459-64
Hood   *Hero and Leander* 108
Keats   *Isabella* 93-6
Lewis C. D.   *Ariadne on Naxos*
Lovelace   *Princess Louisa Painting* 18-21
MacNeice   *Autumn Sequel* XX vi
Prior   *On Beauty* 10ff
Shakespeare   *Two Gentlemen of Verona*
IV iv 163-7
Spenser   *Faerie Queene* VI x 13
— *Antiope, Phaedra, Hippolyta, Hippolytus*
Browning E. B.   *Queen Anelida* 6
Browning R.   *Artemis Prologises* 35-8,
51ff
Fletcher P.   *Purple Island* v 39
Spenser   *Faerie Queene* I v 37-8
Swinburne   *Phaedra*

Thesiphone
See *Tisiphone, Eumenides*
Chaucer   *Troilus and Criseyde* I 6-7,
IV 22-4

Thespia, Thespian   A town of Boeotia near
the foot of Mount *Helicon*, with all the associations of that hill and its spring.
Herrick   *His Farewell to Sack* 29-30

Thesposia, Thesprotia   A coastal part of
Epirus in north-west Greece. The infernal
rivers *Acheron* and *Cocytus* ran through it.
Drayton   *Polyolbion* xxv 31ff

Thessaly, Thessalia, Thessalian   A country
of northern Greece, whose boundaries varied,
but which was broadly between Macedonia,
Epirus and Aetolia, with the Aegean Sea to
the east. It was the reputed site of the flood
in the era of *Deucalion* and also contained
Mounts *Olympus, Pelion* and *Ossa*. In the
plain of *Pharsalia* was fought the battle in
which *Caesar* defeated *Pompey* in 48 BC.
See also *Tessalie*
Chaucer   *Monk's Tale* 3869-73
Keats   *Endymion* i 141-4
Milton   *Paradise Lost* ii 542-4
Swinburne   *Atalanta in Calydon* 566
Thalassius
Vaughan   *Olor Iscanus* 41-2

Thestius   The father of *Leda, Althaea* and
Hypermnestra, also of *Toxeus* and *Plexippus*.
Little is said of him and the mother of the
children is not consistently identified. The
sons were killed at the *Calydonian Boar Hunt*.
Swinburne   *Atalanta in Calydon* 636

Thestylis   A countrywoman's name in the pas-
torals of *Theocritus* and *Virgil*. She is usually
depicted harvesting.
(Theocritus *Idyll* ii;
Virgil *Eclogue* ii)
Milton   *L'Allegro* 88

Thetis   A goddess of the sea, daughter of
Nereus and mother of *Achilles*. She had the
power to change her shape but (after being
rejected by *Neptune* and *Jupiter* as likely to
bring up a son greater than they) she married
Peleus, who bound her to prevent her eluding
him. It was into their marriage feast that *Eris*
threw the apple which led to the Trojan War.
Thetis had children by Peleus but, in some
accounts, burned them to see if they were
immortal. Achilles was saved from this fate
by Peleus. Thetis later plunged him into the
Styx, which made him invulnerable save for
the heel by which she held him. Failing in her
efforts to prevent Achilles from entering the
Trojan War, Thetis bribed *Vulcan* to make
him a special suit of armour. Though she returned to the sea and the *Nereids*, she influenced Achilles' conduct in the War from afar.
When he was killed by *Paris* she and the Nereids
mourned his death and set up a monument
and festival to him. Thetis is 'young', 'fair',
'pearly' and 'silver-footed' in appearance.
(Hesiod *Theogony* 1002-7;
Apollodorus iii 13, *Epitome* iii 26;
Homer *Iliad* i 348-533, xviii 35ff,
Odyssey xxix 15-97;
Ovid *Metamorphoses* xi 217ff)
— *General*
Chaucer   *Legend of Good Women*
2414ff
Drayton   *Polyolbion* v 21-4
Fletcher P.   *The Locusts* i 2
Keats   *Endymion* ii 600-11, iii
1003-5
Lamia i 205-8
Lovelace   *Advice to My Best Brother*
11-15
Triumphs of Philamore 123

Marlowe   *Dido, Queen of Carthage*
130-4, 762-7
Hero and Leander ii 203
Tamburlaine ii 3461-2
Milton   *Comus* 877
Shakespeare   *Troilus and Cressida* I iii
37-40
Shelley   *Prometheus Unbound* III i 33-6
Spenser   *Faerie Queene* IV xi 48,
VI x 22
Mutability Cantos vii 12
Swinburne   *Atalanta in Calydon* 405-9
Yeats   *News for the Delphic Oracle*
— *and Achilles*
Auden   *Shield of Achilles* 65-72
Byron   *Don Juan* iv 4
Coleridge   *To a Friend (Charles Lamb)*
7-12
Spenser   *Ruins of Time* 427-31

Thirty Tyrants   Thirty influential men appointed to draw up a Greek constitution in 404 BC, at the end of the Peloponnesian War. They assumed total power and inaugurated a reign of terror, but within a year were ousted by moderates who, appointing ten governors, restored democracy.

(Xenophon *Hellenica* ii 3-4)
Chaucer   *Franklin's Tale* 1368-78

Thisbe, Thisby
See *Tesbee, Tysbe, Pyramus*
Chaucer   *Legend of Good Women* 261,
778 ff, 805 ff, 862, 896 ff
Parliament of Fowls 288 ff
Donne   *Epigram — Pyramus and Thisbe*
Shakespeare   *Merchant of Venice* V i 7-8
Midsummer Night's Dream
III i 43 ff, 87; V i 56-7,
127 ff, 136 ff

Thoas (1)   King of Aetolia, who gave his army and forty ships in support of the Greeks in the Trojan War. His (unnamed) daughter married *Odysseus* late in life.

(Homer *Iliad* ii 638-44)
See also *Toas*
Shakespeare   *Troilus and Cressida* V v
11-15

Thoas (2)   King of *Lemnos*. When the Lemnian women attempted to kill all the menfolk

of the island, his daughter *Hypsipyle* (to whom he had resigned his crown) saved his life by setting him afloat in a chest.

(Apollodorus I ix 17)
Chaucer   *Legend of Good Women*
1465-8

Tholome
See *Ptolemy (1)*
Chaucer   *Legend of Good Women* 580-2

Thomiris   A queen of the Massagetae who (when her son had been defeated by *Cyrus* the Great of Persia) defeated and killed Cyrus, having his head cut off and immersed in a pot of the blood for which, she said, he thirsted.

(Herodotus i 205 ff)
See also *Thamyris (2)*
Spenser   *Faerie Queene* II x 57
Swinburne   *Masque of Queen Bersabe*

Thon, Thone   The Egyptian doctor whose wife, *Polydamna*, gave *Helen* the anodyne *Nepenthe* for *Menelaus*.
Milton   *Comus* 675-7

Thoosa   A Nymph, daughter of *Phorcys* and mother of *Polyphemus* by *Poseidon*.

(Apollodorus *Epitome* vii 4)
Drayton   *Polyolbion* xx 156-9

Thrace
See *Thracia*
Auden   *Atlantis* 25-30
Chaucer   *Anelida and Arcite* 1-6
Knight's Tale 1638-44

Thracia   A country which generally comprised much of modern Bulgaria. The people were regarded as wild and undisciplined, but of great potential by the Greeks, who civilised them. There is no clear national history, though Thracia was under Macedon from the 4th Century BC. Thrace was seen as a warlike land and the seat of *Mars*. Selected allusions.
See *Trace*
Gray   *Progress of Poesy* 17-18
Marlowe   *Hero and Leander* i 81-2

Thrasea   Publius Clodius, a *Stoic* philosopher in *Nero*'s reign who refused to endorse the Senate's approval of Nero's assassination of his mother *Agrippina*. A victim of conscience, he committed suicide.

(Tacitus *Annals* 21-35)
Gray   *Agrippina* 124-5

Thrasybulus   An Athenian leader and general who was banished by the *Thirty Tyrants* when they seized power at the end of the Peloponnesian War. He set up a force in Phyle, a rocky frontier fortress between Attica and Boeotia, and was instrumental in restoring a form of democracy in 404-403 BC. He was murdered in 388 BC.

(Diodorus Siculus xiv)
Byron   *Childe Harold* ii 74

Thrasymene   A lake in Italy near Perusia, where the Carthaginian *Hannibal* trapped the Roman forces under *Flaminius* and inflicted immense losses in 217 BC.

(Livy xxii)
Drayton   *Polyolbion* xxv 31ff
Marlowe   *Doctor Faustus* 1-2
Shenstone   *Elegies* xix 37-40
Wordsworth   *Memorials of a Tour in Italy* xiii 6-10

Three-formed
See *Persephone*

Thucydides   The major Greek historian, writing in the 5th Century BC. His *History* was of contemporary events (the wars between Athens and Sparta 431-404 BC) and was probably completed by *Xenophon*. Its accuracy has been much debated, but the style is noted for simplicity and for speed of narration.

Auden   *Epistle to a Godson* 32-6
MacNeice   *Autumn Sequel* i
           Hiatus 9-11

Thunderer
See *Jupiter*
Milton   *Paradise Lost* ii 28-9, vi 490-1

Thyads, Thyades   Bacchanals, so called after Thyas, a Bacchant priest.

(Virgil *Aeneid* iv 301-4)
Moore   *Evenings in Greece* 331-4
Swinburne *Prelude* 101-4

Thyestes   Thyestes, son of *Pelops*, raped

Aerope, wife of his brother *Atreus*, because Atreus would not share his throne with him. Atreus banished him and then invited him back, ostensibly in pardon, but in fact to eat the flesh of his own child. This sensational gesture was reputed to have caused the sun to alter its course. Subsequently, Thyestes' daughter (Pelopea) was made pregnant by himself and came to be married to Atreus. She abandoned her son, Aegisthus, in the woods, but he was saved by goats and accepted into the family of Atreus. Atreus caught and imprisoned Thyestes and sent none other than Aegistheus to murder him. But Pelopea, when assaulted, had caught hold of a sword from her unknown assailant and had given it to Aegisthus when he was of age. Thyestes now recognised his own sword in Aegisthus' grasp and, when Aegisthus learnt what had happened, he murdered Atreus with it. Pelopea, discovering her incest, then committed suicide with the sword. Thyestes succeeded to Atreus' throne, but before long he was defeated and exiled.

(Apollodorus ii 4; Seneca *Thyestes*)

Thyestean
See *Thyestes*
Milton   *Paradise Lost* x 687-9

Thyrsis   A shepherd of pastoral verse, notably in the *Idylls* of *Theocritus* and in *Virgil Eclogue VII*, where he is defeated in verse by *Corydon*.

Arnold   *Thyrsis* 77-80
Browning R. *Clive* 112-3
             Ring and the Book v 669-72
Byron   *Mazeppa* 153-4
Collins   *No Longer Aske Me, Gentle Friends* 68
Diaper   *Dryades* 64-70
Gray   *Song II* 1-2
Milton   *L'Allegro* 83-5

Tiber   The principal Italian river, on whose banks is Rome. Select allusions.

Macaulay   *Horatius* 59
Pope   *Windsor-Forest* 355ff
Prior   *Carmen Seculare* 59-60
Thomson   *Liberty* i 267-72
Wordsworth   *Yarrow Revisited* i 61-4

Tiberius   Julius Caesar Augustus Tiberius 42 BC - 37 AD. After a brilliant military career, Tiberius was recognised by *Augustus* as his successor as Emperor. Tiberius had just adopted his nephew *Germanicus* who thus came into the direct line of succession. Augustus died in 14 AD and Tiberius — not without opposition — succeeded him. His character and many events in his reign are problematic and they, like the vacillations of Pilate's governorship of Judea, are the background to the life of Christ. Tiberius followed policies of apparent modesty and discretion — yet he could be arbitrary and dictatorial and, as a hardened soldier, seems to have distrusted the Senate. His reign was marked by insurrections and trials for treason. He was influenced by his adviser, *Sejanus*, who during a period of general terror, helped secure his withdrawal from Rome to Capreae in 26 AD. From here he governed *in absentia*. Meanwhile Germanicus, *Agrippina*, *Nero* and Sejanus committed suicide or were murdered. Tiberius died in 37 and his death was followed by rituals of mingled sorrow and relief. He had revered *Julius Caesar* and refused to allow statues of *Brutus (3)* and *Cassius* at the funeral of *Junia*, wife of Cassius. But how would Julius himself have seen the old man trying to rule an Empire from Capri?

(Suetonius *Caesars* iii 40;
Tacitus *Annals* vi etc.)

Auden	*Whitsunday in Kirchstetten* 19-21
Byron	*Don Juan* xv 49
Jonson	*Sejanus* I i, V i
Masefield	*Letter from Pontus*
Milton	*Paradise Regained* iii 157-60, iv 90-7
Moore	*Corruption* 115-8
Southey	*History* 20-2
Swinburne	*Song for the Centenary of Landor*
Thomson	*Liberty* iii 382 ff

Tibullus   Aulus Albius, Roman love-poet of the 1st Century BC, known mainly from allusions in *Horace* and *Ovid*. His verse was known for extreme simplicity and economy.

Herrick	*To Live Merrily* 41-4
Swift	*Cadenus and Vanessa* 112-3

Ticius   See *Tityus*

Chaucer	*Troilus and Criseyde* i 785-8

Tideaus
See *Tydeus*

Chaucer	*Troilus and Criseyde* v 86-9, 799-804, 932-4, 1485 ff

Timarete   A daughter of the Greek painter Mycon, of the 5th Century BC.
See also *Thamer*

Time   *Chronos* or *Saturn*, traditionally depicted with a sickle (with which Saturn murdered *Uranus*). Selected allusions — there is no single distinctive Classical myth of Time as a god.

Marvell	*To His Coy Mistress* 21-2
Pope	*Temple of Fame* 147-8
Shelley	*Daemon of the World* 319-20
Spenser	*Epithalamion* 281
	Faerie Queene III vi 39
	Mutability Cantos viii 1
Tennyson	*Time, an Ode* 5-7, 27
Wordsworth	*Mary Queen of Scots* 8-12

Timoleon   A Corinthian leader of the 4th Century BC, celebrated for his freeing Greek Sicily from the Carthaginians. He was said to have begun his liberating career by killing his brother, Timophanes, who had become a tyrant in Corinth. But accounts of this episode differ and Timoleon had in fact only recently saved his brother's life in battle.

(Plutarch *Timoleon*;
Diodorus Siculus xvi 65)

Byron	*Siege of Corinth* 58 ff
Pope	*Temple of Fame* 162
Swinburne	*Song for the Centenary of Landor* 24
Thomson	*Winter* 473-5

Timon   A misanthrope of Athens in the time of *Pericles*, associated with the similar *Apemantus*, and with *Alcibiades* the Athenian general who he believed would ruin the state.

(Plutarch *Alcibiades* xvi, *Antony* lxx)

Shakespeare	*Love's Labour's Lost* IV iii 162 ff
	Timon of Athens III iv 15-17; IV iii 52
Spenser	*Daphnaida* 248-9

Timonides   An Ionian, from the island of *Leucas*, who urged *Dion* to free Sicily from *Dionysus II*, and who held rank in Dion's army.
(Plutarch *Dion* xxii)
Wordsworth   *The Prelude* ix 408 ff

Timotheus   A Miletian poet of the 5th Century BC, known mainly for *Persae* (on *Salamis*), a choral composition to which *Euripides* wrote a prologue and which ends with a claim by Timotheus to have revolutionised music. Like many libretti, the poem has little literary merit. The musical innovations were, at least initially, received with displeasure.
(Pausanias III xii 9)
Johnson   *To Miss Hickman* 9-11

Tindarid   Descended from Tyndarus, King of *Lacedaemon*. He was married to *Leda* who, through *Jupiter*, became mother of *Castor*, *Pollux* and *Helen*.
Spenser   *Faerie Queene* IV xi 19

Tiphoeus, Tiphous
See *Typhon*
Fletcher P.   *The Purple Island* xii 22
Marlowe   *Dido Queen of Carthage* 1077-9

Tiresias   A prophet of *Thebes* who lived to a great age, Tiresias was son of a nymph *Chariclo*. Having early in life undergone a temporary change of sex, Tiresias was consulted by *Jupiter* and *Juno* as to the superiority of the sexes and their pleasure in the sexual act. Juno blinded him when he gave the palm to the male sex, but Jupiter in consolation gave him the gift of prophecy and also a sevenfold lifespan. According to other versions, he was blinded for watching the naked *Pallas* bathing on Mount *Helicon*. Pronouncing on how to relieve the curse of war from Thebes, he recommended to *Creon* the sacrifice of his son, Menoeceus, a descendant of *Cadmus* (who had offended *Ares* by killing a dragon guarding water sacred to that god at nearby *Dirce*). This did, indeed, turn Theban fortunes. Tiresias was said to be assisted in his predictions by spirits which he invoked from *Hades*. He died after drinking from a spring which froze his blood, and was buried in pomp by the Thebans. Alternatively, he fell though a hole in the earth opened by *Zeus* in the flight of the Thebans from the Epigoni.
(Apollodorus III 6; Euripides *Phoenissae* 931ff; Homer *Odyssey* xi; Ovid *Metamorphoses* iii 324ff; Pausanias ix 33)
Arnold   *Fragment of an 'Antigone'* 80-7
The Strayed Reveller 135-42, 217-22
Youth of Nature 41-7
Byron   *Don Juan* xiv 73
Cowley   *Nemeaean Ode* 8
Davies, Sir J.   *Orchestra* 567-74
Eliot T. S.   *Waste Land* 218-22, 228-9, 243-6
Milton   *Paradise Lost* iii 34-6
Swinburne   *Tiresias* 4-6, 43-7, 171ff
Tennyson   *Tiresias* 11-17, 38ff

Tirynthian   Of Tiryns, Tirynthus, an Argolian town, ruled for long by descendants of *Perseus*, including *Hercules* − of whom this epithet is common.
(Pausanias II xvi, xxv)
Spenser   *Faerie Queene* VI xii 35

Tisiphone   One of the *Furies*, daughter of *Acheron* and *Nox*, who executed the gods' wish to punish mankind. She had serpents in her hair and brandished a whip.
(Virgil *Aeneid* vi 555, *Georgics* iii 552)
See also *Thesiphone*, *Thesaphone*, *Eumenides*
Marlowe   *Edward II* 2029-321

Titans   The Titans were children of *Uranus* (heaven) and *Ge* (earth). They rebelled against and castrated Uranus and made one of their number (*Saturn*) King. Their names included *Oceanus* (sea and rivers), *Hyperion* (sun), *Rhea* and *Themis* (earth), *Mnemosyne* (memory), *Tethys* (who was also wife of Oceanus), *Phoebe, Coeus, Creus, Theia* and *Chronos* (Saturn). The Titans in turn were overthrown by *Zeus*, son of Saturn, and imprisoned in *Tartarus*. Some of the Titans (Oceanus, Hyperion's son *Helius*, and the Titanesses) are not in accounts of the war in heaven and were presumed to continue their proper role under Zeus. (Milton has the oldest Titan (Oceanus) in the position of Uranus and threatened by his younger brother Saturn.) 'Titan' is often used merely of the Sun (Hyperion).

(Hesiod *Theogony* 207-10, 389-96, 617-735)
— *General*

Byron   *Age of Bronze* 13-18
Chaucer   *Troilus and Criseyde* iii 1463
Hood   *The Elm Tree* 41-2
Noyes   *Drake* iii
Shakespeare   *Cymbeline* III iv 159-64
             King Henry IV pt 1 II iv
             113-5
             Titus Andronicus I i 225-7
Shelley   *Letter to Maria Gisborne* 22-4
             Prometheus Unbound I 117-8,
             445
Spenser   *Faerie Queene* II vii 41
— *War with Zeus*
Bridges   *Prometheus the Firegiver* 632-6
Browning R.   *Paracelsus* V 123-5
Hopkins   *Escorial* 7
Keats   *Endymion* iv 941-4
             Hyperion i 161-6 (*Fall of*
             Hyperion ii 10-16) ii 4-5, 150-5,
             198-201, 212-7
Spenser   *Faerie Queene* III vii 47, V i 9
             Mutability Cantos vi 2, 20, 27
— *for 'Hyperion'*
Henryson   *Testament of Cresseid* 253 ff
Keats   *Hyperion* i 161-6, ii 10-16
Shakespeare   *Romeo and Juliet* II iii 3-4
             Venus and Adonis 176-8
Spenser   *Daphnaida* 468-9
             Faerie Queene I ii 7, iv 8, xi
             31, II iii 1, vi 31, xi 9, III iv
             60, VI iii 13
             Hymn of Heavenly Beauty
             160-5
             Prothalamion 1-4
             Shepherd's Calendar, July
             57-60
— *Titan (Oceanus) and Saturn*
Milton   *Paradise Lost* i 510-12

Titanian, Titanic
See *Titan*
Milton   *Paradise Lost* i 196-8
Shelley   *Hellas* 703-7
             Prometheus Unbound III i 62-3
             Epipsychidion 442-3, 493-5

Tithon, Tithone, Tithonus The husband of
Aurora and brother of *Priam*, Tithonus asked
to be made immortal. But in interceding for
him, Aurora omitted to ask *Zeus* also for such

qualities as youth and beauty. Tithonus thus
found himself condemned to endless senility.
As he could not die, Aurora eventually in pity
made him into a grasshopper, which could
slough off old age with its skin — or shut him
in a cell so that she should not hear his bab-
bling. Tithonus was father of Emathion, *Memnon* and, in some accounts, *Phaethon*.

(Hesiod *Theogony* 984-5; Homeric Hymn
             To Aphrodite (1) 218 ff)
Browning R.   *Pietro of Albano* 381
Fletcher P.   *Piscatory Eclogues* VII 1
             Purple Island III i
Prior   *The Turtle and the Sparrow* 113-4
Shelley   *The Witch of Atlas* 576-83
Spenser   *Epithalamion* 74-7
             Faerie Queene I ii 7, xi 51,
             III iii 20
Tennyson   *The Grasshopper* 5-7
             Tithon 5-6, 60-2
             Tithonus 15 ff

Titus Titus Flavius Vespasianus, Roman
Emperor 79-81 AD. Son of the Emperor *Vespasian*, Titus served him as a ruthless military
right-hand man, amid accusations of claiming
undue power. But his short reign was known
for moderation, pleasantness and generosity.
Unhappily, he died (naturally) within two years
of his accession, having seen Rome through
no easy time of plague and the disaster of
Vesuvius.
Pope   *Essay on Man* ii 195-8, iv 145-8

Tityrus The name of a goatherd or shepherd
in *Eclogues* of *Theocritus* and *Virgil*. It has,
simply, general pastoral associations.
Cowper   *The Task* IV 704-8
Crabbe   *The Village* i 14-16
Diaper   *Dryades* 236-7
MacNeice   *Eclogue by a Five-Barred
             Gate* 73-5
Spenser   *Colin Clout's Come Home
             Again* 1-2
             Shepherd's Calendar, February
             92-3, *June* 81-4, *October*
             55-60
Tennyson   *To Virgil* iv

Tityus The Giant son of *Zeus*, nursed by *Ge*
(Earth) to conceal from *Hera* one of her husband's many illicit amours — with Elara. (Or

Tityus was simply son of Ge). Tityus tried to rape *Leto* (mother of *Artemis* and *Apollo*) at the village of Panopeus as she was on her way to *Delphi*. Hera may have staged the temptation as a trap for him. In any event, Tityus was shot by Artemis and Apollo and condemned to be stretched over nine acres of *Hades*. Two vultures or snakes bit at his heart or liver, which recovered at each new moon.

> (Apollodorus i 4; Homer *Odyssey* xi 576-81;
> Ovid *Metamorphoses* iv 457-8)

Fletcher P. *Purple Island* v 65
Henryson *Orpheus and Eurydice* 296-32, 561ff
Spenser *Faerie Queene* I v 35

Tmolus The name of a Lydian king, mountain and its god. Tmolus appeared with *Midas* as judge of the musical contest between *Apollo* and *Pan*. His head bore a circlet of oak leaves and acorns and he silently listened to their music and sagely favoured Apollo.

> (Ovid *Metamorphoses* xi 153ff)

Housman *Atys* 5-6
Shelley *Hymn of Pan* 10-12

Toas
See *Thoas*
Chaucer *Troilus and Criseyde* iv 137-8

Tomyris
See *Thamyris, Cyrus the Great*
Tennyson *The Princess* v 355-6

Toxeus The brother of *Althaea*, Toxeus was killed by *Meleager* in the *Calydonian Boar Hunt*. In the same family, another Toxeus (son of Althaea) was killed by his father, *Oeneus*, for jumping a ditch, presumably some crucial boundary-line.

> (Apollodorus i 8;
> Ovid *Metamorphoses* viii 437ff)

Swinburne *Atalanta in Calydon* 459, 1555

Trace
See *Thrace*
Chaucer *Legend of Good Women* 2244-50

Trajan Marcus Trajan, Roman Emperor from 98-117AD, was born in Spain, and brought himself by military and administrative merit to the notice of Nerva. Nerva had succeeded *Domitian* as Emperor for two years from 96, and he adopted Trajan and proclaimed him his heir. Trajan was popular and readily accepted, but he soon became involved in war with the Dacians, a German tribe whom Domitian had bought off with tribute as yet unpaid. Trajan defeated them and invaded the Danube lands by means of a famous bridge. He also pursued campaigns against the Parthians and Assyrians, but eventually retired in poor health. In 117 he died of a haemorrhage and was succeeded by Hadrian. The monument, Trajan's Column — a round column with the hero on top —, was built in Rome by the architect Apollodorus (who had also designed the Danube bridge) in 114AD.

> (Pliny *Panegyric*)

Byron *Childe Harold* iv 111
Prior *Ode Inscribed to the Queen* 270-2
Spenser *Ruins of Time* 547-53
Wordsworth *Memorials of a Tour in Italy* xxviii 6-12, 28, 58ff
Pillar of Trajan 25-8

Trasymene
See *Thrasymene*

Trebia A river of Gaul, site of the great victory of *Hannibal* over the Roman Sempronius in 218BC.
Shenstone *Elegies* xix 37-40

Triform
See *Persephone*
Milton *Paradise Lost* iii 730-2

Trinacria, Trinacrian Sicily, so called from its triangular shape.
Belloc *Of Meadows Drowsy* 1ff
Milton *Paradise Lost* ii 60-1

Triple
See *Persephone*

Triptolemus An Eleusinian prince of whose origin there are several explanations. In one, he was son of Attican *Celeus* and Neraea, and was born at Eleusis. *Demeter* gave him a chariot with dragons, with which he sowed her wheat from the sky. He was credited with the invention of the wheel. He was also known as *Demophoon (2)*, but this may have arisen from confusion with another son. As a fertility god, he was the supposed founder of Eleusinian festivals of Demeter.

> (Apollodorus I v 2;
> Ovid *Metamorphoses* v 646 ff)

Bryon	*Age of Bronze* 577 ff
Dryden	*To Sir George Etherege* 30-1
Meredith	*Pastoral* II
Swinburne	*At Eleusis* 186-91

Triton   Originally the son of *Neptune* by *Amphitrite*, Triton had the power to raise storms or to calm the sea by blowing on a conch-shell horn. His became used as a generic name for lesser sea-deities, in form half man and half fish or dolphin, sometimes assisting *Aeolus*. (In the *Aeneid*, Triton and Neptune push *Aeneas'* fleet off the rocks and save it from the enmity of *Juno*.)

> (Apollonius Rhodius iv 1550 ff;
> Hesiod *Theogony* 930-3;
> Ovid *Metamorphoses* i 330-47;
> Pausanias ix 204;
> Virgil *Aeneid* i 144 ff)

Browning R.	*The Two Poets of Croisic* 587-8
Chaucer	*House of Fame* 1596-7
	Legend of Good Women 2414 ff
Crabbe	*To the Monthly Review* 5-9
	The Wish 6
Crashaw	*Upon the Gunpowder Treason* 31-2
Keats	*Endymion* i 205-6, ii 690-1, iii 888-91
	Lamia i 13-16
Marlowe	*Dido Queen of Carthage* 130-4
	Hero and Leander ii 153-8
Marvell	*Last Instructions to a Painter* 543 ff
Milton	*Comus* 873
	Lycidas 89-90
Spenser	*Colin Clout's Come Home Again* 245-51
	Faerie Queene III iv 33, IV xi 12
Wordsworth	*Sonnet 'The World is Too Much With Us'*

Tritonian
See *Tritonis*

Spenser	*Muiopotmos* 265

Triton, Tritonis   A lake and river of modern Tunisia, where *Minerva* had a temple (and hence may be called Tritonia). This was confused with the River Triton in Boeotia, which also was sacred to *Athene*.

> (Diodorus Siculus iii 68-70;
> Herodotus iv 178)

Milton	*Paradise Lost* iv 275-9

Troian
See *Troy*

Chaucer	*Troilus and Criseyde* i 145-7

Troie, Troien
See *Troy*

Chaucer	*Squire's Tale* 305-7
	Troilus and Criseyde i 56-63, iv 120-4, v 599-602
Shakespeare	*Troilus and Cressida* Prologue 16-19

Troilus   The son of *Hecuba* by *Priam* of *Troy* (or by *Apollo*). Troilus is merely mentioned in the *Iliad* as dead before the action of the poem. According to another tradition, he was a youth ill-matched against *Achilles* in battle and killed by him or dragged to death by his own horses. Either way, the story of Troilus and *Cressida* is Medieval rather than Classical, though it has Classical origins. It tells of the love of Trojan Troilus for Cressida (whose father *Calchas*, foreknowing the fall of Troy, has left his daughter there and himself fled to the Greeks). This love is fostered by Cressida's uncle Pandarus as go-between, and shattered when Cressida goes to the Greeks in an exchange of prisoners, where she comes to prefer *Diomedes* to Troilus. The two men meet inconclusively at arms and Troilus is eventually killed by Achilles.

> (Apollodorus iii 32;
> Homer *Iliad* xxiv 257;
> Virgil *Aeneid* i 474-8)

See also *Briseis*, *Troylus*

Chaucer	*Troilus and Criseyde*
Henryson	*Testament of Cresseid* 501-4
Keats	*Endymion* ii 8-13
MacNeice	*The Stygian Banks* vii

Shakespeare　*As You Like It* IV i 87ff
　　　　　　Merchant of Venice V i 3-6
　　　　　　Much Ado About Nothing
　　　　　　V ii 27ff
　　　　　　Troilus and Cressida I i 94,
　　　　　　ii 276-7, III ii 169ff, V ii
　　　　　　169-74
Surrey　*In Winter's Just Return*

Trojans
　Rochester　*Grecian Kindness*

Troy　Identified as the modern Hissarlik
close to the *Hellespont*, where remains not
inconsistent with a city of the third millenium
BC have been found. Troia may be the capital
city of Troas, or a country of which nearby
Ilium was the capital. It was variously called
Dardania, Troia and *Ilion* after the legendary
King *Dardanus* and his successors. It was the
site of the Trojan War, in which the Greeks
sought to repossess *Helen* whom *Paris*, son of
Priam of Troy, had carried away from *Menelaus*
in pursuit of his destiny to marry the most
beautiful woman in the world. The War, if it
happened, probably occurred c.1200BC. (The
walls of Troy were said to have been built by
Phoebus and *Neptune*.)
　　　　　　(Ovid *Metamorphoses* xi 198ff)
See also *Troie*
　Blake　*King Edward III* vi 1ff
　Browning R.　*Ring and the Book* ix
　　　　　　844-5
　Chaucer　*Canon Yeoman's Tale* 972-5
　　　　　　House of Fame 143-8, 151-6
　　　　　　Legend of Good Women 930-3
　Dryden　*To My Lord Chancellor* 17-20
　Keats　*Endymion* ii 8-13
　Kipling　*Ode, Melbourne Shrine* 20-1
　Marlowe　*Dido Queen of Carthage*
　　　　　　403-6
　Milton　*Il Penseroso* 97-100
　Pope　*Rape of the Lock* i 137-8
　　　　　　Temple of Fame 207-9
　Prior　*Ode Inscribed to the Queen* 211-5
　Rosetti D. G.　*Death's Songsters* 1ff
　　　　　　Troy Town 1-7
　Shakespeare　*King Henry VI pt 2* I iv
　　　　　　16-19
　　　　　　King Henry VI pt 3 II i 50-3
　　　　　　Pericles I iv 91-5
　　　　　　Rape of Lucrece 1366-72

　　　　　　Titus Andronicus III i 67-70
　　　　　　Troilus and Cressida, Prologue
　　　　　　7-10
Sidney　*My Mistress Lowers* 18
Spenser　*Faerie Queene* II iii 31, ix 45,
　　　　　　III ix 34, 38, 44, IV xi 19
Surrey　*When Raging Love* 7-12
Swinburne　*Ave Atque Vale* xii
Tennyson　*Oenone* 257-71
Yeats　*Long-Legged Fly*
　　　　No Second Troy
　　　　Parnell's Funeral
　　　　The Rose of the World
　　　　Three Marching Songs ii
　　　　When Helen Lived

Troylus
See *Troilus*
　Chaucer　*Parliament of Fowls* 290-5

Truth
See *Veritas*
Select allusions.
　Milton　*On the Death of a Fair Infant*
　　　　　54

Truth, Hill of
See *Virtue*
　Milton　*Sonnet* ix

Tullia (Tulliola)　The daughter of Tullius
Cicero, Tullia died in giving birth in 45BC.
Her father was overwhelmed with grief and
she was buried in a tomb where, legend has it,
a light burned for 1500 years.
　　　　　　(Plutarch *Cicero*)
　Donne　*Eclogue 1613 (Epithalamion)*
　　　　　215-8

Tullius (Hostilius) (1)　Reputedly the third
king of Rome, in the 7th Century BC. Many
of his exploits were doubtless invented to account for his name, but the story of his capture
and sacking of *Alba* Longa is probably true.
　　　　　　(Livy I 22-5)
　Chaucer　*Wife of Bath's Tale*
　　　　　1165-70

Tullius (2)
See *Cicero*
　Dunbar　*Ryght as the Stern of Day* 66-9

Tullus
See *Amfidius*
  Shakespeare   *Coriolanus* I i 237-8

Tully
See *Cicero*
— *General and Life*
  Byron   *Age of Bronze* 496-9
  Campbell   *Pleasures of Hope* i
  Cowley   *To the Bishop of Lincoln*
       17-20
  Herrick   *His Farewell to Poetry* 75-8
  Moore   *Morality* 74-5
  Pope   *Chorus to Brutus* i 31-2
       Temple of Fame 238-41
  Prior   *The Conversation* 71-3
  Thomson   *Liberty* i 272-7
       Winter 521-2
— *Style and Works*
  Browning R.   *The Bishop Orders His*
       Tomb 76-8
  Burns   *The Author's Earnest Cry and*
       Prayer 79 ff
  Lovelace   *To the Genius of Mr John Hall*
       25-6
  Praed   *To Susan Praed* 113-6
  Prior   *To the Lord Bishop of Rochester*
       20-1
  Shakespeare   *Titus Andronicus* IV i
       12-14

Turnus   A king of the Rutuli who, prompted by *Juno*, tried to drive *Aeneas* out of Italy so that he would not marry *Lavinia* (who was engaged to himself). He was killed by Aeneas, who then married Lavinia.
       (Ovid *Fasti* iv 879-80, *Metamorphoses*
       xiv 451 ff; Virgil *Aeneid* vii 56 ff, xii)
  Chaucer   *Knight's Tale* 1936-46
       Man of Law's Tale 197-202
       House of Fame 451-8, 514-7
  Dryden   *Conquest of Granada* 2, III i
  Marlowe   *Tamburlaine* i 2174 ff
  Milton   *Paradise Lost* ix 13-17
  Pope   *Temple of Fame* 205
  Prior   *On Fleet* 15-18

Tuscan, Tuscany   Toscana (*Etruria*) was a country north-west of Rome, many of whose beliefs and ceremonies Rome inherited. Tuscany was later identified with Florence as the seat of the Renaissance and its values. It

was also famous for wine. Select allusions.
  Collins   *Epistle to Sir Thomas Hanmer*
       47-8
  Keats   *Otho the Great* V 5 120-5

Tyche   Goddess of luck and good fortune, later identified with the Roman *Fortuna*. Tyche was one of the *Fates* or a daughter of *Zeus*, but generally she has no mythology and is not clearly represented as a being. Her workings are blind and obscure — there is some debate as to whether acknowledging her is consistent with belief in the gods. Tyche might be manifest as the fortunes of an individual, virtually his *Daimon*, or again could be the spirit of a city.
       (Hesiod *Theogony* 360;
       Sophocles *Antigone* 1158)

Tydeus   One of the *Seven Against Thebes*, a son of *Oeneus* of *Calydon*. Banished for killing certain relatives, Tydeus went to *Argos*, where he married Deipyle and had a son, *Diomedes (2)*. He was killed in the siege of Thebes after heroic exploits.
  Browning E. B.   *Queen Anelida* 9
  Chaucer   *Anelida and Arcite* 57-63

Tydides
See *Diomedes (2)*
  Pope   *Temple of Fame* 188-9

Typhaean
See *Typhon (Greek)*
  Shelley   *Ode to Naples* 43-6

Typhoean
See *Typhon (Greek)*
  Milton   *Paradise Lost* ii 539-40

Typhoeus
See *Typhon (Greek)*
  Dryden   *Astraea Redux* 37-42
  Spenser   *Faerie Queene* I v 35, III vii 47

Typhon (Egyptian)   The brother of *Osiris*, who attempted Osiris' throne whilst he was abroad. On his return, Typhon would not listen to his pacific brother's arguments, and either hacked him to pieces or threw his body into the Nile in a chest. He was defeated by his mother, *Isis*, and brother, *Horus*.

Typhon (Greek)   Typhon or *Typhoeus*, son of *Tartarus* and *Terra*, was one of the more formidable Classical monsters, having a hundred serpentine heads which emitted flames. He lived in Cilicia, of which *Tarsus* was the capital. He set himself against the combined forces of the gods to avenge their defeat of his brothers, the *Giants*. Eventually he was crushed by *Zeus* and confined beneath *Aetna*, whose eruptions were supposed to represent — as no doubt they explained — his fiery struggles. At one stage of the war, the gods took refuge from him by assuming the forms of birds and animals.

> (Apollodorus i 6; Ovid *Metamorphoses*
> v 325-31, xiv 1ff)

Arnold	*Empedocles on Etna* II i 37ff, 98
Browning R.	*Aristophanes' Apology* 813-5
Keats	*Endymion* iii 243-4
	Hyperion ii 19-22
Marlowe	*Tamburlaine* i 1201ff
Meredith	*The Day of the Daughter of Hades*
Milton	*On the Morning of Christ's Nativity* 236
	Paradise Lost i 198-200
Shakespeare	*Troilus and Cressida* I iii 159-61
Shelley	*Prometheus Unbound* I 209-14
Spenser	*Faerie Queene* V x 10, VI vi 11
	Mutability Cantos vi 15-16, 29
Swinburne	*A Nympholet* 134-6

Tyre   A city on the Phoenician coast. It was captured by *Alexander the Great* in a siege in 332BC. It was the centre of the purple-dyeing industry — the colour being extracted from a local shellfish named Purpura — and a great commercial port noted for its silk. It was for a time free, then a colony of Rome from the 1st Century BC. 'Tyrian' is commonly used for both 'purple' and 'Phoenician'.
See also *Sarra*

Byron	*Childe Harold* i 45

Tyrian
See *Tyre*

Arnold	*The Scholar-Gipsy* 232ff
Browning R.	*Popularity* 26-30
Byron	*Don Juan* xvi 10

Davies, Sir J.	*Orchestra* 619-20
Gray	*On the Death of a Favourite Cat* 16-18
Keats	*Endymion* ii 358-63
Milton	*On the Morning of Christ's Nativity* 204
Pope	*Windsor-Forest* 142
Shakespeare	*Taming of the Shrew* II i 341
Shenstone	*Elegies* vii 22-3
Wordsworth	*Lines Written as a School Exercise* 21-2

Tyro   Tyro, daughter of *Salmoneus* and Alcidice, married her uncle Cretheus, but became infatuated with the River Enipeus, in whose form *Neptune* seduced her. The two sons then born — *Pelias* and *Neleus* — were reared secretly by horse-herders, but eventually discovered their mother and took revenge on her step-mother Sidero, who had mistreated Tyro when news of the birth emerged.

Swinburne	*Atalanta in Calydon* 867-80

Tyrrhene, Tyrrhenian   The Tyrrhene Sea on the west coast of Italy. *Bacchus*, travelling from Icaria to *Naxos*, was kidnapped by Tyrrhene pirates, who steered towards Asia. He transformed the crew into beasts as he waved his ivied wand. The ship came to a stop and was covered in ivy. The pirates leapt overboard and were changed into dolphins. The steersman altered course for Naxos and became a devotee of Bacchus.

> (Ovid *Metamorphoses* iii 629ff)

Belloc	*In Praise of Wine* 37-44
Graves	*The Ambrosia of Dionysus*
Milton	*Comus* 48-9

Tyrtaeus, Tyrtaean   Greek elegiac poet of the 7th Century BC who, being possibly a Spartan general, inspired to victory the Lacedaemonian troops in the siege of Ithome, a Messenian town eventually captured by the Spartans.

Byron	*Hints from Horace* 680-4
Coleridge	*To a Young Lady* 23-4
Dryden	*Amboyna, Epilogue* 1-2
Jonson	*The Vision of Ben Jonson* 68-9

Tysbe
See *Thisbe*

Chaucer   *Legend of Good Women*
           724-8ff

Ulysses   The hero of Homer's *Iliad* and
Odyssey, son and heir of *Laertes*, king of
Ithaca and husband to *Penelope*. He acquired,
when young, a famous bow which he never
used, valuing it so highly that he left it at
home. The contest to draw its string (won by
Ulysses) and win the hand of Penelope, forms
the culmination of the homecoming which
ends the *Odyssey*. Though Ulysses desired
Helen of Sparta, he knew that she would
select the wealthy *Menelaus* for husband. He
therefore bargained with her father that he
(Tyndareus) would persuade his brother
Icarius to give his daughter, Penelope, to
Ulysses. In return Ulysses agreed to handle
any violence arising out of a decision on the
suit for Helen, particularly recommending a
pact among her former suitors to defend
Helen's husband against any harm occurring.
This pact provoked the Trojan War when *Paris*
of *Troy* abducted Helen and in which Ulysses,
despite reluctance, was obliged to join — he
feigned being a ploughman, but *Palamedes* put
his reactions to the test by laying his infant
son in the way of the plough. During the War,
as set out in the *Iliad*, Ulysses distinguished
himself for bravery, shrewdness and eloquence.
The *Odyssey* details his wanderings home to
Ithaca and Penelope after the sack of Troy,
and his recognition (symbolised by drawing
the bowstring) as king of his country. But it
had been prophesied that he would wander
more before old age, and fragments of an epic
of such adventures, the *Telegony*, survive. He
was finally killed, ironically by Telegonus, his
son from *Circe* whom he met during the
Odyssey. His family buried him in Circe's
island of Aeaea. Many by-ways of *Homer's*
two great poems, well conned by any school-
boy, were explored by English poets and most
are still fairly well known. One tale which is
less familiar is his being saved from drowning
by a magic belt given to him by *Leucothea*
(*Odyssey* v 346-7; Keats *Acrostic*).
See also *Odysseus*
— *General and Character*
   Browning E. B.   *The Fourfold Aspect*
                     37-46

              Wine of Cyprus 8
Collins   *Epistle to Sir Thomas Hanmer*
           142-4
Crabbe   *The Library*
Herrick   *No Shipwreck of Virtue* 5-6
Jonson   *Epigram to the Honoured*
           Countess 19-25
           Volpone II i
Milton   *Paradise Lost* ix 13-19
Pope   *Dunciad* ii 340-4
Shakespeare   *King Henry VI pt 3* III ii
               188-93
Shelley   *Hellas* 1076-7
Tennyson   *Ulysses* 6ff, 51-4
— *The Iliad*
Browning R.   *Ring and the Book* ix
               547-50
Cleveland   *Upon an Hermaphrodite*
             49-53
Shakespeare   *King Henry VI pt 3* IV ii
               19-23
               Rape of Lucrece
               1398-1400
               Titus Andronicus I i 379-82
— *The Odyssey*
Davies, Sir J.   *Nosce Teipsum* v 26-9
Jonson   *On the Famous Voyage* 111-4
Keats   *Acrostic* 11-12
         Endymion ii 26-7
Milton   *At a Vacation Exercise* 47-52
          Paradise Lost ii 1019-20
Noyes   *Forty Singing Seamen*
Prior   *Down Hall* 6-10
Rosetti D. G.   *Death's Songsters* 9-12
Spenser   *Faerie Queene* I iii 21
*Homecoming, Penelope and Suitors, Dog
Argus*
Byron   *Don Juan* iii 23
MacNeice   *Day of Returning* ii
Pope   *Argus* 10-15
Spenser   *Faerie Queene* V vii 39

Urania (1) Muse   The daughter of *Jupiter*
and *Mnemosyne*, *Muse* of Astronomy, and so
also of wisdom in the highest senses. Mother
of *Hymenaeus* by *Bacchus* (and also of *Linus*,
who was killed by *Apollo* for rivalling him in
song) she is represented nonetheless as a virgin
in blue and crowned with stars. For Milton
and others, Urania was the name for Christian
inspiration derived but distinguished from
the Muse.

(Hesiod *Theogony* 78; Pausanias ix 26)
Henryson   *Orpheus and Eurydice* 46ff
Keats   *To Charles Cowden Clarke* 40-1
Milton   *Paradise Lost* vii 1-7, 30-1
          *On the Morning of Christ's
          Nativity* 15-16
Shelley   *Fragment, Milton's Spirit* 1-4
Spenser   *Tears of the Muses* 517-28
Swinburne   *Pan and Thalassius*
Tennyson   *In Memoriam* xxx 7
Wordsworth   *For 'The Recluse'* 25-7
          Vernal Ode 75-80

Urania (2)
See *Venus*. Not always distinct from *Urania (1)*.
Keats   *To Charles Cowden Clarke* 40-1
Shelley   *Adonais* 10-14, 28-9, 198-9,
          208-14, 232-5
Wordsworth   *A Morning Exercise* 53-4

Uranus   God of the Sky, son of Earth (*Ge*)
who was daughter of *Chaos*. Uranus married
his mother, Ge, and was father of *Chronos*
(*Saturn*), *Oceanus*, *Hyperion*, the *Titans*, the
Cyclopes and others. He imprisoned all his
children (except the Titans) in the bowels of
the earth and in revenge was castrated by
Chronos, using a sickle provided by Ge. From
the remains of his organs in the sea, there
sprang up *Aphrodite*, and from his blood
appeared the *Furies* and the *Giants*. He is one
of the oldest of gods, devoid of personality.
          (Hesiod *Theogony* 126-210)
Keats   *Hyperion* ii 132-8
Spenser   *Mutability Cantos* vi 27

Uricon   The Roman name for Wroxeter on
Severn, England.

Ursa
See *Arctos*

Valdarno (Val d'Arno)
See *Arno*
Milton   *Paradise Lost* i 286-90

Vacuna   A Sabine goddess of Leisure, of
whom little is known.
          (Horace *Epistles* I x 39;
          Ovid *Fasti* vi 307)

Wordsworth   *Memorials of a Tour in
          Italy* 261-2

Valentinian III   Roman Emperor 425-55AD.
See *Aetius*
Lovelace   *To Fletcher Revived* 14ff

Valeria   A sister of *Publicola*, who urged the
Roman women to plead with *Coriolanus*.
          (Plutarch *Coriolanus* xxxiii)
Shakespeare   *Coriolanus* V iii 64-7

Valerian   Valerius, the legendary husband of
Saint *Cecilia*.
Tennyson   *Amy* 67-72

Valerie
See *Valerius Maximus*
Chaucer   *Monk's Tale* 3909-11

Valerius Maximus   A Roman historian of the
1st Century AD. He dedicated his *Factorum
et Dictorum Memorabilium Libri* to *Tiberius*
soon after the fall of *Sejanus*. The work is a
moralising compendium of earlier writers, particularly *Livy* and *Cicero*, and its rhetorical
manner is no longer attractive, but it was much
used as a source-book in the Middle Ages.
See also *Valerie*
Chaucer   *Wife of Bath's Tale* 1165-70

Varro   Gaius Terentius Varro, consul, general
and statesman of the 3rd Century BC. He was
a commander at *Cannae* where in 216BC the
Romans were heavily defeated by *Hannibal*,
owing partly to a tactical error by Varro. He
fled with the remnants to Canusium and informed the Senate of his defeat. The Senate
and people made a famous vote of thanks for
his service despite its unhappy outcome.
          (Livy xxii 45ff;
          Plutarch *Fabius Maximus* xviii)
Dryden   *Annus Mirabilis* 773-6

Varus   Quintilius Varus was a Roman consul
leading forces in Germany in 10AD when he
was surprised by *Arminius* and his army was
routed. He and several generals committed
suicide.
          (Tacitus *Annals* I iii, lv)
Praed   *Arminius* 19-24

Ventidius   A general who worked up from the ranks with *Julius Caesar*'s favour. After Caesar's assassination, he supported *Mark Antony*, was made consul and was sent to expel the Parthians, which he did with famous victories. He died soon afterwards and was granted a public funeral.

(Plutarch *Antony*)
Dryden   *All for Love* I i

Venus   A minor Roman goddess of gardens, Venus became identified with *Aphrodite*, the Greek goddess of erotic love, beauty and fertility. She was also claimed as grandmother of *Aeneas*' son *Iulus*, the origin of the Julian line. Aphrodite was a daughter of *Zeus* and *Dione*, or sprang from the 'foaming' remains of *Uranus* scattered in the sea by *Chronos* (*Saturn*), his rebelling son. Venus was therefore sometimes depicted as floating on a scallop shell. She was held to have come ashore at *Cypris* (Cyprus) or at *Cythera* (Kythera, an island south of the Peloponnesus), after both of which she is also named. She was married to *Vulcan* but was generally celebrated for her many love-affairs with gods (*Mars, Mercury* and *Neptune* included) and mortals; she was also worshipped as a goddess of warfare and sea-faring. These latter associations probably derive from her Oriental origin, which appears also in her links with *Adonis* in one of her most celebrated love-affairs. *Pausanias* states that she was first worshipped in Assyria. Venus won the golden apple in the Judgment of *Paris*, the cause of the Trojan War, and thereby incurred the implacable enmity of *Hera* (*Juno*). Her power was assisted by a magic belt or *zone* which inspired love even when worn by the most deformed and, worn by Juno, brought about the surrender to her of *Jupiter* (*Iliad* xiv 214ff). She was mother of *Cupid* by Jupiter, Mars or Mercury. She was represented in many attitudes — rising from the sea, posing with Adonis, at her toilet with a mirror, in armour, in a chariot drawn by swans, pigeons or doves wearing her girdle. Rose and myrtle together suggest a modest (or coy) defence of femininity, since Venus was often shrouded in them when washing. Her flower was the white rose, reddened by the blood of Adonis.

(Hesiod *Theogony* 178-206; Homer *Iliad* xiv 214-351; Homeric Hymn *To Aphrodite*; Ovid *Metamorphoses* xii, *Fasti* iv 136ff; Pausanias vi 24ff)
Select allusions.
— *General*

Brooke	*The Goddess in the Wood* 1ff
Byron	*Don Juan* ii 170, v 1, xvi 86
Chaucer	*Knight's Tale* 1098-1102, 1902ff, 1936ff
	Merchant's Tale 1722-3
	Nun's Priest's Tale 4531-6
	Physician's Tale 58-60
	Wife of Bath's Prologue 464
	Complaint of Mars 113-4
	House of Fame 614-9, 1486-9
	Parliament of Fowls 260-70, 652
	Troilus and Criseyde ii 680-3, iii 3-7, 1254-8, v 1016-9
Herbert	*My God, Where Is That Ancient Heat . . .*
Jonson	*Charis* V, 45ff
	To Mary, Lady Worth 11-14
Keats	*Fragment of 'The Castle-Builder'* 38-41
	I Stood Tiptoe Upon a Little Hill 219-20
Kipling	*Samuel Pepys* 16-19
Lamb	*The Female Orators* 14-16
Marlowe	*Dido Queen of Carthage* 838-41
	Hero and Leander i 135-42, 209-14, 299ff, 321-2
Milton	*Comus* 124
Pope	*Spring* 65-8
	Eloisa to Abelard 258-9
	Dunciad ii 209-10, iii 102-4
Praed	*The Modern Nectar* 1-8
Rosetti D. G.	*Jenny*
	Venus Victrix 5-8
Shakespeare	*King Henry VI pt 1* I i 144-5
	Love's Labour's Lost II i 253-5
	Much Ado About Nothing IV i 56-60
	Rape of Lucrece 55-8
Shelley	*Scene from 'Tasso'* 10-13
Sidney	*Arcadia* lxxiii 143-6
	Astrophel and Stella 72, 82
Spenser	*Astrophel* 55-6
	Faerie Queene I i 48, ii 4, vi 16, II vii 55, viii 6, III ix 34, 41,

Marlowe	*Hero and Leander* i 11-15
Marvell	*Elegy on the Death of Lord Villiers* 105 ff
Milton	*Comus* 999-1002
Pope	*Summer* 61-2
Shakespeare	*Passionate Pilgrim* 11
	Venus and Adonis 67-8, 85-90, 163-4, 229-34, 615 ff, 742-6, 1135 ff
Shelley	*Witch of Atlas* 576-83
Spenser	*Faerie Queene* III i 34-8, vi 46-8
Swift	*A Love Song* 9-12
Swinburne	*St Dorothy*
Wordsworth	*Love Lies Bleeding* 12-19

Vergil
See *Virgil*

Verginius Lucius Verginius was a Roman centurion of the 5th Century BC, whose daughter, Verginia, was engaged to the tribune Lucius Icilius. She was, however, desired by a *decemvir*, *Appius Claudius*. He arranged for her to be arrested as the slave of his client *Marcus Claudius*, who then claimed that she had been born in his house, born his slave, and merely palmed off onto Verginius as her father. The hearing — which was, deplorably, by Appius himself — went in favour of Marcus, and so of Appius also. Verginius, being granted words with his daughter, stabbed her, rather than have her submit to the lust of Appius. As in the somewhat parallel case of the Rape of *Lucretia*, a popular uprising followed, and here Appius was either murdered or committed suicide. Marcus also died.

(Livy III 44 ff)

See also *Virginia*, *Virginius*

Shakespeare	*Titus Andronicus* V iii 35-7, 45

Veritas The daughter of *Saturn* and mother of *Virtue*, the goddess Truth was usually represented as a maiden clad in white, elusive and shy.

Verona In ancient times famed principally as the birthplace of *Catullus*. It was not a city of any great size, though on trading routes and having a Roman amphitheatre.

Moore	*To Lord Viscount Strangford* 39-43

Vertumnus
See *Pomona*

Carew	*To my Friend G.N.* 93-4
Keats	*Endymion* ii 444-6
Milton	*Paradise Lost* ix 393-5

Vespasian Titus Flavius Vespasian (79-9 AD, Roman Emperor from 69) was of humble birth and raised himself by his conduct in the Claudian invasion of England in 43-4 AD. After subduing the Jewish rebellion of 67 in *Nero*'s reign — where he ordered the siege of Jerusalem but lamented the burning of the Temple — he invaded Rome in 69 and was adopted by the Senate. Rightly or wrongly, Vespasian has been notorious for greed and extravagance. He sold imperial estates and vastly increased taxation. The uses to which these funds were put, other than a considerable building programme in Rome, are not fully known. Against the accusations have to be set his unassuming personal life and the respect in which he was held for the stability of his reign — symbolised, perhaps, in the fact that he was the first Roman Emperor to die a natural death.

Dryden	*To the Duchess of Ormond* 125-6
Hardy	*Embarcation*
Spenser	*Faerie Queene* II x 52

Vesper
See *Hesper*
Select allusions.

Donne	*Second Anniversary* 197-8
Fletcher P.	*Purple Island* iv 33
Keats	*Song of Four Faeries* 51-5
Spenser	*Mutability Cantos* vi 9

Vesta The goddess of hearth and home (Greek Hestia), daughter of *Saturn* and *Ops*, in whose round temple there burned continuously a flame tended by Vestal Virgins. The extinguishing of this fire was held to portend a national disaster. Vesta was represented robed and veiled, carrying a lamp and spear.

(Hesiod *Theogony* 454; Ovid *Fasti* vi)

Carew	*A Cruel Mistress* 8-11
Keats	*Endymion* iv 701-2

Milton   *Il Penseroso* 23-6
Shelley   *Witch of Atlas* 318-9
Spenser   *Mutability Cantos* vii 26

Vesuvio, Vesuvius   The celebrated volcano of Campania near Naples. It was probably extinct in historical times until its disastrous eruption and earthquake of 79 AD. Then the cities of *Pompeii* and Herculaneum, founded on rich alluvial soil, were buried — and the observer *Pliny* was overcome by fumes and died.

(Diodorus Siculus iv 21;
Virgil *Georgics* ii 224)
Byron   *Age of Bronze* 179-84
Shelley   *Ode to Liberty* 183-4
    The Sensitive Plant iii 1-4
Shenstone   *Elegies* v 37-40

Veto
See *Vetus*
Gray   *Agrippina* 124-5

Veturia
See *Coriolanus*
Collins   *Epistle to Sir Thomas Hanmer*
    127-8

Vetus   Lucius Antistius Vetus was a consul with *Nero* in 55 AD and commanded a Roman army in Germany. He also had a scheme for a canal between the Mediterranean and the North Sea, but was murdered on Nero's orders.

Via Appia
See *Appian Way*
Chaucer   *Second Nun's Tale* 172-3

Virgil   Publius Vergilius Maro, 70-19 BC, the epic and pastoral poet, was born near *Mantua*, educated at Cremona and Rome and rapidly became part of the literary establishment there. He joined the circle of *Catullus* and entered the patronage of *Maecenas*, with the corresponding trust of the Emperor *Augustus*. His principal works are the *Eclogues*, the *Georgics* and the *Aeneid*. From the first he was a model and supreme influence on subsequent literature, establishing the much-lauded life of graduation from pastoral and little things to an epic as a culmination of a

poet's life-work. In point of phrase and details also, his work had an enormous influence on later, particularly English, poetry. Posthumous magical powers were attributed to him, so great was the veneration in which he was held, and these included the ability to cut a long tunnel from his tomb.
See also *Virgilius*
Auden   *Secondary Epic* 47 ff
Browning E. B.   *A Vision of Poets*
    322-34
Butler S.   *Satire upon Plagiaries* 87 ff
Byron   *Don Juan* i 42
Chaucer   *Friar's Tale* 1517-20
    House of Fame 375-80,
    1481-5
    Legend of Good Women 924-7,
    1002-3
    Troilus and Criseyde v 1786 ff
Cowley   *The Motto* 35-8
    The Resurrection 2
Denham   *On Abraham Cowley* 34-40
    Progress of Learning 73-6
    To the Honourable Edward
    Howard 19-33
Dryden   *To Sir Godfrey Kneller*
    152-3
Jonson   *Let Me Be What I Am* 1-2
    The New Inn I i
    The Poetaster V i
Pope   *Windsor-Forest* 227-9
Prior   *Carmen Seculare* 557-8
    The Dove 1-4
    Ode in Imitation of Horace
    110-3
    Satire on Modern Translators
    159-62
Spenser   *Shepherd's Calendar, October*
    55-60
    Sonnet 'That Mantuan Poet's
    Incomparable Spirit'
Suckling   *An Answer to Some Verses*
    5-6
Tennyson   *Poets and their Bibliographies*
    2-4
    To Virgil i, iv, v, vi

Virgilian
See *Virgil*
Arnold   *Geist's Grave* 13-16
Wordsworth   *Memorials of a Tour in*
    Italy 263-9

Virgilius
See *Virgil*
    Chaucer   *House of Fame* 1243-4

Virginia
See *Verginia*
    Chaucer   *Physician's Tale* 7 ff, 14-18,
                  49-51, 107-10, 178-85,
                  207-12, 223 ff
    Macaulay   *Virginia*

Virginius
See *Verginius*
    Chaucer   *Physician's Tale* 1-4, 178-85,
                  207 ff, 254-7
    Macaulay   *Virginia*

Virgo
See *Astraea*
    Spenser   *Mutability Cantos* vii 37

Viriathus   A shepherd who started as a robber and rose to become leader of his own large army. He took over Lusitania and defeated many Roman generals in the 2nd Century BC. He was eventually murdered by his servants, who succumbed to bribery.
        (Livy *Summaries* anno 148 BC ff)
    Wordsworth   *They Seek, Are Sought . . .*
                  10-14

Virtue   Virtue may be described as the summit of a hill with a long and steep path.
        (Hesiod *Works and Days* 286-92)
See also *Virtues*
Selected allusion
    Milton   *Paradise Regained* ii 216-7

Virtues   The principal Roman Virtues were the deities Prudence (pointing to a globe at her feet); Temperance (with a bridle); Fortitude (with a sword); Honesty (with transparent shirt); Modesty (veiled); Clemency (with olive branch); Devotion (with incense); Health (with serpent); Liberty and Gaiety (with myrtle). These were so overlaid by subsequent Christian moralists — not always too clear in the first place — that their place in English poetry as distinct allusion is small. Temples were erected to Virtue and Honour, and you passed through the first before you could see the second. The Christian Fathers distinguished Cardinal

Virtues (Prudence, Temperance, Fortitude, Justice) and Theological Virtues (Faith, Hope and Charity). There were other classifications also. Therefore, he who would claim as Classical (for example) a personified Virtue in English Augustan poetry is treading on dangerous ground. The approach throughout this book has tended towards scepticism.

Vitellius   Aulus Vitellius, 15-69 AD, was of a character not auspicious for long high office. Hailed by his troops as Emperor in 69 AD, he set himself on a path of despotic self-indulgence, modelling himself on *Nero*. He insulted and lost the support of his troops and was a notorious glutton. He had some support against his successor, *Vespasian*, who was irregularly acclaimed by certain provinces before his appointment was ratified by the Senate at the year's end. Vitellius was killed and his body mutilated after he had ruled for just under a year.
        (Plutarch *Galba*; Tacitus *Histories*)
    Byron   *The Irish Avatar* 77-8

Vitruvius   Vitruvius Pollio, a Roman architect in the 1st Century BC. He wrote a comprehensive manual of architecture, on which his fame rests.
    Swift   *The History of Vanbrugh's House*
             35-6

Volsces, Volsci   A tribe from central Italy who threatened the Roman Republic constantly from the 5th to the 3rd Centuries BC. They were subject to Rome by 304 BC and their separate identity was then lost.
See also *Coriolanus*
    Eliot T. S.   *Difficulties of a Statesman*
    Shakespeare   *Coriolanus* I i 226-7

Vulcan   The Roman name for *Hephaestus*, who presided over fire and metalwork. There are various accounts of his origin, but he is usually said to be son of *Juno* and *Jupiter*, the latter of whom flung him out of *Olympus* for trying to release Juno, who had been tied up for insolence. His fall occupied nine days and he landed on the island of *Lemnos*, where he instructed the people in metalwork, building extravagant thrones and apparently animated statues, of which one was *Pandora*, the first

woman on earth. His forge was beneath *Aetna*.
(The very considerable distance between
Lemnos and Aetna no doubt arises from the
mingling of the Greek Hephaestus with the
Roman Vulcan; but any volcano could be a
forge for Vulcan.) Vulcan was deformed and
something of a buffoon. He had numerous
affairs and was married to *Venus*, who was
notoriously faithless to him. His deformity
was ascribed to his having broken a leg in his
fall to Lemnos. He is shown with instruments
such as pincers and hammers. In a celebrated
episode he entrapped Venus and *Mars* in bed
together by entangling them in a net. He gave
Harmonia (Hermione) a present, perhaps a
brooch or necklace, on her marriage to *Cadmus*,
and this was responsible for, or foretold, disasters attending that king's family. His own
children included *Cupid*, *Cecrops* and *Casus*.

(Hesiod *Theogony* 571ff; Homer *Iliad* i 571;
Apollodorus i 3; Pausanias ix 16)

See also *Lemnian*
— *General*

    Chaucer   *House of Fame* 134-9
    Cowley   *The Monopoly* 1
    Davies, Sir J.   *Orchestra* 870-1
    Hood   *Progress of Art* 6
    Jonson   *Execration upon Vulcan* 9-12,
        197ff
    Keats   *Endymion* ii 230-2
        Otho the Great III ii 92-8
    MacNeice   *Birmingham* 7-8
    Milton   *Comus* 653-6
    Rochester   *On Drinking in a Bowl* 1-4
    Shakespeare   *Hamlet* III i 81-2
        Much Ado About Nothing
        I i 155
        Twelfth Night V i 45-7
    Shelley   *Letter to Maria Gisborne* 22-4
        Witch of Atlas 289-94, 641-5
    Spenser   *Faerie Queene* II vii 36, III ix
        19, IV v 3-4
        Muiopotmos 63-4
        Mutability Cantos vii 26
    Swift   *Pethox the Great* 7-8
    Tennyson   *The Princess* iii 55-6
    Wordsworth   *On Seeing a Needlecase in*
        the Form of a Harp 9-13
    Yeats   *A Prayer for My Daughter*
— *and Venus*
    Browning E. B.   *Battle of Marathon* i
        279-83

    Chaucer   *Knight's Tale* 2221-3
— *and Mars*
    Butler S.   *Upon Philip Nye* 97-100
    Chaucer   *Knight's Tale* 2385-92
    Davies, Sir J.   *Orchestra* 491-6
    Drayton   *The Muses' Elizium* vii 123-5
    Jonson   *Sejanus* III i
    Marlowe   *Hero and Leander* i 151-2
— *Pandora and Cadmus*
    Chaucer   *Complaint of Mars* 245ff
    Jonson   *Execration Upon Vulcan* 213-5

Wood-Nymph
See *Dryad*
    Keats   *Endymion* i 939-41
    Milton   *Comus* 120-1
        Paradise Lost v 380-1, ix 386-7
        Paradise Regained ii 294-7
    Shelley   *Prometheus Unbound* iv 508-9
    Spenser   *Faerie Queene* I vi 18

Xanthippe
See *Xantippa*
    Shakespeare   *Taming of the Shrew* I ii
        66-8

Xanthus
See *Scamander*
    Prior   *Ode Inscribed to the Queen* 211-5
    Spenser   *Faerie Queene* III ix 35

Xantippa, Xantippe   *Socrates'* wife, whose
peevishness was legendary. She was said to
have emptied slops on his head and elicited
the philosophical reply that rain follows thunder.

(Jerome *Contra Jovinianum* i 52;
Plato *Phaedo* 60)
See also *Xanthippe*
    Chaucer   *Wife of Bath's Prologue* 727-9

Xenophon   Greek general, philosopher and
historian of c. 427-354 BC. Xenophon began his
military experience in the army of the future
Cyrus II, who fought his brother Artaxerxes
for the succession to *Cyrus the Great*. Cyrus
was defeated at Cunaxa in 401 and Xenophon
supervised the retreat of his large army — as

he himself recorded in *Anabasis*. He knew and was a disciple of *Socrates*, whose influence may be seen in a certain practical and utilitarian stance. Besides *Anabasis* he wrote partly of Cyrus in the moral fiction *Cyropaedia*, and a number of political works and dialogues survive; enough is known of others to establish that Xenophon was an extraordinarily prolific and versatile writer.

Dryden   *Annus Mirabilis* 371-2
MacNeice   *Autumn Journal* viii
            Round the Corner 7-8
Thomson   *Liberty* ii 237-8

Xerxes I   The Persian king who in 480BC assembled a great navy and army to avenge his father *Darius (1)* for the loss of his battle against the Greeks at *Marathon* (490BC). He was himself eventually defeated at *Salamis*. His career and personality are described by *Herodotus*, who includes mention of Xerxes' passion for a Lydian plane tree which he decorated with gold. He was apparently something of an eccentric. He was said to have ordered the *Hellespont* to be given three hundred lashes, and a pair of fetters to be thrown in, when the cable bridges were blown down in a storm. Equally, he had the imagination to replace them with a bridge made of pontoons to support the cables.

(Herodotus vii 31, 35;
Juvenal *Satire* x 198ff)
Browning R.   *Prince Hohenstiel-*
            Schwangau 1028-32
Burns   *A Fragment* 43-6
Butler S.   *Hudibras* II i 845-6
Byron   *Don Juan* i 118
          Isles of Greece 3-4
Cleveland   *Upon the Death of Mr King*
            12
Donne   *Elegy* ix 29-33
Johnson   *Vanity of Human Wishes*
            223-8
Milton   *Paradise Lost* x 306-10
Tennyson   *Exhortation to the Greeks*
            1-2
Thomson   *Liberty* ii 437

Ycarus
See *Icarus*

Ylion
See *Ilium*
   Chaucer   *Legend of Good Women* 935-7
                  Nun's Priest's Tale 4545-51

Ypomedoun
See *Hippomedon*
   Chaucer   *Troilus and Criseyde* v 1502-5

Ysidis
See *Isis*
   Chaucer   *House of Fame* 1843-5

Yole
See *Iole*
   Chaucer   *House of Fame* 397-404

Ypermestre
See *Hypermnestra*
   Chaucer   *Legend of Good Women*
                 267-8, 2563ff, 2656-60,
                 2708-12

Ypocras
See *Hippocrates*
   Chaucer   *Canterbury Tales, Prologue*
                 429-31

Ypolita
See *Hippolyta*
   Chaucer   *Knight's Tale* 860-8

Ysiphile
See *Hypsipyle*
   Chaucer   *Legend of Good Women*
                 263-6, 1465-8, 1542-7,
                 1559-63

Zacynthus   An Ionian island, named after a companion of *Hercules* who, after dying from snake-bite, was buried there. Zacynthus was a meeting point for the troops of *Dion* against *Dionysius II*.
   Wordsworth   *The Prelude* ix 408ff

Zanzis
See *Zeuxis*
   Chaucer   *Physician's Tale* 14-18

Zeno   The Athenian philosopher of the 4th

Century BC who espoused *Cynic* beliefs before developing his own. These became known as *Stoicism* because he taught in the *Stoa Poikile* hall. His philosophy stressed the positive value of virtue, the virtuous mind, as the basis of happiness against which poverty and pain were powerless.

    Moore   *Morality* 31-4

Zenobia   Septimia Zenobia was Princess of Palmyra and second wife of *Odaenathus*, who shared the Roman Emperorship with *Gallienus* in the 3rd Century AD. She possibly had a hand in his murder and on his death called herself Augusta and reigned as Empress in the East, despite the efforts of the true Emperor, Aurelian. She distinguished herself personally in warfare and when defeated by Aurelian in 273 BC she was allowed an honourable and peaceful retirement. The beauty, valour and ruthlessness of Zenobia were much celebrated in the Middle Ages.

See also *Cenobia*
    Tennyson   *The Princess* ii 69-71

Zephyr, Zephyrus   The West Wind, Latin Favonius, son of Astreus and *Aurora*. He married *Chloris* (*Flora*). Zephyr's love for *Hyacinthus* conflicted with that from *Apollo*, and Zephyr killed the youth, but he is himself presented as young, gentle and open, often with flowers.

    (Horace *Odes* i 4; Ovid *Metamorphoses* i 107, x 162ff, *Tristia* I ii 28)

Select allusions.
    Chaucer   *Canterbury Tales, Prologue* 5-7
                     Book of the Duchess 402-9

                   Legend of Good Women 171-4
    Hopkins   *Escorial* 11
    Keats   *Endymion* i 327-31, ii 361-2
    Meredith   *Rape of Aurora*
    Milton   *L'Allegro* 18-19
                 Paradise Lost v 15-17

Zeus
See *Jove*
    Auden   *Under which Lyre* 25
    Bridges   *Prometheus the Fire-Giver* 632-6
    Byron   *Childe Harold* ii 10
    Chaucer   *Troilus and Criseyde* iii 715-20
    Jonson   *And Must I Sing?* 12-15
    Monro H.   *God of the World*
    Tennyson   *Demeter and Persephone* 93-9, 114ff

Zeuxis   A Greek painter of the 4th or 5th Century BC who was noted for the use of shading and subtle variation of colour. His depiction of grapes was said to have deceived birds.

                 (Plato *Protagoras* 318)

See also *Zanzis*
    Cowley   *Ode of Wit* 2
    Skelton   *Garland of Laurel*
    Spenser   *Faerie Queene* III *Prologue* 2

Zoilus   Sophist and grammarian of the 3rd Century BC. As a *Cynic* philosopher he was notorious for his criticisms of *Plato*, *Isocrates* and *Homer*. His work is not extant.

               (Ovid *Remedies of Love* 366)
    Pope   *Essay on Criticism* 464-5
    Spenser   *Sonnet, 'I think in vain'*
    Young   *Night Thoughts* ii

INDEX OF POEMS, POETS
AND REFERENCES

All allusions are listed here under the word which appears in the English text; other allusions to the same subject may be found by the cross-references.

Arnold, Matthew (1822-88)
Alaric at Home 71-2: Capitol
Bacchanalia 24-31: Bacchanals, Iacchus, Maenads
Courage 13-16: Cato (3)
Dover Beach 9ff: Sophocles
Empedocles on Etna I ii 57ff: Pelion, Chiron, Achilles, Peleus; II i 37ff: Typhon, Etna; 74-83: Jove; 84-8: Hebe; 129-33: Phrygian; 132-6: Maeander; 141ff: Marsyas; 201-7: Apollo, Pytho; 327-30: Empedocles; 445ff: Nine; 453-6: Helicon
Epilogue to Laocoon 15-19: Pausanias; 45-8: Galatea, Cyclops
Fragment of an 'Antigone' 39-42: Haemon, Antigone, Creon, Polyneices; 54ff: Aurora, Orion, Euripus, Artemis; 61-4: Parnes, Asopus, Tanagraean; 80-7: Tiresias
Geist's Grave 13-16: Virgilian
To a Gipsy Child 54: Lethaean
Iseult of Brittany 143ff: Caesar G J, Alexander
Isolation 19-24: Luna, Endymion
Lines written on the Seashore 1ff: Naiads
Mycerinus 7-12, 122: Mycerinus
The New Sirens 41-4: Sirens
Palladium 1ff: Palladium
Philomela 5ff: Philomela
The Scholar-Gipsy 206-10: Dido; 232ff: Tyrian
Sonnet to the Hungarian Nation 12-14: Salaminian
The Strayed Reveller 135-42: Tiresias, Asopus; 143-50: Centaurs, Pelion; 182-3: Chorasmian; 217-22: Tiresias; 257-60: Argonauts; 261ff: Silenus; 276-80: Iacchus
Thyrsis 77-80: Thyrsis, Corydon; 82-90: Bion, Proserpine, Orpheus; 91-100: Proserpine; 175ff: Demeter; 182-5: Daphnis, Lityerses
To a Friend 2-4: Homer; 6-8: Epictetus, Arrian, Domitian; 9-14: Sophocles, Colonus
The World and the Quietist 28-32: Darius I (1)
The Youth of Nature 41-7: Tiresias; 75-8: Ida (1 and 2)
Worldly Place 1ff: Aurelius

Auden, Wystan Hugh (1907-1973)
The Age of Anxiety Polyphemus, Orpheus
Anthem for St Cecilia's Day 9-13: Aphrodite
Atlantis 25-30: Thrace; 35-9: Atlantis
Death's Echo 27: Narcissus
Epistle to a Godson 32-6: Thucydides
Fall of Rome 13-16: Cato (2)
For the Time Being Caesar
Homage to Clio 17-18: Aphrodite, Artemis; 66-8: Clio
The Horatians 31-3: Maecenas; 53ff: Flaccus, Pindar; 70-1: Regulus
In Memory of Sigmund Freud 111-2: Eros, Aphrodite
An Island Cemetery 13-16: Alexander
Kairos and Logos 1ff: Caesar
Lakes 25-7: Poseidon
Letter to Lord Byron 161-3: Parnassus; 792-3: Minos
Many Happy Returns 53-6: Saturnalia
Moon Landing 22-4: Hector
New Year Letter Minotaur, Caesars, Plato, Hesperides
Ode to Terminus 47ff: Terminus
Orpheus 1-4: Orpheus
Plains 25-8: Ovid; 64: Tarquin (Sextus)
Secondary Epic 47ff: Virgil, Anchises, Romulus, Augustus
The Shield of Achilles 65-72: Hephaestus, Thetis, Achilles
The Sphinx 1-4: Sphinx
Under Sirius 8-9: Sybil
Under Which Lyre 25: Zeus; 67-72: Apollo, Hermes
Whitsunday in Kirchstetten 19-21: Tiberius

Belloc, Hilaire (1870-1954)
But O Not Lovely Helen 1ff: Helen, Priam, Hector
The Modern Traveller xiv: Regulus
In Praise of Wine 8-13: Bacchus, 37-44: Aufidus, Pelasgian, Tyrrhenian; 56ff: Bacchus, Atlas; 120-4: Bacchus, Ariadne; 135-8: Lenaean; (ii) 15-17: Homer, Odysseus
Of Meadows Drowsy 1ff: Trinacrian, Persephone, Orpheus

To Dives 10ff: Charon
When you to Acheron's Ugly Water Come
  1ff: Acheron

Blake, William (1757-1827)
Auguries of Innocence 97-100: Caesar
Imitation of Spenser 1ff: Apollo, Pan; 15-18:
  Midas; 19ff: Mercurius; 44ff: Pallas,
  Minerva
King Edward III vi 1ff: Brutus (1), Troy;
  55-60: Albion
Mock on, Mock On 9-12: Democritus
The Muses 1ff: Nine

Bridges, Robert (1844-1930)
Demeter 28ff: Pluto, Demeter, Persephone,
  Enna; 328-35: Oceanides, Nereids,
  Persephone; 489-92: Demeter, Daedalus,
  Hephaestus; 563-5: Demeter, Rhea; 575:
  Hermes, Argus, Maia (1); 713-4: Aidoneus;
  763ff: Keleos, Demeter, Demophoon (2);
  873ff: Pluto, Persephone, Demeter
The Growth of Love 31: Phidian; 53: Hector
Ode IV 3: Paphian
Prometheus the Firegiver 90-7: Prometheus,
  Inachus; 206-11: Rhea, Chronos, Ida (1);
  Jupiter; 234-9: Selene, Hyperion; 507-8:
  Prometheus; 562-6: Fates; 632-6:
  Chronos, Iapetus, Hyperion, Thea, Rhea,
  Zeus, Titans; 722-7: Salmoneus, Aeolus;
  931-6: Athamas, Ino; 941-3: Poseidon,
  Pasiphae; 944ff: Actaeon, Artemis; 954-8:
  Lycaon; 961: Cadmus; 962-5: Niobe,
  Leto; 968-72: Sipylus, Achelous, Niobe;
  1163-9: Prometheus
Septuagesima 2-5: Cyclops
A Water-Party 7ff: Narcissus, Hamadryads
Wintry Delights 254ff: Hippocrates

Brooke, Rupert (1887-1915)
Fragments Achilles, Hector, Priam
The Goddess in the Wood 1ff: Venus
Hauntings 9-11: Lethean
It's Not Going to Happen Again 9-10: Styx;
  11-14: Cleopatra, Paris, Helen, Antony
Menelaus and Helen 1ff: Menelaus, Helen,
  Paris
The Old Vicarage, Grantchester 38-42: Faun,
  Naid, Satyr

Browning, Elizabeth Barrett (1806-61)
Aurora Leigh ii 779-82: Iphigenia; v 139-41:

Agamemnon; 169-70: Athos; 399-406:
  Pygmalion; vii 827ff: Jove, Io
The Battle of Marathon 15-20: Hippias,
  Pisistratus, Aeneas, Cytherea, Priam; 35-6:
  Aristides; 142-6: Miltiades; 279-83:
  Venus, Vulcan; 425: Nestor, Pylian;
  668-9: Pan; 670-1: Pluto; 865-71:
  Cleones, Aratus, Sthenelus; 890-5: Hector,
  Helen, Pelides, Andromache; 900-4:
  Priam, Aeneas, Ascanius, Anchises; 962-4:
  Marathonian, Darius; 1412ff: Hippias,
  Datis; 1437ff: Cynegirus
Calls on the Heart iv: Proserpina
Casa Guidi Windows i 731-2: Homer; ii 87-90:
  Caesars, Rubicon
The Claim 3: Jason
Crowned and Buried 19-20: Orestes, Electra
The Dead Pan 1: Hellas, Pan; 6: Naiads; 7:
  Dryads; 8: Oreads; 10: Jove; 11: Juno; 12:
  Apollo, Niobe; 14: Bacchus, Maenads; 15:
  Neptune, Plato; 16: Aphrodite; 17: Loves;
  18: Hermes; 19: Cybele; 29: Dodona; 30:
  Pythia
Flush or Faunus 5ff: Faunus, Satyr, Pan,
  Arcadian
The Fourfold Aspect 37-46: Helen, Achilles,
  Ulysses; 49-50: Admetus
An Island 25: Hellas; 26-7: Pindar, Aeschylus,
  Homer, Meles, Plato
The Lost Bower 33: Dryad; 36: Naiad; 37:
  Pan, Faunus; 56: Oedipus, Colonus
Man and Nature 12-13: Ocean
A Musical Instrument 4: Pan
Portuguese Sonnets 1: Theocritus; 5: Electra;
  11: Aornus; 19: Pindar, Muses
Queen Anelida 6: Hippolyte, Theseus; 8: Mars,
  June, Thebes, Argos; 9: Parthenopaeus,
  Tydeus, Hippomedon, Amphiareus,
  Capaneus, Adrastus, Thebes, Eteocles,
  Polyneices, Seven Against Thebes; 10:
  Creon, Thebes; 12: Lucretia, Penelope
The Soul's Travelling 159-60: Nereids
A Vision of Poets 40-3: Dryad; 204-7: Danae;
  295-7: Homer; 301-9: Aeschylus,
  Euripides, Sophocles; 310-21: Hesiod,
  Pindar, Sappho; 322-33: Theocritus,
  Aristophanes, Virgil; 334-42: Lucretius
Wine of Cyprus 1: Bacchus; 7: Rhea, Paphia,
  Hymettus; 8: Ulysses; 11: Aeschylus,
  Sophocles; 12: Euripides, Theocritus, Bion,
  Pindar; 18: Cassandra, Prometheus

Browning, Robert (1812-89)
Aeschylus's Soliloquy 76-8: Hesperian;
84-90: Hymettus, Ilissus
Apollo and the Fates 11-13: Clotho; 21-5:
Atropos; 52-4: Fates; 156-7: Dionysus,
Semele
Aristophanes' Apology 75 ff: Athenai, Peiraius,
Lysander; 111-2: Phidias; 115-7: Hellas,
Sparta; 120-2: Aeschylus, Sophocles,
Euripides; 176-80: Phrynichus; 193-4:
Admetus, Alcestis; 283-6, 301-3: Euripides;
314-6: Iphigenia, Euripides; 314-8:
Agathon; 419-24: Phaedra; 428-30:
Euripides; 447-51: Aristeides, Miltiades;
490-2: Alcamenes; 511-3: Hercules;
534-8: Hercules; 540-4: Hercules, Megara,
Lukos; 600 ff: Aristophanes; 813-5:
Typhon; 948-9: Melanthius; 1449-55:
Aristophanes; 1677-8: Euripides; 2039-44:
Protagoras; 2077-9: Anaxagoras; 202-4:
Sophist; 3500-6: Sophocles
Artemis Prologises 1-4: Artemis, Hera; 10-12,
13-14: Artemis, Hippolytus, Asclepius;
22-8: Phaedra, Hippolytus, Hippolyta;
35-8, 51 ff: Hippolytus, Poseidon, Theseus;
101-3: Asclepius, Hippolytus; 113-7:
Asclepios, Hippolytus
Balaustion's Adventure 7-10: Nikias; 3709:
Aeschylus, Sophocles, Euripides; 75-7:
Salamis; 77, 130-1: Aeschylus; 132-6:
Euripides, Salamis; 161-3: Bacchus; 201-4:
Socrates, Euripides; 298-304: Euripides;
337-8, 348-9: Bacchaian; 372-6:
Asklepios, Cyclops; 569-72: Alcestis;
1054-9: Hercules; 1076-7: Hercules;
1197-9: Hercules; 1269-72: Faun;
2598-602: Admetus, Alcestis; 2668-71:
Euripides
Bishop Bloughram's Apology 182-3: Euripides
The Bishop Orders His Tomb 76-8: Tully
Christmas Eve 673-6: Scamander; 749-53:
Colossus
Cleon 138-45: Homer, Terpander, Phidias
Clive 112-3: Thyrsis, Chloe
The Dance of Death 47-50: Leander, Hero;
88-91: Pygmalion
A Death in the Desert 279-86: Prometheus,
Aeschylus
Development 54-8: Homer
Echetlos 1-3: Marathon; 25-7: Echetlos;
28-9: Miltiades, Themistocles
Fifine at the Fair 210: Helen, Venus; 218 ff:

Cleopatra; 305-12: Helen; 483: Solon;
1294 ff: Arion
Filippo Baldinucci 397-400: Jupiter, Leda,
Ganymede, Antiope
Imperante Augusto Nato Est 23-32: Octavius;
44-6: Octavius; 154-6: Jupiter, Saturn
Ixion 1-4: Ixion; 28-9: Sisiphus, Tantalus;
37: Ixion; 80-1: Ixion
Old Pictures in Florence 270-3: Chimera
Pan and Luna 48, 65-9: Pan, Luna; 57-9:
Amphitrite; 81-3, 89: Pan, Luna
Paracelsus i 417-9: Stagyrite; v 123-5: Titans;
126-8: Phaeton; 177-80: Galen
Pauline 333-5: Hermes, Proserpine; 435-6:
Plato; 656-60: Andromeda; 919-21:
Lotos Eaters; 963-5: Antigone
Pheidippides 16-17: Pheidippides; 65-9, 72-3:
Pheidippides, Pan; 107 ff: Pheidippides
Pietro of Abano 259-60: Tantalus; 381:
Tithon; 434-5: Geryon
Popularity 26-30: Tyrian, Astarte
Prince Hohenstiel-Schwangau 9 ff: Sphinx,
Lais; 715-8: Atlas, Hercules; 1028-32:
Xerxes; 2080-1: Homer; 1995 ff:
Clitumnian; 2136-40: Clitumnus
The Ring and the Book i 79: Horace; 219-23:
Solon, Romulus; 232-7: Aelian; 868:
Aeacus; 1156-7: Ovidian, Ciceronian; ii
442: Plutus; 1003-4: Helen; 1005-7: Paris;
1167-8: Gordian; 1221-2: Ovid; 1245:
Pontifex Maximus; 1269-70: Canidian;
iii 382-6: Hesperian, Hercules; v 627-9:
Caligula; 669-72: Neaera, Thyrsis; vi
387-8: Catullus; 582: Philomel; 960-3:
Plato, Cephisian; 1168-70: Parian; viii
487-8: Aristotle; 511-6: Aelian; 897-8:
Priam, Hera; 970-1: Ovid; 1227-31:
Galba (2), Horace; ix 187-90: Phrynean,
Lucretia, Tarquin; 225-7: Teian; 400-2:
Lernaean; 527 ff: Venus, Cupid, Moschus;
547-50: Ulysses; 830-3: Nero; 844-5:
Troy; 884-6: Tacitus; 966-70: Hesione;
987-8: Omphale; 1345-8: Aristaeus;
1389-91: Homer; 1541: Phoebus; 1570-2:
Socrates; xi 507: Gorgon, Minerva;
1973-4: Pan
Sordello i 65-8: Aeschylus, Marathon; 927-32:
Apollo; ii 210-11: Perseus, Andromeda;
587-92: Brennus, Manlius; iii 939-42:
Hercules; 950-4: Aeschylus, Marathon,
Plataea, Salamis; v 81-4: Croesus, Pythian;
555-6: Saturn, Chaos

Demetrius I; 267ff: Achilles, Peleus,
Polixena, Priam, Hector; 268-9: Pactolus;
270-2: Sperchius; ii 70-2: Remus; 80-4:
Romulus, Remus; 208-10: Cato (3); II i
103-4: Penates; 110: Brennus; ii 21-2:
Pelides
Don Juan i 6: Horace; 42: Ovid, Anacreon,
Catullus, Sappho, Longinus (2), Virgil;
43: Lucretius (2), Juvenal, Martial; 86:
Medea; 116: Plato; 118: Xerxes; 120:
Aristotle; 127: Prometheus; 159: Achates;
201: Aristotle; ii 64: Atropos; 101: Charon;
142: Aurora; 155: Minotaur, Pasiphae;
170: Venus, Ceres, Bacchus; 205: Sappho;
207: Epicurus, Aristippus; iii 23: Ulysses,
Argus (3); 55: Greece; 74: Psyche; 98:
Horace, Homer; 109: Nero; iv 4: Thetis,
Achilles; 72: Cyclades; v 1: Venus; 6:
Parcae; 61: Semiramis; 96: Venus; vi 4:
Antony; 7: Cato (3); 111: Sallust, Catiline;
vii 79: Homer; 82: Leonidas; 1: Mars,
Bellona; 61: Sylla; 84: Achilles; ix 8:
Epaminondas; x 78: Phaethon; xi 58:
Sporus; xii 19: Plutarch; 78: Marius; xiii
12: Oedipus, Sphinx; 99: Styx; 105:
Dolon; xiv 1: Saturn; 39: Camilla; 72:
Homer, Helen, Menelaus, Paris; 73: Tiresias;
xv 11: Alcibiades; 32: Aristotle; 49:
Brutus (3), Tiberius, Junia; 53: Antony,
Caesar; 66: Lucullus; 73: Sunium,
Hymettus, Diogenes; 85: Socrates; 97:
Minerva; xvi 10: Tyrian; 11: Nessus; 43:
Diogenes; 74: Gordian Knot; 86: Bacchus,
Ceres, Venus
The Dream 12-13: Sibyl
English Bards and Scottish Reviewers 189-93:
Homer, Mars; 265-7: Parnassus Apollo;
287-8: Catullus; 410-14: Sisyphus; 417-21:
Alcaeus; 489ff: Danae; 516-17: Thalia;
564-5: Roscius; 642-3: Petronius; 883-7:
Aonian; 1007-8: Cassandra; 1027-30:
Phidian
Fill the Goblet Again 25-7: Pandora
The Giaour 895-8: Gorgon
Hints from Horace 35: Lethe; 130-1:
Melpomene, Thalia; 347-8: Euphrosyne;
463-4: Democritus; 524-30: Delphi,
Parnassus; 662-6: Orpheus; 667-8:
Amphion; 679-80: Homer; 681-4:
Tyrtaeus; 734-6: Midas; 823ff: Cato (3)
The First Kiss of Love 9-12: Apollo, Nine
The Irish Avatar 77-8: Vitellius

The Island i 83-4: Saturnalia; ii 131-2:
Aphrodite; 191: Nero; 318-21: Caesar,
Cleopatra; 466: Neptune; iii 47-50:
Hercules; iv 259-60: Thermopylae
The Isles of Greece 1: Sappho; 3-4: Marathon,
Salamis, Xerxes; 7: Thermopylae; 10:
Cadmus; 11: Anacreon, Polycrates; 12:
Chersonese, Miltiades
Love's Last Adieu 37-8: Astraea
Manfred II ii 140-1: Croesus; iii 98-102:
Astarte; III iv 10: Coliseum; 29-30:
Caesar, Augustan
Marino Faliero II i 390-1: Alcides; III ii 237-8:
Hydra; 454-5: Gracchus; V i 440-1:
Caligula
Mazeppa 153-4: Thyrsis
An Occasional Prologue 11-13: Roscii
On the Death of Mr Fox 12-16: Atlas,
Hercules
On Hearing that Lady Byron was Ill 35-7:
Clytemnestra; 52-3: Janus
Prometheus 1-7, 26-30, 35, 45-7: Prometheus
The Prophecy of Dante i 104-6: Marius,
Minturnae; ii 108-9: Cambyses; iii 96-7:
Demosthenes; iv 11-16: Prometheus; 41-3:
Apelles, Phidias
Sardanapalus I ii 181: Semiramis; III i 218f:
Alcides, Omphale
The Siege of Corinth 58ff: Timoleon; 225-8:
Helen
To Miss M.S.G. 5-6: Morpheus
To Romance 19-20: Pylades; 49-54: nymphs
The Vision of Judgment 44: Caesar; 46:
Apicius; 79: Cerberus
The Waltz 1-6: Terpsichore; 89-92: Cleopatra
Werner III i 288-9: Sesostris
Written after Swimming from Sestos 1ff:
Leander, Hero, Hellespont

Campbell, Thomas (1777-1844)
Pleasures of Hope i: Plato, Socrates, Nine,
Harmonia, Pythia, Delphian, Hybla,
Scythian, Scipio (1), Tully, Brutus (3);
ii: Idalian, Peace, Syren, Caesar
Song of the Greeks 43-4: Nine, Helicon

Campion, Thomas (d.1619)
Every Dame Affects Good Fortune 13-16:
Astraea
The Peaceful Western Wind 17: Saturn, Cupid
To His Sweet Lute, Apollo 1ff: Apollo,
Midas, Pan

Carew, Thomas (1598-1639)
Coelum Britannicum 587-90: Fortune,
Astraea; 797-800: Lysimachus
The Comparison 19: Leda
A Cruel Mistress 8ff: Vesta
An Elegy on the Death of Dr John Donne
37ff: Orpheus; 65-7: Metamorphoses
A Fly that Flew 13-16: Phaethon
Mediocrity in Love 7-9: Danae
No More, Blind God 1-3: Cupid
Obsequies to a Lady 25-8: Apelles
A Rapture 6-9: Colossus; 35-9: Venus; 81-4:
Danae; 115-8: Lucrece, Lais; 125-30:
Penelope; 130-4: Daphne
To the Countess of Anglesey 7-8: Aeson
To My Friend G.N. 57-60: Amalthea; 61-2:
Ceres; 63-4: Bacchus; 93-4: Vertumnus,
Pomona; 97ff: Bacchus, Ceres
To the Painter 39-42: Pygmalion
Upon a Mole 2-4: Hybla
Upon Mr W. Montague 21-2: Halcion; 25-6:
Boreas
Upon my Lord Chief Justice 15ff: Astraea,
Golden Age
Upon the Sickness of E.S. 17-22: Dian

Chapman, George (1559?-1634?)
Amorous Contention of Phillis and Flora 1:
Tellus; 63: Aeacides; 83: Philomel; 87:
Silenus
Andromeda Liberata Cepheus, Andromeda,
Alcyone, Perseus, Medusa, Enyos, Mercury,
Minerva
Bussy d'Ambois I i 6-9: Colossus; 65-70:
Camillus, Themistocles; 71-5: Epaminondas;
II i 54-9: Hector; IV i 102-8: Chimera,
Peleus, Augean stable; V ii 53-5: Bootes
Epicedium Echidna, Marcellus, Sylla
Hero and Leander (for *Sestiads* i-ii see
Marlowe) iv: Leucote, Dapsilis, Arachne;
v: Hymen, Euchasis; vi: Leucote, Boreas,
Althea, Fates, Lachesis
Hymn to Hymen Hymen
On Sejanus Castalian
Ovid's Banquet of Sense Niobe, Phaethon,
Paris, Cephalus, Delphos, Nisus, Alcides,
Saturnalia
Shadow of Night Gorgon, Calydonian boar,
Amalthea, Argonauts, Promethean,
Orpheus, Saturn, Hercules, Somnus,
Themis, Hyperion, Cytheron, Democrates,
Gorgonean, Cynthia, Hecate, Hesiod,
Euthimya, Alpheus, Lucifera, Chersiphrone,
Herostratus
Tears of Peace Euripus
Vouchsafe, Great Treasurer 8-10: Homer

Chatterton, Thomas (1752-1779)
English Metamorphosis 1-4: Scythians
Fragment 3-4: Heliconian
Resignation 1-2: Parthian
To Mrs Heywood 1-4: Dido

Chaucer, Geoffrey (c1340-1400)
(Line number references are to *The Complete
Works of Geoffrey Chaucer*, ed. F. N. Robin-
son 1957)
Anelida and Arcite 1-6: Mars, Trace, Bellona,
Pallas; 15-20: Polymya, Parnaso, Elycon,
Cirrea; 21: Stace, Corynne; 22-31: Theseus,
Cither, Mars; 36-42: Ipolita; 50-3: Mars,
Juno; 57-63: Amphiorax, Tydeus,
Ipomedon, Parthonope, Campaneus,
Adrastus, Polyneices, Eteocles; 64-6:
Creon; 81-2: Lucresse, Penelope
The Book of the Duchess 70-5: Seys; 107-14:
Alcyone, Juno; 136-46: Morpheus, Seys,
Alcyone; 155-77: Morpheus; 203-14:
Seys, Alcyone; 278-88: Macrobius,
Scipioun; 326-34: Ector, Priamus, Achilles,
Lamedon, Medea, Jason, Paris; 365-8:
Octavian; 402-9: Flora, Zephirus; 511-3:
Pan; 568-73: Ovyde, Orpheus, Dedalus,
Ipocras, Galen; 587-90: Sesiphus; 618-23,
628-34: Fortune; 662-4: Athalus; 666-9:
Pithagores; 709: Tantale; 715-9: Socrates;
725-31: Medea, Jasoun, Phyllis,
Demophoun; 731-6: Dydo, Ecquo,
Narcisus; 981-4: Phoenix; 1055-75:
Alcibiades, Ercules, Alysaunder, Achilles,
Ector, Antylegyus, Polixena, Minerva,
Dares, Phrygius; 1080-2: Penelopee;
1080-4: Lucrece, Livius; 1114-20:
Anthenor; 1167-9: Pictagoras; 1244-9:
Cassandra

(Canterbury Tales)
General Prologue 5-7: Zephirus; 293-6:
Aristotle; 336-8: Epicurus; 429-31:
Esculapius, Deyscorides, Ypocras, Rufus;
741-2: Plato
Canon Yeoman's Tale 972-5: Nineveh, Rome,
Alisaundre, Troy

Clerk's Tale 1189-90: Ekko
Franklin's Tale and Prologue 721: Pernaso;
722: Scithero; 765-6: Cupid; 944-52: Ekko,
Narcisus; 1031-7: Apollo; 1045-8: Lucina,
Neptunus; 1065-70: Lucina, Phoebus;
1072-6: Lucina, Proserpina, Pluto;
1077: Phoebus, Delphos; 1245-7: Phoebus;
1355-6: Fortune; 1368: Thirty Tyrants,
Pheidon; 1379: Mecene, Lacadeomye;
1385-94: Aristoclides; 1399-1404:
Hasdrubal; 1405-8: Lucresse, Tarquin
(Sextus); 1409-11: Milesie; 1414-8:
Habradate; 1423-7: Democion; 1422-30:
Cedasus; 1431-3: Nichanore; 1437-8:
Niceratus; 1439-41: Alcibiades; 1442-4:
Alceste, Penelopee, Homer; 1445-7:
Laodomya, Proteselaus; 1448-50: Brutus,
Porcia; 1451-2: Artemesia; 1454-5: Teuta
The Friar's Tale 1517-20: Virgil
The Knight's Tale 860-8: Theseus, Amazons,
Scithia, Ypolita; 925-6: Fortune; 928-30:
Clemence; 931-3: Cappaneus, Evadne;
938-47: Creon; 959-64: Creon, Theseus;
965-8, 975-80: Theseus, Mars, Minotaur;
998-1102: Venus; 1192-1200: Perotheus;
1329-31: Juno, Thebes; 1385-90:
Mercurie, Argus; 1491-6: Phoebus;
1542-8: Juno, Cadmus, Amphion, Thebes;
1138-44: Thrace; 1679-82: Theseus, Mars,
Diana; 1880: Thebes; 1902-13: Theseus,
Venus, Mars, Diane; 1936-46: Venus,
Citheroun, Narcissus, Hercules, Medea,
Circes, Turnus, Croesus; 1955-62: Venus;
1963-6: Cupido; 1970-5, 1982-4: Mars;
2027-30: Damocles; 2031-5: Julius, Nero,
Antonius; 2041-8: Mars; 2051-72: Diane;
2056-9: Calistopee; 2062-4: Dane;
2065-8: Attheon; 2069-72: Atthalante,
Meleager; 2075-85: Diana; 2081-2: Pluto;
2083-5: Lucina; 2129-47: Lycurgeus;
2214-6: Citherea; 2221-3: Venus,
Vulcanus, Citheron; 2393-4: Stace; 2297-
2303: Diana, Attheon; 2346-7: Diane;
2373-4: Mars; 2385-92: Mars, Venus,
Vulcanus; 2443, 2454-69: Saturneus;
2626-33: Galgopheye; 2684-8: Pluto;
2830-3: Ector; 2905-6: Egeus; 3035-40:
Jupiter
The Manciple's Tale 105-10: Phebus, Phitoun;
113-8: Phebus, Amphioun; 125-9, 130-2:
Phebus; 207-10: Plato; 226-34: Alisaundre;
257-68, 294-7: Phebus

The Man of Law's Tale (Introduction) 25-8:
Seneca; 53-5: Ovide; 64: Dido; 65: Phillis,
Demophoon; 68-9: Leandre, Erro, Naxos;
72-4: Medea, Jason; 77-80: Canacee; 91-3:
Pierides, Muses, Metamorphosios
(The Tale) 197-202: Ector, Achilles,
Pompei, Julius, Thebes, Hercules, Turnus,
Socrates; 288-93: Pirrus, Ilion, Thebes,
Hanybal; 368-9: Semyrame; 400-3: Julius,
Lucan
The Merchant's Tale 1375-6: Senek; 1377:
Catoun; 1715-7: Orpheus, Amphioun;
1718-21: Theodamus; 1722-3: Bacus,
Venus; 2034-41: Priapus, Pluto, Proserpina;
2111-5: Argus; 2125-31: Ovyde, Pyramus,
Tesbee; 2225-36: Pluto; Proserpina;
2232-3: Claudyan
The Miller's Tale 3208: Almageste; 3227-8:
Catoun
The Monk's Tale 2098ff, 3324: Hercules;
3258-92: Centauros, Arpies, Cerberus,
(Nemean) lion; 3293-3300: Busirus,
Diomedes, Hydra, Achelous, Cacus,
Antheus, (Erymanthean) boar; 3309-24:
Dianira, Nessus; 3333-40: Babiloigne;
3437-41, 3501ff, 3517-22, 3541-8:
Cenobia; 3438: Palmyra; 3501-9: Odenake;
3517-22, 3541-8: Aurelian; 3653-7:
Suetonius, Nero; 3705-10: Seneca; 3786-
3810: Antiochus; 3837-50: Alisandre;
3837-40: Darius (I); 3846-7: Philip (II);
3869-74: Caesar, Pompeus, Thessaly;
3887-900: Brutus (3), Cassius, Julius;
3909-11: Lucan, Swetoun, Valerie;
3917-24: Cresus, Cirrus; 3937-50: Jupiter,
Phebus, Cresus
The Nun's Priest's Tale 4130-1, 4163-6:
Catoun; 4133-6: Cipioun, Macrobius;
4328-30: Cresus; 4331-8: Andromacha,
Ector, Achilles; 4418-9: Synon; 4459-62:
Phisiologus; 4531-6: Venus; 4545-51:
Ylion, Pirrus, Priam, Eneydos; 4552-5:
Hasdrubal; 4559-63: Nero
The Pardoner's Tale 492-5: Senec; 579-81:
Attila
The Physician's Tale 1-4: Livius, Virginius;
7-10: Virginia; 14-18: Virginia, Pygmalion,
Zanzis, Apelles; 36-7: Phebus; 49-51:
Virginia, Pallas; 58-60: Bacus, Venus;
107-10: Virginia; 126-9: Apius; 140-1:
Claudius; 178-85: Marcus Claudius,
Virginius, Apius, Virginia; 207ff: Virginia;

267-73: Apius, Claudius
The Second Nun's Prologue and Tale
(**Prologue**) 92-3, 99-101: Cecile;
(**Tale**) 172-3: Via Appia
The Squire's Tale 47: Idus; 48: Phebus; 195:
Poilleys; 204-9: Pegasee, Synon; 232-4:
Aristotle; 236-40: Thelophus, Achilles;
263-5: Phebus; 305-7: Troie; 547-84:
Jason, Paris
The Summoner's Tale 2043-4: Cambyses;
2079-82: Cirus, Babiloigne
The Wife of Bath's Prologue and Tale
(**Prologue**) 180-3: Ptholomee, Almageste;
324-7, 357-60: Argus; 460-3: Metellius;
464, 707-10: Venus; 724-6: Hercules,
Dianyre; 727-9: Socrates, Xantippa;
733-6: Pasiphae; 737-9: Clitermystra;
740-6: Amphiorax, Eriphilem; 757-61:
Latumyus
(**Tale**) 952-77: Myda, Ovyde; 981-2:
Ovyde; 1165-70: Valerius, Tullus Hostilius,
Senek, Boece; 1183-4: Senec; 1192-4:
Juvenal

The Complaint of Mars 24-8: Mars, Venus,
Phebus; 29-35: Mars, Venus; 75-7, 113-4:
Cilenios, Venus, Phebus; 215-7ff: Vulcan,
Harmonia
Complaint Unto Pity 91-5: Herines
The Former Age 33-5: Diogenes; 56-8:
Jupiter, Golden Age
Fortune 17-19: Socrates
The House of Fame (**Book I**) 66-76:
Morpheus, Lete, Cymerie; 103-6: Cresus;
134-9: Venus, Cupid, Vulcan; 143-8:
Aeneas, Troy, Lavyne; 151-6: Troy, Synon;
158-61: Ilion, Priam, Polites, Pirrus;
162-5: Aeneas, Venus; 166-9: Aeneas,
Anchises; 174-88: Aeneas, Creusa, Iulo,
Ascanius; 198-208: Juno, Aeolus; 212-8:
Venus, Aeneas; 234-44: Eneas, Dido;
293-9, 375-82: Dido, Virgile, Eneydos,
Ovyde; 388-94: Demophon, Phyllis;
396-404: Breseyda, Achilles, Paris, Oenone,
Jason, Isiphile, Medea, Ercules, Dyanira,
Yole; 405-20: Theseus, Adriane, Phedra;
427-32: Eneas, Mercurie, Dido; 439-46:
Anchises, Eneas, Palinurus, Dido,
Deiphebus; 451-8: Eneas, Latyne, Turnus,
Lavinia; 461-5: Eneas, Juno, Jupiter, Venus
(**Book II**) 514-17: Scipioun, Turnus;
518-22: Cipris, Parnaso, Elicon; 589-91:

Romulus, Ganymede, Jupiter; 614-19:
Cupido, Venus; 666-8: Cupido; 753-9:
Aristotle, Platon; 914-24: Alixandre,
Scipio, Dedalus, Ykarus; 929-31: Plato;
994-1008: Raven, Bere, Castor, Pollux,
Delphyn, Pleiades (**Book III**) 1094ff:
Apollo; 1201-7: Orpheus, Orion, Eacides,
Chiron; 1229-32: Marcia, Apollo; 1243-4:
Messenus, Virgilius; 1246: Theodomas;
1271-2: Medea, Circes, Calipsa; 1399-
1404: Caliope, Muses; 1412-4: Alexander,
Hercules; 1446: Martes; 1448-50: Saturne;
1456-63: Stace, Achilles; 1464-6: Omer;
1467: Dares; 1475-80: Omer; 1481-5:
Virgile, Aeneas; 1486-9: Venus, Ovide;
1497-1502: Lucan, Julius, Pompe;
1509-12: Claudian, Pluto, Proserpyne;
1571ff, 1586-90: Eolus; 1596-7: Triton;
1636ff: Aeolus; 1678ff: Aeolus; 1843-5:
Ysidis, Herostratus; 1920-22: Dedaly;
2117-20: Aeolus
The Legend of Good Women **Prologue** 110-4:
Agenor, Europa; 171-4: Zephyrus, Flora;
213-9: Cupid, Alceste; 226ff: Cupid
Balade 252-3: Penelopee, Marcia Catoun;
256-60: Lavyne, Lucresse, Polixene,
Cleopatre; 261: Tisbe; 263-66: Hero, Dido,
Laudomia, Phillis, Demophoun, Canace,
Ysiphile, Jasoun; 267-8: Ypermystre,
Adriane; 305-6: Ovyde; 313: Cupid,
Venus; 510ff: Alceste, Ercules, Agaton
Cleopatra 580-2: Tholome, Cleopatra;
588ff: Antonius, Cesar, Octavia; 610-4:
Antonius; 614: Cleopatra; 624-5: Octavyan,
Anthony; 663ff: Cleopatra **Thisbe** 706-8:
Babiloigne, Semyramus; 724ff: Naso,
Piramus, Tysbe; 774-5: Aurora; 778ff:
Piramus, Thisbe, Nynus; 805ff: Thisbe;
823ff: Piramus; 862-8, 896ff: Thisbe
Dido 924-7: Virgil, Mantuan; 928-9:
Naso, Eneydos; 930-3: Troye, Synoun,
Mynerve; 935-7: Ylion; 940-2: Enyos,
Venus, Ascanius; 943-7: Creusa, Anchises;
964-6: Achates; 998-1000: Venus; 1004-7:
Dido, Sytheo; 1017-21: Dido, Aeneas,
Venus; 1023-6: Eneas, Achates; 1061-5:
Dido, Eneas; 1086: Venus, Anchises, Eneas;
1140-4: Cupido, Dido, Eneas; 1168ff:
Dido, Anne; 1198-1201: Dido **Hypsipyle**
1368-70: Jasoun; 1396-1402: Tessalie,
Pelleus, Eson, Jason; 1425-34: Colcos,
Jason, Oetes; 1453-7: Argus, Jason,

Ercules, Agaunautycon; 1465-8: Ysiphele,
Thoas, Ovyde; 1542-7: Jason, Ercules,
Ysiphele; 1559-63: Jason, Ysiphele; 1580-1:
Jason; 1589ff: Jason, Oetes; 1598-1601:
Jason, Medea, Oetes; 1634-6: Jason,
Medea; 1651ff, 1678-9: Jason, Ovyde
Lucrece 1680-3: Tarquinius, Ovyde,
Titus Livius; 1686: Lucresse; 1694-1702:
Ardea, Tarquinius; 1736-42: Lucresse,
Colatyn; 1789-93: Tarquinius, Lucresse;
1853-60: Lucresse; 1861-5: Lucresse,
Brutus, Tarquin **Ariadne** 1886-90:
Mynos, Theseus; 1894-8: Mynos,
Androgeus; 1907-16: Nysus, Mynos,
Scylla (2); 1928ff: Mynos, Minotaur;
1943-7: Egeus, Theseus; 1968-72: Theseus,
Adryane, Phedra; 1985ff: Theseus, Phedra;
2074ff: Theseus, Phedra, Adryane; 2144-8:
Theseus, Mynotaur, Adryane; 2155-60:
Ennopye, Theseus, Adryane; 2170-6:
Adryane, Phedra, Theseus; 2218-20: Naso
Philomela 2223-4: Taurus; 2228ff: Tereus;
2244-50: Trace, Marte, Pandion, Progne,
Imeneus, Juno; 2252: Furies; 2288-94:
Tereus, Philomela; 2309ff: Tereus,
Philomela; 2342ff: Tereus, Philomela,
Progne; 2377: Bacus **Phyllis** 2398-400:
Demophon, Theseus; 2414ff: Demophon,
Neptune, Thetis, Triton, Phyllis; 2424-6:
Phyllis, Ligurges; 2441ff: Demophon,
Theseus, Adryane; 2544-8: Phyllis,
Theseus, Demophon **Hypermestra**
2562ff: Danao, Lyno, Egiste, Ypermystra;
2651-60: Egiste, Ypermystra, Lyno;
2680-1: Zephyrus; 2708ff: Lyno,
Ypermystre
Lenvoy de Chaucer a Scogan 11-12: Venus
The Parliament of Fowls 9ff: Scipioun,
Massynisse, Affrycan; 59-63: Music of the
Spheres; 110-11: Macrobye; 113-6:
Cytherea; 253-9: Priapus; 260-70: Venus;
274-7: Bachus, Ceres, Cypride; 281-4:
Dyane; 286-7: Calyxte, Athalante; 288-94:
Semyramis, Hercules, Biblis, Dido, Thisbe,
Piramus, Paris, Achilles, Cleopatre, Troylus,
Silla, Romulus, Rhea Silvia; 351: Venus;
379-81: Nature; 652: Venus, Cupide
Troilus and Criseyde **(Book I)** 1-2: Troilus,
Priamus; 6-7: Thesiphone; 61-3: Eleyne,
Paris; 56-63: Grekes, Troie; 70: Apollo,
Delphicus; 113: Ector; 145-7: Troian,
Omer, Dares, Dite; 153-4: Palladion;

206-10: Cupid; 453-5: Eleyne, Polixene;
651-5: Paris, Oenone; 659-65: Phebus,
Amete; 699-700: Nyobe; 785-8: Ticius;
848-52: Fortune; 859-61: Cerberus
(Book II) 8-10: Cleo, Muse; 54-6: Phebus,
Bole; 63-6: Proigne; 77: Janus; 101-2:
Edippus, Layus, Thebes; 152-3: Ector;
176-80, 233: Jupiter; 425-7: Pallas;
435-6: Marte, Furies; 593: Mars; 617-8:
Dardanus; 680-3: Venus; 824-6: Antigone;
1062: Minerva; 1396-8: Deiphebus;
1667-8: Eleyne **(Book III)** 3-7: Venus;
45-8: Caliope; 319-82: Agamemnon;
409-11: Polixene, Cassandre, Eleyne;
539-44: Apollo; 617-8: Fortune; 715-20:
Venus, Mars, Saturne, Zeus, Adoun;
722-4: Jove, Europe; 724-5: Mars, Cipris;
726-8: Dane, Phebus; 729-32: Mercurie,
Hierse, Pallas, Aglawros, Diane; 733-5:
Parcae; 1016: Jove; 1254-8: Citherea,
Venus, Imeneus; 1387-93: Crassus, Mida;
1417-8: Lucyfer; 1427-8: Almena; 1463:
Titan; 1494-8: Phebus; 1599-1600:
Flegetoun; 1702-6: Pirous; 1807-10:
Dyane, Cupide, Elicone, Pernaso, Venus,
Muses **(Book IV)** 1ff: Fortune; 22-4:
Herynes, Megera, Alete, Thesiphone; 31-2:
Phebus, Hercules, Lion; 73-7: Calkas;
120-4: Phebus, Neptunus, Troie,
Lameadoun; 173-8: Toas; 197-201:
Juvenal; 300-1: Edippe; 330-2: Calkas;
659-61: Fame; 789-91: Elisos, Orpheus,
Eurydice; 1116-7: Juno; 1138-9: Mirra;
1187-8: Mynos; 1208: Atropos; 1345-8:
Eleyne, Grekis; 1397-8: Apollo; 1459:
Argus; 1534ff: Juno, Athamante, Stix;
1546-7: Atropos; 1548-9: Symois; 1608:
Cynthia; 1683-4: Jupiter **(Book V)**
1-4: Joves, Parcas; 6-7: Lachesis; 8-11:
Phebus, Zephyrus; 86-9: Diomede, Tideus;
207-10: Jove, Apollo, Cupide, Ceres,
Bacus, Cipride; 211-2: Ixion; 276-9:
Phebus; 319-20: Escaphilo; 599-602:
Troie, Juno, Thebes; 638ff: Caribdis;
664-5: Pheton; 652: Latona; 799-804:
Diomed, Tideus; 890-6: Manes, Eleyne;
897-8: Calkas; 932-4: Diomedes, Tideus;
1016-19: Venus, Cynthia, Leoun, Phebus;
1110: Nysus, Scylla (2); 1451ff: Sibille,
Cassandre; 1464-8: Diane, Grekis; 1474-7:
Meleagre, Calydonian Boar Hunt, Atalanta;
1492-3: Tideus, Polymytes, Ethiocles,

Thebes; 1492-3: Hemonydes, Tideus; 1498-9: Archymoris, Amphiorax; 1502-5: Ypomedoun, Parthonope, Capaneus; 1506-8: Ethiocles, Polymyte; 1527ff: Alceste; 1553ff: Ector, Achilles; 1786ff: Virgile, Ovide, Omer, Lucan, Stace; 1812-3: Music of the Spheres

Clare, John (1793-1864)
To the Rural Muse 111-13: Parnassus, Parnass
Written in Prison 10-12: Aesop

Cleveland, John (1613-1658)
Dialogue between Two Zealots 29-30: Cerberus
Parting with a Friend 1-2: Hipolytus
The Rebel Scot 11506: Hyperbolus
Smectymnuus 65-7: Caligula
To Julia 41-2: Pelops
To P. Rupert 109-12: Athos; 161-2: Perseus
Upon an Hermaphrodite 24-6: Regulus; 49-53: Ulysses, Achilles, Lycomedes
Upon a Miser 29-30: Ajax; 54: Hesperian
Upon the Death of M. King 9-10: Helicon; 12: Xerxes; 26-7: Stagirite

Clough, Arthur Hugh (1819-61)
Amours de Voyage i 45-7: Coliseum; iii 85-90: Laodamia, Protesilaus; 229: Sabine, Horace
Trunks for Forest Yield 1ff: Hesperian, Alcinous

Coleridge, Samuel Taylor (1772-1834)
The Destiny of Nations 9-10: Brutus (3), Leonidas; 435-7: Apollo, Python
Domestic Peace 3-8: Halcyon
Fancy in Nubibus 11-15: Homer
Lines to a Beautiful Spring 4-6: Pierian
Lines to a Comic Author 12-14: Momus, Aristophanes
The Nightingale 32ff: Philomela
The Nose 5-8: Prometheus; 10: Phlegethon; 39-40: Pliny
On a Late Connubial Rupture 6-8: Cytherea; 17-8: Siren
The Picture 170-1: Alcaeus, Sappho
Recantation 79-82: Achilles
Religious Musings 222-3: Homer
The Silver Thimble 49-51: Arachne
The Snow-Drop 35-8: Phoenix; 39-40: Lethe
Songs of the Pixies 57: Loves; 104-6: Zephyr

Talleyrand to Lord Grenville 47-8: Midas
To the Author of Poems 41-2: Pomona
To a Friend (Charles Lamb) 7-12: Thetis, Achilles; 20-4: Maecenas
To Sheridan 4: Hymettian
To a Young Lady 23-4: Tyrtaean
A Tombless Epitaph 21-5: Parnassian, Hippocrene

Collins, William (1721-59)
Epistle to Sir Thomas Hamner 15-16: Graces; 21-3: Phaedra; 23-4: Theban, Oedipus; 27-8: Sisters; 30: Menander; 31-2: Muse; 33-4: Ilissus; 37: Maid; 40-1: Arno; 47-8: Tuscan, Athenian; 63: Graces; 71-2: Lucan; 74: Maro; 115-6: Antony; 121-4: Coriolanus; 127-8: Veturia; 142-4: Ulysses
Lines Addressed to a Fastidious Critic 5: Horace; 8: Tuscan; 43-4: Homer
Lines Addressed to a Friend about to Visit Italy 11-12: Augustan
Lines Addressed to James Harris 13: Plato; 29: Pindar
Lines on the Music of Grecian Theatre 1-4: Ptolemy (2); 7, 3-4: Athens; 9-11: Muses
The Manners, an Ode 13-14: Porch; 45: Maids; 46: Satyres; 61-2: Tuscan; 75-6: Cynic
No Longer Ask Me, Gentle Friends 61-4: Damon; 68: Thyrsis
Ode on the Death of Mr Thomson 29-30: Sisters
Ode on the Popular Superstitions of the Highlands of Scotland 1-2: Naiads; 18: Doric; 32: Muse; 138-9, 37: Boreal
Ode to Evening 5, 25: Nymph; 23: Hours
Ode to Fear 26-7: Muse; 30-1: Marathon; 34-5: Hybla; 37: Furies; 38-41: Jocasta; 47: Nymph
Ode to Liberty 1: Sparta; 8-9: Alcaeus; 17-20: Rome; 47: Lydian; 49: Liguria; 64: Nymph; 72: Oreas; 81-2: Mona; 101-2: Muse; 108: Hebe; 109: Albion; 129, 131-4: Concord
Ode to Peace 1-3, 13-15: Peace
Ode to Pity 7: Pella; 13-15: Ilissus; 17-18: Echo; 34: Muse
Ode to Simplicity 11: Attic; 12: Nymph; 13-14: Hybla; 18: Electra; 18-21: Cephisus
On the Use and Abuse of Poetry 1ff: Orpheus; 14: Hymen
The Passions, An Ode for Music 1, 95ff: Music;

Sospetto d'Herode 6: Hydra; 10: Narcissus, Phaethon; 12: Sibill; 34: Alecto; 42: Harpies, Erisicthon, Tantalus, Atreus, Progne, Lycaon, Medusa; 43: Parcae; 44: Minotaurs, Cyclopses, Hydras, Sphinxes; 45: Diomede, Phereus, Therodamus, Busiris, Sylla, Lestrigonians, Procrustes, Scyron, Schinis; 46: Mezentius, Geryon, Phalaris, Ochus, Ezelinus, Nero; 50: Erinnys, Thebes
Upon the Death of Mr Herrys 12 ff: Phoenix
Upon the Gunpowder Treason 29-30: Aeol; 31-2: Triton
The Weeper 14: Tagus

Daniel, Samuel (1562-1619)
Behold what hap 1-4: Pigmalion
The Civil Wars ii 12: Actaeon; 100: Minerva; iii 68: Dioclesian; 73: Marius; iv 15: Hydras; v: Iliads; 62: Paris; vi 26 ff: Prometheus; 30: Nemesis; 31: Pandora; 36: Cadmus; vii 56: Periander; viii 3: Pharsalian; 7: Cato
The Complaint of Rosamond 8 ff: Caron; 379 ff: Amymone; 409-13: Io; 500: Argus (1)
Goe Wailing Verse 1-2: Minerva
Happy in Sleep 9-10: Hydra
Letter from Octavian to Mark Antony 2, 3: Cleopatra
Most Faire and Lovely Maid 1-2: Leander
Read in My Face a Volume of Despairs 1-2: Iliads
To My Brother and Friend John Florio 96-8: Alcibiades
Restore Thy Tresses 12-13: Hyrcan
Whilst Youth and Error 7-12: Actaeon

Davies, Sir John (1569-1629)
Nosce Teipsum v 21-4: Medea; 26-9: Ulysses, Sirens; 33-4: Marius; xxxix 51-2: Apollo; 63-4: Medea, Aeson
Orchestra 1-4: Penelope; 8 ff: Homer; 29 ff: Antinous; 36-40: Terpsichore; 43-5: Tethys, Phoebus; 59-60: Phemius; 123-6: Music of the Spheres; 133-40: Amphion; 449-51: Atlas, Prometheus; 484-7: Leda, Eurotas, Castor, Pollux; 491-6: Venus, Mars, Vulcan; 523-5: Jove; 552-3: Hebe, Muses; 560-3: Caeneus; 567-74: Tiresias; 691: Tereus, Procne; 870-1: Vulcan; 883-4: Mantua

De La Mare, Walter (1873-1956)
Ages Ago 7-12: Helen; 13-18: Cleopatra
The Birth of Venus 21-2: Venus
I Wonder 2-7: Acheron, Cerberus, Lethe
Kismet 24-5: Croesus
Lethe 1-2: Lethe
Mournst Thou Now 5-6: Dryads
Surgery 1-5: Pan
They Told Me 1-4: Pan
Winged Chariot Narcissus, Hesperides
Youth 11: Adonis

Denham, Sir John (1615-1669)
Cooper's Hill 1-4: Helicon, Parnassus; 51-2: Atlas; 193-5: Eridanus; 236-7: Fauns, Sylvans
Friendship and Single Life 40-6: Venus; 93-5: Helen
On Abraham Cowley 34-40: Horace, Virgil, Golden Fleece; 47-8: Pindar; 67-8: Pythagoras
On John Fletcher's Works 7-10: Actaeon
Panegyric on General George Monck 13-14: Fabius; 34-8: Delphos; 46-50: Palladium
The Progress of Learning 2-3: Circean; 5-6: Aeneas; 21-2: Golden Fleece; 23-4: Musaeus, Orpheus; 35-9: Pythagoras, Socrates, Plato, Aristotle; 61-4: Homer; 65-8, 73-6: Augustus, Horace, Virgil; 161 ff: Centaurs, Ixion, Chymera; 186-7: Arachne
To His Mistress 7-8: Prometheus
To the Hon. Edward Howard 17-18: Homer; 19-23: Virgil

Diaper, William (1685-1717)
Brent 122-5: Ovid
Callipaedia iv 27-30: Prometheus; 203-7: Romulus, Remus; 228-33: Socrates
Dryades 64-70: Thyrsis, Silurian, Ariconian; 85-6: Genii; 202-7: Bacchus; 236-7: Tityrus; 302-5: Cadmus; 326-9: Numa; 388-93: Octavius, Mantua; 439-42: Lentulus, Catiline, Cathegus; 504-11: Argus (1), Arachne; 593-4: Hydra; 610-1: Caesar, Philippi; 625-6: Hector
Sea Eclogues i 1-2: Glaucus; 10-12: Tritons, Nereids; 19-20: Cymothoe; ii 11-12: Halcyon; 73-6: Proteus; viii 5-6: Proteus; xii 70: Venus

Donne, John (1572-1631)
The Canonization 21-4: Phoenix
Eclogue 1613 7-8: Flora; 142-5: Phoebus, Phaeton; 215-8: Tullia
Elegy IV (Perfume) 31-4: Colossus
Elegy VIII (Comparison) 19-22: Chaos, Cynthia; 15-16: Ide; 23-4: Proserpine, Jove
Elegy IX (Autumnal) 29-33: Xerxes
Elegy XIII (Julia) 19-20: Tenarus; 23 ff: Orcus
Elegy XVI (On His Mistress) 19-23: Boreas, Orithea
Elegy XVIII (Love's Progress) 27-30: Cupid, Pluto; 60-3: Hellespont, Sestos, Abydos, Loves
Elegy XIX (To His Mistress Going to Bed) 35-8: Atlanta
Elegy XX (Love's War) 17-18: Midas; 25-6: Phao, Sappho
Epigrams, Hero and Leander: Pyramus and Thisbe: Niobe: Mercurius 1-3: Aesop; 7-8: Mercury
Epithalamion Made at Lincoln's Inn 22: Flora
Epithalamion on the Lady Elizabeth 20-6: Phoenixes
A Litany 98-9: Diocletian; 200-1: Music of the Spheres
Love's Deity 15-16: Jove
Love's Exchange 15-18: Cupid
Progress of the Soul 21-2: Janus
Satire III 65-8: Gracchus; 79-81: Truth
Satire IV 129-31: Circe; 197-8: Heracleitus
Satire V 88-9: Aesop
Second Anniversary 27-9: Lethe; 197-8: Hesper, Vesper; 199-200: Argus, Mercury; 283 ff: Caesar, Cicero
To Mr E.G. 1-4: Parnassus
To Mr R.W. 1-5: Morpheus, Phobeter
Upon Mr Thomas Coryat's Crudities 71 ff: Sibyl
A Valediction, Of My Name in the Window 43 ff: Genius
A Valediction, of the Book 5-9: Sibyl, Pindar (1), Lucan, Homer, Corinna, Phantasia
The Will 2-4: Argus

Drayton, Michael (1563-1631)
The Barons Wars ii 6: Cocytus; 43: Achilles; iii 8: Medea; 47: Nereus; 48: Arion; vi 33: Hyacinthus; 35: Io; 36: Mercury, Hebe;
37: Cynthus; 39: Phaethon; 40: Padus, Phaetontiades; 43: Arachne; 47: Morpheus; 69: Ilion
Eclogue IV 9-10: Pierian; 25-8: Hercules; 29-30: Charon; 40: Maro; 45-6: Sybils; 65-6: Jove, Amphitryon; 67-8: Apollo, Oenon; 97-100: Cyclops
Eclogue IX 216-22: Ariadne, Berenice
Elinor Cobham to Duke Humphrey 117-20: Nessus; 178: Bacchus
Endymion and Phoebe 1 ff: Ionia, Archelaus; 9-14: Latmus, Endymion, Silvanus; 30-4: Venus, Mars, Minerva, Alcides; 40-2: Hesperides; 89 ff: Endymion; 137 ff: Endymion, Danae, Aganippa; 165-6: Gordian; 181 ff: Phoebe; 204-5: Amphion; 295-6: Citheron; 331-2: Cynthia; 559-60: Phoebe; 648 ff: Phoebe, Phoebus, Jove; 772 ff: Oreads; 787-9: Hamadryads; 793-5: Dryads; 798-801: Naiads; 803-6: Endymion; 823-8: Phoebe; 859-60: Astraea; 997-8: Musaeus
Henry to Rosamond 85-9: Aeson, Medea
Idea viii 5-8: Prometheus; xix 7-8: Proserpine; xxiii 12-14: Orpheus; xxvii 5-6: Zephyr; xxviii 13-14: Tempe, Helicon
The Muses' Elizium iii 116-20: Helicon, Orpheus, Lynus, Hesiod; 396-402: Thalia; 409-12: Euterpe; 421-2: Terpsichore; 433-6: Erato; 445-8: Caliope; 457-60: Polyhymnia; vii 123-5: Mars, Venus, Vulcan; ix 15-17: Apollo, Sol, Delius, Cynthius; 21-3: Apollo, Delos, Delphos; 32-7: Eos, Ethon, Phlegon, Pirois, Apollo; 41-2: Colatina; 45: Demogorgon; 57-60: Apollo, Hyacinth; 65-8: Apollo, Python; 73-7: Apollo, Cynthus; 77-80: Cragus; x 57: Silvanus
The Owl 82-6: Amphion; 97 ff: Ascallaphus; 223-4: Athens; 267-8: Bellona; 275-80: Ceres, Acheron; 281-6: Orphne, Ascallaphus, Acheron; 286-90: Ascallaphus, Proserpine, Ceres; 298 ff: Nytimine; 672: Promethii; 899-903: Capitol; 919-23: Cadmus; 1060-74: Menelaus, Tenedos, Iliades; 1229-32: Syren
Polyolbion i 309-14: Brut (1); 335 ff: Aeneas, Ascanius, Brut; 406 ff: Brutus (1); v 21-4: Nereus, Thetis, Chiron, Achilles; 83-8: Pegasian, Pierus, Pimpla, Castalia, Pindus, Aganippa, nymphs; xv 7-10: Naiads; 100-6: Diana; 246-8: Rubicon; 267-9:

Tagus; xx 152-4: Saturn, Ops; 156-9: Neptune, Polypheme, Phorcys, Thoosa; 164: Neptune, Chrysaor, Medusa; 165-6: Brontes, Neptune; 167-8: Neptune, Neleus, Nestor; 169-71: Cadmus, Agenor, Neptune; 173-6: Pelasgus, Inachus, Neptune; xxv 31ff: Acherusian, Thesposia, Acheron, Thrasimen, Hannibal; 39-43: Mareotis, Maeotis; 44: Lerna

Rosamond and Henry II 139-42: Diana, Actaeon; 153-8: Amimone, Neptune; 163-6: Io, Argus (1)

The Shepherds Sirena 13-16: Milky Way, Hebe; 182-5: Tagus, Pactolus

To Henry Reynolds 157-8: Ovid

To Himself and the Harp 11-15: Apollo, Nine; 21-5: Pyreneus, Phocian; 36-42: Hebrus, Orpheus, Maia, Mercury

To My Noble Friend Roger Drover 5-8: Olympus, Olympia

Dryden, John (1631-1700)

Absalom and Achitophel II 1123: Hybla

Albion and Albanius i: Augusta, Albion, Acherontic, Charon

All for Love Prologue 21-2: Hectors; I i: Antony, Colossus, Cleopatra, Ventidius; II i: Cleopatra, Fulvia, Octavia, Actium, Cleopatra, Antony, Caesar; III i: Dolabella, Antony, Octavius, Cleopatra, Cydnus; IV i: Cleopatra; V i: Cleopatra

Ambyna-Epilogue 1-3: Tyrtaeus

Annus Mirabilis 17-20: Punick War; 57-60: Proteus; 81-4: Sirens; 193-6: Amazons; 197-8: Scipio (1); 253-6: Patroclus; 329-30: Cacus; 371-2: Xenophon; 629-32: Saturn; 689-92: Cato (2); 773-6: Varro; 925-6: Simois; 993-4: Hydra

Astraea Redux 37-42: Typhoeus, Jove; 45-7: Cyclops; 67-70: Otho, Galba, Piso; 120-2: Portunus; 236-7: Halcyon; 320-3: Augustus

Aureng-Zebe II i: Hercules, Nessus, Bellerophon; IV i: Sabean; V i: Scythian, Helen

Britannia Rediviva 55-8: Alcides; 208-13: Minerva; 334-6: Aristides

Conquest of Granada I III i: Siren, Circe; V i: Antony, Actium

Conquest of Granada II II iii: Achilles; III i: Turnus; ii: Sisyphus

Don Sebastian I i: Hydra; II i: Brutus (3),

Cato (3); III i: Gorgon, Nonacrian, Lethean

Eleanora 193ff: Anchises

Heroic Stanzas (Cromwell) 31-2: Pompey; 77-8: Feretrian; 143-4: Halcyons

The Hind and the Panther ii 48-9: Aesop; iii 6-7: Aesop; 620-1: Boreas; 766ff: Aeneas, Latinus, Lavinia (1); 818: Proteus; 1259-60: Dionysius II (2)

MacFlecknoe 3-6: Augustus; 64-7: Augusta; 112-5: Hannibal; 130-3: Romulus

The Medal 95-8: Phocion, Socrates; 226-7: Cyclop

Oedipus Prologue 1-4: Socrates, Sophocles; *Song iii* 21-4: Alecto; 41-4: Demogorgon

Prologue to the Duchess 14-15: Nereids

Prologue to the University of Oxon 32-5: Lucretian

Religio Laici 14ff: Stagyrite, Epicurus; 78-84: Plutarch, Seneca, Cicero

Song for St Cecilia's Day 48-50: Orpheus; 51-4: Cecilia

Sophonisba, Prologue at Oxford 27-30: Aristotle

Threnodia Augustalis 7-8: Niobe; 26ff: Atlas; 266-7: Camillus; 388-9: Fabius; 446ff: Alcides; 465-71: Ancus, Numa

To the Duchess of Ormond 48-50: Portunus; 125-6: Vespasian; 160-2: Ascanius, Elisa

To John Driden of Chesterton 46: Ceres; 164-6: Hannibal

To the Memory of Mr Oldham 7-10: Nisus (2); 22-3: Marcellus (1)

To My Dear Friend (Congreve) 6-8: Janus; 35-8: Fabius, Scipio (1), Hannibal

To My Honoured Friend (Charleton) 1-4: Stagyrite

To My Honoured Friend (Howard) 39-40: Hercules; 96-8: Rufus (2)

To My Ingenious Friend, Mr Higden 12-15: Horace

To My Lord Chancellor 17-20: Troy; 100-4: Pallas

To the Pious Memory of Mrs Killigrey 29-33: Sappho

To Sir George Etherege 30-1: Triptolemus

The Unhappy Favourite, Epilogue 22-3: Democritus, Heraclitus

Upon the Death of Lord Hastings 15-18: Alexander; 53-4: Pandora; 69-71: Seneca, Cato (3), Numa, Caesar

Dunbar, William (1465-1530)
Quben Merche Wes 33: Eolus; 64-70:
Neptunus, Eolus, Juno
Rygbt as tbe Stern of Day 66-7: Omer; 68-9:
Tullius; 76: Dyane; 77: Cleo; 112-7: Mars,
Saturn, Mercurius; 118-9: Phanus, Priapus,
Janus; 125-6: Pluto

Eliot, Thomas Stearns (1888-1965)
Burbank with a Baedeker Cleopatra
A Cooking Egg 10-12, 29-30: Coriolanus
Difficulties of a Statesman Volscian,
Mantuan (1)
Gerontion Thermopylae
Little Gidding iv Nessus
Mr Apollinax Priapus
Sweeney Erect 1-2: Cyclades; 5-7: Aeolus,
Ariadne
Sweeney Among the Nightingales 35-40:
Agamemnon
The Waste Land 69-70: Mylae; 77-80:
Cleopatra; 97-103: Philomel, Tereus;
174ff: nymphs; 203-6: Tereus; 218-22:
Tiresias; 228-9, 243-6: Tiresias; 263-5:
Ionian; 415-6: Coriolanus

Fletcher, Giles (1549-1611)
Christ's Triumph After Death 23: Janus,
Ganymede
Christ's Triumph Over Death 1: Eridan,
Cedron; 7: Deucalion, Nisus, Phaethon,
Orpheus; 47: Pentheus, Orestes; 66:
Philomel
Christ's Victory in Heaven 68: Eirene
Christ's Victory on Earth 22: Acheron,
Phlegethon; 24: Celeno; 36: Argus (Argo);
40: Ida, Yanthus, Hybla, Rhodope, Tempe,
Adonis Garden, Plato; 49: Circe; 51:
Bacchus
Description of Encolpius 9-10: Rhea; 39-40:
Adonis

Fletcher, Phineas (1582-1650)
The Locusts i 2: Thetis; 23: Erinnys; ii 5:
Proteus; iii 13: Greece; iv 33: Astraea;
v 32: Geryon; 34: Pegasus
Piscatory Eclogues i 1: Halcyon; vi 11:
Diana; vii 1: Tithon; 20: Pan, Jove, Alcides,
Daphne, Hyacinthus; 21: Alcinous,
Pomona, Bacchus, Pallas, Venus
The Purple Island i 9: Peleus; 10: Tiphys; 17:
Maro, Linus, Midas; 18: Bavius, Maevius;

47: Delos, Latona; 49: Bacchus; 51:
Astraea; ii 4: phoenix; 38: Erisicthon;
iii 1: Tithon, Symplegades; iv 8: Haemus;
33: Vesper; v 19: Salmacis, Biblis; 33:
Arachne; 44-5: Daedalus; 61-2: Orpheus,
Eurydice, Calliope; 64-7: Tantal, Ixion;
65: Sisyphus, Tityus, Furies; 66: Cerberus;
67: Eurydice, Orpheus; ix 38: Paris; x 1:
Atlas; 28: Phoenix; 39: Hippolyta; xii 16:
Alcides, Oeneus; 22: Tiphoeus; 35: Alecto;
42: Phineus, Peneus; 66: Alcides, Cerberus
To E.C. 59-61: Circe, Lotos
To My Beloved Cousin 6-10: Philomel, Progne
To My Ever-Honoured Cousin 1-2: Gordian
Knot
Verses of Mourning and Joy 7-9: Philomel,
Tereus; 68-72: Helicon

Goldsmith, Oliver (1730-74)
The Captivity 257ff: Cyrus
Description of an Author's Bedchamber 6:
Muse
The Double Transformation 972: Cupid
Epilogue Spoken by Mr Lee Lewes 27ff:
Aesop
Epilogue to 'The Sister' 17-18: Hebe, Cupids
The Haunch of Venison 109-10: Priam; 115:
Philomel
The Logicians Refuted 5-6: Aristotle
A New Simile 9ff: Mercurius; 51-2: Tartarus
*On a Beautiful Youth Struck Blind with
Lightning* 1-4: Cupid, Narcissus
*On Seeing Mrs . . . Perform in the Character
of . . .* 1: Nine; 9-11: Paphian, Queen of
Love, Jove; 13-14: Jove
On the Death of the Right Honourable . . .
1-2: Muses, Pollio
Prologue to 'Zobeide' 9-11: Scythian
Retaliation 118: Be-Rosciused
Song from 'She Stoops to Conquer' 1ff:
Lethe, Styx
Theseus Did See 1-4: Theseus
Translation of a South American Ode 1:
Enna
The Traveller 5-6: Campania; 159: Caesars;
173: zephyr; 319: Arcadian; 320:
Hydaspis

Graves, Robert (1895-)
Alice 35-6: Apuleius
The Ambrosia of Dionysus 15-16: Tyrrhenian
Cry Faugh! 4-6: Seneca, Plato

Food of the Dead 1-3: Orpheus
In Procession 15: Silenus
Judgment of Paris 1-4: Paris, Aphrodite,
   Helen; 5-6: Helen, Menelaus
Lament for Pasiphae 9-13: Pasiphae
Leda 2-4, 9-10: Leda
The Naked and the Nude 9-10: Hippocratic;
   21-4: Gorgons
New Legends 1ff: Andromeda; 7-11: Atalanta;
   12-15: Proteus; 16-18: Niobe; 19-20:
   Helen
Penthesilea 1-5: Penthesilea, Achilles; 7-10:
   Achilles, Thersites
Purification 23-5: Paphos
Rhea 13-14: Augustus; 14-16: Caesar; 17-18:
   Rhea
To Ogmian Hercules 1-3: Hercules; 4-8:
   Hebe, Megara, Auge, Hippolyte, Deaianira
Troublesome Fame 1-4: Alexander the Great;
   11-14: Octavian, Augustus
The Utter Rim 1: Cerberus
The White Goddess 2: Apollo

Gray, Thomas (1716-71)
Agrippina 14: Britannicus; 38: Agrippina;
   50: Julian; 64ff: Nero; 99-100: Rubellius,
   Sulla; 110: Carbulo; 121-2: Soranus,
   Cassius, Veto, Thrasea; 146-7: Seneca;
   148: Burrus; 161: Antium; 170: Claudius;
   171: Syllani; 189: Helen
The Alliance of Education and Government
   46-7: Scythia
The Character of the Christ-Cross Row 43:
   Proteus
Elegy Written in a Country Churchyard 72:
   Muse
Epitaph on Sir William Williams 3: Muse,
   Grace
Hymn to Ignorance 11: Hyperion; 17:
   Lethean; 37: Sesostris
Lines Spoken by the Ghost of John Dennis
   1-3: Elysian; 3-4: Atropos; 9-10: Tartarean;
   38-9, 44: Pluto; 38-9: Proserpine; 38-40:
   Cleopatra; 50: Artemisia; 51: Alexander
A Long Story 29-30: Amazon; 70: Muses
Ode for Music 1-2: Comus; 9-10: Muse; 29:
   Camus; 31-3: Cynthia
Ode on the Death of a Favourite Cat 16:
   Tyrian; 19: Nymph; 34: Nereid
Ode on the Spring 1: Hours; 5: Attic; 9-10:
   Zephyr
Ode to Adversity 1-2: Jove; 35: Gorgon

The Progress of Poesy 1-2: Aeolian; 2-3:
   Helicon; 9: Ceres; 17-18: Mars, Thrace;
   20-1, 46-7: Jove; 27-8: Idalia; 28-9:
   Cytherea, Loves; 37: Graces; 48: Muse;
   53: Hyperion; 66: Delphi; 68: Ilissus;
   69-70: Maeander; 77-8: The Nine,
   Parnassus; 84-6: Cybele
Song II 1-2: Thyrsis
Sonnet on the Death of Mr Richard West 2:
   Phoebus

Hardy, Thomas (1840-1928)
At the Pyramid of Cestius 5-8, 21-4: Cestius
The Clasped Skeletons 21-4: Antony,
   Cleopatra
The Collector Cleans His Picture 29-30:
   Astarte, Cotytto
Embarcation 1: Vespasian
In St Paul's 17-18: Hebe, Artemisia
In Rome, on the Palatine 1-2: Jove, Livia (1),
   Palatine

Henryson, Robert (1430-1506)
Orpheus and Eurydice 36-7: Euterpe, 38-9:
   Melpomyne; 40-1: Thersycore; 43-5:
   Caliope, Orpheus; 46-7: Clio; 52-3:
   Polimio; 54-6: Talia; 57-70: Urania; 219ff:
   Music of the Spheres; 254-8: Orpheus,
   Cerberus; 261ff: Electo, Mygra,
   Thesaphone, Orpheus; 281-8: Orpheus,
   Tantalus; 296-32: Orpheus, Tityus;
   329-30: Cresus; 365ff: Orpheus, Plato,
   Eurydice, Proserpine; 475-8: Electo,
   Mygra, Thesaphone; 496ff: Ixion; 521-6:
   Tantalus; 561: Tityus
Testament of Cresseid 71-4: Diomeid,
   Cresseid; 106-9: Calchas; 135-6: Venus;
   156ff: Saturn; 197-201: Phoebus; 239ff:
   Mercurius; 253ff: Cynthia, Titan;
   300ff: Saturn, Cresseid; 501-4: Troilus,
   Cresseid
The Want of Wise Men 9-10: Saturnus, Golden
   Age

Herbert, Lord Edward, of Cherbury
(1583-1648)
A Description 36-7: Atlas; 41-4: Venus
To His Mistress for Her True Picture 113-5:
   Minerva

Herbert, George (1593-1633)
The Church 121-3: Caesar

The Church Militant 51-2: Sophisters; 141-2:
  Nero; 205-7: Janus
My God, Where Is That Ancient Heat 1-4:
  Venus

Herrick, Robert (1591-1674)
The Apparition of his Mistress 26-7: Musaeus;
  32-7: Anacreon
Cornubii Flores 56-7: Lucina
The Country Life 51-2: Faunus
Description of a Woman 59-62: Riphean,
  Gordian; 69-73: Hesperides
The Dream 1-6: Fates
A Dream on a Snow 23-4: Hydra
An Epiphalamie 41-50: Domiduca, Juno,
  Hymen, Graces
Good Friday, Rex Tragicus 1-20: Roscius
His Age 106-7: Helen
His Farewell Unto Poetry 67-70: Orpheus,
  Eurydice; 71-4: Demosthenes; 75-8:
  Tully; 83-8: Helicon, Muses
His Farewell to Sack 29-30: Castalian;
  33-6: Thespian
Hymn to Bacchus 1-2: Iacchus
The Invitation 5-6: Sylla
Leander's Obsequies 1-4: Leander
Love Perfumes 5-8: Isis
The New Charm 27-30: Pluto; 31-4: Hecate
No Shipwreck of Virtue 4-5: Ulysses
Not Every Day Fit for Verse 1ff: Sybil
Orpheus and Pluto 23-9: Orpheus, Amphion
The Parcae 5-8: Destinies
The Parting Verse 29-32: Penelope
Song to the Maskers Isis
To Electra 1-6: Jove, Semele; 9-10: Ixion
To His Book 1-4: Absyrtus
To His Friend 3-7: Amphion
To His Mistresses 7-10: Aeson
To His Saviour 1-2: Augean
To Live Merrily 41-4: Tibullus
To the Maids 13-14: Phillis, Demophon
To Myrrha, Hard-hearted 3-4: Jocasta
To the Rt Hon. Mildman 3-4: Sybil
Ultimus Heroum 1-4: Cato (2)
Upon Faunus 1-2: Faunus
Upon Prudence Baldwin 3-7: Aesculapius
The Vine 10-13: Bacchus
The Vision ('Sitting alone . . .') 12-15:
  Diana
The Vision 1-4: Anacreon
The Welcome to Sack 15-17: Ithaca; 49-50:
  Iphiclus; 61: Cassius; 92: Daphne

When He Would Have His Verses Read
  Cato (2)
Women Useless 1ff: Cadmus

Hood, Thomas (1799-1845)
Autumn 19-20: Proserpine
Bianca's Dream 5: Dryads
The Departure of Summer 24-7: Aurora
The Elm Tree 7-8: Dryad, Nymph; 23: Pan;
  41-2: Laocoon, Titans
Hero and Leander 1: Philomel, Niobe, Sappho,
  Hero; 3: Abydos, Sestos; 10: Lethe; 18:
  Hellespont, Styx; 36: Naiad, Nereid, Syren,
  Hero; 42: Hero, Scylla; 45: Leander; 108:
  Ariadne, Theseus; 116: Hero
Hymn to the Sun 3: Python; 5: Delphic,
  Phoebus
Love and Lunacy 37: Niobe
Love's Champion 6ff: Leander, Hero,
  Sappho
To the Moon 20ff: Latmian, Endymion, Dian
Ode to Richard Martin 78-9: Centaur
The Progress of Art 5: Nestor; 6: Bacchus,
  Pallas, Vulcan, Dian
The Two Swans 15: Argus

Hopkins, Gerard Manley (1844-89)
Andromeda 1, 9: Andromeda, Perseus; 14:
  Gorgon
Escorial 7: Doric, Titan; 11: Paris, Antinous,
  Ceres, Python, Zephyr, Hyacinthus
A Vision of Mermaids Hector

Housman, Alfred Edward (1859-1936)
Atys 1-2: Hermes; 5-6: Tmolus; 8-15:
  Croesus, Atys
Crossing Along the Nighted Ferry 1-4: Lethe
Epithalamion 1-4: Hymen; 13-14: Oeta
Look Not in My Eyes 9-15: Hyacinthus
On Wenlock Edge 5-8: Uricon
Tarry Delight, So Seldom Met 4-7: Sestos,
  Hero, Leander

Johnson, Samuel (1709-84)
Festina Lente 9ff: Orestes, Flaminius (2);
  17-20: Fabius (Maximus)
On Colley Cibber 1: Augustus, Maro
To Miss Hickman Playing on the Spinet 9-11:
  Timotheus
The Vanity of Human Wishes 49-52:
  Democritus; 223-8: Xerxes; 269-70:
  Orpheus; 313-4: Solon, Croesus

Jonson, Ben (1572-1637)
The Alchemist I i: Jason; II i: Elephantis;
   IV i: Danae, Aesculapius; iii: Pythagoras
And Must I Sing? 4-6: Hercules; 10-12:
   Bacchus; 13-15: Pallas, Hephaestus, Zeus
Charis V 45 ff: Paris, Venus, Juno, Minerva
Catiline I i: Catiline, Sylla, Charon; III iii:
   Charybdis; IV i: Catiline, Cicero; V v:
   Lentulus, Catiline
Cynthia's Revels I i: Narcissus, Echo, Actaeon,
   Niobe; V ii: Paeons, Maia; iii: Niobe,
   Cynthia, Artemis, Midas
Dedication of the King's New Cellar 13-15:
   Bacchus; 25-8: Bacchus, Apollo,
   Hippocrene
Epigram on Sir Edward Coke 15-17: Solon
Epigram to the Honoured Countess 19-25:
   Penelope, Ulysses
Epistle to Elizabeth 49-50: Helen; 51ff:
   Achilles, Idomen, Ajax, Homer; 77-9:
   Orpheus
Epithalamion 89-90: Juno
Execution Upon Vulcan Vulcan, Pandora
Expostulation with Inigo Jones 5-6: Architas
Helen, Did Homer Never See 3-5: Sappho;
   5-8: Anacreon; 17-20: Ovid, Corinna (2)
If Men and Times Were Now 37-41: Minerva,
   Giants, Medusa
Inviting a Friend to Supper 29-33: Horace,
   Anacreon
Let Me Be What I Am 1-4: Virgil, Horace,
   Anacreon
Love is Blind 1-8: Cupid
The Magnetic Lady I i: Archimede; V ii:
   Aesculapius
The New Inn I i: Virgil, Aeneas; III ii:
   Hesperian
A New Year's Gift 9-10: Janus; 28-30: Pales,
   Pan
Ode Allegoric 19-20: Dircaean, Pindar;
   99-101: Cycnus
An Ode, To Himself 9-10: Clarius
Ode to James, Earl of Desmond 8-10:
   Cynthius; 40-6: Brontes, Steropes,
   Peracmon
On the Famous Voyage 50-5: Alcides; 77-8:
   Castor, Pollux; 81-4: Briareus, Hydra,
   Scyllas (1 and 2), 111-4: Ulysses,
   Polyphemus; 141-5: Acheron
A Panegyre 20-7: Themis, Dice, Eunomia,
   Irene
The Poetaster I i: Callimachus (2), Menander,

Accius; III i: Nestus; V i: Virgil
The Sad Shepherd I i: Scamander
Sejanus I i: Tiberius, Cato (2), Brutus (3),
   Germanicus, Alexander, Sejanus,
   Rhadamanth; II i: Livia (2), Drusus (1),
   Sejanus, Augusta (2), Apicata; ii: Sejanus,
   Agrippina (1), Germanicus; III i: Oedipus,
   Sphinx, Vulcan, Livius, Livia (2), Sejanus;
   IV v: Jove, Gemonies; V i: Sinon, Tiberius,
   Sejanus; x: Phlegra, Sejanus
The Staple of News IV i: Charybdis, Apicius
Swell me a Bowl 1-3: Lyaeus
That Love's a Bitter Sweet 19-23: Midas
To Benjamin Rudyerd 1-4: Saturn
To Doctor Empiric 1-2: Aesculape
To Edward Alleyn Roscius, Aesopus
To George Chapman 1-2: Hesiod
To the Ghost of Martial 1-4: Martial,
   Domitian
To His Lady, Then Mrs Cary 3-8: Phoebus,
   Daphne
To the Immortal Memory of that Noble Pair
   1-8: Saguntum, Hannibal
To Inigo 13-14: Colossus
To My Lady Worth 11-14: Idalian, Venus,
   Diana
To Mrs Philip Sidney 3-8: Cupid
To My Chosen Friend . . . 1-2: Caesar,
   Pompey; 14-16: Lucan; 16-17: Phoebus,
   Hermes
To Penshurst 76-80: Penates
To Shakespeare 31-7: Aeschylus, Euripides,
   Sophocles, Pacuvius, Accius, Seneca; 51-4:
   Aristophanes, Terence, Plautus
To Sir Henry Savile 1-4: Pythagoras, Tacitus;
   13-16: Minerva; 22-3: Sallust
To Sir Horace Vere 3-4: Horace
To Sir Robert Wroth 47-50: Comus, Saturn
To William Roe 12-14: Aeneas
The Vision of Ben Jonson 31-2: Minerva;
   68-9: Tyrtaeus
Volpone I i: Aeson; II i: Ulysses; III iv:
   Nestor; V i: Acrisius

Keats, John (1795-1821)
Acrostic 3-5: Apollo; 11-12: Ulysses; 15:
   Nine
After Dark Vapours 9-12: Sappho
Ah, Woe Is me . . . 11: Favonian
Apollo to the Graces 1-3: Apollo, Graces
As Hermes Once 1-4: Hermes, Argus, Delphic;
   7-12: Ida, Tempe, Io, Jove

Bards of Passion and of Mirth 9-12: Elysian, Dian, fawns

Blue! 'Tis the Light of Heaven 1-4: Cynthia, Hesperus

Calidore 113-5: Mercury; 154: Philomel; 161-2: Hesperus

The Cap and Bells 1-3: Hydaspes; 246-9: Argus; 618-21: Mercury; 634-5: Pegasus

Endymion (Book I) 35-7: Endymion; 64-5: Latmos; 77-8: Pan; 95-9: Apollo; 139-40: Arcadian; 139-44: Apollo, Thessaly; 157-8: Leda; 169-70: Ganymede; 175-7: Elysian; 190-2: Endymion; 205-6: Triton; 232-5: Pan; 236-7: Hamadryads; 243-6: Pan, Syrinx; 263-4: faun, satyre; 271-2: naiads; 278: Pan, Satyr; 290: Pan, Dryope; 305-6: Lycaean; 308-11: Ionian; 317-9: Thermopylae; 327-31: Hyacinthus, Zephyr; 337-43: Niobe; 346-8: Argonauts, Neptune; 350-3: Apollo; 362-3: Vesper; 371-3: Elysium; 378-84: Mercury; 408-9: Peona; 493-5: Dryope; 497-500: Delphic; 510: Paphian; 511-4: Dian, Actaeon; 525-6: Endymion; 529-31: Lucifer; 549-52: Sun; 554-5, 624-30: Diana; 554-60: Morpheus; 554-63: Mercury; 561-2: Night; 579-80: Milky Way; 592-3: Neptune; 604-5: Olympus; 613-9: Diana; 624-6: Venus; 670-1: Oread; 684-6: Hesperus; 789-90: Apollo; 793-4: Orpheus; 862: Latona; 880-4: Neptune; 888-9: Cupid; 939-41: wood-nymph; 943-6: Proserpine; 947-54: Echo; 965-6: Delos; 966-9: Echo (Book II) 8-13: Troy, Troilus; 22-3: Themistocles; 24-5: Alexander; 26-7: Ulysses, Cyclops; 36-8: Muse; 81-2: Delphi; 98ff: naiad; 106-9: Amphitrite; 116-9: Meander; 164-70: Orphean, Eurydice; 169-74: Cynthia; 179-82: Cynthia, Cupids; 189-93: Cynthia; 195-8: Deucalion, Orion; 230-2: Vulcan; 260-2: Dian; 299-300: Endymion; 302-8: Diana; 317-8: zephyr; 358-60: Arion; 358-63: Apollo, Ionian, Tyrian; 361-2: Zephyrus; 373: Carian; 385-6: Cupids; 396-400: Apollonian; 418-27: Cupids; 429: Latmian; 441-4 Ariadne; 444-6: Vertumnus, Pomona; 446-9: Amalthea, Jupiter; 452-3: Hesperides; 458-78: Venus, Adonis; 473-6: Jove; 492: Cythereas; 516-29: Venus, Adonis; 536-41: Cupid; 558-9:

Mars; 585-6: Aetnean; 608-11: Thetis; 640-4: Cybele; 657-8: Jove; 674-5: Music of the Spheres; 689-90: Atlas; 690-1: Triton; 692-4: Dian, nymph; 695-7: Aurora; 717-23: Helicon; 723-9: Muses, Apollo; 761: Ida, Venus; 782-5: Olympus, Diana; 790-1: Minerva; 788-803: Pallas; 809-10: ambrosial; 832-9: Phoebus; 866-8: Aeolian; 874-5: Alecto; 875-7: Hermes, Argus; 895-7: Pan, Golden Age; 911: Olympian, Jove; 948-52: Alpheus, Arethusa; 961: Oread, Diana; 963-71: Alpheus, Arethusa; 983-7: Diana; 988-90: Alpheus, Arcadian; 993-4: Saturn; 1001-4: Sol; 1005-12: Alpheus, Arethusa, Diana, Latmian (Book III) 30-40: Ceres; 40-9: Chaos, Apollo, Diana, Muses; 70-1: Tellus; 72-4: Cynthia; 78: Vesper; 81-2: Neptune 97-9: Cynthia, Leander, Orpheus, Pluto; 111-4: Aurora; 121-3: Morpheus; 126-9: Saturn; 131-3: Nox; 193-200: Glaucus; 210-13: Glaucus, Neptune, Nymphs; 232-3: Echo; 238-9: Neptune; 241-2: Sirens; 243-4: Typhon; 251-2: Fates; 269-71: Tartarus; 277-9: Diana; 310: Glaucus; 311: Carian; 352-5: Neptune, Glaucus; 364-5: Aethon; 399-404: Scylla, Glaucus, Circe; 405-6: Hercules, Oeta; 411-4: Glaucus, Circe; 415-7: Aeaea; 425-8: Circe, Elysium; 449: Latmos; 459: Circe; 460-2: Amphion, Scylla; 463-4: Apollo; 473-4: Pluto; 503-6: Stygian; 529-31: Python, Boreas; 536: fauns, nymphs, satyrs, centaurs; 580-1: Atropos; 590-9: Glaucus; 618-23: Circe, Scylla; 633-5: Aeolus; 682-5: Atlas; 711-2: Endymion; 718-27: Neptune; 728-31: Mars; 775-82: Glaucus, Scylla; 785-8: Apollo; 807-10: Glaucus, Scyllas, Neptunus; 833-43: Neptune; 847-9: Memphis, Babylon, Nineveh; 850-4: Iris, Paphian; 862-5: Neptune, Cupid, Venus; 866-71: Neptune, Jove; 888-93: Triton, Nereids, Sirens, Neptune, Cupid, nectarous; 893-7: Venus, Scylla, sea-nymph; 898-902: Nais; 917-9: Cythera, Cupid, Adonis; 924-6: nectar; 937-40: Muses; 944-5: Neptune; 951-3: Aeolus; 955-9: Apollo, Neptune; 973-7: Cupid, Cytherea; 983-7: Cupid; 993-7: Oceanus; 999-1000: Doris, Nereus; 1001-2: Amphion; 1003-5: Amphitrite, Thetis; 1010-5: Neptune, Nereids

Bacchus; 211-2: Pluto; 216-9: Lycius, Lamia; 223-5: Cenchreas, Egina; 46-50: Orpheus, Eurydice; 265-70: Pleiad, Music of the Spheres; 279-83: Lamia; 304-6: Lamia; 316-20: Venus, Adonis; 324-7: Lamia; 329-33: Pyrrha; 363-5: Apollonius; 386-7: Aeolian **(Part ii)** 78-81: Apollo, Python; 159-62: Apollonius; 186-8: Ceres; 296-300: Apollonius, Lamia; 305-8: Lycius

Lines on the Mermaid Tavern 1-4: Elysium

Lines Rhymed in a Letter from Oxford 2: Doric

Not Aladdin magian 23-8: Lycidas, Oceanus; 42: Proteus

Ode on a Grecian Urn 5-7: Tempe; 41-3: Attic

Ode on Indolence 9-10: Phidian

Ode on Melancholy 1-4: Lethe, Proserpine; 6-7: Psyche

Ode to a Nightingale 1-4: Lethewards; 7: Dryad; 11-13: Flora; 15-19: Hippocrene; 31-3: Bacchus; 36-7: Moon

Ode to Apollo 1-6: Apollo; 14: Maro; 34-5: Aeolian; 42-3: Apollo, Nine

Ode to May 1-3: Hermes, Maia, Baiae

Ode to Psyche 24-9: Psyche, Olympus, Phoebe, Vesper; 40-3: Psyche, Olympians; 56-7: Dryads

Oh, How I Love, on a Fair Summer's Eve . . . 3-4: zephyrs

On a Leander 9-11: Leander, Hero

On First Looking into Chapman's Homer 3-4: Apollo; 5-6: Homer

On Leaving some Friends 11-12: Music of the Spheres

On Peace 8: nymph; 9: Europa

On Receiving a Laurel Crown from Leigh Hunt 1-3: delphic

On Seeing a Lock of Milton's Hair 2: Music of the Spheres; 17-18: Delian

On Sitting Down to read 'King Lear' . . . 1-2: Siren; 13-14: Phoenix

On the Sea 1-4: Hecate; 13-14: sea-nymphs

On the Story of Rimini 5-6: Hesperus

On Visiting the Tomb of Burns 8-10: Minos

Otho the Great I i 93-5: Minerva; 132-4: Hymen; II i 130-1: Mars; III ii 41-3: Apollo; 92-8: Vulcan; IV i 81-7: Hesperian; ii 30-5: Night; V v 23-4: Orphean, Amphion; 28-30: Psyche, Cupid; 120-5: Iberian, Calabrian, Tuscan, Aetna, Bacchus

Sleep and Poetry 11-15: Sleep; 56-61: Apollo; 63-7: nymphs; 71-5: Meander; 101-2: Flora, Pan; 167-71: Jove; 171-7: Music of the Spheres; 178-80: Muses; 181-3: Apollo; 185-7: Pegasus; 231-5: Polyphemes; 238-47: Muses; 248-51: myrtle, Paphos; 302-4: Dedalian; 324-6: Bacchus, Ariadne; 348: Sleep; 360-3: fauns, satyrs; 371-2: nymphs, Diana; 381-4: Sappho

Song of the Four Fairies 31: Zephyr; 46-7: Sun; 51-5: Vesper

Spenser! A jealous honourer of thine . . . 5-10: Phoebus

Spirit Here That Reignest 15-20: Momus, Comus

To Apollo 1-12: Apollo; 13-16: Jupiter; 25-6: Pleiades

To a Young Lady Who Sent Me a Laurel Crown 5-7: Apollo; 11-13: Caesars

To B. R. Haydon 5-8: Heliconian

To Charles Cowden Clarke 6: Naiad, zephyr; 23-7: Helicon; 40-1: Urania; 44-5: Apollo; 623: Atlas; 68: Clio; 92-3: Cynthia

To Emma Mather 1-2: Flora; 13-14: zephyr

To George Spencer 1-4: Apollo

To Georgina Augusta Wylie 11-14: Grace, Apollo

To George Felton Mathew 17-23: Lydian, Phoebus, Aurora, naiad; 31-4, 53-6: Muse; 76-8: Helicon; 78-83: Diana; 79-86: Apollo

To Homer 1-4: Cyclades; 5-8: Homer, Jove, Neptune, Pan; 13-4: Homer, Dian

To J. H. Reynolds Esq. 5-9: Alexander, Socrates

To Kosciusko 1-4: Music of the Spheres

To Leigh Hunt Esq. 5-8: nymphs, Flora; 11-12: Pan

To Mary Frogley 26-30: Loves; 35-6: Muses; 167-8: Thalia; 39-40: Graces

To My Brother George 4-5: Music of the Spheres; 9-12, 43-5: Apollo

To My Brother George ('Many the wonders') 10-12: Cynthia

To Me Who Has Been Long in City Pent 9-10: Philomel

To the Ladies Who Saw Me Crowned 6-7: halcyon

Welcome Joy and Welcome Sorrow 1-2: Lethe, Hermes; 16-17: Cleopatra; 20-4: Muses (2), Saturn, Momus

Where's the Poet? 1-7: Plato
Woman, When I Behold Thee Flippant, Vain 13-14: Leander
Written in Disgust of Vulgar Superstition 5-7: Lydian
You say you love 6-9: Cupid

Kingsley, Charles (1819-75)
Andromeda 37-40: Hero, Hephaestos; 53 ff: Andromeda, Orpheus; 80-2: Andromeda; 136-8: Nereus; 238-41, 262-4: Perseus, Andromeda; 358 ff: Perseus, Medusa; 440-2: Hephaestos
Elegiacs 3-4: Achilles
Frank Leigh's Song 1: Megaera; 11-12: Ixion
Ode Performed in the Senate House 106-10: Clio
Sappho 16-19, 29-31: Sappho

Kipling, Rudyard (1865-1936)
The Bees and the Flies 1-8: Aristaeus, Proteus, Virgil, Cyrene
The Fabulists 1-4: Aesop
Ode — Melbourne Shrine 20-1: Troy
Our Fathers of Old 41-4: Galen, Hippocrates
Romulus and Remus 9-12: Romulus
Samuel Pepys 16-19: Venus, Liber; 23-7: Nine, Clio
The Second Voyage 11: Venus; 17-18: Paphos; 28: Hesperides
A Song of Travel 1-4: Hero, Leander

Lamb, Charles (1775-1834)
Leisure 13-14: Atlas
The Ballad-Singers 24-5: Pyracmon; 30-3: Rhodope, Orpheus, Proserpine, Orcus, Sisyphus
The Female Orators 14-16: Venus, Demosthenic, Cicero; 17-8: Ate
The Three Graves 7-8: Clotho
Written at Cambridge 12-3: Stagyrite

Lawrence, David Herbert (1885-1930)
Anaxagoras 1-4: Anaxagoras
Attila 1-3: Attila
Autumn Sunshine 1ff, 24-9: Persephone
Bavarian Gentians 3 ff: Persephone, Demeter
The Body of God 4-5: Helen
Don Juan 1-2: Isis
Eagle in New Mexico 32-4: Damocles
Eloi, Eloi 90-2: Erinnyes
Late at Night 21ff: Bacchae, Iacchos

Leda 1ff: Leda
Medlars and Sorb-Apples 40-2: Orpheus; 53-5: Dionysus
Middle of the World 4-5: Dionysus
Name the Gods! 10-11: Priapus
Narcissus 4ff: Narcissus
Purple Anemones 1ff: Pluto; 18-21: Proserpine; 23 ff: Enna, Proserpine; 62 ff: Ceres
Self-Sacrifice 7: Venus
Spiral Flame 18-19: Aphrodite
St John 62-5: Phoenix
They Say the Sea is Loveless 555: Dionysus
Tommies in the Train 8-13: Danae
Tortoise Shell 19-20: Pythagoras
The Universe Flows 10-11: Cleopatra
We Have Gone Too Far 35-6: Hesperides

Lewis, Cecil Day (1904-72)
The Antique Heroes 25-8: Odysseus, hydras
Ariadne on Naxos Ariadne, Theseus, Pasiphae, Minotaur
Baucis and Philemon Baucis, Philemon, Hermes, Zeus
Elegy for a Woman Unknown 2: Delos
Hero and Saint 11-16: Heracles, Bellerophon
A Letter from Rome Catullus, Nero, Colosseum
The Magnetic Mountain 6: Sirens
Pegasus 13-8: Pegasus, Helicon; 79-84: Pegasus; 100-2: Pegasus, Bellerophon
The Perverse 9-12: Pygmalion
Psyche 28-30: Psyche; 71-80: Cupid, Psyche
A Time to Dance Orpheus
Transitional Poem 7: Homer, Cassandra, Helen; 12: Priapus; 18: Scamander, Achilles, Helen; 19: Achilles, Helen; 31: Artemis

Lovelace, Richard (1618-58)
Advice to My Best Brother 11-15: Thetis, Dione; 25-6: Ixion
Against the Love of Great Ones 10-14: Ixion; 21-4: Semele
Amarantha 105-10: Europa, Io
Cupid Far Gone 25-30: Olympus, Charon, Argos, Cerberus
Female Glory 11-12: Phoenix
Ode, Calling Lucasta 4-5: Cimmerian
Ode to Lucasta 13-16: Silenus
On Sannazar 35-6: Lucan; 101-2: Berenice; 209: Parnassus

On the Best Comedy of Mr Fletcher 25-30: Cleopatra
Orpheus to Beasts 1ff: Eurydice
Painture 1-2: Pliny; 26-7: Cerberus, Hydra
Paris's Second Judgment 5-6: Juno; 7-8: Venus; 9-10: Minerva
Princess Louisa Drawing 1ff: Cupid, Echo; 14-17: Syrinx, Pan; 18-21: Ariadne, Theseus; 22-5: Iphis, Anaxarete; 26-8: Leucothoe; 28-33: Daphne; 34-7: Venus, Adonis
The Snail 43-4: Scythians
To Fletcher Revived 14ff: Aetius, Valentinian III; 28-32: Alcides
To the Genius of Mr John Hall 25-6: Tully; 45-50: Hierocles
To My Friend Mr E. R. 40-4: Aeson, Minerva; 59-62: Parnassus
To My Noble Kinsman T.S. 13-18: Amphion
The Triumphs of Philamore 21-2: Regulus; 35-8: Deucalion; 97-8: Phaeton; 23: Neptune, Thetis

Macaulay, Lord Thomas Babington (1800-59)
Horatius 1: Porsenna, Tarquin; 6: Clitumnus; 12: Mamilius; 16: Tarpeian; 23: Lucumo; 47, 24: Porsenna, Mamilius, Tarquin (Sextus); 27ff: Horatius; 30: Herminius, Spurius Lartius; 54ff, 59: Tiber; 65: Horatius
Lake Regillus 2-3: Regillus; 11: Mamilius; 12: Sextus; 15: Calabrian, Herminius; 28: Mamilius
The Prophecy of Capys 1: Amulius; 6: Romulus and Remus
Virginia Appius Claudius, Virginia, Lucrece, Scaevola, Virginius

MacNeice, Louis (1907-63)
Autumn Journal viii: Xenophon; ix: Alcibiades, Venus, Menander; xii: Plato; xviii: Lethe, Styx; xx: Socrates; xxi: Cecrops; xxiv: Lethe, Rubicon
Autumn Sequel i: Thucydides, Pnyx; iv: Dido; xi: Jason, Medea; xix: Pheidias, Alcibiades, Socrates, Melos, Athens; xx: Pactolus; xxvi: Ariadne, Theseus
Birmingham 7-8: Vulcan
Cock o' the North i: Meleager, Leonidas; ii: Meleager; iii: Adonis
Day of Returning ii: Penelope, Ulysses, Argus (3); iii: Cyclops

Eclogue by a Five-Barred Gate 15-6: Theocritean; 21-3: Thanatos; 73-5: Tityrus, Damon
Flavours in the Internal i: Hymettus, Delphi
Hiatus 9-11: Corcyra
The Island ii: Calypso, Hermes; iv: Calypso, Hermes, Cadmus
Leaving Barra 9-13: Atlantis
Memoranda to Horace ii: Flaccus, Maecenas, Augustus, Regulus; iv: Flaccus
Round the Corner 7-8: Xenophon
The Stygian Banks vii: Socrates, Troilus, Stygian
Suite for Recorders 9-12: Hellespont

Marlowe, Christopher (1564-93)
Dido Queen of Carthage 12-15: Jupiter, Ganymede, Juno; 34-7: Juno, Venus; 66-7: Epeus; 96-9: Ascanius, Rome; 104-8: Hector, Rhea Silvia, Rome; 130-4: Triton, Thetis, Cymothoe; 258-9: Lares; 288-9: Baucis; 298-301: Niobe; 311-2: Pygmalion; 403-6: Troy, Sinon, Antenor; 418-9: Myrmidons; 438-44: Sinon, Epeus; 496ff: Hector; 612-7: Ascanius; 719-25: Dido, Aeneas; 762-7: Achates, Thetis; 838-41: Juno, Venus; 1013-5: Pean; 1039ff: Aeneas, Dido; 1068-72: Apollo, Atlas; 1077-9: Tiphons, Iarbus; 1105ff: Iarbus, Dido; 1137ff: Anna, Iarbus; 1153-7: Aeneas; 1175-80: Aeneas, Dido; 1419-24: Hybla; 1465-6: Deucalion; 1651ff: Icarus, Orion (2), Dido; 1700ff: Dido, Hannibal
Doctor Faustus 1-2: Thrasymene; 104-5: Jove; 142-5: Musaeus (1); 146-7: Agrippa; 170-2: Delphian; 587-8: Penelope; 639-41: Amphion; 791-5: Olympus; 815-7: Maro; 1035-8: Alexander; 1328-31: Helen, Ilium; 1341-7: Helen, Semele, Arethusa; 1478-80: Apollo
Edward II 6-9: Leander; 10-11: Elisium; 61ff: Dian, Actaeon; 143-5: Hilas; 467-70: Circe, Hymen; 474-7: Jove, Juno, Ganymede; 609-10: Cyclops; 689-94: Ephestion, Hilas, Patroclus, Octavius, Alcibiades; 852ff, 1574-8: Danae; 2029-32: Tisiphon; 2385-6: Aristorchus
Hero and Leander (Sestiad i) 1-5: Hellespont, Abydos, Sestos; 5-8: Hero, Apollo; 11-16: Hero, Venus, Adonis; 37ff: Hero; 51-3: Leander, Abydos, Musaeus (2); 55-8: Colchos, Leander; 59-65: Cynthia, Circe,

285

Jove, Pelops, Leander; 73-6: Leander,
Narcissus; 77-8: Hippolytus; 81-2: Leander,
Thracian; 91-3: Sestos, Adonis; 96-102:
Phaethon; 114: Ixion, centaurs; 35-42:
Venus, Proteus, Bacchus, Sestos; 145-6:
Danae; 147-8: Ganymede, Jove, Juno;
149-50: Europa, Iris; 151-2: Mars, Vulcan;
154-6: Sylvanus, Cyparissus; 187-91:
Hero, Leander, Cupid, Acheron; 209-14:
Venus, Hero; 299 ff: Venus, Hero; 321-3:
Pallas, Venus; 347-50: Morpheus; 369-74:
Cupid; 386 ff: Io, Argus (1), Hebe; 447-8:
Destinies; 455-8: Saturn, Ops, Stygian,
Jove; 473-5: Destinies, Hermes, Midas
(Sestiad ii) 45-8: Salmacis, Hero; 74-6:
Hero, Tantalus; 120: Alcides; 153-8:
Leander, Neptune, Triton, Ganymede;
179-80: Helle; 203: Thetis; 260-3: Hero,
Diana, Actaeon; 297-300: Hercules,
Hesperides, Leander; 303-7: Mars, Erycine;
322-5: Hero, Dis; 327-31: Apollo,
Hesperus
See also under *Chapman, George*
The Jew of Malta 20-1: Draco; 22-6: Phalaris;
174-6: Iphigen, Agamemnon; 674-7:
Morpheus; 1400 ff: Alexander, Hydra,
Hebon, Cocytus; 1808-10: Jason, Bacchus;
1812-4: Adonis; 2139-43: Aesop
The Massacre at Paris 58-9: Hymen; 1005:
Caesar
Tamburlaine **(Part i)** 44-5: Persepolis; 73-4:
Paris, Helen; 137-8: Cyrus; 283-5:
Rhodope (1); 269-90: Pegasus; 333-6:
Avernus, Cerberus; 436-40: Pylades,
Orestes; 463-5: Atlas; 616 ff: Cyclopian;
899-901: Harpy; 983-4: Orcus; 1035-7:
Muses, Pierides, Minerva, Neptune;
1030-40: Juno; 1062-6: Auster, Aquilon;
1201ff: Typhon; 1238-9: Hydra; 1250-3:
Caesar, Pharsalia; 1417-8: Erebus; 1571-6:
Meleager, Calydonian Boar, Cephalus,
Themis; 1646-7: Jason; 1656-61: Avernus,
Lerna; 1920-1: Flora; 1999-2001: Cocytus;
2036-9: Stygian; 2174 ff: Turnus, Lavinia,
Aeneas; 2245-8: Styx, Charon; 2291-2:
Juno, Jove; 2296: Latona, Diana; 2310-1:
Alcides **(Part ii)** 2351-3: Polypheme;
2537-40: Pygmalion, Io; 2539-43: Phoebus;
2944-7: Orcus; 3054-8: Helen, Tenedos,
Homer; 3059-63: Lesbia, Corinna; 3080-3:
Janus; 3100-4: Mausolus; 3202-4: Hades;
3229-32: Bellona; 3461-2: Cynthia, Thetis;

3537-9: Semiramis; 3566-70: Hector,
Achilles; 3898-900: Hermes; 3991-5:
Egeus; 4011 ff: Pluto, Proserpina; 4090-2:
Ilion; 4101-2: Hyrcania; 4207-10: Cerberus;
4400-1: Cimmerian; 4621 ff: Clymene,
Phaethon; 4631-4: Hippolytus

Marvell, Andrew (1621-78)
The Character of Holland 97-8: Athos; 137-8:
Hydra
Damon the Mower Damon
Elegy on the Death of Lord Villiers 97-104:
Hector, Achilles; 105 ff: Venus, Adonis
Epigram on Two Mountains 11-12: Pelion,
Ossa, Pindus
The First Anniversary 49 ff: Amphion
Flecknoe 117 ff: Nero; 151-2: Perillus
The Garden 27-9: Daphne; 30-1: Syrinx
Last Instructions to a Painter 543 ff: Neptune,
Aeolus, Tritons
Letter to Dr Ingelo 49-50: Hercules,
Nemean
The Loyal Scot 63-4: Pegasus; 67-8: Curtius
Mourning 19-20: Danae
The Nymph Complaining 96-100: Heliades
Thyrsis and Dorinda 31-7: Elysium
Tom May's Death 90-7: Phlegethon, Cerberus,
Ixion, Megaera
To that Renowned Man . . . Graphologist
1ff: Bellerophontean; 42-4: Palamedes
The Unfortunate Lover 45-8: Ajax
Upon Appleton House 37-40: Romulus;
427-8: Alexander; 753 ff: Tempe, Idalian,
Elysian
Upon the Death of Lord Hastings 43-6:
Hymenaeus
Upon the Death of the Lord Protector 232-7:
Janus

Masefield, John (1878-1967)
Arthur and his Ring Saturn
Cassandra 6 ff: Cassandra
Clytemnestra 4 ff: Helen, Paris, Agamemnon,
Priam; 31 ff: Iphigenia
The Horse Epeios
A King's Daughter Helen, Menelaus
Letter from Pontus Ovid, Agrippa, Postumus,
Tiberius
The Rider at the Gate 17 ff: Caesar
Roses are Beauty 6-7: Sphinx
Shopping in Oxford Helicon
The Spearman Achilles, Paris, Deiphobus

The Tale of Nireus 7-9: Nireus; 32-9:
Menelaus, Nireus, Helen, Paris

Meredith, George (1828-1909)
Antigone Polyneices, Antigone
The Appeasement of Demeter Demeter,
Proserpine
Bellerophon Bellerophon, Hippocrene
Cassandra Cassandra
The Comic Spirit Astarte
Daphne Daphne, Thessalian, Tempe, Peneian,
Pindus, Arethusa, Daphne
The Day of the Daughter of Hades Enna,
Proserpine, Pluto, Aetna, Typhon
Empedocles Empedocles
The Empty Purse Phalaris, Attis, Cybele
A Garden Idyll, Arachne
Idomeneus Idomeneus
The Labourer Heracles
London by Lamplight Circe
Milton Hellespont
Pastoral II Triptolemus, Ceres, Proserpine
Periander Melissa
Phaethon Phoebus, Phaethon
The Rape of Aurora Flora, Zephyr, Aurora,
Apollo
Solon Solon, Peisistratus
South West Wind Aeolian
Swathed round in Mist Ida, Tenedos, Olympus
The Two Marks Melpomene, Thalia
Youth in Memory Persephone

Milton, John (1608-74)
Arcades 20-3: Latona, Cybele, Juno; 28-31:
Arcady, Alpheus, Arethusa; 32-3: Nymphs;
43-4: Genius, Jove; 61-4: Sirens; 63-70:
Music of the Spheres, Necessity, Fates; 97:
Ladon; 98: Lycaeus, Cyllene; 100:
Erymanth; 102: Maenalus; 106: Syrinx
At a Solemn Music 1-2: Sirens
Comus 1-2: Jove; 1-6: Daemons; 16-17:
Ambrosial; 17-21: Jove, Neptune, Pluto;
46-7, 54-5: Bacchus; 46-50: Aeaea; 48-9:
Tyrrhene; 50-2: Circe; 54-8, 63-70:
Comus; 63-7: Circe; 82-4: Iris; 93-4:
Hesper; 95-7: Helios; 111-4: Music of the
Spheres; 120-1: wood-nymphs; 124:
Venus; 128-36: Cotytto, Hecate, Stygian;
172-6: Pan; 188-90: Phoebus; 230ff:
Echo; 230-3: Meander; 233-5: Nightingale;
252-5: Circe; 256-7: Elysium, Scylla,
Charybdis; 290: Hebe; 331-5: Chaos;

341-2: Arcas, Cynosure; 393-7: Hesperian;
421-3: Nymph; 441-6: Diana, Cupid;
447-9: Minerva, Gorgon; 476-80: Apollo,
nectar'd; 515-7: Chimera; 519-20: Bacchus,
Circe, Comus; 335-6: Hecate; 552-4:
Night; 602-5: Acheron, Harpies, Hydras;
636-7: Moly; 653-6: Vulcan, Cacus; 661-3:
Daphne, Apollo; 675-7: Nepenthe, Thone,
Helen, Polydamna; 701-2: Juno; 706-9:
Stoick, Cynick; 802-5: Jove, Erebus,
Saturn; 821-3: Meliboeus; 835: Nereus;
837-40: Nectar'd, Asphodil, Ambrosial;
867-70: Oceanus, Neptune, Tethys; 871:
Nereus; 872: Carpathian; 873: Triton;
874: Glaucus; 875-6: Leucothea, Melicerta;
877: Thetis; 878-80: Parthenope, Sirens,
Ligea; 883-4: Nymphs; 920-1: Amphitrite;
922-3: Anchises; 962-5: Mercury, Dryads;
977-1011: Elysian Fields; 981-3: Hesperus,
Hesperides; 986-7: Graces, Howres; 989-91:
Zephyrs; 992-9: Iris, Hyacinth; 999-1002:
Adonis, Venus; 1004-8: Cupid, Psyche;
1019-21: Music of the Spheres
Epitaph on the Marchioness of Winchester
17-22: Hymen, cypress; 25-30: Lucina,
Atropos; 55-6: Helicon; 57-9: Came
Il Penseroso 9-10: Morpheus; 11-18: Memnon,
Himera; 16-21: Cassiopeia, Nereids; 23-6:
Vesta, Saturn; 28-30: Ida, Jove; 47-8:
Muses, Jove; 56-62: Philomel; 59-60:
Cynthia; 68-92: Plato; 93-6: daemons;
97-100: Thebes, Pelops, Troy, Melpomene;
103-4: Musaeus; 103-8: Orpheus, Pluto;
121-5: Cephalus; 134-5: Sylvan; 136-8:
Nymphs; 146: Sleep; 154: Genius
L'Allegro 1-3: Cerberus, Stygean; 1-10:
Cimmerian; 11-13: Euphrosyne; 13-16:
Graces, Venus, Bacchus; 18-19: Zephyr,
Aurora; 25-6: nymph; 28-30: Hebe; 36:
nymph, Oread; 59-62: Sun; 83-5: Corydon,
Thyrsis; 88: Thestylis; 125-6: Hymen;
135-6: Lydian; 143-50: Orpheus, Elysian,
Pluto, Eurydice
Lycidas 1-3: laurels, myrtles, ivy; 8-10:
Lycidas; 15: Sisters, Aganippe; 30-1:
Hesperus; 34-5: Satyrs, Fauns; 36:
Damoetas; 52-4: Mona; 55: Deva; 58-63:
Calliope, Orpheus, Hebrus, Lesbian; 66:
Muse; 66-8: Amaryllis; 68-9: Neaera; 70ff:
Fame; 75-6: Atropos; 75-8: Phoebus; 82-3:
Jove; 85-7: Arethuse, Mincius; 89-90:
Triton, Neptune; 93-7: Hippotades; 98-9:

Panope; 103-4: Camus; 106: Hyacinth;
132-3: Alpheus, Muse; 138: Sirius; 159-60:
Bellerus; 164: Arion; 172-5: Nectar;
182-5: Genius; 189: Dorick
On the Death of a Fair Infant 8-9: Aquilo,
Orithyia; 23-8: Apollo, Hyacinth, Eurotas,
Spartan; 38-40: Elisian Fields; 43-4:
Olympus; 47-9: Giants, nectar'd; 50-1:
Astraea; 54: Truth
On the Morning of Christ's Nativity 15-16:
Urania; 18-19: Sun; 46-52: Peace; 68:
halcyon; 72-4: Lucifer; 85-90: Pan;
101-2: Cymbria; 125-35: Music of the
Spheres; 135: Age of Gold; 141-4: Truth,
Astraea; 176-8: Apollo, Delphos; 184-6:
Genius; 107-8: Nymphs; 191: Lars,
Lemures; 200-1: Ashtaroth; 203: Hammon;
204: Tyrian, Thamuz; 213: Orion,
Memphian; 226: Typhon; 235-6: Night
On Shakespeare 10-12: Delphick
Paradise Lost (Book i) 6-8: Muse; 376, 9-10:
Chaos, 12-15: Aonian; 72-3: Hades;
196-8: Titanian; 198: Jove, Giant, Briareos;
198-200: Typhon; 230-3: Pelorus; 239-40:
Stygian; 266: Lethe; 286-9: Tuscan;
286-90: Valdarno; 302-4: Etrurian;
304-6: Orion; 307: Busiris, Memphis;
386-7: Jehovah; 438-9: Astarte, Astoreth;
439-41: Sidonian; 446ff: Thammuz,
Adonis (River); 464: Azotus; 462-3:
Dagon, Azotus; 467-8: Rimmon; 477-9:
Osiris, Isis, Orus; 508-10: Ionian; 510-12:
Titan, Saturn; 512-4: Jove, Rhea; 514-5:
Creet, Ida; 514-7: Olympus; 517-9:
Delphian, Dodona, Doric; 519-20: Saturn,
Adria, Hesperian; 543: Chaos, Night;
549-51: Dorian; 576-9: Phlegra; 575-6:
Pygmy; 577-9: Thebes, Ilium; 713-5:
Doric; 739-40: Ausonia; 740ff: Mulciber;
741-2: Jove; 745-6: Lemnos; 769: Taurus;
777-9: Giant-Sons; 777-81: Pigmean
(Book ii) 14-15: Virtues; 28-9: Jupiter;
68-70: Tartarean; 73-4: Lethe; 149-50:
Night; 173-4: Jupiter; 231-3: Chaos;
244-5: Ambrosial; 305-7: Atlantean; 506:
Stygian; 529-30: Olympian, Pythian;
539-40: Typhoean; 539-44: Alcides,
Oechalia, Thessalian, Lichas, Oeta, Euboic
Sea; 578: Acheron; 577: Styx; 579-80:
Cocytus; 580-1: Phlegethon; 582-3: Lethe;
592-4: Serbonian; 604-8: Lethean; 610-3:
Medusa, Gorgonian; 612-4: Tantalus;

626-8: Gorgons, Hydras, Chimeras; 653-5:
Cerberean; 659-61: Scylla, Calabria,
Trinacrian; 662-5: Hecate; 671: Furies;
757-8: Minerva; 858: Tartarus; 874-6:
Stygian; 879-83: Erebus; 894-6: Night,
Chaos; 903-4: Barea, Cyrene; 907-9:
Chaos; 920-4: Bellona; 939-40: Syrtis;
943-7: Amiraspian, Gryfon; 959-61:
Chaos, Night; 963-4: Orcus, Ades; 964-7:
Demogorgon, Rumor; 1001-2: Night;
1016-18: Argo; 1019-20: Ulysses,
Charybdis; 1037-9: Chaos (Book iii)
13-4: Stygian; 17-8: Orphean, Chaos,
Night; 19-21: Muse; 26-9: Muses; 34-6:
Thamyris, Maeonides, Tiresias, Phineus;
358-9: Elisian; 419ff: Chaos, Night;
431-2: Imaus; 431-6: Hydaspes; 464-5:
Giants; 469-71: Empedocles; 471-3:
Cleombrotus; 557-60: Andromeda; 567-9:
Hesperian; 600-3: Hermes; 603-5: Proteus;
730-2: triform (Book iv) 162-3: Arabia,
Sabean; 211-12: Seleucia; 218-20:
Ambrosial; 237-40: Nectar; 248-51:
Hesperian; 260-3: myrtle, Venus; 266-7:
Pan, Graces, Proserpin, Dis, Ceres; 272-5:
Daphne, Orontes, Castalian Spring; 275-9:
Nyseian, Triton (River), Ammon, Amalthea,
Bacchus, Rhea; 301-3: Hyacinthin; 327-30:
Zephyr; 331-2: Nectarin; 347-9: Gordian;
460-8: Narcissus; 497-500: Jupiter, Juno;
605-6: Hesperus; 665-7: Night, Chaos;
692-4: laurel, myrtle; 695-7: Acanthus;
705-8: Pan, Silvanus, nymph, Faunus;
709-11: Hymenean; 714-9: Pandora,
Japhet, Hermes, Jove, Epimetheus,
Prometheus; 763-4: Cupid; 979-82: Ceres
(Book v) 5-6: Aurora; 15-7: Zephyrus,
Flora; 55-7: Ambrosia; 139-40: Sun;
166-9: Phosphorus, Sun; 175-8: Moon;
264-5: Cyclades, Delos, Samos; 272-4:
Phoenix, Egyptian Thebes; 285-6: Maia;
292-4: Elysian fields; 303-7: nectarous;
338: Earth, Pontus, Alcinous; 377-9:
Pomona; 380-1: wood-nymph; 380-2:
Ida, Paris; 558-60: Sun; 577-9: Chaos;
632-5: Nestor; 642-3: Ambrosial; 685ff:
Night; 707-8: Morning Star; 659-60:
Lucifer (Book vi) 2-4: Hours; 52-4:
Tartarus; 53-5: Chaos; 331-3: nectarous;
406: Night; 474-5: ambrosial; 490-1:
Jupiter; 761-2: Victory (Book vii) 1-6:
Urania; 3-4: Olympian, Pegasean; 5-7:

Olympus; 16-9: Bellerophon, Aleian; 30-1:
Urania; 32-3: Bacchus; 33-8: Orpheus,
Rhodope, Calliope; 90-3: Chaos; 98-9:
Sun; 104-6: Vesper; 102-3: Nature; 131-3:
Lucifer; 211ff: Chaos; 366: Phosphor;
373-5: Pleiades; 574-81: Milky Way;
604-5: Giants **(Book viii)** 60-1: Graces;
60-2: Venus; 162: Sun; 518-20: Evening
Star; 630-2: Hesperian **(Book ix)** 13-9:
Achilles, Hector, Turnus, Lavinia, Neptune,
Juno, Odysseus, Aeneas; 20-4: Muse; 48-50:
Hesperus; 76-8: Pontus Maeotis; 80-3:
Orontes; 217-9: roses, myrtle;
386-7: wood-nymph, Oread, Dryad;
386-90: Delia; 393-5: Pales, Pomona,
Vertumnus; 393-6: Ceres, Proserpina, Jove;
426-32: myrtle, rose; 439-41: Gardens of
Adonis, Alcinous, Laertes; 626-7: myrtles;
670-2: Athens, Rome; 1060: Herculean;
1110-1: Amazonian **(Book x)** 230-3:
Chaos; 282-3: Chaos; 289-91: Cronian
Sea; 293-6: Delos; 293-7: Gorgonian;
306-10: Xerxes, Susa, Memnonian,
Hellespont; 316-8: Chaos; 347-9: Chaos;
425-6: Lucifer; 443-5: Plutonian; 452-4:
Stygian; 476-7: Night, Chaos; 519-26:
Amphisbaena, Cerastes, Hydrus, Ellops,
Dipsas; 527-31: Python, Gorgon, Ophiusa,
Pythian; 558-60: Megaera; 580-4: Ophion,
Eurynome, Olympus, Saturn, Ops, Dictaean;
635-7: Chaos; 687-9: Thyestean; 699-705:
Boreas, Notus, Eurus, Zephyr **(Book xi)**
9-14: Deucalion, Pyrrha, Theseus; 127-9:
Janus; 129-31: Argus; 129-33: Arcadian,
Hermes; 133-5: Leucothea; 185: Jove;
240-4: Meliboean, Sarra, Iris; 279:
Ambrosial; 402: Atlas; 410-11: Geryon;
587-8: Evening Star; 589-91: Hymen
(Book xii) 422-3: Morning Star
Paradise Regained **(Book i)** 294: Morning
Star; 333-4: Fame; 456-9: Delphos;
478-80: sylvan; 499-501: Night
(Book ii) 138-9: Graces; 182-8: Calisto,
Clymene, Daphne, Semele, Antiopa,
Amynome, Syrinx; 188-91: Apollo,
Neptune, Jupiter, Pan, satyr, faun, sylvan;
196-8: Pellean; 199-200: Africa; 213-5:
Venus, Jove; 216-7: Virtue; 294-7: wood-
nymphs; 344-7: Pontus, Lucrine Bay;
350-3: Ganymede, Hylas; 353-6: Diana,
Naiades, Amalthea; 355-7: Hesperides;
363-5: Flora; 445-9: Quintius, Fabricius,

Curius, Regulus **(Book iii)** 31-4: Philip II,
Cyrus; 31-6: Scipio, Pompey, Mithridates;
39-42: Caesar; 82-7: Alexander, Romulus;
96-9: Socrates; 100-4: Scipio; 157-68:
Tiberius; 275-8: Nineveh, Ninus,
Salamanassar; 280: Babylon, Cyrus; 284-8:
Persepolis, Bactra, Ecbatana, Hecatompylos;
288-9: Susa, Choaspes; 289-91: Emathian,
Parthian, Seleucia, Nisibis; 294-7: Parthian,
Arsaces, Antioch; 299-302: Parthia,
Ctesiphon, Scythian, Sogdiana; 317-8:
Hyrcanian, Iberian, Caucasus; 363-7:
Parthian, Antigonus, Hyrcanus; 383-5:
Rome **(Book iv)** 31: Septentrion; 45-7:
Rome; 47-9: Capitol, Tarpeian Rock;
50-5: Palatine; 67-70: Appian Road,
Aemilian, Syrene; 70-1: Meroe; 90-7:
Tiberius, Caprene, Sejanus; 116-9: Setia,
Cales, Falerne; 117-9: Chios; 238-43:
Athens; 244-5: Academe, Plato, Attic;
247-9: Hymettus, Ilissus; 251-3: Alexander,
Aristotle, Lyceum, Stoa; 256: Aeolian,
Dorian; 259-60: Melisigenes, Homer,
Phoebus; 273-80: Socrates, Peripatetics,
Epicurean, Stoic; 293-4: Socrates; 296:
Sceptics; 300-6: Stoicism; 562-6: Antaeus,
Irassa, Alcides; 572-6: Sphinx, Ismenian;
587-90: Ambrosial
Samson Agonistes 12-13: Dagon; 133:
Chalybean; 434ff: Dagon; 711-9: Tarsus,
Tartessus; 1150-1: Dagon; 1699-1707:
Phoenix
The Passion 22-3: Phoebus; 29-34: Night
Song on May Morning 1-2: morning star
Sonnets 8 *(Captain or Colonel)* Emathian,
Pindarus, Euripides, Electra, Athenian;
9 *(Lady, That in the Prime)* Truth;
11 *(A Book Was Writ)* Quintilian;
12 *(I Did But Prompt the Age)* Latona,
Apollo, Artemis; 13 *(To Mr H. Lawes)*
Midas, Phoebus; 15 *(On the Lord General
Fairfax)* Hydra; 17 *(To Sir Henry Vane)*
Epeirot, African; 20 *(Lawrence of Virtuous
Father)* Attic, Favonius, Tuscan;
21 *(Cyriack, Whose Grandsire)* Themis,
Euclid, Archimedes; 23 *(Methought I Saw)*
Alcestis, Heracles, Admetus

Monro, Harold (1879-1932)
Children of Love 15-8: Cupid
God of the World 1: Zeus

Moore, Thomas (1779-1852)
Aspasia 7-14: Aspasia
Cephalus and Procris 17-22: Cephalus and Procris
Corruption 115-8: Capreae, Tiberius
Cupid and Psyche 5ff: Cupid, Psyche
A Dream of Antiquity 23-5: Epicurus; 52-6: Hyrcanian; 85-6: Teian
Evenings in Greece **(Part i)** 52-4: Patmos; 131-8: Sappho, Leucadia; 331-4: Thyads, Peneus; 551-2: Eleusis **(Part ii)** 79-80: Naxos, Lesbian; 451-5: Harmodius, Hymettus, Helle
The Fall of Hebe 16ff: Lyaeus; 70-4: Hebe; 97-100: Eleusinian
The Genius of Harmony 44-5: Orphic; 60-2: Pangean, Orpheus
The Grecian Girl's Dream 41-2: Leontium, Epicurus; 44-5: Pythias, Aristotle; 46-7: Socrates, Aspasia; 48-51: Theano, Pythagoras
Hero and Leander 7-12: Leander, Hero
Hymn of a Virgin of Delphi 5-8: Delphi, Tempe; 49-52: Plistus
Intolerance 74: Danae
Morality 31-4: Zeno; 36-43: Aristippus; 74-5: Tully
Nature's Labels 5-8: Plato, Stagyrite
The Philosopher Aristippus 38-42: Ascra, Nine, Castalia
Rhymes on the Road iii 1-4: Hippomenes; 13-4: Astraea; xii 13: Attic; xiii 55-8: Palmyra, Persepolis
The Sale of Loves 1-4: Paphian, Loves
The Sceptic 26-7: Epicurus
The Summer Fete 77-82: Epicurus; 659ff: Sappho; 785-90: Hippocrene
To George Morgan 3-5: Anacreon
To The Invisible Girl 39-42: Numa, Socrates
To Joseph Atkinson 31ff: Heraean
To Lord Viscount Strangford 1-4: Crotona, Pythagoras; 39-43: Verona, Catullus
To Mrs Henry Tighe 29-32: Psyche
A Vision of Philosophy 25-8: Orpheus

Noyes, Alfred (1880-1958)
At Dawn 1-2: Hesper-Phosphor; 49: Hesper, Hours; 58-61: Naiad, nymph, Oceanides
Black Bill's Honeymoon 1: Hyrcania
The Burning Boughs 13-16: Oread, Bacchus
Drake Exordium Aeneas, Homer; i: Penelope; ii: Erebus; iii: Titan, Laocoon, Hecate; xii: Charon
Euterpe 1-4: Euterpe, Helicon; 27-32: Euterpe
Forty Singing Seamen 3-8: Ulysses, Polyphemus
Helicon 1-4: Helicon, Nine
Memories of the Pacific Coast 5-8: Hesperian
Mount Ida 2-3: Muses, Ida (2); 85-8: Ganymede, Ida (2); 113-6: Hylas; 121-2: Theocritus; 138-44: Hesperian, Juno, Dian, Aphrodite
Niobe 11-15: Niobe, Promethean
A Spring Hat 1-6: Sabine
Tales from The Mermaid vii: Lais; x: Amphion
The Tramp Transfigured 152-5: Ovid, Proteus

Owen, Wilfred (1893-1918)
Antaeus 1ff: Antaeus, Heracles, Eurystheus
To a Comrade in Flanders 1-4: Lethe, Styx

Pope, Alexander (1688-1744)
Acis and Galatea, Chorus 4-8: Polypheme
Argus 10-15: Argus (3)
Autumn 5-6: Mantuan, Hylas, Aegon; 7-8: Terence, Plautus, Menander; 15-6: Hylas; 55: Aegon; 89-92: Love
Chorus to 'Brutus' i 31-2: Tully; ii 7-8: Marcus, Brutus (3); 15-16: Brutus (3), Porcia, Cassius (2), Junia; 21-4: Hymen, Cynthia
The Dunciad (Text A) **(Book i)** 7-8: Pallas, Jove; 159-60: Horace, Maro **(Book ii)** 79-83: Jove; 89-90: Cloacina; 135-6: Codrus; 165: Jove; 209-10: Venus, Paris, Achilles; 307ff: Hylas; 314-9: Styx, Lethe, Alpheus, Arethuse; 340-4: Ulysses, Argus **(Book iii)** 2-4: Cimmerian; 102-4: Pan, Venus, Phidias, Apelles; 123-6: Berecynthia; 239-40: Cynthia; 311-2: Aeschylus; 343-5: Argus, Hermes; 349-51: Stagyrite
Elegy to the Memory of an Unfortunate Lady 59-60: Loves
Eloisa to Abelard 258-9: Venus
Epilogue to Jane Shore 30-4: Cato (3), Plutarch; 36-7: Cato (3)
Epilogue to Satires 11ff: Horace; 73-4: Ciceronian; 98: Nepenthe; 120: Cato (3)
Epistle to Dr Arbuthnot 3-4: Parnassus; 69-72: Midas; 116: Horace; 117: Alexander; 209-10: Cato (2); 231: Apollo
Epistle to Henry Cromwell 70-4: Tiberius Gracchus, Caius Gracchus, Septimuleius;

74-8, 102-3: Cato (3), Aristophanes
Epistles I 81-4: Caesar; 212: Catiline; 213:
   Caesar, Servilia; 216-7: Caesar, Scipio;
   218-9: Lucullus; III 3-4: Momus; 127-8:
   Didius; 295: Gorgon; IV 69ff: Nero
Essay on Criticism 34-5: Maevius; 94-7:
   Parnassus; 124-5: Homer; 129: Mantuan;
   130ff: Maro, Homer; 179-80: Homer;
   215-6: Pierian; 271-2: Aristotle; 341-3:
   Parnassus; 366ff: Zephyr, Ajax, Camilla;
   464-5: Homer, Zoilus; 514-5: Parnassus;
   645-8: Stagyrite, Maeonian; 653-6: Horace;
   665-6: Dionysius; 667-8: Petronius;
   669-70: Quintilian; 675-80: Longinus (2);
   709-11: Latium
Essay on Man **(Epistle i)** 41-2: Jove; 155-6:
   Catiline; 201-6: Music of the Spheres,
   Zephyr **(Epistle ii)** 23-6: Plato; 195-8:
   Nero, Titus; 199-202: Decius, Catiline,
   Curtius **(Epistle iv)** 145-8: Caesar, Titus;
   207-8: Lucrece; 220: Alexander; 233-6:
   Aurelius, Socrates; 244-6: Rubicon; 257-8:
   Marcellus (2), Caesar
Imitation of Cowley 22-4: Daphne
A Lady Singing to Her Lute 9-10: Orpheus
Letter to Cromwell 2-4: Elysian, Asphodel
Lines from Alcander VIII 1-2: Phoenix; 2-4:
   Argus, Briareus
The Messiah 3-6: Pindus, Aonian; 99-100:
   Cynthia
Ode for Musick 1-4: Muses; 25ff: Morpheus;
   35ff: Amphion; 37-41: Orpheus, Argo,
   Pelion; 49-50: Phlegethon; 51-6:
   Orpheus; 66-70: Sysiphus, Ixion, Furies;
   71ff: Orpheus, Eurydice, Proserpine; 72-5:
   Asphodel, Elysian; 111: Haemus,
   Bacchanals; 131-4: Orpheus, Cecilia
Of a Lady Who Could not Sleep II 7-10:
   Narcissus; V 1-4: Cytherea
On Burnet and Ducket 5-8: Amphisbaena
Prologue to Addison's 'Cato' 23-4: Cato (3);
   33-5: Cato (3), Caesar; 39-40: Cato (2)
The Rape of the Lock (First Edition)
   (Canto i) 13-14: Sol; 137-8: Troy
   (Canto ii) 92-5: Aeneas, Dido, Anna;
   126-7: Jove; 168-71: Proculus, Romulus
A Rhapsody 1-6: Pegasean, Parnassian,
   Aganippe
A Simile 1-3: Maeotis
Spring 3-4: Muses; 6: Albion; 61: Pactolus;
   65-8: Venus, Idalia, Ceres, Hybla, Diana,
   Cynthus; 102: Pleiads

Summer 50: Satyrs, Pan; 59-60: Elysium;
   61-2: Venus, Adonis, Diana; 65-6: Ceres;
   81-4: Orpheus
The Temple of Fame 27-30: Parian; 59-60:
   Atlas; 80: Perseus; 81-2: Alcides, Hesperian;
   83-4: Orpheus; 85-8: Amphion, Cythaeron;
   95-6: Ninus, Cyrus; 124-6: Scythian;
   147-8: Time; 151-2: Alexander; 155-7:
   Caesar, Minerva; 162: Timoleon; 163-4:
   Scipio (1); 165-7: Aurelius; 170-1: Socrates;
   172-3: Aristides; 176: Phocion, Cato (3);
   177: Brutus (3); 188ff: Tydides, Hector,
   Patroclus; 200-3: Mantuan, Homer; 205:
   Latian, Turnus; 207-9: Aeneas, Anchises,
   Troy; 212-5: Pindar (1); 222-5: Horace,
   Ausonian, Pindar (1), Alcaeus, Sapphick;
   229-31: Augustus; 232-7: Stagyrite;
   238-41: Tully; 265-9: Fame; 270-3:
   Nine; 296-7: Fortune
To Belinda 5-8: Helen, Homer; 19-22:
   Lucrece
To the Author of a Poem 9-10: Orpheus; 18-9:
   Bavius, Maevius; 20: Codrus, Chaerilus
Upon a Girl of Seven Years Old 3-6: Pallas,
   Venus
Weeping 13-18: Phaeton
Windsor-Forest 12-4: Chaos; 33-6: Olympus;
   37-40: Pan, Flora, Pomona, Ceres; 142:
   Tyrian; 159-62: Arcadia, Diana; 165ff:
   Diana, Cynthus; 198ff: Arethusa; 227-9:
   Po, Virgil; 257-8: Scipio (1), Atticus; 316:
   Belerium; 335-6: Augusta; 355ff: Tiber,
   Hermes; 377-8: Augusta; 429-30: Peace
Winter 11-12: Alexis, Dryads; 21-4: Muses,
   Nymphs, Sylvans, Loves, Adonis; 41-4:
   Echo; 49ff: zephyrs; 69ff: Daphne (2);
   87: Boreas
A Winter Piece 1-4: Boreas

Praed, Winthrop Mackworth (1802-39)
Arminius 2-5: Arminius; 19-24: Varus,
   Arminius
The Bridal of Belmont 252-8: Parian,
   Phidias
The County Bell 536-8: Daedalus; 608-12:
   Aphrodite
Lillian ii 26-30: Cupid
Love at a Rout 1-7: satyrs, nymphs, fauns,
   Cupid
The Modern Nectar 1-8: Bacchus, Venus;
   51-4: Pactolus; 59-60: Hebe
To Susan Praed 113-6: Pompey, Tully

Prior, Matthew (1664-1721)
Alma **(Canto i)** 136 ff: Lucretius; 389-93:
   Venus, Cupid; 398-404: Horace; 486-8:
   Antonius, Actium **(ii)** 91ff: Paris, Atrides
Carmen Seculare 1: Janus; 26-7: Latium;
   31-4: Sabine, Romulus; 35-6: Numa;
   40-1: Brutus (2); 42-3: Fabius Maximus;
   52-3: Julius; 54-5: Augustus; 59-60:
   Tiber; 205-6: Pindar (1); 212-3: Pegasus;
   257-8: Astraea; 290-1: Bellerophon,
   Lycian; 299-300: Chromius, Theron;
   318-9: Janus; 454-5: Atrides; 472-3:
   Argo; 557-8: Virgil, Aeneas, Latian
Chloe Hunting 17-8: Cynthia
The Conversation 71-3: Tully
Cupid and Ganymede 1-4: Anacreon; 11-2:
   Danae; 17-8: Cupid, Paris
Democritus and Heraclitus 1-2: Democritus;
   3-4: Heraclitus
The Dove 1-4: Virgil; 19-20: Heraclitus
Down Hall 1-4: Jason, Aeneas; 6-10: Ulysses,
   Penelope
Epilogue to 'Lucius' 9 ff: Phaon, Sappho
Epilogue to 'Phaedra' 11-13: Ismena
Henry and Emma 343-4: Thalestris
The Ladle 101ff: Amphitryon, Alcmena
Ode in Imitation of Horace 110-13: Virgil,
   Homer
Ode in Memory of George Villiers 14: Bellona;
   35-8: Pythagoras; 55-9: Proserpine
Ode Inscribed to the Queen 1ff: Augustus,
   Horace; 211-5: Brutus (1), Xanthus, Troy;
   271-2: Trajan; 281-3: Aeneas, Latian
On Beauty 10ff: Theseus, Paris, Jason,
   Antony, Lucrece, Alcides, Omphale, Lais
On the Coronation of James II 15-16: Argo
On Fleet 15-8: Hector, Capaneus, Turnus,
   Ajax
The Padlock 1-4: Danae
Pallas and Venus 1-2: Paris
A Pindaric 65-7: Saturnian, Golden Age
Prologue Spoken at Court 33-6: Perseus,
   Andromeda, Minerva
Protagenes and Apelles 17-8: Protagenes,
   Apelles
Satire on Modern Translators 53-4: Mantuan,
   Lucretius; 79-80: Ovid; 111-3: Ovid,
   Hannibal; 159-62: Virgil, Homer, Horace,
   Pindar (1)
To Charles Montague 2: Maeander
To the Countess Dowager of Devonshire
   41-4: Rhea

To the Earl of Dorset 38-40: Janus; 41-4:
   Hymen
To the Lord Bishop of Rochester 5-6:
   Phaeton; 20-1: Tully, Catiline
To Mr Howard 5ff: Apelles, Ammon
The Turtle and the Sparrow 113-4:
   Tithonus
The Wedding Night 1-2: Alcmena, Alcides
Written in an Ovid 1-4: Ovid

Raleigh, Sir Walter (1552-1618)
Epitaph on Sidney 57-60: Hannibal, Cicero,
   Scipio (1)
Of Spenser's 'Faerie Queene' 13-14: Homer
The Shepherd's Praise of Diana 9-12: Diana

Rochester, John Wilmot, Earl of (1648-80)
Could I but Make My Wishes 9-10:
   Phaethon
Epilogue to Love In The Dark 38: Cathegus
Grecian Kindness 1-6: Greeks, Trojans
The History of Insipids 61-4: Pompey,
   Caesar
On Drinking in a Bowl 1-4: Vulcan, Nestor
Tunbridge Wells 33-4: Scylla, Charybdis

Rosetti, Dante Gabriel (1828-82)
Aspecta Medusa 1-5: Amdromeda, Perseus,
   Gorgon
The Garden of Nineveh 10-14: Nineveh
Cassandra I 2ff: Cassandra; 9-11: Andromache,
   Hector
Cassandra II 9-14: Paris
Death's Songsters 1ff: Troy; 9-12: Ulysses,
   Sirens
Hero's Lamp 1ff: Hero, Leander, Anteros
Jenny Venus, Priapus, Danae
The Kiss 5-8: Orpheus
Pandora 1-4: Pandora
Tiber, Nile and Thames 1ff: Cicero,
   Fulvia
Troy Town 1-7: Troy, Helen; 92-9: Paris
Venus Victrix 1-2: Juno; 5-8: Venus

Sassoon, Siegfried (1886-1967)
Preface to Satirical Poems 1ff: Phoenix
Solar Eclipse 8ff: Daphne, Apollo

Scott, Sir Walter (1771-1832)
From 'Ann of Grierstein' Sisters Nine
From 'Waverley' Hyrcanian
Saint Cloud 10-11: Naiads

Shakespeare, William (1564-1616)

All's Well That Ends Well I iii 66-9: Helen, Priam; 107ff: Diana; 141-3: Iris; 200-4: Dian; II i 96-7: Pandarus; 160-1: Apollo; iii 72-4: Dian; III iv 8-11: Mars; 13-4: Juno; IV iii 233-4: Nessus, Hercules; V iii 101-4: Plutus

Antony and Cleopatra I i 12-3: Antony; 31-2, 41: Fulvia; ii 97-100: Labienus; 123-5: Fulvia, Cleopatra; 177-9: Pompeius Sextus; 179-84: Pompey, Pompeius Sextus; iii 27-9: Fulvia; 49-52: Pompeius Sextus; 64-5: Cleopatra, Fulvia; iv 4-5: Antony; 48-51: Menecrates, Menas; v 23: Atlas; 25-6: Cleopatra; 27-8: Phoebus; 70-2: Isis, Caesar, Antony; II i 11-16: Lepidus; 26-7: Lethe; 40: Fulvia; 41-2: Antonius (Lucius); 98: Fulvia; 202ff: Cleopatra, Cupids, Nereides; 230-2: Caesar, Cleopatra; iii 39-41: Antony, Octavia; v 38-41: Fury; 95-6: Narcissus; vi 15: Cassius; 16: Brutus; 62-4: Caesar; 69-70: Apollodorus, Cleopatra, Caesar; 116-9: Octavia, Cleopatra, Antony, Caesar, Augustus; vii 65-7: Pompeius Sextus; III i 1-3: Crassus, Ventidius; 3-5: Pacorus, Orodes, Crassus; 17-20: Sossius; 33: Parthia; ii 15: Lepidus; 34-6: Antony; iii 18-21: Octavia; v 12-4: Octavia; vi 3-6: Caesarion, Cleopatra, Antony; 31-2: Pharsalia; 47ff: Actium, Antony; x 17-21: Antony, Cleopatra; xi 35-9: Augustus, Cassius, Brutus, Antony; xiii 82-5: Cleopatra; 117-20: Cneius, Pompey (2), Cleopatra, Caesar; 148-50: Hipparchus; IV viii 26-9: Phoebus; xii 37-8: Octavia, Cleopatra; xiii 1-3: Telamon, Calydonian Boar; xiv 38-41: Ajax, Cleopatra; 57-60: Neptune; 51-3: Dido, Aeneas, Cleopatra, Antony; 99-101: Antony; xv 47-8: Proculeius; V i 1: Dolabella; 17-8: Antony; 32-3, 61-3: Proculeius; ii 301-3: Cleopatra; 307-8, 355-6: Antony, Cleopatra

As You Like It I ii 27-30: Fortune; iii 120-1: Ganymede; II vii 5-6: Music of the Spheres; III ii 135-9: Helen, Cleopatra, Atalanta, Lucretia; iii 5-6: Ovid; IV i 87ff: Troilus; 90ff: Hero, Leander; 137-9: Dian; 189ff: Cupid; V i 27ff: Caesar; iv 135-8: Juno, Hymen

The Comedy of Errors V i 331-3: genius

Coriolanus I i 6: Marcius; 50: Menenius

Agrippa; 94-5: Menenius; 212-4: Brutus (2), Sicinius Velutus; 226-7: Volsces, Aufidius; 234-5: Cominius; 237-8: Lartius, Tullus; 258-60: Coriolanus; I iii 39-43: Hecuba, Hector; 82-3: Penelope; iv 57-62: Coriolanus, Cato (3); vi 36-8: Lartius; ix 63-5: Coriolanus, Marcius; II i 85: Deucalion; 107-10: Galen; 142: Tarquin, Coriolanus; 153-6: Marcius, Coriolanus; 204-8: Phoebus; ii 85ff: Coriolanus, Tarquin; iii 235-42: Marcius, Numa, Hostilius, Publius, Quintus, Censorinus; III i 91-7: Hydra; 211-3: Marcius, Tarpeian; 255-8: Jove, Neptune, Coriolanus; ii 1-6: Coriolanus, Tarpeian; IV i 15-8: Hercules; ii 51-3: Juno; vi 66-7: Aufidius, Marcius; 99-100: Hercules; V iii 29-31: Olympus; 64-7: Dian, Valeria, Publicola; iv 20-1: Coriolanus, Alexander; 31ff: Aufidius, Coriolanus

Cymbeline I vi 19-20: Parthian; 132-3: Diana; II 11-12: Tarquin, Lucrece; 13-6: Cytherea; 35: Gordian Knot; 43-5: Philomel, Tereus; iv 17-23: Caesar; 68-71: Cleopatra, Antony, Cydnus; 80-2: Dian; III i 21-6, 47-9: Caesar; iv 55-9: Aeneas, Sinon; 159-64: Juno, Titan; IV ii 50-2: Juno; 115-6: Hercules; 172-4: Zephyrs; 253-4: Thersites, Ajax; 309-12: Martial, Mercurial, Jovial, Hercules; 314-5: Hecuba; 349-52: Jove; V iv 30-4: Jove, Mars, Juno; 94-6: Jove; 97-8: Elysium; v 81-2: Augustus; 179-81: Dian; 186-91: Phoebus; 426-31: Jupiter; 458-61: Augustus

Hamlet I i 113-6: Julius; 117-20: Neptune; ii 149: Niobe; iv 81-3: Nemean lion; v 32-4: Lethe; II ii 428ff: Aeneas, Dido, Priam; 483-6: Cyclops, Mars, Pyrrhus, Priam; 551-5: Hecuba; III ii 81-2: Vulcan; 251-2: Hecat; 383-6: Nero; iv 55-63: Mars, Jove, Hyperion, Mercury; V i 202-6: Alexander; 207-10: Caesar; 245-8: Pelion, Olympus

Julius Caesar I i 37ff: Pompey; 68-70: Lupercal; ii 28-9: Brutus, Antony; 31-4: Cassius, Antony; 46ff: Brutus; 100ff: Caesar, Cassius, Aeneas, Anchises; 115-8: Caesar, Cassius; 135-8: Caesar, Colossus; 185-8: Cicero; 194-5: Cassius; 251-3: Caesar; II i 52-4: Tarquin; 63-9: Genius; 83-5: Erebus; 156ff: Antony; 295: Portia; ii 44-7: Caesar; III i 30: Casca; 246-7:

109-15: Cadmus, Hercules; V i 10-13:
Helen; 48-9: Bacchanals; 49-50: Muses;
56-7: Pyramus, Thisby; 127ff: Pyramus,
Thisby; 136-7: Ninus; 139ff: Pyramus,
Thisby; 197: Shafulus, Procrus; 276-9:
Furies, Fates; 327-32: Fates
Much Ado About Nothing I i 32: Cupid; 155:
Cupid, Vulcan; 233: Cupid; iii 8-9:
Saturn; II i 221-6, 329ff: Hercules; iii
171-2: Hector; III i 20-3: Cupid; ii 7ff:
Cupid; IV i 56-60: Dian, Venus; 315:
Hercules; V ii 27ff: Leander, Troilus; iii
26-7: Phoebus; iv 43-7: Jove, Europa
Othello I ii 33: Janus; iii 142-5:
Anthropophagi; 268-70: Cupid; II i 185-6:
Olympus; iii 90: Chaos; 293-4: Hydra;
III iii 358-60: Jove; 390-2: Dian; iv 70-2:
Sibyl; V i 10-13: Promethean
The Passionate Pilgrim 4, 6: Cytherea, Adonis;
8: Phoebus; 9: Cytherea, Adonis; 11:
Adonis, Venus, Mars; 16: Juno, Jove; 20:
Philomela, Tereus, Pandion
Pericles, Prince of Tyre (Prologue) 17ff:
Antiochus; I i 6-9: Jove, Lucina; 27-9:
Hesperides; 104: Jove; 145-7: Antiochus;
ii 106-8: Destinies; iv 22-4: Tharsus; 92-5:
Troyan horse; II ii 30: Juno; iv 5-10:
Antiochus; v 8-12: Diana, Cynthia; III i
10-14: Lucina; 35-7: Neptune; IV i 14-8:
Tellus; 47-9: harpy; vi 2-4: Priapus; 16-7:
Neptune; V i 225-8: Music of the Spheres;
iii 1-6: Dion; 70-1: Dian
The Rape of Lucrece 1-7: Ardea, Tarquin
(Sextus), Collatium, Collatine, Lucrece;
15-8: Collatine; 55-8: Venus; 155-8:
Tarquin (Sextus); 254-9: Collatinus,
Lucrece; 264-6: Narcissus; 316-21, 477-82:
Tarquin, Lucretia; 552-3: Pluto, Orpheus;
673ff: Tarquin, Lucretia; 855-61: Tantalus;
939ff: Fortune; 1079-80: Philomel,
Lucrece; 1127ff, 1291-3: Lucrece,
Collatinus; 1366-72: Priam, Helen, Ilion,
Troy; 1398-1400: Ulysses, Ajax; 1401ff:
Nestor; 1437-8: Simois, Dardan; 1447-9:
Hecuba, Priam, Pyrrhus; 1473-5: Paris;
1490-1: Paris, Priam; 1520-2: Sinon,
Priam; 1541-6: Sinon; 1723-9: Lucrece;
1732ff: Lucretius, Brutus (2); 1811-4,
1850-5: Tarquin (Sextus), Lucrece
Romeo and Juliet I i 132-9: Aurora; 206-9:
Cupid, Dian; iv 4-6: Cupid; II ii 159-63:
Echo; iii 3-4: Titan; v 3-8: Cupid; III ii

1-4: Phoebus, Phaethon; v 18-9: Cynthia
The Sonnets 5: Phoebus; 53: Adonis, Helen;
55: Mars; 119: Siren; 153: Cupid, Dian;
154: Cupid
The Taming of the Shrew (Induction) 47-51:
Adonis, Cytherea; 52-3: Io; 55-7: Daphne,
Apollo; I i 31-3: Stoics, Ovid, Aristotle;
147-9: Anna, Dido; 162-5: Agenor,
Europa; ii 66-8: Sibyl, Florentius,
Xantippe; 240-1: Leda, Helen; II i 251-2:
Dian; 206-7: Lucrece; 341: Tyrian; III i
50-1: Aeacides
The Tempest I i 200-5: Jove, Neptune;
396ff: nymphs; II i 70-77: Dido, Aeneas,
Carthage; 161: Golden Age; IV i 22-3:
Hymen; 27-31: Phoebus, Night; 60ff:
Ceres; 70-4: Juno; 76-81: Iris; 87-90:
Venus, Cupid, Dis, Proserpina; 92-4:
Venus, Cupid, Hymen, Paphos; 97-100:
Mars, Venus, Cupid; 127-33: Naiads;
V i 33-5: nymphs
Timon of Athens I i 62-3: Apemantus; 276ff:
Plutus; II ii 152: Lacedaemon; III iv 15-17:
Timon; IV iii 52: Timon; 381-4: Dian
Titus Andronicus I i 5-6: Saturninus; 10-14:
Bassianus; 21-6: Andronicus; 52: Lavinia;
71-5: Andronicus; 79-80: Priam; 86-9:
Styx; 131-2: Scythia; 136-8: Hecuba,
Polymnestor; 173-8: Solon; 193-7:
Andronicus; 225-7: Saturnine, Titan;
315-7: Phoebe; 335: Pantheon; 379-82:
Ajax, Ulysses; 415-8: Andronicus,
Lavinia; II i 15-7: Prometheus; 108-9:
Lucrece; iii 21-6: Ovid, Aeneas; 42-3:
Philomel; 55-9: Dian; 61-4: Dian, Actaeon;
226ff: Pyramus; 235-6: Cocytus; iv 22ff:
Lavinia, Tereus; 37ff: Tereus, Philomel,
Cerberus, Orpheus; III i 54-5: Rome;
67-70: Troy; IV i 12-4: Tully, Cornelia;
20-1: Hecuba; 42ff: Ovid, Lavinia,
Philomel, Tereus; 64-5: Lucrece; 105-6:
Sibyl; ii 93-7: Enceladus, Alcides; iii 11-6:
Pluto; 37-41, 43-5: Acheron; 45-6:
Cyclops; iv 63ff: Coriolanus; V ii 54-7:
Hyperion; 195-6: Philomel, Progne; iii
35-7: Verginius; 45ff: Verginius, Lavinia;
80-7: Aeneas, Dido, Priam, Sinon
Troilus and Cressida (Prologue) 7-10: Troy,
Helen, Menelaus, Paris; 11-3: Tenedos;
16-9: Dardan, Tymbria, Helias, Chetas,
Troien, Atenorides; I i 94: Troilus, Cressid,
Pandar; 99-103: Cressida, Pandar; 110-11:

Paris, Menelaus; ii 4-5: Hector; 28-9: Ajax, Briareus; 276-7: Troilus, Pandar, Cressida; iii 37-40: Boreas, Thetis; 54-5: Agamemnon; 61: Nestor; 146-50: Achilles, Patroclus; 159-61: Typhon; 162-3: Achilles; 188-90: Ajax; 193-5: Thersites; 228-30: Phoebus; 291-2: Nestor; 316: Achilles; 378-9: Myrmidon; II i 31-4: Ajax, Achilles, Cerberus, Proserpina; ii 81-2: Helen; 76-80: Paris, Hesione, Helen; 110-12: Cassandra; 163-7: Aristotle; 199-202: Helen; iii 167-71: Achilles; 239-42: Milo; 245-6: Nestor; III ii 7-12: Charon, Troilus, Stygian; 169 ff: Troilus; 180 ff: Cressid; iii 196-200: Plutus; 209-13: Pyrrhus (2); 274: Agamemnon; IV i 70-4: Helen; ii 98-9: Cressida; v 6-9: Aquilon; 142-5: Neoptolemus; 185-6: Perseus; 280-3: Diomed; V ii 105-6: Cressid; 154-8: Diomed, Cressida; 169-74: Diomed, Troilus, Neptune; iii 51-5: Mars, Priamus, Hecuba; 83-6: Hecuba, Andromache, Hector; v 6-11: Polydamas, Menon, Margarelon, Doreus, Epistrophus, Cedius; 11-15: Polixenes, Amphimacus, Thoas (1), Palamedes; 30-4: Achilles, Patroclus, Myrmidons; ix 4-6: Hector, Achilles; x 3-5: Hector; 17-9: Hector, Priam, Niobes

Twelfth Night I i 19-23: Actaeon; ii 3-4: Elysium; 15-6: Arion; II v 86, 97: Lucrece; III i 48-50: Pandarus; IV ii 49-50: Pythagoras; V i 45-7: Vulcan

The Two Gentlemen of Verona I i 21-5: Leander, Hellespont; II v 37-8: Elysium; III i 117-20: Hero, Leander; 153-5: Phaethon, Merops; ii 75-81: Orpheus; IV iv 163-7: Ariadne, Theseus

Venus and Adonis 87-8: Venus, Adonis; 97-101: Venus, Mars; 109-10, 153-4: Venus; 161-2: Narcissus; 176-8: Titan, Hyperion; 229-34: Venus; 421-4: Adonis; 599-600: Tantalus, Elysium; 615 ff: Venus, Adonis; 724-6: Dian, Elysium; 727-30: Cynthia; 1055 ff: Adonis; 1135 ff: Venus; 1189-94: Venus, Paphos

The Winter's Tale II ii 182-4: Delphos; III i 8-10: Delphos; 142 ff: Apollo, Delphos; IV iii 34-5: Mercury; iv 1-3: Flora; 25-30: Jupiter, Neptune, Apollo; 115-24: Proserpina, Dis, Cytherea, Phoebus, Juno; 421-2: Deucalion; V i 37-40: Apollo, Delphos; 153-4: Neptune

Shelley, Percy Bysshe (1792-1822)

Adonais 10-14: Adonis, Venus, Urania; 28-9: Urania, Venus; 64: Adonis; 127-32: Echo; 140-4: Phoebus, Hyacinth, Narcissus; 166-7: Chaos; 190: Adonis; 195-8: Echo; 198-9: Urania, ambrosial; 208-14: Urania; 249-51: Pythian, Apollo; 268-9: Ierne; 274-9: Actaeon; 289-94: Dionysus; 316, 336 ff, 370-1: Adonis; 414: Vesper; 492-5: Adonais

Alastor 242-3: Parthian; 672-5: Medea

Arethusa 1-3: Arethusa; 19-24: Alpheus, Erymanthus; 37-45: Arethusa; 49-51: Alpheus; 73-8: Alpheus, Arethusa, Enna; 82-7: asphodel, Ortygian, Alpheus, Arethusa

Charles The First IV 8-10: Evening Star

The Daemon of the World 53-5: genii; 56-8: Daemon; 69-70: Hesperus; 244-50: Music of the Spheres; 288-91: Necessity; 311-5: Erebus; 319-20: Time; 325-7: Chaos

Dirge for the Year 1-4: Hours; 11 ff: Hours

Epipsychidion 53: Muse; 185-9: Elysian; 220-4: Hesper; 241-4: Chaos; 422-8: Ionian, Elysian, Golden Age; 484-95: Titanic; 502-7: Parian; 536-40: Elysian; 541-2: Ionian

Fiordispina 78-82: Elysian

Fragment — A Tale Untold 3: daedal

Fragment — Milton's Spirit 1-4: Uranian

Fragment of a Fragment on Satire 29-30: Parthian

Fragment written for 'Hellas' 8-9: Alpheus, Arethuse, Doris; 10-12: Sun; 15-16: Alpheus, Arethusa, Doris

Hellas (**Prologue** 2-3: Chaos; 4-5: Plato); 52-7: Thermopylae, Marathon, Philippi; 65-61: Atlantis; 161-4: Demonesi; 230-4: Apollo, Pan, Jove; 682-6: Athens; 688-91: Thermae, Asopus (2); 703-7: Orphic, Titanian; 733-4: Athens; 793-5: Dodona; 901-5: Hour; 926-8: Elysian; 992-5: Rome, Atlantis; 1002-7: Amphionic; 1036-41: Hesperus; 1060-3: Golden Age; 1068-71: Peneus, Morning Star, Tempes, Cyclads; 1072-3: Argo; 1074-5: Orpheus; 1076-7: Ulysses, Calypso; 1080-4: Laian, Sphinx, Thebes; 1084-7: Athens; 1094: Saturn, Jupiter

Hymn of Apollo 1: Hours; 5-6, 23 ff: Apollo

Hymn of Pan 10-12: Tmolus, Pan; 13-5: Peneus, Tempe, Pelion; 18-24: Sileni,

The Retrospect 106-7: Echo
The Revolt of Islam 84-8: Amphion; 308-10:
    Vesper; 352-60: Chaos, Morning Star;
    1419: Mother of the Months; 2089-91:
    Lethean; 2101-4: Athos, Samothrace;
    2299: Earth; 2326-30: Orion; 2499,
    2714-6: Tartarian; 2905-7: Symplegades;
    2940-4: Hesperian; 3080-3: Nautilus;
    3111-4: Crotona; 3160-2: Scythian;
    3379-87: Amphisbaena; 3650-2: Scythian;
    4288-92: Hydra; 4726-7: Elysian; 4761-4:
    Cyclopean
Rosalind and Helen 402-9: Lethean; 701-3:
    Python; 1302-3: Arctos
Scene from 'Tasso' 10-13: Venus, Adonis
The Sensitive Plant i 21: Naiad; 29: nymph;
    33-4: maenad; 49-54: asphodels; 108-9:
    Elysian; iii 1-4: Vesuvius, Baiae
Song of Proserpine Earth, Hours, Proserpine,
    Enna
To a Star 8-11: Favonius
To Jane 73-5: Elysian
The Triumph of Life 93-5: Janus; 270-2:
    Proteus; 356-9: Iris, Nepenthe; 413-20:
    Lucifer; 440: Iris; 463: Lethean
The Witch of Atlas 55-7: Atlas, Atlantides;
    73-7: Mother of the Months; 105-8:
    Silenus; 109-10: Dryope, Faunus; 113-8:
    Pan; 121-3: nymph, Ocean; 130: Garamant;
    133-5: Pigmies, Polyphemes, Centaurs,
    Satyrs; 185-9: Saturnian; 217-9, 226-7:
    Hamadryads, Oreads, Naiads; 275-7:
    asphodel; 289-94: Vulcan, Venus, Apollo;
    297: Cupid, Chaos; 316ff: Evan; 318-9:
    Vesta, Homer; 450-3: Hydaspes; 481-5:
    Arion; 505-11: Moeris, Mareotic; 510-12:
    Osirian; 576-83: Aurora, Tithon, Venus,
    Proserpina; 587-90: Dian, Endymion;
    635-8: Apis; 641-5: Cyclopses, Vulcan;
    646-8: Memphis, Amasis
The Woodman and the Nightingale 68-70:
    Dryads

Shenstone, William (1714-63)
Anacreontic 29: Pierian
The Charms of Precedence 79-84: Lucian,
    Elysium, Charon
Economy ii 123-8: Ilium, Aeneas; iii 30-2:
    Ariadne
Elegies I 1-2: Augusta; 23-4: Aonia; 40-4:
    Loves, Graces; V 37-40: Maro,
    Parthenope (2), Vesuvio; VI 15ff: Philomel,

Damon, Tereus; VII 22-3: Tyrian; VIII
    61-4: Phoebus, Cyrian; XIV 39-40: Ladon;
    XVI 69-70: Saturn; XVII 65-8: Marius;
    XIX 17-8: Thalia; 37-40: Hannibal,
    Cannae, Thrasimene, Trebia; XXII 69-70:
    Paean
The Judgment of Hercules 125-8: Cleopatra,
    Cydnus; 188-9: Bacchus; 278-81:
    Favonius
Love and Music 7-9: Orpheus, Pluto
The Progress of Taste iii 11ff: Naiads, Oreads,
    Dryads
The Ruined Abbey 264-5: Stygian, Erebus;
    296-8: Cacus
Song 9-10: Venus, Loves
To the Virtuosi 13-14: Camilla; 33-6:
    Domitian

Sidney, Sir Philip (1554-86)
Lyrics from 'Arcadia 18 11-12: Cupid; 13-4:
    Cupid, Argus (1), Io; 20 9-10: Cupid;
    26 5ff: Apollo, Latona, Python; 62 77ff:
    Cupid; 63 37: Pan; 73 143-6: Venus,
    Paris; 74 19-20: Nestor; 75 29:
    Hyacinth, 109-11: Atropos
Astrophel and Stella (nos. of Sonnets) 4:
    Cato (2); 13: Cupid, Jove, Mars, Ganymede;
    15: Parnassus; 24: Tantal; 32: Morpheus;
    33: Paris, Helen; 35: Nestor; 63: Pean; 68:
    Amphion; 72: Venus, Dian; 74: Aganippe,
    Tempe; 82: Narcissus, Helen, Paris,
    Esperian; 83: Orpheus, Amphion
Espilus and Therion 7-12: Pan, Hercules,
    Omphale
My Mistress Lowers 6-7: Stygian; 18: Troyan;
    44-5: Hannibal
The Nightingale 1ff: Philomela, Tereus
Pastoral 13-16: Orpheus
A Shepherd's Tale 349-50: Tartars; 409-12:
    Creusa (1), Medea

Skelton, John (1460-1529)
Against the Scots Thalia
The Garland of Laurel Helicon, Aechines,
    Demosthenes, Orpheus, Amphion, Phoebus,
    Daphne, Theocritus, Bacchus, Ennius,
    Macrobius, Dryads, Muses, Pierides, Iopas,
    Argia, Thamarys (2), Zeuxis, Apelles,
    Penelope
A Laud and Praise Astraea, Adrastus
Philip Sparrow Acheron, Alecto, Medusa,
    Cerberus, Andromache, Sulpicia, Croesus,

Medea, Melanchaetes, Actaeon, Phoenix, Helicon, Hannibal, Scipio (1), Hector, Penelope (*Commendation*) Arethusa, Tagus, Flora, Cicero (*Addition*) Hercules, Hesperides, Hercules, Diomedes (1), Geryon, Cocytus, Charon
Upon the Dolorous Death of the . . . Earl of Northumberland 8-9: Clio; 120ff: Atropos

Smart, Christopher (1722-71)
Apollo and Daphne Daphne
Epistle to John Sherratt 4: Plato; 11-12: Demosthenes, Plato
Prologue to 'A Trip to Cambridge' Pindus

Southey, Robert (1774-1843)
History 20-2: Tiberius; 28-31: Cato (2)
Hymn to the Penates 7-13: Penates; 12-13: Juno, Pallas; 80-1: Dryads; 82: Oreads; 144-8: Apega; 229-34: Brutus (2)
Roderick i 26-30: Kronos, Briareus, Bacchus, Hercules; ii 213-6: Berecynthian; xvi 199-203: Charon, Achilles; 212-4: Oread, Dryad
Thalaba i 12: Persepolis, Jove; vi 21: Orpheus
Waterloo 3: Erebus

Spenser, Edmund (1558?-99)
Amoretti (nos. of Sonnets) 1: Helicon; 4: Janus; 16: Loves; 23: Penelope; 24: Pandora; 26: Moly; 28: Daphne; 34: Helice; 35: Narcissus; 38: Arion; 44: Argonauts, Orpheus; 60: Cupid; 77: Hercules, Hesperides, Atalanta; 86: Furies
Astrophel 1: Arcady; 55-6: Venus
Colin Clouts Come Home Again 1-2: Tityrus; 245-51: Triton, Proteus; 765-70: Cupid; 801-4: Venus; 803-4: Gardens of Adonis; 805-12: Cupid; 919-22: Stesichorus
Daphnaida 11-3: Muses; 14-21: Fates, Proserpina, Stygian; 22-5: Sun; 108-9: Venus; 162-6: Nemean lion; 218-9: Astraea; 248-9: Timon; 463-6: Eurydice, Proserpina; 468-9: Titan, Hyperion; 474-6: Philumene
Epithalamion 1-3, 14: Muses; 16-7: Orpheus, Eurydice; 25-9: Hymen; 37-40: Nymphs; 74-7: Tithonus, Phoebus; 92-5: Hesperus; 98-102: Hours; 103-9: Graces, Venus; 121-6: Phoebus; 140ff: Hymen; 148-50: Phoebe; 255-7: Bacchus, Hymen, Graces;

281: Time; 285-92: Evening Star; 305-10: Maca, Jove, Tempe, Acidalian; 326-30: Jove, Alcmena, Tirynthian; 372: Cynthia; 377-81: Cynthia, Endymion; 390-7: Juno
The Faerie Queene (references are in order of Book, Canto, Stanza) **(Book I) Prologue** 1-2: Muse, Clio; 3: Cupid; 4: Phoebus; i 23: Phoebus; 32: Sun; 36: Morpheus; 37: Proserpina, Cocytus, Demogorgon, Styx; 39: Morpheus, Tethys, Cynthia, Night; 40: Gates of Sleep; 43: Hecate; 48: Venus, Hymen, Flora, Graces; ii 1: Phoebus; 2: Proserpine; 4: Venus; 6: Hesperus; 7: Aurora, Tithonus, Titan, Hyperion; 10: Proteus; 29: Phoebus; 33: Boreas; iii 21: Ulysses, Calypso; 31: Tethys, Orion, Nereus, Sirius; 32: Neptune; 36: Lethe, Furies; iv 8: Titan; 9: Phaethon, Phoebus; 11: Pluto, Proserpina, Jove; 16: Aurora; 17: Flora, June, Jove, Argus; 44: Morpheus; v 2: Phoebus; 20: Night, Phoebus; 22: Night, Jove, Demogorgon; 28: Night; 32: Pluto; 33: Acheron, Phlegethon; 34: Cerberus; 35: Ixion, Sisyphus, Tantalus, Tityus, Typhoeus, Theseus; 36: Aesculapius, Hippolytus; 37-8: Phaedra, Neptune; 39: Phaedra, Diana, Hippolytus, Aesculapius; 43: Aesculapius; 47: Croesus, Antiochus; 48: Ninus, Ammon, Alexander; 49: Tarquin, Romulus, Lentulus, Scipio, Hanniball, Sulla, Marius, Caesar, Pompey, Antonius; 50: Semiramis, Sthenoboea, Cleopatra; vi 6: Phoebus; 7: fawns, satyrs, Sylvanus; 15: fawns, satyrs, Bacchus, Cybele, Dryope; 16: Venus, Diana; 17: Sylvanus, Cyparisse; 18: woody nymphs, Hamadryades, Naiades, satyrs; vii 4-5: nymph, Diane, Phoebe; 9: Earth, Aeolus; 13: Furies; 17: Alcides, Lerna, Hydra; 29: Phoebus; 29-30: Hesperus; 34: Phoebus, Cynthia; 44: Tartary; viii 9: Jove; 21: Pegasus; xi 5: muse, Clio, Phoebus, Mnemosyne; 6: Clio, Mars; 27: Hercules, Nessus, Centaur; 30: Hebrus; 31: Phoebus; 33: Titan, Hyperion; 41: Cerberus; 51: Aurora, Tithone; xii 2: Phoebus; 7-8: Diana, nymphs; 21: morning star **(Book II)** i 53: Cynthia, Lucina; 55: Bacchus, Nymph; ii 6: Flora; 7: Faunus, Arethusa; 8: Diana; 29: Erinnys; 46: Orion; iii 1: Titan, Hyperion; 31: Diana, Eurotas, Cynthus, Nymphs, Penthesilea, Amazons,

Priam, Troy, Pyrrhus; iv 41: Phlegethon, Iarre, Herebus; v 22: Stygian; 29: zephyrus; 31: poplar, Olympicke, Jove, Alcides, Nemea; 37: Furies; vi 10: Neptune, Jove; 31: Titan; 35: Mars, Cupidoes, Venus; 50: Jove, Phlegethon; vii 5: Mulciber; 20-1: Pluto; 23-4: Celeno, Pluto; 28: Arachne; 36: Vulcan; 41: Titan; 52: Socrates, Critias; 53-5: Proserpina; 54: Hercules, Atlas, Hesperides; 55: Acontius, Ate, Idaean, Paris, Venus, Helen; 56: Cocytus; 58: Tantalus; viii 5: Phoebus; 6: Cupid, Idaean, Venus, Graces; 20: Aetna, Styx; ix 10: Phoebus; 18: Cupides; 21: Nine; 29: Aetna; 32: Port Esquiline; 45: Cadmus, Thebes, Alexander, Hector, Troy; 56-7: Nine, Assaracus, Nestor, Inachus; x 3: Maeonian, Phoebus, Jove, Ossa, Phlegraean; 6: Albion; 9: Brutus, Assaracus; 47-9: Caesar; 51: Claudius; 52: Vespasian; 54-5: Bunduca; 56: Semiramis, Thomiris, Hysiphil; 57: Severus, Carausius, Allectus; 58: Allectus, Asclepiodotus; 70: Prometheus; 71: Gardens of Adonis; xi 9: Titan; 43: Jove; xii 6: Tartare; 13: Delos, Latona, Juno, Apollo, Artemis; 22: Neptune; 23: Hydraes; 26: Tethys; 31: Sirens, Muses; 33: Zephirus; 39: Venus; 41: Caduceus, Mercury, Stygian, Orcus, Furyes; 44-5: Jason, Medea, Argo, Creusa; 47: Genius; 48: Agdistes; 50: Flora; 52: Rhodope, Tempe, Daphne, Phoebus, Ida, Parnasso, Muses; 65: morning star, Cyprian, Aphrodite; 77: Arachne

(Book III) Prologue 2: Zeuxis, Praxiteles, daedal; 4: nectar, Cynthia; i 34-8: Venus, Adonis; 39: Cupid; 40: Lydian; 43: Cynthia; 51: Ceres, Lyaeus; 58: Atlas, Pleiades; ii 20: Phao, Ptolemy; 26: Cupid; 32: Aetna; 41: Biblis, Pasiphae; 44-5: Cephisus, Narcissus; iii 1-3: Love; 4: Phoebus, Mnemnosyne, Clio; 20: Aurora, Tithonus; 54: Bunduca; iv 2: Homer, Penthesilee, Camilla, Orsilochus; 10: Neptune; 19: Nereus; 25: Proteus; 32: Neptune; 33: Triton; 37: Proteus; 41: Apollo, Pindus, Paeon (1); 42: Neptune; 43: Tryphon; 51: Hesperus; 55: Night, Herebus, Cocytus; 60: Titan; vi 2: Jove, Venus, Phoebus, Graces; 11: Venus, Cupid; 13-14: Cupid; 17-18: Diane, ambrosia; 24: Venus, Mars, Stygian; 27: Lucina; 29: Venus, Adonis, Paphos,

Cytheron, Gnidus; 36-7: Chaos; 39: Time; 44: Phoebus, Aeolus; 45: Hyacinthus, Phoebus, Narcissus; 46: Adonis, Venus, Stygian; 49-50: Adonis, Cupid, Psyche, Venus; vii 11: Diane; 26: Myrrha, Daphne; 41: Olympus; 47: Titans, Typhoeus; 61: Alcides; viii 6: Riphoean; 30: Proteus, Neptune; 37: Proteus, Panope; 41: Proteus; ix 7: Argus; 19: Vulcan; 22: Minerva, Encelade, Hemus, Gorgonian; 30: Bacchus; 34: Helen, Troy, Ilion, Paris, Lacedaemon, Venus; 35: Helene, Scamander, Xanthus; 36: Paris, Oenone, Ida; 36-7: Pari(u)s, Pari/os; 38: Troy; 41: Anchises, Venus, Aeneas; 42: Latium, Latinus; 43: Latinus, Iulus, Alba, Romulus; x 1-3: Phoebus, Aurora; 5: Cupid; 12-3: Helen; 44-8: satyrs; xi 1: Proserpine; 29-30: Cupid; 30-5: Jove; 30: Helle, Europa; 31: Danae; 32: Leda; 33: Semelee, Juno, Alcmena; 34: Asteria, Ganymede; 35: Antiopa, Aegin(a), Menemnosyne, Persephone, Cupid; 36: Phoebus, Cupid, Mars, Venus, Daphne; 37: Hyacinth, Phoebus, Coronis; 38: Clymene, Phaethon, Phebus, Cupid; 39: Isse, Admetus; 40-2: Neptune, Melantho; 41: Bisaltis; 42: Iphimedia, Aeolus, Arne, Deucalion, Amphitrite, Medusa, Pegasus; 43: Saturn, Erigone, Cheiron, Phillira; 47: Iris; xii 7: Ganymede, Hylas, Alcides; 22: Cupid **(Book IV)**
Prologue 3: Socrates, Critias; 4-5: Venus, Cupid; i 19: Ate; 22: Babylon, Thebes, Rome, Ilion, Juno, Minerva, Venus, Paris, Alexander; 23: Lapithes, Centaures, Alcides, Argonauts; ii 1: Phlegeton, Orpheus; 47: Demogorgon, Chaos; 47-8: Fates, Clotho, Lachesis, Atropos; iii 32: Stygian; 42: Maia, Mercury, Caduceus; 43-4: Nepenthe; v 3-4: Venus, Vulcan, Lemno(s); 5: Venus, Mars, Acidalian, Graces; 37: Brontes, Pyracmon, Lipari; vi 1: Phebus; 14: Jove, 20: Pactolus; vii 1: Cupid; 22: Myrrh, Daphne; 30: Latona, Diana, Niobe; ix 2: Cupid; 23: Aeolus, Neptune, Canace, Chaos; x 5: Venus, Paphos; 27: Hercules, Hylas, Theseus, Pirithous, Pylades, Orestes, Damon, Pythias; 30: Diane; 34: Concord; 40: Phidias, Pericles; 42: Cupid; 44-7: Venus; 58: Cerberus, Orpheus, Eurydice, Pluto; xi 4: Styx; 6: Tryphon; 11: Neptune,

Medusa, Perseus, Andromeda; 666-70:
Mercurie
The Shepheardes Calendar **Januarye** 17: Pan;
66, 73-4: Phoebus **Februarie** 91-3:
Tityrus; 226: Boreas **March** 16-7: Flora,
Maia; 23: Lethe; 79-84: Cupid
April 41-5: Muses, Parnasse, Helicon;
50-1: Syrinx, Pan; 86-90: Latonae, Niobe,
Cynthia; 100-5: Calliope, Muses
Maye 27-33: Flora; 51-4, 109-14: Pan
June 28-32: Pan, Phoebe, Parnasse,
Muses; 56-7: Calliope; 65-72: Muses,
Pan, Phoebus; 81-4: Tityrus; 102-4:
Menalcas **Julye** 49-52: Pan; 57-60: Ida,
Titan; 63-4: Phoebe, Endymion; 77-8:
fauns, sylvans; 143-4: Pan; 145-8: Paris,
Ida, Helen; 153-5: Argus **August** 183-6:
Nightingale **September** 203: Argus
October 11-12: Argus; 25-30: Orpheus,
Eurydice, Cerberus, Pluto; 55-60: Tityrus,
Virgil, Maecenas; 61-2: Maecenas, Augustus;
106-8: Bacchus, Phoebus; 112-4: Bellona
November 13-16: Phoebus; 53:
Melpomene; 141: Philomele; 146-7: Muses;
148-9: Fates; 178-9: Elisian; 193-6:
nectar, ambrosia **December** 3-4: Tityrus;
5: Pan
Sonnets (Dedicatory to 'The Faerie Queene')
Those Prudent Heads Rome, Muses,
Ennius, Africane, Maro, Augustus; *To You,*
Right Noble Lord Atlas; *Receive Most*
Noble Lord Heliconian; *Most Noble Lord,*
the Pillar Parnasso; *In Vain I Think* Zoilus;
That Mantuan Poet's Incomparable Spirit
Virgil, Maecenas, Augustus
Teares of the Muses 1-12: Muses, Apollo,
Helicon, Phaethon; 13-18: Calliope,
Palici; 55-8: Muses, Jupiter, Castalie,
Parnassus; 97-8: Clio; 107-8, 151-7:
Melpomene; 163-8: Megera, Persephone,
Melpomene; 175-80: Thalia, Graces;
256-8: Cim(m)erians; 271-5: Muses,
Helicon, Castalian; 289-92: Euterpe;
379-84: Erato; 396-402: Cytheree, Cupid;
403-6: Graces, Venus, Muses; 427-33:
Calliope; 447-8: Irus, Inachus; 457-62:
Calliope, Bacchus, Hercules; 517-28:
Urania; 547-55: Polyhymnia; 577-9:
Pandora
Visions of the World's Vanitie 43: Jove;
145-8: Capitol

Stevenson, Robert Louis (1850-94)
After Reading 'Antony and Cleopatra' 9-12:
Cleopatra
As One Who Having Wandered 17-22:
Melampus
Et Tu In Arcadia 6-7: Achilles; 20-5: Chiron,
Pelethronian, Pan
I Whom Apollo Sometime Visited 1-3: Apollo
Madrigal 5-8: Cytherea; 9-12: Hero
Still I Love to Rhyme 5-6: Apollo
To H. F. Brown 1ff: Elysian, Styx
To My Father 7-8: Pharos
You Know the Way to Arcady 1-4: Arcady

Suckling, Sir John (1609-42)
An Answer to Some Verses 5-6: Homer,
Virgil
His Dream 7-10: Paris, Atlanta
Love and Debt 9: Croesus; 11-2: Ovid
The Metamorphosis 1-4: Cupid; 10: Narcissus,
Apollo, Danae
A Prologue to a Masque 7-10: Helicon,
Parnassus
Song 1-6: Cupid

Surrey, Henry Howard, Earl of (1515-47)
Divers Thy Death 11-4: Pyramus
The Great Macedon 1-2: Macedon, Darius (2)
In Winter's Just Return Boreas, Troilus
So Cruel Prison 1-4: Priam
When Raging Love 7-12: Troy, Iphigenia;
13ff: Helen

Swift, Jonathan (1667-1745)
Answer to a Scandalous Poem 99: Mercury
Apollo to the Dean 93-4: Prometheus
Cadenus and Vanessa 112-3: Tibullus; 136-7:
Lucina
Description of a Salamander 44-5: Pliny
Description of Mother Ludwell's Cave 1-2:
Parnassus, Aonian; 11-12: Pomona,
Minerva, Flora; 47: Camilla; 55-6: Sybil
An Elegy on Mr Demar 7-8: Pluto
The Fable of Midas 1ff: Midas; 33-40: Midas,
Pactolus
The History of Vanbrugh's House 35-6:
Vitruvius
A Love Song 5-8: Arcadians; 9-12: Venus,
Adonis, Cyprian; 23-4: Morpheus; 25-6:
Meander
A Motto 1-4: Jason
Ode to Athenian Society 8-10: Parnassus;

Masque of Queen Bersabe Semiramis, Hesione, Chersonese, Thomyris, Pasiphae, Sappho, Messalina, Erigone
Memorial Verses 17: Lethean; 30: Pierian; 49: Persephone
A Nympholet 134-6: Etna, Typho
On the Cliffs 48-9: Erinnyes; 152 ff: Agamemnon, Clytemnestra, Cassandra; 171: Cassandra; 279-83: Sappho; 315-6: Sappho, Leucadian; 353-8: Sappho; 380-3: Sappho, Lesbos; 423: Mnemosyne
Pan and Thalassius Pan, Urania
Phaedra Phaedra, Hippolyta, Hippolytus, Ate, Theseus
Prelude 101-4: Bassarid, Thyades; 115-20: Cotys, Edonian
Proserpine 16-20: Proserpine
St Dorothy Gaditane, Adonis, Mars
Sapphics 9 ff: Aphrodite, Loves; 23-7: Sappho
Satia Te Sanguine 9-14: Sappho
Song for the Centenary of Landor 12: Nestor; 15: Simonides, Hymettian; 18: Oenone; 20: Tiberius; 23: Medea; 24: Thermopylae, Leonidas, Timoleon; 29: Alpheus, Ladon; 37: Aspasia, Pericles; 40: Scipio (1); Hannibal; 41: Ammon, Alexander; 42: Semiramis; 46: Cleopatra, Caesarion; 47: Theocritus, Catullus; 49: Homer, Laertes
Song of Italy Promethean
Statue of Victor Hugo 12: Pindar (1); 22: Phidias
Thalassius 12-15: Oread; 18-20: Cymothoe
Tiresias 4-5: Tiresias, Antigone; 17-8: Cadmus, Harmonia; 43-7: Tiresias; 67-70: Dircean, Oedipus, Seven Against Thebes; 73-6: Pentheus, Cithaeron, Agave; 85-90: Laius, Oedipus; 171 ff: Tiresias, Chariclo; 306-8: Maenads; 309-14: Sphinx-like, Cadmean; 314: Semele
Tristram of Lyonesse **(Prelude)** Helen, Hero, Dido, Mars, Cleopatra, Phaethon

Tennyson, Alfred, Lord (1809-92)

Adeline 15-16: Naiad; 51-4: Saturn
Amphion 17-20, 49-52: Amphion
Amy 67-71: St Cecilia, Valerian
Antony to Cleopatra 9-10: Antony, Cleopatra; 24-6: Actium
Babylon 21-4: Cyrus
The Burial of a Love 1: Cupid
The Coach of Death 2-4: Phoebus; 181-4: Dionys; 191-2: Saturn, Jove

The Death of Oenone 14-18: Oenone, Paris; 23-9: Paris, Oenone; 70-5: Gorgon, Oenone; 102-6: Oenone, Paris
Demeter and Persephone 13 ff: Pluto, Persephone, Demeter; 26-8: Hades, Phlegethon; 35-9: Aidoneus, Enna, Proserpine; 80-6: Fates; 93-9: Zeus, Pluto, Persephone, Demeter; 114 ff: Zeus, Persephone, Demeter, Pluto; 150-1: asphodel
Did Not Thy Roseate Lips 15-16: Merope; 21-30: Sibyl
The Druid's Prophecies 1-4: Mona; 29-32: Galba, Otho; 53-6: Severus (2); 57-60: Mona; 73-6: Rome
A Dream of Fair Women 105-12: Iphigenia; 137-42: Cleopatra; 141-2: Mark Antony; 145-6: Cleopatra, Antony, Canopus
To E.L. 1-2: Illyrian
Exhortation to the Greeks 1-2: Xerxes; 17-18: Plataea
The Gardener's Daughter 135-6: Hebe
Hendecayllables 9-12: Catullus
Hero to Leander 38-41: Hero, Leander
The Hesperides 24-8: Hesperides; 83: Hesper, Phosphor
I Dare Not Write an Ode 1-2: Pimplaea; 3-4: Astraea
Ilion, Ilion 3-6: Scamander, Simois, Ida (2), Ilion
In Memoriam xxiii 10-12: Pan; 22-4: Argive, Arcady; xxxvii: Urania, Parnassus, Melpomene; xliv 9-12: Lethean; cxviii 25-8: Faun; cxxi 1-2, 9-12, 17-18: Hesper, Phosphor
The Last Tournament **(Idylls)** 320-4: Orpheus
Leonine Elegiacs 11-13: Hesper(us), Sappho
The Lotos Eaters 28 ff, 153-5: Lotos-Eaters; 169-70: Elysian, asphodel
The Lover's Tale i 294-7: Mercury; 463-7: Music of the Spheres, Aeolian; iv 17-18: Aetna
Lucretius 14-19: Lucretius (2); 37-9, 47-50: Sylla (2); 85 ff: Venus, Endymion, Adonis, Paris; 93-4: Empedocles, Calliope; 116-20: Epicurus, Lucretius, Memmius; 124-6: Apollo, Delius, Hyperion; 147-9: Plato; 159-60: Harpies; 181-3: Faunus, Picus, Numa; 188-9: Oread; 192 ff: satyr; 217-8: Epicurean; 224: Heliconian; 235-40: Lucretia, Collatine; 259-64: Lucretius,

Ixionian, Fury; 273-4: Lucretius
Mariana in the South 89-90: Hesper
On a Mourner 31-5: Aeneas
Oenone 1-2: Ida (2); 10-11: Gargarus; 57-61:
Paris; 64-5: Paris, Hesperian; 65 ff: Paris,
Oenone, Oread, Ida; 126: Paris; 181-3:
Paris, Aphrodite; 170-1: Aphrodite,
Idalian, Paphian; 217 ff: Eris, Oenone;
257-61: Cassandra, Oenone, Troy
The Palace of Art 97-9: St Cecily; 110-12:
Egeria, Numa; 117-20: Europa; 121-4:
Ganymede; 137-40: Homer, Ionian; 164:
Plato; 169-72: Memnon
The Pallid Thunderstricken 1-6: Pactolus
Parnassos 8: Music of the Spheres; 17-8:
Pierian
Persia 13-6: Cyrus; 17-23: Alexander; 26-32:
Alexander, Thais, Persepolis; 41-2:
Pactolus; 47-50: Cunaxa; 59-60: Cydnus
Pierced Through with Knotted Thorns 36-8:
Dionys
Poets and their Bibliographies 2-4: Virgil;
5-6: Horace; 7-8: Catullus
The Princess (Book i) 19: Galen (Book ii)
13-4: Muses, Graces; 64-5: Egeria, Sabine;
66: Semiramis; 67: Artemisia; 68: Rhodope;
69-71: Cl(o)elia, Cornelia, Zenobia,
Aurelian, Agrippina, Palmyrene; 108:
Lycian; 114: Lucumo; 262-8: Brutus (2);
318-21: Danaid; 322-5: Aspasia; 420:
Astraean (Book iii) 10-11: Iris; 55-6:
Ganymede, Vulcan; 284-6: Diotima,
Socrates; 323-7: Elysian; 329-34: Corinna,
Pindar (1) (Book iv) 99-101: Ithacensian;
184-8: Actaeon; 352-3: Niobean; 417-9:
Cassiopeia, Persephone (Book v) 355-6:
Tomyris, Cyrus (Book vii) 107-11:
Oppian, Cato (2); 112: Hortensia
Religion Be Thy Sword 5-8: Acestes
Rifle Clubs 5-8: Charon
Semele 11ff: Semele, Bacchus
On Sublimity 40: Dian
The Talking Oak 66-8: Cupid; 206-8: Dryad
Third of February, 1852 45-8: Thermopylae
Timbuctoo 31-6: Acropolis
Time, An Ode 5-7, 27: Time
Tiresias 11-17: Ares, Cadmus, Dirce, Tiresias;
38 ff: Tiresias; 93-5: Ares; 108 ff: Ares,
Cadmus; 134-7: Moeneceus; 143-4:
Sphinx; 158-9: Moeneceus
Tithon 5-6, 60-2: Tithon; 53: Ilion
Tithonus 15 ff: Tithonus

The Two Voices 194-5: Ixion; 349-51:
Lethe
Ulysses 6 ff: Ulysses; 10-11: Hyades; 33-4:
Telemachus; 51-4: Ulysses
To Virgil i: Virgil, Ilion, Dido; iv: Virgil,
Tityrus; v: Virgil, Pollio; vi: Virgil
Where Is the Giant of the Sun 1ff: Colossus;
22-7: Memnon

Thomas, Dylan (1914-53)
Greek Play in a Garden 4-8: Electra, Orestes,
Agamemnon; 17-20: Electra; 23-4:
Clytemnestra, Agamemnon; 25-8: Electra
My Hero Bears His Nerves 11-13: Venus
The Morning, Space for Leda 1-4: Leda;
29-33: Leda

Thomas, Edward (1878-1917)
The Sun Used to Shine 15-17: Hades

Thomson, James (1700-48)
The Castle of Indolence Canto i, xvii:
Scipio (1); xxvii: Nepenthe; xl: Aeolian
Harp
Liberty (Part i) 26-30: Liberty; 267-72:
Tiber, Horace; 272-7: Tully (*Part ii*)
85-9: Greece; 111-9: Sparta, Lycurgus;
138-40: Hymettus; 183-5: Marathon;
223 ff: Socrates; 236-7: Plato; 237-8:
Xenophon; 241-2: Epicurus; 306: Mars;
315-9: Apelles; 437: Xerxes (Part iii)
37 ff: Pythagoras; 127-9: Brennus, Cannae;
166-75: Regulus; 257 ff: Flaminius (1);
382 ff: Tiberius; 430-1: Marius, Sylla;
475-6: Caesar; 490-7: Caesars
(Part iv) 163-7: Python, Phoebus
(Part v) 201-6: Brutus (3), Caesars;
419-21: Scipio (1); 425-8: Tully, Catiline
The Seasons (Spring) 52-7: Maro; 456-7:
Mantuan (Summer) 663-6: Pomona;
853-5: Pan; 1300-8: Paris, Ida (2);
1491-3: Aristides, Cato (2), Cincinnatus;
1625-9: Amphitrite (Autumn) 1-4:
Doric; 516-7: Maia; 770-2: Deucalion;
798: Atlas; 1316-9: Haemus, Tempe
(Winter) 439 ff: Socrates; 406-52: Solon;
453-8: Lycurgus (3), Thermopylae,
Leonidas; 458-63: Aristides; 464-70:
Cimon; 473-5: Timoleon; 478-84:
Phocion; 491-2: Aratus; 493-7:
Philopoemen; 510: Camillus; 511:
Fabricius; 512: Cincinnatus; 517-20:

Scipio (1); 521-2: Tully; 523: Cato (2);
524-6: Brutus (3)
To Amanda 18-20: Zephyrs, Hours, Graces
To the Memory of Lord Talbot 73-6: Astraea

Vaughan, Henry (1622-95)
The Charnel House 16-7: Lucian
An Elegy 7-11: Flora
In Amicum Foeneratorem 30-2: Parnassus,
Tempe, Hippocrene
Monsieur Gombauld 51-2: Endymion
Olor Iscanus 1-2: Apollo, Eurotas; 3-4:
Orpheus, Hebrus; 15-18: Genii; 41-2:
Thessaly
To His Retired Friend 11-14: Brennus; 37:
Domitian
To My Ingenuous Friend R.W. 39-42: Lethe

Wordsworth, William (1770-1850)
Advance, Come Forth 6-9: Echo
Beguiled into Forgetfulness 60-3: Ceres
Departing Summer Hath Assumed 37-9:
Alcaeus; 46-8: Sappho
Descriptive Sketches 31-2: Memnon; 287-8:
Marathonian; 340ff: Genii
Dion 7-12: Dion, Plato; 42-3: Ilissus; 72-6:
Boreas, Maenalus
Ecclesiastical Sonnets I 6: Diocletian; 20:
Venus, Bacchus; 24: Cecilia; III 4: Platonic
Epistle to George Beaumont 38-43: Muse,
Olympus, Phoebus
Evening Voluntaries vii 26ff: Minerva, owl
An Evening Walk 72-3: Sabine, Bandusia
The Excursion ii 251: Janus; iii 347ff:
Epicureans; 756-9: Golden Age; iv 602ff:
Belus; 745-9: Cephisus; 872-6: oreads;
877-9: zephyrs; 886-7: Pan; vi 539-45:
Prometheus, Tantalus, Thebes; viii 220ff:
Archimedes
For 'The Recluse' 25-7: Urania; 35-40:
Chaos, Erebus
The Haunted Tree 21-7: Hamadryad
The Idiot Boy 342-6: Muses
I Find It Written of Simonides 12-14:
Simonides
Isle of Man 6-9: sea-nymphs
It is No Spirit 4ff: Hesperus
Laodamia 19-24: Laodamia, Protesilaus;
43-7: Protesilaus; 65-7: Parcae, Stygian;
70-2: Erebus; 79-84: Hercules, Alcestis,
Medea, Aeson; 140-2: Laodamia; 155-7:
Laodamia, Protesilaus

Lines Written as a School Exercise 20: Hebe;
21-2: Tyrian, 69-70: Elysian
Look at the Fate of Summer Flowers 14:
Arcady
Love Lies Bleeding 12-9: Adonis, Venus
Mary Queen of Scots 8-12: Time
Memorials of a Tour, 1820 i 3ff: Nereid; xi
7-14: Orphean, Argo; xxv 10: Ganymede;
75-8: Astraea; xxxii 30-3: Neptune,
Cereal, Salii; 33-6: Corybantian, Cybele;
xxxiv 9-10: Elysian
Memorials of a Tour in Italy, 1837 i 255-7:
Sabine, Bandusian; 261-2: Vacuna; 263-9:
Parthenope, Virgilian; iii 1-4: Capitolean,
Tarpeian; vi 7-14: Clio, Mnemosyne;
xiii 6-10: Thrasymene, Flaminius (2);
xxviii: (The Pillar of Trajan); 6-12, 28,
58-64, 67-9: Trajan
Memorials of a Tour in Scotland, 1803 i 10-12:
Chaos; xv 1-4: Hours
Memorials of a Tour in Scotland, 1813 ii 37-42:
Leonidas, Marathonian
A Morning Exercise 53-4: Urania
Oak of Gernica 1-5: Dodona
Ode, 1814 93-8: Marathon; 111ff: Pierian
Ode on May Morning 1-4: Flora
Ode to Lycoris 5-8: Dian, Cupid
Once Could I Hail 13-8: Dian, Proserpine
On Seeing a Needlecase in the Form of a Harp
5-8: Minerva; 9-13: Minerva, Arachne,
Vulcan; 29-30: sylphs
The Power of Music 1-4: Orpheus, Pantheon
The Power of Sound 76-80: Lydian, Graces;
129-44: Arion, Amphion; 145ff: Pan,
Fauns, Satyrs, Silenus
The Pillar of Trajan 6-12, 28, 58-64, 67-9:
Trajan
The Prelude **(Book i)** 190-4: Sertorius;
231-3: Orphean **(Book iv)** 13-16: Charon;
113-4: Venus **(Book vii)** 83-4: Tartarean;
500-2: Aurora; 531-4: Aeolian; 538-9:
Minerva **(Book viii)** 181-4: Pan, Lucretilis
(Book ix) 408ff: Dion, Eudemus,
Timonides, Dionysius II, Zacynthus;
456-61: Satyrs **(Book x)** 198-92:
Aristogiton, Harmodius, Brutus (3); 435:
Archimedes; 437ff: Theocritus, Comates;
464-6: Arethuse
Protest Against the Ballot 11-14: Pandorian
The River Duddon i 1-4: Latian, Sabine,
Horace, Bandusia; x 13-14: Loves; xii 6:
Naiads; xx 7ff: Bacchanal; xxii 2-3: Dian

To the River Greta 5-7: Cocytus
A Roman Master Stands 1-4: Flaminius
Rural Illusions 13-7: Flora
The Russian Fugitive 176-84: Phoebus, Daphne
To the Same Flower (Daisy) 25-6: Cyclops
Sonnets Dogmatic Teachers 7-9: Genius;
 From the Dark Chambers 2-7: Bellerophon;
 I heard (alas . . .) 6-11: Swan, Apollo;
 Lady, I rifled . . . 1-7: Parnassian, Dian,
 Lethe; *Pelion and Ossa* Pelion, Ossa,
 Olympus, Parnassus; *A Volant Tribe of
 Bards* 1-2: zephyrs; *The World is Too
 Much With Us* 9-14: Proteus, Triton;
 When Haughty Expectations 10-14:
 Emathian, Theban; *With How Sad Steps*
 13-4: Cynthia; *When Philoctetes* 1-4:
 Philoctetes, Lemnian
They Seek, are Sought 10-14: Viriathus, Sertorius
Those Breathing Tokens 90-5: Horace;
 102-5: Horace, Sabine, Bandusia
The Triad 8-14: Naiad, Dryad, Ida, sea-nymph;
 45-51: Juno; 80-4: Phoebus; 98 ff:
 Euphrosyne, Terpsichore, Idalian
To the Clouds 74: Protean, Cyclades
To Enterprise 144-6: Philomela
Vernal Ode 75-80: Muse, Urania, Clio;
 127-30: Tartarean, Golden Age
The Waggoner ii 81-2: Rubicon; iv 7-10:
 Muse; 108-13: Apollo
When, far and wide . . . 9-14: Marathon,
 Flaminius, Pelion
The Wishing-Gate 40-2: Genius
Written in a Blank Leaf of Ossian 37-44:
 Orpheus, Musaeus; 79-82: Maeonides
Written in a Grotto 10-15: Endymion
Yarrow Revisited i 61-4: Tiber; xi 1-3:
 Arcadian; xxvi 6-9: Persepolis

Wyatt, Sir Thomas (1503-42)
Farewell Love 3: Senec, Plato
Jopas' Song Dido, Aeneas, Juno, Atlas, Jopas
Love with Unkindness 24-7: Terence; 31-5:
 Lucrece, Tarquinius; 45-6: Venus
Tagus, Farewell 5: Brutus (1)
Though this the Port 5-7: Citherea

Yeats, William Butler (1865-1939)
Among School-Children ii: Ledaean, Plato;
 iv: Ledaean; vi: Plato, Aristotle, Alexander,
 Pythagoras

Beautiful Lofty Things Pallas
Conjunctions Mars, Venus
Coole Park and Ballylee Homer
Crazy Jane Reproved Europa
The Delphic Oracle Upon Plotinus Plotinus,
 Rhadamanthus, Plato, Minos, Pythagoras
The Double Vision of Michael Robartes
 Helen
A Full Moon in March (Song) Pythagoras
The Herne's Egg Ovid, Danae, Leda
His Bargain Plato
Lapis Lazuli Callimachus (1)
The Leaders of the Crowd Helicon
Leda and the Swan Leda, Agamemnon
Long-Legged Fly Caesar, Helen, Troy
Lullaby Paris, Helen, Leda, Eurotas
Mad as the Mist and Snow Cicero, Homer
A Man Young and Old vi Helen, Hector
Meditations in Time of Civil War i: Homer,
 Juno; iii: Juno
Michael Robartes and the Dancer Athene
The Municipal Gallery Revisited Antaeus
News for the Delphic Oracle Plotinus, Peleus,
 Thetis
Nineteen Hundred and Nineteen 1: Phidias
No Second Troy Troy, Helen
On a Picture of a Black Centaur Saturnian
Parnell's Funeral iii: Troy, Helen
A Prayer for My Daughter Helen, Venus,
 Vulcan
The Rose of the World Troy, Helen
The Saint and the Hunchback Alexander,
 Alcibiades, Augustus
The Scholars Catullus
Song of the Happy Shepherd Arcady, Chronos
Statues Pythagoras, Phidias
Three Marching Songs ii: Troy, Helen
The Tower i: Plato, Plotinus; iii: Plato,
 Plotinus
Two Songs from a Play i: Athene, Dionysus;
 Argo; ii: Platonic, Doric
Under Ben Bulben iv: Phidias
Upon a Dying Lady Petronius
Vacillation iii: Lethean; vii: Homer
When Helen Lived Helen, Paris, Troy

Young, Edward (1683-1765)
The Best Argument for Peace Augustus
Epistle to Lord Lansdowne 1-2: Augustus,
 Numa
The Instalment Ajax
The Last Day ii: Cannae

Young, Edward

Letter to Mr Tickell Dido
The Merchant (**Prologue**) Pindarics,
  Anacreontics; i: Attic; ii: Zephyr, Eurus,
  Notus, Boreas; iii: Pindar (1); v: Aeolus
Night Thoughts i: Maionides; ii: Esculapian,
  Iris, Favonius, Parthian, Hyblean, Bacchus,
  Zoilus; iii: Cynthia, Endymion, Circean,
  Cimmerean; iv: Aonion, Meander, Socrates;
v: Castalia, Plato, Cleopatra; vi: Nero,
  Delphos; vii: Bellerophon, Pyrrhus; viii:
  Epicurus, Demosthenes; ix: Cassandra
Ocean Paean, Nereids, Arion, nymphs
The Old Man's Relapse Augustus
Resignation Thalia, Helicon, Styx
Sea Piece (**Dedication**) Arion; 1: Minerva
The Universal Passion i: Homer